The Book of Monasteries

Letter from the General Editor

The Library of Arabic Literature makes available Arabic editions and English translations of significant works of Arabic literature, with an emphasis on the seventh to nineteenth centuries. The Library of Arabic Literature thus includes texts from the pre-Islamic era to the cusp of the modern period, and encompasses a wide range of genres, including poetry, poetics, fiction, religion, philosophy, law, science, travel writing, history, and historiography.

Books in the series are edited and translated by internationally recognized scholars. They are published as hardcovers in parallel-text format with Arabic and English on facing pages, as English-only paperbacks, and as downloadable Arabic editions. For some texts, the series also publishes separate scholarly editions with full critical apparatus.

The Library encourages scholars to produce authoritative Arabic editions, accompanied by modern, lucid English translations, with the ultimate goal of introducing Arabic's rich literary heritage to a general audience of readers as well as to scholars and students.

The publications of the Library of Arabic Literature are generously supported by Tamkeen under the NYU Abu Dhabi Research Institute Award G1003 and are published by NYU Press.

Philip F. Kennedy
General Editor, Library of Arabic Literature

كتاب الديارات

أبو الحسن عليّ بن محمّد
المعروف
بالشابشتي

LIBRARY OF
المكتبة
ARABIC
العربية
LITERATURE

The Book of Monasteries

Al-Shābushtī

Edited and translated by
Hilary Kilpatrick

Volume editor
Tahera Qutbuddin

NEW YORK UNIVERSITY PRESS
New York

NEW YORK UNIVERSITY PRESS
New York

Library of Congress Cataloging-in-Publication Data

Names: Shābushtī, ʿAlī ibn Muḥammad, -998, author. | Kilpatrick, Hilary, editor, translator. | Shābushtī, ʿAlī ibn Muḥammad, -998. Diyārāt.
Title: 880-01 The book of monasteries = Kitāb al-diyārāt / al-Shābushtī ; edited and translated by Hilary Kilpatrick.
Other titles: Diyārāt. English | 880-02 Kitāb al-diyārāt
Description: New York : New York University Press, 2023. | Includes bibliographical references and index. | In English and Arabic. | Summary: "A literary anthology of poetry and anecdotes related to Christian monasteries of the medieval Middle East"-- Provided by publisher.
Identifiers: LCCN 2022050287 | ISBN 9781479825769 (hardcover) | ISBN 9781479825752 (ebook) | ISBN 9781479825721 (ebook)
Subjects: LCSH: Monasteries--Middle East--Early works to 1800. | Monasteries--Middle East--Poetry--Early works to 1800. | LCGFT: Poetry.
Classification: LCC BX385.A1 S513 2023 | DDC 271/.8156--dc23/eng/20221118

LC record available at https://lccn.loc.gov/2022050287

New York University Press books are printed on acid-free paper, and their binding materials are chosen for strength and durability.

Series design by Titus Nemeth.

Typeset in Tasmeem, using DecoType Naskh and Emiri.

Typesetting and digitization by Stuart Brown.

Manufactured in the United States of America
c10 9 8 7 6 5 4 3 2 1

Table of Contents

To the peoples of Iraq and Greater Syria,
whose ancestors came together in and around
al-Shābushtī's monasteries

Acknowledgements

My first thanks go to the late Kūrkīs ʿAwwād, whose edition of the single manuscript of the *Diyārāt* helped me throughout the preparation of my own edition. In particular his supplying dots where the copyist had been economical with them, his corrections of some erroneous pointing, and his supplying parallel texts spared me much time. It is only right to mention, as he did, the help he received from two colleagues of his, the late Muṣṭafā Jawād and Kāẓim al-Dujaylī. رحمهم الله رحمة واسعة.

The Staatsbibliothek in Berlin kindly made available to me images of Wetzstein 1111, the only known manuscript of the *Kitāb al-diyārāt*, and my son George Waardenburg (Lausanne/Bern) made superior photocopies of it. Antoine Scrivo (Épalinges/CH) painstakingly rebound my copy of ʿAwwād's edition, saving it from a fate worse than that of the MS. Their logistical support was essential.

Boris Liebrenz (Leipzig) generously shared his expertise on manuscripts with me, elucidating Wetzstein 1111's marginal notes. Lorenzo Capezzone (Rome) sent me a copy of his *Il Libro dei Monasteri*, an abridged version of the *Diyārāt*, while Jack Tannous (Princeton) made available for me his unpublished partial annotated translation of the text. I am grateful to all of them.

Katia Zakharia (Lyon) sent me an article she had prepared for publication and her notes on the *Diyārāt* as a set text for the *agrégation* examination. Geert Jan van Gelder (Haren/NL) and Thomas Bauer (Münster) commented on knotty points of Arabic poetry. Remke Kruk (Leiden) elucidated bird and plant names for me; Salam Rassi (Oxford) gave me Syriac references; Anna Livia Beelaert (Leiden) threw light on a Persian celebration; Matthew Gordon (Oxford, OH) identified a Turkish caliphal companion and gave me references; Carsten Walbiner (Bonn/Beirut) provided books and bibliographical indications; Haci Osman Gündüz (Cambridge, Mass.) organized for me copies of works which were out of reach; Youhanna Nessim Youssef (Stockholm) answered queries about Coptic matters. Other colleagues who helped me with questions include Dmitry Morozov (Moscow), Thomas Carlson (Stillwater, OK) and Muhsin

Musawi (New York). Letizia Osti (Basel/Milan) kindly gave me the run of her collection of Abbasid sources.

I am much obliged to Madeleine Voegeli (Basel), who solved my problems of layout for the Arabic poetry, and to my son Johannes Waardenburg (Naples/Lausanne), who helped me likewise with the layout of the Arabic poetry index. Michael Athanson (Oxford) prepared the maps with creative professionalism and I am very grateful to him.

Of the Library of Arabic Literature team, Tahera Qutbuddin (Chicago), my project editor, provided invaluable help with the poetry and she made constructive comments throughout. Chip Rossetti (New York) regularly put his extensive experience as Editorial Director of the series at my disposal. Julia Bray (Oxford) gave me useful advice. Bilal Orfali cast a last critical eye over the poetry. It was splendid to have their backing.

Finally, colleagues too many to mention encouraged me in the four years when I was working on this project and sometimes felt I would never manage it. I thank them all.

Introduction

Twenty-first-century readers of al-Shābushtī's late-tenth-century *Book of Monasteries* are likely to be taken aback on several counts. The monasteries in it belong to Christian communities unfamiliar to most people outside the Middle East. The characteristics generally associated with monasteries and their inhabitants—withdrawal from the world, prayer, and asceticism—are seldom mentioned, and no striking monastic figure emerges from the book.[1] By contrast, al-Shābushtī's monasteries inspire poets because of the beauty of their settings and the opportunities they provide for enjoying wine and having fun, innocent and not so innocent. Poetry thus forms a major part of the book. Moreover, some important political personalities and events are indirectly linked with monasteries, and they too appear in this book, as do scenes of festive court life and gruesome murders.

Al-Shābushtī and His Anthology

The compiler of this many-sided work, Abū al-Ḥasan ʿAlī ibn Muḥammad al-Shābushtī al-Kātib, was a state scribe of Persian origin;[2] Shābushtī, an unusual name, is explained as meaning "support of the king, chamberlain" in Persian. His date of birth is unknown, but he probably grew up and had his education in Baghdad, which from 334/945 was ruled under the authority of the Abbasid caliphs by the Būyids, a Shiʿi dynasty from northwestern Iran. The tenth and early eleventh centuries were a time of great cultural achievement,[3] and the author and his book fit well into this period. From *The Book of Monasteries*, it is clear that al-Shābushtī traveled in Iraq, southern Anatolia, and Syria. Then, like many other cultivated scribes and administrators in this period, he moved to Egypt. In Cairo, the newly founded capital of the Shiʿi Fatimid state, he became one of the caliph al-ʿAzīz's (r. 365–86/975–96) court companions, his reader and his librarian. The Fatimid palace library came to be known as one of the most splendid in the Muslim world, and al-Shābushtī no doubt played a part in developing it. His death date is given as either 388/998 or 390/1000.

Al-Shābushtī is credited with other works besides *The Book of Monasteries*. One was on deliverance after hardship, another on the classes of jurisprudents, and a third, *Al-Tawqīf wa-l-takhwīf* (*Attention Arrested and Apprehension Inspired*),[4] apparently warned against the horrors of hell. He also left correspondence, including maxims and a collection of poetry. None of these texts have survived.

The Book of Monasteries is one of several works compiled on this subject in the fourth/tenth century, but is the only one still extant, albeit in a truncated form. It is probably also the last. The other writers listed as having compiled a book of monasteries with poems about them are Saʿīd ibn Hishām (d. ca. 390/1000) and his brother Muḥammad (d. 380/990), known together as the Khālidiyyān; Abū al-Faraj ʿAlī ibn al-Ḥusayn al-Iṣbahānī (d. ca. 363/972); al-Sarī al-Raffāʾ (d. 362/973); and ʿAlī ibn Muḥammad al-Shimshāṭī (d. after 376/987).[5] The two Khālidī brothers, librarians at the Hamdanid court in Aleppo, were poets who also compiled several anthologies of poetry. Al-Sarī al-Raffāʾ, their bitter rival, moved between the courts of Mosul, Aleppo, and Baghdad; as well as a collection of his own poetry and his lost book on monasteries, he left one extant poetic anthology. Al-Shimshāṭī, the tutor of the Hamdanid princes in Mosul, left an extant anthology of poetry arranged by topic and including some prose accounts, and a lost philological work. His lost *Book of Monasteries* included some thirty entries on monasteries. Al-Iṣbahānī, a man of wide interests, was a musicologist, historian, man of letters, and poet working in Baghdad.[6] An attempt has been made to reconstruct his *Book of Monasteries* on the basis of excerpts and references in other texts.[7]

Although it is far from convincing,[8] this reconstruction, taken together with quotations from the other books of monasteries mentioned above, as they are found in later works, gives an idea of what these texts may have contained: a description of a monastery's setting, followed by poetry about it and sometimes anecdotes about people who frequented it. If they were poets, further quotations of their verses are included. When a monastery provides healing or has some extraordinary feature, these are mentioned. In al-Shābushtī's book, the treatment of Egyptian monasteries conforms to this pattern.

Parts of al-Shābushtī's *Book of Monasteries* are lost, including the preface where he would have explained what his purpose was and, if the book had been commissioned, who had commissioned it. He could also have answered other questions in it, such as where and when the book was compiled. Very likely, he collected material for it over several years. The fact that he includes obscure poets from geographically distant regions suggests that this was a project he worked on during his travels and completed after he arrived in Egypt.[9] Furthermore, he might have referred to other books of monasteries he knew of. It is conceivable that his *Book of Monasteries* was intended as a contribution from the Fatimid domains to the genre.

Nonetheless, he appeared to have innovated in several ways, as far as can be judged from a comparison of his *Book of Monasteries* with the fragments of the others that have survived.[10] First, his book has a wide geographical scope, starting with monasteries in Baghdad, going up the Tigris into the mountains of southeastern Anatolia, moving across to Palestine and Syria, and then following the Euphrates down to the old Christian center of Ḥīrah. The short section on Egyptian monasteries, which is almost entirely devoted to poetry, follows, and the book concludes with notes on monasteries where wondrous events and healing take place. The settings for the anecdotes and poetry al-Shābushtī quotes take the reader far afield, for instance to Azerbaijan (§22.3) and Khurasan (§13 and passim), where Christian monasteries were thin on the ground.

Second, as one of his medieval biographers points out, he draws on many kinds of sources.[11] He provides a sample of types of prose text, such as a letter of condolence (§§13.11–15), jokes and witty retorts (§§10.4–10, §§20.6–10), tales of battles (§§13.44–46, §§24.10–11), accounts of court intrigues and extravagant festivities (§§13.60–62, §§14.3–14, §§15.14–15), and rhetorical jousts (§§18.7–8). He sometimes uses a monastery as a starting point for a historical section; the most striking example of this is when he sketches the lives of four generations of the Ṭāhirid family, curiously in reverse chronological order (§§13.6–66). The material he has brought together includes short statements side by side with tersely told incidents and more elaborate longer narratives. Frequent dialogues give the accounts vividness and immediacy. Al-Shābushtī is a transmitter of good, plausible, choicely formulated stories. They may convey a moral lesson and often have some historical value. He is not, however, concerned with the historians' search for "true facts."[12]

The poetry al-Shābushtī quotes is also varied. Some of it describes the natural settings of the monasteries; in an age before photography and in a culture where figurative art was not widely practiced, such paintings in words served as a record of places, much like eighteenth-century genre painting in Europe. Other poems celebrate meetings with attractive young people of either sex in monasteries, the vicissitudes of love affairs, or the provocations of well-known libertines. Wine and, less often, song belong to the repertoire of these scenes, which often end on a nostalgic note: "Those were the days, my friend / We thought they'd never end."[13] A detailed study of where the different types of poetry occurs in the notices on the monasteries concluded that wine poetry dominates in the passages directly linked to the monasteries, whereas elsewhere in the notices poetry of love and nostalgia is frequent.[14] But al-Shābushtī also includes samples of genres unconnected with monasteries and the goings-on in them, such as panegyric (§13.45, §§22.4–5), elegy (§§13.32–33, §14.14), satire (§1.14, §12.11), poems exchanged between friends (§§9.6–19), reflections on the transience of power (§30.4, §32.2, §32.4), and contentment with one's lot (§36.6, §36.9, §36.12). Poetry was a mode of communication about anything from the sublime to the ridiculous to the utilitarian, and al-Shābushtī's book reflects this; even a request for tax exemption could be put into verse (§13.29).[15]

Al-Shābushtī's wide-ranging interest in poetry extends even to its form. All traditional Arabic poetry is metrical, and the meter as a rule remains constant throughout the poem. But al-Shābushtī includes unique examples of nonmetrical poetry, which, it has been suggested, were not proof of incompetence on the part of the poet al-Muʿtamid (he also composed acceptable metrical poetry) but an experiment in innovation (see §12.3, §12.6, §12.12–13, and the note to the translation). His example was not, however, followed before modern times.

As the above sketch of the contents shows, *The Book of Monasteries* is much more than its title suggests. One can see it as a pocket anthology of Arabic literature from the coming of Islam to the compiler's own time. Arabic anthologies are not haphazard collections of anecdotes and poetry, but are organized on a variety of principles. Poetry anthologies may focus on the works of one poet or a group of poets, perhaps from a particular period or region, or on poetic themes and motifs.[16] Prose anthologies may bring together, for instance, anecdotes illustrating traits of character or genres such as speeches or letters. And many anthologies combine poetry and prose.[17] Al-Shābushtī's *Book of Monasteries* uses monasteries ordered geographically as a frame for a rich variety of poetry and prose.

Apart from his conception for *The Book of Monasteries*, al-Shābushtī's contribution is essentially behind the scenes. The sketches of the monasteries and their surroundings, which he almost certainly wrote, and which set the scene for the subsequent prose and poetry, make up a tiny part of the book. All the poetry is by others. Some of the prose texts—for instance, the letter of condolence and its reply—have been quoted verbatim; others, such as the pithy jokes, have a fixed form. For longer historical accounts, al-Shābushtī sometimes mentions informants, such as ʿUbaydallāh ibn ʿAbdallāh ibn Ṭāhir or Abū ʿAbdallāh ibn Ḥamdūn, whom he could not have met. Whether their information was transmitted to him orally or in writing he does not say. He may have revised or polished their versions, but it is impossible to determine precisely his contribution to the final wording.

Al-Shābushtī and Shiʿism

A minor theme in *The Book of Monasteries* is the tensions and conflicts between Sunnis and Shiʿis, an aspect to which an irate reader of the manuscript has drawn attention. He has erased the word "cursing" (that is, cursing ʿĀʾishah) in the account of the Battle of the Camel that is attached to the Monastery of Mount Tabor (§24.11). Cursing ʿĀʾishah, the Prophet's wife, for her hostility to his daughter Fāṭimah, his son-in-law ʿAlī, and their descendants, and for her political involvement came to be a vocal expression of Shiʿi disapproval of the Sunnis. The same reader has erased a line in a poem that al-Shābushtī mistakenly ascribes to Ibn al-Rūmī as being an elegy for Muḥammad ibn ʿAbdallāh, a prominent member of the Ṭāhirid family (§13.32). In fact, it is by a lesser poet and commemorates the death of al-Ḥasan ibn Zayd, ʿAlid ruler of Ṭabaristān. Whether al-Shābushtī has made an honest mistake or attempted to smuggle commemoration of a prominent Shiʿi leader into the book is not clear.

Other passages, such as the confrontation between Muʿāwiyah and the widow of ʿAmr ibn al-Ḥamiq (§§18.6–8); the reference to Abū ʿAlī ibn Jamhūr's transmitting narratives about the family of the Prophet (§35.9); and ʿAbdallāh ibn Dāwud al-Khuraybī's question about inheritance, which could be understood as an affirmation of Shiʿi claims to leadership of the Community (§10.13),[18] point to al-Shābushtī entertaining Shiʿi sympathies. Yet, while his move to Cairo shows that he was not hostile to the Ismāʿīlī branch of Shiʿism—the doctrine followed by the rulers of Egypt from 358/969 on—there is no evidence that he adhered to it. However, he might have revealed his views in the lost preface to *The Book of Monasteries*.

The Christian Religious Background: Syriacs, Melkites, and Copts

For al-Shābushtī, monasteries are a way into the religious community that made up about half the population of the Abbasid Empire in his time.[19] To explore this further, it is necessary to consider the situation of monasteries, and of Christianity more generally, in the fourth-/tenth-century Middle East.

Looking back from the twenty-first century, it is tempting to read into the situation of Middle Eastern Christianity over a thousand years ago features that only appeared later. In Egypt and the Fertile Crescent at the end of the fourth/tenth century, Christianity was probably still the majority religion, even if it was unevenly distributed and politically subordinate to Islam.[20] When Baghdad was founded in 145/762, the Christians in the surrounding villages were conscious of having four centuries of history behind them, during which they had suffered several savage persecutions by the Sassanians, and this gave them a "tranquil assurance" in their encounters with Muslims.[21] Some important cities might have a Muslim majority, but the countryside must still have been largely Christian. Monasteries were not Christian islands in a Muslim sea.

The Middle Eastern Christians who appear in *The Book of Monasteries* belonged to four churches. The Syriac tradition was represented by the Church of the East in Iraq, Persia, and further east,[22] and by the Syrian Orthodox Church in Syria and western Iraq, referred to by al-Shābushtī respectively as Nestorians and Jacobites. The Melkites, chiefly in Syria, Palestine, and Egypt, were Chalcedonians, while the Copts in Egypt, whom al-Shābushtī never mentions by name, although he includes some of their monasteries, shared the beliefs of the Syrian Orthodox. The divisions go back mainly to the Fourth Ecumenical Council (Chalcedon, AD 451), where the fundamental issue of the nature of Christ was debated.[23] According to the council's definition, adhered to by the Melkites, Christ, both God and man, was incarnate in two natures. The Copts and the Syrian Orthodox, however, held that Christ was incarnate in one nature alone, hence the name "Miaphysite" applied to their churches. The Church of the East represented the Christian tradition that had developed independently in the Sassanian Empire and spread as far as China; although long associated with the beliefs of Nestorius, its view of Christ's nature was in fact very close to that of the Chalcedonians.

Al-Shābushtī shows no interest in the theological divisions between the churches. He does, however, note differences in organization between the monasteries of the Syrian Orthodox and Melkites, which have administrators, on the one hand, and those of the Church of the East, which do not, on the other (§43.2). And he mentions the unusual phenomenon of a Melkite monk who had installed himself in a Church of the East monastery and was administering it (§16.1). Given the doctrinal closeness between the two churches concerned, such an arrangement was possible; it would have been unthinkable for members of the Church of the East and the Syrian Orthodox Church to be involved together in this way.[24] Another detail al-Shābushtī provides, without linking it to a specific church, concerns two monasteries where the monks owned their cells and could sell them to each other (§35.1, §36.1).[25]

Al-Shābushtī's notions of church history and traditions are limited to mentioning people and events referred to in the Bible, as well as founders of monasteries and saints to whom monasteries were dedicated. For Syro-Palestinian monasteries, he indicates historical or legendary connections with the life of Christ (mentioning an unspecified connection of Christ with the monastery, §23.1; indicating the place where the Transfiguration took place, confusing it with Christ's post-Resurrection appearances , §24.1). He relates prophets to the places where several monasteries stand (the mountain where Noah's ark came to rest, §48.1; the village where Moses was born, §37.2; Mount Sinai, the place of Moses's encounter with God, §49.1; Nineveh, the city of Yūnus (Jonah), §19.1). He identifies two founders (both women) of monasteries (Ushmūnī, §6.1; Hind bint al-Nuʿmān, §32.1) and two patron saints (Mār Tūmā, §44.1; Mār Bākhūs, §45.1).[26] Admittedly, several monasteries are named after their patron saint, making further mention of him or her superfluous.

As someone outside the Christian community, what al-Shābushtī is best informed about are the monasteries' patronal feasts, occasions on which non-Christians could join in the festivities, albeit for their own reasons. The Sundays of Lent were celebrated in some monasteries (§1.2; §11.1), while Palm Sunday (§18.2), the Veneration (or Feast) of the Cross (§35.1), and unspecified feasts were celebrated in others (§31.1; §41.1; §53.1). Monasteries attracted members of all communities when they had a healing spring or were known for treating a particular disease (rabies, §42.1; skin complaints, §43.2, §46.1; scrofula, §50.1). Al-Shābushtī also reports strange and marvelous features of monasteries, known to Christians and Muslims alike (scarabs gathering on the eve of the monastery's feast, §41.1; resistant stone door, raven guardians, §45.1; expandable roof, §48.1; holy fire, §49.1; hornbills, §53.1). He is generally silent about Christian rituals, although he mentions Christians receiving communion (§2.1, §13.3, §41.1).

Some of his poets refer to this too (§12.2, §49.2), and also to the chanting of the monks (§6.5, §15.1, §34.1, §37.3, §40.2) and the clappers used to summon monastics to church services (§6.5, §15.1, §23.2, §27.1, §34.1, §37.3).

What were the attractions of monasteries for Muslim poets and bons vivants? Several scholars have commented on the presence of wine as a magnet; Christians need wine for the Eucharist and so it was bound to be available in monasteries.[27] Monasteries also dispensed hospitality to travelers. After an arduous journey across difficult terrain, it was a relief to stop where one could be sure of a welcome, and some visitors appear to have revisited a monastery later. The monasteries' settings were certainly also a draw; not for nothing does al-Shābushtī start the section on each monastery with a sketch of its attractive grounds.[28] Most monasteries were outside cities; they were peaceful havens far from the violent power struggles of Baghdad and Samarra, and places where visitors could behave freely without incurring criticism.[29]

Classical Arabic literature includes a multitude of anecdotes about generally Muslim poets, musicians, handsome attendants, gifted singers, and wine set in urban palaces or private houses and a vast corpus of poetry produced in and about these gatherings.[30] Monasteries were thus not essential for drinking parties. Besides, the connection between wine and love poetry, so often illustrated in al-Shābushtī's text, has roots in early poetry outside a monastery context.[31] What distinguished monasteries, however, in addition to their often rural surroundings and their well-maintained grounds and buildings, was the fact that everyone was welcome. Monasteries were also centers of Syriac learning and culture, and Muslim visitors may have sensed this even though al-Shābushtī makes no reference to it.[32] Their religious aura may indeed have added spice to transgressive behavior.[33] But it is worth remembering that convivial gatherings at the monasteries of Ḥīrah in which rulers, courtiers, and poets took part predate the Muslim conquest,[34] and Muslims could feel they were continuing this tradition.

Given that conversion to Islam was an ongoing process, some Muslims would have had family or friends who, as Christians, attended services at monasteries. Al-Shābushtī provides the example of the vizier Ṣāʿid ibn Makhlad, a convert who reached the top of his profession, while his brother ʿAbdūn, who remained a Christian, took refuge in a monastery after his brother's disgrace (§35.10, §35.14).[35] Al-Shābushtī carefully points out that the Muslims only attended festivals for the accompanying fun, but this is disingenuous. In an environment where conversion occurred for a variety of reasons, mostly unconnected with doctrinal conviction or profound spiritual experience, converts to Islam continued to maintain ties to the Christian community, employ Christian symbols, and observe Christian rituals.[36] Attendance at patronal and other feasts was open to all who lived within walking or riding distance of a monastery, providing occasions for men and women of many backgrounds to mix freely.[37] Areas outside monasteries could also be the venue for celebrations by Christians and Muslims together. The historian, geographer, and traveler al-Masʿūdī, who attended the Feast of the Epiphany in Egypt some years before al-Shābushtī was writing, reports that the ruler, Muḥammad ibn Tughj al-Ikhshīd, ordered lamps to be lit for the festivities, which were an occasion of general rejoicing beside the Nile.[38]

Monasteries and Historical Memory

Apart from their attractiveness for Muslims of al-Shābushtī's time and earlier, monasteries provided a link to the past—a past that reached back before the coming of Islam. Several sections in *The Book of Monasteries* record historical or legendary events, starting with prophecies of the end of the Sassanian Empire and the conquest of Ḥīrah. The latter is portrayed chiefly through the encounters of Hind, daughter of the last Lakhmid king, with three central figures in the early Muslim history of Iraq: al-Ḥajjāj ibn Yūsuf, governor from 75/694; Saʿd ibn Abī Waqqāṣ, conqueror of Iraq in 13/637; and al-Mughīrah ibn Shuʿbah, governor of Kufa from 41/661 (§§32.1–6).[39] Each meeting has its own character: al-Ḥajjāj expels Hind from her convent and seeks to impose the tax for non-Muslims; Saʿd treats her with respect; and al-Mughīrah, true to his reputation as a womanizer, proposes marriage but is turned down and made a laughing stock. At least two of these meetings are obviously legendary, but together they illustrate different attitudes to the Christian former elite and salient traits of the governors concerned.

About the historicity of another event from this early period, the Battle of the Camel (36/656), there is no doubt (§§24.10–11). In this early episode of the First Civil War, al-Shābushtī's perspective is that of the supporters of ʿAlī in Basra, who sacrificed their lives to deny entry to the city to those demanding revenge for ʿUthmān's murder. To include this episode in his book, he has attached it to the section on the monastery of Mount Tabor. This he begins with several quotations of verses on nature and wine by a poet who is a distant descendant of the martyr in Basra, and the poet's genealogy provides the transition to the heroic ancestor. Further indication of al-Shābushtī's sympathy for the family of the Prophet appears in the section on al-Aʿlā Monastery, near which was the grave of ʿAmr ibn al-Ḥamiq, a supporter of ʿAlī who was hunted down and killed by a relative of Muʿāwiyah. Al-Shābushtī recounts the confrontation between the caliph and ʿAmr's widow, just released from prison. She gives as good as she gets and the caliph grants her the fare back home (§§18.6–8).

The last account from the Umayyad era in *The Book of Monasteries* takes up almost the whole of the section on the Bactrians' Monastery (§§25.1–5). It relates the split between al-Walīd ibn ʿAbd al-Malik and ʿAlī ibn ʿAbdallāh ibn al-ʿAbbās, grandfather of the first two Abbasid caliphs, and then the refutation of the claim by Abū Muslim, the leader of the Abbasid revolution, that he was an Abbasid himself. Here the main Umayyad character, al-Walīd, is portrayed critically.

In the portions on the Abbasid period, al-Shābushtī makes no secret of his sympathy for the Ṭāhirids, to whom he devotes the longest section in the book, 20 folios of the 135 the manuscript now contains. An unusual feature of this section is that it traces the family's history in reverse chronological order, starting with the cultured but politically rather ineffectual ʿUbaydallāh ibn ʿAbdallāh, and ending with his grandfather, Ṭāhir ibn al-Ḥusayn, founder of the family's empire-wide fortunes. Where caliphs are concerned, the anecdotes al-Shābushtī includes give most space to those who presided over a rich court culture of poetry and music—Hārūn al-Rashīd (r. 170–193/786–809), al-Maʾmūn (r. 196–218/812–33), al-Muʿtaṣim (r. 218–27/833–42), and al-Mutawakkil (r. 232–47/847–61)—though their successors up to al-Muktafī (d. 295/908) are not neglected.

Al-Shābushtī does not try to produce coherent historical accounts. He himself may have been at a loss to understand the forces at play in the violent and chaotic period following al-Mutawakkil's death, which he mentions. Rather, he chooses heroic or spectacular incidents, illustrations of caliphal extravagance, and events that gave rise to memorable poetry. As can be seen from the marginal comments of an owner-reader of the manuscript (translated in the endnotes to the relevant sections), some of his information still resonated five centuries later as mythicized recollections of a Golden Age. Al-Shābushtī uses these accounts not to teach history but to convey moral and philosophical lessons: the transitoriness of power, the virtues of generosity and tolerance, the effectiveness of eloquence in prose and poetry, and the fleeting nature of pleasure and beauty. Always in the background is the knowledge that at the Day of Judgment people will be held responsible for their acts. With his references to the transitoriness of this life and its pleasures and the coming of the Day of Judgment, al-Shābushtī's message perhaps unintentionally concurs with the teachings of the monks whose monasteries he describes.

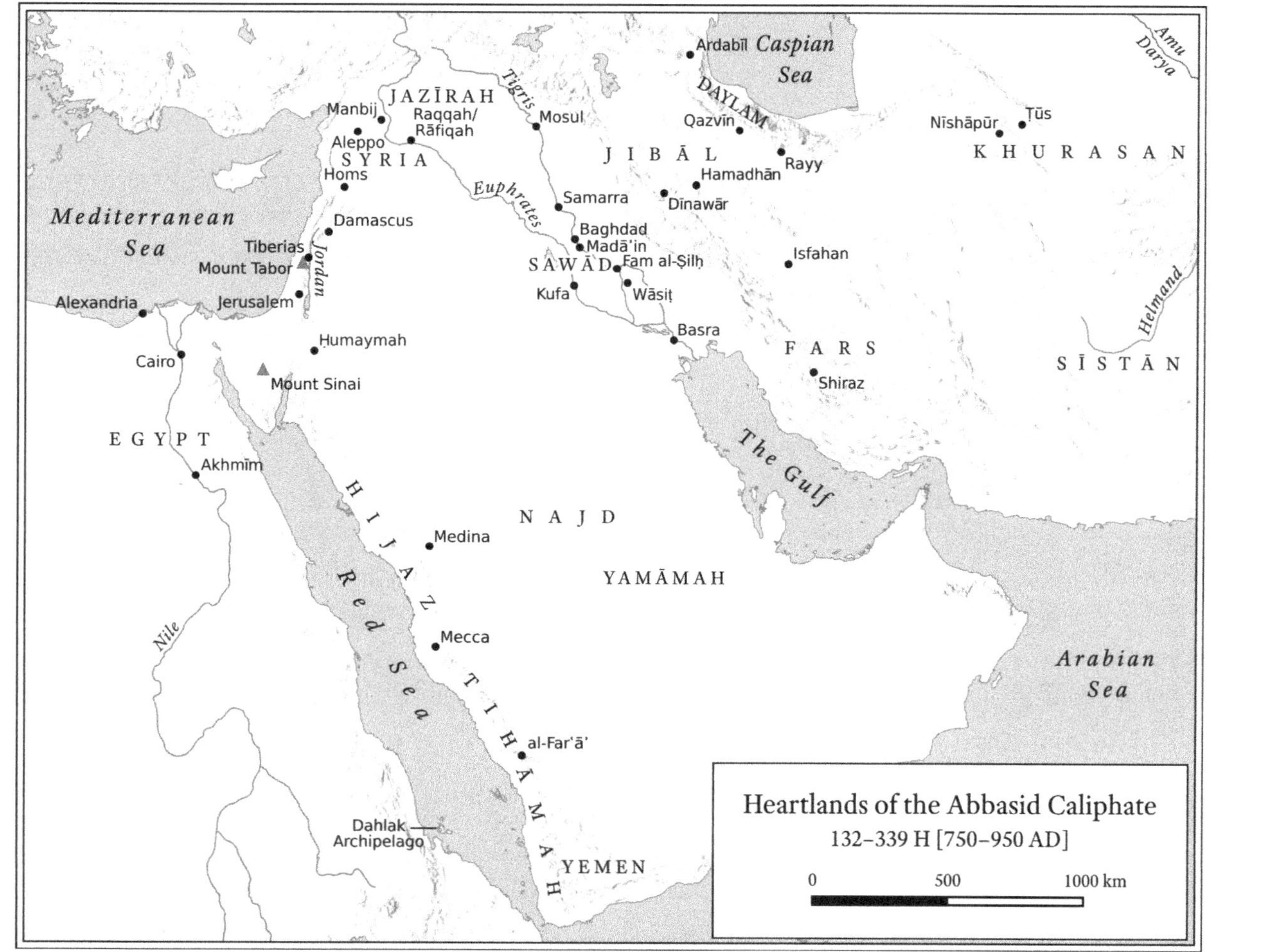

Heartlands of the Abbasid Caliphate
132–339 H [750–950 AD]
0
500
1000 km
Mediterranean Sea
Caspian Sea
Arabian Sea
The Gulf
Red Sea
Amu Darya
Tigris
Euphrates
Jordan
Nile
Helmand
JAZĪRAH
SYRIA
EGYPT
HIJAZ
TIHĀMAH
YEMEN
NAJD
YAMĀMAH
SAWĀD
JIBĀL
DAYLAM
FARS
KHURASAN
SĪSTĀN
Ardabīl
Qazvīn
Rayy
Nīshāpūr
Ṭūs
Mosul
Samarra
Hamadhān
Dīnawār
Baghdad
Madā'in
Fam al-Ṣilḥ
Wāsiṭ
Kufa
Basra
Isfahan
Shiraz
Manbij
Raqqah/
Rāfiqah
Aleppo
Homs
Damascus
Tiberias
Mount Tabor
Jerusalem
Alexandria
Cairo
Humaymah
Mount Sinai
Akhmīm
Medina
Mecca
al-Far'ā'
Dahlak
Archipelago

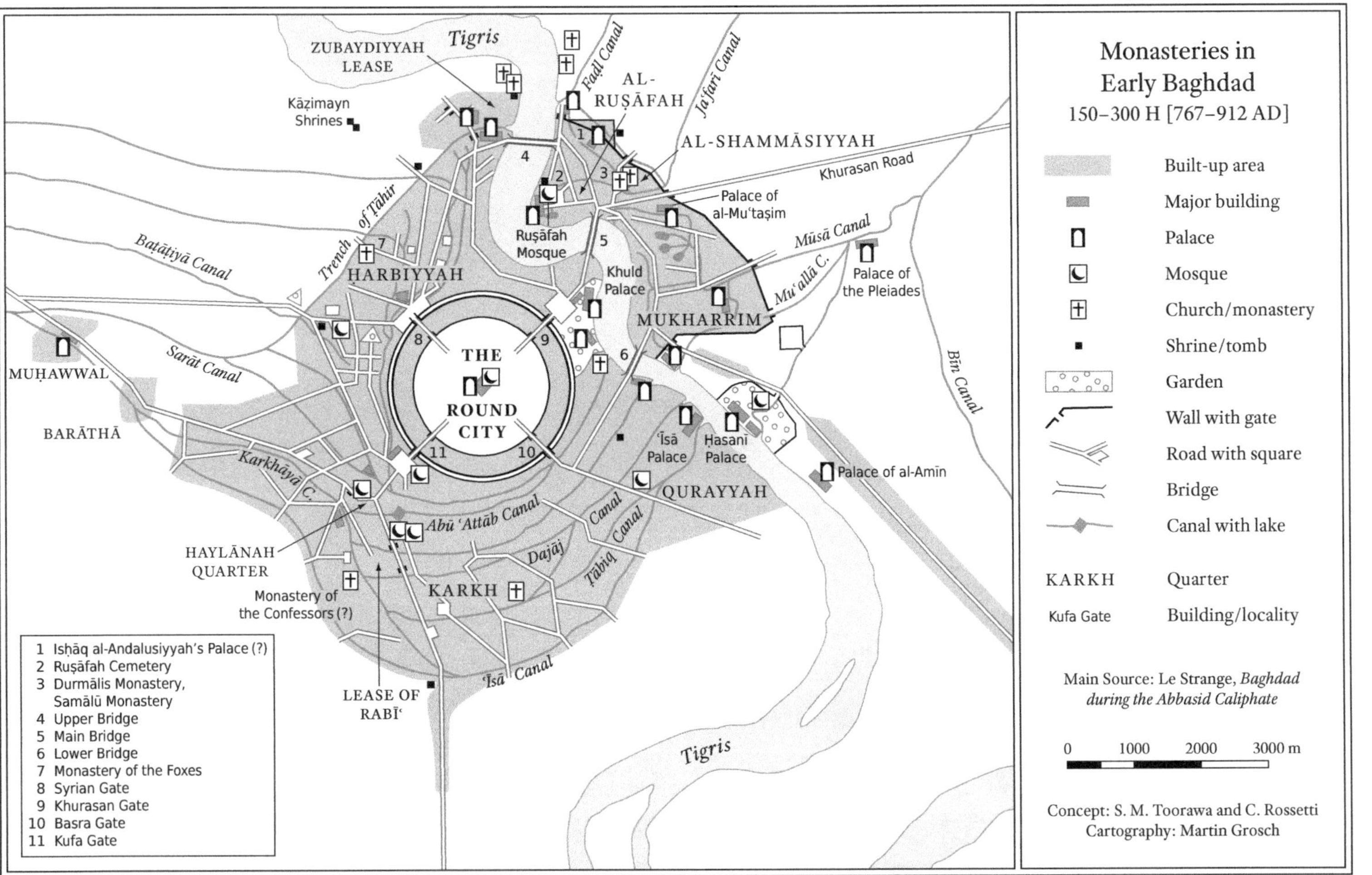
Monasteries in Early Baghdad
150–300 H [767–912 AD]
Built-up area
Major building
Palace
Mosque
Church/monastery
Shrine/tomb
Garden
Wall with gate
Road with square
Bridge
Canal with lake
KARKH
Quarter
Kufa Gate
Building/locality
Main Source: Le Strange, *Baghdad during the Abbasid Caliphate*
0
1000
2000
3000 m
Concept: S. M. Toorawa and C. Rossetti
Cartography: Martin Grosch
Tigris
ZUBAYDIYYAH LEASE
Kāẓimayn Shrines
Faḍl Canal
AL-RUṢĀFAH
Ja'farī Canal
AL-SHAMMĀSIYYAH
Khurasan Road
Palace of al-Mu'taṣim
Ruṣāfah Mosque
Mūsā Canal
Mu'allā C.
Palace of the Pleiades
Khuld Palace
MUKHARRIM
Trench of Ṭāhir
Baṭāṭiyā Canal
ḤARBIYYAH
THE ROUND CITY
MUḤAWWAL
Sarāt Canal
Bīn Canal
BARĀTHĀ
'Īsā Palace
Ḥasanī Palace
Palace of al-Amīn
Karkhāyā C.
QURAYYAH
Abū 'Attāb Canal
Canal
Canal
Dajāj
Ṭābiq
HAYLĀNAH QUARTER
Monastery of the Confessors (?)
KARKH
'Īsā Canal
LEASE OF RABĪ'
Tigris
1 Isḥāq al-Andalusiyyah's Palace (?)
2 Ruṣāfah Cemetery
3 Durmālis Monastery, Samālū Monastery
4 Upper Bridge
5 Main Bridge
6 Lower Bridge
7 Monastery of the Foxes
8 Syrian Gate
9 Khurasan Gate
10 Basra Gate
11 Kufa Gate

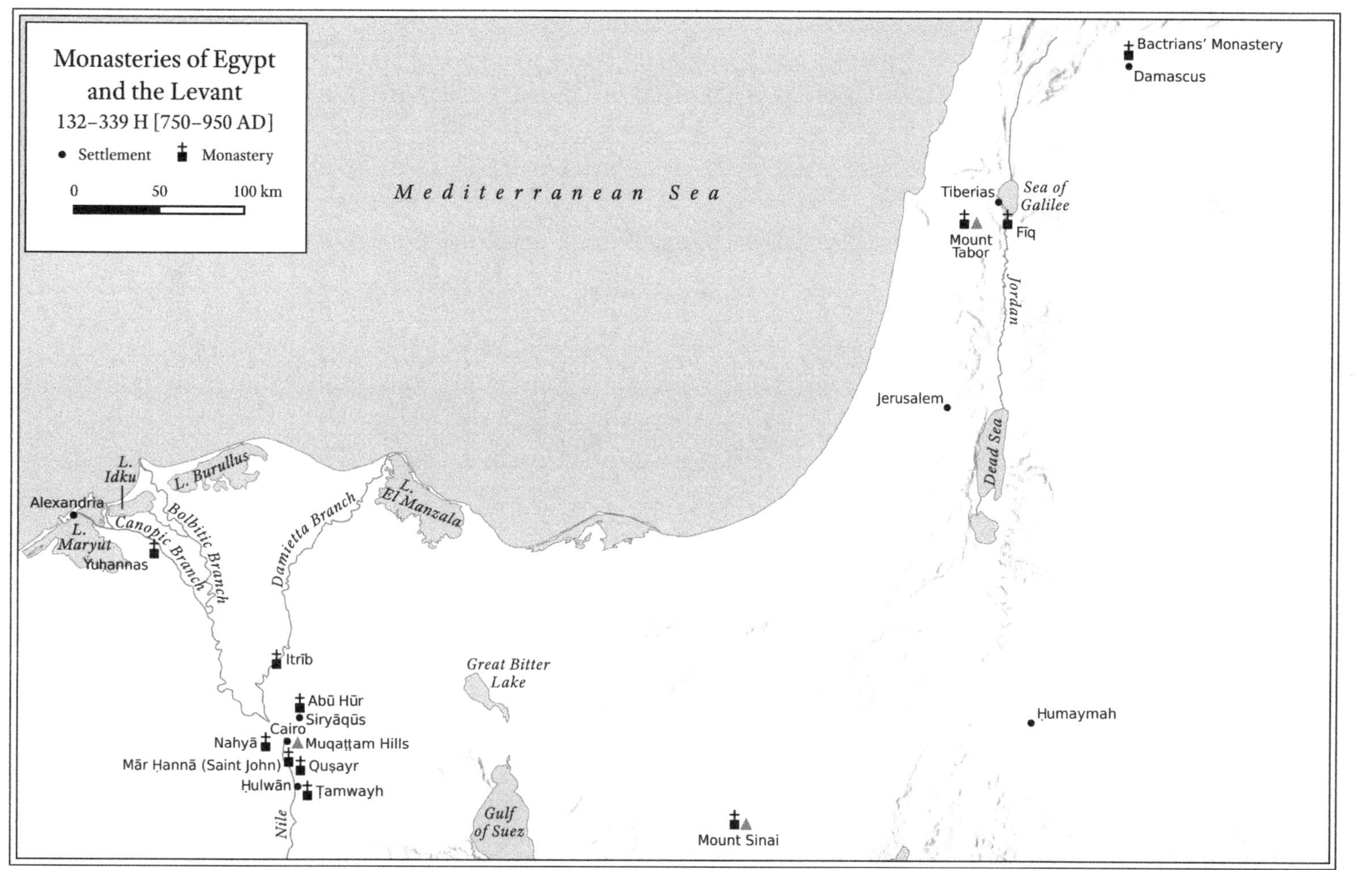
Monasteries of Egypt and the Levant
132–339 H [750–950 AD]
Settlement
Monastery
0
50
100 km
Mediterranean Sea
Bactrians' Monastery
Damascus
Tiberias
Sea of Galilee
Mount Tabor
Fīq
Jordan
Jerusalem
Dead Sea
L. Idku
L. Burullus
Alexandria
L. Maryut
Yuhannas
Canopic Branch
Bolbitic Branch
Damietta Branch
L. El Manzala
Itrīb
Great Bitter Lake
Abū Hūr
Siryāqūs
Cairo
Nahyā
Muqaṭṭam Hills
Mār Ḥannā (Saint John)
Quṣayr
Ḥulwān
Ṭamwayh
Nile
Gulf of Suez
Mount Sinai
Ḥumaymah

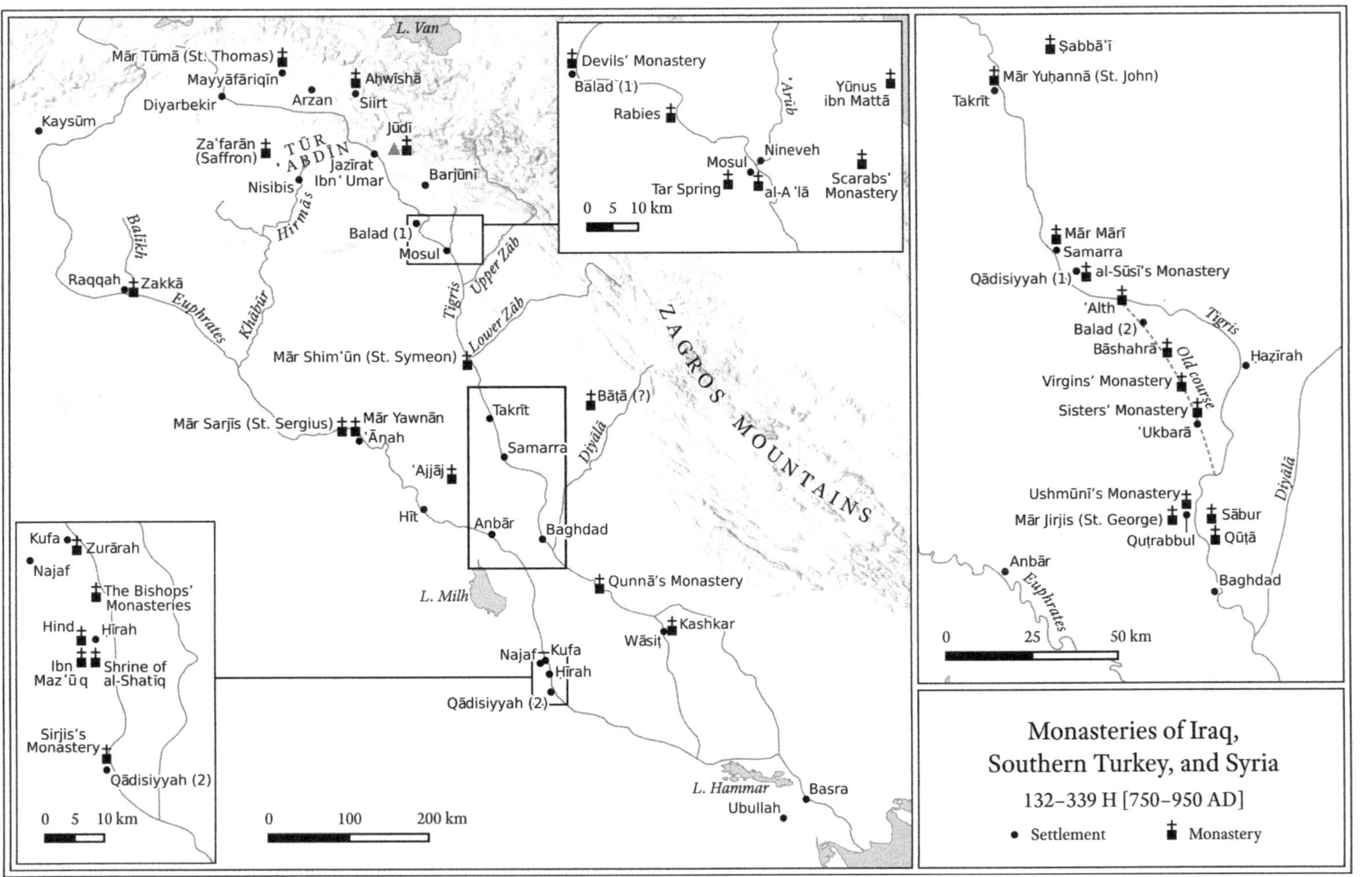

Monasteries of Iraq, Southern Turkey, and Syria
132–339 H [750–950 AD]
Settlement
Monastery
L. Van
Mār Tūmā (St. Thomas)
Mayyāfāriqīn
Arzan
Aḥwīshā
Siirt
Diyarbekir
Kaysūm
Jūdī
Za'farān (Saffron)
ṬŪR 'ABDĪN
Jazīrat Ibn 'Umar
Barjūnī
Nisibis
Hirmās
Balīkh
Balad (1)
Mosul
Raqqah
Zakkā
Euphrates
Khābūr
Tigris
Upper Zāb
Lower Zāb
Mār Shim'ūn (St. Symeon)
ZAGROS MOUNTAINS
Takrīt
Bāṭā (?)
Mār Sarjīs (St. Sergius)
Mār Yawnān
'Ānah
Samarra
Diyālā
'Ajjāj
Hīt
Anbār
Baghdad
L. Milh
Qunnā's Monastery
Kashkar
Wāsiṭ
Najaf
Kufa
Ḥīrah
Qādisiyyah (2)
L. Hammar
Basra
Ubullah
0 100 200 km
Devils' Monastery
Balad (1)
Rabies
'Arūb
Yūnus ibn Mattā
Nineveh
Mosul
Tar Spring
al-A'lā
Scarabs' Monastery
0 5 10 km
Kufa
Zurārah
Najaf
The Bishops' Monasteries
Hind
Ḥīrah
Ibn Maz'ūq
Shrine of al-Shatīq
Sirjis's Monastery
Qādisiyyah (2)
0 5 10 km
Ṣabbā'ī
Mār Yuḥannā (St. John)
Takrīt
Mār Mārī
Samarra
Qādisiyyah (1)
al-Sūsī's Monastery
'Alth
Balad (2)
Tigris
Bāshahrā
Old course
Ḥazīrah
Virgins' Monastery
Sisters' Monastery
'Ukbarā
Diyālā
Ushmūnī's Monastery
Mār Jirjis (St. George)
Quṭrabbul
Sābur
Qūṭā
Anbār
Euphrates
Baghdad
0 25 50 km

Note on the Text

The Edition

Only one manuscript of al-Shābushtī's *Kitāb al-Diyārāt* is known. It is Berlin ar. 8321 in the Staatsbibliothek zu Berlin (Preussischer Kulturbesitz), which formed part of the collection acquired by Johann Gottfried Wetzstein while he was Prussian consul in Damascus (1848–62). The colophon reads:

تمّ كتاب الديارات بحمد الله وعونه وقوّته وحسن توفيقه ووافق الفراغ منه في ليلة صباحها يوم الخميس السادس عشر من شهر ربيع الآخر سنة إحدى وثلاثين وستّمائة.

كتبه العبد الفقير إلى رحمة الله عبد الحليم بن محمّد بن عبد الوهّاب ابن عربي الدمشقيّ المعروف جدّه بالنحويّ وهو يسأل الله أن يغفر ذنوبه ويستر عيوبه.

والحمد لله ربّ العالمين وصلّى الله على محمّد سيّد المرسلين وعلى آله وصحبه أجمعين وسلّم تسليمًا كبيرًا إلى يوم الدين.

God be praised, *The Book of Monasteries* was successfully completed with His help and strength on the eve of Thursday, Rabi al-Thani 16, 631 [January 19, 1234].

It was copied by ʿAbd al-Ḥalīm ibn Muḥammad ibn ʿAbd al-Wahhāb ibn ʿArabī al-Dimashqī, whose grandfather (or forefather) was known as "the Grammarian." He asks God to forgive his sins and cover up his faults.

Praise be to God, Lord of the Worlds, and His blessings upon Muḥammad, the Prince of prophets, his family, and all his Companions. And blessings upon them until the Day of Judgment.

The manuscript consists of 135 folios with fifteen lines to a page and is incomplete, with an unknown number of quires missing at the beginning and at least one missing in the middle. There was almost certainly a heading for the first and longest section in the book, on the monasteries in Iraq, al-Jazīrah, Syria, and Palestine, to match the headings for Egypt and the monasteries known for wonders and healing later on. Folio 135b has been used for writing exercises. The manuscript has been rebound, and occasionally a marginal note has been cut.

The manuscript [الأصل] is clearly and legibly written in brown ink. It occasionally has catchwords. There are very few corrections. There is one small lacuna on folio 7 due to a tear. A reader of a different sectarian persuasion has erased words in two places. Diacritical points are sometimes lacking, particularly in combinations including *bā'*, *tā'*, *thā'*, *yā'*, or *nūn*. Vowels are often supplied. In the writing of numbers, superscript *alif* is usually omitted and the word *ālāf* is consistently written as *alf*. Final *hamzah* is omitted, as is the bearer of medial *hamzah* at times. Final *alif maqṣūrah* is often replaced by *alif*. *Alif al-wiqāyah* occurs frequently. In the prose passages, there are occasional Middle Arabic traits in gender agreement or case endings; it cannot be ascertained whether these stem from the author or the copyist. Where I have made them conform to standard usage in the edition, I have given the manuscript's version in a footnote. Errors in number have been silently corrected, as have errors in pronoun agreement. Stylistic or syntactic Middle Arabic traits have been retained, with a footnote confirming their existence in the manuscript. Names of Syriac origin are given as they appear in the manuscript. The word *mār* ("Saint"), a borrowing from Syriac, is spelt variously *mār*, *mar*, or *mā* in the headings. The manuscript spelling is retained in the headings but in the translation Mār is used consistently.

A mark in red ink of the owner and reader, Sirāj al-Dīn ʿAbd al-Raḥmān Aḥmad ibn Aḥmad ibn Muḥammad al-Zarʿī al-Anṣārī al-Ḥanafī, on the last page is dated 927/1520–21.[40] Red ink has also been used, probably by this owner, to add sporadic overlinings, catchwords, commas, and dots singly or in triangles; he also makes marginal comments using both red and black ink. Other marginal comments in black ink appear to be from at least two hands, one of which may be the copyist's, and folio 108a has a note in Turkish. I have not mentioned the marginal interjection *qif* ("stop!") as a sign of appreciation, but brief marginal indications of contents and comments conveying the reader's appreciation of certain passages are given in the notes.

The *Kitāb al-Diyārāt* was edited and annotated by Kūrkīs ʿAwwād ([عواد]). This edition helpfully supplies diacritical points missing in the manuscript, and it has made my task much easier. ʿAwwād was working from photos of the manuscript and sometimes he misread it; he also occasionally omitted words or even phrases. He often supplements the MS with additional phrases from parallel texts. I have not followed him in this, nor have I noted where my reading differs from his. I have, however, mentioned instances where I have adopted his reading. Where possible, I have identified citations of verses in *akhbār* and poetry.

I have followed the LAL guidelines about marking the vowels, and so have often omitted vowels given in the prose sections of the manuscript. I have added *hamzat al-qaṭʿ* and lexical *shaddah*. *Waṣlah*s are only given in the poetry.

*Isnād*s in this text are the exception, not the rule. When an *isnād* mentions more than one name, I have put it on a separate line. A single name for a source, however, is incorporated into the main text.

Prose and poetry passages restored in damaged parts of the manuscript on the basis of readings in other texts are listed here, as are emendations derived from such texts.

§1	Heading دير دُرمالس absent from the manuscript.
§1.13	Absent from the manuscript, completed from Yāqūt, *Muʿjam al-udabāʾ*, 167–68. (The edition has continuous pagination.)
§2.12	A tear in the manuscript, completed from Arazi, *Amour divin et amour profane dans l'Islam médiéval à travers le Dīwān de Khālid al-Kātib*, 256, no. 44.
§2.13	A tear in the manuscript, completed from Arazi, *Amour divin et amour profane*, 256, no. 44.
§7.1	Emendation supplied by ʿAwwād on the basis of the meter and al-Iṣbahānī, *Kitāb al-Aghānī* 7:200.
§12.2	Emendation from al-Sūdānī, *Jaḥẓah al-Barmakī: al-adīb al-shāʿir*, 271.
§12.2	Two lines absent in the original, added from Yāqūt, *Muʿjam al-buldān*, 2:524.
§13.32	A line erased in the manuscript (f. 53r). It and the accompanying three verses are wrongly attributed to Ibn al-Rūmī. They are by the state secretary Abū Ghamr al-Ṭamrī, mourning al-Ḥasan ibn Zayd, ruler of Ṭabaristān (d. 270/884) (al-Marzubānī, *Muʿjam al-shuʿarāʾ*, 463).
§13.35	Words partially erased on f. 53v.
§13.45	Emendation from al-Ṭabarī, *Taʾrīkh al-rusul wa-l-mulūk*, 8:622.

§19.1	Emendation from Yāqūt, *Muʿjam al-buldān*, 2:543.
§24.11	A word partially erased on f. 92v.
§26.13	Emendation from al-Iṣbahānī, *Aghānī* 5:175.
§30.2	Emendation from al-Tawḥīdī, *al-Baṣāʾir wa-l-dhakāʾir*, 1:195.
§30.7	Emendation from Ibn Faḍlallāh al-ʿUmarī, *Masālik al-abṣār fī mamālik al-amṣār*, 1:285.
§32.1	Emendation from Ibn Faḍlallāh al-ʿUmarī, *Masālik al-abṣār*, 1:324.
§33.11	Emendation from al-Iṣbahānī, *Aghānī*, 7:49.
§37.3	Emendations from al-Najjār, *Shuʿarāʾ ʿabbāsiyūn mansiyyūn*, 6:29.

The Translation

The material al-Shābushtī includes varies widely in tone and style, from the elaborate, balanced periods of formal letters of condolence, to apparently straightforward historical narrative, to the crude repartee of singing girls and their boyfriends. I have endeavored to reflect these differences in my rendering. The translations of poetry are freer than those of prose. Arabic poetry rhymes, and I have searched for rhymes in English to correspond, although I have not often been successful. I have paid attention to rhythm, trying to create an echo of the meters of Arabic verse.

One problem that often occurred was how to translate "monastery." It is a difficult word to work into poetry, and I have frequently replaced it with "convent," which, while nowadays associated more with women's communities, historically applied to establishments of either monks or nuns.

The relationship expressed in a monastery's name may be possessive, locative, or dedicative. Depending on the type of relationship, I have adopted different styles of translation. Here are the various styles, with examples: for founders of monasteries, "Sābur's Monastery"; for beings associated with monasteries, "the Monastery of the Foxes," "the Monastery of the Confessors"; for a saint to whom the monastery is dedicated, "the Monastery of Saint George"; and for places, either "Durmālis Monastery" or "the Monastery at ʿAlth," depending partly on euphony. While Arabic *dayr* is consistently translated as "monastery" in the prose passages, at times it has been retained in the poetry for the sake of rhythm.

As in the edition, chains of transmission of authorities have only been set apart in the translation when more than two names are mentioned. Al-Shābushtī's attitude to citing his sources is extraordinarily casual, and such chains are the exception.

Many passages are introduced with *qāla* ("he said"), without it being clear who is speaking. One may see such instances of *qāla* as marking a new paragraph or introducing a new anecdote rather than referring to a specific speaker. In such cases, I have generally omitted *qāla*. When several poems by the same poet are quoted, each one introduced by *wa-qāla*, I have grouped them under a heading such as "Here are some poems he composed," rather than introducing each one with "and he said."

I have transliterated the names of saints and personalities of the Syriac tradition in the form in which they appear in al-Shābushtī's text. If they have a recognized equivalent in English, I have given it in brackets when the name is first mentioned.

Notes to the Introduction

1 These characteristics of monks can be found in Arabic texts by Muslims treating ascetic and mystical subjects, and also in wisdom literature and some belles lettres. See, for a discussion of the various significances they have, Mourad, "Christian Monks in Islamic Literature: A Preliminary Report on Some Arabic *Apothegmata Patrum*."

2 See al-Shābushtī, *Kitāb al-Diyārāt*, ed. ʿAwwād, 23–30, for the medieval accounts of his life and writings.

3 Kennedy, *The Prophet and the Age of the Caliphates: The Islamic Near East from the Sixth to the Eleventh Century*, 173. Kennedy's book is a readable and reliable introduction to the first four centuries of Muslim rule in the Middle East.

4 The translation is Jack Tannous's from an unpublished paper.

5 I follow the order given by Yaiche in *Les "livres des couvents", un genre littéraire arabe médiéval: L'élite musulman et le couvent chrétien* with his explanation of this chronology (118–19). Yaiche (221–23) includes a further book, Muḥammad ibn al-Ḥasan ibn Ramaḍān al-Naḥwī's *Kitāb al-Diyarah* (or *al-Dabrah*), of which nothing has survived but which is mentioned by Ibn al-Nadīm in the *Fihrist*, 29, and by Yāqūt in *al-Khazal wa-l-da'l bayn al-dūr wa-l-dārāt wa-l-diyarah*, 1:249. Since his only other title in the *Fihrist* is on names of wine and derived juices, and since he is classified in the section on writers on grammar and language, it is unlikely that his book, whatever its title, had much in common with the five works mentioned here.

6 The widely held belief that al-Iṣbahānī was connected with the court in Aleppo is a later invention (Kilpatrick, *Making the Great Book of Songs: Composition and the Author's Craft in Abū l-Faraj al-Iṣbahānī's Kitāb al-Aghānī*, 19–20).

7 Al-ʿAṭiyyah, ed., *al-Diyārāt li-Abī al-Faraj al-Iṣbahānī.*

8 Zakharia, "Le moine et l'échanson ou le *Kitāb al-diyārāt* d'al-Šābuštī et ses lecteurs," 61n10.

9 Compilations in particular could sometimes take years to complete. Abū al-Faraj al-Iṣbahānī is rumored to have worked on his great *Book of Songs* (*Kitāb al-Aghānī*) for fifty years; at all events, he never finished it (Kilpatrick, *Making the Great Book of Songs*, 30).

10 Yaiche, *Les "livres des couvents,"* 107–219, presents the excerpts from these books quoted in later sources.

11 Ibn Khallikān, *Wafayāt al-aʿyān*, 3:319.

12 The conventions of premodern Arabic historical writing (systematic indications of written or oral sources, the author's or compiler's comments on the veracity of his material, and the quotation of alternative accounts of the same event) are conspicuously absent from *The Book of Monasteries*.

13 Katia Zakharia aptly uses the refrain of Mary Hopkin's song, of which this is the first line, as the epigraph for her article.

14 Zakharia, "'Un paradis sans éternité': Note sur la poésie et les poètes cités dans le *Kitāb al-Diyārāt* (Livre sur les couvents) de Šābuštī (m. 388/998)," 12–13, 16–18.

15 See Gruendler, "Verse and Taxes: The Function of Poetry in Selected Literary *Akhbār* of the Third/Ninth Century," 96–104, for a discussion of this anecdote and the correlation between poetic and monetary currency.

16 See, for the types of poetry anthologies, Orfali, *The Anthologist's Art: Abū Manṣūr al-Thaʿālibī and His Yatīmat al-dahr*, 10–33.

17 See, for examples, Kilpatrick, "Anthologies, Medieval" in *Encyclopedia of Arabic Literature*, 94–96. Detailed studies of some individual and highly diverse anthologies are found in Orfali and El Cheikh (eds.), *Approaches to the Study of Pre-Modern Arabic Anthologies*.

18 Particularly in the early Abbasid period, the issue of leadership of the Muslim community was expressed in terms of the right to inherit. Marwān ibn Abī Ḥafṣah, an Abbasid loyalist, refuted ʿAlid claims in a famous line of poetry recited before al-Mahdī, which, according to some reports, led a Shiʿi supporter to murder him. The line ran "How could it be—no, it cannot be—that the children of daughters are heirs to their uncles" (*Aghānī*, 10:89, 94–95).

19 Of other religious communities, Jews are mentioned a handful of times as vintners and tavern keepers. Zoroastrians are also mentioned as vintners, and a crypto-Zoroastrian masquerades as a Christian, while Zoroastrianism as the official religion of the Sassanians is once recalled. Though Manichaeism was a widespread religion at the time, it only appears in a passing reference to a Manichaean monastery.

20 Although precise data do not exist, the consensus among historians now is that Islam became the majority religion in the Middle East later than was traditionally thought. Tannous, *The Making of the Medieval Middle East: Religion, Society, and Simple Believers*, chaps. 11 and 12, discusses the subject of conversion in detail. Cf. also Kennedy, *The Prophet and the Age of the Caliphates*, 173–74; and, for the conditions favoring conversion, Ellenblum, "Demography, Geography, and the Accelerated Islamisation of the Eastern Mediterranean."

21 Allard, "Les Chrétiens à Baġdād," 376.

22 This church has often but erroneously been labeled "Nestorian." See, for example, Winkler, "Terminology."

23 Melling and Parry, "Christology."

24 The conflicts between the Syrian Orthodox Church and the Church of the East during the sixth and seventh centuries are set out in Jullien, "S'affirmer en s'opposant: Les polémistes du Grand Monastère (VIe–VIIe siècle)."

25 These monasteries, Qunnā and Kaskar, belonged to the Church of the East, whose monks built their own cells after a period of probation (Baumer, *The Church of the East: An Illustrated History of Assyrian Christianity*, 130, quoting the canons of the sixth-century Abbot Dadisho).

26 Al-Shābushtī notes that another monastery was originally dedicated to Mār Mikhā'īl before becoming known for Bactrian camels kept there (§25.1).

27 Zakharia, "Le moine et l'échanson," 70; Tannous, *The Making of the Medieval Middle East*, 466; Atiya, "Some Egyptian Monasteries According to the Unpublished MS. of al-Shābushtī's *Kitāb al-diyārāt*," 4. Wine was also available in taverns kept by Christians and Jews, but these seem often to have been sordid places (cf. §28.2).

28 This is a standard element found in other *Books of Monasteries* (Yaiche, *Les "livres des couvents,"* 17, 105, 175, 186).

29 Inside a city, riotous behavior could call down the ire of the authorities, as the fate of Abū ʿAlī ibn al-Rashīd shows (§§5.3–4). *Pace* Sizgorich, "The Dancing Martyr: Violence, Identity, and the Abbasid Postcolonial," 11, although the police chief judged Abū ʿAlī to be a disgrace to the caliphal family and the Muslim community, the neighbors who complained about him are not specified as Muslims.

30 References to such gatherings in *The Book of Monasteries* include §5.16, §7.7, §9.11, and §33.13.

31 Dmitriev, "The Symbolism of Wine in Early Arabic Love Poetry: Observations on the Poetry of Abū Ṣakhr al-Hudhalī," discussing the poetry of Abū Ṣakhr al-Hudhalī.

32 As Yaiche observes (*Les "livres des couvents,"* 243–44, 248–49), al-Shābushtī often mentions crowds attending the monasteries. The monasticism of the Church of the East was notable for engagement with the civic life of villages, towns, and cities, and for constant interaction with laypeople of every kind (Harvey, "Monasticism," 293–94). For more on monasteries as a center of Syriac culture and learning, see the survey in Debié, "Livres et monastères en Syrie-Mésopotamie d'après les sources syriaques."

33 It has been argued recently that the view of Christianity and Christians found in the books of monasteries is "postcolonial"—namely, that of Muslim men of the imperial Abbasid elite who desire to see themselves reflected in the desiring gaze of their submissive non-Muslim subjects (Sizgorich, "The Dancing Martyr"). His interpretation

is informed by a simplistic view of early Islamic history as one of "the brutality of the Arab conquests" that subjugated the Christians (14). The social dynamics involved were far more complex and included differentiation according to ethnic origin and class. Cf. §§33.15–17 and the discussion of it in Lagrange, "Une affair de viol."

34 Yaiche, *Les "livres des couvents,"* 49–52.

35 Ṣāʿid was extremely competent, whereas his brother is portrayed as slightly ridiculous and lacking appropriate qualifications for his position. This is just as likely to reflect a real incompetence as anti-Christian bias; "jobs for the boys" is a universal phenomenon. Interestingly, al-Shābushtī does not mention a possible motive contributing to the hostility to Ṣāʿid and ʿAbdūn that is found in other sources: ʿAbdūn's success in restoring the patriarchal seat of the Church of the East just outside Baghdad after it had been vandalized (Fiey, *Chrétiens syriaques sous les Abbasides surtout à Bagdad (749–1258)*, 115–16; Sourdel, *Le vizirate ʿAbbāside de 749 à 936 (132 à 324 de l'Hégire)*, 321–22).

36 Tannous, *The Making of the Medieval Middle East*, 386–89.

37 See n. 31 above.

38 Al-Masʿūdī, *Murūj al-dhahab wa-maʿādin al-jawhar*, 2:69–70 = §779–80.

39 This and the section on the Bactrians' Monastery (§25) are the only two sections in the main part of the book that do not begin with a descriptive poem.

40 The note, in the margin of the manuscript, reads:

أنهاه مطالعة متملكه سراج الدين عبد الرحمٰن بن أحمد بن أحمد بن محمد الزرعيّ الأنصاريّ الحنفيّ في ٩٢٧.

("Its owner, Sirāj al-Dīn ʿAbd al-Raḥmān ibn Aḥmad ibn Aḥmad ibn Muḥammad al-Zurʿī al-Anṣārī al-Ḥanafī, completed the perusal of it in 927.")

كتاب الديارات

The Book of Monasteries

[ديـر دُرمالســـ]

١،١ [. . .][1] الدار التي بناها الديلمي أحمد بن بويه بباب الشمّاسيّة وموقعه أحسن موقع وهو نزه كثير البساتين والأشجار وبقربه أجمة قصب وهو كبير آهل برهبانه وقسّانه والمتبتّلين فيه وهو من البقاع المعمورة بالقصف والمقصودة بالتنزّه والشرب.

٢،١ وأعياد النصارى ببغداد مقسومة على ديارات معروفة منها أعياد الصوم. فالأحد الأوّل منه عيده دير العاصية وهو على ميل من سَمالو والأحد الثاني دير الزُريقيّة والأحد الثالث دير الزَنْدَورد والأحد الرابع دير دُرمالَس هذا. وعيده أحسن عيد يجمع نصارى بغداد إليه ولا يبقى أحد ممّن يحبّ اللّهو والخلاعة إلّا تبعهم. ويقيم الناس فيه الأيّام ويطرقونه في غير الأعياد.

٣،١ ولأبي عبد الله بن حمدون النديم فيه

يَا دَيْرَ دُرمَالَسَ مَا أَحْسَنَكْ   وَيَا غَزَالَ ٱلدَّيْرِ مَا أَفْتَنَكْ
لَئِنْ سَكَنْتَ ٱلدَّيْرَ لَا سَيِّدِي   فَإِنَّ فِي جَوْفِ ٱلْحَشَا مَسْكَنَكْ
وَيْحَكَ يَا قَلْبُ أَمَا تَنْتَهِي   عَنْ شِدَّةِ ٱلْوَجْدِ بِمَنْ أَحْزَنَكْ
اِرْفَقْ بِهِ بِٱللهِ يَا سَيِّدِي   فَإِنَّهُ مِنْ حَيْنِهِ مَكَّنَكْ

٤،١ وكان من خبر هذا الشعر ما ذكره أحمد بن خالد الصَّرِيفينيّ قال كنّا عند أبي عبد الله بن حمدون في الوقت الذي نفاه فيه المتوكّل فتذاكرنا الديارات وطيبها وحسنها في الأعياد واجتماع الناس إليها فقال قد والله شهّيتني لحضور هذه المواضع والتفرّج فيها والتسلّي بها فأيّ دير منها قد حضر عيده فقلت دير دُرمالَس وغداً عيده

[1] هذا بداية المخطوط والأصل ناقص.

The Durmālis Monastery

. . .[1] the palace built by Aḥmad ibn Buwayh the Daylamite at the Shammāsiyyah Gate. It is delightful and excellently situated, surrounded by many gardens and trees, and with a reed bed close by. It is large and well populated with resident monks, priests, and other celibates. It is well equipped for revelry, and people go there to stroll about and drink. 1.1

In Baghdad, the Christian holidays are celebrated at different well-known monasteries. During the season of Lent, the first Sunday is celebrated at the ʿĀṣiyah Monastery, which is over a mile (a little less than two kilometers) from Samālū; the second at the Zurayqiyyah Monastery; the third at the Zandaward Monastery; and the fourth at this monastery, Durmālis. It is a splendid feast attended by all the Christians of Baghdad, and everyone who enjoys amusement and debauchery follows them to it. People stay there for several days. They even go there when there is no feast. 1.2

The caliph's boon companion Abū ʿAbdallāh ibn Ḥamdūn composed this poem about it: 1.3

> O for the beauty of Durmālis's Cloister,
> O for the charm of the monastery's fawn!
> If, master, you seem to dwell in a cell,
> your home is deep in my breast.
> Alas, my heart, can't you forgo
> your passion for him who has grieved you?
> Show him mercy, for God's sake, master,
> for he's left you his life to barter.

The story of this poem was told by Aḥmad ibn Khālid al-Ṣarīfīnī: We were visiting Abū ʿAbdallāh ibn Ḥamdūn after al-Mutawakkil had banished him. We reminisced about monasteries, how pleasant they are and how beautiful during festivals when people gather in them. Abū ʿAbdallāh said, "By God, you've made me want to visit these places, look around, and take my mind off my problems. Which monastery celebrates its feast about now?" I replied, 1.4

قال فعلى بركة الله وأعددت جميع ما نحتاج إليه ويصلح لمثله وبكّرنا إلى الدير ونظرنا إلى اجتماع الناس وتعييدهم وانصرف من انصرف وأقمت معه في الدير ذلك اليوم ومن غده وجلسنا منه مجلساً يشرف على تلك البساتين والمزارع فشرب وطابت نفسه وطرب وحضره من أحداث الموضع مَن كان يقضي لنا الحاجة ويجيئنا بالطرفة والتحيّة فشغف بهم واستطاب وقته منهم وقال الأبيات المتقدّمة.

٥،١ وكان سبب نفي المتوكّل له أنّ الفتح بن خاقان كان يعشق شاهك خادم المتوكّل واشتُهر الأمر فيه حتّى بلغه وله فيه أشعار منها

أَشَاهَكُ لَيْلِي مُذْ هَجَرْتَ طَوِيلُ   وَعَيْنِي دَماً بَعْدَ ٱلدُّمُوعِ تَسِيلُ
وَبِي مِنْكَ وَٱلرَّحْمٰنِ مَا لَا أُطِيقُهُ   وَلَيْسَ إِلَى شَكْوَى إِلَيْكَ سَبِيلُ
أَشَاهَكُ لَوْ يُجْزَى ٱلْمُحِبُّ بِوُدِّهِ   جُزِيتُ وَلٰكِنَّ ٱلْوَفَاءَ قَلِيلُ

٦،١ وكان أبو عبد الله يسعى فيما يحبّه الفتح فعرف المتوكّل الخبر فقال له إنّما أردتك وأدنيتك لتنادمني ليس لتقود على غلماني فانكر ذلك وحلف يميناً حنث فيها فطلّق من كانت حرّة وأعتق من كانت مملوكة ولزمه حجّ ثلاثين سنة فكان يحجّ في كلّ عام. قال فأمر المتوكّل بنفيه إلى تكريت فأقام بها أيّاماً ثمّ جاءه زرافة بالليل على البريد فظنّ أنّه لمّا شرب وسكر أمر بقتله فلمّا دخل عليه قال جئت في شيء ما كنت أحبّ أن أجيء في مثله. قال وما هو قال أمر أمير المؤمنين بقطع أذنك وقال قل له لست أعاملك إلّا كما يَعمل الفتيان. فرأى ذلك أسهل ممّا ظنّه من القتل. فقطع غضروف أذنه من خارج ولم يستقصّه وجعله في كافور معه وانصرف.

"Durmālis's Monastery. Its feast is tomorrow." "With God's blessing! Let's go." I prepared everything we would need as was appropriate for someone in his station, and we set off early to the monastery. We saw the people gather and celebrate the feast. Then some of the company left, but I stayed with him in the monastery that day and the next. We sat in a room overlooking the gardens and fields. Abū ʿAbdallāh drank some wine, cheered up, and went into raptures. Some local youths came to take care of our needs, bringing us presents and sweet-smelling bouquets, and he was much taken by them. They were the reason he had a wonderful time and composed the poem above.

Al-Mutawakkil banished Abū ʿAbdallāh because al-Fatḥ ibn Khāqān had a passion for Shāhak, al-Mutawakkil's servant. The news got about and reached Abū ʿAbdallāh, who made Shāhak the subject of several poems, such as: 1.5

> Shāhak, when you'd left, the night dragged on
> and my eyes shed tears—tears of blood.
> God knows my feelings for you are past bearing
> but I've no way to reach you with my pleading.
> Shāhak! If a lover were requited for his love
> I'd be rewarded. But are debts ever paid in full?

Abū ʿAbdallāh made it his business to carry out al-Fatḥ's wishes. Al-Mutawakkil summoned him when he came to hear of it. "I sought you out and placed you close to me to keep me company, not to be a pimp for my servants." Abū ʿAbdallāh denied any wrongdoing and swore an oath in which he perjured himself. Consequently, he had to divorce his freeborn wives and set his concubines free. He was also obliged to perform the pilgrimage for thirty years, so he used to make it every year.[2] Al-Mutawakkil exiled him to Takrit and he spent a few days there. Then one night, Zurāfah came to him as part of the government messenger service.[3] Abū ʿAbdallāh thought that the caliph was drunk and ordered him to be killed. When the officer entered his presence, he said, "I've come for a purpose I'd rather not have come for." "What's that?" "The caliph gave the order to cut off your ear and sent you this message: 'I'm just treating you like a brigand.'"[4] Abū ʿAbdallāh realized that this punishment was much milder than the execution he had feared. Zurāfah cut off the outer cartilage of his ear without perforating the eardrum, placed it in camphor he'd brought with him, and left. 1.6

١،٧ ثمّ حُدر أبو عبد الله إلى بغداد إلى منزله فأقام به مدّة. قال أبو عبد الله فلقيت إسحاق بن إبراهيم الموصليّ بعدما كُفّ بصره فسألني عن أخبار الناس والسلطان فأخبرته ثمّ شكوت إليه غمّي بقطع أذني فجعل يسلّيني ويعزّيني ثمّ قال لي من المتقدّم اليوم عند أمير المؤمنين والخاصّ من ندمائه فقلت محمّد بن عمر. فقال لي ومن هذا الرجل وما مقدار أدبه وعلمه فقلت أمّا أدبه فلا أدري ولكنّي أخبرك بما سمعت منه منذ قريب. حضرنا الدار يوم عقد المتوكّل لأولاده الثلاثة فدخل مروان بن أبي حفصة فأنشده قصيدته التي يقول فيها

بَيْضَاءُ فِي وَجَنَاتِهَا وَرْدٌ فَكَيْفَ لَنَا بِشَمِّهْ

١،٨ فسُرّ بذلك سرورًا شديدًا وأمر فنثر عليه بدْرةَ دنانير وأن تُلقط وتُطرح في حجره. وأمره بالجلوس وعقد له على اليمامة والبحرين. فقال يا أمير المؤمنين ما رأيت كاليوم قطّ ولا أرى أبقاك الله ما دامت السموات والأرض فقال محمّد بن عمر هذا بعد عمر طويل إن شاء الله. فقال لي إسحاق ويلك جزعت على أذنك وغمّك قطعها لِمَ حتّى تسمع مثل هذا الكلام. ويلك لو أنّ لك مكّوك آذان أيش كان ينفعك مع هؤلاء.

١،٩ قال وأعاده المتوكّل إلى خدمته وكان إذا دعا به قال له على جهة المزاح يا أبا عبيد. ولمّا رضي عنه قال له هل لك في جارية أهبها لك فأكبر ذلك وأنكره فوهب له جارية يقال لها صاحب من جواريه حسنة كاملة الآداب إلّا أنّ بعض الخدم ردّ السبطانة على فمها وقد أرادت أن ترميه فصدع إحدى ثنيّتيها فاسودّت فشانها ذلك عنده وحمل معها كلّ ما كان لها وكان شيئًا عظيمًا كثيرًا. فلمّا مات أبو عبد الله تزوّجت صاحب بعض العلويّين. قال عليّ بن يحيى المنجّم فرأيته في النوم وهو يقول لي

Then Abū ʿAbdallāh was brought down to his house in Baghdad, where he stayed for a time. He recounted this incident: I met Isḥāq ibn Ibrāhīm al-Mawṣilī after he had lost his sight. He asked me news of people and the palace, which I gave him, and after that I complained to him, telling him how miserable I was about my ear being cut off. He comforted and consoled me, and then he asked, "Which of the caliph's companions is taking precedence nowadays and enjoying his favor?" "Muḥammad ibn ʿUmar." "Who is this man, and how polite and knowledgeable is he?" "I know nothing about his manners. But I can tell you what I heard about him recently. We were at the palace on the day of the investiture of al-Mutawakkil's three sons. Marwān ibn Abī Ḥafṣah entered and declaimed the poem in which he says: 1.7

pale, with roses in her cheeks. How can we ever breathe their scent?[5]

"Al-Mutawakkil was overjoyed with it. He ordered a purse of dinars[6] to be poured over him, picked up, and placed in his lap; told him to be seated; and made him commander over Yamāmah and Baḥrayn. Marwān responded, 'I've never seen a day like this, sire, and—may God give you long life—I shall not see another, as long as heaven and earth exist.' Whereupon Muḥammad ibn ʿUmar said, 'After a long life, God willing.'" Isḥāq said to me, "Good God! You're complaining about your ear being cut off, but why on earth are you upset? So you can hear things like this? Damn it, even if you had a thousand ears, what good would they do you with people like this?" 1.8

Then al-Mutawakkil restored Abū ʿAbdallāh to his service. Every time he spoke to him, he would call him Abū ʿUbayd[7] as a joke. After his pardon, he asked him, "Would you like me to give you one of my slave girls?" Abū ʿAbdallāh thought he was exaggerating and didn't believe him, but al-Mutawakkil gave him one of his slave girls, called Ṣāḥib.[8] She was beautiful and extremely well mannered, but a servant had broken one of her front teeth: Ṣāḥib had been taking aim with a blowpipe and the servant had pushed it into her mouth. The tooth turned black, and that ruined her appearance in al-Mutawakkil's eyes. He sent all her belongings with her, a huge quantity of things. After Abū ʿAbdallāh died, she married one of the ʿAlids. ʿAlī ibn Yaḥyā al-Munajjim said he saw Abū ʿAbdallāh in a dream, declaiming: 1.9

أَبَا عَـلِيٍّ مَا تَـرَى ٱلْعَجَائِبَـا   أَصْبَحَ جِسْمِي فِي ٱلتُّرَابِ غَائِبَـا
وَٱسْتَبْدَلَتْ صَاحِبُ بَعْدِي صَاحِبَـا

١٠،١ ولأبي عبد الله شعر جيّد ومن شعره يعاتب عليّ بن يحيى

مَنْ عَذِيرِي مِنْ أَبِي حَسَنٍ   حِينَ يَجْفُونِي وَيَصْرِمُنِي
كَانَ لِي خِلاًّ وَكُنْتُ لَهُ   كَٱمْتِزَاجِ ٱلرُّوحِ بِٱلْبَدَنِ
فَوَشَى وَاشٍ فَغَيَّرَهُ   وَعَلَيْهِ كَانَ يَحْسُدُنِي
إِنَّمَا يَزْدَادُ مَعْرِفَةً   بِوِدَادِي حِينَ يَفْقِدُنِي

١١،١ قال اتّصل بنجاح بن سلمة أنّ أبا عبد الله بن حمدون يذكره ويتنادر به بين يدي المتوكّل. فلقيه يوماً فقال له أبا عبد الله قد بلغني ذكرك لي بحضرة أمير المؤمنين بغير الجميل ولم يَخْفَ عليّ قولك إذا خلوت أتراني أحبّه وقد فعل بي ما فعل. والله ما وضعت يدي على أذني إلّا تجدّدت له بغضة في قلبي فقال ابن حمدون الطلاق له لازم إن كان قال هذا قطّ وامرأته طالق إن ذكرتك بغير ما تحبّه أبداً.

١٢،١ قال كان إبراهيم بن محمّد بن مدبّر يلاعب أبا عبد الله بالنرد فإذا غلبه شيئاً دفعه إلى كرديّة المغنّية جارية محمّد بن رجا. فغلبه يوماً عشرين ديناراً فأخذها منه ودفعها إليها فكتب إليه أبو عبد الله بعد ذلك

تَقْضِي ٱلْحُقُوقَ بِمَالِي   وَأَنْتَ تَعْرِفُ حَالِي
إِنْ دَامَ هٰذَا عَلَيَّ   أَفْقَرْتَنِي وَعِيَالِي

١٣،١ وكان حمدون بن إسماعيل ينادم المعتصم ثمّ الواثق بعده وكان يعابث المتوكّل في ذلك الوقت وجاءه مرّة بحيّة في كمّه وأخرج رأسها تعريضاً بأمّه شجاع وكان ذلك يعجب الواثق. قال فلمّا مات الواثق نادم المتوكّل قال فلمّا كان في بعض الأيّام أمر

Oh, Abū ʿAlī, marvels have no end.
My body's out of sight,
hidden in the ground.
My friend Ṣāḥib's replaced me
with a new friend.

Abū ʿAbdallāh produced fine poetry, such as these verses reproaching ʿAlī ibn Yaḥyā: 1.10

Who'll plead my case to Abū Ḥasan when he snubs me and cuts me dead?
He and I were close, inseparable like body and soul,
Till someone defamed me and filled him with envy.
He'll know well how true a friend I am—when he loses me.

Najāḥ ibn Salamah happened to hear that Abū ʿAbdallāh ibn Ḥamdūn was talking about him and making fun of him in al-Mutawakkil's presence. One day he met him and said, "Abū ʿAbdallāh, I've heard that you speak unkindly of me in the caliph's presence. I know that you say in private, 'Do you think I can love him after what he did to me? By God, hatred wells up in my heart every time I put my hand on my ear.'" Ibn Ḥamdūn replied, "I deserve to get divorced if I ever said this. And I swear I'll repudiate my wife if I ever say anything about you that you dislike." 1.11

Ibrāhīm ibn Muḥammad ibn Mudabbir used to play backgammon with Abū ʿAbdallāh, and he would give all his winnings to Kurdiyyah, the singing girl belonging to Muḥammad ibn Rajāʾ. One day he won twenty dinars, which he gave her. So Abū ʿAbdallāh wrote to him: 1.12

You pay your dues with my cash
when you know the state I'm in.
If this losing streak keeps on
you'll beggar my kith and kin.

Ḥamdūn ibn Ismāʿīl was a court companion of al-Muʿtaṣim and then of al-Wāthiq. In those days, he used to tease al-Mutawakkil. Once he came to him with a snake hidden in his sleeve and pulled out its head, alluding to al-Mutawakkil's mother's name, Shujāʿ.[9] Al-Wāthiq liked that a lot. After al-Wāthiq's death, Ḥamdūn became a companion of al-Mutawakkil. One day, al-Mutawakkil summoned Farīdah, his brother al-Wāthiq's slave girl—she was a peerless 1.13

المتوكّل بإحضار فريدة جارية أخيه الواثق وكانت من الحسن والإحسان على ما لم يُر مثله وقال للخدم إن لم تجئ فجيئوني برأسها. فأُحضرت ودُفع إليها عود فغنّت غناءً يشبه الندبة والمرثية فأسمعها وأمرها أن تغنّي غيره فبكت وغنّت غناءً شجيًّا بحزن فزاد[1] ذلك في طيب غنائها فوجم حمدون للرقّة الّتي تداخلته. فغضب المتوكّل ورأى أنّه فعل ذلك بسبب أخيه الواثق حزنًا عليه وكان يبغض كلّ من مال إليه. فأمر بنفيه إلى السند وضربه ثلاثمائة سوط. فسأل أن يكون الضرب من فوق الثياب لضعفه عن ذلك فأجيب إلى ذلك. وأقام منفيًّا ثلاث سنين.

١٤،١ قال دعا إبراهيم جماعة من المغنّين[2] فيهم جحظة وقاسم بن زرزور وكان فيها عمّه أبو محمّد بن حمدون فجعل إبراهيم يحاكي واحدًا واحدًا من المغنّين[3] فقال له عمّه لا تحاك جحظة ولا يكن بينك وبينه عمل فلم يقبل وحاكاه فلم يزل جحظة يحتال في شيء يكتب فيه إلى أن وجد رقعة فكتب فيها

حَصَلْتَ عَلَى حِكَايَةِ مَنْ يُغَنِّي   فَحَاكِ لَنَا ٱلْعَجُوزَ إِذَا تَغَنَّتْ
وَحَاكِ لَنَا لَبِيباً إِذْ أَتَاهَا   فَأَعْطَاهَا ٱلْقُمُدَّ كَمَا تَمَنَّتْ

وكان لبيب غلام أبيه وكانت أمّه تعشقه فلمّا قرأ الرقعة ارتعدت يده فقال له عمّه ألم أقل لك عقرب لا تقرب.

١٥،١ وحكى جحظة عن إبراهيم بن القاسم زرزور أنّ لاكهكيفيّ[4] كان حسن الغناء مجيدًا وكان يحسد إبراهيم بن أبي العُبيس على غنائه وشجا صوته فلمّا مات إبراهيم فكانت وفاته في أيّام المكتفي دخلت على لاكهكيفيّ والدموع في عينيّ فقال ما لك قلت مات إبراهيم قال بسلام. والله لو لم يمت لقتلته.

---

١ الأصل مطموس. ٢ الأصل: مغنيين. ٣ الأصل: مغنيين. ٤ كذا في الأصل.

beauty and singer—and said to the servants, "If she refuses, bring me her head." When present, with a lute in her hands, she sang a song that sounded like a dirge or a lament. He swore at her and told her to sing something else. She wept and sang a sad, moving song, which made her singing even more beautiful. Ḥamdūn stood speechless, overwhelmed by its loveliness. Al-Mutawakkil fell into a rage, thinking that his reaction was out of grief for his brother al-Wāthiq. (Al-Mutawakkil hated anyone who sided with his brother.) He exiled Ḥamdūn to Sind and sentenced him to three hundred lashes. Ḥamdūn asked to remain clothed for the beating because he was too weak to bear it otherwise, and his request was granted. He spent three years in exile.[10]

Ibrāhīm[11] had invited a number of singers, including Jaḥẓah and Qāsim ibn Zarzūr. His uncle Abū Muḥammad ibn Ḥamdūn was there too. When Ibrāhīm started to mimic the singers, one by one, his uncle warned him, "Don't imitate Jaḥẓah and don't get on the wrong side of him." But he took no notice and mimicked him. Jaḥẓah looked for something to write on, and he wrote on a slip of paper: 1.14

You've managed to mimic the singers;
now mimic your old woman as she sings,
And mimic Labīb when he comes to her
and gives her the fuck she longs for.

Labīb was Ibrāhīm's father's servant and his mother had taken a fancy to him. When he read the note, his hand started to shake. His uncle said to him, "What did I tell you? Give a scorpion a wide berth."

Jaḥẓah recounted the following anecdote he had heard from Ibrāhīm ibn al-Qāsim ibn Zarzūr: 1.15

Lākahkīfī had a good voice and sang well, but he envied Ibrāhīm ibn Abī ʿUbays his singing and his moving voice. When Ibrāhīm died—it was during al-Muktafī's caliphate—I went to see Lākahkīfī with tears in my eyes. He asked, "What's the matter?" I said, "Ibrāhīm's died." "Good riddance," he retorted. "By God, I'd have killed him if he hadn't died."

دير سمالو

وهـذا الدير شرقيّ بغداد بباب الشمّاسيّة على نهر المهديّ وهناك أرحية للماء وحوله بساتين وأشجار ونخل والموضع نزه حسن العمارة آهل بمن يطرقه وبمن فيه من رهبانه. وعيد الفصح ببغداد فيه منظر عجيب لأنّه لا يبقى نصرانيّ إلّا حضره وتقرّب فيه ولا أحد من أهل التطرّب واللّهو من المسلمين إلّا قصده للتنزّه فيه. وهو أحد متنزّهات بغداد المشهورة ومواطن القصف المذكورة. ١،٢

ولمحمّد بن عبد الملك الهاشميّ فيه ٢،٢

وَلَرُبَّ يَوْمٍ فِي سَمَالُو تَمَّ لِي ... فِيهِ ٱلسُّرُورُ وَغُيِّبَتْ أَحْزَانُهُ
وَأَخٍ يَشُوبُ حَدِيثَهُ بِحَلَاوَةٍ ... يَلْتَذُّ رَجْعَ حَدِيثِهِ نُدْمَانُهُ
جَعَلَ ٱلرَّحِيقَ مِنَ ٱلْمُدَامِ شَرَابَهُ ... وَٱلْمُحْسِنَاتُ مِنَ ٱلْأَوَانِسِ شَانُهُ
بَكَرَتْ عَلَيَّ بِهِ ٱلزِّيَارَةُ فَٱغْتَدَى ... طَرِبًا إِلَيَّ وَسَرَّنِي إِتْيَانُهُ
فَأَمَرْتُ سَاقِينَا وَقُلْتُ لَهُ ٱسْقِنَا ... قَدْ حَانَ وَقْتُ شَرَابِنَا وَأَوَانُهُ
فَتَلَاعَبَتْ بِعُقُولِنَا نَشَوَاتُهُ ... وَتَوَقَّدَتْ بِخُدُودِنَا نِيرَانُهُ
حَتَّى حَسِبْتُ لَنَا ٱلْبِسَاطَ سَفِينَةً ... وَٱلدَّيْرَ يَرْقُصُ حَوْلَنَا حِيطَانُهُ

ولخالد الكاتب فيه ٣،٢

يَا مَنْزِلَ ٱلْقَصْفِ فِي سَمَالُو ... مَا لِيَ عَنْ طِيبِكَ ٱنْتِقَالُ
وَاهًا لِأَيَّامِكَ ٱلْخَوَالِي ... وَٱلْعَيْشُ صَافٍ بِهَا زُلَالُ
تِلْكَ حَيَاةُ ٱلنُّفُوسِ حَقًّا ... وَكُلُّ مَا دُونَهَا مُحَالُ

The Samālū Monastery

This monastery is east of Baghdad at the Shammāsiyyah Gate on the Mahdī Canal, where the water mills are. Surrounded by gardens, trees, and palm groves, it is delightful and well cultivated, frequented by visitors as well as the monks who live there. At Easter in Baghdad, it is an amazing sight, because every Christian goes there to receive communion and Muslims who enjoy music making and fun all head for it to enjoy the surroundings. It is one of the best-known places for outings from Baghdad and is famous for the revelry it offers. 2.1

Muḥammad ibn ʿAbd al-Malik al-Hāshimī composed these verses about it: 2.2

How many days have I spent in Samālū,
where delight is sovereign, banishing sorrow
With a brother who laces his words with sweetness,
making his friends want to hear them again!
He chooses not wine[12] but nectar to drink,
spending his time with fine singing girls.
In the early morning he came to visit,
overjoyed to see me, as I was to see him.
"Cupbearer," I said, "pour out the wine;
for a morning's drink this is the time."
Its heady vapors played with our brains,
its fire was setting our cheeks ablaze,
Till I thought the carpet we sat on a ship
and the monastery's walls were dancing around us.

Khālid the Scribe has a poem on it too: 2.3

Samālū, home of revelry,
your charms I can't ever leave.
Oh, for the days gone by there,
with life untroubled in joy.
That's the life of true spirits;
anything less is absurd.

٤،٢ وهو أبو القاسم خالد بن يزيد الكاتب وكان مليح الشعر رقيقه لا يقول إلّا في الغزل ولا يتجاوز الأربعة أبيات ولا يزيد عليها ولم يكن له شعر في مدح ولا هجاء. وذكر ميمون ابن حمّاد قال دخل عليّ يوماً أبو عبد الله بن الأعرابيّ فقلت يا أبا عبد الله سمعت من شعر هذا الغُلَيم شيئاً قال من هو قلت خالد بن يزيد. قال لا وأنا لأحبّ ذلك. فصِح به .فجاء حتّى وقف فقلت أنشِدْ أبا عبد الله شيئاً من شعرك فقال إنّما أقول في شجون نفسي لا أمدح ولا أهجو . فقلت أنشِدْه فأنشده

أَقُولُ لِلسُّقْمِ عُدْ إِلَى بَدَنِي حُبّاً لِشَيْءٍ يَكُونُ مِنْ سَبَبِكْ

فقال ابن الأعرابيّ حسبك يا غلام فقد خُيِّل إليّ أنّ الرقّة قد جُمعت لك في هذا البيت.

٥،٢ قال جحظة حدّثني خالد الكاتب قال لم أشعر إلّا ورسول إبراهيم بن المهديّ قد وافاني فدخلت إليه فإذا برجل أسود مُشفَرانيّ قد غاص في الفراش. فاستجلسني فجلست فقال أنشِدْني شيئاً من شعرك فأنشدته

رَأَتْ مِنْهُ عَيْنِي مَنْظَرَيْنِ كَمَا رَأَتْ مِنَ ٱلْبَدْرِ وَٱلشَّمْسِ ٱلْمُضِيئَةِ بِٱلْأَرْضِ
عَشِيَّةَ حَيَّانِي بِوَرْدٍ كَأَنَّهُ خُدُودٌ أُضِيفَتْ بَعْضُهُنَّ إِلَى بَعْضِ
وَنَاوَلَنِي كَأْساً كَأَنَّ رُضَابَهَا دُمُوعِي لِمَا صَدَّ عَنْ مُقْلَتِي غَمْضِي
وَوَلَّى وَفِعْلُ ٱلسُّكْرِ فِي حَرَكَاتِهِ مِنَ ٱلرَّاحِ فِعْلُ ٱلرِّيحِ بِٱلْغُصْنِ ٱلْغَضِّ

٦،٢ وزحف حتّى صار في ثلثي المصلّى ثمّ قال يا بُنيّ شبّه الناس الخدود بالورد وشبّهت أنت الورد بالخدود. زدني فأنشدته

His full name was Abū l-Qāsim Khālid ibn Yazīd the state scribe. He composed fine, delicate poems but only on love, and only in quatrains, never longer. He did not compose panegyrics or satires. Maymūn ibn Ḥammād related: One day Abū ʿAbdallāh ibn al-Aʿrābī came to see me. I asked him, "Abū ʿAbdallāh, have you heard anything of this kid's poetry?" "Who is he?" "Khālid ibn Yazīd." "No. I'd like to. Summon him." He stood before us, and I told him, "Recite some of your poetry to Abū ʿAbdallāh." "But I only talk about my personal sorrows, I don't praise or satirize anyone." "Recite to him all the same." And this is what he recited: 2.4

I tell the disease, Come back to my body
for love of something you've caused.

Then Ibn al-Aʿrābī said, "That's enough, my boy. I think you've put into this verse the very essence of delicacy."

Jaḥẓah said that Khālid the Scribe told him: All of a sudden, a messenger sent by Ibrāhīm ibn al-Mahdī came for me. I was admitted into his presence and saw him, sunk deep in the cushions, a swarthy man with thick lips. He told me to sit down and I did so. He asked me to recite and I complied: 2.5

In two forms my eyes espied him,
moon and light-spreading sun.
That evening his greeting was roses,
like cheeks added one to another.
He gave me a cup filled with tears
pressed from my eyes by my grief.
Then he turned, swaying from the wine,
a tender bough in the breeze.

Ibrāhīm edged two-thirds of the way over the carpet. Then he said, "My boy, people have compared cheeks with roses, but you have compared roses with cheeks. Recite something else." 2.6

عَاتَبْتُ نَفْسِي فِي هَوَا كَ فَلَمْ أَجِدْهَا تَقْبَلُ
وَأَجَبْتُ دَاعِيَهَا إِلَيْكَ وَلَمْ أُطِعْ مَنْ يَعْذُلُ
لَا وَٱلَّذِي جَعَلَ ٱلْوُجُو هَ لِحُسْنِ وَجْهِكَ تَمْثُلُ
لَا قُلْتُ إِنَّ ٱلصَّبْرَ عَنْكَ مِنَ ٱلتَّصَابِي أَجْمَلُ

وزحف حتّى صار خارج المصلّى ثمّ قال زدني فأنشدته ٧،٢

عِشْ فَحُبِّيكَ سَرِيعًا قَاتِلِي وَٱلضَّنَى إِنْ لَمْ تَصِلْنِي وَاصِلِي
ظَفَرَ ٱلْحُبُّ بِقَلْبٍ دَنِفٍ بِكَ وَٱلسُّقْمُ بِجِسْمٍ نَاحِلِ
وَبَكَا ٱلْعَاذِلُ لِي مِنْ رَحْمَتِي فَبُكَائِي لِبُكَاءِ ٱلْعَاذِلِ

فصاح وقال يا بُليق كم لي معك من العين قال ستّمائة وخمسون ديناراً. قال اقسمها بيني وبينه واجعل الكسر كاملاً للغلام.

وذكر أحمد بن صدقة المغنّي قال اجتزت بخالد الكاتب يوماً فقلت له اعمل لي أبياتاً أغنّي فيها أمير المؤمنين يعني المأمون قال فأيّ حظّ لي في ذلك تأخذ أنت الجائزة وأحصل أنا على الإثم. فحلفت له أنّه إن وصلني بشيء قاسمته إيّاه فقال لي أنت أنذل[1] من ذاك ولكن أذكِرْه بي فلعلّه أن يصلني بشيء. قلت أفعل فأنشدني ٨،٢

تَقُولُ سَلَا فَمَنِ ٱلْمُدْنِفُ وَمَنْ عَيْنُهُ أَبَدًا تَذْرِفُ
وَمَنْ قَلْبُهُ قَلِقٌ خَافِقٌ عَلَيْكَ وَأَحْشَاؤُهُ تَرْجُفُ

فحفظت الشعر وعملت فيه لحناً وحضرنا عند المأمون من الغد وكان بينه وبين بعض حظاياه هجرة فوجّهت إليه بتفّاحة مكتوب عليها بالغالية سلوتَ وابتدأت أغنّي ٩،٢

١ الأصل: انذل.

I blamed my soul for your passion,
but I found it didn't agree.
I obeyed its call to adore you,
ignoring all words of blame.
No! By Him who made all faces
bow down before the beauty of your face,
I'll not say endurance is lovelier
than the love that sets my soul on fire.

He edged forward till he was no longer on the carpet. Then he said, "Recite more." 2.7

Live! Love for you will soon be my death.
I'll pine away if you show me no kindness.
Love has conquered a heart sick for you,
and sickness has conquered a body worn thin.
Out of pity the blamer weeps over me.
I weep for the blamer's weeping.

He called out, "Bulayq! How much cash have you got with you?" "Six hundred and fifty gold dinars." "Divide them between him and me, and give him all the small coins."

This anecdote comes from Aḥmad ibn Ṣadaqah the singer: I looked in on Khālid al-Kātib one day and said to him, "Compose some poetry for me to set to music and sing for the caliph" (meaning al-Ma'mūn). "What's in it for me? You'll get the reward and I'll get the blame." I swore that I would share any gift the caliph gave me. He said, "You're too mean to do that. But mention me to him—perhaps he'll give me something." "Very well." Then he recited: 2.8

You say, "He got over it." But who's thin and pale?
Whose eyes are always brimming with tears?
Whose heart is worried and anxious for you,
shaking and trembling in fear?

I committed the poetry to memory and composed a setting for it. The next day, we had an audience with al-Ma'mūn. He'd had a tiff with one of his concubines, and she'd sent him an apple with "You're over it" written in dark 2.9

بشعر خالد فلمّا غنّيته إيّاه انقلبت عيناه ودارتا في أمّ رأسه وظهر الغضب في وجهه وقال لكم على حرمي أصحاب أخبار. فقمت إعظاماً لما شاهدته منه وقلت أعيذ أمير المؤمنين بالله أن يظنّ بعبده هذا الظنّ وأنزّه داره أن يكون لأحد عليها صاحب خبر. قال فمن أين عرفت خبري مع جاريتي حتّى غنّيت في معنى ما بيننا. فحدّثته حديثي مع خالد فلمّا انتهيت إلى قوله أنت أنذل من ذلك قال أشهد أنّك كذاك وأسفر وجهه وقال ما أعجب هذا الاتّفاق وأمر لي بخمسة ألف درهم ولخالد بمثله.

ومن مليح شعر خالد ١٠،٢

كَبِدُ ٱلْمُسْتَهَامِ كَيْفَ تَذُوبُ   مَا تُقَاسِي مِنَ ٱلْعُيُونِ ٱلْقُلُوبُ
بَدَنُ ٱلْمُسْتَهَامِ كَيْفَ تَرَاهُ   شَجَنٌ مَا لَهُ سِوَاهُ طَبِيبُ
أَيْنَ أَيْنَ ٱلرُّقَادُ يَا مُقْلَتَيَّ مَنْ   حَرُّ أَحْشَائِهِ عَلَيْهِ رَقِيبُ
يَا مَكَانَ ٱلْهَوَى خَلَوْتَ مِنَ ٱلصَّبْرِ   فَمَا لِلسُّلُوِّ فِيكَ نَصِيبُ

ومن مليح شعره

وَلَمْ أَدْرِ مَا جُهْدُ ٱلْهَوَى وَبَلَاؤُهُ   وَشِدَّتُهُ حَتَّى وَجَدْتُكَ فِي قَلْبِي
أَطَاعَكَ طَرْفِي فِي فُؤَادِي فَخَانَهُ   لِطَرْفِكَ حَتَّى صَارَ فِي قَبْضَةِ ٱلْحُبِّ

ومن شعره وفيه لحن ١١،٢

وَمَا ٱسْتَعَارَ ٱلْحُسْنُ مِنْ وَجْهِهِ   وَٱلْغُصْنُ ٱلنَّاعِمُ مِنْ قَدِّهِ
لَقَدْ تَعَاتَبْنَا بِأَبْصَارِنَا   فِيمَا جَنَاهُ ٱلْخُلْفُ مِنْ وَعْدِهِ
حَتَّى تَجَارَحْنَا بِتَكْرَارِنَا   لِلَّحْظِ فِي خَدِّي وَفِي خَدِّهِ

perfume oil. I started to sing Khālid's verses, and when I'd finished his eyes goggled and rolled in their sockets. Furious, he asked, "Do you have spies in my harem?" I stood up, horrified at his reaction, and answered, "God forbid that the caliph should suspect his servant of such a thing. His palace is too majestic to be spied upon." "Then how did you know what had been going on between me and my concubine so as to sing about it?" I told him about my meeting with Khālid, and when I got to Khālid's saying "You're too mean to do that," he commented, "I can confirm that," and his face cleared. He added, "What an extraordinary coincidence this is." He ordered me to be given five thousand dirhams[13] and he ordered the same for Khālid.

Here is one of Khālid's fine poems: **2.10**

How does the lover's soul melt away?
With the heart tormented by glances.
How then does the lover's body look?
Pure grief that no doctor but he can treat.
Where does sleep come to a man's eyes
when his passion spies on him?
Abode of love, you've lost all patience
and in you comfort has no part.

And another one:

Love's violence, travail, and grief I knew
only once you entered my heart.
My sight obeyed you,
gave my soul to your eyes,
and it fell into love's hand.

This poem of his was set to music: **2.11**

By the charm that beauty borrowed from his face
and the slender branch took from his frame!
We gave each other looks of reproach
about the promise he never kept
Till our glances, so often exchanged,
wounded both our cheeks, his and mine.

وله أيضاً ١٢،٢

مَا عَلَى ٱلْغَضْبَانِ لَوْ كَانَ[١] أَرْضَى وَرَثَى لِي مِنْ تَمَادِي مَرَضِي
قَالَ لِي لَمَّا تَشَكَّيْتُ[٢] ٱلْهَوَى اِحْمَدِ ٱللهَ كَذَا كَانَ قُضِي
قُلْتُ حَاشَى ٱللهَ أَنْ يَقْضِيَ بِذَا بَلْ قَضَاهُ صَاحِبُ ٱلْوَجْهِ ٱلْوَضِي
أَنْتَ شَرَّدْتَ رُقَادِي ظَالِمًا فَٱجْعَلِ ٱلْإِنْصَافَ مِنْهُ عِوَضِي

وله أيضاً

رَحَلْتُمْ فَكَمْ مِنْ أَنَّةٍ بَعْدَ زَفْرَةٍ مُبَيِّنَةٍ لِلنَّاسِ شَوْقِي إِلَيْكُمُ
وَقَدْ كُنْتُ أَعْتَقْتُ ٱلْجُفُونَ مِنَ ٱلْبُكَا فَقَدْ رَدَّهَا فِي ٱلرِّقِّ حُزْنِي عَلَيْكُمُ

له أيضاً

زَارَنِي فِي مُوَرَّدٍ مِثْلَ خَدَّيْهِ وَعَقْدُ فُصُولِهِ ٱلْكَافُورُ
لَيْلَةً لَمْ يَكُنْ سِوَى قِصَرِ ٱللَّيْلَةِ فِيهَا عَيْبٌ وَلَا تَقْصِيرُ

١٣،٢ قال جحظة كنت يوماً عند عبد الله بن المعتزّ فطلبت نعلي فلم أجده فجعلت أقول

يَا قَوْمُ مَنْ لِي بِنَعْلِي أَوْ فِي مُصَحَّفِ نَعْلِي

فسار هذا البيت حتّى رواه الصبيان. قال ودعاني عبيد الله يوماً فأبطأت عنه فكتب إليّ

لَا تَهْجُرُ ٱلْأُمَرَاءُ مَنْ يَعْدُو عَلَى فَرَسِ ٱلْحَ . . . . ٱلْقِيرَاطِ[٣]

فكتب إليه جحظة

---

١ الأصل مطموس. ٢ الأصل مطموس. ٣ الأصل مطموس.

And here are a few more of his poems: 2.12

What if, though angered, he'd satisfied me,
pitying my long-lasting sickness.
He said, when I lamented my passion,
"God be praised. This is your fate."
But I: "God's far above such a decree.
It comes from one with a radiant face."
Unjustly you've chased away my rest;
requite me with just sentence against it.

You are gone. What sighing, what sobs
proclaim to the world my longing!
My eyelids I'd freed from the fetters of tears;
now my sorrow for you has enchained them again.

He came to me in a mantle rosy as his cheeks,
his limbs swathed in dazzling white,
On a night without blemish or fault
but that it was all too fleeting.

Jaḥẓah said: When I was visiting ʿAbdallāh ibn al-Muʿtazz one day, I looked for my sandal and couldn't find it, so I exclaimed: 2.13

Men, who'll find me my sandal
or else buy me a mount?

The line caught on till it was even on the street urchins' lips. Then one day ʿUbaydallāh summoned me. I took my time coming, so he wrote to me:

Princes don't break with those who ride
shanks' mare a little way.[14]

And I replied:

مَنْ كَانَ خَادِمَ مِثْلِكُمْ فَجَوَادُهُ فَرَسُ ٱلْحَفَاءِ وَدَيْنُهُ طَسُّوجُ

قال جحظة كنت أعشق جارية من القيان يقال لها شروين فسكرت عندي ليلة فخرئت ١٤،٢
في سطلي وحُميديّتي وانصرفت فكتبت إلى الهُداهديّ

قَدْ زَارَنِي خِلٌّ أُسَرُّ بِهِ حُلْوُ ٱلشَّمَائِلِ رَاجِحُ ٱلْعَقْلِ
فَبِحَقِّ شَرْوِينَ ٱلَّتِي خَرِئَتْ فِي ٱلطَّسْتِ وَٱلْإِبْرِيقِ وَٱلسَّطْلِ
إِلَّا أَتَيْتَ مُبَادِراً عَجِلاً وَأَرَحْتَ مِنْ نَكَدٍ وَمِنْ مَطْلِ
حَتَّى أَرَاكَ إِذَا سَكِرْتَ وَقَدْ شَارَكْتَهَا فِي ذٰلِكَ ٱلْفِعْلِ

ولجحظة إلى ابن طرخان يدعوه ١٥،٢

لَنَا يَا أَخِي زَلَّةٌ وَافِرَهْ وَقِدْرٌ مُعَجَّلَةٌ حَاضِرَهْ
وَمَا شِئْتَ مِنْ خَبَرٍ طَيِّبٍ وَنَادِرَةٍ بَعْدَهَا نَادِرَهْ
وَرَاحٍ تُرِيكَ إِذَا صُفِّقَتْ سَنَا ٱلْبَرْقِ فِي ٱللَّيْلَةِ ٱلْمَاطِرَهْ
وَمُحْسِنَةٍ لَمْ يَخُنْهَا ٱلصَّوَابُ وَزَامِرَةٍ أَيَّمَا زَامِرَهْ

لَسْتُ أَدْرِي أَيْنَ ٱلْفُؤَادُ مُقِيماً يَا مَكَانَ ٱلْفُؤَادِ أَيْنَ ٱلْفُؤَادُ
دَفَعَتْهُ ٱلْأَحْشَاءُ عَمَّا يَلِيهَا فَأَذَابَتْهُ حُرْقَةٌ وَٱتِّقَادُ

وله ١٦،٢

نَأَيْتَ فَلَمْ يَنْأَ عَنْهُ ٱلضَّنَى وَعُدْتَ فَعَادَ إِلَى نُكْسِهِ
وَفَارَقَهُ ٱلصَّبْرُ فِي يَوْمِهِ لِمَا فَاتَهُ مِنْكَ فِي أَمْسِهِ
وَمُسْتَوْحِشٍ آنِسٍ بِٱلْبُكَاءِ عَلَى قَلْبِهِ وَعَلَى إِنْسِهِ
يَرِقُّ هَوَاهُ لِأَحْشَائِهِ وَيَرْثِي لَهُ ٱلشَّوْقُ مِنْ نَفْسِهِ

A servant of men like you has shanks' mare as a mount and debts in
dimes.

Another story of Jaḥẓah's: I was in love with a singing girl called Sharwīn. One night she got drunk at my house and shat in my dipper and spittoon before she left. Al-Hudāhidī wrote to me: 2.14

I had a visitor, a dear friend,
a fine character wise in his ways.
Now you owe it to Sharwīn, who shat
in the dipper, the bowl, and the jug.
Hurry and visit, dropping excuses and delays,
and I'll see you as drunk as she,
Making a mess on the rug.

Jaḥẓah sent an invitation to Ibn Tarkhān: 2.15

My friend, we've food aplenty
and a pot bubbling away,
As much good talk as you like,
and an endless supply of jokes.
The wine, when poured, is like
a lightning flash on a rainy night.
Our singer's a mistress of modes;
the flute player is superb.

I don't know where my heart's gone; it's not in its place.
My bosom has driven it out; it's caught fire and now is ablaze.[15]

Another of his poems: 2.16

You left, but his sickness did not leave.
You came back and again he fell ill.
He's lost all patience today
since he missed yesterday's meeting.
Lonely, a friend to weeping
for his heart and his beloved—
His love bleeds for his heart
and his longing laments his soul.

دير الثعالب

١،٣ وهـذا الدير ببغداد بالجانب الغربيّ منها بالموضع المعروف بباب الحديد وأهل بغداد يقصدونه ويتنزّهون فيه ولا يكاد يخلو من قاصد وطارق وله عيد لا يتخلّف عنه أحد من النصارى والمسلمين. وباب الحديد أعمر موضع ببغداد وأنزهه لما فيه من البساتين والشجر والنخل والرياحين ولتوسّطه البلد وقربه من كلّ أحد فليس يخلو من أهل البطالات ولا يخلّ به أهل التطرّب واللذاذات فمواطنه أبدًا معمورة وبقاعه بالمتنزّهين مشحونة وقد قالت الشعراء في الدير وباب الحديد وفبرونيا[1] فأكثروا ووصفوا حسن تلك المواضع فأطنبوا.

٢،٣ ولابن دهقانة الهاشميّ فيه

دَيْرُ ٱلثَّعَالِبِ مَأْلَفُ ٱلضُّلَّالِ ... وَمَحَلُّ كُلِّ غَزَالَةٍ وَغَزَالِ
كَمْ لَيْلَةٍ أَحْيَيْتُهَا وَمُنَادِمِي ... فِيهَا أَغَنُّ مُقَطَّعَ ٱلْأَوْصَالِ
سَمِحٌ يَجُودُ بِرُوحِهِ فَإِذَا مَضَى ... وَقَضَى سَمَحْتُ لَهُ وَجُدْتُ بِمَالِي
وَمُنَعَّمٍ دِينُ ٱبْنِ مَرْيَمَ دِينُهُ ... غَنِجٌ يَشُوبُ مُجُونَهُ بِضَلَالِ
سَقَّيْتُهُ وَشَرِبْتُ فَضْلَةَ كَأْسِهِ ... فَشَرِبْتُ مِنْ عَذْبِ ٱلْمَذَاقِ زُلَالِ

٣،٣ وابن دهقانة هذا من ولد إبراهيم بن محمّد بن عليّ بن عبد الله بن عبّاس ويُعرف بأبي جعفر محمّد بن عمر. وله شعر مليح وذكر جحظة أنّه أنشده

أَحِينَ قَطَعْتُ لَكَ ٱلْوَاصِلِينَ ... وَجُدْتُ عَلَيْكَ وَلَمْ أَبْخَلِ
غَدَرْتَ وَأَظْهَرْتَ لِي جَفْوَةً ... وَجُرْتَ عَلَيَّ وَلَمْ تَعْدِلِ
أَأَطْمَعُ فِي آخِرٍ مِنْ هَوَاكَ ... وَلَمْ تَرْعَ لِي حُرْمَةَ ٱلْأَوَّلِ

[1] الأصل: وقبرونيا.

The Monastery of the Foxes

This monastery is in the western part of Baghdad at the place known as the Iron Gate. The people of Baghdad go there for outings, and it is hardly ever empty of visitors and passersby. It has a festival no Christian or Muslim misses. The Iron Gate is the best-cultivated and most pleasant part of Baghdad because of its gardens, trees, palms, and foxes' basilicum.[16] Besides, it is in the center of the city and close to everyone, so people with time on their hands visit it, as do those who enjoy music making and revelry. Its grounds are well kept and always thronged with people. Poets have composed many verses about the monastery, the Iron Gate, and Fabrūniyā, describing at length the beauties of the place. 3.1

Here is a poem by Ibn Dihqānah al-Hāshimī on it: 3.2

The Foxes' Monastery is the home of the errant,
a place to meet gazelle-like boys and girls.
Oft have I spent there a night with my friend,
pouring wine into cups, skillfully watered,
Yielding its spirit freely till the last drop ran out.
I forgave it then and paid more than I owed.
For a sweet young follower of Mary's Son,
flirtatious, wanton, yet at times coy,
I poured wine, then sipped the dregs of his glass,
and had in my mouth the taste of nectar.

Ibn Dihqānah was a descendant of Ibrāhīm ibn Muḥammad ibn ʿAlī ibn ʿAbdallāh ibn ʿAbbās. His given name was Abū Jaʿfar Muḥammad ibn ʿUmar. He is the author of fine poetry, such as these verses, which Jaḥẓah recalled him reciting to him: 3.3

Ha! When I came between you and your friends
and showered you with gifts, ever generous,
You played me false and treated me harshly,
acting the tyrant, doing me wrong.
Why should I want the conclusion of your love
when you showed no respect for its beginning?

٤،٣ وذكر جحظة أنّه كان والي البصرة في أيّام الزنج وأنّه أخذ من الناجم بها ثلاثين ألف دينار وسلّم إليه البصرة. وكان جحظة يكثر عنده ولا يغبّه. قال فتأخّرت عنه في وقت من الأوقات لعارض عرض لي فوجّه إليّ يدعوني فكتبت إليه أنا والله عليل

وَلَيْسَ بِتَزْوِيقِ ٱللِّسَانِ وَصَوْغِهِ   وَلٰكِنَّهُ قَدْ خَالَطَ ٱللَّحْمَ وَٱلدَّمَا

فوجّه إليّ بخمسين ديناراً وخلعة وقال هذا يزيل العلّة فبحياتي إلّا جئتني فمضيت إليه.

٥،٣ وذكر جحظة أنّه كان ينادم المعتمد والموفّق وكان عظيم الخلق ثقيل الجسم وكان إذا قام الخليفة ورجع وقام[١] الندماء نام هو وقال هذا عوض القيام لما لم يكن يقدر عليه. وكان أكولاً وكان يقول قد أكلت حتّى زمنت وأريد أن آكل حتّى أموت.

٦،٣ ومن شعره

فَلَوْ أَنَّ فِي جَزَعِي رَاحَةً   لَأَصْبَحْتُ أَجْزَعَ مَنْ يَجْزَعُ
سَأَصْبِرُ جُهْدِي عَلَى مَا تَرَى   وَإِنْ عِيلَ صَبْرِي فَمَا أَصْنَعُ

٧،٣ وللناشئ يذكر باب الحديد وفبرونيا[٢]

مَا جَلِيدٌ يَوْمَ ٱلنَّوَى بِجَلِيدِ   بَعُدَتْ وَٱلْمَزَارُ غَيْرُ بَعِيدِ
خَبَّرَتْ عَنْ ضَمِيرِهَا عَبَرَاتٌ   صِرْنَ عَوْنًا عَلَى ٱلْفُؤَادِ ٱلْعَمِيدِ
يَا لَيَالِي ٱللَّذَّاتِ بِٱللهِ عُودِي   بَيْنَ فَبْرُونِيَا[٣] وَبَابِ ٱلْحَدِيدِ
بَيْنَ تِلْكَ ٱلرُّبَى وَقَدْ نَسَجَ ٱلْوَبْلُ بِكَفِّ ٱلرَّبِيعِ رَيْطَ ٱلْبُرُودِ
خَدُّهُ ضِدُّ صُدْغِهِ مِثْلَ مَا ٱلْوَعْدُ إِذَا مَا ٱخْتَبَرْتُ ضِدُّ ٱلْوَعِيدِ
طَلَبَ ٱلطَّبْلُ طَائِلَاتٍ مِنَ ٱلزَّمْرِ وَعَادَ ٱلسُّرُورُ إِذْ عَادَ عُودِي

١ الأصل: ورجع قام. ٢ الأصل: وقبرونيا. ٣ الأصل: قبرونيا.

Jaḥẓah mentioned that Ibn Dihqānah was the governor of Basra at the time of the Zanj uprising.[17] In return for thirty thousand dinars from its ringleader, he handed over the city to him. Jaḥẓah spent a lot of time with Ibn Dihqānah and would visit him every day. He recounted: One time I had not been to see him for some reason or other, so he sent me an invitation. I wrote back: 3.4

I'm ill, by God! It's not a joke or a lie.
I'm affected in my flesh and blood.

He sent me fifty dinars and a robe of honor, saying, "This will cure the illness. Come to me, please!" Which I did.

Jaḥẓah also said that Ibn Dihqānah was a court companion of al-Muʿtamid and al-Muwaffaq. Being large and heavily built, he would lie down when the caliph rose to retire and the courtiers stood up. He explained that as a substitute for standing up, which was beyond him. He was a compulsive eater and used to say, "I've eaten and made myself seriously ill, but I intend to go on eating till I die." 3.5

Here is one of Ibn Dihqānah's poems: 3.6

If my anguish brought relief,
I'd be the greatest lover in anguish.
I'll do my utmost to endure this.
But if my patience runs out—must I languish?

And here is a poem by al-Nāshiʾ mentioning the Iron Gate and Fabrūniyā: 3.7

The cold cannot match the coldness of the day you parted.
She's far off, though she's not far away.
Her tears betrayed her hidden feelings,
bringing solace to the tormented heart.
Come back, by God, nights of delight
between Fabrūniyā and the Iron Gate,
On those slopes where the rain wove
with spring's hand a patterned veil,
Its cheek as unlike its temple
as a promise is unlike a threat.
The tambourine asked favors from the flute,
and joy returned with the strains of the lute.

ومن رقيق شعره ٨،٣

لَمْ أَسْلُ عَنْكَ وَلَمْ أَخُنْكَ وَلَمْ يَكُنْ   فِي ٱلْقَلْبِ مِنِّي لِلسُّلُوِّ مَكَانُ
لٰكِنْ رَأَيْتُكَ قَدْ مَلَلْتَ مَوَدَّتِي   فَعَلِمْتُ أَنَّ دَوَاءَكَ ٱلْهِجْرَانُ

This is another delicate poem of his: 3.8

I didn't tire of you or act untrue—
  my heart had no room for consolation.
When I saw you were weary of my love,
  I knew a break was the only cure.

دير الجاثليق

وهذا الدير يقرب من باب الحديد وهو دير كبير حسن نزه تحدق به البساتين ١،٤
والأشجار والرياحين وهو يوازي دير الثعالب بالنزهة والطيب وعمارة الموضع لأنّهما في بقعة واحدة وهو مقصود مطروق لا يخلو من المتنزّهين فيه والقاصدين له وفيه رهبانه وقسّانه ومن يألفه من أهل الخلاعة والبطالة. وقالت الشعراء فيه ووصفته ولمحمّد بن أبي أميّة الكاتب فيه وفيه لحن خفيف رمل

لَهْفِي عَلَى قَمَرٍ فِي ٱلدَّيْرِ مَسْجُونِ　　فِي صُورَةِ ٱلْإِنْسِ فِي مَكْرِ ٱلشَّيَاطِينِ
وَٱللهِ مَا أَبْصَرَتْ عَيْنِي مَحَاسِنَهُ　　إِلَّا خَرَجْتُ لَهُ طَوْعًا مِنَ ٱلدِّينِ

وله في هذا الدير أيضاً ٢،٤

تَذَكَّرْتُ دَيْرَ ٱلْجَاثَلِيقِ وَفِتْيَةً　　بِهِمْ تَمَّ لِي فِيهِ ٱلسُّرُورُ وَأَسْعَفَا
بِهِمْ طَابَتِ ٱلدُّنْيَا وَتَمَّ سُرُورُهَا　　وَسَالَمَنِي صَرْفُ ٱلزَّمَانِ وَأَنْصَفَا
أَلَا رُبَّ يَوْمٍ قَدْ نَعِمْتُ بِظِلِّهِ　　أُبَادِرُ مِنْ لَذَّاتِ عَيْشِيَ مَا صَفَا
أُغَازِلُ فِيهِ أَدْعَجَ ٱلطَّرْفِ أَهْيَفَا　　وَأُسْقَى بِهِ مِسْكِيَّةَ ٱلطَّعْمِ قَرْقَفَا
فَسُقْيًا لِأَيَّامٍ مَضَتْ لِي بِقُرْبِهِمْ　　لَقَدْ أَوْسَعَتْنِي رَأْفَةً وَتَعَطُّفَا
وَتَعْسًا لِأَيَّامٍ رَمَتْنِي بِبَيْنِهِمْ　　وَدَهْرٍ تَقَاضَانِي ٱلَّذِي كَانَ أَسْلَفَا

ومحمّد بن أبي أميّة هذا أحد المتقدّمين في الشعر رقيق الطبع حسن التصرّف ٣،٤
فيه غريب المعاني وأكثر شعره في الغزل وكان هو وأخوه يكتبان للفضل بن الربيع

The Monastery of the Catholicos[18]

This monastery is close to the Iron Gate. It is large, beautiful, and pleasant, surrounded by gardens, trees, and sweet basil. It is as attractive, fragrant, and well cultivated as the Monastery of the Foxes, since they are in the same area. It attracts passersby and visitors, and people regularly go on outings to it. It houses monks and priests, as well as libertines and those with time on their hands to frequent it. Poets have composed verses about it and described it. Here, for instance, is a poem by Muḥammad ibn Abī Umayyah the scribe, which has a musical setting in the light *ramal* rhythmic mode:[19] 4.1

I grieve for a moon, a captive of the cloister,
human in form, in cunning a devil.
By God, when my eye fell on his beauty,
I yielded and freely abandoned my faith.

He has another poem on this monastery: 4.2

The Catholicos's Monastery I recall, and companions
with whom I spent times of utter delight.
With them my joy of the world was complete,
and fate was at peace with me, fair in its dealings.
How many days in the shade of the convent
I spent, the pleasures of life pure,
Flirting with a slim, black-eyed beauty
pouring me sparkling musk-scented wine.
Blessed be the days I spent in their company,
rich in affection and in kindness.
Cursed be the days that forced me away
when fate required I repay its loan.

This Muḥammad ibn Abī Umayyah was a first-rate poet, sensitive and accomplished, going in for unusual images. Most of his poetry was on love. 4.3

وهو عمّ أبي حشيشة الطنبوريّ. ومن مليح شعره

رَأَيْتُكَ حِلْيَتِي دُنْيَا وَدِينِ   حَيَاةً لِلضَّجِيعِ وَلِلْقَرِينِ
بَدَا لِي بَعْدَمَا سَبَقَتْ يَمِينِي   بِهَجْرِكَ أَنْ أُكَفِّرَ عَنْ يَمِينِي

وله

لَمْ أَسْلُ عَنْكَ وَلَمْ أَخُنْكَ وَلَمْ يَكُنْ   فِي ٱلْقَلْبِ مِنِّي لِلسُّلُوِّ مَكَانُ
لٰكِنْ رَأَيْتُكَ قَدْ مَلِلْتَ مَوَدَّتِي   فَعَلِمْتُ أَنَّ دَوَاءَكَ ٱلْهِجْرَانُ

ومن رقيق شعره ٤،٤

يَا غَرِيبًا يَبْكِي لِكُلِّ غَرِيبِ   لَمْ يَذُقْ قَبْلَهَا فِرَاقَ ٱلْحَبِيبِ
عَزَّهُ ٱلصَّبْرُ فَٱسْتَرَاحَ إِلَى ٱلدَّمْعِ   وَفِي ٱلدَّمْعِ رَاحَةٌ لِلْقُلُوبِ
لَيْتَ يَوْمًا أَرَاكَ فِيهِ كَمَا كُنْتَ قَرِيبًا فَأَشْتَكِي مِنْ قَرِيبِ

وله

رُبَّ يَوْمٍ مِنْكَ لَا أَنْسَاهُ لِي   أَوْجَبَ ٱلشُّكْرَ وَإِنْ لَمْ تَفْعَلِ
أَقْطَعُ ٱلدَّهْرَ بِظَنٍّ حَسَنٍ   وَأُجَلِّي غَمْرَةً مَا تَنْجَلِي
وَأَرَى ٱلْأَيَّامَ لَا تُدْنِي ٱلَّذِي   أَرْتَجِي مِنْكَ وَتُدْنِي أَجَلِي
كُلَّمَا أَمَّلْتُ يَوْمًا صَالِحًا   عَرَضَ ٱلْهِجْرَانُ دُونَ ٱلْأَمَلِ

ومن نادر شعره ٥،٤

لَأُقِيمَنَّ مَأْتَمًا عَنْ قَرِيبٍ   لَيْسَ بَعْدَ ٱلْفِرَاقِ غَيْرُ ٱلنَّحِيبِ
ظَلَمَتْنِي فِيكَ ٱلْخُطُوبُ فَلَمْ أَقْوَ عَلَى أَنْ أَرُدَّ ظُلْمَ ٱلْخُطُوبِ

He and his brother ʿAlī were secretaries of al-Faḍl ibn al-Rabīʿ. And he was the uncle of Abū Ḥashīshah the pandore[20] player. One of his fine poems is:

I held you an adornment for world and for faith,
    life for your companion and for your bedfellow;
After I'd sworn to leave you
    I repented and did penance for my oath.

Another one:

I didn't tire of you or act untrue—
    my heart had no room for consolation.
When I saw you were weary of my love
    I knew a break was the only cure.[21]

This is one of his poems of sentiment: 4.4

O stranger weeping for every stranger,
    you've never felt what it's like to part from a friend.
Patience worn out, you've sought rest in tears,
    for weeping brings the heart rest.
I wish I might see you one day nearby
    as before, to complain of your nearness.

Here is another:

Many a day with you I'll never forget,
    yet you never thanked me for them!
Now I pass my time with auspicious thoughts,
    laying bare heedlessness not disclosed.
Time, I see, brings no closer my hope of you—
    it's the end of my life it brings close.
I hope for a favorable day,
    but separation blights my hopes.

This is one of his excellent pieces: 4.5

I'll hold a wake before long.
    After separation, only wailing is left.
Destiny wronged me in you,
    and I was too weak to ward off its injustice.

رَبِّ مَا أَوْجَعَ ٱلْهَوَى لِلْقُلُوبِ ثُمَّ لَا سِيَّمَا فِرَاقَ ٱلْقُلُوبِ
لَمْ أَكُنْ أَعْرِفُ ٱلْفِرَاقَ فَأَقْدَمْتُ عَلَيْهِ غِرًّا بِلَا تَجْرِيبِ

وله أيضاً ٦،٤

ٱلْيَوْمَ أَثْكَلَنِي صَبْرِي فِرَاقُكُمُ كَذَاكَ أَعْظَمُ شَيْءٍ فَقْدُ مَعْشُوقِ
وَكُنْتُ فِي فُسْحَةٍ مِنْ قَبْلِ بَيْنِكُمُ فَٱلْيَوْمَ صِرْتُ مِنَ ٱلْأَحْزَانِ فِي ضِيقِ
وَٱغْتَالَنِي زَمَنٌ قَدْ كُنْتُ آمَنُهُ تَعْسًا لِغُدْرَتِهِ مِنْ بَعْدِ تَوْثِيقِ
إِنِّي عَلَى ٱلْعَهْدِ لَمْ أَنْقُضْ مَوَدَّتَكُمْ يَا مَنْ يَرَى حَسَنًا نَقْضَ ٱلْمَوَاثِيقِ

وله

مَا ذَاقَتِ ٱلنَّفْسُ عَلَى شَهْوَةٍ أَلَذَّ مِنْ وُدِّ صَدِيقٍ أَمِينِ
مَنْ فَاتَهُ وُدُّ أَخٍ صَالِحٍ فَذٰلِكَ ٱلْمَغْبُونُ حَقَّ ٱلْيَقِينِ

وله وهو من مليح شعره ٧،٤

فَيَا شَوْقُ لَا تَنْفَدْ وَيَا دَمْعُ فِضْ وَزِدْ وَيَا شَوْقُ رَاوِحْ بَيْنَ جَنْبٍ إِلَى جَنْبِ
وَيَا عَاذِلِي لُمْنِي وَيَا عَابِدُ ٱفْتِنِي عَصَيْتُكُمَا حَتَّى أُغَيَّبَ فِي ٱلتُّرْبِ
إِذَا كَانَ رَبِّي عَالِمًا بِسَرِيرَتِي فَمَا ٱلنَّاسُ فِي عَيْنِي بِأَعْظَمَ مِنْ رَبِّي

وله يصف روضة ٨،٤

فِي جِنَانٍ كَأَنَّمَا نُشِرَتْ فَوْ قَ ثَرَاهَا حَرِيرَةٌ خَضْرَاءُ
أَعْيُنُ ٱلنَّرْجِسِ ٱلْجَنِيِّ نُجُومٌ وَٱخْضِرَارُ ٱلرِّيَاضِ فِيهَا سَمَاءُ
لِلثَّرَى تَحْتَهَا سُبَاتٌ وَلِلْمَا ءِ خَرِيرٌ وَلِلْغُصُونِ غِنَاءُ

Oh God, how much pain love inflicts on the heart,
but it's nothing compared to the beloved's departure.
Knowing nothing of separation, in innocence
I risked it, without any experience.

He also composed these poems: 4.6

Your parting today has robbed me of endurance.
It's awful to lose one's beloved like this.
Before you left I lived a life of ease,
now my sorrows have crowded in on me.
Time has attacked me when I thought I was safe.
Cursed be its treachery after I'd trusted it.
I've been faithful, true to your love,
you who so easily broke our tryst.

To the desiring soul nothing tastes sweeter
than the love of a faithful friend.
Not to know a true brother's love
is to be duped and ill-omened.

This is one of his fine poems: 4.7

Longing, tire not! Tears, well up and flow!
Yearning, roam from place to place!
Critics, warn me; believers, counsel me—
I'll disobey you to the grave.
If the secrets of my heart my Lord knows well,
I see none who over my Lord can excel.

Here is his description of a meadow: 4.8

In gardens as if covered in green silk outspread,
where eyes of wondrous narcissi
Shine like stars in a sky of emerald meadows,
while the earth beneath slumbers
To the murmur of water
and the song of the branches.

وله ٩،٤

فَهَا أَنَا مُغْضٍ فِي رِضَاكَ وَصَابِرٌ   عَلَى مِثْلِ مَصْقُولِ ٱلذُّبَابَيْنِ قَاضِبِ
وَمُنْتَزِحٌ عَمَّا كَرِهْتَ وَجَاعِلٌ   رِضَاكَ مِثَالًا بَيْنَ عَيْنِي وَحَاجِبِي

وله

كَمْ فَرْحَةٍ كَانَتْ وَكَمْ تَرْحَةٍ   تَخَرَّصَتْهَا لِيَ فِيكَ ٱلظُّنُونْ
إِذَا قُلُوبٌ أَظْهَرَتْ غَيْرَ مَا   تُضْمِرُهُ أَنْبَتَكَ عَنْهُ ٱلْعُيُونْ

وله

يُصَعِّدُ فِي ٱلْحَشَا نَفَسًا   وَيَسْهَرُ إِنْ فَتًى نَعَسَا
يَظَلُّ يُعَالِجُ ٱلزَّفَرَا   تِ إِنْ أَغْفَى وَإِنْ جَلَسَا
غَذَا بِٱلشَّوْقِ مُهْجَتَهُ   وَعَلَّلَ نَفْسَهُ بِعَسَى
مُحِبٌّ صَيَّرَ ٱلشَّكْوَى   إِلَى جُلَسَائِهِ أُنُسَا

وكان أبو بكر محمّد بن القاسم الأنباريّ يختم أماليه في مجالسه بمقطوع من شعر ابن أبي أميّة استحساناً له واستعذاباً لألفاظه ويقرّظه دائماً ويصفه. ١٠،٤

Here are more poems: 4.9

Here am I, eager to please you, long-suffering,
as if grasping a bright double-edged sword,
Eschewing what you loathe, and
willing to give up my eyes just to satisfy you.

What joy I knew, and what sorrow
when suspicion of you entered my mind.
If the heart reveals one thing and conceals another,
its true feelings the eyes will betray.

He heaves the deepest of sighs,
Stays awake when others are nodding,
Utters moans when drowsy or dozing,
Feeds his mind with longing,
Gives himself hope with "Perhaps"—
A lover who's turned his plaint
Into friendship with his fellows.

Abū Bakr Muḥammad ibn al-Qāsim al-Anbārī used to conclude his dicta- 4.10
tions in his teaching sessions with a quotation from Ibn Abī Umayyah's poetry because he admired it and appreciated the poet's diction. He always praised him and spoke highly of him.

ديـر مُديان

١٫٥ وهـذا الدير على نهر كرخايا ببغداد. وكرخايا نهر يشقّ من المحوّل الكبير ويمرّ على العبّاسيّة ويشقّ الكرخ ويصبّ في دجلة. وكان قديمًا عامرًا والماء فيه جاريًا ثمّ انطمّ وانقطعت جريته بالبثوق التي انفتحت في الفرات. وهو دير حسن نزه حوله بساتين وعمارة ويُقصد للتنزّه والشرب ولا يخلو من قاصد وطارق وهو من البقاع الحسنة النزهة.

٢٫٥ وللحسين بن الضحّاك فيه

حُثَّ ٱلْمُدامَ فَإِنَّ ٱلْكَأْسَ مُتْرَعَةٌ ... مِمَّا يَهِيجُ دَوَاعِي ٱلشَّوْقِ[1] أَحْيَانَا
إِنِّي طَرِبْتُ لِرُهْبَانٍ مُجَاوِبَةٍ ... بِٱلْقُدْسِ بَعْدَ هُدُوِّ ٱللَّيْلِ رُهْبَانَا
فَاسْتَنْفَرَتْ شَجَنًا مِنِّي ذَكَرْتُ بِهِ ... كَرْخَ ٱلْعِرَاقِ وَإِخْوَانًا وَأَشْجَانَا
فَقُلْتُ وَٱلدَّمْعُ فِي عَيْنَيَّ مُطَّرِدٌ ... وَٱلشَّوْقُ يَقْدَحُ فِي ٱلْأَحْشَاءِ نِيرَانَا
يَا دَيْرَ مُدْيَانَ لَا عُرِّيتَ مِنْ سَكَنٍ ... مَا هِجْتَ مِنْ سَقَمٍ يَا دَيْرَ مُدْيَانَا
هَلْ عِنْدَ قَسِّكَ مِنْ عِلْمٍ فَيُخْبِرُنِي ... أَنْ كَيْفَ يُسْعِدُ وَجْهُ ٱلصَّبْرِ مَنْ بَانَا
سُقْيًا وَرَعْيًا لِكَرْخَايَا وَسَاكِنِهِ ... بَيْنَ ٱلْجُنَيْنَةِ وَٱلرَّوْحَاءِ مَنْ كَانَا

٣٫٥ قال وكان أبو عليّ بن الرشيد يلازم هذا الدير ويشرب فيه وكان له قيان يحملهنّ[2] إليه ويقيم به الأيّام لا يفتر عزفًا وقصفًا. وكان شديد التهتّك وكان من يجاور الموضع يشكون ما يلقونه منه. فانتهى الخبر إلى إسحاق بن إبراهيم الطاهريّ وهو خليفة

[1] الأصل: (الحزن) وردت فوق هذه الكلمة. [2] الأصل: يحملهم.

The Monastery of the Confessors[22]

This monastery is on the Karkhāyā Canal in Baghdad. The Karkhāyā Canal branches off from the great canal in al-Muḥawwal, passes al-ʿAbbāsiyyah, cuts through Karkh, and flows into the Tigris. At first it was well maintained and the water flowed through it, but then it was covered over and stopped flowing when breaches were made in the Euphrates embankment. It is beautiful and pleasant, surrounded by gardens and cultivated land. People visit it to walk there and to drink, and it has many visitors and passersby. It is a beautiful place for an outing. 5.1

Al-Ḥusayn ibn al-Ḍaḥḥāk composed this poem about it: 5.2

Bring on the wine, for the cup flows over,
 brimming with pangs of nostalgia.
I delight to hear Jerusalem's monks
 answering each other after night's silence.
They've roused grief and sorrow in me as I remember
 Karkh of Iraq, and my good friends there.
As the tears well up in my eyes and longing
 strikes fire in my heart and burns,
I cry, "Dayr Mudyān, as long as you rouse lovesickness,
 may you always be peopled, Dayr Mudyān."
Does your priest know—and can he tell me—
 how acceptance can bring joy to one who's left you?
May rain and prosperity bless Karkhāyā and its people
 who dwell between the mill and the garden.

It is reported that Abū ʿAlī ibn al-Rashīd would constantly go to this monastery to drink. He took singing girls there, and would listen to music and carouse for days. He was utterly shameless, and those who lived in the neighborhood complained of the nuisance he caused. Isḥāq ibn Ibrāhīm al-Ṭāhirī, who was the representative of the authorities in Baghdad, came to hear of it. He sent a message to Abū ʿAlī, rebuking him for his behavior and forbidding 5.3

السلطان ببغداد فوجّه إليه يُقبّح له فعله وينهاه عن المعاودة لمثله فقال وأيّ يد لإسحاق عليّ وأيّ أمرله فيَّ. أتراه يمنعني من سماع جواريّ والشرب بحيث أشتهي.

٤،٥ فلمّا أتاه هذا القول منه أحفظه وأمهل حتّى إذا كان الليل ركب إلى الموضع وأحاط به من جميع جهاته وأمر أن يُفتح باب الدير ويُنزَل به على الحال التي هو عليها فأُنزل به وهو سكران في ثياب مصبّغة وقد تضمّخ بالخلوق. فقال سوءة لك رجل من ولد الخلافة على مثل هذه الحال ثمّ أمر ففرش بساط على باب الدير وبُطح عليه وضربه عشرين درّة وقال إنّ أمير المؤمنين لم يولّني خلافته حتّى أضيّع في الأمور وأهلها ولا حتّى أدعك وغيرك من أهله تعرّونه وتفضحونه وتخرجون إلى ما خرجت إليه من التبذّل والشهرة وهتك الحرمة وإخراجهم إلى الديارات والحانات. وفي تأديبك صيانة للخلافة وردع لك ولغيرك عن هذه الفضيحة. ثمّ أمر بعمّاريّات كانت معه فأركب فيها مع حرمه وردّه إلى داره. فبلغ ذلك المعتصم فكتب إليه يصوّب رأيه وفعله ويأمره أن لا يرخّص لأحد من أهل بيته في مثله.

٥،٥ وأمّ أبي عليّ هذا تُعرف بشكل. وكان الرشيد قد اشتراها وصاحبة لها تُعرف بشذر في يوم واحد فحملت شذر وولدت أمّ أبيها فحسدتها شكل وبلغ بها الحسد إلى أمر عظيم من العداوة حتّى اشتُهر ذلك. وحملت شكل وولدت أبا عليّ وماتت أمّاهما وبقيت العداوة بين أبي عليّ وأمّ أبيها حتّى بلغ الأمر إلى أن تهاجيا بالأشعار وشاع أمرهما في جميع آل الرشيد. فلمّا قُتل الأمين وورد المأمون إلى بغداد جلس يوماً وعمّه إبراهيم بن المهديّ وأبو إسحاق أخوه والعبّاس ابنه وتذاكروا العداوة التي بين هذين فقال لقد سمعت بخبر عداوتهما بخراسان ولقد هممت أن أصلح بينهما.

٦،٥ ووجّه فأحضر أمّ أبيها وأقبل يعاتبها وهي مطرقة لا تردّ جواباً ثمّ أمر بإحضار أبي عليّ فلمّا رأته أمّ أبيها تنقّبت وسترت وجهها فقال المأمون كنت مسفرة فلمّا

him from committing the same offence again. Abū ʿAlī burst out, "And what authority has Isḥāq over me? How can he order me about? Will he be able to stop me listening to my singing girls and drinking where I like?"

When Isḥāq heard this, he was furious. He waited until it was night, and 5.4
then rode to the place and had it surrounded on all sides. He ordered the monastery's gate to be opened and Abū ʿAlī to be fetched as he was. He was brought down drunk, dressed in gaudy, brightly dyed clothes and daubed with perfume paste.[23] Isḥāq said to him, "Shame on you! A man of the caliph's family in a state like this!" He had a carpet rolled out at the gate of the monastery and Abū ʿAlī thrown on it and given twenty blows with a blackjack. Then he said, "The Commander of the Faithful did not make me his deputy for me to mismanage and neglect his affairs. Nor did he want me to let you or any other member of his family shame him with extravagance and with the scandal you've created. You've even dishonored your womenfolk by taking them to monasteries and taverns. Your punishment will serve to preserve the caliphate's reputation and deter everyone from such shameful actions." He loaded Abū ʿAlī and his womenfolk into some palanquins he had brought and sent him home. When al-Muʿtaṣim heard about it, he wrote to Isḥāq, approving of his decision and the action he had taken, and instructed him never to allow any member of his family to behave in such a way.

Abū ʿAlī's mother was called Shikl. Al-Rashīd had bought her and another 5.5
girl called Shadhr on the same day. When Shadhr became pregnant and gave birth to Umm Abīhā, Shikl became jealous of her. Her jealousy reached such a pitch of hostility that it became common knowledge. Then she became pregnant and gave birth to Abū ʿAlī. Though both the mothers died, the enmity between Abū ʿAlī and Umm Abīhā lived on, to the point where they attacked each other in verse and all of al-Rashīd's family were familiar with the situation. After the death of al-Amīn, when al-Maʾmūn had entered Baghdad, he was sitting one day with his uncle Ibrāhīm ibn al-Mahdī, his brother Abū Isḥāq, and his son al-ʿAbbās, and they mentioned the enmity between Abū ʿAlī and Umm Abīhā. Al-Maʾmūn said, "I learned of their enmity in Khurasan, and I'm resolved to reconcile them."

He sent for Umm Abīhā, and when she arrived he began to reprimand her, 5.6
while she said nothing and stood with downcast eyes. Then he sent for Abū ʿAlī. When Umm Abīhā saw him, she put on her veil and covered her face. Al-Maʾmūn said, "You were unveiled, but when your brother came, you covered your face."

حضر أخوك تنقّبت. قالت والله يا أمير المؤمنين لسفوري بين يدي عبد الله بن طاهر وعليّ بن هشام أوجب من سفوري لأبي عليّ فوالله ما هو لي بأخ ولا للرشيد بابن فقد قال الله عزّ وجلّ في قريش ﴿ٱلَّذِىٓ أَطْعَمَهُم مِّن جُوعٍ وَءَامَنَهُم مِّنْ خَوْفٍ﴾. قال ابن عبّاس آمنهم من البرص والجذام وهو والله أبرص وما هو إلّا ابن فلان الفرّاش.

٧.٥ فأمر المأمون أخاه أبا إسحاق فجلدها حدّاً فقالت سوءة يا أمير المؤمنين أن تحدّ أختك لابن الفرّاش وسننت على بنات الخلفاء الحدّ. فوالله لقد ظننتُ أنّ أمره يستتر. فأمّا الآن فوالله ليتناقلنّه الرواة وليتحدّثن به إلى أن تقوم الساعة. ونهضت فقال المأمون قاتلها الله فلو كانت رجلاً لكانت أقعد بالخلافة من كثير من الخلفاء. وقلّد أبا عليّ الصلاة على جنائز أولاد الخلفاء ليدرأ عنه العيب.[1]

٨.٥ ونرجع إلى ذكر إسحاق بن إبراهيم ونورد طرفاً من أخباره في حزمه وضبطه بقدر ما يليق بالكتاب. إسحاق هذا هو ابن أخ طاهر بن الحسين ويُكنّى أبا الحسين وكان المأمون اصطنعه وولّاه خلافة عبد الله بن طاهر بحضرته لمّا أخرج عبد الله إلى خراسان وكان أشدّ الناس تقدّماً عنده واختصاصاً به. فذكر عبد الله بن خرداذبه أنّه حضر مجلس المأمون يوماً وقد عرض عليه أحمد بن أبي خالد رقاعاً فيها رقعة قوم متظلّمين من إسحاق بن إبراهيم فلمّا قرأها المأمون أخذ القلم وكتب على ظهرها ما في هؤلاء الأوباش إلّا كلّ طاعن واشٍ. إسحاق غرسي بيدي ومن غرسته أنجب ولم يخلف. لا أُعدي عليه أحداً. ثمّ كتب إلى إسحاق رقعة فيها من مؤدّب مشفق إلى حصيف متأدّب يا بُنيّ من عزّ تواضع ومن قدر عفا ومن راعى أنصف ومن راقب حذر. وعاقبة الدالّة غير محمودة والمؤمن كيّس فطن. والسلام.

١ الأصل: (ألا رحم الله تعالى أمير المؤمنين عبد الله المأمون ما كان أوسع علمه وأغزر عقله في أمره وتقليده لأبي عليّ في الصلاة على الجنائز من أولاد الخلفاء) وردت في الهامش.

She replied, "I swear by God, Commander of the Faithful, that it's more proper for me to be unveiled in the presence of ʿAbdallāh ibn Ṭāhir and ʿAlī ibn Hishām than in the presence of Abū ʿAlī. For, by God, he's not my brother or al-Rashīd's son. Almighty God revealed about the Quraysh: «Who has fed them against hunger and given them security against fear»[24] and Ibn ʿAbbās glossed that 'He has given them security against leprosy and elephantiasis.' He's a leper, and he's simply the son of one of the house servants."

On al-Maʾmūn's orders, his brother Abū Isḥāq beat her the number of lashes mandated for false accusation.[25] She said, "Commander of the Faithful, it's disgraceful for you to have inflicted this beating on your sister because of the son of a house servant and to have imposed Qur'anic punishments on daughters of the caliphs. By God, I thought his condition was a secret, but now, by God, the story will be told and people will speak of it until the Day of Judgment." She stood up and went out. Al-Maʾmūn said, "God damn her. If she were a man, she'd be much better qualified for the caliphate than many caliphs." He appointed Abū ʿAlī to lead the prayers at the funerals for members of the caliphal family, to avert disgrace from him.[26] 5.7

Coming back to Isḥāq ibn Ibrāhīm, we will relate some instances of his decisiveness and control of affairs, as are appropriate to the nature of this book. He was the nephew of Ṭāhir ibn al-Ḥusayn and his teknonym was Abū l-Ḥusayn. Al-Maʾmūn took him into his service and, in the presence of ʿAbdallāh, whom he was sending to govern Khurasan, appointed him ʿAbdallāh ibn Ṭāhir's deputy. Isḥāq enjoyed the greatest favor with al-Maʾmūn and was his closest associate. ʿAbdallāh ibn Khurdādhbih related that one day when he was attending al-Maʾmūn's court, Aḥmad ibn Abī Khālid presented the caliph with some documents, including a petition from people complaining that Isḥāq ibn Ibrāhīm had treated them unjustly. When al-Maʾmūn had read it, he took his pen and wrote on the back of it: "This rabble are mere traitors and mud-slingers. Isḥāq I have nurtured with my own hands, and those whom I nurture turn out excellently and do not disappoint." Then he wrote a note to Isḥāq, as follows: "From a sympathetic tutor to a discriminating pupil: My boy, the mighty should show humility, the powerful should forgive; those who impose regulations should act justly and those who supervise should show caution. Capriciousness comes to a bad end, but the believer is perspicacious and shrewd. Farewell." 5.8

٩،٥ وولي إسحاق للمأمون ثمّ للمعتصم ثمّ للواثق ثمّ للمتوكّل ومات في أيّام المتوكّل فأقام ابنه محمّداً مكانه فلبث يسيراً ومات فاستُدعي محمّد بن عبد الله بن طاهر من خراسان ورُدّ إليه ما كان إلى إسحاق.

١٠،٥ وذكروا أنّ بعض ولد الرشيد وكان له موضع من النسب ومكان من المعرفة والأدب مرض ببغداد مرضاً طال ولم يقدر على الركوب فاشتهى التفرّج والتنزّه في الماء فأراد أن يبني زلّالاً يجلس فيه فمنعه إسحاق وقال هذا شيء لا نحبّ أن يُعمل مثله إلّا بأمر أمير المؤمنين وإذنه. فكتب إلى المعتصم يستأذنه في ذلك فخرج الأمر لإسحاق بإطلاقه له فكتب إسحاق ورد عليّ كتاب من أمير المؤمنين بإطلاق بناء زلّال لم يُحدّ لي طوله ولا عرضه فوقفت أمره إلى أن أستطلع الرأي في ذلك. فكتب إليه يحمده على احتياطه ويحدّ له ذرع الزلّال.

١١،٥ قال ولمّا انتقل المعتصم إلى سرّ من رأى كان الناس في يوم الموكب يغشون دار المأمون ويقعدون فيها على سبيلهم في حياته إجلالاً للسلطان وتعظيماً لأمره فانصرف محمّد بن إسحاق في يوم من الأيّام الحارّة وقد أطال الركوب واجتاز بدار المأمون وقد فتل قلنسوته على رأسه مستتراً بها من الشمس فبلغ أباه ذلك فضربه معاقباً له على اجتيازه بباب الخليفة متبذّلاً.

١٢،٥ وذكر عبد الله بن خرداذبه أنّه خرج يوماً من بين يدي المأمون في أثر إسحاق ابن إبراهيم حتّى إذا صار إلى الدهليز الثاني وقف ووقف القوّاد والناس لوقوفه ثمّ قال أين خليفة عليّ بن صالح وكان عليّ ذلك الوقت صاحب أمر الدار والمرسوم بالحجبة فأتي بخليفته فضربه مائة مقرعة ثمّ قال الحبس. ثمّ قال هاتوا خليفة صاحب البريد فأُتي به فضربه مائة مقرعة ثمّ قال الحبس. ثمّ دعا بعليّ بن صالح وبصاحب البريد وقال لهما تقلّدان خلافتكما في دار الخليفة من يضيّع الأمور ويهملها. كنتما بهذا الأدب أحقّ من هذين. فقالا وما كان من أمرهما الذي أنكرتَه أيّها الأمير

Isḥāq governed Baghdad for al-Ma'mūn, al-Mu'taṣim, al-Wāthiq, and finally al-Mutawakkil. He died during the caliphate of al-Mutawakkil, who appointed his son, Muḥammad, to succeed him. Muḥammad died shortly thereafter, and then Muḥammad ibn ʿAbdallāh ibn Ṭāhir was summoned from Khurasan and entrusted with the office Isḥāq had occupied. 5.9

One of al-Rashīd's sons, a man of noble descent on his mother's side and noted for his knowledge and culture, fell ill in Baghdad. The illness dragged on and he was unable to ride. He wanted to get out and take a trip on the river, so he decided to have a light boat built that he could sit in. Isḥāq, however, blocked the plan, saying, "We wouldn't wish to approve this without the caliph's knowledge and permission." He wrote to al-Muʿtaṣim for permission, and the answer came back that he could go ahead. He wrote to the man: "I have received a letter from the Commander of the Faithful granting permission for the boat to be built, but he did not specify its length and breadth. So I've halted the project until I can consult him about that." Al-Muʿtaṣim wrote to him praising him for his caution and setting out the boat's dimensions. 5.10

When al-Muʿtaṣim moved to Samarra, people went to al-Ma'mūn's palace on days when there were processions and took their seats there as they had done when he was alive, out of deference to the state and glorification of its prestige. One hot day, Muḥammad ibn Isḥāq was going home after he had been in the saddle a long time, and passed by al-Ma'mūn's palace. To protect himself from the sun, he had wound his headdress round his head. When his father heard, he punished him with a beating for passing the caliph's gate dressed in such a slovenly fashion. 5.11

Ibn Khurdādhbih recounted that he left al-Ma'mūn's presence one day hard on Isḥāq ibn Ibrāhīm's heels. When Isḥāq reached the second anteroom, he came to a stop. All the commanders and the others present stood up when he stopped. Then he asked, "Where is ʿAlī ibn Ṣāliḥ's deputy?" ʿAlī was then in charge of the palace administration and responsible for the chamberlains. His deputy was produced. Isḥāq struck him a hundred times, and said, "Prison." Then he ordered, "Bring me the deputy of the man in charge of the postal service," struck him a hundred times, and said, "Prison." Calling for ʿAlī ibn Ṣāliḥ and the manager of the postal service, he said to them, "You have appointed as your deputies in the caliph's palace two incompetent and negligent men. You deserve this punishment more than they do." They replied, "What did they do to merit your disapproval, sire?" "The manager of the postal service was seated 5.12

فقال صاحب البريد يقعد في دار الخليفة فيضحك ويقهقه وصاحب الدار جالس لا ينكر ثمّ خرج. قال فكنت أدخل الدار بعدها فلا أرى فيها ضاحكاً.

١٣.٥ قال ودخل إسحاق في يوم نوروز إلى المتوكّل والسمّاجة بين يديه وعلى المتوكّل ثوب وشي مثقل وقد كثر أصحاب السمّاجة حتّى قربوا منه للقط الدراهم التي تُنثر عليهم وجذبوا ذيله. فلمّا رأى إسحاق ذلك ولّى مغضباً وهو يقول أفّ وتفّ فما تُغني حراستنا المملكة مع هذا التضييع. ورآه المتوكّل وقد ولّى فقال ويلكم رُدّوا أبا الحسين فقد خرج مغضباً. فخرج الحجّاب والخدم خلفه ودخل وهو يسمع وصيفاً وزرافة كلّ مكروه حتّى وصل إلى المتوكّل فقال ما أغضبك ولِمَ خرجت فقال يا أمير المؤمنين عساك تتوهّم أنّ هذا الملك ليس له من الأعداء مثل ما له من الأولياء. تجلس في مجلس يبتذلك فيه مثل هؤلاء الكلاب حتّى يجذبوا ذيلك وكلّ واحد منهم متنكّر بصورة منكرة فما يؤمن أن يكون فيهم عدوّ قد احتسب نفسه ديانةً وله نيّة فاسدة وطويّة رديّة فيثب بك فمتى كان يستقال هذا ولو أخليت الأرض منهم فقال يا أبا الحسين لا تغضب فوالله لا تراني على مثلها أبداً. فبُني للمتوكّل بعد ذلك مجلس مشرف ينظر منه إلى السمّاجة.

١٤.٥ وذكر موسى بن صالح بن شيخ أنّه كلّم إسحاق بن إبراهيم في امرأة من أهله وسأله النظر لها فقال يا أبا محمّد من قصّة هذه المرأة ومن حالها ومن بعلها فوالله إن زال يصفها حتّى تحيّرتُ. قال أبو البرق الشاعر كان إسحاق يُجري عليّ أرزاقاً فأنشدته يوماً فسألني عن عيالي وما أحتاج إليه لهم. ثمّ قال لي تحتاج عيالك في كلّ شهر من الدقيق كذا ومن كذا كذا فما زال يخبرني بشيء من أمر منزلي جهلته وعلمه هو.

١٥.٥ قال وورد على إسحاق كتاب من المعتصم وهو جالس يشرب ومعه محمّد بن راشد الخنّاق وكان خصيصاً به أثيراً عنده. فما فرغ من قراءة الكتاب حتّى قال سياط وعقابين وجلّادين. فأُحضر ذلك فأمر محمّد بن راشد فأقيم من مجلسه وشُقّ عنه ونصب

in the caliph's palace, laughing and guffawing, and the palace administrator was sitting there without reproving him." Then Isḥāq left. Ibn Khudādhbih added, "After that, when I entered the palace, I didn't see anyone laughing."

One Nauruz festival, Isḥāq went to visit al-Mutawakkil and saw the masked players[27] in front of him. The caliph was wearing a heavily brocaded robe. The players had crowded together and come up to him to pick up the dirhams he was scattering among them, and they were pulling at the edge of his robe. When Isḥāq saw that, he left in anger, saying, "Fie! What's the use of our guarding the empire with these dissolute goings-on!" Al-Mutawakkil, seeing that he had gone out, said, "Damn it! Bring back Abū l-Ḥusayn. He's left in anger." So the attendants and servants went after him, and he came back, heaping all kinds of curses on Waṣīf and Zurāfah until he reached al-Mutawakkil. The caliph asked, "What made you angry? Why did you go away?" Isḥāq replied, "Commander of the Faithful, perhaps you imagine that this realm does not have as many enemies as it does friends. You hold an audience where dogs like these can make up to you, pulling at your robe, each wearing an ugly mask. How can one be sure that one of them is not an enemy ready to sacrifice his life for some religious conviction, driven by an evil purpose and wicked intention to attack you? Even if you rid the world of your enemies, would he abandon his aim?" Al-Mutawakkil responded, "Don't be angry. By God, you'll never see me in such a situation ever again." After that, he had a dais constructed from which he could look down on the players. 5.13

According to Mūsā ibn Ṣāliḥ, he spoke to Isḥāq ibn Ibrāhīm about a female member of his family, asking him to take an interest in her. Isḥāq replied, "Abū Muḥammad, this woman's story, her situation, and her husband are . . ." And Mūsā went on: "He described her in such detail I was amazed." The poet Abū l-Barq said, "Isḥāq used to pay me a regular wage. One day I recited a poem to him and he asked me about my household and what I needed for their upkeep. He went on, 'Your household needs this much flour each month, this much of this and this much of that.' And he continued to tell me things about my household that I didn't know, but he did." 5.14

While sitting drinking with Muḥammad ibn Rāshid the executioner, an intimate and valued friend of his, Isḥāq received a letter from al-Muʿtaṣim. He read the letter and said, "Whips, two whipping posts, and two hangmen." When they arrived, he had Muḥammad ibn Rāshid pulled to his feet, stripped of his robe, and attached to the two posts, while Muḥammad was asking, "Prince, 5.15

في العقابين وهو يقول أيّها الأمير ما حالي وما قصّتي فقال الحُقّ الجوهر الذي كان لفلان من صفته كيت وكيت تُحضرنيه الساعة وإلّا أتيت على نفسك. فذهب يتلكأ فقال أوجعوا فلمّا أحسّ بالضرب قال أنا أحضره أيّها الأمير. قال وحقّ أمير المؤمنين لا برحت مكانك أو تحضره. فأحضره لوقته فلمّا رآه إسحاق سرّي عنه وأسفر وجهه وقال هاتوا ثيابًا فأُتي بخلعة فألبسها وردّه إلى موضعه وأجاب عن الكتاب وأنفذ الحقّ لوقته إلى المعتصم فقال محمّد أيّها الأمير ما أبعد ما بين الفعلين. فقال ويحك وفّيت الخدمة والنصيحة حقّها ووفّيت المودّة بعد ذلك حقّها.

وذكر أبو حشيشة الطنبوريّ قال كنت يومًا في منزلي إذ طرق الباب صاحب بريد ١٦،٥
وقال أجب فلمّا قال أجب علمت أنّه أمر عال فلبست ثيابي ومضيت معه حتّى دخلنا دار إسحاق بن إبراهيم فعدل بي إلى ممرّ طويل فيه حجر متقابلة تفوح من جميعها روائح الطعام. فأُدخلت حجرة منها وقُدّم إليّ طعام في نهاية النظافة وطيب الراحة فأكلت وجاؤوني بثلاثة أرطال فشربت وأحضروني صندوقًا فيه طنابير فاخترت طنبورًا منها وأصلحته على الطريقة وأُخرجت من الموضع إلى حجرة لم أرَ أحسن منها وإذا في مجلسها رجلان جالسان على أحدهما قباء مُلحم وقلنسوة سمّوريّة وعلى الآخر ثياب خزّ وستارة مضروبة فسلّمت وأُمرت بالجلوس فجلست فقال لي صاحب السمّوريّة غنّ فغنّيت

مَـا أَرَانِي إِلَّا سَأَهْجُرُ مَنْ لَيْـــسَ يَرَانِي أَقْوَى عَلَى ٱلْهِجْرَانِ
مَـلَّنِي وَاثِقًـا بِحُسْنِ وَفَـائِي   مَا أَضَـرَّ ٱلْوَفَا عَلَى ٱلْإِنْسَانِ

فغنّيته فشرب رطلًا ونقر الستارة وقال غنّوه فغُنّي الصوت أحسن غناء في الدنيا ١٧،٥
وخلت أنّ البيت يرقص فقال لي كيف ترى قلت قد والله يا مولاي بغّضوا إليّ هذا

what's wrong? What have I done?" Isḥāq simply said, "The jeweled amulet case belonging to so-and-so, which looks like such and such. Produce it for me immediately, or it will be the end of you." Muḥammad started to apologize profusely, but Isḥāq ordered, "Make him feel it!" When Muḥammad felt the lash, he said, "I'll bring it, Prince." "By the obligation I owe the Commander of the Faithful, you won't leave here until you produce it." So he had it brought immediately. When Isḥāq saw it, he relaxed and his face cleared. "Bring clothes," he commanded. A robe of honor[28] was brought and was put on Muḥammad. Isḥāq took him back to his dwelling, answered the letter, and sent the amulet case to al-Muʿtaṣim straightaway. Muḥammad remarked, "Prince, what an enormous difference there is between these two actions." Isḥāq answered, "I fulfilled the obligations of counsel and service—and afterward I paid friendship its due."

Abū Ḥashīshah the pandore player had this story: One day when I was at home, 5.16
a messenger from the postal service knocked at the door. "Obey the order," he said. I could tell from his words it was important. So I got dressed and set off with him. We entered Isḥāq ibn Ibrāhīm's palace and I was taken into a long passage with rooms on each side, from each of which I could smell food. I was taken into one of the rooms and brought food, excellent and delicious, which I ate. Then they brought me three measures of wine, which I drank, and a box containing pandores. I chose one and tuned it. Then I was taken off to the most beautiful room I had ever seen. Two men were in the sitting area, one wearing a coat of blended silk and a sable hat, and the other a robe of pure silk. Part of the room was curtained off. I greeted the men and was told to sit, which I did. The wearer of the sable hat said to me, "Sing something," and I sang:

I'm doomed to part from the one
  who thinks I'm unable to.
She's tired of me, sure of my loyalty.
  What harm loyalty inflicts!

When I had finished, the man drank and tapped on the curtain, saying, 5.17
"Sing." The song was performed so beautifully it was out of this world, and I felt as though the room were dancing. He asked, "How do you find it?" "Sir, they've made me hate this song. I now find it ugly." He laughed and asked me to repeat it three times, each time drinking a measure of wine. Then he asked,

الصوت وسمّجوه في عينيّ. فضحك واستعادنيه ثلاث دفعات يشرب في كلّ دفعة منها رطلاً ثمّ قال أتعرفني قلت لا قال أنا إسحاق بن إبراهيم وهذا محمّد بن راشد الخنّاق ووالله لئن ظهر حديث هذا المجلس منك لأضربنّك ثلاثمائة سوط. قم إذا شئت. فقمت من بين يديه فلحقني الغلام بصرّة فيها ثلاثمائة دينار فاجتهدت أن يأخذ منها شيئاً فأبى.

١٨،٥ وذكر عمرو بن بانة قال وجّه إليّ إسحاق بن إبراهيم في آخر النهار فصرت إلى داره ودخلت عليه وهو جالس في طارمة ملبّسة بالخزّ على دجلة وقد انبسط القمر على الروشن وعلى دجلة وهو من أحسن منظر رأيت قطّ والمغنّون[١] جميعاً بين يديه وبذل جالسة وراء مقطع في الطارمة فلم يزل جالساً بموضعه ونحن بين يديه إلى أن نودي بالفجر فقام وقمنا وقال لنا الغلمان انصرفوا فنزلنا إلى الشطّ ودعونا بسميريّة فجلسنا فيها جميعاً وقلت لهم إنّ منزلي أقرب من منازلكم فاجعلوا مقامكم اليوم عندي ففعلوا. وحصلنا في المنزل فطلبت فيه شيئاً يؤكل فلم أجد فأمرت بإحضار المائدة فأُحضرت فارغة وطرحت في وسطها مائة درهم صحاحاً وقلت يوجّه كلّ واحد منكم فيشتري له ما يريد فما كان بأسرع من أن امتلأت بكلّ شيء فأكلنا وشربنا ومرّ لنا يوم طيّب وتفرّقنا آخر النهار وفي قلوبنا غصص ممّا فعله بنا إسحاق وما فاتنا من تلك الليلة الحسنة في ذلك الموضع الحسن.

١٩،٥ فمضيت بعد ذلك إلى بذل وسألتها عن السبب فيما فعله فقالت قد سألته عن ذلك فقال ويحك أنا أشتهي الشرب في مثل هذه الليلة منذ سنة وأدافع نفسي به فلمّا حصل لي جميع ما أريده واشتهيته أردت أن أري نفسي سلطاني عليها وقهري لها ومنعها ممّا تحبّه لئلاّ تقودني إلى ما تريد ففعلت ما رأيت.

٢٠،٥ وكان مع ذلك حسن المروءة كريم النفس. فذكر أبو حشيشة قال دعاني في بعض الأيّام فصرت إليه وجلست أغنّيه وعليه درّاعة خزّ خضراء لم أر أحسن منها قطّ. فجعلت

١ الأصل: والمغنّيون.

"Do you know me?" "No." "I'm Isḥāq ibn Ibrāhīm and this is Muḥammad ibn Rāshid the executioner. By God, if ever you let on about this meeting, I will give you three hundred lashes. You can go now." I got up and left his presence. The servant caught up with me to give me a purse of three hundred dinars. I tried to get him to take some but he refused.

ʿAmr ibn Bānah recalled: Isḥāq ibn Ibrāhīm sent for me at the end of the day. 5.18
I arrived at his palace and was shown in. He was sitting in a pavilion hung with silk, overlooking the Tigris. The moon was shining through the lattice window and on the Tigris, and it was the most beautiful sight I have seen. All the singers were with him, and Badhl was sitting behind a screen in the pavilion. He did not budge, with us arranged in front of him, until the dawn prayer was called. Then he stood up, as did we. He said, "The servants have gone." So we went down to the riverbank and called for a pleasure boat. We all took our seats and I said, "My house is closer than yours, so let's spend the day at my house." They agreed, and we arrived home. I looked for something to eat and, not finding anything, I ordered the servants to bring the table, which arrived bare. I put a hundred solid dirhams on the table and said, "Each of you can go and buy what you want." In no time at all the table was covered with all kinds of food. We ate and drank and passed an excellent day. At the end of the day, we parted with heavy hearts because of how Isḥāq had treated us and because we were missing that beautiful night and lovely place.

Later on I went to see Badhl and asked her the reason for his behavior. She 5.19
said, "I asked him, and he replied, 'Damn it, I've been wanting to drink on a night like that for a whole year and I've been resisting my inclination. When everything I wanted and desired came together, I wanted to show my soul my mastery and domination over it and my ability to prevent it from doing what it wanted, so that it would not induce me to follow its own desires. And so I did what you saw.'"

Still, he was generous and high-minded. Abū Ḥashīshah related: One day, 5.20
Isḥāq invited me to his house. I was sitting singing to him, and he was wearing a green silk outermantle, more beautiful than any I had seen. I stared at it and he understood why. He summoned his wardrobe master and said, "Some

أنظر إليها وفطن بنظري فدعا بالخازن وقال كانوا جاؤونا منذ أيّام بعشرة أثواب خزّخضر هذا أحدها فجئني ببقيّتها فأحضر تسعة أثواب يتجاوز حسنها كلّ وصف فأعطانيها فبعت من رذالها الثوب بمائة دينار.

وقال طرق أحمد بن يوسف الكاتب إسحاق بن إبراهيم فقدّم إليه كلّ شيء حسن من ٢١،٥
الأطعمة والآلة وضُربت الستائر وأُحضرت الفواكه والنبيذ ومرّ يوم لم يكن مثله. ثمّ سأل أحمد أن يكون عنده من الغد فقال أحمد يفوتني الصيد. فأحضر جارية وغلاماً وفرساً لم ير أحسن منهم وقال هذا صيدك غداً ثمّ تصنّع له من الغد فرأى أحمد شيئاً لم ير مثله قطّ. وقال له إسحاق أمس كان فتوّة واليوم مروّة.

وكان المأمون يصير إليه إلى داره فيقيم عنده الأيّام هو وغلمانه وحشمه أنساً به وثقةً ٢٢،٥
بمكانه.

واجتازت[١] يوماً زبيدة في دجلة في حرّاقتها فصعدت إلى دار إسحاق لبعض حاجتها فعرض عليها إسحاق الطعام فأمرت بإحضاره فعجبت ممّا رأت وممّا قُدّم. وقالت والله ما كانت لي حاجة إليه وإنّما أردت أن أختبر مروّته فوجدته أتمّ الناس مروّة. هذا من غير تصنّع لي ولا علم بمجيئي.

١ الأصل: (مرور الستّ زبيدة على مسكن إسحاق فدخلت إليه لتنظر مروءته) وردت في الهامش.

days ago they brought us ten green silk garments and this is one of them. Bring me the others." The wardrobe master brought nine garments, indescribably beautiful, and Isḥāq gave them to me. I sold the least valuable robes for one hundred dinars apiece.

Another anecdote: Aḥmad ibn Yūsuf the secretary visited Isḥāq ibn Ibrāhīm unexpectedly. He entertained him with all kinds of good food and accoutrements. The curtains were drawn for singing, fruit and wine were brought, and they spent a splendid day. Then Isḥāq asked Aḥmad if he would visit him the next day, at which Aḥmad said, "I won't get anything out of it."[29] Isḥāq produced a slave girl, a servant, and a horse, all of surpassing beauty, and said, "This will be your catch tomorrow." He spared no pains the next day, and Aḥmad had an unforgettable time. Isḥāq said to him, "Yesterday was nobility, today is generosity." 5.21

Al-Ma'mūn used to visit Isḥāq in his palace and spend days with him—he, his servants, and his suite—out of pleasure in his company and confidence in his standing. 5.22

Zubaydah was out on the Tigris in her boat one day,[30] and she disembarked and came up to Isḥāq's palace to conduct some business. Isḥāq suggested she have something to eat, and she ordered the food to be brought. She was amazed at what she saw and what was put on the table. She said later, "By God, I didn't need the food but I wanted to test his generosity. And I found him the most generous of mortals. For this was without taking any special pains for me and with no advance knowledge that I was coming."[31]

دير أشموني

١،٦ وأشموني امرأة بُني الدير على اسمها ودُفنت فيه وهو بقُطْرَبُّل غربيّ دجلة وعيده اليوم الثالث من تشرين الأوّل وهو من الأيّام العظيمة ببغداد يجتمع أهلها إليه كاجتماعهم إلى بعض أعيادهم ولا يبقى أحد من أهل التطرّب واللعب إلّا خرج إليه فمنهم في الطيّارات ومنهم في الزبازب والسميريّات كلّ إنسان بحسب قدرته ويتنافسون فيما يظهرونه هنالك من زيّهم ويباهون بما يعدّونه لقصفهم ويعمرون شطّه وأكنافه وديره وحاناته وتُضرب لذوي البسطة منهم الخيم والفساطيط وتعزف عليهم القيان فيظلّ كلّ إنسان منهم مشغولاً بأمره ومكبّاً على لهوه. فهو أعجب منظر وأنزهه وأطيب مشهد وأحسنه. وهناك أيضاً دير يُسمّى دير الجرجوث وحوله بساتين ومزارع ومن ضاق به دير أشموني[1] عدل إليه.

٢،٦ قال جحظة خرجت في عيد من أعياد أشموني إلى قطربّل فلمّا وصلت إلى الشطّ مددت عيني لأنظر موضعاً خالياً أصعد إليه أو قوماً ظرافاً أنزل عليهم فرأيت فتيَين من أحسن الناس وجوهاً وأنظفهم لباساً وأظرفهم آلة فقدّمت سميريّتي نحوهم وقلت أتأذنون في الصعود إليكم فقالوا بالرحب والسعة. فصعدت وقلت يا غلام طنبوري ونبيذي. فقالا أمّا الطنبور فنعم وأمّا النبيذ فلا. فجلست مع أحسن الناس أخلاقاً وأملحهم عشرة وأخذنا في أمرنا ثمّ تناولت الطنبور وغنّيت بشعر لي

سُقْياً لِأَشْمُونِي وَلَذَّاتِهَا ... وَٱلْعَيْشِ فِيمَا بَيْنَ جَنَّاتِهَا
سُقْياً لِأَيَّامٍ مَضَتْ لِي بِهَا ... مَا بَيْنَ شَطَّيْهَا وَحَانَاتِهَا
إِذِ ٱصْطِبَاحِي فِي بَسَاتِينِهَا ... وَإِذْ غُبُوقِي فِي دِيَارَاتِهَا

[1] الأصل: الشموني.

Ushmūnī's Monastery

Ushmūnī is a woman after whom the monastery was named and who is buried there. The monastery is at Quṭrabbul to the west of the Tigris. It celebrates its patronal feast on the thirteenth of October, and that is a major occasion in Baghdad, when people gather as they do for some other festivals. None of those who enjoy revelry and entertainment fail to attend. Some travel by rapid skiffs, others by small boats or launches with rowers, each according to his means, and they vie with one other in what they wear and bring for amusement. They occupy the riverbank, the slopes, the monastery, and the taverns; tents or awnings are set up for the better-off; and singing girls make music for them. Everyone attends to his own affairs and concentrates on his own pleasure. It is the most marvelous and attractive sight, and the pleasantest and loveliest scene. In that same place, there is another monastery, the Jarjūth Monastery, surrounded by gardens and fields, and those who grow weary of Ushmūnī's Monastery go there. 6.1

Jaḥẓah recounted: I went to Quṭrabbul on one of Ushmūnī's feast days, and 6.2
when I arrived at the bank I looked back and forth to find an empty space where I could go ashore and an elegant group I could join. I saw two young men, handsome, nicely dressed, and well provided for, so I maneuvered my boat toward them and asked, "Will you allow me to come up and join you?" They replied, "You are most welcome." I went ashore and summoned my servant: "Boy, my pandore and my wine." "The pandore is fine," they said, "but no need for the wine." I took my seat beside them, men of excellent character and delightful companionship, and we set about enjoying ourselves. I took up the pandore and sang a song of mine:

> May the memory of Ushmūnī and its pleasures stay fresh,
>   and the time I have spent in its gardens.
> May the memory of the days remain fresh
>   that I've spent by its banks and in its taverns,
> And the morning wine in its gardens I've drunk,
>   and the evening draft in its convents.

٣،٦ فنعر القوم وشربوا بالأرطال وشربتُ وطاب لنا الوقت ثمّ قلتُ لأحدهما فداك ما أرى في هذا الجمع أرقّ منكما طبعاً ولا أرق نبيذاً. فقال لي مجيباً

شَـرَابِي رَقِـيقٌ كَمَا قَدْ رَأَيْـتَ وَدِبْسُهُـمُ بِذُبَابٍ يُسَاطْ

وأشار إلى القوم ثمّ قال

فَكَـيْفَ أَكُونُ نَظِيرًا لَهُـمْ أَبِنْ لِي بِعَقْلِكَ . . . ضُرَاطْ[1]

ثمّ قال أزيدك قلت لا. ومرّ لنا أطيب يوم وأحسنه.

٤،٦ قال محمّد بن المؤمّل الطائيّ كنت مع أبي العتاهية في سميريّة ونحن سائرون إلى أشموني فسمع غناءً طرب له فقال لي تحسن ترقص قلت نعم. فقال قم بنا نرقص. قلت نحن في سميريّة وأخاف أن نغرق. قال وإن غرقنا نكون ماذا أليس نكون شهداء الطرب.

٥،٦ وللثروانيّ فيه

اِشْـرَبْ عَـلَى قَـرْعِ ٱلنَّوَاقِيسِ فِي دَيْرِ أُشْمُونِي بِتَـغْـلِيسِ
لَا تَخْفِ كَأْسَ ٱلشُّرْبِ وَٱللَّيْلُ فِي حَــدِّ نَعِيـمٍ لَا وَلَا بُؤْسِ
إِلَّا عَلَى قَــرْعِ ٱلنَّوَاقِيسِ أَوْ صَوْتِ قُسَّانٍ وَتَشْمِيسِ
فَإِنَّمَا ٱلشَّيْءُ بِأَسْـبَابِهِ وَمُحْكَمُ ٱلْوَصْفِ بِتَأْسِيسِ
فَهٰكَذَا فَٱشْرَبْ وَإِلَّا فَكُنْ مُجَـاوِرًا بَعْضَ ٱلنَّوَاوِيسِ

١ كذا في الأصل.

My companions bellowed and drank a few measures of wine, I did too, and we had an excellent time. Then I said to one of them, "May my life be your ransom. I cannot see anyone in this gathering with a finer nature than you two, or finer wine." He answered: 6.3

My wine is refined, as you have seen,
while their syrups are mixed with flies.

And he gestured toward the people round about:

How can you think that I'm like them?
Use your great brain, or else fart mayhem!

Then he asked, "Shall I go on?" "No." And we spent a splendid day.

An incident told by Muḥammad ibn al-Mu'ammil al-Ṭā'ī: I was with Abū 6.4
l-ʿAtāhiyah in a launch making for Ushmūnī's when he heard singing, which sent him into ecstasy. He asked me, "Can you dance well?" I replied, "Yes." "Then let's get up and dance." "We're in a boat and I'm afraid we'll be drowned." "If we are, so what? Won't we be martyrs to ecstasy?"

Al-Tharwānī composed these verses on the monastery: 6.5

Drink to the sound of the clappers,[32]
as dawn comes to Ushmūnī's Convent.
Don't spurn the glass of wine at night's end
in happiness, not in misery,
Except for the beat of the clappers
and the chant of the priests and deacons.
Things have their causes. A good description
should have a firm foundation.
And so drink away, and if not,
go live next to a graveyard.

قال كتب يحيى بن كامل إلى عبد الملك بن محمّد الهاشميّ في يوم أشموني ٦،٦

ٱليَوْمَ أُشْمُونِي أَبَا ٱلْفَضْلِ وَهْوَ عَجِيبٌ طَيِّبُ ٱلظِّلِّ
وَأَنْتَ لِلْيَوْمِ صَرِيعٌ فَمَا تَصْنَعُ يَحْيَى يَا أَبَا ٱلْفَضْلِ

فوجّه إليه بما ركبه وصار إليه وعرف الجمّاش الخبر فكتب إليه

قُولَا لِعَبْدِ ٱلْمَلِكِ ٱلْمَاهِرِ وَلِٱبْنِ عَمِّ ٱلْمُصْطَفَى ٱلطَّاهِرِ
أَمَا تَرَى ٱلْيَوْمَ وَأَحْوَالَهُ تَدْعُو إِلَى حَثِّكَ بِٱلدَّائِرِ
عِيدٌ وَغَيْمٌ زَارَ فِي يَوْمِنَا فَقُمْ بِحَقِّ ٱلْعِيدِ وَٱلزَّائِرِ
وَٱلْيَوْمَ أُشْمُونِي فَبَادِرْ بِنَا نَحُثُّهَا فِي يَوْمِنَا ٱلزَّاهِرِ
حَبَسْتَ يَحْيَى ثُمَّ أَغْفَلْتَنِي أَحُلْتَ عَنْ جَمَّاشِكَ ٱلشَّاعِرِ

فوجّه إليه وأحضره ومرّ لهم يوم طيّب.

ولأبي الشبل البرجميّ فيه ٧،٦

شَهِدْتُ مَوَاطِنَ ٱللَّذَّاتِ طُرًّا وَجُبْتُ بِقَاعَهَا بَحْرًا وَبَرًّا
فَلَمْ أَرَ مِثْلَ أُشْمُونِي مَحَلًّا أَلَذَّ لِحَاضِرِيهِ وَلَا أَسَرَّا
بِهِ جَيْشَانِ مِنْ خَيْلٍ وَسُفْنٍ أَنَاخَا فِي ذُرَاهُ وَٱسْتَقَرَّا
كَأَنَّهُمَا زُحُوفٌ وَغًى وَلَكِنْ إِلَى ٱللَّذَّاتِ مَا كَرًّا وَفَرًّا
سِلَاحُهُمَا ٱلْقَوَاقِزُ وَٱلْقَنَانِي وَأَكْوَاسٌ تَدُورُ هَلُمَّ جَرًّا
وَضَرْبُهُمَا ٱلْمَثَالِثُ وَٱلْمَثَانِي إِذَا مَا ٱلضَّرْبُ فِي ٱلْحَرْبِ ٱسْتَحَرَّا
وَأَسْرُهُمَا ظِبَاءُ ٱلدَّيْرِ طَوْعًا إِذَا أُسْدُ ٱلْحُرُوبِ أُسِرْنَ قَسْرَا
لَقَدْ جَرَّتْ لَنَا ٱلْهَيْجَاءُ خَيْرًا إِذَا مَا جَرَّتِ ٱلْهَيْجَاءُ شَرَّا

Yaḥyā ibn Kāmil wrote to ʿAbd al-Malik ibn Muḥammad al-Hāshimī on Ushmūnī's feast day: 6.6

Today's Ushmūnī's feast, Abū l-Faḍl;
it's marvelous and delightful
And you dearly love this day.
But what will Yaḥyā do, Abū l-Faḍl?

So ʿAbd al-Malik sent Yaḥyā a mount and he rode to his house. Al-Jammāsh came to hear of this and he wrote to ʿAbd al-Malik:

Ask the canny ʿAbd al-Malik,
and ask the Chosen One's pure cousin,
"Don't you think this kind of day
calls for you standing a round?"
A feast and a thirst, two visitors today.
By the truth of feast and visitor, come!
It's Ushmūnī's day, hurry!
On her feast day, wine will abound.
You've kept Yaḥyā by you
but I'm ignored in your démarche.
Can it be that you've dropped
your poet al-Jammāsh?

Upon which ʿAbd al-Malik fetched him, and they spent a fine day together.

Abū l-Shibl al-Burjumī composed this poem about the monastery: 6.7

I've visited all pleasure's playgrounds on land and by sea,
but found no more joy and delight than at Ushmūnī's mansion.
By its slopes two hosts of horses and boats moored and tied,
wheeling and turning like troops in battle, simply out for diversion,
Their weapons—bowls, flasks, and cups—passed round again and again,
sounding all the lutestrings together if blows fall in the heat of conflict,
Their captives the monastery's gazelles, while in war lions fall prisoner;
this fray has been good to us, while in battle evil is the verdict.

وكان أبو الشبل هذا من الطيّاب وله شعر مليح وطبع رقيق وكان منعكفاً على ٨،٦
الشرب لا يفارقه ولا يوجد إلّا سكران وكان يتطرّح في الديارات والحانات ومواطن
اللّهو لا يغبّها ولا يتأخّر عنها. وكانت بينه وبين محمود الورّاق مودّة وكانا لا يفترقان.
وذكر أبو الشبل قال صرت أنا ومحمود إلى قطربّل فدعونا الخمّار وقلنا إيتنا ببنت عشر
قد أنضجها الهجير. فجاءنا بها. فقلنا اسقنا فسقانا فقلنا اشرب واسقنا فقال أنا مسلم
وكان يهودياً قد أسلم فقال لي محمود قوم يكون الخمّار عندهم مسلماً متحرّجاً وهم عند
الخمّار كفّار. أترى لله فيهم حاجة.

قال كان أبو الشبل يعاتب خنساء قينة هشام الضرير النحويّ وكانت تقول الشعر ٩،٦
فعبث بها يوماً وأفرط فغضبت وقالت ليت شعري بأيّ شيء تدلّ. أنا والله أشعر
منك ولئن شئت لأهجونّك حتّى أفضحك. فأقبل عليها وقال

خَنْسَاءُ قَدْ أَفْرَطَتْ عَلَيْنَا فَلَيْسَ مِنْهَا لَنَا مُجِيرُ
تَاهَتْ بِأَشْعَارِهَا عَلَيْنَا كَأَنَّمَا نَاكَهَا جَرِيرُ

فخجلت وانقطعت عن جوابه.

ولأبي الشبل في جارية سوداء كان يهواها فعوتب عليها وكان مولعاً بالسودان ١٠،٦

غَدَتْ بِطُولِ ٱلْمَلَامِ عَاذِلَةٌ تَعْذِلُنِي بِٱلسَّوَادِ وَٱلدَّعَجِ
وَيْحَكِ كَيْفَ ٱلسُّلُوُّ عَنْ غُرَرٍ مُقَيَّرَاتِ ٱلْوُجُوهِ كَٱلسَّبَجِ
يَحْمِلْنَ بَيْنَ ٱلْأَفْخَاذِ أَسْنِمَةً يَطِيرُ أَوْبَارُهَا مِنَ ٱلْوَهَجِ
لَا عَذَّبَ ٱللهُ مُؤْمِنًا بِهِمِ غَيْرِي وَلَا حَانَ مِنْهُمُ فَرَجِي
فَإِنَّنِي بِٱلسَّوَادِ مُبْتَهِجٌ وَلَسْتُ بِٱلْبِيضِ جِدَّ مُبْتَهِجِ

Abū l-Shibl was an excellent person, a composer of fine poetry with a delicate talent. He was a compulsive drinker and never gave it up; indeed, he was always to be found drunk. He was a regular customer at monasteries, taverns, and places of entertainment, never absent for long. He was a close friend of Maḥmūd the Bookseller; in fact, they were inseparable. He related: One day, Maḥmūd and I went to Quṭrabbul. We called the tavern keeper and gave him our order: "Bring us a wine ten years old that has been fermented by the hot sun." When he produced it, we asked him to pour it out and he did so. Then we said, "Have a drink, and pour us another round." "I'm a Muslim." (He was a Jew who had converted to Islam.) So Maḥmūd said to me, "When people have a wine seller who's a pious Muslim—while they are unbelievers in his eyes—do you think God has any use for them?" 6.8

Abū l-Shibl used to scold Khansā', blind Hishām the Grammarian's singing girl, who also composed poetry. One day he teased her and went too far, and she angrily retorted, "If only I knew what you are trying to prove! I'm a better poet than you, and if I want to, I can lampoon you and ruin your reputation." He looked at her and said: 6.9

Khansā''s gone too far,
she'll find no one to support her.
She's boasted of her poems,
as though she'd been fucked by Jarīr.

Khansā' was too abashed to reply.

This is a poem by Abū l-Shibl on a black slave girl he was in love with. This earned him many rebukes but he was crazy about black girls. 6.10

A scold has fired her full stock of rebuke at me,
blaming me about duskiness and ink-black eyes.
Damn it, how can I be consoled for pearls
with pitch-black faces like small shells.
Between their thighs they have mounds
where the hair burns with the fire of hell.
May God torment no other believer with them,
or cause my organ to wither.
For I'm mad about black; white women leave me cold.

وله في جارية كان يحبّها اسمها تبر ١١،٦

لِمْ تُنْصِفِي يَا سَمِيَّةَ ٱلذَّهَبِ تَتْلَفُ نَفْسِي وَأَنْتِ فِي لَعِبِ
يَا بِنْتَ عَمِّ ٱلْمِسْكِ ٱلذَّكِيِّ وَمَنْ لَوْلَاكِ لَمْ يُحْتَنَ وَلَمْ يَطِبِ
نَاسَبَكِ ٱلْمِسْكُ فِي ٱلسَّوَادِ وَفِي ٱلـ ـطِّيبِ فَأَكْرِمْ بِذَاكَ مِنْ نَسَبِ

He had a black slave girl he loved who was called Tibr.[33] 6.11

You've treated me unfairly, namesake of gold,
you're killing my soul just for fun.
You're the cousin of strong-scented musk,
but for you who'd gather it—it would be scentless.
In blackness and perfume, musk's your kin!
What a splendid kinship!

ديـر سـابـر

١٫٧ وهـذا الدير ببزوغى[1] وهي بين المزرفة والصالحيّة في الجانب الغربيّ من دجلة. وهي عامرة نزهة كثيرة البساتين والفواكه والكروم والحانات والخمّارين معمورة بأهل التطرّب والشرب وهي موطن من مواطن الخلعاء. والدير حسن عامر لا يخلو من متنزّه فيه ومتطرّب إليه.

٢٫٧ وللحسين بن الضحّاك فيه

وَعَوَاتِقٍ بَاشَـرْتُ بَيْنَ حَـدَائِقٍ   فَفَضَضْتُهُنَّ وَقَدْ حَسُنَّ صِحَاحَـا
أَتْبَعْتُ وَخْزَةَ تِلْكَ وَخْزَةَ هٰذِهِ   حَتَّى شَـرِبْتُ دِمَاءَهُنَّ جِرَاحَـا
أَبْـرَزْتُهُنَّ مِنَ ٱلْخُدُورِ حَوَاسِرًا   وَتَرَكْتُ صَوْنَ حَرِيمِهِنَّ مُـبَاحَـا
فِي دَيْرِ سَابُرَ وَٱلصَّبَاحُ يَلُوحُ لِي   فَجَمَعْتُ بَدْرًا وَٱلصَّبَاحَ وَرَاحَـا
فَٱذْهَبْ بِظَنِّكَ كَيْفَ شِئْتَ فَكُلُّهُ   مِمَّا ٱقْتَرَفْتُ تَغَـطْرُسًا وَجِمَاحَـا

٣٫٧ وكان الحسين بن الضحّاك من الأدباء الشعراء وأهل الخلاعة والمجون وبالخليع يُعرف ونادم جماعة من خلفاء بني العبّاس منهم الأمين والمعتصم والواثق والمتوكّل. فأمّا المأمون فإنّه لم يدخل إليه ولم يختلط به وذاك أنّه رثى الأمين فقال فيه

هَـلَّا بَقِيتَ لِسَـدِّ فَاقَـتِـنَا   فِينَا وَكَانَ لِغَـيْرِكَ ٱلتَّـلَـفُ
قَدْ كَانَ فِيكَ لِمَنْ مَضَى خَلَفٌ   فَٱلْيَوْمَ أَعْوَزَ بَعْدَكَ ٱلْخَـلَـفُ

فلمّا ورد المأمون إلى بغداد أمر بأن تُثبت له أسماء من يصلح لمنادمته من أهل الأدب فأُثبت له قوم ذُكر فيهم الحسين بن الضحّاك فقال أليس القائل وَكَانَ لِغَيْرِكَ ٱلتَّلَفُ

[1] كذا في عوّاد. الأصل: بابروعى.

Sābur's[34] Monastery

This monastery lies in Bazūghī, which is between Mazrafah and Ṣāliḥiyyah to the west of the Tigris. The village is well cultivated, attractive, and has many gardens, orchards, vineyards, and taverns with wine merchants that are frequented by those who want to amuse themselves and drink. It is a place where libertines gather. The monastery is beautiful and well maintained, regularly visited by people on outings or in search of amusement. 7.1

Al-Ḥusayn ibn al-Ḍaḥḥāk has a poem on it: 7.2

Old jars of wine I took in gardens, breaking their seal
 when they'd matured untouched,
The sting of one following the sting of another
 till I'd wounded myself with their blood.
I brought them out unveiled from their boudoirs
 and didn't keep their sanctuary inviolate.
In Dayr Sābur, as dawn appeared,
 I coupled the moon with daybreak and wine.
Think what you like—they're only a few
 of the deeds I did haughtily in defiance.

Al-Ḥusayn ibn al-Ḍaḥḥāk was a poet, a man of letters, dissolute and frivolous. He was known as the Libertine. He was the boon companion of several Abbasid caliphs, among them al-Amīn, al-Muʿtaṣim, al-Wāthiq, and al-Mutawakkil. He was not granted audience by al-Ma'mūn, however, and had no contact with him, because of his elegy for al-Amīn, in which he said: 7.3

Would that you'd stayed with us to fulfill our needs,
 and another had met his end.
You were worthy of those gone by;
 after you there can be no successor.

When al-Ma'mūn arrived in Baghdad, he asked for a list to be drawn up of men of culture suitable to be his companions. Al-Ḥusayn ibn al-Ḍaḥḥāk was

والله لا رأى وجهي إلّا على قارعة الطريق. فلم يحظ طول أيّام المأمون بشيء.

٤،٧ وقد كان وقت خدمته المتوكّل ضعف كثيرًا فكتب إليه يستعفيه من الخدمة فقال

أَسْلَفْتُ أَسْلَافَكَ فِيمَا مَضَى   مِنْ خِدْمَتِي إِحْدَى وَسِتِّينَا
كُنْتُ ٱبْنَ عِشْرِينَ وَخَمْسٍ فَقَدْ   وَفَّيْتُ بِضْعًا وَثَمَانِينَا
إِنِّي لَمَعْرُوفٌ بِضُعْفِ ٱلْقُوَى   وَإِنْ تَجَلَّدْتُ أَحَايِينَا
وَإِنْ تَحَمَّلْتُ عَلَى كِبْرَتِي   خِدْمَةَ أَبْنَاءِ ٱلثَّلَاثِينَا
هَدَّتْ قُوَايَ وَوَهَتْ أَعْظُمِي   وَصِرْتُ فِي ٱلْعِلَّةِ عَزُّونَا
وَخِفْتُ أَنْ يَعْجَلَ بِي مُعْجِلٌ   إِلَى ٱلَّتِي تُعْيِي ٱلْمُدَاوِينَا

٥،٧ عزّون هذا الذي ذكره نديم كان للمعتصم ثمّ نادم المتوكّل. وذكر عزّون هذا قال كنّا مع المعتصم في بعض متنزّهاته فٱحتجنا[1] أن نخوض نهرًا وكان معنا الحسين[2] بن الضحّاك فكاد أن يغرق فقبض المعتصم على عضده وحمله من السرج حتّى عبر به النهر إشفاقًا عليه.[3]

٦،٧ وكان الحسين مستهترًا بالخدم جدًّا ولم يقصر عن ذاك حتّى مات. قال المتوكّل أنشدني الحسين قوله

فَلَوْ شِئْتَ تَيَسَّرْتَ   كَمَا سُمِّيتَ يَا يُسْرُ
وَلَا وَٱللهِ لَا تَبْـرَ   حُ أَوْ يَنْصَرِمِ ٱلْأَمْرُ
فَإِمَّا ٱلْمَنْعُ وَٱلذَّمُّ   وَإِمَّا ٱلْبَذْلُ وَٱلشُّكْرُ
فَدَعْنِي مِنْ مَوَاعِيدِ   كَ إِذْ حَيَّنَكَ ٱلدَّهْرُ
فَقُلْتُ أَيُّهُمَا كَانَ   فَقَالَ ٱلْبَذْلُ وَٱلشُّكْرُ

١ الأصل: (فٱحتجنا) وردت مرّتين. ٢ الأصل: حسين. ٣ الأصل: (أقول انظر إلى أخلاق المعتصم أمير المؤمنين مع علوّ شرف نفسه كيف خشي على تكدّر مجلسه من النكد لمّا تحقّق غرق أحد جلسائه فأنقذه بنفسه وحمله من سرجه بنفسه ولم يسأل أحدًا من أتباعه فعل ذلك) وردت في الهامش.

one of them, and the caliph asked, "Isn't he the one who said, '. . . and another had met his end?' By God, he'll not see my face unless it's from the roadside." And al-Ḥusayn received no rewards during al-Ma'mūn's rule.

At the time when he was in al-Mutawakkil's service, he had become weak from old age, and he wrote to the caliph asking to be excused from attendance: 7.4

Full sixty-one years I lent my service to your fathers,
When I was twenty-five, and now I've passed fourscore.
People know I've lost my strength, robust though I sometimes seem,
Forcing myself to serve you like a youth despite my age.
My strength is failing, my bones are brittle, I'm sick like 'Azzūn—
I fear I'll be hastened to the illness no doctor can treat.

This 'Azzūn whom he mentions was a boon companion of al-Mu'taṣim and then of al-Mutawakkil. 'Azzūn relates: We were with al-Mu'taṣim on one of his trips and we needed to ford a river. Al-Ḥusayn ibn al-Ḍaḥḥāk, who was with us, almost drowned, but out of fear for his life al-Mu'taṣim grabbed him by the upper arm and carried him from his saddle until they had crossed the river.[35] 7.5

Al-Ḥusayn was quite shameless where servants were concerned, and he stayed that way until he died. Al-Mutawakkil related that al-Ḥusayn recited to him one of his poems: 7.6

If you wanted, you'd be compliant, like Yusr, your name;[36]
No, by God, don't leave till the matter's decided.
Either refusal and blame, or generosity and thanks.
Don't come with your promises, fate's fixed you a time.
Tell me, which will it be? He said, "Generosity and thanks."

قال أبو عبد الله بن حمدون كنّا عند المتوكّل في يوم نوروز والهدايا تُعرض عليه وفيها تماثيل من عنبر وكان شفيع الخادم واقفاً وعليه أقبية مورّدة ورداء مورّد وهو فيها من أحسن الناس فجعل المتوكّل يدفع إلى شفيع قطعةً قطعةً من ذلك العنبر ويقول اِدفعها إلى الحسين[1] واغمز يده. وكان آخرما دفع إليه وردةً حمراء حيّاه بها فأنشأ يقول ٧،٧

وَكَٱلْوَرْدَةِ ٱلْبَيْضَاءِ حَيَّا بِحُمْرَةٍ مِنَ ٱلْوَرْدِ يَسْعَى فِي غَلَائِلَ كَٱلْوَرْدِ
لَهُ عَبَثَاتٌ عِنْدَ كُلِّ تَحِيَّةٍ بِكَفَّيْهِ يَسْتَدْعِي ٱلْخَلِيَّ إِلَى ٱلْوَجْدِ
تَمَنَّيْتُ أَنْ أُسْقَى بِكَفَّيْهِ شَرْبَةً تُذَكِّرُنِي مَا قَدْ نَسِيتُ مِنَ ٱلْعَهْدِ
سَقَى ٱللّٰهُ دَهْرًا لَمْ أَبِتْ فِيهِ لَيْلَةً مِنَ ٱلدَّهْرِ إِلَّا مِنْ حَبِيبٍ عَلَى وَعْدِ

فأمره المتوكّل أن يسقيه وقال قد أعطيناك أمنيّتك.

وكان الحسين ينادم صالح بن الرشيد فشرب معه مرّةً في متنزّه باري وهي من أعمال كلواذا وكان له هناك بستان حسن جليل وسوره باقٍ إلى الآن وآثاره. وقال يصف البستان وصبوحهم فيه وهي من مليح شعره ٨،٧

أَمَا نَاجَاكَ بِٱلنَّظَرِ ٱلْفَصِيحِ وَأَنَّ إِلَيْكَ مِنْ قَلْبٍ قَرِيحِ
فَلَيْتَكَ حِينَ تَهْجُرُهُ ضِرَارًا مَنَنْتَ عَلَيْهِ بِٱلْقَتْلِ ٱلْمُرِيحِ
بِحُسْنِكَ كَانَ أَوَّلُ حُسْنِ ظَنِّي أَمَا يَنْهَاكَ حُسْنُكَ عَنْ قَبِيحِ
وَمَا يَنْفَكُّ مُتَّهَمًا لِنُصْحِي بِنَفْسِي نَفْسُ مُتَّهَمٍ نَصِيحِ
أُحِبُّ ٱلْفَيْءَ مِنْ نَخَلَاتِ بَارِي وَجَوْسَقَهَا ٱلْمُشَيَّدَ بِٱلصَّفِيحِ

[1] الأصل: حسين.

Abū ʿAbdallāh ibn Ḥamdūn recalled: We were at al-Mutawakkil's palace one Nauruz when the gifts were being presented to him. They included figurines of ambergris.[37] Shafīʿ the eunuch stood there looking extremely handsome in a rose-colored coat with a rose-colored cloak over it. Al-Mutawakkil started to hand Shafīʿ the ambergris figurines, piece by piece, saying, "Give them to al-Ḥusayn and touch his hand lightly." The last thing he handed him was a red rose with which Shafīʿ greeted al-Ḥusayn, at which the poet recited: 7.7

Like a white rose, his greeting was a rose that was red;
  clad in a rose-colored gown,
Gesturing with his hands at each greeting,
  inviting the fancy-free to love.
I wished his hand would pour me wine
  to remind me of the past I'd forgotten.
O for the time when I spent every night
  with a promise to meet a beloved!

Al-Mutawakkil ordered Shafīʿ to pour al-Ḥusayn some wine, saying, "I've given you what you wanted."

Al-Ḥusayn was a boon companion of Ṣāliḥ ibn al-Rashīd. One day he was drinking with him during an outing to Bārī, which is in the district of Kalwādhā. Ṣāliḥ owned a beautiful, magnificent garden there; its wall is still standing to this day and its ruins can be viewed. Al-Ḥusayn composed this poem about the garden and their drinking there. It is a fine piece: 7.8

Didn't my eloquent gaze address you
  and my wounded heart complain to you?
When you parted from me jealously, if only
  you'd granted me death—and peace.
At first I valued you for your beauty.
  Does your beauty not deter you from evil?
Yet a good friend is accused because of the
  counsel he gave my soul.
I love the shade of the palm trees of Bārī
  and its palace built on a slope,

وَيُعْجِبُنِي تَنَاوُحُ أَيْكَتَيْهَا إِلَيَّ بِـــرِيحِ حُوذَانٍ وَشِيحِ
وَلَنْ أَنْسَى مَصَارِعَ لِلسُّكَارَى وَنَادِبَةَ ٱلْحَمَامِ عَلَى ٱلطُّلُوحِ
وكَأْسٍ فِي يَمِينِ عَقِيدِ مُلْكٍ تَزِينُ صِفَاتِهِ غُرَرُ ٱلْمَدِيحِ
صَدِيحُ مُدَامَةٍ هَوِيَتْ صَرِيحًا وَهَلْ تُزْرِي ٱلصَّرِيحَةُ بِٱلصَّرِيحِ
أَلَا يَا عَمْرُو هَلْ لَكَ فِي ٱلصَّبُوحِ هَلُمَّ إِلَى صَفِيَّةِ كُلِّ رُوحِ
فَقَامَ عَلَى تَخَاذُلِ مُقْلَتَيْهِ وَسَلْسَلَ بِٱلسَّنِيحِ وَبِٱلْبَرِيحِ
وَأَتْبَعَ سَكْرَةً سَلَفَتْ بِأُخْرَى وَخَلَّى ٱلصَّحْوَ لِلْحَزِّ ٱلشَّحِيحِ

وذكر عمرو بن بانة قال كنّا عند صالح بن الرشيد في بستانه هذا ومعنا الحسين ابن الضحّاك وحولنا من النرجس أمر عظيم وقد طلع القمر على الشجر والنور ووقتنا من أحسن وقت رئي وخادم لصالح كان يحبّه يسقيه فقال للحسين قل في مجلسنا هذا شيئاً يتغنّى به ابن بانة. فقال وأشار إلى الخادم ٩،٧

وَصَفَ ٱلْبَدْرُ حُسْنَ وَجْهِكَ حَتَّى خِلْتُ أَنِّي وَمَا أَرَاكَ أَرَاكَا
وَإِذَا مَا تَنَفَّسَ ٱلنَّرْجِسُ ٱلْغَضُّ تَوَهَّمْتُهُ نَسِيمَ نَشَاكَا
خُدَعٌ لِلْمُنَى تُعَلِّلُنِي فِيكَ بِإِشْرَاقِ ذَا وَبَهْجَةِ ذَاكَا
لَأَدُومَنَّ مَا حَيِيتُ عَلَى ٱلْوُدِّ لِهَاذَا وَذَاكَ إِذْ حَكَيَاكَا

قال عمرو فغنّيت فيه ومرّ لنا أطيب وقت وأحسنه.

قال الحسين بن الضحّاك كنت جالساً في داري يوم شكّ وقد أفطر المأمون وأمر الناس بالإفطار فجاءني رقعة الحسن بن رجاء يقول فيها ١٠،٧

The trees swaying in the wind, wafting toward me
 scents of sage and water lily.
I won't forget the drunkards' collapse
 with the dove cooing dolefully in the acacias,
And a cup in the hand of a scion of royalty,
 his traits adorned with pearls of praise,
A frank devotee of wine, which loves frankness—
 and how could one frankness look down on another?
"Come, ʿAmr, do you feel like a drink in the morning?
 Let's turn to the purest spirit of all."
He rose, though his gaze faltered,
 and made good omens follow bad,
One bender coming after another,
 with sobriety put off till the wine had run out.

A recollection of ʿAmr ibn Bānah: We were with Ṣāliḥ ibn al-Rashīd in this garden of his, and al-Ḥusayn ibn al-Ḍaḥḥāk was one of our company. We were surrounded by beds of daffodils, and the risen moon shone on the trees and flowers. We were having the most delightful time imaginable. A servant of Ṣāliḥ whom he loved was pouring wine for him, and Ṣāliḥ said to al-Ḥusayn, "Compose a poem about this gathering, which Ibn Bānah can set to music and sing." Al-Ḥusayn gestured to the servant and said: 7.9

The moon described your face's beauty
 till I thought I saw you—but no.
The perfume wafting from the tender daffodils
 seemed like the scent of your youth.
Time after time my hopes that you've come are deceived
 by the light of the moon and these flowers in their splendor,
Yet while I live, to the moon and the flowers
 I'll stay true for as long as they resemble you.

ʿAmr continued: I set it to music and sang it, and we had a wonderful time.

Al-Ḥusayn ibn al-Ḍaḥḥāk recounted: I was sitting at home on a Day of Doubt.[38] 7.10
Al-Ma'mūn had breakfasted and ordered people to eat. I received a note from al-Ḥasan ibn Rajāʾ in which he'd written:

هَـزَزْتُكَ لِلصَّبُوحِ وَقَدْ نَهَـانِي   أَمِـيرُ ٱلْمُؤْمِـنِينَ عَنِ ٱلصِّـيَامِ
وَعِنْدِي مِنْ بَنَاتِ ٱلْكَرْخِ عَشْرٌ   يَطِيبُ بِهِمْ مُصَافَحَـةُ ٱلْمُـدَامِ
وَمِنْ أَمْـثَالِهِنَّ[1] إِذَا ٱنْتَشَيْنَـا   نَـرَانَا نَجْتَـنِي ثَمَـرَ ٱلْحَـرَامِ
فَكُنْ أَنْتَ ٱلْجَوَابَ فَـلَيْسَ شَيْءٌ   أَحَبَّ إِلَيَّ مِنْ حَـذْفِ ٱلْكَلَامِ

١١،٧ فوردت عليّ رقعته وقد أرسل إليّ محمّد بن الحارث بن بسخُنَّر غلاماً له نظيف الوجه ومعه ثلاثة غلمان أقران حسان ورقعة منشورة قد ختم أسفلها مثل المناشير فيها

سِرْ عَلَى ٱسْمِ ٱللهِ يَا أَحْـسَنُ مِنْ غُصْنِ لُجَيْنِ
فِي ثَلَاثٍ مِنْ بَنِي ٱلرُّو   مِ إِلَى دَارِ حُسَـيْنِ
أَشْخِصِ ٱلْكَهْلَ إِلَى مَوْ   لَاكَ يَا قُـرَّةَ عَيْـنِي
أَرِهِ ٱلْعُنْفَ إِنِ ٱسْتَعْـصَى وَطَالِبْهُ بِدَيْنِ
وَدَعِ ٱللَّفْـظَ وَخَاطِبْـهُ بِغَمْزِ ٱلْحَاجِبَيْنِ
وَٱحْذَرِ ٱلرَّجْعَةَ مِنْ وَجْـهِكَ فِي خُفَّيْ حُنَيْنِ

فمضيت مع غلام محمّد بن الحارث وتركت المضيّ إلى الحسن.

[1] الأصل: أمثالِهِم.

I'm prodding you to a morning drink;
    the caliph's forbidden the fast.
I've ten jars, daughters of Karkh,
    which I'll ply you with, excellent wine.
And ten more when we're drunk—
    let's cull the fruits of sin.
So be my answer and come. I like nothing more
    than avoiding cutting out words.

When his note arrived, Muḥammad ibn al-Ḥārith ibn Buskhunnar had already sent me a good-looking servant accompanied by three others like him, with a note folded and sealed at the bottom like an official document. It said: 7.11

Go in God's name, you beauty, you slender branch of silver,
Take three Byzantine boys to the house of al-Ḥusayn.
Bring the fellow to your master, my darling.
Treat him roughly if he demurs, demand payment of a debt.
Don't use words with him, just give him a wink,
And beware of your fate if you come back without him.

So I went off with Muḥammad's servant and disregarded al-Ḥasan's note.

ديـر قوطــا

وهــذا الدير بالبردان على شـاطئ دجلة وبين البردان وبغداد بسـاتين متّصـلة ومتنزّهات متتابعة منها إلى بلشكر ثمّ إلى المحمّديّة ثمّ إلى الطولونيّ الصغير ثمّ إلى الطولونيّ الكبير ثمّ إلى البردان كلّ ذلك بساتين وكروم وشجر ونخل. والبردان من المواضع الحسنة والبقاع النزهة والأماكن الموصوفة وهي كثيرة الطرّاق والمتنزّهين. وهذا الدير بها وهو يجمع أحوالاً كثيرةً منها عمارة البلد وكثرة فواكهه ووجود جميع ما يُحتاج إليه فيه. ومنها أنّ الشراب هناك مبذول والحانات كثيرة ومنها أنّ في هذا الموضع ما يطلبه أهل البطالة والخلاعة من الوجوه الحسان والبقاع الطيّبة النزهة فليس يكاد يخلو. ١،٨

ولعبد الله بن العبّاس بن الفضل بن الربيع فيه ٢،٨

يَا دَيْرَ قُوطَا لَقَدْ هَيَّجْتَ لِي طَرَبَا　　أَزَاحَ عَنْ قَلْبِيَ ٱلْأَحْزَانَ وَٱلْكُرَبَا
كَمْ لَيْلَةٍ فِيكَ وَاصَلْتُ ٱلسُّرُورَ بِهَا　　لَمَّا وَصَلْتُ لَهَا ٱلْأَدْوَارَ وَٱلنُّخَبَا[1]
فِي فِتْيَةٍ بَذَلُوا فِي ٱلْقَصْفِ مَا مَلَكُوا　　وَأَنْفَقُوا فِي ٱلتَّصَابِي ٱلْمَالَ وَٱلنَّشَبَا
وَشَادِنٍ مَا رَأَتْ عَيْنِي لَهُ شَبَهًا　　فِي ٱلنَّاسِ لَا عَجَمًا مِنْهُمْ وَلَا عَرَبَا
إِذَا بَدَا مُقْبِلًا نَادَيْتُ وَا طَرَبَا　　وَإِنْ مَضَى مُعْرِضًا نَادَيْتُ وَا حَرَبَا
أَقَمْتُ بِٱلدَّيْرِ حَتَّى صَارَ لِي وَطَنًا　　مِنْ أَجْلِهِ وَلَبِسْتُ ٱلْمِسْحَ وَٱلصُّلُبَا
وَصَارَ شَمَّاسُهُ لِي صَاحِبًا وَأَخًا　　وَصَارَ قِسِّيسُهُ لِي وَالِدًا وَأَبَا
ظَبْيٌ لَوَاحِظُهُ فِي ٱلْعَاشِقِينَ ظُبًى　　فَمَنْ دَنَا مِنْهُ مُغْتَرًّا بِهَا ضَرَبَا
إِنْ سُمْتُهُ ٱلْوَصْلَ أَبْدَى جَفْوَةً وَنَبَا　　أَوْ سُمْتُهُ ٱلْعَطْفَ وَلَّى مُعْرِضًا وَأَبَى

[1] كذا في عوّاد؛ الأصل: النحبا.

The Monastery of Qūṭā (the Flock)[39]

This monastery stands in Baradān on the banks of the Tigris. Between Baradān and Baghdad lies an uninterrupted series of gardens and pleasure grounds, running from Balashkur to Muḥammadiyyah to Lesser Ṭūlūnī, Greater Ṭūlūnī, and then Baradān, with gardens, vineyards, orchards, and palm trees. 8.1

Baradān is a lovely, attractive place, and is often talked of. It attracts many visitors and people going on outings. The monastery there shares many of its qualities: well cultivated, with an abundance of fruits and everything else one could need. For instance, wine is to be had and there are numerous taverns. Pleasure-seekers and profligates find there the beautiful faces and pleasant surroundings they look for. It is almost never deserted.

ʿAbdallāh ibn ʿAbbās ibn al-Faḍl ibn al-Rabīʿ composed this poem about it: 8.2

Qūṭā Convent, you've sent me into raptures,
smoothing sorrow and trouble from my heart.
How many nights brought me unbroken joy,
when I brought together songs and toasts
With men who gave all they owned for pleasure,
squandering goods and chattels for love!
A young beauty, whose like I'd not seen
anywhere, among Persians or Arabs—
When he came to me I cried, "Oh joy!"
when he turned away, "Woe is me!"
I stayed at the convent till it became home
for his sake, even wearing the habit and cross:
The deacon became my friend and my brother;
the priest was my father in body and spirit.
A gazelle with fawn-like glances that dealt blows to lovers
when they wandered toward him, losing their way.
If I tried to approach him, he shunned me.
If I showed him affection, he turned away haughtily.

وَإِنْ شَكَوْتُ إِلَيْهِ طُولَ هِجْرَتِهِ   وَمَا أُلَاقِيهِ مِنْ إِبْعَادِهِ قَطَبَا
وَٱللهِ لَوْ سَامَنِي نَفْسِي سَمَحْتُ بِهَا   وَمَا بَخِلْتُ عَلَيْهِ بِٱلَّذِي طَلَبَا

٣،٨ وكان عبد الله هذا من الأُدباء الظرفاء وكان صاحب غزل ومجون كثير التطرّح في الديارات والحانات والاتبّاع لأهل اللّهو والخلاعة. وله شعر مليح يُغنّى فيه ويتغنّى هو أيضاً فيه وفي غيره. وقال له محمّد بن عبد الملك الزيّات يوماً أنشِدني من شعرك قال وما قدر شعري أيّها الوزير قال ألست الّذي يقول

وَشَادِنٍ رَامَ إِذْ مَرَّ   فِي ٱلشَّعَانِينِ قَتْلِي
يَقُولُ لِي كَيْفَ أَصْبَحْتَ كَيْفَ يُصْبِحُ مِثْلِي

من يقول هذا يقول ما مقدار شعري.

٤،٨ قال وكان عبد الله يعشق عَساجِ جارية عمّته رُقيّة فقالت له بَذل الكبيرة أرني عساج فإمّا عذرتك وإمّا عذلتك قال فدعاها إلى منزله وحضرت بذل فابتدت عساج فغنّت

أَإِنْ خُنْتُمُ بِٱلْغَيْبِ عَهْدِي فَمَا لَكُمْ   تُدِلُّونَ إِدْلَالَ ٱلْمُقِيمِ عَلَى ٱلْعَهْدِ
صِلُوا وَٱفْعَلُوا فِعْلَ ٱلْمُدِلِّ بِوَصْلِهِ   وَإِلَّا فَصُدُّوا وَٱفْعَلُوا فِعْلَ ذِي ٱلصَّدِّ

فأتت فيه بكلّ شيء حسن فقال لبذل كيف ترين يا ستّي فقطعت عساج الغناء وقالت يا عبد الله تشاور فيّ فوالله ما شاورت فيك حين وددتك فنعرت بذل وقالت أحسنت والله يا عبد الله عذرتك.

٥،٨ ومن شعر عبد الله

اِسْقِنِي ٱلرَّاحَ قَدْ خَلَعْتُ ٱلْعِذَارَا   وَتَحَمَّلْتُ فِيكَ قَالًا وَقِيلَا
اِسْقِنِي طَارِدَ ٱلْهُمُومِ وَلَا تَمْزُجْ مِنْهُ ٱلْغَدَاةَ إِلَّا قَلِيلَا

If I complained he'd left me alone,
  and spoke of my pain, he simply frowned.
Oh God, if he asked me, I'd give my life willingly,
  and I'd not grudge him what he'd asked.

ʿAbdallāh was an elegant man of letters, much given to love affairs, and frivolous, a regular visitor to monasteries and taverns, spending time with pleasure-seekers and libertines. He has fine poetry, which has been set to music. He himself composed settings for poetry, both his own and that of others. 8.3

Muḥammad ibn ʿAbd al-Malik al-Zayyāt said to him one day, "Recite me some of your poetry." He replied, "Vizier, what's my poetry worth?" Al-Zayyāt exclaimed, "Aren't you the author of:

A young beauty who sought to kill me on Palm Sunday
  by asking, 'How are you this morning?' What could I answer?

"Does the man who's composed this ask, 'What's my poetry worth?'"

ʿAbdallāh had fallen in love with ʿAsālij,[40] his aunt Ruqayyah's slave girl. 8.4
Badhl the Elder said to ʿAbdallāh, "Show me ʿAsālij. Either I'll approve or reprove." So he invited ʿAsālij to his house when Badhl was present, and ʿAsālij started to sing:

Oh! If you've betrayed me behind my back,
  why make a show of keeping faith?
Meet me and act as if you're happy to meet,
  or else turn away like those who keep aloof.

She performed it excellently and he asked Badhl, "What's your opinion, madam?" ʿAsālij broke off the song, complaining, "ʿAbdallāh, are you asking someone's opinion about me? By God, when I fell in love with you I didn't ask anyone's opinion!" Badhl shouted with laughter. "Well done, ʿAbdallāh, by God! I approve."

Here is some of ʿAbdallāh's poetry: 8.5

Pour me the wine, I've let myself go and suffered for you all kinds of
    gossip;
Pour me the chaser of cares, and go easy with the water this morning.

ومن شعره

يَا حَبَّذَا يَوْمِي بِٱلدَّالِيَهْ   نَشْرَبُهَا قُفْصِيَّةً صَافِيَهْ
مَعْ كُلِّ قَرْمٍ مُتْلِفٍ مَالَهُ   لَمْ يَبْقَ فِي ٱلدُّنْيَا لَهُ بَاقِيَهْ
فَخُذْ مِنَ ٱلدُّنْيَا وَلَذَّاتِهَا   فَإِنَّمَا نَحْنُ بِهَا عَارِيَهْ

قال وكتب عبد الله إلى صديق له يدعوه جُعلت فداك أنا وقلم وأنت أعلم.
وكان عبد الله يعشق جارية نصرانيّة ويهيم بها فله فيها ٦،٨

فَتَنَتْنَا صُورَةٌ فِي بِيعَةٍ   فَتَنَ ٱللهُ ٱلَّذِي صَوَّرَهَا
زَادَهَا ٱلنَّاقِشُ فِي تَحْسِينِهَا   أَنَّهُ إِذْ صَاغَهَا نَصَّرَهَا

وله فيه لحن.
وكانت مصابيح جارية الأحدب المقيّن تغني بهذا الصوت وتغنّي في كثير من شعره ٧،٨
وكانت أروى الناس له وأعرفهم بغنائه وكانت موصوفة بالحسن والإحسان وكان
عبد الله يهواها. وممّا غنّت فيه من شعر عبد الله

أَلَا ٱصْبَحَانِي يَوْمَ ٱلشَّعَانِينِ   مِنْ قَهْوَةٍ عُتِّقَتْ بِكَرْكِينِ
عِنْدَ أُنَاسٍ قَلْبِي بِهِمْ كَلِفٌ   وَإِنْ تَوَلَّوْا دِينًا سِوَى دِينِي

ولعبد الله في مصابيح وكان قال هذا الشعر وغنّى فيه وهي حاضرة فأخذته عنه وغنّت فيه أيضاً متيّم الهشاميّة

إِنِّي عَشِقْتُ عَدُوَّةً   فَسَقَى ٱلْإِلٰهُ عَدُوَّتِي
وَفَدَيْتُهَا بِأَقَارِبِي   وَبِأُسْرَتِي وَبِجِيرَتِي
جُدِلَتْ كَجَدْلِ ٱلْخَيْزُرَا   نِ وَثُنِّيَتْ فَتَثَنَّتِ
وَٱسْتَيْقَنَتْ أَنَّ ٱلْفُؤَا   دَ يُحِبُّهَا فَأَدَلَّتِ

And another:

Oh for my day at The Vine, drinking a pure wine from Qufṣ
With peers who squander their fortune till they've nothing left in the
world.
Partake of the world and its pleasures, for we're on loan to it.

ʿAbdallāh wrote an invitation to a friend: "I'd give my life to ransom you! Qalam's[41] at my side. What do you decide?"

ʿAbdallāh fell in love with a Christian girl. Besotted with her, he composed these verses: 8.6

An image in church has enraptured us.
May God enrapture its painter.
What's even more lovely is
that he's painted a Christian.

And he set them to music.

Maṣābīḥ,[42] the slave of al-Aḥdab, the dealer in singing girls, used to sing this song and many other compositions by ʿAbdallāh. She was the main transmitter of his poetry and most knowledgeable about his settings. She was known for her beauty and her fine performances, and ʿAbdallāh loved her. One of his poems that she sang was: 8.7

Friends, on Palm Sunday,
pour me old wine from Karkīn
With someone I love,
though her religion's not mine.

Here are verses ʿAbdallāh composed on Maṣābīḥ and set to music. He sang them in her presence and she learned them from him. Mutayyam[43] al-Hishāmiyyah also sang them.

I've fallen in love with a foe. May God shower blessings on my foe.
My kith and kin and my neighbors—I'd ransom their lives for her.
She's firm and upright as cane, but bend her and she'll yield.
Sure of the love in my heart, now she's all flirtation.

قال وغاضبت مصابيحُ عبدَ الله بن العبّاس في شيء بلغها عنه فرام أن يترضّاها فأبت فكتب إليها رقعة يحلف أنّه ما أتى شيئاً ممّا أنكرته ويدعو على من ظلم فلم تجبه عن شيء ممّا كتبه ووقّعت تحت الدعاء على الظالم آمين ولم تزد على ذلك فكتب إليها ٨،٨

أَمّـا سُـرُورِي بِٱلْجَوَا ... بِ فَلَيْسَ يَفْنَى مَا بَقِينَا
وَأَسَـرُّ حَرْفٍ فِيهِ لِي ... آمِينَ رَبَّ ٱلْعَالَمِينَا

ومن شعره ٩،٨

ذَهَبٌ فِي ذَهَبٍ رَا ... حَ بِهِ غُصْنُ لُجَيْنِ
فَأَتَتْ قُرَّةُ عَيْنٍ ... بِيَدِي قُرَّةِ عَيْنِ
قَمَرٌ يَحْمِلُ شَمْساً ... مَرْحَباً بِٱلنَّيِّرَيْنِ
أَلِفَا سُكْرَيْنِ إِلْفَيْ ... نِ مَعاً مُؤْتَلِفَيْنِ
لَا جَرَى بَيْنِي وَلَا بَيْ ... نَهُمَا طَائِرُ بَيْنِ
بَلْ غَنِيْنَا مَا بَقِينَا ... أَبَداً مُعْتَنِقَيْنِ
فِي صَبُوحٍ وَغَبُوقٍ ... لَمْ نَبِعْ نَقْداً بِدَيْنِ

Maṣābīḥ had been angered by something she heard about ʿAbdallāh ibn al-ʿAbbās. He sought to propitiate her but she was unrelenting. He wrote her a note in which he swore that he had not done anything that would have displeased her and he cursed those who had wronged him. She did not reply to his note—under his curse of the people who had injured him, she added "Amen." Nothing more. So he wrote to her: 8.8

I will stay delighted at your answer for as long as we live.
The word that delights me most is "Amen" to the Lord of the Worlds.

This is another poem by ʿAbdallāh: 8.9

Gold on gold, brought by a silver branch—
A heart's desire bearing my heart's desire.
A moon with the sun in its hand. Welcome to heaven's two lights!
Friends of both friendly carousals, ever in close accord,
May no bird of ill omen come to part us.
No! A long as we're alive, let us stay entwined,
Drinking at dawn and dusk, with no care for the future.

ديرمَرجُرجس

هــذا الدير بالمَزرَفة وهو أحد الديارات والمواضع المقصودة والمتنزّهون من أهل بغداد يخرجون إليه دائماً في السميريّات لقربه وطيبه وهو على شاطئ دجلة والعروب بين يديه والبساتين محدّقة به والحانات مجاورة له. وكلّ ما يحتاج إليه المتنزّهون حاضر فيه. والمَزرَفة من أحسن البلاد عمارة وأطيبها بقعة وبها من البساتين ما ليس لبلد من البلدان. ١،٩

ولأبي جفنة القرشيّ فيه وكان من الخلعاء ومدمني الشرب والمتطرّحين في الديارات والحانات ولم يكن يخلو من غلمان مُرْد بعضهم يخدمه وبعضهم يغنّيه ٢،٩

تَرَنَّمَ ٱلطَّيْرُ بَعْدَ عُجْمَتِهِ   وَٱنْحَسَرَ ٱلْبَرْدُ فِي أَزِمَّتِهِ
وَأَقْبَلَ ٱلْوَرْدُ وَٱلْبَهَارُ إِلَى   زَمَانِ قَصْفٍ يَمْشِي بِرُمَّتِهِ
مَا أَطْيَبَ ٱلْوَصْلَ إِنْ نَجَوْتُ وَمَا[1]   يَلْسَعُنِي هَجْرُهُ بِحُمَّتِهِ
وَمِثْلَ لَوْنِ ٱلنَّجِيعِ صَافِيَةً   تَذْهَبُ بِٱلْمَرْءِ فَوْقَ هِمَّتِهِ
نَازَعْتُهَا مَنْ سَدَاؤُهُ أَبَدًا   فِي ٱلْعِشْقِ وَٱلْفِسْقِ مِثْلَ لُحْمَتِهِ
فِي دَيْرِ مَرْجُرْجِسٍ وَقَدْ نَفَحَ ٱلْـ   ـفَجْرُ عَلَيْنَا أَرْوَاحَ زَهْرَتِهِ
أُرِيدُ مِنْهُ وَلَيْسَ يَمْنَعُنِي   مِنْ ذٰلِكَ ٱلشَّيْءِ غَيْرُ حِشْمَتِهِ
وَفَى بِمِيعَادِهِ وَزَوْرَتِهِ   وَكُنْتُ أَوْفَى لَهُ بِذِمَّتِهِ

ومن مليح شعره ٣،٩

وَمُعَرِّسٍ طَلَبَ ٱلصَّبُوحَ وَإِنَّنِي   لَفَتًى يُوَافِقُنِي ٱلصَّبُوحُ بُكُورَا

١ كذا في عوّاد؛ الأصل: ولم.

The Monastery of Mār Jirjis (Saint George)

This monastery stands in Mazrafah. The monastery and its surroundings draw visitors, and people from Baghdad are always going on outings to it by boat, because it is close by and attractive. It is built on the banks of the Tigris, the floating water mills are in front of it, gardens surround it, and there are taverns close by. Everything pleasure-seekers might want is to be found there. Mazrafah is very well cultivated and beautiful, and it has gardens unlike those anywhere else. 9.1

Abū Jafnah al-Qurashī, who was a libertine, a steady drinker, and a frequenter of monasteries and taverns, always in the company of beardless boys to serve him and sing to him, composed these verses: 9.2

The birds, long silent, sing,
  and the cold has been led away.
Roses and blossoms have come forward,
  all for a season of pleasure.
How good is a meeting if I'm well,
  not stung by fever when he's left me.
A pure wine, the color of blood,
  transporting the drinker beyond his cares,
I've shared with one who in debauchery
  and love gave measure for measure,
In Mār Jirjis's Convent, when the dawn
  wafted the scent of its flowers.
He didn't withhold what I wanted
  except when too diffident.
He kept his promise and came,
  and I kept my share of the pact.

Here is another fine poem of his: 9.3

I'm a traveler who asks for a morning drink,
  for I like wine in the morning;

وَقَرَعْتُ صَافِيَةً بِمَاءِ سَحَابَةٍ فَشَجَيْنَ حِينَ قَرَعْتُهُنَّ سُرُورَا
فَشَرِبْتُ ثُمَّ سَقَيْتُهُ فَكَأَنَّمَا سَبْسَبْتُ فَوْقَ لَهَاتِهِ كَافُورَا
وَفَتًى يُدِيرُ عَلَيْكَ فِي طَرَبَاتِهِ خَمْرًا تُوَلِّدُ فِي ٱلْعِظَامِ فُتُورَا
وَإِذَا رَشَفْتَ بِمَرْشَفَيْكَ رُضَابَهَا كَتَبَ ٱلْعُقَارُ بِحُسْنِ وَجْهِكَ نُورَا
مَا زِلْتُ أَشْرَبُهَا وَأَسْقِي صَاحِبِي حَتَّى رَأَيْتُ لِسَانَهُ مَكْسُورَا
مِمَّا تَخَيَّرَتِ ٱلتُّجَارُ بِبَابِلٍ أَوْ مَا تَعَتَّقَهُ ٱلْيَهُودُ بِسُورَا

وله ٤،٩

وَمُزْوَرِّ وَجْهٍ لَمْ يَرَ ٱلنَّاسُ مِثْلَهُ أَدَرْتُ عَلَيْهِ ٱلْكَأْسَ لَمَّا تَغَضَّبَا
يُؤَاخِذُنِي إِنْ رُمْتُ فِي ٱلْخَدِّ قُبْلَةً وَيُعْرِضُ عَنِّي كُلَّمَا قُلْتُ مَرْحَبَا
وَلَوْلَا ٱلَّذِي يَرْتَجُّ تَحْتَ إِزَارِهِ لَأَلْسَعْتُهُ مِنِّي إِذَا صَدَّ عَقْرَبَا
أَدَرْتُ عَلَيْهِ قَهْوَةً بَابِلِيَّةً تُرِيكَ حُمَيَّاهَا عَلَى ٱلْكَأْسِ كَوْكَبَا
إِذَا شَجَّهَا ٱلسَّاقِي بِمَاءٍ تَدَرَّعَتْ عَلَى ٱلْمَزْجِ سِرْبَالًا مِنَ ٱلدُّرِّ مُذْهَبَا

وللنميريّ فيه ٥،٩

نَزَلْتُ بِمَرْمَا جِرْجِسٍ خَيْرَ مَنْزِلٍ ذَكَرْتُ بِهِ أَيَّامَ لَهْوٍ مَضَيْنَ لِي
تَكَنَّفَنَا فِيهِ ٱلسُّرُورُ وَحَفَّنَا فَمِنْ أَسْفَلٍ يَأْتِي ٱلسُّرُورُ وَمِنْ عَلِ
وَسَالَمَتِ ٱلْأَيَّامُ فِيهِ وَسَاعَفَتْ وَصَارَتْ صُرُوفُ ٱلْحَادِثَاتِ بِمَعْزَلِ
يُدِيرُ عَلَيْنَا ٱلْكَأْسَ ظَبْيٌ مُقَرْطَقٌ يَحُثُّ بِهَا كَاسَاتِهَا لَيْسَ يَأْتَلِي
فَيَا عَيْشُ مَا أَصْفَى وَيَا لَهْوُ دُمْ لَنَا وَيَا وَافِدَ ٱللَّذَاتِ حُيِّيتَ فَٱنْزِلِ

I mixed a pure wine with water from heaven,
 and in joy they both sang out loud.
I drank, and poured him a cup as if
 I was dripping camphor on his raging thirst.
A joyful youth passes round the wine
 that fills the body with lethargy;
If you sip the froth with your lips,
 the liquor lights up your face.
I drank and poured for my friend
 till I saw his tongue stumbling
From the vintage pressed by Babylon's merchants
 or stored long by the Jews of Sūrā.

And these verses are by him: 9.4

I poured wine for a falsehearted boy,
 with a peerless face when he feigned anger,
Scolding me for trying to kiss his cheek,
 and turning away when I said, "Welcome."
If it hadn't been for the quivering in his loincloth,
 I'd have had him stung with a scorpion for his snub.
I gave him Babylonian wine to drink,
 which ignited the cup with stars.
When the cupbearer mixed the cup with water,
 it was dressed in chain mail of golden pearls.

Here is a poem by al-Numayrī: 9.5

I had a splendid stay at Mār Jirjis's,
 recalling past days of leisure.
Gaiety enveloped us
 with pleasure from all sides.
Fate was our friend, helping us along;
 destiny's blows were far.
A fawn in a tunic poured us wine,
 tirelessly refilling our cups.
What a perfect life! Pleasure, stay with us!
 To the bringer of joys, stop here! Live long!

٦،٩ وهو أبو الطيّب محمّد بن القاسم النميريّ وكان من أهل الأدب والفضل مليح الشعر رقيق الطبع وكانت له حال ونعمة وكان يكثر الشرب في الديارات والحانات ويلذّ له ذلك. وكان عبد الله بن المعتزّ يأنس به ولا يفارقه وكانت تجري بينهما مكاتبات ومناقضات في الشعر ومداعبات طيّبة ونحن نذكر طرفًا منها.

٧،٩ قال عبد الله بن المعتزّ كتب إليّ النميريّ يوماً وقد دعوته

رَأَيْتُكَ تَدْعُونِي إِلَى ٱلشُّرْبِ مُعْتِمًا وَتَقْطَعُ عَنِّي ٱلشُّرْبَ وَٱللَّيْلُ مُمْتِعُ
فَإِمَّا شَرِبْتَ ٱلرَّاحَ لَيْلَكَ كُلَّهُ وَإِمَّا شَرِبْتَ ٱلرَّاحَ وَٱلشَّمْسُ تَلْمَعُ
فَأَيَّهُمَا آثَرْتَ وَفَّيْتَ حَقَّهُ وَذَاكَ ٱلَّذِي تَهْوَاهُ شُرْبٌ مُخَلَّعُ

قال وكتبت إليه في يوم عيد ولم يكن جاءني ذلك اليوم

بِأَبِي هَلْ حَلَا بِعَيْنِكَ شَيْءٌ هُوَ أَسْلَاكَ يَا خَلِيلِي بَعْدِي
طَعْمُ كَأْسِي مُرٌّ إِذَا لَمْ تَزُرْنِي وَهْوَ حُلْوٌ إِذَا رَأَيْتُكَ عِنْدِي

فكتب إليّ

سَيِّدِي أَنْتَ لَمْ تُرِدْنِي فَمَاذَا حِيلَتِي إِذْ بُلِيتُ مِنْكَ بِصَدِّ
يَعْلَمُ ٱللهُ مَا أُقَاسِيهِ[١] مِنْ شَوْ قِي وَمِنْ حَسْرَتِي وَغَمِّي بِبُعْدِي

٨،٩ قال عبد الله وكتبت إليه مرّة أدعوه فكتب إليّ عندي قوم ولعلّي أتخلّص منهم. وعلّق الوعد فكتبت إليه

يَا مَنْ يُسَوِّفُ[٢] وَعْدِي لَوْ شِئْتَ جِئْتَ بِمَرَّهْ
فَٱسْقُطْ عَلَيْنَا سُقُوطًا وَلَا تُرَفْرِفْ لِغُدْرَهْ

١ الأصل: أُقَاسِي. ٢ الأصل: يُسَرِّف.

Al-Numayrī's full name was Abū l-Ṭayyib Muḥammad ibn al-Qāsim al-Numayrī. He was a man of culture and virtue, a good poet with a delicate talent, a man of high rank and wealth. He enjoyed frequenting monasteries and taverns to drink. ʿAbdallāh ibn al-Muʿtazz enjoyed his company and was inseparable from him. They used to write to each other, competing in poetry and playful jokes. We shall mention some of them here. 9.6

ʿAbdallāh ibn al-Muʿtazz recalled: One day when I sent an invitation to al-Numayrī, he wrote to me: 9.7

I see you're inviting me for a drink after twilight,
and you'll break up the party when the night's at its height;
Either you should spend the whole night drinking
or else you should drink when the sun is high.
Whichever you prefer, give it its due.
But what you're after is quaffing cut short.

I wrote to him one feast day when he had not visited me:

By heaven! Has something caught your eye,
my friend, and made you forget me?
The wine in my cup is bitter when you're not here,
but how sweet it is when you're with me.

So he wrote back to me:

Sire, you didn't want me. What was I to do,
since I'd suffered your rejection?
God knows the longing I endure,
the grief and regret, since I'm far from you.

One day I wrote him an invitation, and he wrote back: "I have visitors, but perhaps I'll be able to get rid of them." He didn't fulfill his promise, so I wrote: 9.8

You've put off your promise to me;
If you'd wanted, you'd have come like a shot.
Drop in to see us straightaway;

فَإِنْ ضَبَطْتُ بِسَاقِيكَ بَعْدَ هٰذِي ٱلْمَرَّهْ
لَأَحْبِسَنَّكَ عِنْدِي عَلَى أَذًى وَمَضَرَّهْ

قال عبد الله وكتب إليّ النميريّ في آخر شعبان

يَا أَبَا ٱلْعَبَّاسِ قَدْ شَمَّرَ شَعْبَانُ إِزَارَهْ
وَمَضَى يَسْعَى فَمَا يُلْحِقُ إِنْسَانٌ غُبَارَهْ
فَٱغْدُ نَشْرَبْ صَفْوَةَ ٱلدَّنِّ وَنَسْلُبْهُ[1] وَقَارَهْ
وَإِذَا مَا ذُكِرَ ٱلْعَقْلُ شَرِبْنَا يَادِكَارَهْ

٩،٩ قال وكتب إليّ وقد تأخر اجتماعنا

بِكُمِ ٱلْمَوْتُ فِي ٱلْجَمَاعَةِ خَيْرٌ مِنْ حَيَاةٍ فِي وَحْشَةٍ وَٱنْفِرَادِ
عَرَّفُونِي ٱجْتِمَاعَهُمْ يَوْمَهُمْ ذَا وَٱسْتَبَدُّوا عَلَيَّ فِي ٱلْمِيعَادِ
وَٱلْحَرِيرِيُّ رَأْسُهُمْ وَبِحَسْبِي بِٱلْحَرِيرِيِّ رَأْسَ كُلِّ فَسَادِ
إِنْ رَأَى قَيْنَةً تَبَرْقَشَ لِلْعِشْقِ وَأَرْخَى جَنَاحَهُ لِلسِّفَادِ
وَتَصَدَّى لَهَا وَحَرَّكَ عِطْفَيْهِ وَرَاقَتْ لِشَهْوَةِ ٱلْأَوْلَادِ

فاعتذرت إليه وسألته المصير إلينا فجاءنا.

١٠،٩ قال عبد الله وكتب إليّ

إِذَا غِبْتُ لَمْ أُطْلَبْ وَإِنْ جِئْتُ لَمْ أَصِلْ وَلَلْعَتْبُ أَوْلَى بِي وَلَسْتُ بِعَاتِبِ
سَأَصْبِرُ لِلشَّوْقِ ٱلْمُبَرِّحِ كَارِهًا وَأَرْقُبُ يَوْمًا صَالِحًا فِي ٱلْعَوَاقِبِ
وَمَا كُلُّ مَنْ صَاحَبْتُهُ مِثْلَ قَاسِمٍ فَقِسْهُ وَفَكِّرْ فِي سَبِيلِ ٱلذَّوَاهِبِ

[1] الأصل: نسلمه.

Don't wrap yourself in apology's cloak.
If I get my hands on you after this,
You won't be able to leave, whatever's amiss.

Al-Numayrī wrote to me on the last day of Shaban:[44]

Abū l-ʿAbbās, Shaban's up and running.
So swift no one can catch him.
Come, let's drink the best of the cask,
To rob him of his solemnity.
If anyone even mentions a clear mind,
Let's raise a glass to its memory.

He wrote to me, when a meeting between us had been put off: 9.9

How much better is death in company than life alone and lonely?
They told me the day we'd meet, then went off and left me alone.
Al-Ḥarīrī was their chief—the source of every vice, I know.
If he sees a singing girl, he's ready for love, dropping his pants for sex.
He'll make for her all aquiver, but she's unmoved at his childish desire.

So I apologized and asked him to come, which he did.
And he wrote me: 9.10

If I'm absent no one asks for me; if I come I'm not let in.
    Blame would be justified, but I'm not a blamer.
I'm patient against my will, exhausted by longing,
    waiting for a day with a favorable outcome.
Not all the friends I've had are like Qāsim.
    Take his measure and think of good times past.

قال وكتب إليّ في يوم خميس صُمته

أَبَا ٱلْعَبَّاسِ يَا خَيْرَ ٱلأَنَامِ   تَصُومُ وَلَيْسَ ذَا يَوْمَ ٱلصِّيَامِ
فَهَلْ لَكَ فِي مُدَامٍ أَخٍ ظَرِيفٍ   يُسَاعِدُ فِي ٱلْحَلَالِ وَفِي ٱلْحَرَامِ

١١٫٩ قال كتب إليّ النميريّ يستبطئ رسولي ويعتذر من تأخّره عنّي ويذكر أنّه اشتغل بعمارة بستانه. فأجبته أمّا ما ذكرت من تأخّر رسولي عنك للسؤال عن خبرك في هذه الأيّام والتفقّد لك فإنّي رأيتك قلتَ قول القائل خذ اللصّ من قبل أن يأخذك وإلّا فما قصّرت في السؤال عنك والبعثة إليك ولكنّ ما أقول لمن نكس عليله فلم يعده واشتاق إليه فلم يزره مشتغلاً بطروق الحانات والديارات وركوب الزلالات ومغازلة القيان ومعاقرة ابنة الدنان جامعاً بين طرفي نهاره بغبوق لا يهدأ سامره وصبوح لا يفتر باكره في عسكري لهو واحد يخبط الماء بمجاديفه وآخر يقرع الأرض بخيله ووجيفه. وسألت عن خبري في هذه الأمطار فما عسيت أن أقول في المنّة الواجب لله تعالى الشكر عليها إذ تخطّتنا بعد أن سلّت سيفها وخفنا حيفها.

١٢٫٩ قال عبد الله وكتب إليّ النميريّ

أَمِيرٌ كُنْتُ أَرْجُوهُ لِدَهْرِي   إِذَا مَا نَابَ بِٱلْخَطْبِ ٱلْجَلِيلِ
مَرِضْتُ فَلَمْ يَعُدْنِي مِنْ سَقَامِي   وَتَاهَ عَنِ ٱلْعِيَادَةِ وَٱلرَّسُولِ
وَمَا بِي حَاجَةٌ تَدْعُو إِلَى مَا   أَذِلُّ بِهِ لِذِي ٱلنَّيْلِ ٱلْمُنِيلِ
وَلَا لِمُتَوَّجٍ بِٱلْمُلْكِ يُزْهِي   إِذَا مَا كُنْتُ أَقْنَعُ بِٱلْقَلِيلِ

فكتبت إليه رقعة في آخرها

فِي كُلِّ يَوْمٍ طَاعَةٌ وَعِصْيَانْ
وَمَلَلٌ وَمَلَقٌ وَهِجْرَانْ
خَلَائِقٌ كَأَنَّهُنَّ غِيلَانْ

He wrote to me on a Thursday when I was fasting:

Abū l-ʿAbbās, you best of men,
you're fasting but it's the wrong day.
Why not enjoy a friend's wine, which helps,
whether there's a fiat or a ban?

Al-Numayrī wrote to me, complaining of the lateness of my messenger and excusing himself for not coming to see me. He explained he was occupied with work in his garden, so I replied, "You mention my messenger's delay in coming to see you and ask after you and your latest news—that looks to me like the person who says, 'Catch the thief before he catches you.' I've certainly not neglected to ask after you or send messengers. But what should I say to someone who has not visited his sick friend when he's had a relapse and who has not gone to see him when the friend missed him? Instead, he has been taken up with going to taverns and monasteries, taking boat trips, flirting with singing girls, and imbibing the daughter of the vine. He divides his days between an evening glass with a tireless storyteller and a morning draft with an unflagging companion, in two camps of revelers, one striking the water with its oars, the other pounding the earth with its horses' hooves. 9.11

"You asked how I have kept during these rainy days. What can I say about this gift for which we should thank God? The days had unsheathed their swords and we were fearful of the harm they could do, but they have moved on and passed us."

Al-Numayrī wrote to me: 9.12

A prince whose help I had hopes of, if ever disaster struck.
I fell ill, but he didn't visit me, too proud to come or send for news.
Though content with little, I've no reason to humble myself
Before a proud man crowned with power, a dispenser of favors.

So I replied:

Each day we see obedience and rebellion,
Boredom, flattery, and separation.
Qualities like demons in action.

قال ودعوته ليوم أسميته فتأخّر رسولي عنه فكتب إليّ

دَعوتَنَا وبَـــــدا لكَ   نِكَ فِي ٱسْتِهِ مَنْ وَفَى لَكْ

قال وكتب إليّ النميريّ ١٣،٩

بَـرَّحَ بِي ٱلشَّوْقُ إِلَى ٱلشُّرْبِ   مَعْ سَـيِّدٍ يَهْرُبُ مِنْ قُرْبِي
وَلَمْ أَكُنْ أَعْهَدُهُ جَافِياً   فَـصَارَ يَجْفُونِي بِلاَ ذَنْبِ
وَٱللّٰهِ مَا أَعْرِفُ لِي عِنْدَهُ   ذَنْباً سِوَى ٱلْإِفْرَاطِ فِي ٱلْحُبِّ
وَإِنَّنِي مَا سُؤْتُـهُ سَـاعَـةً   فِي حَاضِرِ ٱلْجِدِّ وَلَا ٱللَّعْبِ

فكتبت إليه

يَا أَيُّهَا ٱلْجَافِي وَيُسْتَجْفَى   لَيْسَ تَجَنِّيكَ مِنَ ٱلظَّرْفِ
إِنَّكَ وَٱلشَّوْقَ إِلَيْنَا كَمَنْ   يُؤْمِنُ بِٱللّٰهِ عَلَى حَرْفِ
مَحَوْتَ آثَـارَكَ مِنْ وُدِّنَا   غَيْرَ أَسَاطِيرِكَ فِي ٱلصُّحْفِ
وَإِنْ تَجَشَّمْتَ لَنَا زَوْرَةً   يَوْماً تَحَامَلْتَ عَلَى ضَعْفِ

قال وكتب إليّ ١٤،٩

أَتَيْتُكَ مَسْرُوراً فَطَابَ لِي ٱلشُّرْبُ   وَنَالَتْ مُنَاهَا عِنْدَكَ ٱلْعَيْنُ وَٱلْقَلْبُ
فَجَارَتْ عَلَيَّ ٱلْكَأْسُ حَتَّى هَجَرْتُهَا   ثَلَاثَـةَ أَيَّامٍ كَمَا ٱسْتَوْجَبَ ٱلذَّنْبُ

فكتبت إليه

عَلَامَ هَجَرْتَ ٱلْكَأْسَ إِذْ جَارَ حُكْمُهَا   وَلَا لَهْوَ إِلَّا أَنْ يَكُونَ لَهَا ٱلذَّنْبُ
أَدَامَ لَكَ ٱللّٰهُ ٱلسُّرُورَ وَدَامَ لِي   بِكَ ٱلْعَيْشُ وَٱلنَّعْمَاءُ وَٱتَّصَلَ ٱلْقُرْبُ

I sent him an invitation for a specific day, but my messenger did not arrive in time, so he wrote me:

You invited us and changed your mind.
Fuck your true friend in the ass.

Al-Numayrī wrote to me: 9.13

I'm worn out with longing to drink,
with a noble who shuns my company.
I'm not used to his coldness.
Without reason, he's treating me harshly.
By God, the only thing I've done wrong
is to exaggerate in my love.
I've never once harmed him,
whether seriously or in jest.

And I wrote back:

You scorn, yet your scorn is unjust,
your charges false and lacking in style.
If you say you miss us,
you're like a believer with a wavering faith.
You've erased your traces
from our friendship,
except for stories people tell;
Should you ever embark on a visit,
it'll be out of weakness.

He also wrote to me: 9.14

I came to you gladly. We had a fine drinking bout.
My heart and my eyes rejoiced to see you.
But the wine did me wrong, so I left off for three days—
just enough time to atone for my sin.

And I wrote back:

Why did you leave the cup when it wronged you?
If wine's not at fault, there's no pleasure.
May God keep you in gladness and grant me
your nearness in this life of leisure.

قال عبد الله بعثت إلى النميريّ يوم جمعة رسولاً وقلت له اركب معنا إلى الصلاة ١٥،٩
فوجده الرسول قد اصطبح فقال له قل له أنا أصلّي مذ صلاة الغداة فكتبت له

يَا مَنْ يُصَلِّي صَلَاةً فِيهَا لِإِبْلِيسَ طَاعَهْ
إِنْ كُنْتَ تَقْبَلُ شُكْرِي فَٱلشُّكْرُ فِي ذَا رَقَاعَهْ

قال وكتبت إليه وقد اعتللت فلم يعدني ١٦،٩

ٱلْحَمْدُ لِلّٰهِ حَتَّى أَنْتَ تَجْفُونِي بَعْدَ ٱلصَّفَاءِ جَفَاءً لَيْسَ بِٱلدُّونِ
قَدْ كُنْتُ مُنْتَظِرًا هٰذَا لَجِئْتَ بِهِ وَلَيْسَ خَلْقٌ عَلَى غَدْرٍ بِمَأْمُونِ

فكتب يعتذر بشغل كان له واعتلال مركبه فكتبت إليه

لَا تَعْتَذِرْ قَدْ عَرَفْنَا كَ سَوْفَ تَفْعَلُ فِعْلَكْ
ذَكَرْتَ شُغْلًا فَهَلَّا جَعَلْتَنِي بَعْضَ شُغْلِكْ
وَلَمْ يَكُنْ لَكَ عَيْرٌ فَكُنْتَ تَرْكَبُ نَعْلَكْ

قال فكتب إليّ

إِنْ كُنْتُ أَذْنَبْتُ ذَنْبًا فَقَدْ وَثِقْتُ بِفَضْلِكْ
وَقَدْ أَتَيْتُكَ مَشْيًا كَمَا قَضَيْتَ بِعَدْلِكْ

وجاءني ماشياً.

قال النميريّ كان عبد الله بن المعتزّ يعيب العشق كثيراً إلى أن صار يقول هو طرف ١٧،٩
من الحمق وإذا رأى منّا مطرقاً أو مفكّراً اتّهمه بهذا المعنى ويقول وقعت والله يا فلان

On another occasion, on a Friday, I sent a message to al-Numayrī: "Ride with us to the Friday prayer." The messenger found that he had already been drinking that morning. He said to the messenger, "Tell him I've been praying since the early morning prayer." 9.15

I wrote back:

You who pray a prayer in submission to what's devilish,
Though you accept thanks from me, to thank you for that is foolish.

I wrote to him when I had fallen ill and he had not visited me: 9.16

Praise be to God! Even you have shown contempt—
no little contempt—to me after friendship.
It's what I expected, and it's what you have done.
Who is safe from betrayal?

He replied, excusing himself because he had some business and his mount was ill, so I wrote back to him:

Don't excuse yourself. We know you.
You'll always do what you want.
You mentioned business—
why didn't you make me a part of it?
And if you had no mount,
why not ride your shoes?

He replied:

If I've made a mistake,
in your mercy I have confidence;
I'll come to you on foot,
obeying your just sentence.

And he came on foot.

Al-Numayrī is the authority for the following story: ʿAbdallāh ibn al-Muʿtazz used to consider love a great failing; he even said it was a kind of stupidity. When he saw one of us pensive, with eyes downcast, he would accuse him of it and say, "By God, you've fallen. You've become stupid and feebleminded." 9.17

وقلّ عقلك وسخفت إلى أن رأيناه قد حدث به سهو شديد وفكر دائم إلى أن كانت تبدر منه الأبيات في معنى العشق. فمرّة يقول

أَسَـرَ ٱلْحُبُّ أَمِـيرًا   لَمْ يَكُنْ قَبْلُ أَسِـيرَا
فَٱرْحَمُوا ذُلَّ عَـزِيـزٍ   صَارَ عَبْدًا مُسْتَجِيرَا

ومرّة يقول

عَقْلُ ٱلْمُحِبِّ سَاهِي
فِي قَلْبِـهِ ٱلدَّوَاهِي

فقلت جعلني الله فداك هذه أشياء قد كنت تعيب أمثالها منّا ونحن ننكرها الآن ١٨،٩
منك. فيرجع تصنّعاً ثمّ لا يلبث أن تبدر منه بادرة فقال مرّة

مَكْتُومُ يَا أَحْسَنَ خَلْقِ ٱللهِ   لَا تَتْرُكِينِي هٰكَذَا بِٱللهِ

ثمّ تنفّس فقلت

قَدْ ظَفِرَ ٱلْعِشْقُ بِعَبْدِ ٱللهِ   وَٱنْهَتَكَ ٱلسِّتْرُ بِحَمْدِ ٱللهِ
فَقُـلْ لَهُ سَـمِّ لَنَـا بِٱللهِ   هٰذَا ٱلَّذِي تَهْوَى بِحَقِّ ٱللهِ

فضحك وقال لا ولا كرامة فكتبت إليه من غد

بَكَتْ عَيْـنُهُ وَشَكَا حُـرْقَـةً   مِنَ ٱلْوَجْدِ فِي ٱلْقَلْبِ مَا تَنْطَفِي
فَقُـلْتُ لَهُ سَـيِّدِي مَا ٱلَّذِي   أَرَى بِكَ قَـالَ سَقَـامٌ خَفِيّ
فَقُـلْتُ أَعِشْقٌ فَقَالَ ٱقْتَصِرْ   عَلَى مَا تَـرَاهُ أَمَا تَكْتَـفِي

Then we noticed that he was very absentminded and always lost in thought. Finally he began to utter verses about love. Once he said:

Love has made captive a prince who was never before in subjection.
Pity a mighty man's fall; he's a slave now, asking protection.

And another time:

The lover's mind is distracted,
His heart's a prey to disaster.

So I said, "May God make me your ransom! You used to reproach us for 9.18
these kinds of things, and now here we are, blaming you for them." At that he made an effort and pulled himself together. But then he would burst out, saying once:

Hidden, my feelings, loveliest of God's creatures.
By God, don't leave me thus.

Then he sighed, and I said:

'Abdallāh's been seized by love!
His defenses are down, thank the Lord.
Tell him, by God's truth,
to name us the one he loves.

He laughed and said, "No, certainly not." So the next day I wrote to him:

His eyes shed tears, and he bemoaned
the unquenched fire of love in his heart.
So I said to him, "Sire, what's this I see in you?"
He answered, "A hidden sickness."
"Not love?" I asked. He said, "Be satisfied
with what you see. Isn't that enough?"

فكتب إليّ ١٩،٩

يَا مَنْ يُحَدِّثُ عَنِّي بِظَنِّ سَمْعٍ وَعَيْنِ
إِنْ كُنْتَ تَخْطُبُ سِرِّي فَٱرْجِعْ بِخُفَّيْ حُنَيْنِ

فكتبت إليه

هَيْهَاتَ حَظَّكَ وَٱللّٰهِ أَنْ تَبُوحَ بِعِشْقِكْ
دَعْ عَنْكَ خُفَّيْ حُنَيْنٍ وَٱحْرِصْ عَلَى حَلِّ رِبْقِكْ
تَعَالَ نَحْتَالُ فِيمَا تَهْوَى بِرِفْقِي وَرِفْقِكْ

ثمّ صرت إليه فأخبرني بقصّته فسعيت له بلطف الحيلة وأعانني بحزم الرأي إلى أن فاز بالظفر وأدرك البغية.

He wrote to me: 9.19

> You talk of me because of what you've seen and heard—
> If you think you'll learn my secret, your hopes will be dashed.

And I wrote back:

> You'll have no luck, by God, just speaking of your love!
> Instead of dashing hopes, try to puzzle out something.
> Come, let's find a solution with your finesse and mine.

Then I went to see him and he told me the whole story. Helped by his resolution, I employed my cunning, and he achieved his goal.

دير باشهرا[1]

١٠،١ وهــذا الدير على شاطئ دجلة وهو دير حسن عامر نزه كثير البساتين والكروم وهو أحد المواضع المقصودة والديارات المشهودة والمنحدرون من سرّ من رأى والمصعدون إليها ينزلونه فمن جعله طريقاً بات فيه وأقام به إن طاب له ومن قصده أقام الأيّام في ألذّ عيش وأطيبه وأحسن مكان وأنزهه.

١٠،٢ ولأبي العيناء فيه وكان نزله وأقام به أيّاماً واستطابه وقال فيه

نَـزَلْنَا دَيْـرَ بَاشَهْـرَا　　عَـلَى قَسِّيسِـهِ ظُهْـرَا
عَـــلَى دِينِ يَشُوعِيٍّ[2]　　فَمَا أَفْـتَى وَمَا أَسْـرَا
فَأَوْلَى مِنْ جَمِيلِ ٱلْفِعْــلِ مَا يَسْتَعْبِدُ ٱلْحُرَّا
وَسَــقَّانَا وَرَوَّانَا　　مِنَ ٱلصَّافِيَةِ ٱلْعَذْرَا
وَطَابَ ٱلْوَقْتُ فِي ٱلدَّيْرِ　　فَرَابَطْـنَا بِهِ عَشْـرَا
وَسُقِّينَا بِهِ ٱلشَّمْسَا　　وَأُخْدِمْـنَا بِهِ ٱلْبَدْرَا
وَأَحْيَتْ لَذَّةُ ٱلْكَأْسِ　　وَلٰكِنْ قَتَّلَتْ سُكْرَا
وَنِلْنَا كُلَّ مَا نَهْوَا　　هُ مِنْ لَذَّاتِنَا جَهْرَا
تَصَابَيْنَا وَغَنَّيْنَا　　وَأَرْغَمْنَا بِهِ ٱلدَّهْرَا
فَنِكْنَا وَتَهَتَّكْنَا　　وَمِثْلِي هَتَكَ ٱلسِّتْرَا
وَقَدْ سَاعَدَنَا رَبَّنْ　　طَوْعًا مِنْهُ لَا جَبْرَا
جَزَاهُ ٱللهُ عَنْ خَيْرٍ　　بِهِ قَابَلَنَا خَيْرَا
فَقَدْ أَوْسَعْتُهُ شُكْرًا　　كَمَا أَوْسَعَنَا بِرَّا

---

١ الأصل: (النوادر الواقعة في هذا الدير لطيفة جدًّا. يجب على المسامر حفظها واستحضارها فإنّ النفس تشرف بوقائع الأفاضل) وردت في الهامش. ٢ الأصل: ايسوع.

Bāshahrā Monastery (The House of Vigils)[45]

This monastery stands on the banks of the Tigris. It is fine, well maintained, and pleasant, with large gardens and vineyards. It is famous and a well-known destination for visitors. People traveling down from Samarra or coming upriver stop there, and those who pass it on their way spend the night there and may stay longer. Those who make it their destination beguile days in the best, most delightful way and in very beautiful and pleasant surroundings. 10.1

Abū l-ʿAynāʾ stopped there, stayed some days, and appreciated the place, composing this poem about it: 10.2

Stopping one noon at Bāshahrā Convent, we met the priest,
A believer in Jesus, not doctrinaire or laying down rules,
But showing such kindness as to enthrall noble souls.
He gave us a drink, quenching our thirst with pure, unmingled wine.
We enjoyed life in the convent so much that we stayed ten days,
With the moon as our attendant, drinking wine as bright as the sun,
Given life by the cup's delight, but killed by intoxication.
We were granted all the pleasures we wanted, with no need to hide.
Singing, carefree as children, we were masters of destiny,
Indulging fancies with no fear of disgrace—I went too far,
Helped along by Brother,[46] quite willingly and unforced,
May God reward him well for all the good he did us.
My thanks equal the generosity he showed us.

٣،١٠ وكان أبو العيناء من الطيّاب وكان المتوكّل يعجب بكلامه وسرعة جوابه ونوادره وعمي على رأس أربعين سنة من عمره وممّا يدلّ على ذلك قول أبي عليّ البصير فيه

قَدْ كُنْتُ خِفْتُ يَدَ ٱلزَّمَا　　نِ عَلَيْكَ إِذْ ذَهَبَ ٱلْبَصَرْ
لَمْ أَدْرِ أَنَّكَ بِٱلْعَمَى　　تَغْنَى وَيَفْتَقِرُ ٱلْبَشَرْ

وكان حسن الشعر جيّد العارضة مليح الكتابة والترسّل خبيث اللسان في سبّ الناس والتعريض بهم. ونحن نذكر طرفاً من أخباره بمقدار لا يخرج إلى الإطالة ولا يخلّ بالشرط.

٤،١٠ قال المتوكّل لأبي العيناء ما أشدّ شيء مرّ عليك في ذهاب بصرك قال فوات رؤيتك يا أمير المؤمنين مع اجتماع الناس على جمالك. وقال له يوماً يا محمّد إلى كم تمدح الناس وتذمّهم قال ما أساؤوا وأحسنوا.

وقال له عبيد الله بن سليمان قد أمرنا لك بشيء في هذا الوقت فخذه واعذر. قال لا أفعل أيّها الوزير إذا كنت في النكبة تعتذر وفي الدولة تعتذر فمتى لا تعتذر.

٥،١٠ قال وسأل صاعد بن مخلد كتاباً يكتبه له إلى مصر فجعل يقول إلى مصر يا أبا العيناء إلى مصر فقال وما استبعادك أعزّك الله لي مصر والله لما في صناديقك أبعد عليّ ممّا في مصر.

ودخل إلى أبي الصقر فقرّب مجلسه وأدناه فقال أيّها الوزير تقريب الوليّ وحرمان العدوّ. ودخل عليه يوماً فقال ما أخّرك عنّا يا أبا عبد الله قال سُرق حماري قال وكيف سُرق قال لم أكن مع اللصّ فأعرف كيف سرقه. ثمّ جاءه بعد مدّة فقال ما أخّرك عنّا يا أبا عبد الله فقال منّ العواري وذلّة المكاري. فأمر له بخمسين ديناراً.

Abū l-ʿAynāʾ was a pleasant fellow. Al-Mutawakkil enjoyed his conversation, his jokes, and the quickness of his repartee. He went blind in his early forties, as these verses of Abū ʿAlī al-Baṣīr show: 10.3

When you lost your sight,
  I feared time's hand was against you,
Not knowing blindness would enrich you,
  while others are down and out.

He was a good poet, eloquent, with a fine style in writing and correspondence, and a mordant tongue in insulting and attacking people. We include here a selection of anecdotes about him, which is not too long, so as not to go against the plan of the book.

Al-Mutawakkil asked Abū l-ʿAynāʾ, "What's the worst experience you have had from losing your sight?" He replied, "Not being able to see you, Commander of the Faithful, when everyone agrees on how handsome you are." 10.4

The caliph asked him one day, "Abū Muḥammad, how long do you go on praising or blaming people?" "As long as they continue to behave badly or well."

ʿUbaydallāh ibn Sulaymān once said to Abū l-ʿAynāʾ, "We've ordered that you be given something now. Take it and accept my apologies." He answered, "No, I won't, Vizier. You apologize when you're in disgrace, you apologize when you're in power. When don't you apologize?"

Abū l-ʿAynāʾ asked Ṣāʿid ibn Makhlad to write him a letter of recommendation for a position in Egypt. "For Egypt, Abū l-ʿAynāʾ, for Egypt!" he exclaimed. Abū l-ʿAynāʾ rejoined, "And why should my interest in Egypt surprise you, may God grant you honor? By God, it's easier for me to get to Egypt than to the contents of your coffers!" 10.5

Abū l-ʿAynāʾ was admitted to Abū l-Ṣaqr, who allowed him to draw close. So Abū l-ʿAynāʾ said, "Vizier, this is bringing a friend close and keeping an enemy at bay."

One day when he went to see him, Abū l-Ṣaqr asked, "What kept you from visiting us, Abū ʿAbdallāh?" "My donkey was stolen." "How did it happen?" "I wasn't with the thief to see how he stole it." A while later he went to see him again, and the vizier asked, "What kept you from visiting us, Abū ʿAbdallāh?" "A mountain of debts and the muleteer's contempt." So he gave him fifty dinars.

قال دخل أبو العيناء يوماً إلى محمّد بن عبد الملك الزيّات فلم يرفع طرفه إليه ولا كلّمه. فقال إنّ من حقّ نعمة الله عليك لمّا أهّلك له في الحال التي أنت عليها أن تجعل البسطة لأهل الحاجة إليك خُلقاً فإن أوحش انقبض عن المسئلة وبكثرة السؤال مع النجح يدوم السرور وبقضاء الحاجات تدوم النعم. فقال له محمّد إنّي أعرفك فضولياً كثير الكلام. ترى أنّ طول لسانك يمنع من تأديبك إذا زللت وأمر به إلى الحبس. فكتب إليه أبو العيناء من الحبس قد علمت أنّ الحبس لم يكن لذنب تقدّم إليك ولكن أحببت أن تريني قدرتك عليّ لأنّ كلّ جديد يستلذّ ولا بأس أن ترينا من عفوك ما أريتنا من قدرتك فأمر بإطلاقه. ٦،١٠

فلقيه بعد مدّة طويلة على الطريق فحبس محمّد دابّته وقال ما أراك أبا عبد الله تواصلنا بحسب أنجائنا لك فقال أبو العيناء أمّا المعرفة بعنايتك فمتأكّدة ولكنّني أحسب الذي جدّد ٱستبطاءك لي فراغ حبسك ممّن فيه فأردت أن تعمره بي.

قال ودخل على رجل قد عُزل عن عمل كان يتولّاه فقال لئن قبحت عليك النعمة لقد حسنت بك النقمة قال ولِمَ ذاك قال لأنّي سألتك أحقر من قدرك فرددتني بأقبح من وجهك ثمّ قال ٧،١٠

قُلْ لِزَيْدٍ بْنِ صَاعِدٍ   جَاءَكَ ٱلْعَزْلُ فِي لَطَفْ
فَٱجْرَعِ ٱلْهَمَّ وَٱصْتَبِرْ   فَعَلَى رَبِّكَ ٱلْخَلَفْ
أَنْتَ أَيْضاً إِذَا وَلِيتَ فَلَا تُكْثِرِ ٱلصَّلَفْ

قال اجتاز ابن بدر بأبي العيناء وهو على بابه جالس فقال هذا منزلك أبا عبد الله قال نعم. فإن شئت أن ترى سوء أثرك فيه فانزل.

قال ومرّ بدار عبد الله بن منصور يوماً فقال لغلامه أيّ شيء خبر أبي محمّد قال كما تحبّ. قال فما لي لا أسمع الصراخ في الدار.

Abū l-ʿAynāʾ was admitted to Muḥammad ibn ʿAbd al-Malik al-Zayyāt, but the vizier did not raise his eyes to him or address him. So Abū l-ʿAynāʾ said, "Seeing that God has granted you this favor and that you occupy this position, you should make it your second nature to welcome petitioners. If they feel slighted, they do not dare to ask. There is lasting happiness, when many petitions are granted, and benefits persist when needs are fulfilled." Muḥammad responded, "I know that your behavior is excessive and you talk a great deal. Do you think your garrulousness will prevent you being disciplined when you have committed a fault?" And he sent him to prison. 10.6

Abū l-ʿAynāʾ wrote to him from prison: "I realize my imprisonment is not because I offended you earlier. Rather, it's because you wanted to demonstrate to me the power you have over me. Every novelty causes pleasure, so there's nothing to prevent you from showing me your capacity to forgive as you did your power." At which Muḥammad ordered his release.

Much later, Abū l-ʿAynāʾ met Muḥammad in the street. Muḥammad reined in his horse and said, "Abū ʿAbdallāh, I haven't observed you visiting us, as would be consistent with our releasing you." Abū l-ʿAynāʾ answered, "I am very well aware of your concern for us, but I expect that your calling on me to stop now is because your prison is empty and you want to lodge me there."

One day Abū l-ʿAynāʾ visited a man who had been dismissed from a governorship he held. He said, "Good fortune made you ugly: adversity becomes you." "Why?" "I asked you for something beneath your worth and your refusal was uglier than your face." Then he recited: 10.7

Tell Zayd ibn Ṣāʿid,
  "Your dismissal has been kind.
So swallow your cares and bear up.
  God will take care of the rest.
If you get a new appointment,
  avoid insults when speaking your mind."

Ibn Badr passed Abū l-ʿAynāʾ while he was sitting by the doorway of his house. Ibn Badr asked, "Is this your house, Abū ʿAbdallāh?" "Yes, and if you want to see the bad impression you leave on it, you can dismount."

Abū l-ʿAynāʾ passed ʿAbdallāh ibn Manṣūr's house one day. He asked his servant, "What's the news of Abū Muḥammad?" "He's just as you would wish," he replied. "Then why don't I hear the house full of the wails of the bereaved?"[47]

قال وذكر أبو العيناء ميمون بن إبراهيم فقال لو تأمّل رجل أفعاله فاجتنبها لاستغنى ٨،١٠
عن الآداب أن يطلبها.

قال أبو العيناء قال لي محمّد بن مكرّم أما تعرفني قلت بلى ولكن معرفة أرثي لك منها.

وقال له محمّد بن مكرّم يوماً يا أبا عبد الله كلّ شيء لك من الناس حتّى أولادك.

وقال أبو العيناء رأيت ابن مكرّم فرأيت بطنه بطن حبلى ونفَسه نفس ولهى ٩،١٠
ومخاطه مخاط ثكلى وفي استه الداهية العظمى. وقال له ابن[١] مكرّم يوماً يا أبا
عبد الله هو ذا تصوم معنا في هذا الشهر شيئاً وكان شهر رمضان فقال وتدعنا
العجوز نصوم.

قال رجل لعبيد الله بن سليمان إن رأيت أعزّك الله أن تُخرج لي رزقاً فقال ممّن ١٠،١٠
الرجل ليخرج الرزق على قدر ذاك قال من ولد آدم. فقال أبو العيناء احتفظ أعزّك الله
بهذا النسب فقد انقطع أصله.

قال اجتمع الجاحظ وأبو العيناء عند الحسن بن وهب فقال له الجاحظ علمت أنّ محمّد بن عبد الله أحسن من عمرو بن بحر وأبو عبد الله أحسن من أبي عثمان ولكنّ الجاحظ أحسن من أبي العيناء. فقال أبو العيناء هيهات جئت إلى ما يخفى من أمورنا ففضّلتني عليك فيه وإلى ما يُعرف ففضّلت نفسك فيه. إنّ أبا العيناء يدلّ على كنية والجاحظ يدلّ على عاهة والكنية وإن سمجت أصلح من العاهة وإن ملحت.

قال أبو العيناء عشقتني امرأة بالبصرة من غير أن تراني وإنّما كانت تسمع عذوبة ١١،١٠
كلامي فلمّا رأتني استقبحتني وقالت قبّحه الله أهذا هو. فكتبتُ إليها

وَنُبِّئْتُهَا لَمَّا رَأَتْنِي تَنَكَّرَتْ وَقَالَتْ ذَمِيمٌ أَحْوَلٌ مَا لَهُ جِسْمُ
فَإِنْ تُنْكِرِي مِنِّي ٱحْوِلَالاً فَإِنَّنِي أَدِيبٌ أَرِيبٌ لَا عَيِيٌّ وَلَا فَدْمُ

١ الأصل: وقال له مكرّم.

Abū l-ʿAynāʾ observed of Maymūn ibn Ibrāhīm: "Contemplate Maymūn's actions and avoid them—you won't need to try to acquire good manners." 10.8

Abū l-ʿAynāʾ said, "Muḥammad ibn Mukarram asked me, 'Don't you know me?' 'Yes indeed,' I replied, 'but I'm sorry for you that I have that sort of knowledge.'"

Muḥammad ibn Mukarram remarked to Abū l-ʿAynāʾ one day, "Abū ʿAbdallāh, people have given you all you have, including your children."

Abū l-ʿAynāʾ recalled, "I saw Muḥammad ibn Mukarram—his belly was swollen like a pregnant woman's, he panted like a woman crazy with love, and his nose was covered in snot like a bereaved woman. His backside was an utter disaster." 10.9

Ibn Mukarram asked Abū l-ʿAynāʾ once, "Abū ʿAbdallāh, will you be fasting with us at all this month?" It was the month of Ramadan. He replied, "Do you think my old woman will let me fast?"[48]

A man submitted a request to ʿUbaydallāh ibn Sulaymān: "Would it please you to award me a pension, may God keep you?" So as to award him the appropriate amount, ʿUbaydallāh asked, "What's your genealogy?" "I'm descended from Adam," he answered. "Take good care of this genealogy," commented Abū l-ʿAynāʾ, "because its origin is lost." 10.10

Al-Jāḥiẓ and Abū l-ʿAynāʾ met at al-Ḥasan ibn Wahb's house. Al-Jāḥiẓ said to Abū l-ʿAynāʾ, "I recognize that 'Muḥammad ibn ʿAbdallāh' is better than 'ʿAmr ibn Baḥr' and 'Abū ʿAbdallāh' is better than 'Abū ʿUthmān,' but 'al-Jāḥiẓ' is certainly preferable to 'Abū l-ʿAynāʾ.'" Abū l-ʿAynāʾ retorted, "Not a bit of it. You've touched on matters that are private and recognized my superiority, and on matters that are public knowledge and considered yourself superior. 'Abū l-ʿAynāʾ' (father of the girl with very black eyes) is a teknonym, whereas 'al-Jāḥiẓ' (the goggle-eyed) denotes a physical defect. Even if a teknonym is ugly, it's better than a physical defect, funny though that may be."

Abū l-ʿAynāʾ related: A woman in Basra fell in love with me without seeing me. She had simply heard how well I expressed myself. When she saw me, she thought I was ugly and said, "God damn! Is this him?" So I wrote to her: 10.11

She heard about me but snubbed me on sight,
saying, "Ugly, squinting, with a miserable body!"
Maybe you don't like my squint,
but I'm cultured and clever,
Not a fuddy-duddy or a stuttering dolt.

فوقّعت في الرقعة يا عاضّ بظر أمّه لديوان الرسائل أردتك.

ولأبي العيناء في عليّ بن الجهم ١٢،١٠

أَرَادَ عَلِيٌّ أَنْ يَقُولَ قَصِيدَةً بِمَدْحِ أَمِيرِ ٱلْمُؤْمِنِينَ فَأَذَّنَا
فَقُلْتُ لَهُ لَا تَعْجَلَنْ بِإِقَامَةٍ فَلَسْتُ عَلَى طُهْرٍ فَقَالَ وَلَا أَنَا

أبو العيناء قال أتيت عبد الله بن داود الخُرَيبيّ فسألته أن يحدّثني فاستصغرني وقال اذهب فتحفظ القرآن قلت قد حفظته قال اقرأ من رأس ستّين من يونس فقرأت العشر فقال أحسنت اذهب فتعلّم الفرائض قلت قد حفظتها قال فأيّما أقرب إليك عمّك أو ابن أخيك قلت ابن أخي قال ولِمَ ذاك قلت لأنّ هذا من ولد أبي وهذا من ولد جدّي قال أحسنت اذهب فتعلّم العربيّة قلت قد فعلت وتعلّمت منها ما فيه كفاية قال فلِمَ قال عمر يا لَلّهِ يا لِلمسلمين قلت لأنّ الأوّل استغاثة والثاني نداء. فقال لو كنت محدّثًا أحدًا في سنك لحدّثتك. ١٣،١٠

قال أبو العيناء دخلت على أبي أحمد عبيد الله بن عبد الله بن طاهر وكان يومًا صافيًا وقوم بين يديه يلعبون بالشطرنج فقال يا أبا عبد الله إنّا نلعب في ندب إلى أن ندرك طعامنا ففي أيّ الحزبين تحبّ أن تكون قلت في حزب الأمير أيّده الله فإنّه أعلى وأبهى فغُلبنا فقال أبو أحمد يا أبا عبد الله قد غُلبنا وقد أصابك بقسطك عشرون رطلًا ثلجًا فقلت أحضره أيّها الأمير ووثبت فصرت إلى أبي العبّاس بن ثوابة فأقرأته السلام من أبي أحمد وقلت له إنّه يتشوّقك وأراد أن يكتب إليك رقعة فخاف مراوغتك فوجّهني رسولًا وحمّلني رسالةً ولسنا نفترق إلّا بحضرته. فركب معي وجئنا فلمّا ١٤،١٠

She wrote on the back of the letter: "You motherfucker, did you think I wanted to give you a job in the chancery?"

Abū l-ʿAynāʾ composed these verses about ʿAlī ibn al-Jahm: 10.12

ʿAlī meant to praise the caliph in a poem,
so he recited the call to prayer.[49]
I said, "Don't hurry with the second call. I'm not pure."
He said, "Nor me neither."

Another tale told by Abū l-ʿAynāʾ: I went to ʿAbdallāh ibn Dāwud al-Khuraybī 10.13 and asked him to transmit traditions of the Prophet to me. He was unimpressed with me, and said, "Go and learn the Qurʾan by heart." I said, "I've already done so." Then he said, "Recite from the beginning of verse sixty of the Surah of Jonah." So I recited those ten verses. "Well done," he said. "Now go and study the rules for dividing estates."[50] "I've learned them." He asked, "Which is closer to you, your uncle or your nephew?" I answered, "My nephew." "And why is that?" I replied, "Because my nephew is a descendant of my father, while my uncle is a descendant of my grandfather."[51] He said, "Well done. Now go and study the Arabic language." I answered, "I've done that and learned enough of it." He asked, "So why did ʿUmar[52] say, 'O God!' and 'O Muslims!'?" "The first is an appeal for help, and the second is a battle cry."[53] Then he said, "If I were to transmit traditions to anyone of your age, I'd transmit them to you."

Abū l-ʿAynāʾ related another experience of his: I went to visit Abū Aḥmad 10.14 ʿUbaydallāh ibn ʿAbdallāh ibn Ṭāhir. It was a beautiful day and there were people playing chess in his presence. He said to me, "Abū ʿAbdallāh, we're playing for wagers until our food is brought, so which team would you like to join?" "The prince's team, God grant him aid, for it is more eminent and illustrious." We were beaten, and Abū Aḥmad said, "Abū ʿAbdallāh, we've lost. For your stake, you must produce some seventeen pounds (eight kilos) of ice." "I'll bring them, Prince," I replied, and rushed off. I went to Abū l-ʿAbbās ibn Thawābah, conveyed to him Abū Aḥmad's greetings, and said, "He's very keen to see you. He wanted to write you a note, but he was afraid that you would come up with some trick, so he sent me as a messenger and gave me a note to carry. We will only part ways when we reach him." He set off with me on

وقفت بين يديه قلت أيّها الأمير قد جئتك بجبل همذان ثلجًا فاقتص منه ما قُمِرنا والعب مع أصحابك في الباقي. فضحك حتّى استلقى وسأل ابن ثوابة عن القصّة فعُرِّف الخبر فلمّا وقف عليه شتمني وانصرف.

١٥،١٠ قال أبو العيناء دخلت على المتوكّل ودعوت له وكلّمته فاستحسن خطابي وقال لي بلغني أنّ فيك شرًّا فقلت يا أمير المؤمنين إن يكن الشرّ ذكر المحسن بإحسانه والمسيء بإساءته فقد زكّى الله جلّ وعزّ وذمّ فقال في التزكية ﴿نِعۡمَ ٱلۡعَبۡدُ إِنَّهُۥٓ أَوَّابٌ﴾ وقال في الذمّ ﴿هَمَّازٍ مَّشَّآءِۭ بِنَمِيمٍ مَّنَّاعٍ لِّلۡخَيۡرِ مُعۡتَدٍ أَثِيمٍ عُتُلِّۭ بَعۡدَ ذَٰلِكَ زَنِيمٍ﴾ فذمّه تعالى اسمه وقد قال الشاعر

إِذَا أَنَا بِٱلۡمَعۡرُوفِ لَمۡ أَثۡنِ دَائِبًا وَلَمۡ أَشۡتِمِ ٱلۡجِبۡسَ ٱللَّئِيمَ ٱلۡمُذَمَّمَا
فَفِيمَ عَرَفۡتُ ٱلۡخَيۡرَ وَٱلشَّرَّ بِٱسۡمِهِ وَشَقَّ لِيَ ٱللّٰهُ ٱلۡمَسَامِعَ وَٱلۡفَمَا

وإن كان الشرّ كفعل العقرب التي تلسع النبيّ والذمّي بطبع لا يميّز[1] فقد صان الله عبدك عن ذلك.

١٦،١٠ وقال لي وبلغني أنّك رافضيّ فقلت يا أمير المؤمنين وكيف أكون رافضيًّا وبلدي البصرة ومنشأي في مسجد جامعها وأستاذي الأصمعيّ وليس يخلو[2] من إرادة دين أو دنيا. فإن أرادوا دينًا فقد أجمع المسلمون على تقديم من أخّروا وإن أرادوا دنيا فأنت وآباؤك أمراء المؤمنين لا دنيا إلّا معك.

فقال كيف داري هذه فقلت رأيت الناس بنوا دورهم في الدنيا وأنت جعلت الدنيا في دارك. فقال لي ما تقول في عبيد الله بن يحيى فقلت العبد لله ولك منقسم بين طاعته وخدمتك يؤثر رضاك على كلّ فائدة وما عاد بصلاح رعيّتك على كلّ لذّة. فقال ما تقول في صاحب البريد ميمون بن إبراهيم وكان عرف أنّي وجدت

١ الأصل: يتميز. ٢ كذا في الأصل ولعلّ كلمة سقطت هنا.

horseback and we arrived. When I entered Abū Aḥmad's presence I said to him, "Prince, I have brought you this block of ice, so take what we lost at gambling, and play with your friends for the rest." Abū Aḥmad laughed so much he collapsed. Ibn Thawābah asked what was going on, so we told him, and when he understood he cursed me and left.

Abū l-ʿAynāʾ also recalled: After I was admitted to al-Mutawakkil's presence, I prayed for blessings on him and delivered a speech. The caliph appreciated it and said to me, "I've heard that you can be offensive." I replied, "Commander of the Faithful, if being offensive is mentioning a benefactor with his good deeds and a malefactor with his evil ones, God, the mighty and glorious, has praised and blamed. As praise, He said, «How excellent a servant! He was penitent»,[54] and as blame, «Backbiter, spreader of slander, hinderer of good, transgressor, sinner, greedy, moreover ignoble».[55] The Almighty has led the way. And a poet said: 10.15

If I didn't praise the well-doer
or curse the wretched, vulgar wrongdoer
How would I know good and evil by their names?
God would split my ears and my mouth.

"And if the scorpion was evil when it stung both the Prophet and the non-Muslim without distinction, at least God has protected me, your servant, from that."[56]

Al-Mutawakkil went on, "I've heard that you are a heretical Shiʿi." "How could I be a Shiʿi, when I come from Basra, grew up in its Friday mosque, and my teacher was al-Aṣmaʿī? There are people who seek either right belief or power. If they want belief, the Muslims have agreed to give precedence to those whom they kept back,[57] while if they want power, you and your forefathers are the caliphs, and there is no power without you." 10.16

Then al-Mutawakkil said, "What do you think of this palace of mine?" I replied, "I've seen people who built their houses in the world, but you have put the world in your house." "And what do you think of ʿUbaydallāh ibn Yaḥyā?" "He is the servant of both you and God, divided between obeying God's commandments and serving you. He prefers satisfying you to any personal profit and prefers the welfare of your subjects to any pleasure." "And what's your opinion of the head of the postal service, Maymūn ibn Ibrāhīm?" (He knew that

عليه في تقصير وقع بي منه فقلت يا أمير المؤمنين يد تسرق واست تضرط هو مثل يهوديّ قد سرق نصف جزيته فله إقدام بما أدّى ومعه إحجام لما بقي. إساءته طبيعة وإحسانه تكلّف.

١٧،١٠ فقال إنّي أريدك لمجالستي فقلت لا أطيق ذاك ولا أقوى عليه وما أقول هذا جهلاً بما لي في هذا المجلس من الشرف ولكنّي رجل محجوب والمحجوب تختلف إشارته ويخفى عليه إيماؤه. ويجوز عليّ أن أتكلّم بكلام غضبان ووجهك راضٍ وبكلام راضٍ ووجهك غضبان ومتى لم أميّز بين هذين هلكت. قال صدقت ولكن تلزمنا. قلت لزوم الفرض الواجب فوصلني بعشرة آلاف درهم. وقال لي يوماً وقد دخلت إليه يا محمّد ما بقي في المجلس أحد إلّا اغتابك عندي فقلت

إِذَا رَضِيَتْ عَنِّي كِرَامُ عَشِيرَتِي   فَلَا زَالَ غَضْبَانًا عَلَيَّ لِئَامُهَا

١٨،١٠ وهو أبو عبد الله محمّد بن القاسم بن خلّاد بن ياسر بن سليمان وأصله من اليمامة من بني حنيفة أنفسهم وكان مسكنه بالبصرة ثمّ انتقل إلى بغداد وانتجع سرّ من رأى ولقي المتوكّل وأقام بها. وكان حسن الكتّابة بليغ الخطابة مليح الشعر طلق اللّسان بالذمّ والاستبطاء سريع الجواب حاضر النادرة لا يقام له. وقال المتوكّل أشتهي أنادم أبا العيناء لولا أنّه ضرير فبلغ ذلك أبا العيناء فقال إن أعفاني أمير المؤمنين من رؤية الأهلّة وقراءة نقوش الخواتيم فإنّي أصلح له. قال وحجب محمّد بن مكرّم أبا العيناء ثمّ كتب يعتذر منه فكتب إليه أبو العيناء تحجبني مشافهة وتعتذر إليّ مكاتبة.

١٩،١٠ وأخباره كثيرة ولكنّا أوردنا بمقدار ما يحتمله الكتاب ويقتضيه الشرط ولا يخرج قارئه إلى الملل. وكتب ابن مكرّم إلى أبي العيناء عندي سكباج ترعب المجنون

I was angry with Maymūn because I'd suffered from negligence on his part.) I answered, "Commander of the Faithful, he's a hand that steals and an ass that farts. He's like a Jew who has stolen half the money he was supposed to collect in taxes. He boasts of what he has paid and keeps quiet about the rest. Evil comes naturally to him and when he does good, he's shamming."

Al-Mutawakkil then said, "I'd like you to sit with me at court." "It's not in my power; it's beyond me. I don't say this out of ignorance of the honor that attending court would confer on me. But I'm a man whose eyes are veiled. Those who are sightless may be out of step in their advice and not notice gestures. I might speak as if angry while you were pleased, and as if glad while you were angry. And to fail to distinguish between these moods would be the end of me." "You are right," he said, "but keep us company." "I will," I replied, "as a binding obligation." Then he gave me ten thousand dirhams. 10.17

One day, when I had gone to attend al-Mutawakkil, he said to me, "Muḥammad, there's no one at the audience who has not slandered you to me." I recited:

> If the nobles of my tribe are content with me,
> let the base ones be angry.

Abū l-ʿAynāʾ's name was Abū ʿAbdallāh Muḥammad ibn al-Qāsim ibn Khallād ibn Yāsir ibn Sulaymān. His family was from al-Yamāmah and were members of the Banū Ḥanīfah tribe by blood. He used to live in Basra but then moved to Baghdad. He went to Samarra to make money, met al-Mutawakkil, and settled there. He wrote well, and was an eloquent speaker and a fine poet. He was ready to blame and complain when kept waiting, was quick in repartee, and always had a joke up his sleeve. No one could stand up to him. 10.18

Al-Mutawakkil said, "I'd like to have Abū l-ʿAynāʾ as a companion, but he's blind." When Abū l-ʿAynāʾ heard that, he said, "If the Commander of the Faithful will let me off spotting new moons and reading inscriptions on rings, I'm his man."

Muḥammad ibn Mukarram kept Abū l-ʿAynāʾ from seeing him, but then he wrote to apologize to him. Abū l-ʿAynāʾ wrote back: "He keeps me at a distance orally and apologizes in writing."

There are many anecdotes about him, but we wanted to include only as much as the book would take without violating its plan and boring the reader. 10.19

وحديث يطرب المحزون وإخوانك المجازون[1] فلا تعلو عليّ وأتون. فأجابه أبو العيناء ﴿قَالَ ٱخْسَـُٔواْ فِيهَا وَلَا تُكَلِّمُونِ﴾ .

١ الأصل: المحازون.

Ibn Mukarram wrote to Abū l-ʿAynāʾ: "I've a dish of *sikbāj*[58] that will amaze a madman, talk that will delight a sad man, and old friends from your clan. So don't be proud—come to me unbowed." At which Abū l-ʿAynāʾ replied, "«Go away into it and do not speak to me.»"[59]

دير الخوات

١،١١ هذا الدير بعكبرا وهو دير كبير عامر يسكنه نساء مترهّبات متبتّلات فيه وهو وسط البساتين والكروم حسن الموقع وعيده الأحد الأوّل من الصوم يجتمع إليه كلّ من يقرب منه من النصارى والمسلمين فيعيّد هؤلاء ويتنزّه هؤلاء. وفي هذا العيد ليلة الماشوش وهي ليلة تختلط النساء بالرجال فلا يردّ أحد يده عن شيء ولا يردّ أحد أحدًا عن شيء. وهو من معادن الشراب ومنازل القصف ومواطن اللّهو.

٢،١١ وللناجم أبي عثمان فيه[١]

آحِ قَلْبِي مِنَ ٱلصَّبَابَةِ آحِ ... مِنْ جَوَارٍ مُزَيَّنَاتٍ مِلَاحِ
وَفَتَاةٍ كَأَنَّهَا غُصْنُ بَانٍ ... ذَاتِ وَجْهٍ كَمِثْلِ نُورِ ٱلصَّبَاحِ
أَهْلَ دَيْرِ ٱلْخَوَاتِ بِٱللهِ رَبِّي ... هَلْ عَلَى عَاشِقٍ قَضَى مِنْ جُنَاحِ

٣،١١ وكان أبو عثمان هذا راوية ابن الروميّ وهو مليح الشعر رقيق الطبع جيّد المعاني في وصف الخمر والأغاني والغزل. ومن مليح شعره

أَدِرْ يَا سَلَامَةُ كَأْسَ ٱلْعُقَارِ ... وَضَاهِ بِشَدْوِكَ شَدْوَ ٱلْقَمَارِي
وَخُذْهَا مُعَتَّقَةً مُزَّةً ... تَصُبُّ عَلَى ٱللَّيْلِ ثَوْبَ ٱلنَّهَارِ
يُنَازِعُهَا ٱلْخَدُّ جِرْيَالَهَا ... فَيُهْدِيهِ لِلْعَيْنِ يَوْمَ ٱلْخُمَارِ

١ الأصل: (أبو عثمان الناجم) وردت في الهامش.

The Sisters' Monastery

The Sisters' Monastery is in ʿUkbarā. It is large and well maintained, inhabited by women who live the monastic life and are celibate. It stands in the midst of gardens and vineyards, and is well situated in a delightful spot. Its patronal festival is the first Sunday of Lent, when everyone who lives close by, Christians and Muslims, gather there. The Christians celebrate the feast and the Muslims enjoy themselves. The Night of Māshūsh[60] falls during this feast. It is a night when women and men mix freely, no one observes any restraint, and no one imposes restrictions on anyone else. The monastery produces wine and is a place of revelry and enjoyment. 11.1

Al-Nājim Abū ʿUthmān has this poem on it: 11.2

Ah, my heart, for love!
  Ah, for bejeweled beauties!
Girls like slender boughs,
  faces like the light of the morn.
People of the Sisters' Convent,
  by the Lord God!
A lover's met his death—
  what wrong has he done?

This Abū ʿUthmān was the transmitter of Ibn al-Rūmī's poetry, a fine poet, sensitive, using excellent imagery to describe wine, singing, and love. One of his fine poems is: 11.3

Salāmah, vie in your song
  with the turtledove's coo,
And pass around the cups of wine
  matured with a full bouquet,
  clothing the night in the robe of day.
Our cheeks take their crimson from it,
And with a hangover they pass the color to the eye.

ومن مليح شعره

سَلَامَةَ بْنَ سَعِيدٍ يُجِيدُ حَثَّ ٱلرَّاحِ
إِذَا تَغَنَّى زَمَرْنَا عَلَيْهِ بِٱلْأَقْدَاحِ

وله ٤،١١

مَا نَطَقَتْ عَاتِبٌ وَمِزْهَرُهَا إِلَّا وَبِتْنَا[1] بِٱللَّهْوِ وَٱلْفَرَحِ
لَهَا غِنَاءٌ كَٱلْبُرْءِ فِي جَسَدٍ أَضْنَاهُ طُولُ ٱلسَّقَامِ وَٱلتَّرَحِ
تَعْبُدُهُ ٱلرَّاحُ فَهِيَ مَا نَطَقَتْ إِبْرِيقُنَا سَاجِدٌ عَلَى ٱلْقَدَحِ

وله

مَا نَطَقَتْ عَاتِبٌ وَمِزْهَرُهَا إِلَّا طَلَبْنَا بِٱلرَّاحِ نُعْمِلُهَا
تَطْلُبُ أَوْتَارُهَا ٱلْهُمُومَ بِأَوْ تَارٍ فَمَا تَسْتَفِيقُ تَقْتُلُهَا

وله وفيه لحن ٥،١١

مَا دَعَانِي ٱلشَّوْقُ إِلَّا أَذْرَتِ ٱلْعَيْنُ دُمُوعَا
إِنَّمَا أَبْكِي لِأَنِّي صِرْتُ لِلْحُبِّ رَبِيعَا
أَحْسَنَ ٱلنَّاسِ وَأَوْلَى ٱلنَّاسِ بِٱلْحُسْنِ جَمِيعَا
مَا أَرَى لِي عَنْ حَبِيبِي أَبَدَ[2] ٱلدَّهْرِ نُزُوعَا

١ الأصل: وبعنا. ٢ الأصل: ابدا.

Here is another fine poem of his:

Salāmah ibn Saʿīd[61] pours wine well and swiftly;
When he sings, we clink our cups in harmony.

And another: 11.4

Every time we hear ʿĀtib and her lute,
our time is full of fun and rejoicing.
Her singing's a cure for a body
weakened by sickness and grief.
She only needs to sing for the wine to bow down
and kneel in the cup in adoration.

And another:

Every time we hear ʿĀtib and her lute,
we call for wines and put them to work.
Her strings call out our cares
with cords that never fail to kill them.

This poem of his has a musical setting: 11.5

When longing calls me,
tears well up in my eyes;
I weep because I've become
the springtime for my love,
The loveliest of beings,
most suited to beauty.
Never, I believe,
will I abandon my beloved.

ديـر العـلْث

١٫١٢ والعَلْث قرية على شاطئ دجلة في الجانب الشرقيّ منها وبين يديها من دجلة موضع صعب ضيق المجاز كثير الحجارة شديد الجرية تجتاز فيه السفن بمشقّة. وهذه المواضع تُسمّى الأبواب وإذا وافت السفن إلى العَلْث أرست بها فلا يتهيأ لها الجواز إلّا بهادٍ من أهلها يكترونه فيمسك السكّان ويتخلّل بهم تلك المواضع فلا يحطّها حتّى يتخلّص منها. وهذا الدير راكب دجلة وهو من أحسن الديارات موقعاً وأنزهها موضعاً يُقصد من كلّ بلد ويطرقه كلّ أحد ولا يكاد يخلو من منحدر ومصعد. ومن دخله لم يتجاوزه إلى غيره لطيبه ونزهته ووجود جميع ما يحتاج إليه بالعَلْث وبه.

٢٫١٢ ولجحظة فيه

أَيُّهَا ٱلْمَالِحَانِ بِٱللهِ جُدَّا وَٱصْلِحَا لِي ٱلشِّرَاعَ وَٱلسُّكَّانَا
بَلِّغَانِي هُدِيتُمَا ٱلْبَرَدَانَا وَٱبْرِزَا لِي[1] مِنَ ٱلدِّنَانِ دِنَانَا
وَٱعْدِلَا بِي إِلَى ٱلْقَبِيصِيَّةِ ٱلزَّهْرَاءِ عَلِّي أُفَرِّجُ ٱلْأَحْزَانَا
وَإِذَا مَا أَقَمْتُ حَوْلًا تَمَامًا فَٱقْصِيَا بِي إِلَى كُرُومِ أَوَانَا
وَٱنْزِلَا بِي إِلَى شَرَابٍ عَتِيقٍ عَتَّقَتْهُ يَهُودُهُ أَزْمَانَا
رَقَّ حَتَّى حَسِبْتُهُ خَدَّ مَنْ أَبْدَلَنِي مِنْ وِصَالِهِ هِجْرَانَا
وَٱحْطُطَا لِي ٱلشِّرَاعَ بِٱلدَّيْرِ بِٱلْعَلْثِ لَعَلِّي أُعَاشِرُ ٱلرُّهْبَانَا
وَظِبَاءً يَتْلُوْنَ سِفْرًا مِنَ ٱلْإِنْجِيلِ بَاكَرْنَ سَحْرَةً قُرْبَانَا
لَابِسَاتٍ مِنَ ٱلْمُسُوحِ ثِيَابًا جَعَلَ ٱللهُ تَحْتَهَا أَغْصَانَا[2]

---

١ في الأصل: وَٱنْزِلَا بِي. ٢ سقط هذا البيت من الأصل.

The Monastery in ʿAlth

The village of ʿAlth is on the east bank of the Tigris. In front of it a stretch of the Tigris flows through rough country, narrow and stony, with a very fast current, and it is difficult for boats to navigate. That place is called the Gates. When boats arrive at ʿAlth, they dock and go no farther unless they have secured the services of a pilot. He works the rudder and steers them through the passage, only taking his hands from the rudder when he has taken them through that stretch of the river. 12.1

The monastery rises above the Tigris. It is a beautiful, delightful site, and people from all over come and visit it, including people traveling up or down the river. Those who enter it go no farther, for it is lovely and pleasant, and everything one needs can be had there or in ʿAlth itself.

Jaḥẓah composed this poem on it: 12.2

Sailors! By God, stir yourselves.
 Trim the sails and set the rudder!
Bring me, God keep you, to Baradān
 and open jar after jar,
Then to Qabīṣah the Radiant,
 where maybe I can cast off my sorrows,
And after a full year there,
 take me to Awānā's vineyards,
Letting me stop for an ancient wine
 long matured by the Jews,
Its taste so fine I thought it the cheek
 of one who loved me and left me.
Then lower the sails at ʿAlth's Convent
 and let me spend time with the monks
And gazelles who recite from the Gospels
 and take communion at daybreak
Clad in hair shirts under which God
 has hidden young branches,

خَفِـرَاتٍ حَتَّى إِذَا دَارَتِ ٱلْكَأْ سُ كَشَـفْنَ ٱلنُّحُورَ وَٱلصُّلْبَـانَا

وللمعتمد ٣،١٢

يَا طُولَ لَيْـلِي بِفَمِ ٱلصِّلْحِ أَتْبَـعْتُ خُسْـرَانِي بِٱلرِّبْحِ
لَهْفِي عَلَى دَهْرٍ لَنَا قَدْ مَضَى بِٱلْقَصْرِ وَٱلْقَاطُولِ وَٱلشِّلْحِ
بِٱلدَّيْرِ بِٱلْعَلْثِ وَرُهْبَانُهُ بَيْنَ ٱلشَّعَـانِينِ إِلَى ٱلدِّنْحِ

وكان للمعتمد شعر جيّد وشعر غير موزون[1] وربّما قال الأبيات فيصحّ بعضها ويفسد باقيها وكان يعطيه المغنّين فيعملون عليه ألحانًا فيغيب عيبه في التقطيع والألحان إلّا على خاصّة الناس.

قالت بدعة كان المعتمد يوجّه بشعره إلى عريب لتصوغ له الألحان فكانت تقول ويلي كم أغنّي في حروف ألف با تا ثا.

٤،١٢ قال الصوليّ أنشدني عبد الله بن المعتزّ من شعره الموزون

ٱلحَــمْدُ لِلّٰهِ رَبِّي مَلَكْتُ مَالِكَ قَلْبِي
فَصِرْتُ مَوْلًى لِمُلْكِي وَصَارَ مَوْلًى لِحُبِّي

ومن شعره لمّا أكثر الموفّق نقله من مكان إلى مكان

أَلِفْتُ ٱلتَّبَاعُدَ وَٱلْغُرْبَـهْ فَفِي كُلِّ يَوْمٍ أَطَا تُرْبَـهْ
وَفِي كُلِّ يَوْمٍ أَرَى حَادِثًا يُؤَدِّي إِلَى كَبِـدِي كُرْبَـهْ
أَمَـرَّ ٱلزَّمَانُ لَنَا طَعْـمَهُ فَمَا إِنْ نَرَى سَاعَةً عَذْبَـهْ

وهذا شعر جيّد صحيح في معناه ومن شعره الموزون

١ في الأصل: شعرًا جيّدًا وشعرًا غير موزون.

Shy till when the wine has gone round,
 they bare their breasts and show their crosses.[62]

And al-Muʿtamid composed this poem on it: 12.3

O for my long night at Fam al-Ṣilḥ,
 when I drank Khosroes's wine as a winner;
O how I look back on the time
 we passed at Qaṣr, Qāṭūl, and Shilḥ,
And—from Palm Sunday to Epiphany—
 with the monks of the Convent of ʿAlth.[63]

Al-Muʿtamid composed some excellent poetry, and also some that had no recognizable meter. Sometimes he made poems that were part metrical and part unmetrical.[64] Then the singers would come and compose settings for them, and the musical periods and the melodies hid their shortcomings from all but the cognoscenti. Bidʿah recalled that al-Muʿtamid used to send his poetry to ʿArīb for her to set to music, and she would complain, "Alas, how can I set the alphabet to music?"

Al-Ṣūlī is the authority for the following narrative: ʿAbdallāh ibn al-Muʿtazz 12.4
recited to me some of al-Muʿtamid's metrical poetry:

Praise be to God my Lord,
 for I own the queen of my heart.
Now I'm possessed by my slave,
 and she's possessed by my love.

And this is a poem he composed when al-Muwaffaq kept moving him from place to place:

I'm a stranger now, far from loved ones;
Every day I tread foreign earth,
Exposed to distressing events.
Time's taste has turned bitter in my mouth—
Will it ever again become sweet?

This is fine poetry, aptly expressing the theme. Another of his metrical poems:

بُليتُ بِشَادِنٍ كَٱلْبَدْرِ حُسْنًا يُعَذِّبُنِي بِأَنْوَاعِ ٱلْجَفَاءِ
وَلِي عَيْنَانِ دَمْعُهُمَا غَزِيرٌ وَنَوْمُهُمَا أَقَلُّ مِنَ ٱلْوَفَاءِ

وذكر الصوليّ أنّ المكتفي أخرج إليهم مدائح مكتوبة بالذهب من شعر المعتمد فكان فيها من الموزون ٥،١٢

طَالَ وَٱللهِ عَذَابِي وَٱهْتِمَامِي وَٱكْتِئَابِي
بِغَزَالٍ مِنْ بَنِي ٱلْأَصْفَرِ لَا يَعْنِيهِ مَا بِي
أَنَا مُغْرًى بِهَوَاهُ وَهْوَ مُغْرًى بِٱجْتِنَابِي
وَإِذَا مَا قُلْتُ صِلْنِي كَانَ لَا مِنْهُ جَوَابِي

وكان فيها أيضاً

عَجَّلَ ٱلْحُبُّ بِفُرْقَهْ فَبِقَلْبِي مِنْهُ حُرْقَهْ
مَالِكٌ بِٱلْحُبِّ رِقِّي وَأَنَا أَمْلِكُ رِقَّهْ
إِنَّمَا يَسْتَرْوِحُ ٱلصَّبُّ إِذَا أَظْهَرَ عِشْقَهْ

وللمعتمد شعر غنّت فيه شارية في طريقة الرمل ٦،١٢

تَأَنَّيْتُ بِٱلْحُبِّ دَهْرًا طَوِيلًا فَلَمْ أَرَ فِي ٱلْحُبِّ يَوْمًا سُرُورَا

وممّا غنّت فيه من شعره

يَا نَفْسُ وَيْحَكِ مَا لَكِ إِنِّي لَأُنْكِرُ حَالَكِ

وله

I'm tortured by a fawn lovely as the moon,
Who punishes me with rebuffs of all kinds.
My eyes shed incessant streams of tears.
He doesn't keep his promises,
And they sleep even less.

Al-Ṣūlī related that al-Muktafī showed them panegyrics by al-Muʿtamid 12.5
written in gold. One of the metrical ones was:

By God! Torture, cares, and sorrow have long been my lot,
caused by a Byzantine fawn careless of my feelings.
I'm obsessed with love for him, and he with avoiding me.
If I say, "Be generous," "No!" is his reply to me.

Another of these poems is:

Love brought swift separation, and my heart was rent.
Love improved your fortune, while enthrallment is all I own.
A lover only knows peace when he's declared his passion.

This is a verse by al-Muʿtamid, which Shāriyah made a setting for in the 12.6
ramal rhythmic mode:[65]

I've suffered in love for an age!
  I've not seen one day of joy.

Another of his verses that she set to music is:

My soul, alas! What troubles you?
  I'm ignorant of your state.

Another poem of his:

أَصْبَحْتُ لَا أَمْلِكُ دَفْعًا لِمَا   أُسَامُ مِنْ خَسْفٍ وَمِنْ ذِلَّهْ
تَمْضِي أُمُورُ ٱلنَّاسِ دُونِي وَلَا   يُشْعَرُ بِي فِي ذِكْرِهَا قِلَّهْ
إِذَا ٱشْتَهَيْتُ ٱلشَّيْءَ وَلَّوْا بِهِ   عَنِّي وَقَالُوا هَاهُنَا عِلَّهْ

٧،١٢ قال طلب المعتمد ثلاثمائة دينار يصل بها عريباً وقد حضرت عنده فلم توجد فطلب مائتي دينار فلم توجد فبكى وقال

أَلَيْسَ مِنَ ٱلْعَجَائِبِ أَنَّ مِثْلِي   يَرَى مَا قَلَّ مُمْتَنِعًا عَلَيْهِ
وَتُوخَذُ بِٱسْمِهِ ٱلدُّنْيَا جَمِيعًا   وَمَا مِنْ ذَاكَ شَيْءٌ فِي يَدَيْهِ
إِلَيْهِ تُحْمَلُ ٱلْأَمْوَالُ طُرًّا   وَيُمْنَعُ بَعْضَ مَا يُجْبَى إِلَيْهِ

٨،١٢ وكان لمّا فوّض الأمر إلى أخيه أبي أحمد واستروح إلى كفايته القيام بها وتفريغه للّهو والشرب واللعب وترك النظر في شيء من أمر المملكة أو المسئلة عنه طمع أبو أحمد واستبدّ بالأمر وغلب على المملكة ورام المعتمد بعد ذلك تغيير الحال فعزّه وأعوزه وامتنع عليه وطمع الناس جميعاً فيه إذ رأوه مغلوباً على أمره ورأوا لا ضرّ ولا نفع في يده.

٩،١٢ وذكر إسحاق بن مروّح[١] أنّ مفلحًا وجّهه إلى المعتمد وقال قل له قد سمعت هزارًا جارية أمير المؤمنين فأعجبتني وأحببت أن أملكها ورأيت بدرًا الجلّنار فأعجبني فأحببت أن أملكه فليوجّه بهما أمير المؤمنين إليّ. فأدّيت الرسالة إلى المعتمد بعد أن استأذنته فيها فلمّا سمعها غضب وخرق ثيابه وقال هكذا يفعل العبيد بالموالي يغصبونهم على حريمهم وغلمانهم وتكلّم بأشياء عظيمة فخرجنا فردّنا وقد سكن ثمّ قال مثل أبي صالح

١ الأصل: بروح.

I cannot brush aside
The base humiliations I suffer.
People conduct their affairs without me;
My absence is not felt.
If I want something,
It's withheld from me,
And they say, "There's a reason."

Al-Muʿtamid asked for three hundred dinars to give ʿArīb when she had come to visit him, but they could not be had. So he asked for two hundred dinars, and they could not be had either. Then he said: 12.7

How amazing that a man like me
    sees a small sum withheld;
The whole world's in his name,
    but he holds none of it in his hands.
All revenues come to him—
    and he's not even allowed a fraction!

Al-Muʿtamid took it easy when he entrusted the government to his brother Abū Aḥmad. Confident of Abū Aḥmad's capacity to govern, he could devote himself to entertainment, pleasure, and fun without having to examine or inquire into affairs of state. But Abū Aḥmad monopolized power and took control of the entire empire, so when al-Muʿtamid wanted to alter the situation it proved impossible. He was powerless, lived under restrictions, and was taken advantage of by everyone when they saw he had no influence and could neither harm nor help them. 12.8

Isḥāq ibn Murawwiḥ related that Mufliḥ sent him to al-Muʿtamid with this message: "Tell him that I heard Hazār, the Commander of the Faithful's singing girl, perform. I was amazed at her and I'd like to own her. I saw Badr al-Jullanār[66] and found him handsome, and I'd like to own him. Let the Commander of the Faithful have them sent to me." I conveyed the message to al-Muʿtamid with his permission. When he heard it, he flew into a rage and tore his clothes. "Is this how slaves treat their masters?" he exclaimed. "Abducting their womenfolk and seizing their servants!" And he swore terrible oaths. We left the room, but he called us back when he had calmed down and said, "A request 12.9

لا يُردّ عن طلبته. قد أمرت بحمل هزار مع كسوتها وفرشها وجواريها وجميع ما لها. فأمّا بدر الجلّنار فقد وقع على خدمتنا وله منّا موضع. فقل له يسعفنا بتركه. فعدت إلى مفلح فأخبرته بطرف من الأوّل وبالآخر وكان على الخروج إلى البصرة لحرب صاحب الزنج فقال يا أبا إسحاق قد حصلت هزار وإذا رجعنا من هذه الحرب أخذنا بدر الجلّنار منه شاء أم أبى. فخرج فأصابه سهم فمات.

وكان المعتمد من أسمح آل العبّاس وكان يُمثّل بينه وبين المستعين ويقال ما ولي أسمح منهما وكان جيّد التدبير فهماً بالأمور فلمّا فُوّض أمره وغُلب على رأيه نقصت حاله عند الناس. ١٠،١٢

قال محمّد بن عبيد الله بن يحيى بن خاقان بعث بي أبي إلى المعتمد في شيء فقال لي اجلس فاستعظمت ذاك فردّ الأمر عليّ فاعتذرت بأنّه لا يجوز لي فقال لي يا محمّد إنّ أدبك في القبول منّي خير من أدبك في خلافي.

ظلم بعض أسباب موسى بن بغا محمّد بن عليّ الكاتب المعروف بباذنجانة فلمّا مات موسى هجاه فقال ١١،١٢

مَاتَ قَسُّ ٱلدَّيْـرِ مُوسَى   لَعَنَ ٱلرَّحْـمٰنُ مُوسَى
فَلَقَـدْ كَـانَ ضَعِيفاً   فِي تُقَى ٱللهِ خَسِيسَا
فَسُرُورِي مُطْـلَقٌ وَٱلْـحُزْنُ قَدْ صَارَ حَبِيسَا

فبلغ هذا الشعر المعتمد فنقضه فقال

مَاتَ خَيْرُ ٱلنَّاسِ مُوسَى   رَحِـمَ ٱلرَّحْمٰنُ مُوسَى
فَلَقَـدْ كَـانَ جَلِيلاً   عَـالِيَ ٱلْقَـدْرِ رَئِيسَا
أَطْـلَقَ ٱلْحُزْنَ وَخَـلَّى   فَـرَحِي وَقْـفاً حَبِيسَا

from someone like Abū Ṣāliḥ cannot be refused. I've ordered Hazār to be conveyed to him along with her wardrobe, her furnishings, her maids, and all that she owns. But I need Badr al-Jullanār to serve me, and I'm fond of him. So ask Abū Ṣāliḥ to do us a favor by letting us keep him." I went back to Mufliḥ and reported part of al-Muʿtamid's first reply and the whole of his second one. Mufliḥ was just leaving for Basra to fight the leader of the Zanj, so he said, "Abū Isḥāq, we've got Hazār, and when we come back from this campaign we'll take Badr al-Jullanār from him, whether he likes it or not." He marched out, was struck by an arrow, and died.

Al-Muʿtamid was one of the most easygoing of the ʿAbbāsid family. He was **12.10**
compared to al-Mustaʿīn and it was said that they were the most easygoing caliphs ever. He managed affairs very well and understood them, but his status declined when he delegated his power, and his opinions were ignored.

Muḥammad ibn ʿUbaydallāh ibn Yaḥyā ibn Khāqān recalled: For some reason my father sent me to al-Muʿtamid, and al-Muʿtamid said, "Sit down." I was too astonished at his invitation to accept it, but he repeated it. I excused myself, saying, "It's not fitting." So he said, "Muḥammad, it's better manners to accept my invitation than to go against me."

One of Mūsā ibn Bughā's underlings wronged Muḥammad ibn ʿAlī the secre- **12.11**
tary, known as Aubergine. When Mūsā died, Muḥammad lampooned him:

Mūsā, the convent's priest, has died. God curse him.
He was a feeble man, of contemptible piety.
My joy at his death is boundless—sorrow is imprisoned.

When al-Muʿtamid heard these verses, he composed a rebuttal:

Mūsā, the best of men, has died. God have mercy on him.
He was powerful, much respected, a true leader.
Sorrow has free rein—it's imprisoned my joy.

ومن شعره المرذول قوله[١] ١٢،١٢

مَا لِي وَهٰـذَا ٱلْهَوَى مَا لِي   لَوْ أَمْكَنَنِي ٱفْتَدَيْتُهُ بِمَالِي
وَهٰذَا ٱلْحَبِيبُ مَا يُوَاصِلُنِي   فَأَنَا مَعَ هِجْرَانِهِ فِي قِتَالِ
بَدَا لِي عَلَى مَا أَرَى فِي حُبِّهِ   وَكُنْتُ وَٱللهِ مَا بَدَا لِي

وله من هذا الفنّ

مَنْ قَالَ إِنِّي أَعْشَقُ لَوْ صَوَّرُوا   ٱلْحُبَّ لَكَانَ رَجُلًا أَحْمَقْ
أَدُورُ ٱلسُّطُوحَ فَلَا أَرَاهُ   كَأَنَّنِي سِنَّوْرٌ أَبْلَقْ
تَمَنَّيْتُ مِنْ شَوْقِي إِلَيْهِ   أَنْ أَطْلَعَ عَلَيْهِ فَأَكُونَ لَقْلَقْ
هَوَى ٱلنَّاسِ مُجْتَمِعٌ عِنْدِي   وَهَوَاهُمْ عَلَيْهِمْ مُفَرَّقْ

قال فكتب الراضي بخطّه تحت هذه الأبيات

لَمْ يَقُلْ ذَا ٱلشِّعْرَ إِلَّا   جَاهِلٌ بِٱلشِّعْرِ أَحْمَقْ
أَوْ مُصَابٌ ذُو جُنُونٍ   ضَائِعُ ٱلْفِكْرَةِ أَبْلَقْ

ومن شعره ١٣،١٢

عَجِبْتُ مِنْ هٰذَا ٱلْحُبِّ لَا   يُجَارَى بِهِ ٱلْمَحْلُوبُ
أَرَاكَ يَا ظَالِمُ لَا تُرِيدُنِي   هٰذَا وَٱللهِ هَوًى مَقْلُوبُ
أَنْتَ فِي حُسْنِكَ يُوسُفُ   وَأَنَا فِي ضُرِّي يَعْقُوبُ
لَسْتُ أَعْنِي يَعْقُوبَ ٱلصَّفَّارَ   أَنْتَ ٱلصَّفَّارُ مَصْلُوبُ

١ الأصل: (من الأشعار المرذولة للمعتمد) وردت في الهامش.

Here is one of his poems that critics reject as unmetrical: **12.12**

How, oh how can I deal with this love?
If I could, I'd give all I own for it
And this beloved who ignores me—
his avoidance kills me.
I'd renounced his love,
or so I thought, but by God I've not!

And another poem of the same kind:

Whoever said I was in love,
if they imagined it, he was stupid.
I wander over the roofs
without seeing my love,
like a black-and-white cat.
From longing I want
to catch sight of him;
then I'll be a stork.
Within me I combine all men's love,
while among them it is divided.

Under these verses, al-Rāḍī wrote in his own hand:

The composer of these verses was either stupid
and knew nothing of poetry,
Or was insane, afflicted with madness,
deluded, and crazy.

Here are two more of his unmetrical poems: **12.13**

This love amazes me—
the beloved's feelings
are not mirrored.
I see you don't want me, tyrant!
By God, it's a love back-to-front.
You are Joseph in your beauty,
while in my pain I'm Jacob;

وله

عَشِقْتُ إِنْسَانًا بِكَسْكَرْ　　وَجْهُهُ كَالْقَمَرِ ٱلْأَزْهَرْ
فَلَمَّا شَكَوْتُ إِلَيْهِ هَوَاهُ　　طَأْطَأَ رَأْسَهُ وَفَكَّرْ
هُوَ ٱلذَّهَبُ ٱلْإِبْرِيزُ فِي حُسْنِهِ　　وَهُوَ ٱلْيَاقُوتُ ٱلْأَحْمَرْ
مَنْ دَلَّنِي عَلَيْهِ فَلَهُ عِنْدِي　　كُلُّ مَا تَمَنَّى وَقَدَّرْ
لَمَّا ظَنَنْتُهُ بِيَدِي حَاصِلًا　　لَا شَكَّ تَرَكَنِي وَشَمَّرْ

قال ودخل يوماً الجوسق فرأى طائراً فصاده فقال الموفّق ما رأيت أحسن منه فهبه لي يا أمير المؤمنين فأعطاه إيّاه فلمّا حصل في يده أفلت وجعل يصفق بجناحيه ويطير فضحك المعتمد ضحكاً شديداً وقال ١٤،١٢

دَخَلْتُ يَوْمًا ٱلْجَوْسَقَا　　فَٱصْطَدْتُ طَيْرًا أَبْلَقَا
أَخَذَهُ مِنِّي ٱلْمُوَفَّقَا　　فَحِينَ أَخَذَهُ صَفَقَا
وَطَارَ مِنْهُ فَرَقَا

قال ولمّا شخص أبو أحمد إلى البصرة والجيش معه وبقي المعتمد بسرّ من رأى قال

مُهِمٌّ مُهِمٌّ مُهِمٌّ مُهِمٌّ　　وَأَمْرٌ فَظِيعٌ وَأَمْرٌ صُرُمْ
أَيَحْسُنُ أَنْ تَذْهَبُوا كُلُّكُمْ　　وَأَقْعُدُ فِي ٱلْبَيْتِ كَنِّي[1] حُرُمْ
وَيَمْضِي ٱلْأَمِيرُ أَبُو أَحْمَدٍ　　وَيُضْرَبُ بِٱلطَّبْلِ كُرْدُمْ كُدُمْ

قال وخرجت بثرة على قدم بدر غلامه فأُخبر بذلك فاغتمّ فلمّا كان بعد عتمة خرج إلى حجرته عائداً له وقال ١٥،١٢

١ لفظة عاميّة عراقية بمعنى كأنّي.

Not Jacob the Coppersmith.
That's you, coppersmith on the cross.[67]
I loved someone in Kaskar,
with a face like a radiant moon.
When I complained to him of my love,
he pondered and looked down.
He's pure gold in his beauty;
he's the ruby, deepest red.
Anyone who brings me to him can have
whatever reward he wants, and more.
Yet when I thought he'd yield a return,
he took to his heels and fled.

Al-Muʿtamid entered the Jawsaq Palace one day and saw a bird, which he caught. Al-Muwaffaq said, "I've never seen a lovelier bird. Give it to me, Commander of the Faithful." **12.14**

He did so, but when al-Muwaffaq took hold of it, it escaped, flapped its wings, and flew off. Al-Muʿtamid laughed like anything and said:

One day I came to the Jawsaq
And caught a piebald bird.
Al-Muwaffaq took it from me,
But it beat its wings
And flew away in panic.

When Abū Aḥmad set out for Basra with the army while al-Muʿtamid stayed in Samarra, he said:

Such important business!
A terrible affair's come about!
Is it right that you all go off,
and leave me at home like a woman?
Prince Abū Aḥmad marches off,
and the drums beat "Kedum, kedum."

A pustule erupted on the leg of Badr, al-Muʿtamid's servant, and al-Muʿtamid was informed of it. He was upset, and after nightfall he visited him in his room. He said: **12.15**

عُـدْتُـهُ بَعْـدَ ٱلْعَتَـمْ لِعِلَّةٍ حَـادِثَةٍ عَلَى ٱلْقَدَمْ
مَضَيْتُ أَمْشِي فِي ٱلظُّلَمْ وَحْـدِي فَلَا خَلْقٌ عَلِمْ

وله

رَمَـضَـانُ أَتَاكَ بِحَزْمٍ مِسْقَرٍ فَٱقْعُـدْنَ خَلْفَ بَابِكُنَّ وَتَكَسَّرْ
لِسَيْنِ بُسْـتَانِ سَرْهَكَ فِيهِ يَأْكُلُ ٱللَّحْمَ بَارِدًا حِينَ يَشْطُرْ
وَٱلرَّثِيثَا وَٱلْجُنْدُ مَعَـهُ دَقُوقًا وَٱلطَّلَعْلَعُ وَقِشْرُ ٱلْبَيْضِ ٱلْأَحْمَرْ

I visited him after nightfall
    when he had a sore leg.
I found my way in the dark,
    with no one any the wiser.

And another of his poems:[68]

Ramadan has arrived . . .
So sit behind your doors and . . .
    . . . in a garden. . .
    eating slices of cold meat.
And the . . . and the soldiers with him
    in broad daylight, with . . . and
    peeling red eggs.

ديرالعذارى

وهذا الدير أسفل الحظيرة على شاطئ دجلة وهو دير حسن عامر حوله البساتين والكروم وفيه جميع ما يحتاج إليه ولا يخلو من متنزّه يقصده للشرب واللّعب وهو من الديارات الحسنة وبقعته من البقاع المستطابة وإنّما سُمّي بديرالعذارى لأنّ فيه جوارٍ متبتّلات عذارى هنّ سكّانه وقطّانه فسُمّي الدير بهنّ. ١،١٣

وذكر يموت بن المزرّع عن الجاحظ قال حدّثني ابن فرج التغلبيّ أنّ قوماً من بني تغلب أرادوا القطع على مال السلطان فأتهم المعاينة فأعلمهم أنّ السلطان قد نذر بهم فساروا ثمّ أزمعوا على الاستخفاء في ديرالعذارى فصاروا إلى الدير ففُتح لهم فما استقرّوا حتى سمعوا وقع حوافر الخيل في طلبهم. فلمّا أمنوا وجاوزتهم الخيل خلا كلّ واحد منهم بجارية هي عنده عذراء فإذا القسّ قد فرغ منهنّ فقال بعضهم في ذلك ٢،١٣

وَأَلْوَطَ مِنْ رَاهِبٍ يَدَّعِي بِأَنَّ ٱلنِّسَاءَ عَلَيْهِ حَرَامُ
يُحَرِّمُ بَيْضَاءَ مَمْكُورَةً وَيُغْنِيهِ فِي ٱلْبَضْعِ عَنْهَا غُلَامُ
إِذَا مَا مَشَى غَضَّ عَنْ طَرْفِهِ وَفِي ٱلدَّيْرِ بِٱللَّيْلِ مِنْهُ عُرَامُ
وَدَيْرُ ٱلْعَذَارَى فُضُوحٌ لَهُنَّ وَعِنْدَ ٱللُّصُوصِ حَدِيثٌ تَمَامُ

وفي بغداد أيضاً دير يُعرف بديرالعذارى في قطيعة النصارى على نهر الدجاج[١] وسُمّي بذلك لأنّ لهم صوم ثلاثة أيّام قبل الصوم الكبير يُسمّى صوم العذارى فإذا انقضى ٣،١٣

١ الأصل: الزجاج.

The Virgins' Monastery[69]

This monastery lies below Ḥaẓīrah on the banks of the Tigris. It is beautiful, well appointed, and surrounded by gardens and vineyards. It has everything one needs, and is never without visitors coming to drink and have fun there. It is a fine monastery in splendid surroundings. It is called "the Virgins' Monastery," taking its name from celibate virgins who live there. 13.1

Yamūt ibn al-Muzarriʿ cited al-Jāḥiẓ who had it from Ibn Faraj al-Taghlibī: 13.2

Some men of the Banū Taghlib wanted to seize government money as it was being transported, but their scouts told them that the authorities had learned of their plan. They moved off and decided to hide in the Virgins' Monastery. They were given admission, but hardly had they begun to relax when they heard the sound of horses' hooves in pursuit. When they were sure they were safe and the horses had passed, each paired with a woman whom he imagined to be a virgin, but it turned out the priest had already been with them all. A poet has said:

What a pervert the monk is
 who says women are forbidden him,
Calls a fair comely girl taboo,
 and does it with a boy instead of a pussy.
He walks with lowered eyes,
 but has wild nights in the convent.
It's the Virgins' Monastery—
 but they're nothing but hussies.
The bandits can tell you all about it.

In Baghdad there is also a monastery called the Virgins' Monastery in the Christians' concession on the Poultry Canal. It acquired that name because the Christians have a three-day fast before Lent, which is called the Virgins' 13.3

الصوم اجتمعوا إلى هذا الدير تعبّدوا وتقرّبوا. وهو دير حسن طيّب.

ولابن المعتزّ في دير العذارى المقدّم ذكره ٤،١٣

خَلِيلَيَّ قُمْ حَتَّى نَمُوتَ مِنَ ٱلسُّكْرِ بِحَانَةِ خَمَّارٍ مَمَاتًا بِلَا قَبْرِ
وَنَشْرَبَ مِنْ كَرْخِيَّةٍ ذَهَبِيَّةٍ وَنَصْفَحَ عَنْ ذَنْبِ ٱلْحَوَادِثِ وَٱلدَّهْرِ
أَلَا رُبَّ أَيَّامٍ مَضَيْنَ حَمِيدَةً بِدَيْرِ ٱلْعَذَارَى وَٱلصَّوَامِعِ وَٱلْقَصْرِ
وَكَمْ مِنْ لَيَالٍ مُسْعِدَاتٍ لِذِي ٱلْهَوَى جَسَرْتُ عَلَى ٱللَّذَّاتِ فِيهِنَّ بِٱلْجِسْرِ
خَلِيلَيَّ فَلَا تَطْلُبْ فَلَاحِي وَخَلِّنِي فَمَا لِي عَلَى مَا لُمْتَنِي فِيهِ مِنْ صَبْرِ

ولبعضهم فيه

قَامَ عُذْرِي فِي طَيِّ دَيْرِ ٱلْعَذَارَى حِينَ أَبْصَرْتُ عَاشِقِيهِ حَيَارَى
فِتْنَةٌ عَمَّتِ ٱلْخَلَائِقَ وَٱسْتَوْ لَتْ عَلَى مُسْلِمِيهِمِ وَٱلنَّصَارَى

قال ولمّا خرج عبيد الله بن عبد الله بن طاهر من بغداد إلى سرّ من رأى وكان المعتزّ ٥،١٣
استدعاه نزل هذا الدير فأقام به يومين واستطابه وشرب فيه ثمّ قال هذه الأبيات

مَا تَرَى طِيبَ وَقْتِنَا يَا سَعِيدُ زَمَنٌ ضَاحِكٌ وَرَوْضٌ نَضِيدُ
وَرِيَاضٌ كَأَنَّهُنَّ بُرُودٌ كُلَّ يَوْمٍ لَهُنَّ صَبْغٌ جَدِيدُ
وَكَأَنَّ ٱلشَّقِيقَ فِيهَا عَشِيقٌ وَكَأَنَّ ٱلْبَهَارَ صَبٌّ عَمِيدُ
وَكَأَنَّ ٱلْغُصُونَ مَيْلًا قُدُودٌ وَكَأَنَّ ٱلنَّوَارَ فِيهَا عُقُودُ
وَكَأَنَّ ٱلثِّمَارَ وَٱلْوَرَقَ ٱلْخُضْرَ ثِيَابٌ مِنْ تَحْتِهِنَّ نُهُودُ

Fast.[70] When it is over, they gather in this monastery, celebrate the liturgy, and receive communion. It is a fine and beautiful monastery.

Ibn al-Muʿtazz composed this poem on the Virgins' Monastery mentioned earlier: 13.4

Come, my friends, let's drink till we die
in a tavern where the owner will leave us unburied.
Drinking a golden wine from Karkh,
absolving the sins of the hazards of fortune.
How many laudable days we've spent
in the Virgins' Monastery, its cells and the castle!
How many nights helpful to lovers
I dared to devote by the bridge to pleasure!
Friends, leave me, don't seek my welfare;
the passion you blame me for I can't endure.

And these are some verses by another poet:

I'd an excuse for a gazelle in the Virgins' Convent,
when I saw its lovers bewildered,
Seduction spread throughout mankind,
Muslims and Christians alike falling victim.

When ʿUbaydallāh ibn ʿAbdallāh ibn Ṭāhir left Baghdad to go to Samarra, in response to al-Muʿtazz's summons, he spent two days in this monastery. He liked it and enjoyed some of its wine. And he composed this poem: 13.5

Saʿīd, remember the good time we've spent,
days of joy in well-kept gardens,
In meadows like cloaks spread out,
each day a different hue.
Anemones were our beloveds,
oxeyes their persistent suitors;
Branches like slender figures swayed,
garlanded with spring flowers;
Green foliage was draped
around the fruits
like garments concealing breasts.

فَٱسْقِنِيهَا رَاحًا تُرِيحُ مِنَ ٱلْهَمِّ وَتُبْدِي سُرُورَنَا وَتُعِيدُ
وَٱحْثُثِ ٱلْكَأْسَ يَا سَعِيدُ فَقَدْ حَثَّكَ نَايٌ بِهَا وَحَرَّكَ عُودُ
وَٱفْتَرِعْ عِذْرَةَ ٱللَّذَاذَاتِ فِي دَيْرِ ٱلْعَذَارَى فَعَلَّهَا لَا تَعُودُ

٦،١٣ وعبيد الله من أحسن الناس أدبًا وشعرًا وتصرّفًا في سائر العلوم مع كرم نفس وحسن خلق. ولمّا وصل عبيد الله من سفرته المذكورة إلى المعتزّ أمره بالمقام عنده في ذلك اليوم فأقام.

قال عبيد الله فأرسل المعتزّ إلى شارية أن تخرج فتعالت عليه فقال عندي من يحبّ أن يسمعك وأحبّ لك وله ذلك ولا بدّ من حضورك. فخرجت فجلست خلف الستارة ثمّ قالت لولا الزائر ما جئت. فأوّل صوت غنّته

غَشِيتُ ٱلْمَنَازِلَ بِٱلْأَنْعَمِ كَمُنْعَرَجِ ٱلْوَشْمِ فِي ٱلْمِعْصَمِ

ثمّ غنّت بعده

لَقَدْ رَاعَنِي لِلْبَيْنِ صَوْتُ حَمَامَةٍ عَلَى غُصْنِ بَانٍ جَاوَبَتْهَا حَمَائِمُ

٧،١٣ فقال لي المعتزّ كيف تسمع قلت أسمع شيئًا حظّ العجب منه أكثر من حدّ الطرب فاستحسن هذا الكلام منّي. ثمّ أسمعني زمر زُنام الزامر وقد ضعف وأرعش وأزمنه النقرس وأراني الآلة التي عملها أحمد بن موسى المهندس من صفر يرسل فيها الماء فيسمع لها زمر السرناي. ثمّ أدخلني إلى شبّاك وأمر أن يجمع بين السبع والفيل فرأيتهما كيف يتواثبان ثمّ قال لي أذكر أنّي أريتك اليوم أربعة أشياء طريفة قلت نعم يا سيّدي قال أيّها أظرف عندك قلت غناء شارية. فقال صدقت.

٨،١٣ قال جحظة دخلت على عبيد الله بن عبد الله بن طاهر يومًا فجاءه مشيخة فأمرهم بالجلوس عن يمينه وجاءه كهول فأمرهم بالجلوس عن شماله ودخل أحداث فوقفوا بين

Pour the wine, rid us of care,
 and call forth our joy again,
Hurry, Saʿīd, and pass the cups,
 urged on by the flute and the lute.
Make the most of pleasure
 in the Virgins' Monastery,
 for it may never return.

ʿUbaydallāh was a most cultured man, a poet, familiar with all branches of knowledge, noble of spirit and upright. After this journey, al-Muʿtazz asked him to spend the rest of the day with him, so he did. 13.6

ʿUbaydallāh takes up the story: Al-Muʿtazz sent a message to Shāriyah summoning her, but she snubbed him. So he said, "I have a visitor who wants to hear you, and I'd like that for both of your sakes. You must come." Then she came and took her seat behind the curtain, saying, "If it weren't for the visitor, I wouldn't have come." The first song she sang was:

I came with the herds to the abandoned campsite,
 its traces like lines of tattoo on a wrist.

And then she sang:

Startled by a dove's coo, echoed by her sisters
 in the ben tree's branches, I feared a parting.

Al-Muʿtazz asked me, "What do you think?" I replied, "What I've heard amazes me even more than the ecstasy it inspired." He approved of this answer. 13.7

Then he made me listen to the playing of Zunām the flautist, whose body trembled because he had become feeble and was plagued by gout. He showed me the machine made by Aḥmad ibn Mūsā[71] the Engineer, with a pipe through which water flows, producing the sound of a flute. He took me to a window and ordered lions and elephants to be assembled in the same space, and I saw how they tried to attack each other. Then he said to me, "Now, I've shown you four curiosities." "Yes, sire." "And which of them is the finest, in your opinion?" "Shāriyah's singing," I replied. "You're right," he concurred.

Jaḥẓah related: One day I was visiting ʿUbaydallāh ibn ʿAbdallāh ibn Ṭāhir when some elderly men arrived. He told them to be seated on his right. Then 13.8

يديه ولم يأمرهم بالجلوس فسألته عنهم فقال هؤلاء بنيّ وأومأ إلى الشيوخ وهؤلاء بنوهم وأومأ إلى الكهول وهؤلاء بنوهم وأومأ إلى الأحداث. قلت بنوك لأمّ أو لأمّهات قال أمّ جميعهم شاجي. وأنشد

زَرَعْتُ وَشَاجِي بَيْنَنَا فِي شَبِيبَتِي غِرَاسَ ٱلْهَوَى فَٱعْتَمَّ بِٱلثَّمَرِ ٱلْعَذْبِ
فَشَابَ بَنُو شَاجِي لِظَهْرِي وَأَدْرَكُوا وَشَابَ بَنُوهُمْ وَهْيَ مَالِكَةٌ قَلْبِي

قال وهي معي مذ سبعين سنة.

٩،١٣ وكان بعض المنجّمين حكم بموته قبلها فماتت قبله فقال

فَيَا عَجَبًا مِنِّي وَمِمَّنْ رَعَيْتُهُ بِأَوْكَدِ أَسْبَابِ ٱلْهَوَى وَرَعَانِي
وَكُنْتُ أُرَجِّي أَنْ أَكُونَ فِدَاءَهُ فَلَمَّا أَتَى وَقْتُ ٱلْحِمَامِ فَدَانِي

١٠،١٣ وذكر ابن قدامة قال حضرت جنازة شاجي فلمّا انصرفنا دخلت مع عبيد الله مساعداً له ومؤنساً وهو مطرق ودموعه تجري على خدّيه فلم أر باكياً أحسن منه ثمّ رفع رأسه وأقبل علينا فقال

يَمِينًا بِأَنِّي لَوْ بُلِيتُ بِفَقْدِهَا وَبِي نَبْضُ عِرْقٍ لِلْحَيَاةِ وَلِلنُّكْسِ
لَأَوْشَكْتُ قَتْلَ ٱلنَّفْسِ عِنْدَ فِرَاقِهَا وَلٰكِنَّهَا مَاتَتْ وَقَدْ ذَهَبَتْ نَفْسِي

قال ثمّ حضرت معه لزيارة قبرها فلمّا همّ بالانصراف قال

some men in their prime came in and he had them sit on his left. Finally, some youths came in and stood before him, without him telling them to be seated. I asked him who they were, and, gesturing to the elderly men, he said, "These are my sons"; gesturing to the men in their prime, he said, "and these are their sons"; and gesturing to the youths, "and these are *their* sons." "Your sons by one mother or several?" I inquired. "The mother of all of them is Shājī," he said, and then he recited:

> "In my youth I sowed love's seeds with Shājī,
> and the harvest came rich and sweet.
> Our sons became men, and their sons too,
> with Shājī still the queen of my heart.

"We've been together for seventy years."

An astrologer had predicted that he would die before her, but she died first 13.9
and he spoke these verses:

> Strange! I cherished my love so dearly,
> And my love cherished me.
> I'd hoped to save her with my life,
> But when the time came,
> She gave her life for me.

Ibn Qudāmah related: I attended Shājī's funeral and when we separated, I went 13.10
back with ʿUbaydallāh to his house to support him and keep him company. He was speechless, with tears running down his cheeks; I never saw a more handsome mourner. Then he raised his head, turned to us, and said:

> I swear that had I known her loss
> while my pulse was still beating,
> To keep me alive and suffering,
> I'd have nigh killed myself
> when she left me.
> But she's dead and my soul
> has already departed.

I was with him when he visited her grave, and when he was about to leave, he said:

مَنْ زَارَ دَارَ أَحِبَّةٍ لِحَيَاتِهِمْ وَلِمَا يُؤَمِّلُ مِنْ لِقَاءٍ يُقْدَرُ
فَلْيَأْتِ دَارَ أَحِبَّةٍ سَكَنُوا ٱلْبِلَى كَرَمًا وَحِفْظًا وَٱللِّقَاءُ ٱلْمَحْشَرُ

قال ومات ابن لعبيد الله من[1] شاجي فزار قبره ثمّ أنشد

أَيَا مَجْمَعَ ٱلْأَحْبَابِ بَعْدَ تَفَرُّقٍ أَرَاكَ قَرِيبًا وَٱلتَّلَاقِي شَاسِعَا
فَيَا عَجَبًا أَنِّي أَزُورُكَ مُكْرَهًا وَفِيكَ ٱلْأُلَى أَهْوَى وَأَجْفُوكَ طَائِعَا

قال الصوليّ[2] لمّا ماتت شاجي جزع عليها عبيد الله الجزع الذي لم يُرمثله فرثاها ١١،١٣
جماعة من الأدباء ورثاها عبيد الله بعدّة قصائد فكان أحسن ما مرّ بي في ذلك
رسالة لعبد الله بن المعتزّ إليه وجوابها من عبيد الله بن عبد الله وكانت نسخة التعزية
اتّصل[3] بي أعزّك الله خبر المصيبة فوالله لقد أشركني الهمّ بها معك وألمني منها ما
ألمك فصبرًا يا أخي على حكم القدر ونهضًا عن عثرة الجزع وثباتًا للمحنة وشكرًا لمفيد
النعمة بتقديم الحُرم وتحصيل الأجر على حسن الصبر وإن كانت

جَلِيلَةُ حَظٍّ مِنْ عَفَافٍ وَمِنْ تُقًى وَقُمْرِيَّةٌ فِي ذِرْوَةِ ٱلْغُصْنِ تَسْجَعُ
تَوَلَّتْ وَلَوْ لَمْ تُطْعِمِ ٱلْأَرْضَ غَيْرَهَا كَفَتْهَا وَلَٰكِنْ لَا أَرَى ٱلْأَرْضَ تَشْبَعُ

وقد أطال الله إمتاعك بها منذ وهبها لك وجعل فقدها لمثوبتك التي هي أكبر منها ١٢،١٣
إذا ارتجعها منك ومثلك أيدك الله لا يُحضّ على حفظ دينه لأنّك تعلمه وترغب فيه

١ الأصل: بن. ٢ الأصل: (قف على هذه التعزية الغريبة) وردت في الهامش. ٣ الأصل: (رسالة التعزية أرسلها ابن المعتزّ إلى عبيد الله بن طاهر) وردت في الهامش.

Let him who visits the abode
of loved ones during their life,
not hoping for a meeting foreordained,
Visit his loved ones
when they dwell in the earth,
Nobly to remember them,
till the Last Day's meeting.

One of ʿUbaydallāh's sons by Shājī died, and when he went to visit the grave he declaimed:

You who unite loved ones after they have parted,
I find you close, though the meeting's far away.
Strange! Though my loved ones are with you,
my visits are forced, my avoidance voluntary.

Al-Ṣūlī reported: When Shājī died, ʿUbaydallāh was more distressed than anyone had ever seen before. Many men of letters mourned her, and ʿUbaydallāh himself composed a number of elegies on her. One of the finest pieces I saw was a letter ʿAbdallāh ibn al-Muʿtazz wrote to ʿUbaydallāh and his reply. Here is the text of the letter of condolence: 13.11

God give you strength! I have heard the news of the calamity. By God, it has made me share your distress and given me as much pain to bear as yours. Have patience in bearing Fate's verdict, brother; rise above the misstep of affliction, stand firm in this trial, and thank the Bestower of Favors that He has allowed your wife to precede you and allowed you to receive a reward for your noble endurance, though she was

A gift of fortune, a consort chaste and pious,
a dove cooing high in the branches.
Gone! She was enough for the earth to take—
but the earth is voracious.

God granted you long years to enjoy her after He had given her to you. He has made her loss an occasion for you to receive a reward greater than you would merit if He were to return her 13.12

وتسارع إليه لكنّ المصائب ربّما عصفت بالجازع حتّى يذكر أو يُذكّر فيراجع الرضا بحكم من لا يجور ويسبق الصبر على المصيبة مختاراً للسلوة التي لا بدّ من أن يصير إليها اضطراراً. وربّ خيرة مرّة وحميد في مكروه وهو الدهر الذي نعرفه ولا يؤتى من غرّة به. هذه سجيّته وبهذا تقدّمت سيرته كذلك حتّى يرث الله الأرض ومن عليها وهو ﴿خَيْرُ ٱلْوَٰرِثِينَ﴾.

ولولا علّة عائقة عن لقائك أعزّك الله لصرت إليك بدلاً من كلّ كتاب ورسول وقضيت بذلك حقّك ورأيته من واجبك. وربّ حاضر لم يحضر ودّه وغائب لم يغب عمّا عنا. وأعظم الله أجرك وأجزل ثوابك ودلّ على سبيل العزاء قلبك وكفاك مكارهك ووفّقك لما يوافقك ورحم التي تُوفّيت وجعل ما اتّصلت به من الآخرة خيراً ممّا انقطعت عنه من الدنيا و﴿إِنَّا لِلَّهِ وَإِنَّآ إِلَيْهِ رَٰجِعُونَ﴾.

فأجابه عبيد الله بن عبد الله أطال الله بقاء السيّد المؤمّل للدنيا والدين وابن السادة المنعمين والخلفاء الراشدين والآباء المنتجبين وزاد الله السيّد تشريفاً وتفضيلاً وأدام له العزّ والسعادة والكرامة والغبطة والسلامة وجدّد له النعم الظاهرة والمنن المترادفة وجعلني من كلّ سوء ومكروه فداءه وقدّمني إلى كلّ مرهوب ومحذور قبله. ١٣،١٣

to you. A man like you, may God fortify you, does not need to be reminded to observe the precepts of your religion, because you know them, desire to follow them, and hasten to observe them. But calamities may sometimes shake those who are stricken, until they remember or their memory is prompted. Then, by the decree of Him who is never unjust, they recover their equanimity. Fortitude precedes disaster, preferring consolation, which the bereaved will undoubtedly obtain. Many a good thing is bitter, and many an adversity hides something commendable. This is destiny as we know it. It does not take us unawares: this is its nature and this is how it has been and will be until God shall inherit the earth and those who are on it. He is «the best of inheritors».[72]

Illness prevents me from being with you, God keep you! Otherwise I would have come in person rather than sending a letter. Thus, I would have fulfilled my obligation to you—I would have considered it your due. But how often the visitor comes without friendship, and how often a person who is absent is only too aware of what you suffer. May God increase your reward, recompense you generously, and guide your heart toward consolation. May He protect you from adversity and lead you to what is beneficial. May He have mercy on the departed, making the hereafter she has arrived at better than this world whence she has been taken. «We are God's and to God we shall return.»[73]

This is ʿUbaydallāh's reply: 13.13

May God grant long life to the prince, hope of the world and the faith, descendant of generous lords, rightly guided caliphs, and excellent ancestors. May God increase him in honor and precedence. May God perpetuate his glory, happiness, nobility, rapture, and health, and may He bestow on him ever-new public favors and gifts without cease. May He direct at me any evil or adversity that might befall him, and put me forward to face every terror and danger before him.

The prince's letter—may God give him long life—has arrived, abounding in affection, merits, and generous favors, and exemplary in its refinement and charms without number. I received

وصل كتاب السيّد أطال الله بقاءه مملوءًا بالبرّ والفضل والإنعام والتطوّل وفوائد الأدب وجوامع المحاسن. فتلقّيته بحقّه من الإعظام والشكر والمعرفة بعلوّ قدره وارتفاع درجته وارتقاء رتبته في حسن التأليف واتّفاق المعاني وجليل الصواب وجميل الخطاب ولقد رفع الله الأدب والعلم ونواظر أهلهما بالسيّد أيّده الله بعنايته[1] وقدرته. فأمّا المشاركة فمعهودة من تفضّله حتّى لو قلت إنّ التعزية بهذه المصيبة التي لحقتني لو شوفه بها وعزّى عنها جرى الأمر مجراه ووضع القصد في أحقّ مقاصده.

وأمّا الصبر فهو الذي لا بدّ منه اضطرارًا أو اختيارًا ١٤،١٣

إِذَا مَا أَصَابَتْ ذَا حَيَاةٍ مُصِيبَةٌ فَقَابَلَهَا مِنْهُ ٱلتَّحَمُّلُ وَٱلصَّبْرُ
فَمَا بَعُدَتْ مِنْ أَنْ تَحَوَّلَ نِعْمَةً يَحِقُّ عَلَيْنَا ٱلْحَمْدُ لِلّٰهِ وَٱلشُّكْرُ

وأمّا الجزع فما أصاب وأوجع وألمّ وروّع فلا محيد عنه وإذا لم يتعدّ العين والقلب إلى البدن واللسان فخطبه أسهل.

وشكر المولى المخفِّف للمحن والمتمِّم للنعم المفزع في النوائب والعصمة في المصائب. ولو كان طول الإمتاع أعزّ الله السيّد يسلي لا يسلو عنه إلّا لمن[2] ساعده ووهى عقده لما عمل عليه مميّز نظّار ولو كان على أشدّ المضض وأمرّ الغصص ولوعة الأبد ودوام الكمد. وأقول

أَسَـرُّ أُمُورِ ٱلدَّهْـرِ صَارَ أَغَمَّـهَا وَكُـلُّ جَدِيـدٍ صَارَ بَعْدَكَ بَالِيَـا
فَـأَعْجَبُ مِنْ شُهْـدٍ تَحَوَّلَ عَلْقَـمًا وَمِنْ ضَاحِكٍ لَمْ يَعْدُ أَنْ ظَلَّ بَاكِيَـا

١٥،١٣ وأمّا السلوة أعزّ الله السيّد فليست من فعل الأحرار المخلصين لا في محيا ولا في مماة وإنّما هو اغتنام الاحتساب واتّصال الأكباد والعياذ بالله من فقد العزاء وفقد

---

١ الأصل: بعنايه. ٢ كذا في الأصل.

it with due honor and gratitude, recognizing its value and high degree. I am conscious of its superb and fine composition, the appropriateness of the ideas it conveys, the rightness of its sentiments, and the beauty of its style of address. God has honored letters and learning through the prince, and men of culture look up to him, may God support him with His solicitude and strength. His sympathy is a sign of his beneficence, which I am accustomed to. So may I say that if the condolence I have received for this calamity that has befallen me has been expressed in speech and is consolation for my loss, then things have taken their normal course and the intended purpose has been achieved.

As for patience, it is essential, whether it is forced on us or we choose it. 13.14

When calamity strikes a mortal man
and he meets it with patience and fortitude,
It may well be changed to a favor,
for which we praise God and thank Him.

As for distress, what has befallen me, causing me grief, pain, and dismay, cannot be avoided. If it confines itself to the eyes and the heart, without affecting the tongue and the rest of the body, it is easier to bear. To thank God who lightens sorrows and bestows all favors is a refuge in trials and a protection in tribulations. Even if the memory of long-lasting delight were a consolation—may God fortify the prince—there is only consolation when one receives sympathy.[74] This is agreed on by those of discernment and perspicacity, even when they themselves are suffering extreme misery, bitter grief, and endless pain and sorrow. As I have put it:

Fate's greatest delights have turned bitter;
with your parting, everything new has become old.
How amazing the honey that has turned to gall,
the man who laughed but now only weeps.

Consolation—may God keep the prince—is not a deed done by noble and sincere friends, either for life or death, but an occasion to add something in one's favor for the Day of Judgment and 13.15

أجره. وبالله يا سيّدي إنّ الشخص لخاشع وإنّ الطرف لدامع وإنّ القلب لحرّان موجع. ولقد صادفت هذه الحال بدنًا ما فيه عضو صحيح. أسقام متطاولة ومصيبة موصولة بما بقي من الزمن

وَبَيْنَا ٱلْفَتَى يَبْكِي وَيَنْدُبُ شَجْوَهُ   وَمَأْلُوفُهُ إِذْ صَارَ يُبْكَى وَيُنْدَبُ

وأمّا ما ذكره السيّد جعلني فداه من أمر العلّة التي لا كانت ولا سمع لها بذكر أبدًا فإنّه لولاها لكان وكان ممّا لا ينطلق بذكره اللسان وأنا أعيذه بالله العظيم الذي فضله بكلّ خلق كريم من تعسّف الفعل الذي لا يجزي أدناه أقصى الشكر ما سلف من المخاطبة والمشاركة ما بلغ أقصى منازل الشرف وحاول أعلى مآثر الفخر وأنا أفاوض السيّد أطال الله بقاءه الشيء بعد الشيء ممّا نطق به الحزن وأبثّه إيّاه. فمن ذلك

وَقَفْتُ عَلَى ٱلْأَحْبَابِ وَٱلتُّرْبُ دُونَهُمْ   بِنَفْسِي وُجُوهٌ تَحْتَ تِلْكَ ٱلْمَقَابِرِ
وَمَثَّلَ لِي مَا نَالَ مِنْ حُسْنِهَا ٱلْبِلَى   فَسُبْحَانَ رَبِّ عَالِمٍ بِٱلسَّرَائِرِ

ثمّ بعث إليه بعدّة قصائد قالها فيها.

قال ولمّا اختلّت حال عبيد الله بعث إليه المعتضد يسأله أن يفسح لشاجي في زيارته ١٦،١٣
فشقّ ذلك عليه واحتجّ بأنّها عليلة ومختلّة الهيئة فلجّ في طلبها حتّى ظهر منه تهديد له فبعث بها إليه فذكر عنها أنّها قالت احتقرت نفسي حين دخلت على جواريه لما رأيت

to unite hearts. May God protect us from receiving no consolation and losing our recompense! By God, Prince, this person is humble, his eyes are full of tears, his heart is burning with pain. The disaster has struck a body that cannot function properly, suffers lasting sickness, and endures calamities related to the remaining time accorded him,

While a man weeps and laments his distress,
as he is wont to do since his birth.

And about the illness the prince mentioned—may God inflict this illness upon me. May it cease to exist and never be mentioned. Else he would have been here, and there would have been no reason to speak of it. I ask him to seek refuge with Almighty God, who bestows His favors on every noble being, from the vexation of the deed that falls far short of the enormous gratitude we feel for earlier conversations and meetings. These meetings were the pinnacle of honor and the peak of glory. In return, I will send the prince—God grant him long life—poems that voice my sorrow, one after another. Here is one:

I stood by my beloveds' graves,
separated from them by dust.
For those faces beneath the stones
I'd give my life.
I pictured the decay
their beauty has suffered.
Praise to the Lord who knows
the secrets of all hearts.

And he sent him a number of poems he composed about her.

When ʿUbaydallāh's situation had become precarious, al-Muʿtaḍid asked 13.16
him to allow Shājī to visit him. ʿUbaydallāh was disturbed by the request[75] and he made excuses for her, saying she was unwell and not in good shape. Al-Muʿtaḍid insisted she come. He even threatened ʿUbaydallāh, so he sent her to him. She is said to have said, "I despised myself when I met his slave girls because of the jewels and fine clothes I saw they were wearing. And they

عليهنّ من حليّهنّ وحللهنّ وحقروني هم[١] أيضاً حتّى غنّيت وغنّين فانتقل إعظامي لهنّ إليّ منهنّ فلمّا خرجتُ حمل معها المعتضد عشرة ألف درهم وكسوة وطيب فجاءت شاجي وعبيد الله واله فلمّا رآها سري عنه ثمّ قال لها هل رأيتِ شيئاً لم تريْ مثله عندنا فاستحسنتِه فقالت لا والله إلّا عوداً من عود وذلك أنّه محفوراً لا مبنيّاً فاستظرفته.

قال وكان ممّا صنعته وغنّته ذلك اليوم للمعتضد ١٣،١٧

مَاذَا ٱسْتَعَارَ ٱلْحُسْنُ مِنْ وَجْهِهِ وَٱلْغُصْنُ ٱلنَّاعِمُ مِنْ قَدِّهِ
لَقَدْ تَعَاتَبْنَا بِأَبْصَارِنَا فِيمَا جَنَاهُ ٱلْخُلْفُ مِنْ وَعْدِهِ
حَتَّى تَجَارَحْنَا بِتِكْرَارِنَا لِلَّحْظِ فِي قَلْبِي وَفِي خَدِّهِ
فَأَدْرَكَ ٱلثَّأْرَ وَأَدْرَكْتُهُ وَسَرَّنِي بِٱلصَّدِّ عَنْ صَدِّهِ

وكان ممّا غنّته أيضاً

هُوَ ٱلدَّهْرُ لَا يُعْطِيكَ إِلَّا تَعِلَّةً وَلَا يَأْخُذُ ٱلْمَوْهُوبَ إِلَّا تَغَشُّمَا
عَزَاءً إِذَا مَا فَاتَ مَطْلَبُ هَالِكٍ وَصَبْرًا إِذَا كَانَ ٱلتَّصَبُّرُ أَحْزَمَا

قال أبو عليّ محمّد بن العلاء الشجريّ لمّا تقلّد عبيد الله بن سليمان الوزارة للمعتضد ١٣،١٨
دفع عبيد الله بن عبد الله بن طاهر إليّ رقعة سألني عرضها على عبيد الله بن سليمان فكان فيها

أَبَى دَهْرُنَا إِسْعَافَنَا فِي نُفُوسِنَا وَأَسْعَفَنَا فِيمَنْ نُجِلُّ وَنُعْظِمُ
فَقُلْتُ لَهُ نُعْمَاكَ فِيهِمْ أَتِمَّهَا وَدَعْ أَمْرَنَا إِنَّ ٱلْمُهِمَّ ٱلْمُقَدَّمُ

١ كذا في الأصل.

despised me too. But when we all sang, my admiration for them gave way to their admiration for me." When she left, al-Muʿtaḍid sent ten thousand dirhams, clothes, and perfume with her. She came back to find ʿUbaydallāh on tenterhooks, but when he saw her he relaxed. He asked her, "Did you see anything there you admired that we cannot match?" "No," she replied, "except for a lute. It was made of a single piece of hollowed-out wood, and had not been assembled. I thought it elegant."

One of her settings she sang to al-Muʿtaḍid that day was: 13.17

By the charm that beauty borrowed from his face,
and the slender branch took from his frame!
We gave each other looks of reproach
about the promise he never kept
Till our glances, so often exchanged,
wounded both our cheeks, his and mine.[76]
Then he took his revenge and so did I;
gladly I saw him rebuff his adversary.

And another was:

Fate gives only to distract you,
and its gifts behave unjustly.
So, patience when a mortal misses his goal,
patience, when patience is the wisest course.

Abū ʿAlī Muḥammad ibn al-ʿAlāʾ al-Shajarī related the following: When 13.18
ʿUbaydallāh ibn Sulaymān was appointed al-Muʿtaḍid's vizier, ʿUbaydallāh ibn ʿAbdallāh ibn Ṭāhir gave me a note, asking me to show it to him. The text was:

Fate has refused to help us directly,
but it's helped us through those we admire and honor.
I said to it, "Complete your favors to them,
and forget our affairs. What's important has come before."

فاستحسن عبيد الله بن سليمان ما كتب به وقال أما ترى كيف تلطّف لشكوى حاله ثمّ أخذ جميع رقاعه فوقع له فيها بجميع ما أحبّ.

١٩،١٣ قال وقال أبو العيناء يوماً لعبيد الله أسكت[١] أيّها الأمير أم أقول. قال إن سكتّ كفيت وإن قلت أصغي إليك وإنك تتقرّب منّا إذا احتجنا إليك وتبعد عنّا إذا احتجت إلينا.

ومن شعره قوله

لَعَمْرِي لَئِنْ حَدَّثْتُ نَفْسِيَ أَنَّنِي ... أَفُوتُكَ إِنَّ ٱلرَّأْيَ مِنِّي لَعَازِبُ
لِأَنَّكَ مِنِّي بِٱلْمَكَانِ ٱلْمُحِيطِ بِي ... مِنَ ٱلْأَرْضِ أَنَّى ٱسْتَنْهَضَتْنِي ٱلْمَذَاهِبُ

٢٠،١٣ ذكر أبو عليّ الأوارجي أنّ أبا بكر محمّد بن السريّ السرّاج النحويّ كان يحبّ جارية من القيان فأنفق عليها مالاً جزيلاً فلمّا ورد المكتفي من الرقّة خرج الناس ينظرون إليه فخرجت أنا وهو وأبو القاسم عبد الله الموصليّ فجلسنا على روشن دار ابن جهشيار لنراه فلمّا وافى ونظرنا إليه استحسنّاه كلّنا. وكان أبو بكر السرّاج واجداً على هذه الجارية ومغاضباً لها فقال قد حضرني شيء فاكتب فكتبت

قَايَسْتُ بَيْنَ جَمَالِهَا وَفِعَالِهَا ... فَإِذَا ٱلْمَلَاحَةُ بِٱلْخِيَانَةِ لَا تَفِي
وَٱللهِ لَا كَلَّمْتُهَا وَلَوَ ٱنَّهَا ... كَٱلشَّمْسِ أَوْ كَٱلْبَدْرِ أَوْ كَٱلْمُكْتَفِي

٢١،١٣ ثمّ مضى للحديث مدّة طويلة وكان أبو عبد الله محمّد بن إسماعيل زنجيّ الكاتب يهوى قينة وهو إذ ذلك يكتب لأبي العبّاس بن الفرات وكان يحدّثه بحديثه معها ولا يحتشمه. وكان اجتماعها معه في كلّ يوم جمعة لأنّه كان يوم نوبته في داره. قال أبو عليّ فحدّثني زنجيّ قال غدوت يوم سبت على أبي العبّاس بن الفرات فقال لي ما كان خبرك أمس فحدّثته باجتماعنا فقال لي فما كان صوتك فقلت

---

١ كذا في الأصل.

ʿUbaydallāh ibn Sulaymān appreciated what he had written and commented, "Don't you see how subtle he is in complaining about his situation?" He had all the notes ʿUbaydallāh ibn ʿAbdallāh had written collected together, and he endorsed all his requests.

Abū l-ʿAynāʾ asked ʿUbaydallāh one day, "Should I keep silence, Prince, or 13.19
should I speak?" "If you keep silence, it's satisfactory, but if you speak, I will listen. You approach us when we need you, but stay far when you need us."

Here is a poem by ʿUbaydallāh:

By my life, if I thought I'd ever escape from you,
my mind would be wandering.
You are where I am on earth,
no matter where my paths have taken me.

According to Abū ʿAlī l-Awārijī: Abū Bakr Muḥammad ibn al-Sarī al-Sarrāj 13.20
the Grammarian was in love with a singing girl and spent huge sums on her. When al-Muktafī arrived from Raqqa, everyone came out to see him.[77] I, Abū Bakr, and Abū l-Qāsim ʿAbdallāh al-Mawṣilī went out and took our seats in Ibn Jahshiyārī's oriel window to see him, and as he passed we looked at him and we all admired him. Abū Bakr ibn al-Sarrāj was irritated and angry with this singing girl, and he said, "I've just thought of something. Write it down." So I wrote:

I've suffered from her beauty and her deeds;
betrayal can't be paid for by beauty.
By God, I won't ever speak to her, even if
she were the sun, the moon, and al-Muktafī.

A long time after this, Abū ʿAbdallāh Muḥammad ibn Ismāʿīl Zanjī the Sec- 13.21
retary was in love with a singing girl. At that time, he was working for Abū l-ʿAbbās ibn al-Furāt, and he used to talk to him frankly about his relationship with her, hiding nothing. She met him on Fridays, because that was the day he spent at home. Zanjī told me:

"On Saturday morning, when I presented myself before Abū l-ʿAbbās ibn al-Furāt, he asked me, 'What news of yesterday?' So I told him about our meeting. Then he asked, 'And what was the song you listened to?' I said:

قَايَسْتُ بَيْنَ جَمَالِهَا وَفِعَالِهَا

فقال لي أبو العبّاس لمن هذا الشعر قلت لعبد الله بن المعتزّ. ثمّ ركب أبو العبّاس ابن الفرات إلى الوزير القاسم بن عبيد الله فحدّثه بهذا الحديث وأنشده الشعر وسار معه إلى الثريّا ثمّ انصرف عنه فجلس في ديوانه فلمّا علم أن قد قرب انصرافه خرج فتلقّاه فلمّا لقيه حدّثه أنّه أنشد المكتفي الشعر وأنّه سأله عن قائله فعرّفه أنّه لعبيد الله ابن عبد الله بن طاهر. قال فأمرني أن أحمل إليه ألف دينار فقلت إنّما قلت لك إنّ الشعر لعبد الله بن المعتزّ فنسبته إلى ابن طاهر فقال والله ما وقع لي إلّا أنّك قلت إنّه لعبيد الله وهذا رزق رزقه الله عبيد الله لا حيلة لأحد فيه. قال زنجيّ فلمّا انصرف أبو العبّاس حدّثني بهذا الحديث وقال خذ أنت الدنانير وامضِ بها إلى عبيد الله وقل له هذا رزق بعثه الله إليك من حيث لم تحتسب فحملت إليه الدنانير وحدّثته الحديث فحمد الله وشكر أبا العبّاس فكان هذا من الاتّفاق العجيب.

٢٢،١٣ وكان عبيد الله يقول من صحب السلطان وخدمه احتاج أن يدخل أعمى ويخرج أخرس.[١]

ومن شعره

إِذَا أَنْتَ لَمْ تَفْضُلْ عَلَى ذِي مَوَدَّةٍ وَكُنْتَ وَإِيَّاهُ بِمَنْزِلَةٍ سَوَا
فَلَا تَكُ ذَا تِيهٍ عَلَيْهِ وَإِنَّمَا يُعَاقَبُ بِٱلذَّنْبِ ٱلْفَتَى لَا عَلَى ٱلرِّضَا

وقال أيضاً

أَلَا إِنَّ قَلْبِي مِنْكَ بَعْدَ ٱلَّذِي مَضَى لَمَلْآنُ مِنْ أَمْرَيْنِ يَخْتَلِفَانِ
هَوًى مِنْكَ يَتْلُوهُ أَذًى لَكَ وَٱلْأَذَى عَدُوُّ ٱلْهَوَى لَنْ يُوجَدَا بِمَكَانِ

---

١ الأصل: (أقول لا خصوصيّة للسلطان بل كلّ كبير ينبغي على الكمال مصاحبته وحفظ السرّ) وردت في الهامش.

I've suffered from her beauty and her deeds.

"'Who's the composer?' he asked. I replied, "Abdallāh ibn al-Muʿtazz.' Then Abū l-ʿAbbās ibn al-Furāt rode off to the vizier al-Qāsim ibn ʿUbaydallāh, told him the story, and recited the poetry to him. Abū l-ʿAbbās accompanied him to the Thurayyā Palace and then left him to go to his own office. When Abū l-ʿAbbās knew that the time for the vizier to leave was approaching, he came out to meet him, and al-Qāsim told him that he had recited the poetry to al-Muktafī, and when al-Muktafī asked who it was by, he said, "Ubaydallāh ibn ʿAbdallāh ibn Ṭāhir.' At that, al-Muktafī ordered, 'Take him one thousand dinars.' Zanjī objected: 'But I told you it was by ʿAbdallāh ibn al-Muʿtazz and you've ascribed it to Ibn Ṭāhir.' 'I only heard that you said it was by ʿUbaydallāh. This is a gift from God to ʿUbaydallāh, and no one can change that.'"

Zanjī went on: "When Abū l-ʿAbbās left work, he told me the story and said to me, 'You take the dinars, bring them to ʿUbaydallāh's house, and say to him, "This is a gift God has given you unexpectedly."' So I took him the dinars and told him the story. He said, 'God be praised,' and he thanked Abū l-ʿAbbās." It was an extraordinary accident.

ʿUbaydallāh used to say, "He who keeps company with the ruler and serves **13.22**
him needs to come into his presence blind and leave it dumb."[78]

Here is some of ʿUbaydallāh's poetry:

If you're not more eminent
than one who loves you
But you are both of equal standing,
don't treat him with contempt.
Punishment's for offenses,
not when there's satisfaction.

After what you did,
my heart is home to two opposites:
Your love, and then the pain you inflicted.
Pain is love's enemy—
they never meet in one place.

وقال أيضاً ٢٣،١٣

كَفَاكَ عَنِ ٱلدُّنْيَا ٱلدَّنِيَّةِ مُخْبِرًا غِنَى بَاخِلِيهَا وَٱفْتِقَارِ كِرَامِهَا
وَأَنَّ رِجَالَ ٱلنَّفْعِ تَحْتَ مَدَاسِهَا وَأَنَّ رِجَالَ ٱلضُّرِّ فَوْقَ سِنَامِهَا

وقال أيضاً

وَقَالُوا غَدًا يَنْأَى فَمَا أَنْتَ صَانِعُ فَمَا هُوَ إِلَّا أَنْ تَفِيضَ ٱلْمَدَامِعُ
بَلَى زَفَرَاتٌ بَيْنَهُنَّ تَنَفُّسٌ يُقَطِّعْنَ قَلْبِي وَٱلْهُمُومُ ٱلنَّوَازِعُ
وَذُلٌّ وَإِطْرَاقٌ وَفِكْرٌ وَحَسْرَةٌ وَأَعْظَمُ مِنْهَا مَا تُجِنُّ ٱلْأَضَالِعُ

قال عبد الله بن المعتزّ كتبت إلى عبيد الله بن عبد الله بن طاهر حين ولي ابنه خلافة مؤنس[1] على شرط بغداد ٢٤،١٣

فَرِحْتُ بِمَا أَضْعَافُهُ دُونَ قَدْرِكُمْ وَقُلْتُ عَسَى قَدْ هَبَّ مِنْ نَوْمِهِ ٱلدَّهْرُ
فَتَرْجِعُ فِينَا دَوْلَةٌ طَاهِرِيَّةٌ كَمَا بَدَأَتْ وَٱلْأَمْرُ مِنْ بَعْدِهِ ٱلْأَمْرُ
عَسَى ٱللّٰهُ إِنَّ ٱللّٰهَ لَيْسَ بِغَافِلٍ وَلَا بُدَّ مِنْ يُسْرٍ إِذَا مَا ٱنْتَهَى ٱلْعُسْرُ

فأجابه عبيد الله بن عبد الله

فَنَحْنُ لَكُمْ إِنْ مَسَّنَا ضَيْمُ جَفْوَةٍ وَمِنَّا عَلَى لَأْوَائِهَا ٱلصَّبْرُ وَٱلْعُذْرُ
فَإِنْ رَجَعَتْ مِنْ نِعْمَةِ ٱللّٰهِ دَوْلَةٌ إِلَيْنَا فَمِنَّا عِنْدَهَا ٱلْحَمْدُ وَٱلشُّكْرُ

ولعبيد الله شعر كثير وأخبار ظريفة اخترنا منها ما يليق بغرض الكتاب ولا يخرج إلى حدّ الإطالة. وكانت وفاة عبيد الله بن عبد الله بن طاهر ليلة السبت لاثنتي عشرة ٢٥،١٣

[1] كذا في عوّاد؛ الأصل: يونس.

It tells you enough about this world of ours— 13.23
the wealth of misers and the poverty of benefactors.
Those who do good it tramples upon,
those who do harm ride high on its back.

They said, "Tomorrow she's leaving.
What'll you do then?"
Right away my eyes flood with tears,
sighs and moans wound my heart,
pierced by sorrows.
Humiliation, silence, cares,
regrets, and above all, the emotions
surging in my bosom.

ʿAbdallāh ibn al-Muʿtazz recalled: I wrote to ʿUbaydallāh ibn ʿAbdallāh ibn Ṭāhir when his son was appointed deputy to Muʾnis, the commander of the Baghdad police: 13.24

I rejoiced at something far beneath your rank,
and said, "Maybe fate's awakened from its sleep
And we'll have the Ṭāhirids in power again
as they were before, though matters take their course.
God grant—God's not heedless—[79]
when hardship ends, ease will surely come."[80]

And ʿUbaydallāh replied:

We stay true, though harsh injustice strike us,
enduring and excusing in adversity.
If by God's grace power returns to us,
we'll give Him praise and gratitude.

ʿUbaydallāh composed much poetry and there are many interesting anecdotes about him. We have made a selection appropriate for the purpose of this book and kept it within bounds. ʿUbaydallāh died on Saturday night, the twelfth of Shawwal in the year 300 [May 5, 913]. When he died, Shaghab,[81] al-Muqtadir 13.25

ليلة خلت من شوّال سنة ثلاثمائة. ولمّا تُوفّي وجّهت شغب والدة المقتدر بأمّ موسى القهرمانة إلى ولده وحرمه فعزّتهم عنها وكفّنته بكفن حظيريّ[1] وتصدّقت في جنازته بألف دينار وألف درهم وقامت بجميع أمورهم.

٢٦،١٣ وأمّا أخوه محمّد بن عبد الله بن طاهر فكان كريماً سريّاً جواداً سمحاً حسن الأخلاق مع أدب وحسن معرفة وافتنان في سائر العلوم وضبط وسياسة وتقدّم في التدبير. وكان المتوكّل استدعاه من خراسان لمّا مات إسحاق بن إبراهيم الطاهريّ ومحمّد ابنه وولّاه خلافته ببغداد فأقرّ أخاه طاهر بن عبد الله على خراسان وكان أكبر إخوته.

٢٧،١٣ وذكر الشاه بن ميكال أنّ بعض البزّازين عرض على محمّد بن عبد الله بن طاهر ثوبي وشي فعرفهما أنّهما من ثيابه فأحضر إبراهيم بن هارون النصرانيّ قهرمانه فأمره أن يحضر الثوبين اللذين من صفتهما كيت وكيت فذكر أنّه لا يعرفهما وأنّه رجع إلى الإحصاء فلم يجدهما فيه ورجع إلى الديوان فوجدهما ثابتين فيه وكانا ابتيعا بألف وخمسمائة دينار فسألت عن الخبر فأخبرت أنّ الكاتب في الخزانة أباعهما وأسقط من الإحصاء عددهما. فأمر بحبس الكاتب وقال لإبراهيم ويلك تستكتب من يقدم هذا الإقدام فحلف أنّه ما وقف على مثل هذه الحال منه ولا عرف له مثل هذه الزلّة. فقال إن كان الأمر كذلك فليُطلق وأمر له بخمسمائة دينار وقال له تعفّف بهذه فإنّي أظنّ الخلّة حملتك على ذلك وردّ الثوبين على التاجر وأطلقه.

٢٨،١٣ قال وكنّا يوماً عند إسحاق بن إبراهيم بن مصعب فقدمت المائدة وكان قد تقدّم بعمل هريسة فقدمت إليه الهريسة فنظر إليها فرأى شعرة فأومأ إلى بعض غلمانه بشيء لم نفهمه فما لبث أن جاء بطيفوريّة عليها مكبّة فوضعها ورفع المكبّة

[1] كذا في عوّاد؛ الأصل: خطير.

bi-llāh's mother, sent Umm Mūsā, the head of her household, to his children and womenfolk to convey her condolences. She provided him with a fine Ḥaẓīrī[82] shroud, distributed one thousand dinars and one thousand dirhams at the funeral, and took care of all the family's needs.

I turn now to his brother, Muḥammad ibn ʿAbdallāh ibn Ṭāhir, who was noble, firm, generous, conciliatory, and a man of probity. Cultured and knowledgeable, he was well grounded in all branches of learning, and in the exercise of power and policy. He was also an excellent administrator. Al-Mutawakkil had summoned him from Khurasan after the deaths of Isḥāq ibn Ibrāhīm al-Ṭāhirī and Isḥāq's son Muḥammad. He made him his deputy in Baghdad and appointed Ṭāhir ibn ʿAbdallāh, his oldest brother, governor of Khurasan. 13.26

Al-Shāh ibn Mīkāl related that a cloth merchant offered two brocade robes to Muḥammad ibn ʿAbdallāh ibn Ṭāhir. He recognized them and knew they were his, so he summoned his majordomo, Ibrāhīm ibn Hārūn the Christian, and told him to bring the two robes, which he described, from his wardrobe. Ibrāhīm said he couldn't recall them. He had consulted the inventory, where he couldn't find them, so he turned to the accounts, where he saw an entry that they had been sold for fifteen hundred dinars. Al-Shāh made inquiries and learned that the clerk of the wardrobe had put them up for sale and removed them from the inventory. Muḥammad ibn Ṭāhir had the clerk imprisoned. He rebuked Ibrāhīm, saying, "Damn it, do you appoint men who do this sort of thing?" Ibrāhīm swore that he had never discovered him acting like this before or noticed him making any error. "In that case," said Muḥammad, "release him." He gave the clerk five hundred dinars with the words, "Take this and behave yourself. I think you were driven to it by poverty." He also returned the two robes to the merchant and let him go. 13.27

Al-Shāh ibn Mīkāl also told the following story: One day we were at Isḥāq ibn Ibrāhīm ibn Muṣʿab's place when the table was prepared. A dish of harīsah had been ordered, and when it was brought in Isḥāq looked at it and noticed a hair. He made a gesture to one of his attendants, which we didn't understand. Soon after, a dish was brought in with a cover, and when the cover was raised, the cook's hand, covered in blood, lay in the dish. We raised our hands in horror. 13.28

فإذا يد الطبّاخ بدمها في الطيفوريّة. فرفعنا أيدينا وتنغّص أكلنا ممّا ورد علينا وقمنا وليس منّا أحد ينتفع بنفسه. ثمّ اجتمعنا بعد ذلك بدهر على مائدة محمّد بن عبد الله بن طاهر وكان قد تقدّم بإصلاح لون اشتهاه فعُمل له وجاء به الطبّاخ بنفسه حرصاً على التقرّب من قلبه فلمّا قرب منه عثر بعجلته فأفلت الطيفوريّة على محمّد فصارت ثيابه وما تحته من فرش آية. فقام للوقت فغيّر ثيابه واغتسل وعاد إلينا بوجه طلق لم يؤثّر فيه ما جرى وجلس على المائدة ثمّ قال عليّ بفلان الطبّاخ فجيء به وهو لا يشكّ في حلول النقمة فقال له أحسبنا قد رعناك. أنت حرّ لوجه الله جلّ وعزّ وفلانة الجارية لك وقد زوّجتكها وأمر له بصلة وكسوة فأقبلنا بالدعاء له وتعجّبنا من فعله وذكرنا فعل إسحاق.

قال[1] كان ابن أبي فنن ويُكنّى أبا عبد الرحمٰن شاعراً مطبوعاً وكانت له ضيعة في ٢٩،١٣
قطيعة محمّد بن عبد الله بن طاهر وكان الحاشر يضير إليه فيؤذيه وربّما أشخصه فكتب إلى محمّد يشكو الحاشر وما تلقّى منه من الإعنات

أَبَنِي حُسَيْنٍ إِنَّنِي أَصْبَحْتُ فِي كَنَفِ ٱلْأَمِيرِ
وَلَنَا مَعَايِشُ فِي قَطِيعَتِهِ عَلَى ٱلْمَاءِ ٱلنَّمِيرِ
وَبَنَيْتُ بَيْتاً وَسْطَهُ سَمَّيْتُهُ بَيْتَ ٱلسُّرُورِ
فَإِذَا جَلَسْتُ إِزَاءَهُ وَشَرِبْتُ مِنْ حَلَبِ ٱلْعَصِيرِ
قُلْتُ ٱلْعَفَا لَمَّا رَوِيتُ عَلَى ٱلْخَوَرْنَقِ[2] وَٱلسَّدِيرِ
لَوْلَا تَرَدُّدُ حَاشِرٍ كَٱلْكَلْبِ فِي يَوْمٍ مَطِيرِ
فَإِذَا بَدَا لِي وَجْهُهُ أُخْرِجْتُ صِفْراً مِنْ سُرُورِي
فَهَلِ ٱلْأَمِيرُ بِجُودِهِ مِنْ قُبْحِ طَلْعَتِهِ مُجِيرِي

---

١ الأصل: (ابن أبي فنن من الشعراء المفلقين) وردت في الهامش. ٢ الأصل: الحرونق.

The sight had taken away our appetite, so we got up and left and the day was ruined for us.

Years later, we were gathered for a meal at Muḥammad ibn ʿAbdallāh ibn Ṭāhir's. A dish that he especially liked had been ordered, and when it was ready the cook brought it in himself out of a desire to curry favor with his master. As he got close to him, he tripped in his haste and the dish landed on Muḥammad. His clothes and the furnishings where he was sitting were a sight to be seen! He got up immediately and went out, changed his clothes, washed, and came back to us looking cheerful and completely unaffected by what had happened. He took his seat at the table and said, "Bring me the cook." The cook was fetched, certain it was his last hour. But Muḥammad said, "I'm sure we've scared you. You are a freeman for the sake of God, almighty and glorious is He. I'm giving you so-and-so the slave girl and marrying you to her." He also gave him money and clothes. We turned to him, calling down blessings on him, amazed at his behavior. And we recalled how Isḥāq had acted.

Another anecdote: Ibn Abī Fanan, surnamed Abū ʿAbd al-Raḥmān, who was a **13.29**
gifted poet, owned property in Muḥammad ibn ʿAbdallāh ibn Ṭāhir's concession.[83] The official responsible for the corvée used to come and tyrannize him, sometimes even summoning him. So he wrote to Muḥammad ibn ʿAbdallāh complaining of the official and his ill-treatment:

> Sons of Ḥusayn, the prince has taken me under his wing.
> I've property in his fief on the sweet-water canal;
> I've built a house there, which I call the House of Joy,
> And I sit before it, savoring wines anything but banal,
> Untroubled that al-Khawarnaq and al-Sadīr are no more.
> But when the corvée master, like a dog on a rainy day,
> Shows his face, I have no joy left.
> Can't the prince in his generosity
> Keep his ugly mug away?

فلمّا قرأ محمّد الأبيات وقّع تحتها قد أجزناك أبا عبد الرحمٰن وأمرنا باحتمال خراجك وكان مبلغه ثمانية آلاف درهم ووجّه إليه بألف دينار وحلف عليه أن يقبلها وكان ابن أبي فنن لا يقبل من أحد شيئاً وكان حسن الحال مستقلاً.

٣٠،١٣ ولمحمّد بن عبد الله من الأفعال الكريمة ما يطول الشرح بذكرها وفيما ذكرناه كفاية. ومن مليح شعره قوله[١]

قَالَتْ بِنَاظِرِهَا أَقْبِلْ فَقُلْتُ لَهَا ... بِٱلدَّمْعِ لَبَّيْكِ يَا سَمْعِي وَيَا بَصَرِي
حَتَّى إِذَا عَلِمَتْ أَنْ قَدْ كَلِفْتُ بِهَا ... أَوْمَتْ إِلَيَّ بِدَمْعٍ غَيْرِ مُسْتَتِرِ
يَا كَاتِمِي خِيفَةَ ٱلْوَاشِي مَحَبَّتَهُ ... إِنِّي وَعَيْشِكِ أَقْرَأُهُ مِنْ نَظَرِ[٢]
قُولِي بِطَرْفِكِ مَا تَهْوَيْنَ أَعْرِفُهُ ... وَٱسْتَنْطِقِي نَاظِرِي يُخْبِرْكِ بِٱلْخَبَرِ

٣١،١٣ كان مولد محمّد بن عبد الله سنة تسع ومائتين في الليلة التي فُتحت في صبيحتها كيسوم وفيها وُلد عبيد الله بن خاقان وأحمد بن إسرائيل والحسن بن مخلد وكلّهم ولي الوزارة. ومات محمّد يوم السبت لثلاث عشرة خلت من ذي القعدة سنة ثلاث وخمسين ومائتين وسنّه أربع وأربعون سنة وكانت وفاته من بثرة خرجت في حلقه. وتوفّي والقمر في الكسوف وكان يقول إذا تمّ الكسوف وبدأ في الانجلاء متّ فكان كذلك. واستخلف أخاه عبيد الله فأقرّه المعتزّ ووجّه إليه بالخلع مع مفلح خليفة باكياك. وكان طاهر بن محمّد نازعه الأمر وأعانه مواليه والعامّة حتّى جاءت الرسل والخلع فاستقرّ الأمر لعبيد الله.

١ الأصل: (يحفظ) وردت في الهامش. ٢ الأصل: النظر.

When Muḥammad read the verses, he wrote beneath them: "We'll protect you, Abū ʿAbd al-Raḥmān. We've ordered your tax to be covered." It amounted to eight thousand dirhams. And he sent him one thousand dinars, making him swear to accept them, for Ibn Abī Fanan never accepted anything from anyone. He was well off and independent.

Muḥammad's acts of generosity would take too long to recount—we have given enough examples. Here is a fine poem of his:[84] 13.30

With her glance she said, "Come!"
and I, in tears, "I come,
O my ears and my eyes."
When she knew I loved her,
she beckoned to me,
not veiling her tears.
"You who've hidden your love
for fear of slander,
I swear I read it in your eyes."
Let your glance say what you want
and I'll know it.
Ask my eyes to speak
and they'll tell what I feel.

Muḥammad ibn ʿAbdallāh was born in the year 209 [823–24] in the night before the morning when Kaysūm was conquered. ʿUbaydallāh ibn Yaḥyā ibn Khāqān, Aḥmad ibn Isrāʾīl, and al-Ḥasan ibn Makhlad were born that same night too, and they all became viziers. Muḥammad died on Saturday the fourteenth of Dhu'l-Qadah, 253 [November 15, 867], at the age of forty-four. His death was caused by the eruption of a pustule in his throat. He died during an eclipse of the moon; he used to say, "When the eclipse has reached its peak and started to decline, I will die," and so it was. He appointed his brother ʿUbaydallāh as his successor, and al-Muʿtazz confirmed this, sending him robes of honor via Mufliḥ, Bākiyāk's deputy. Ṭāhir ibn Muḥammad contested this appointment and was supported by his dependents and the common people, but ʿUbaydallāh's position was secured when the messengers and the robes of honor arrived.[85] 13.31

ولابن الروميّ يرثي محمّد بن عبد الله بن طاهر ٣٢،١٣

بَاتَ ٱلْأَمِيرُ وَبَاتَ بَدْرُ سَمَائِنَا هٰذَا يُوَدِّعُنَا وَهٰذَا يَكْسِفُ
قَمَرٌ رَأَى قَمَرًا يَجُودُ بِنَفْسِهِ فَبَكَى أَخَاهُ أَخٌ مُوَاسٍ مُنْصِفُ
فَتَكَتْ بِهِ ٱلْأَيَّامُ وَهْيَ عَلِيمَةٌ أَنْ سَوْفَ يُتْلَفُ مُنْهُ مَا لَا يُخْلَفُ

وقال فيه

وَسَأَلْتُ عَنْهُ فَقِيلَ بَاتَ لِمَا بِهِ قُلْتُ ٱلنَّدَى لَا شَكَّ بَاتَ لِمَا بِهِ
وَكَأَنَّمَا ضَنَّ ٱلزَّمَانُ عَلَى ٱلْوَرَى بِبَقَائِهِ أَوْ هَابَهُ فَبَدَا بِهِ
فَلِمَنْ أَصُونُ مَدَامِعِي مِنْ بَعْدِهِ وَلِمَنْ تُرَى تَنْهَلُّ مِنْ أَسْبَابِهِ
لِصَوَابِهِ لِخِطَابِهِ لِجَوَابِهِ لِشَبَابِهِ لِلْغُرِّ مِنْ آدَابِهِ

ولعبيد الله أخيه فيه ٣٣،١٣

كَسَفَ ٱلْبَدْرُ وَٱلْأَمِيرُ جَمِيعًا فَٱنْجَلَى ٱلْبَدْرُ وَٱلْأَمِيرُ عَمِيدُ
عَاوَدَ ٱلْبَدْرَ نُورُهُ لِتَجَلِّيهِ وَنُورُ ٱلْأَمِيرِ مَا لَا يَعُودُ

وقال

ذَكَرْتُ أَخِي مِنْ غَيْرِ نِسْيَانِ ذِكْرِهِ وَلٰكِنَّهَا حَالٌ تَزِيدُ وَتَنْقُصُ
عَلَى حَسَبِ أَخْلَاقِ ٱلزَّمَانِ وَإِنَّهُ لَيَصْحَبُنِي عَيْشٌ عَلَيْهِ مُنَغَّصُ

ولمّا مات محمّد بن عبد الله بن طاهر اشتدّ وجد المعتزّ عليه وكان رأى أنّ الأتراك ٣٤،١٣
يهابونه من أجله ولمكانه فقال فيه

This is part of an elegy Ibn al-Rūmī composed on Muḥammad ibn ʿAbdallāh ibn Ṭāhir: 13.32

Night has fallen on the prince,
night has fallen on the moon in our sky;
He has bidden us farewell, the moon is eclipsed.
The moon saw another moon depart this life,
A brother justly commiserating weeps for his friend.
Fate has destroyed him, knowing full well
That he has no successor.

And here is another elegy:

I asked after him. They told me, "His illness has killed him."
I said, "His illness has killed generosity,"
As if Fate grudged mankind his staying alive,
or feared him and took him far away.[86]
Whom shall I keep my tears for after him?
For which of his qualities do they flow?
His judgment, his eloquence, his ready wit,
his youth, his brilliant culture?

His brother ʿUbaydallāh composed these lines on him: 13.33

The moon and the prince were both eclipsed.
The moon now shines; the prince is in shadow.
The moon has risen, luminous again.
The prince's light has gone forever.

And these:

I recall my brother, not forgetting his memory,
but it's a humor that waxes and wanes
According to destiny's mood. The life I live now
is troubled forever by his loss.

When Muḥammad ibn ʿAbdallāh ibn Ṭāhir died, al-Muʿtazz grieved for him especially intensely because he saw that it was thanks to Muḥammad and his standing that the Turks stood in awe of him. He composed these verses: 13.34

ذَهَبَتْ بَهْجَةُ ٱلْخِلَافَةِ عَنَّا حِينَ أَضْحَى مُحَمَّدٌ فِي ٱلْقُبُورِ
عَنْ قَلِيلٍ نَكُونُ أَحْدَاثَ دَهْرٍ عَنْ سَنَا نَارِهَا يَشِبُّ ٱلسَّعِيرُ

قال وأمّا سليمان بن عبد الله بن طاهر فكان ابن أخيه محمّد بن طاهر أنفذه إلى العراق في سنة خمس وخمسين ومائتين خليفة له فأمضى المعتزّ ذلك وعزل عبيد الله فأقرّه أيّاماً وخرج إليه عبيد الله فخلع عليه وولّاه شرطة بغداد وعزل سليمان ابن عبد الله فدخل عبيد الله إلى بغداد ومعه خلق عظيم من الأولياء والقوّاد فتلقّاه الناس وفرحوا بولايته. وخرج سليمان قبل وصول أخيه إلى البردان فأقام بها إلى أن ورد موسى بن بغا من الجبل فرُدَّ إليه أمر الشرطة ببغداد وسرّ من رأى وأمر السواد وعزل سليمان وذلك في سنة سبع وخمسين ومائتين. فتسلّم عبيد الله الولاية في جمادى الأولى. ٣٥،١٣

ثمّ اضطرب أمر الطاهريّة بخراسان ودخل يعقوب بن الليث نيسابور فلمّا قرب منها وذلك في سنة ثمان وجّه محمّد بن طاهر إليه يستأذنه في تلقّيه فلم يأذن له فبعث بعمومته وأهل بيته فلقوه ودخل نيسابور ونزل طرفاً من أطرافها. فركب إليه محمّد بن طاهر ولقيه في مضربه فأقبل يوبّخه على تفريطه في عمله ثمّ وكّل به وبأهل بيته وكتب إلى الحضرة يذكر أنّه على السمع والطاعة والضبط لما يتولّاه ويطعن على محمّد. فردّ الموفّق عليه أقبح ردّ وأعلمهم أنّه لا يقارّهم على ذلك. ثمّ أقبل يعقوب بن الليث إلى بغداد وسار المعتمد نحوه فالتقوا وكان الموفّق في المقدّمة وموسى بن بغا في الميمنة ومسرور البلخيّ في الميسرة[١] وذلك يوم الأحد لسبع خلون من رجب وكان يوم شعانين. فقُتل من الأولياء خلق كثير واشتدّت الحرب وكشف الموفّق عن رأسه وقال أنا الغلام الهاشميّ ثمّ صارت الدائرة على يعقوب فانهزم أقبح هزيمة واتّبعهم الموفّق وموسى بن بغا فقتلوا ٣٦،١٣

١ الأصل: (المعركة بين يعقوب بن الليث وبين الخليفة بالقرب من بغداد) وردت في الهامش.

The caliphate's splendor left us
when Muḥammad went to dwell in the grave.
Before long we'll be the fuel of destiny,
a flame flaring from the glow of its fire.

Muḥammad ibn Ṭāhir ibn ʿAbdallāh sent his nephew Sulaymān ibn ʿAbdallāh ibn Ṭāhir to Iraq in the year 255 [869] as his deputy. Al-Muʿtazz approved the appointment and dismissed ʿUbaydallāh ibn Ṭāhir. He recognized Muḥammad for a few days, but then ʿUbaydallāh visited him and he gave him a robe of honor and appointed him military commander of Baghdad, dismissing Sulaymān. ʿUbaydallāh entered Baghdad with a large crowd of high officials and army commanders. Everyone welcomed him, delighted with his appointment. Sulaymān had left the city for Baradān before his brother entered it, and he stayed there until Mūsā ibn Bughā arrived from Jibāl. Then Mūsā was again given military command of Baghdad, Samarra, and the region south of Baghdad, Sulaymān having been dismissed. This was in the year 257 [871], and ʿUbaydallāh was made governor in Jumada al-Awwal [March]. 13.35

The Ṭāhirids faced unrest in Khurasan, with Yaʿqūb ibn al-Layth entering Nīshāpūr. When he approached the city in the year 258 [872], Muḥammad ibn Ṭāhir requested a meeting, but Yaʿqūb did not agree. Then Muḥammad sent his uncles and other relatives and they met him. After Yaʿqūb entered Nīshāpūr, camping on the outskirts, Muḥammad rode out and met him in his tent. Yaʿqūb started to upbraid him for his negligence as an administrator, then he appointed an agent to take charge of him and his family. He wrote to the caliph assuring him of his complete obedience and his firmness in administering what would be entrusted to him, and he leveled accusations against Muḥammad. Al-Muwaffaq replied to him in the ugliest fashion, announcing that he did not accept the arrangement they had made. 13.36

Yaʿqūb then advanced toward Baghdad, and al-Muʿtamid marched out to meet him. When the armies met, al-Muwaffaq was leading the vanguard, with Mūsā ibn Bughā on the right wing and Masrūr al-Balkhī on the left wing. It was Sunday the ninth[87] of Rajab [April 12, 876]—Palm Sunday, in fact. Many high officials were killed, and as the battle raged, al-Muwaffaq bared his head and shouted, "I'm the Hāshimite champion!" Then the tide turned against Yaʿqūb and he suffered a crushing defeat. Al-Muwaffaq and Mūsā pursued his army and inflicted great carnage. They flooded the land behind the fugitives and more

مقتلةً عظيمةً وأُطلق عليهم الماء فغرق أكثر ممّن قُتل. وكان محمّد بن طاهر معه مثقّلاً بالحديد فأُطلق من حديده وخُلع عليه وأُنزل دار عمّه محمّد بن عبد الله بن طاهر ورُدّ إليه عمله بخراسان وأُطلق له خمس مائة ألف درهم. ورجع المعتمد إلى بغداد وسار الموفّق إلى واسط وعقد لعبيد الله على الحرمين.

٣٧،١٣ وورد الخبر بموت يعقوب بن الليث وقيام أخيه عمرو وأُخذت البيعة على عمرو وقُلّد خراسان وفارس وكرمان وسجستان وإصبهان والسند. وكتب عمرو إلى عبيد الله بتوليته الشرطة خلافة له ووجّه إليه بخلع وعمود ذهب وأمضى الموفّق ذلك وخلع على عبيد الله أيضاً.

٣٨،١٣ ومات سليمان بن عبد الله بن طاهر سنة ستّ وستّين ومائتين في المحرّم فوقف أخوه عبيد الله على قبره متّكئاً على سيفه وقال

ٱلنَّفْسُ مِنِّيَ تَرْقَى فِي مَرَاقِيهَا وَدَمْعَةُ ٱلْعَيْنِ تَجْرِي فِي مَجَارِيهَا
لِبُقْعَةٍ مَا رَأَتْ عَيْنِي كَمِثْلَتِهَا[١] وَلَا كَكَثْرَةِ أَحْبَابٍ ثَوَوْا فِيهَا

ثمّ استخلف صاعد بن مخلد أبا عبد الله محمّد بن طاهر بن عبد الله بن طاهر على مدينة السلام في سنة سبعين ومائتين فقبض على عمّه عبيد الله وحبسه. ثمّ استخلف المعتضد غلامه بدراً على مدينة السلام وانقرض أمر الطاهريّة منها ومن خراسان. وكان لسليمان شعر مليح وأدب وفهم ومعرفة.

٣٩،١٣ وأمّا عبد العزيز بن عبد الله بن طاهر فكان أصغر إخوته وكان له أدب وفهم وشعر مليح. فمن شعره إلى أخيه عبيد الله وكان أخواه عبد الله وسليمان حبساه

قَدْ كُنْتُ أَحْسِبُ أَنِّي مِنكَ إِنْ نَزَلَتْ إِحْدَى ٱلنَّوَائِبِ بِي آوِي إِلَى جَبَلِ
حَتَّى إِذَا وَقَعَ ٱلْأَمْرُ ٱلَّذِي وَجَبَتْ فِي مِثْلِهِ نُصْرَتِي مِنْ غَيْرِ مَا فَشَلِ

١ الأصل: كيعليها.

were drowned than were killed. Muḥammad ibn Ṭāhir had accompanied Yaʿqūb, loaded with chains, and he was released from his fetters, given a robe of honor, and lodged in the house of his uncle, Muḥammad ibn ʿAbdallāh ibn Ṭāhir. He was reinstated as governor of Khurasan, with a grant of five hundred thousand dirhams. Al-Muʿtamid returned to Baghdad while al-Muwaffaq marched to Wāsiṭ, where he appointed ʿUbaydallāh governor of the Two Holy Cities.

Then news came of Yaʿqūb's death and his brother ʿAmr's emergence. 13.37
ʿAmr swore allegiance to the caliph and was invested with the governorship of Khurasan, Fars, Kirman, Sīstān, Isfahan, and Sind. He then wrote to ʿUbaydallāh, appointing him his deputy in command of the police and sending him robes of honor and a golden staff. Al-Muwaffaq endorsed the appointment and also gave ʿUbaydallāh robes of honor.

Sulaymān ibn ʿAbdallāh ibn Ṭāhir died in the year 266 in Muharram 13.38
[August–September 879]. His brother ʿUbaydallāh stood by his grave, leaning on his sword, and declaimed:

My soul ascends to the heights,
while my tears flow and furrow my cheeks
For a place as small as any I've ever seen,
where so many loved ones rest.

Subsequently, Ṣāʿid ibn Makhlad appointed Abū ʿAbdallāh Muḥammad ibn Ṭāhir ibn ʿAbdallāh ibn Ṭāhir governor of Baghdad in the year 270 [883–84], and Muḥammad ibn Ṭāhir arrested and imprisoned his uncle ʿUbaydallāh. Then al-Muʿtaḍid appointed his equerry Badr governor of Baghdad, and the Ṭāhirids' power there and in Khurasan decreased. Sulaymān composed good poetry, and he was a man of culture, intelligence, and knowledge.

The youngest of the brothers was ʿAbd al-ʿAzīz ibn ʿAbdallāh ibn Ṭāhir. He was 13.39
cultured, intelligent, and a good poet. This is a poem he sent to his brother ʿUbaydallāh when he had been imprisoned by two other brothers, ʿAbdallāh and Sulaymān.

I used to think, if misfortune struck me,
that I'd find you a tower of strength.
But when the blow fell and you had a duty
to help me without fail,

أَسْلَمْتَنِي لِخُطُوبِ ٱلدَّهْرِ تَلْعَبُ بِي   مَا هٰكَذَا كَانَ تَقْدِيرِي وَلَا أَمَلِي
لَوْ كُنْتُ فِي بَلَدٍ نَائِي ٱلْمَحَلِّ لَمَا   بَالَيْتُ عَثْرَةَ أَيَّامِي وَمِثْلُكَ لِي
إِنِّي أَخُوكَ ٱلَّذِي قَدْ كُنْتَ تَأْلَفُهُ   مَا حُلْتُ عَنْ عَهْدِكُمْ يَوْمًا وَلَمْ أَزَلِ
إِنِّي أَخُوكَ وَإِنَّ ٱللّٰهَ مُطَّلِعٌ   عَلَى ٱلسَّرَائِرِ فَٱقْطَعْ بَعْدُ أَوْ فَصِلِ

ومن شعره أيضاً إلى أخيه لمّا حُبس وكان اتُّهم بأنّه[1] كاتب الخجستانيّ فكتب من ٤٠،١٣
الحبس يحلف على بطلان ذلك وكتب آخر الرقعة بهذه الأبيات

تَقُولُ وَقَدْ رِيعَتْ سُلَيْمَى بِحَبْسِي   كَمَا رَاعَ ثُكْلٌ فَاجِعٌ أُمَّ وَاحِدِ
أَبَى ٱلدَّهْرُ إِلَّا أَنْ يَنُوبَكَ صَرْفُهُ   كَعَادَتِهِ ٱلنَّكْرَاءِ فِي كُلِّ مَاجِدِ
فَقُلْتُ لَهَا غُضِّي عَلَيْكِ فَإِنَّمَا   تُصِيبُ ٱلرِّجَالَ صَائِبَاتُ ٱلشَّدَائِدِ
وَلَا تَعْجَبِي لِلْحَبْسِ وَيْحَكِ وَٱعْجَبِي   لِأَنْكَرِ مَا حَدَّثْتُهُ فِي ٱلْمَشَاهِدِ
حُبِسْتُ لِحَرْبٍ مَا شَهِدْتُ كِفَاحَهَا   وَأَصْبَحَ سَجَّانِي أَخِي وَٱبْنُ وَالِدِي

ومن مليح شعره

يَا أَيُّهَا ٱلْقَمَرُ ٱلْمُنِيرُ ٱلزَّاهِرُ   ٱلْمُشْرِقُ ٱلْحَسَنُ ٱلْبَهِيُّ ٱلْبَاهِرُ
أَبْلِغْ شَبِيهَتَكَ ٱلسَّلَامَ وَهَنِّهَا   بِٱلنَّوْمِ وَٱعْلِمْهَا بِأَنِّي سَاهِرُ

وكان المعتضد يستحسن هذا الشعر فغنّى فيه في طريقة خفيف الرمل وكان أحد أصواته.

١ كذا في عوّاد؛ الأصل: وكان بأنّه.

You left me to be fate's plaything—
against all hope and expectation.
Living far away, I'd not heed fate's trials
with a man like you beside me.
I'm your brother, you loved me,
I've kept faith with you till now.
I'm your brother. God knows men's hearts.
So either sever our ties or restore them!

In another letter he sent to his brother from prison, after being accused of having corresponded with al-Khujistānī, he swore that that was untrue, and at the bottom of the paper he wrote: 13.40

Stricken by my imprisonment,
like the bereaved mother of an only child,
Sulaymā cried, "Fate refuses to spare you its blows.
Thus does it treat the illustrious."
I answered, "Hush! The arrows of misfortune
strike only men of worth.
Damn it, don't let prison astound you
but be astounded at the terrible tale I tell.
I'm a prisoner because of a war I never fought;
my jailors are both my father's sons."

Another good poem of his is:

You bright radiant moon,
shining in beauty,
dazzling in splendor,
Greet your likeness,
wish her a good sleep,
and tell her I'm wide awake.

Al-Muʿtaḍid admired this poem, for which he made a setting in the light *ramal* mode. It was one of his noteworthy compositions.

وذكر أبو عبد الله بن حمدون أنّ محمّد بن عبد الله بن طاهر كان يجب المتوكّل بسرّ من ١٣،٤١
رأى شهرين ثمّ ينحدر إلى بغداد فيقيم بها شهرين ويخلفه خلفاؤه بسرّ من رأى فقدمها قدمة أخذ فيها معه أخاه عبد العزيز وكان قد اشترى جارية لها من قلبه محلّ فاشتدّ عليه فراقها. فسألني أن أستأذن أخاه له في الرجوع إلى بغداد على أن يعطيني شهريّاً كنت رأيته تحته ففعلت فأذن له. فأعطاني الشهريّ ثمّ أنشدني هذا الشعر

أَقُولُ لَمَّا هَاجَ قَلْبِي ٱلذِّكْرَى   وَٱعْتَرَضَتْ وَسْطَ ٱلسَّمَاءِ ٱلشِّعْرَى
كَأَنَّهَا يَاقُوتَةٌ فِي مِدْرَى   مَا أَطْوَلَ ٱللَّيْلَ بِسُرَّ مَنْ رَا
يَا رَبُّ فَكَّ كَفَكَاكِ ٱلْأَسْرَى   فَإِنْ تَجُدْ لِي بِنَجَاةٍ أُخْرَى
أَجْعَلُ أَدْنَى خَطَوَاتِي بُصْرَى   حَتَّى أَؤُوبَ بِٱلْمَطَايَا حَسْرَى
كَأَنَّهَا مِنَ ٱلْكَلَالِ سَكْرَى   ثُمَّ أَعِيشُ مِثْلَ عَيْشِ كِسْرَى

ولم يدخل بغداد من ولد عبد الله بن طاهر غير هؤلاء الأربعة محمّد وعبد الله وسليمان وعبد العزيز. ١٣،٤٢

فأمّا عبد الله بن طاهر فكان من سروات الناس أدباً وفضلاً وسياسةً وتدبيراً وسخاءً وكرماً. وكان المأمون تبنّاه وربّاه وكان مولده سنة اثنتين وثمانين ومائة وذكر أبو أحمد عبيد الله أنّ أباه عبد الله بن طاهر انصرف ليلة من دار المأمون وذلك بعد خروج طاهر إلى خراسان وكان قد غلب عليه النبيذ. فبات في القبّة الطاهريّة من دار طاهر بمدينة السلام فتعلّق طرف من الخيش وقد يبس بالشمعة فاحترقت القبّة واحتمل عبد الله فأُخرج منها. واتّصل الخبر بطاهر فكتب إلى عبد الله يعذله ويؤنّبه ويقول لو ورد الخبر بوفاتك كان أسهل عليّ من وروده بفضيحتك وأن يبلغ بك النبيذ مبلغاً لا تحسّ معه باحتراق موضع أنت فيه ويأمره بالتجهّز والخروج إليه. فأقلق عبد الله ذلك وكتمه جميع الناس وختم الكتاب وجعله تحت مصلّاه.

Abū ʿAbdallāh ibn Ḥamdūn related: Muḥammad ibn ʿAbdallāh ibn Ṭāhir would spend two months in Samarra as al-Mutawakkil's chamberlain and then go down to Baghdad, spending two months there, with his deputies replacing him in Samarra. Once when he went there, he took with him his brother ʿAbd al-ʿAzīz, who had just bought a slave girl of whom he was very fond. He found it hard to be separated from her, so he asked me to request his brother's permission for him to return to Baghdad. In return he would give me a mixed-breed-horse I had seen him riding. I did so, and he gave me the horse. Then he recited: 13.41

I say, as memories move my heart
and the Dog Star rises
like a gemstone in a diadem,
"Long are the nights in Samarra!"
O Lord, free me like a captive,
and if you grant me further release,
I'll direct my first steps to Buṣrā.
Then with weary mounts, as if drunk from fatigue,
I'll come back and live like Khosroes!

Among ʿAbdallāh ibn Ṭāhir's sons, only these four, Muḥammad, ʿUbaydallāh, Sulaymān, and ʿAbd al-ʿAzīz, ever visited Baghdad. 13.42

ʿAbdallāh ibn Ṭāhir was outstanding in culture, virtue, political and administrative skills, generosity, and nobility. Al-Maʾmūn had taken him under his wing and educated him. He was born in the year 182 [798].

Abū Aḥmad ʿUbaydallāh ibn ʿAbdallāh mentioned that one night after Ṭāhir had set out for Khurasan, ʿAbdallāh ibn Ṭāhir, ʿUbaydallāh's father, left al-Maʾmūn's palace, having drunk too much. He settled down for the night in the Ṭāhirid dome in their palace in Baghdad, but part of the linen wall hangings, which were dry, touched the candle and the dome caught fire. ʿAbdallāh was carried out of the fire. When the news reached Ṭāhir, he wrote to ʿAbdallāh blaming and scolding him, saying, "If I had heard the news of your death, it would have been easier to bear than hearing of this scandal and that you get so drunk that you are not even aware the place you are in is on fire." And he ordered him to get ready to set out to join him. This disturbed ʿAbdallāh, and he hid the news from everyone, sealing the letter and putting it under his prayer mat.

١٣،٤٣ وتبيّن الهمّ عليه فسأله المأمون عن خبره فكتمه ثمّ سأل من يخصّه فأعلمه أنّ كتاباً ورد عليه لا يعلم ما فيه. فأقسم عليه المأمون في إحضار الكتاب فأحضره. فكتب المأمون إلى طاهر يعاتبه على ما فعل ويعلمه منزلته عنده وإحلاله محلّ الولد وأنّه لا يد لطاهر عليه إلّا بحقّ خلافته فإن صرفه عنها فليس له أن يزعجه عن الحضرة. فأجاب طاهر بالشكر لتطوّله إذ كان هذا محلّه عنده وأُعيد بناء القبّة. فلم تزل إلى أن نقضت في سنة ثلاث وتسعين ومائتين.

١٣،٤٤ وخرج عبد الله إلى الشام في سنة تسع ومائتين لمحارب نصر بن شبث إلى أن ظفر به.

قال عبيد الله بن عبد الله حدّثني نصير وياسر وجماعة من مشايخ موالينا أنّ أبا العبّاس عبد الله بن طاهر لمّا أشرف على كيسوم تحصّن بها نصر بن شبث وركب من الغد وقد عبّأ جيشه للقاء فوافى نصراً وقد خرج من الحصن فصفّ بإزائه وواقفه إلى الليل على غير حرب ثمّ أوقد نصر النيران فشاور عبد الله قوّاده فقالوا هذا الليل فننصرف ونبيت في معسكرنا ثمّ نغاديه الحرب فقال إنّ انصراف المحارب نكوص ولست أبرح من موضعي. فنزل وكان يُحَمّ حمّى رِبْع وكان نوبتها تلك الليلة فوعك وعكاً شديداً فالتمس ما يدفئه فلم يكن معهم فقال احفروا حفيرةً فحفروها بأسيافهم[١] وأمر أن يُجمع التبن من مخالي الدوابّ فيُلقى في الحفيرة ففعل ذلك ثمّ جلس فيها. وجاءت السماء بهطل وودق[٢] شديد فقال استروني بتراسكم فلم نزل كذلك ليلتنا أجمع نستره حتّى أصبح وصلّينا وصلّى.

١٣،٤٥ وأعاد سلاحه وركب فرسه وتطرّف ونحن معه. فنظر فإذا ليس خارج الحصن أحد فقال خدعنا الخبيث وأوهمنا أنّه يبيت بإزائنا ودخل حصنه ووكّل به من يوقد

١ كذا في عوّاد؛ الأصل: فقالوا آحفروا حفيرةً بأسيافهم. ٢ كذا في عوّاد؛ الأصل: وبق.

People could see that he was worried, and al-Maʾmūn asked him what was wrong, but he said nothing. So al-Maʾmūn asked someone close to ʿAbdallāh, who told him that a letter had arrived for him but he did not know its contents. Al-Maʾmūn made ʿAbdallāh swear to produce the letter, which he did. Then al-Maʾmūn wrote to Ṭāhir, criticizing him for what he had done, reminding him of ʿAbdallāh's standing with himself, and pointing out that he treated him like a son. Ṭāhir therefore had no influence over ʿAbdallāh except by right of being al-Maʾmūn's deputy. If al-Maʾmūn had removed ʿAbdallāh from his father's authority, it was not for Ṭāhir to drive ʿAbdallāh away from the caliphal presence. Ṭāhir wrote back thanking al-Maʾmūn for his generosity, in view of the position ʿAbdallāh occupied with him. The dome was rebuilt and remained standing until the year 293 [905]. 13.43

In the year 209 [824], ʿAbdallāh set out for Syria, where he fought and vanquished Naṣr ibn Shabath. 13.44

According to ʿUbaydallāh ibn ʿAbdallāh, who had it from Nuṣayr, Yāsir, and several other elderly clients of his family who had witnessed the event: When Abū l-ʿAbbās ʿAbdallāh ibn Ṭāhir approached Kaysūm, Naṣr ibn Shabath entrenched himself there. The next day ʿAbdallāh prepared his army for combat and advanced, appearing before Naṣr, who had come out of the fortress. He drew up his army facing Naṣr's and confronted him without giving battle until nightfall. Then Naṣr lit fires, and ʿAbdallāh conferred with his commanders. They advised, "Let's go off tonight, spend the night in our camp, and attack him early tomorrow morning." He countered, "If a combatant leaves, it means he's retreating. I'll not budge," and he dismounted. He suffered from quartan fever and a bout occurred that night. He had a high fever and looked for something to keep him warm, but they had nothing. He said, "Let's dig a trench," and they dug it with their swords. He ordered them to collect the straw from the animals' forage bags and throw it into the trench. When that was done, he settled himself in the trench. Then it started to rain and the rain came down in torrents. He said, "Protect me with your shields," and we did so, protecting him the whole night. When morning came, we prayed and so did he.

He took up his weapons again and mounted his horse to reconnoiter, with us accompanying him. We looked, and there was no one outside the fortress. He said, "The cunning fellow has outwitted us, making us think he was spending the night drawn up against us. He went back into the fortress and had the 13.45

النيران والساعة يخرج عليكم بحدّته فخذوا حذركم. ودعا العزيز[1] فقال امضِ في ألفي فارس فأريحوا واستريحوا وسمّى لهم موضعاً يكونون فيه ولا يبرح منكم أحد أو يأتيه طاهر بن إبراهيم بن مدرك برسالتي. فإذا أتاك فإن قدرت أنت وأصحابك أن تكونوا في أجنحة الطير حتّى توافوني فافعلوا فمضى. ولم يستتمّ الكلام حتّى خرج نصر وحمل عليهم فبرز إليه عبد الله يقدم أصحابه فلم تزل الكرّات بينهم والجلاد وعبد الله يفدّي أصحابه ويعدهم ويرمي نفسه كلّ مرمًى إلى أن صارت الشمس في كبد السماء وكلّ مَن معه وتبيّن فيهم الضعف والعجز فأرسل إلى العزيز يأمره بالإسراع فوافى فلمّا رأى نصر ومن معه الرايات السود والأسود السود وكان عبد الله أوّل من اتّخذها جزعوا وتبيّن فيهم الفشل. وقال عبد الله للعزيز شأنك وأصحابك نحو القوم. فلم يكن إلّا ساعة حتّى انهزم نصر وجاء إلى حصنه فدعا أبو العبّاس بالنقّابين وأمر بنصب العرّادات والمجانيق والسلاليم واطّلعوا فلم يروا في الحصن أحدًا وإذا نصر قد نقب نقباً من وراء الحصن وخرج منه. وأمر الرجال ففتحوا الباب ودخل فغنم وأصحابه جميع ما في الحصن وبُشّر في ذلك الوقت وهُنّئ بالفتح فأنشده عوف بن محلّم الخزاعيّ

اُشْكُرْ لِرَبِّكَ يَوْمَ ٱلْحِصْنِ نِعْمَتَهُ   فَقَـدْ حَبَاكَ بِعِزِّ ٱلنَّصْرِ وَٱلظَّفَرِ

وهي قصيدة طويلة.

٤٦،١٣ ومضى نصر فلجأ إلى جبال لم تحصّنه فعاد بالأمان فكتب عبد الله إلى المأمون بخبره فكتب إليه أعطه الأمان على أن يطأ بساط أمير المؤمنين وينفذ فيه حكمه. فرضي بذلك ووجّه به عبد الله مع محمّد بن الحسن بن مصعب إلى حضرة المأمون.[2] قال وكان نصر قد كبر فرآه المأمون وغلامان له يحملانه على السرج فقال نصر يحمله اثنان فقال نعم يا أمير المؤمنين ولا ينزله مائتان.

[1] الأصل: القرير. والتصويب من الطبريّ. [2] الأصل: (لمّا ظفر المأمون بنصر بن شبث) وردت في الهامش.

people inside it keep fires going, and soon he'll be coming to attack us in full fury. Be on full alert!" He summoned al-ʿAzīz and said, "Take two thousand horsemen to this place"—mentioning the name—"and let the horses rest and take some rest yourselves. Let no one leave until Ṭāhir ibn Ibrāhīm ibn Mudrik brings a message from me. When he comes, take the wings of a bird, you and your company, and join me as soon as you can." He rode off, and no sooner had he finished speaking than Naṣr marched out and attacked them. Taking the lead, ʿAbdallāh engaged him in combat, and they charged and exchanged blows, with ʿAbdallāh sacrificing himself for his companions, encouraging them with promises and taking all kinds of risks. Then, when the sun was high overhead and his companions were tiring, enfeebled, and visibly exhausted, he sent Ṭāhir to al-ʿAzīz, ordering him to come quickly. When he arrived and Naṣr and his comrades saw the black banners and the black lions—ʿAbdallāh was the first to adopt them[88]—they took fright, realizing that they had lost the day. ʿAbdallāh said to al-ʿAzīz, "Now it's up to you. Fall on them!" And in no time Naṣr was routed, retreating into his fortress. ʿAbdallāh summoned the sappers and ordered the catapults, mangonels, and ladders to be brought. But when they scaled the walls, they found no one inside, because Naṣr had dug a tunnel at the rear of the fortress and escaped through it. ʿAbdallāh gave the order for his men to open the gate and enter, and they seized everything in the fortress. The good news was dispatched and ʿAbdallāh was congratulated on the victory. ʿAwf ibn Muḥallim al-Khuzāʿī declaimed this to him:

> Give thanks to your Lord for His favor on the Day of the Fortress;
> He showered on you the glory of victory and conquest.

It is a long poem.

Naṣr fled to the mountains, which did not offer him a refuge, so he came 13.46
back after he had obtained a safe conduct. ʿAbdallāh wrote to al-Maʾmūn to explain his situation, and he answered, "Grant him amnesty, on condition that he comes to tread the caliph's carpet and submits to his judgment." Naṣr agreed, so ʿAbdallāh dispatched him with Muḥammad ibn al-Ḥasan ibn Muṣʿab to appear before al-Maʾmūn.[89]

Naṣr had grown old, and when al-Maʾmūn saw him being lifted into his saddle by two servants, he said, "Naṣr needs two men to lift him!" "Yes, Commander of the Faithful," he responded, "but two hundred men can't bring him down."

٤٧،١٣ ثمّ سار عبد الله بن طاهر إلى مصر في سنة عشر وفتحها واستأمن إليه ابن السريّ وأقام بها إلى سنة إحدى عشرة وقدم على المأمون وقد أصلح البلد وجبى أمواله واستقامت أحواله. فتلقّاه أبو إسحاق والعبّاس بن[1] المأمون وقدم معه بالمتغلّبين كانوا على مصر.

٤٨،١٣ قال وقال المأمون يوماً هل تعرفون رجلاً يزيد على جميع أهل دهره نزاهة وحسن سيرة فقال عليّ بن صالح صاحب المصلّى ما أعلم أحداً له[2] مثل هذا النعت إلّا عمر ابن الخطّاب. فقال المأمون اللّهمّ غفراً لم أرد قريشاً فأمسك القوم. فقال المأمون ذاك عبد الله بن طاهر وليّته مصر وأموالها جمّة فوجد لعبيد الله بن السريّ ما تقصر عنه الصفة فما تعرّض منه لدينار ولا لدرهم ولم يخرج من مصر إلّا بعشرة آلاف دينار وثلاثة أفراس وحمارين لكنّه غرس يدي وخرّيج أدبي ولأنشدنّكم أبياتاً في صفته ثمّ أنشد

حَلِيـمٌ مَعَ ٱلتَّقْوَى شُجَـاعٌ مَعَ ٱلرَّدَى ... نَـدٍ حِينَ لَا يَنْدَى ٱلسَّحَابُ سُكُوبُ
شَدِيدُ مَنَاطِ ٱلْقَلْبِ فِي ٱلْمَوْقِفِ ٱلَّذِي ... بِـهِ لِقُـلُوبِ ٱلْعَالَمِـينَ وَجِيبُ
فَتًى هُوَ مِنْ غَـيْرِ ٱلتَّخَـلُّقِ مَـاجِـدٌ ... وَعَنْ غَـيْرِ تَأْدِيبِ ٱلرِّجَـالِ أَدِيبُ

٤٩،١٣ فأقام قبل المأمون سنة ثمّ سيّره إلى بابك وقد كان ظهر وعظمت شوكته فأقام بإزائه سنة وكان شرط على المأمون أنّه إن ظفر ببابك رجع على الباب فكان مقامه بحضرة المأمون ويختار بخلافته على خراسان من أحبّ من إخوته. فأقام بالدينور تسعة أشهر يستعدّ لقتال بابك فبينا هو كذلك إذ ورد على المأمون كتاب صاحب نيسابور يذكر أنّ المارقة أغارت على قرية منها يقال لها الحمراء على طريق الجادّة وأنّهم أحرقوا وسبوا وقتلوا النساء والأطفال. فعظم ذلك على المأمون ودعا إسحاق بن إبراهيم وهو خليفة عبد الله بن طاهر على الشرطة ويحيى بن أكثم وبعث بهما إلى عبد الله وكتب معهما

١ الأصل: ابنى. ٢ كذا في عوّاد؛ الأصل: أحداً مثل.

After that, ʿAbdallāh departed for Egypt in the year 10 [825], and when he conquered it, Ibn al-Sarī asked for amnesty. He stayed there until the year 11 [826], when he presented himself before al-Maʾmūn, having restored order to the country, collected the taxes, and established a proper administration. He was met by Abū Isḥāq al-Muʿtaṣim and al-ʿAbbās, al-Maʾmūn's son, and he brought with him those who had been in power in Egypt and had been defeated. 13.47

One day al-Maʾmūn asked, "Do you know of someone who surpasses all the men of his time in his self-control and excellent lifestyle?" ʿAlī ibn Ṣāliḥ, the Master of the Prayer Carpet,[90] volunteered, "I know no one who corresponds to this description except ʿUmar ibn al-Khaṭṭāb." Al-Maʾmūn responded, "God forgive me, I didn't mean a member of the Quraysh," and everybody fell silent. Then al-Maʾmūn said, "It's ʿAbdallāh ibn Ṭāhir. I appointed him governor of Egypt and all its revenue. He discovered Ibn al-Sarī's unimaginable shortfall, but he didn't accept a single dinar or dirham from him, and when he left, he took ten thousand dinars, three horses, and two donkeys, no more. He's a plant I nurtured and the product of my education. I'll recite you some verses describing him: 13.48

> Judicious and pious, courageous, openhanded,
> showering bounty when clouds withhold their rain,
> stouthearted where wise men feel fear,
> a champion, glorious without pretense,
> refined without need of any instruction."

ʿAbdallāh spent a year in attendance on al-Maʾmūn, and then the caliph sent him to combat Bābak, who had raised a rebellion and become very powerful. He campaigned against him for a year. He had stipulated to al-Maʾmūn that if he vanquished the rebel, he would return to the palace and remain a member of al-Maʾmūn's entourage, with the ability to choose whichever brother he wanted to deputize for him in Khurasan. He spent nine months in Dīnawār in preparation for the campaign against Bābak, and while he was there al-Maʾmūn received a letter from the governor of Nīshāpūr with the news that the heretics[91] had attacked a village called al-Ḥamrāʾ on the main Khurasan road, burning and killing, and taking the women and children prisoner. Al-Maʾmūn was very worried, and he summoned Isḥāq ibn Ibrāhīm, ʿAbdallāh ibn Ṭāhir's 13.49

كتاباً بخطّه إلى عبد الله يُقسم عليه أن يحوّل مضربه من وجه بابك إلى وجه خراسان فإنّ خراسان أهمّ من المملكة كلّها بعد الحضرة وأن يشير عليه بمن يبعث به إلى بابك. فامتثل ما أمره به وأشار بعليّ بن هشام وكاتب من بخراسان بما أحبّ وقدّم أخاه محمّد بن طاهر على مقدّمته ووافاه عليّ بن هشام فوافقه على الطريق في محاربة بابك. ومضى لوجهه إلى خراسان حتّى وافى نيسابور وكتب إلى المأمون أنّ أمير المؤمنين أنهضني إلى هذا الثغر بسبب ما قد غلب عليه من أمر الحمراء وما أحدثه المارقة بها وأنّي وافيت بنيسابور فوجدت ما حولها عشّ المارقة ووجدتها أهمّ الكور والمهمّ أبدأ وأرى. قال فأعجب المأمون من الكتاب بهذه اللفظة ولم يزل الكتّاب يتذاكرونها بينهم. وكان مقامه بخراسان إلى أن توفّي بها خمس عشرة سنة.

٥٠.١٣ وذكر ابن جدّان عن الجلوديّ قال جلس عبد الله يوماً بخراسان أنصف فيه من وجوه القوّاد وأمراء الأجناد وضرب الأعناق وقطع الأيدي والأرجل وعقد العقود فلمّا زالت الشمس دخل داره. قال الجلوديّ وكنت أقرب من قلبه وأدلّ عليه فتلقّاه الخدم فأخذ هذا قباه وأخذ آخر خفّه وآخر رانه وبقي في غلالة وسراويل فرفع الغلالة على كتفه وجعل يقول

ٱلنَّشْـرُ مِسْكٌ وَٱلْوُجُوهُ دَنَا   نِيرُ وَأَطْرَافُ ٱلْبَنَانِ عَنَمْ

قال فاغتظت عليه ونزعت ثوبه عن عاتقه ورددته إلى حاله وقلت له تجلس اليوم مجلس الإسكندر ودارا بن دارا وتفعل الساعة فعل علّويه ومخارق. قال فنظر إليّ نظر الجمل الصؤول وردّ ثوبه على كتفه وقال

لَا بُدَّ لِلنَّفْسِ إِذْ كَانَتْ مُصَرَّفَةً   إِلَى ٱلتَّنَقُّلِ مِنْ حَالٍ إِلَى حَالِ

deputy in command of the police, and Yaḥyā ibn Aktham, dispatching them to ʿAbdallāh with a letter written in his own hand begging him to change his route from Bābak to Khurasan, for apart from the caliphal palace Khurasan was the most important place in the empire. He asked him to advise him whom to send to fight Bābak. ʿAbdallāh obeyed, and suggested ʿAlī ibn Hishām. He exchanged letters with the officials in Khurasan about his policy there. He put his brother Muḥammad in charge of the advance troops, and when ʿAlī ibn Hishām joined him they agreed on how to fight Bābak. Then he set off for Khurasan. From Nīshāpūr, he wrote to al-Maʾmūn: "The Commander of the Faithful sent me to this frontier post because of his great concern about al-Ḥamrāʾ and what the rebels did there. I arrived in Nīshāpūr and found the surrounding countryside a hotbed of rebels, with Nīshāpūr a real hornet's nest. The important thing now is to make a start and see what happens." Al-Maʾmūn appreciated his use of this expression, and the secretaries often quoted it among themselves. ʿAbdallāh spent fifteen years in Khurasan, until he died there.

Ibn Jaddān told the following on the authority of al-Jallūdī: While ʿAbdallāh was in Khurasan, one day he dispensed justice for his chief commanders and army captains, ordering executions and the amputation of hands and feet, and concluding contracts. When the sun went down, he entered his palace—al-Jallūdī added, "I was very close to his heart and familiar with him"—and was met by his servants; one took his cloak, another his slippers, and a third his leggings. He was left in his tunic and drawers. He hitched the tunic up on his shoulder and started to repeat: 13.50

Women's breath
  smells of musk,
Faces are golden coins,
  fingertips jujubes.

I lost my temper with him, and pulled down his tunic and straightened it, saying, "You've been sitting all day like Alexander and Darius the son of Darius, and now you're behaving like ʿAllūya and Mukhāriq." He gave me a look like a rabid camel, hitched up his tunic again, and said:

When a person is put under pressure,
  he must change from one state to another.[92]

٥١،١٣ ولمّا مات المأمون أقرّ المعتصم عبد الله بن طاهر على خراسان وإسحاق بن إبراهيم على خلافته ببغداد وكان سيّئ الرأي فيه فكتب إليه أمّا بعد عافانا الله معاً فقد كانت في نفسي عليك حزازات غيّرها بقاء الانتقام عليك لك وقد بقيت منها هنات أخاف منها عليك فلا تقدم وحسبك ممّا أنا منطوٍ عليه لك إظهاري إيّاك ما في ضميري والسلام.

٥٢،١٣ قال الفضل بن مروان ذكر المعتصم يوماً عبد الله بن طاهر فنال منه وتابعته الجماعة ووصفوه بسوء الطاعة وأنا حاضر فقمت وقلت اكتب له في القدوم فإنّه لا يمسي حتّى يشخص فقال اجلس واكتب إليه بالخبر. فكتب إلى المعتصم كتاباً أنفذه درج كتابي إليه وسألني أن أوصله من يدي إلى يده ففعلت. فقرأه المعتصم وأقبل يسألني عن الحرف بعد الحرف فأفتح عليه فإذا هو قد كتب يحلف أنّ الكتاب لو ورد عليه بالشخوص لما أمسى حتّى يشخص.

٥٣،١٣ قال أبو العميثل دخلت على عبد الله بن طاهر فقال إنّك لنازح الأدؤر قليلاً ما ترى ومدّ يده إليّ فقبّلتها فقال ما عققتني به أكثر ممّا بررتني. قلت بماذا قال بخشونة شاربك. قلت إنّ شوك القنفذ لا يضرّ برثن الأسد. قال هذا والله أحبّ إليّ من مدح مائة قافية وأمر لي بعشرة آلاف درهم.

٥٤،١٣ وكانت وفاة عبد الله بن طاهر في سنة ثلاثين ومائتين في أيّام الواثق. وذكر أحمد ابن أبي دؤاد أنّ محمّد بن عبد الملك أشار على الواثق لمّا ورد الخبر بوفاة عبد الله بن طاهر أن يخرج إسحاق بن إبراهيم بن مصعب إلى خراسان مكان عبد الله فأجابه إلى ذلك وأمره أن يكتب كتبه وينظر في تجهيزه ووجّه إليّ الواثق فحضرت الدار فرأيت محمّد بن عبد الملك وإسحاق بن إبراهيم جالسين ومحمّد يكتب الكتاب فلمّا رآني أقلبه فتفاءلت أنّ الذي هما فيه سينقلب. ودخلت إلى الواثق فذكر لي خبر وفاة عبد الله

When al-Ma'mūn died, al-Muʿtaṣim confirmed ʿAbdallāh ibn Ṭāhir as governor of Khurasan and Isḥāq ibn Ibrāhīm as his deputy in Baghdad, but he had a low opinion of ʿAbdallāh. He wrote to him: "Now may God forgive us both. I used to be overcome by waves of anger toward you, but your revenging yourself upon yourself has changed that. What I feel now is petty resentment, but I fear for you because of it, so do not come to court. Where my attitude to you is concerned, be content that I have revealed my feelings.[93] Farewell." 13.51

Al-Faḍl ibn Marwān related: Al-Muʿtaṣim one day slandered ʿAbdallāh ibn Ṭāhir, and the rest of the company followed suit, describing him as disloyal. I was there, and I got up and said, "Send him a letter summoning him to Baghdad. When he gets it, he'll set off the same day." Al-Muʿtaṣim said, "Sit down and write to him about our exchange." ʿAbdallāh wrote back a letter to al-Muʿtaṣim, which he folded into the letter I had sent him, asking me to put it into the caliph's hand, which I did. Al-Muʿtaṣim read it and asked me what it meant, word by word, and I explained it. As it turned out, ʿAbdallāh had sworn in his letter that if a letter containing a summons had arrived, he would have set out before evening. 13.52

Abū l-ʿUmaythil recalled: I entered ʿAbdallāh ibn Ṭāhir's audience hall and he said, "You're somewhat distant, don't you think?" He stretched out his hand to me and I kissed it. He remarked, "You've shown me more disobedience than filial piety." "How's that?" I asked. "With the roughness of your mustache." I responded, "The hedgehog's prickles can't harm the lion's claws." "I like this better than the praise of a hundred poems," he said, and he ordered that I be given ten thousand dirhams. 13.53

ʿAbdallāh ibn Ṭāhir died in the year 230 [844–45] in the reign of al-Wāthiq. 13.54

Aḥmad ibn Abī Du'ād remembered: When the news of ʿAbdallāh's death arrived, Muḥammad ibn ʿAbd al-Malik advised al-Wāthiq to dispatch Isḥāq ibn Ibrāhīm ibn Muṣʿab to Khurasan in his stead. Al-Wāthiq accepted the suggestion, ordering him to draw up the documents and organize his equipment. Al-Wāthiq then summoned me, and when I entered the palace, I saw Muḥammad ibn ʿAbd al-Malik and Isḥāq ibn Ibrāhīm sitting together, with Muḥammad writing the letter of appointment. When he saw me, he turned it over, and I saw that as an omen that their plan would be overturned. I entered al-Wāthiq's presence and

ابن طاهر وأنّه قد عمل على إخراج إسحاق إلى خراسان وأن يضمّ إليه خمسة آلاف رجل من الجند ويطلق أرزاقهم وأن يطلق لإسحاق خمسة آلاف ألف درهم معونة فقلت يا أمير المؤمنين إسحاق رهينة القوم عندك فإن أخرجته لم يكن في يدك من القوم شيء والجند فأنت محتاج إلى الزيادة فيهم فكيف تفرّقهم لا سيّما مع ما تنفق فيهم وإخراج هذه الأموال لا وجه له. وهاهنا ما هو خير من ذلك قال وما هو قلت طومار بدرهمين تكتب فيه إلى طاهر بن عبد الله بن طاهر بالتعزية عن أبيه وبتجديد الولاية له وتربح ما تنفقه وتكون قد أتممت الصنيعة عند عبد الله وولده وأحسنت الخلافة فيهم. فقال الصواب ما قلت. وأمر محمّد بن عبد الملك بذلك والإضراب عمّا كان عمل عليه. كانت مدّة حياة عبد الله بن طاهر ثمانياً وأربعين سنة.

١٣،٥٥ وأمّا طاهر بن الحسين فكان من سروات الناس وذوي الرأي والبأس. سمّاه المأمون ذي اليمينين فكان يكتب ويكاتب بها. وسأل المعتصم جماعة من خواصّه عن معنى تسمية طاهر بذي اليمينين فلم يعرفوه فقال محمّد بن عبد الملك معناه ذو الاستحقاقين استحقاق بالجدّة ودنوّ في الدولة وكان أحد النقباء واستحقاق ما له في دولة المأمون. قال الله تعالى ﴿لَأَخَذْنَا مِنْهُ بِٱلْيَمِينِ﴾ أي بالاستحقاق. وقال الشاعر

إِذَا مَا رَايَةٌ رُفِعَتْ لِمَجْدٍ تَلَقَّاهَا عَرَابَةُ بِٱلْيَمِينِ

١٣،٥٦ ذكر جبهان الشيعيّ قال كان الحسين بن مصعب جيّد الرأي حسن الإصابة بالظنّ. قال كنت يوماً في دار عليّ بن عيسى بن ماهان وقد أمر بطاهر بن الحسين فشُدّ بحبل إلى سارية فقال لي الحسين أما ترى هذا المشدود يعني ابنه ليقتلنّ صاحب هذا القصر. فجرى هذا القول عندي مجرى الهزل ثمّ كان من أمرهما ما كان فعجبت من

he told me the news of ʿAbdallāh ibn Ṭāhir's death, adding that he had taken steps to have Isḥāq sent to Khurasan, accompanied by five thousand soldiers, with their pay assured and Isḥāq to receive five million dirhams' worth of support. I exclaimed, "Commander of the Faithful, Isḥāq guarantees the people's submission to you. If you send him away, you'll have no power over them. You need to increase the army, so how can you divide it, especially with what you'll spend on it? There's no sense in paying out these sums. I have a better suggestion." "What is it?" he asked. "Take a roll of parchment costing two dirhams and use it to write to Ṭāhir ibn ʿAbdallāh ibn Ṭāhir, offering your condolences on his father's death and transferring the governorship to him. You'll get a return on what you spend, and you'll have bestowed the utmost favor on ʿAbdallāh and his descendants and improved the caliphate's standing with them." "What you've said is quite right," al-Wāthiq said, and he ordered Muḥammad ibn ʿAbd al-Malik to carry it out and stop what he was working on.

ʿAbdallāh lived forty-eight years.

Ṭāhir ibn al-Ḥusayn was outstanding, a man of judgment and courage. 13.55
Al-Ma'mūn called him "he of the two right hands," and he signed his letters with this epithet and was addressed thus as well. Al-Muʿtaṣim asked a group of his close associates why Ṭāhir was called "he of the two right hands," and they did not know the reason. Muḥammad ibn ʿAbd al-Malik said, "It means 'possessing two merits, one of pursuing a right policy and fidelity to the Abbasid cause'"—he was one of its principal proselytizers—"'and the other of having helped al-Ma'mūn to establish himself as caliph.' Almighty God has said, «We would have seized him by the right hand»[94]—that is, by his merit. And as the poet said:

> If a standard was raised in glory,
> ʿArābah seized it
> with the might of his right hand."[95]

A recollection of Jabhān the Shiʿi: Al-Ḥusayn ibn Muṣʿab had good judgment 13.56
and his suppositions turned out correct. I was in ʿAlī ibn ʿĪsā ibn Māhān's palace one day when he had ordered Ṭāhir ibn al-Ḥusayn to be tied up with a rope to a pole. Al-Ḥusayn said to me, "Take a look at this fellow tied up here. He'll surely kill the owner of this palace." I took it to be a joke, but then

قول الحسين. قال ولمّا أنفذ الأمين عليّ بن عيسى بن ماهان في الجيوش إلى خراسان لأخذ المأمون وإنفاذه إليه عقد المأمون لطاهر بن الحسين على أربعة آلاف ووجّهه إلى الريّ لحرب عليّ بن عيسى فكتب إليه عليّ بن عيسى أن يقيم له الميرة ولم يكن يظنّ أنّه يحاربه.

٥٧،١٣ قال عبيد الله بن عبد الله بن طاهر حدّثني عبد الرحمٰن بن فهم عن عمّه قال شخصت أريد المأمون فدفعت إلى عسكر طاهر يوم الوقعة فرأيته يعبئ الصفوف ويذهب ويجيء وبيده كسر من خبز ومع غلام له كوز من رصاص فيه ماء فقلت أيّها الأمير ليس هذا وقت أكل. قال معذرة إليك وإلى من لا يعرف خبري. ما دخل جوفي طعام مذ ثلاث لشغلي بهذا الأمر. وتخوّفت أن أحتاج إلى نفسي فتخونني في هذا الوقت ففعلت ما رأيت. فقلت الأمير أخبر بما يعاني.

٥٨،١٣ قال عبيد الله وحدّثني جماعة من شيوخنا قال لمّا أقبل جيش عليّ كان صاحب علمهم حاتم الطائيّ وكان قد ضُرب ثمانمائة حتّى ذهب لحم أَلْيَتيه وكان عظيم الخلق شديد البأس وكان له أربعة غلمان يحملونه حتّى يقعد في سرجه فإذا استوى في سرجه عُدّ بألف فارس.

قال طاهر فجعلته وكدي وحملت عليه فلمّا دنوت منه إذا به مكفّرًا في الحديد لا تخلص إليه الضربة فرأيت أمرًا هالني فقلت ليس إلّا أن أضربه على البيضة فإن عمل السيف فيها وإلّا فهو التلف. فجمعت يديَّ ثمّ ضربته على رأسه فقددت البيضة والرأس حتّى نشب السيف بين ثناياه.

٥٩،١٣ قال فلمّا قُتل حاتم اضطّرب القوم وكان عليّ بن عيسى راكبًا في قبّة فنزل عنها وقُدم إليه شهريّ أصدأ أرجل ليركبه فطعنه داود سياه قبل أن يتمكّن في سرجه فقتله وهو لا يعرفه وصار إلى طاهر فقال قد قتلت قاضي العسكر ثمّ أتى برأسه فنادى

things happened between them the way they did, and I was amazed at what al-Ḥusayn had said.

When al-Amīn sent ʿAlī ibn ʿĪsā ibn Māhān with the armies to Khurasan to capture al-Maʾmūn and dispatch him to him, al-Maʾmūn gave Ṭāhir ibn al-Ḥusayn command over four thousand men and sent him to Rayy to fight ʿAlī. ʿAlī had written to Ṭāhir demanding he provide supplies; he was not expecting Ṭāhir to fight him.

ʿUbaydallāh ibn ʿAbdallāh ibn Ṭāhir got this account from ʿAbd al-Raḥmān ibn Fahm, who had it from his uncle: I had set out to go to al-Maʾmūn and I pushed on till I reached Ṭāhir's camp. It was the day of the battle, and I saw him marshaling the troops and going back and forth with a piece of bread in his hand, while a servant of his was holding a tin jug of water. I said, "Prince, this is not a time to eat." "I beg your pardon," he said, "and the pardon of those who don't know the state I'm in. For three days I haven't eaten anything because I've been so consumed with this business. I was afraid my strength would fail me when I needed it most, so I'm doing what you see." I responded, "The prince knows best what he is going through." 13.57

ʿUbaydallāh also cited elderly members of the family: When ʿAlī's army advanced, the standard-bearer was Ḥātim al-Ṭāʾī.[96] He had suffered a flogging of eight hundred lashes and so he had no flesh left on his buttocks. He was corpulent but very brave, so he had four servants who lifted him into the saddle, and when he was sitting firmly, he was worth a thousand horsemen. 13.58

Ṭāhir said, "I set my sights on him and charged. Up close, I saw he was covered in chain mail and there was no way a blow could reach him. It was a terrifying sight. I thought, 'The only thing is to strike him on the helmet. Either the sword cuts through it, or it's the end of me.' I clasped my hands round the sword and struck him on the crown, splitting the helmet and his head, and the sword stuck in his front teeth."

The army was alarmed by the killing of Ḥātim. ʿAlī ibn ʿĪsā had been riding in a palanquin, but he came down and a fine bay with a white sock was brought up for him to ride. Before he was settled in the saddle, Dāwud Siyāh struck him and killed him, without knowing who he was. He went to Ṭāhir and said, "I've killed the army's judge," but then ʿAlī's head was brought and Ṭāhir's herald proclaimed, "Anyone who takes anything can keep it, and those who 13.59

منادي طاهر من أخذ شيئاً فهو له وبرئت الذمّة ممّن سفك الدماء. وكتب إلى المأمون وذي الرياستين كتابي ورأس عليّ بن عيسى بين يديّ وخاتمه في إصبعي والسلام. ثمّ سار طاهر إلى بغداد فكان من أمره ما كان.

١٣،٦٠ قال وكان المأمون عند دخوله إلى بغداد قد سخط على محمّد بن العبّاس الطوسيّ فاستعاذ بطاهر بن الحسين وكان له صديقاً وسأله سؤال المأمون في الصفح عنه فدخل طاهر إلى المأمون وهو يشرب فسقاه رطلاً وأمره بالجلوس فقال ليس لصاحب الشرط أن يجلس بين يدي سيّده. فقال المأمون ذاك في مجلس العامّة فأمّا في مجلس الخاصّة فالجلوس له مطلق. ثمّ سقاه رطلين آخرين وتغرغرت عيناه فقال له طاهر لِمَ تبكي[1] يا أمير المؤمنين لا أبكى الله عينيك وقد دانت لك البلاد وأذعن لك العباد وصرت إلى المحبّة في كلّ أمورك. فقال لأمر في ذكره ذلّ وفي ستره حزن وما يخلو أحد من شجو فتكلّمْ بحاجة إن كانت لك. فقال يا أمير المؤمنين محمّد بن أبي العبّاس فأقله وارضَ عنه. قال قد رضيت عنه وأمرت بصلته وردّ مرتبته ولولا أنّه ليس من أهل الأنس لأحضرته.

١٣،٦١ فشكر ذلك ودعا للمأمون وانصرف وقد شغل قلبه بكاؤه. فقال لمروان بن جبغويه كاتبه إنّ للكتّاب لطافة وأهل خراسان يتعصّب بعضهم لبعض فخذ معك ثلاث مائة ألف درهم فأعطِ الحسين الخادم مائتي ألف وكاتبه محمّد بن هارون مائة ألف وتسأله أن يسأل أمير المؤمنين لِمَ بكى. ففعل ذلك فلمّا خلا الحسين بالمأمون من غد وطابت نفسه سأله عن سبب بكائه. فقال له ولِمَ سألت عن ذلك فقال لغمّي به وتنغّصي من أجله. فقال هو شيء إن خرج من رأسك قتلتك. فقال يا سيّدي ومتى أخرجت سرًّا فقال لمّا رأيت طاهراً ذكرت أخي وما ناله من الذلّة فخنقتني العبرة فاسترحت إلى الإفاضة ولن يفوت طاهراً منّي ما يكره.

١٣،٦٢ فأخبر محمّد بن هارون طاهراً بذلك فركب طاهر إلى أحمد بن أبي خالد وهو الوزير فقال إنّ المعروف عندي غير ضائع والثناء منّي ليس برخيص فغيّبني عن عين

[1] الأصل: تبك.

shed blood will not be held responsible." Ṭāhir wrote to al-Ma'mūn and Dhū al-Riyāsatayn:[97] "I'm writing to you with ʿAlī's head in front of me and his ring on my finger. Farewell." Then Ṭāhir marched to Baghdad and his subsequent history is well known.

At the time when al-Ma'mūn entered Baghdad he was incensed against Muḥammad ibn Abī l-ʿAbbās al-Ṭūsī. Muḥammad turned to Ṭāhir, who was a friend of his, for help, asking him to request a pardon from al-Ma'mūn. When Ṭāhir went to see al-Ma'mūn he was drinking, and he poured Ṭāhir a measure and told him to take a seat. Ṭāhir objected, "It's not for the chief of police to sit in his master's presence." Al-Ma'mūn replied, "That's in a public gathering, but in private he's free to sit." He poured him two more measures, and his eyes filled with tears. Ṭāhir asked, "Why are you weeping, Commander of the Faithful? May God never give you cause to weep. The country has submitted to you, the servants have been subjugated, and you have achieved what you wanted in all your affairs." Al-Ma'mūn said, "Because of something that is humiliating to talk about and distressing to hide. Everyone knows some sorrow. Mention a request, if you have one." "Commander of the Faithful, Muḥammad ibn Abī l-ʿAbbās is in the wrong. Pardon him and restore him to your favor." "He's pardoned. I'm giving him a gift and reinstating him to his rank. I'd summon him if he were good company." 13.60

Ṭāhir thanked al-Ma'mūn, invoked God's blessings, and left, his mind occupied with the caliph's weeping. He said to his secretary, Marwān ibn Jabghūyah, "Secretaries know how to be subtle. And there's a clannishness among the Khurasanis. Take three hundred thousand dirhams and give Ḥusayn the Eunuch two hundred thousand and his secretary Muḥammad ibn Hārūn one hundred thousand, and tell Ḥusayn to ask the Commander of the Faithful why he wept." Marwān carried out the order and the next day, when Ḥusayn was with al-Ma'mūn and the caliph was in a good mood, he asked him why he had wept. Al-Ma'mūn said, "Why do you ask?" "Because I'm sad and upset about it." "If you breathe a word of it, I'll kill you." Ḥusayn protested, "Sire, when have I ever revealed a secret?" "When I saw Ṭāhir, I remembered my brother and the humiliation that befell him, and I was choked with tears. But I relaxed and let them flow. Sooner or later I'll do something horrible to Ṭāhir." 13.61

Muḥammad ibn Hārūn passed the information on to Ṭāhir, who rode off to see Aḥmad ibn Abī Khālid, the vizier. "No favor done me is forgotten," he 13.62

أمير المؤمنين. فقال له بكّر إليّ غداً فإنّي سأفعل. فغدا عليه وغدا ابن أبي خالد على المأمون فلمّا وصل إليه قال إنّي ما نمت البارحة. قال ولِمَ ويحك قال لأنّك ولّيت غسّان بن عبّاد خراسان وهو ومَن معه أكلة رأس فأخاف أن يخرج عليه خارجيّ فيصطلمه قال لقد فكّرت فيما فكّرت فيه فمن ترى. قال طاهر بن الحسين. قال يا أحمد هو والله خالع فلم يزل به حتّى أجابه ودعا بطاهر من ساعته فعقد له وشخص من يومه فنزل بستان خليل بن هشام وذلك يوم الجمعة لليلة بقيت من ذي القعدة سنة خمس ومائتين.

قال فلمّا حصل طاهر بن الحسين بخراسان وكانت الشراة قد كثرت هناك واستبدّ أمرهم فكتب إليه المأمون كتباً كثيرة تحثّه على مناهضتهم وينكر عليه تضجّعه في أمرهم فكتب طاهر يذكر غلظ أمرهم وقوّة شوكتهم وأنّه يحتاج إلى زيادة عدّة في رجاله ليلقاهم فأحفظ ذلك المأمون فكتب إليه يغلظ له ويقول لهممت أن أردّك إلى حيث أبيك. ٦٣،١٣

فذكر كلثوم بن ثابت بن أبي سعد وكان يتقلّد البريد على طاهر بن الحسين بخراسان أنّه جلس بالقرب من المنبر لمّا تبيّن ما حدث من طاهر عند ورود ما ورد عليه. فخطب فلمّا بلغ إلى ذكر الخليفة قال اللّهمّ أصلح أمّة محمّد بما أصلحت به أولياءك واكفها مؤونة من بغى فيها وحشد عليها بلمّ الشعث وحقن الدماء وصلاح ذات البين. فعلمت أنّي أوّل مقتول لأنّي لم أكن أقدر على ستر الخبر ولم يكن يستتر كتابي عن طاهر فحملت نفسي على أن كتبت فأتى الله من صنعه بقرب وفاة طاهر بما لم أحتسبه. ٦٤،١٣

ولمّا ورد الخبر على المأمون بذلك شقّ عليه ودعا أحمد بن أبي خالد وقال له قد كنت ٦٥،١٣
قلت لك في طاهر لمّا أشرت بتقليده خراسان ما كنت أعلم به فضمّنت ما يكون وبالله

said to him, "and my praise does not come cheaply. Get me out of the Commander of the Faithful's sight." "Come to me tomorrow morning early. I'll take care of it."

The next day Aḥmad ibn Abī Khālid went to see al-Ma'mūn, and when in his presence he said, "I couldn't sleep last night." "Why on earth not?" "Because you have appointed Ghassān ibn ʿAbbād governor of Khurasan. He and his people are easygoing, and I'm afraid that a Kharijite will revolt against him and overthrow him." Al-Ma'mūn responded, "You've had the same idea I've had. Who would be suitable?" "Ṭāhir ibn al-Ḥusayn." "But Aḥmad, he'll throw off his allegiance, by God." Aḥmad kept on at al-Ma'mūn until he secured his agreement. He summoned Tāhir immediately and gave him the letter of appointment. Ṭāhir left straightaway and established a temporary camp in Khalīl ibn Hishām's garden. It was Friday,[98] the twenty-ninth of Dhu'l-Qadah in the year 205 [May 6, 821].

When Ṭāhir ibn al-Ḥusayn arrived in Khurasan, the Kharijites had acquired 13.63
many followers there and were a force to be reckoned with. Al-Ma'mūn wrote him many letters urging him to fight them and denouncing his lack of action against them. Ṭāhir replied, pointing out their fierceness and bravery, and saying that he needed to expand his army to fight them. That angered al-Ma'mūn, who wrote back with insults and threats, saying, "I'm thinking of sending you to join your father."

Kulthūm ibn Thābit ibn Abī Saʿd, who headed the postal service in Khurasan 13.64
under Ṭāhir, told how he was sitting near the pulpit when it emerged that Ṭāhir had taken the decision he'd taken, after he had received this message from al-Ma'mūn. Ṭāhir delivered the Friday sermon, and when he came to the point of mentioning the caliph he said, "O God, grant Muḥammad's community prosperity, as You have done to those close to You, and preserve it from the harm caused by those who act tyrannically toward it and mobilize force against it. Reunite it, save it from bloodshed, and heal the discord within it."[99] Kulthūm said, "I knew I would be the first to be killed, because I couldn't keep quiet about this sermon, and couldn't keep my actions from Ṭāhir. I forced myself to write, but God granted me an unexpected favor when Ṭāhir died soon after."

Al-Ma'mūn was disturbed by the news of the sermon. He summoned 13.65
Aḥmad ibn Abī Khālid and said, "When you advised me to appoint Ṭāhir

لئن لم تتلطّف لإصلاح أمره كما كنت لفساده[١] لأضربنّ عنقك. فأهدى ابن أبي خالد إلى طاهر هدايا وألطافاً وفيها كامخ أبيض مسموم لعلمه بإعجابه به فلمّا وصلت الهدايا إلى طاهر أكل من الكامخ بتدارج مشويّة فمات بعد يومين.

وكان مولد طاهر بن الحسين في المحرّم سنة تسع وخمسين ومائة ووفاته سنة سبع ومائتين. ٦٦،١٣

ولمّا مات شغب الجند بخراسان وانتهبوا خزائن طاهر فقلّد المأمون مكانه طلحة ابنه ووجّه بأحمد بن أبي خالد إلى خراسان ليعاونه في إصلاح الأمر فصار إلى هناك وأصلح الأمور وسكّن اضطرابها ووجّه إليه طلحة ثلاثة آلاف ألف درهم وعروضاً بألفي ألف درهم ووهب لإبراهيم بن العبّاس كاتبه خمسة آلاف درهم.

١ الأصل: فساده.

governor of Khurasan I told you what I knew about him, and you vouched for his actions. By God, I'll have you beheaded if you don't find a way to make sure that he acts properly, just as you enabled him to spread iniquity." Then Ibn Abī Khālid sent presents and different kinds of gifts to Ṭāhir, including a certain white vinegar sauce he was very fond of. It was poisoned, and when he ate it as an accompaniment to roasted pheasant, he died two days later.[100]

Ṭāhir ibn al-Ḥusayn was born in the year 159 [775–76] and he died in the year 13.66
207 [822–23].

When Ṭāhir died, the soldiers went on the rampage and plundered his treasury. Al-Ma'mūn appointed his son Ṭalḥah to succeed him and sent Aḥmad ibn Abī Khālid to Khurasan to help him restore order. On his arrival, Aḥmad restored order and put down the disturbance. Thereupon Ṭalḥah sent him three million dirhams and other goods worth two million dirhams, and he gave his secretary, Ibrāhīm ibn al-ʿAbbās, five thousand dirhams.

ديـر السوسيّ

١،١٤ وهـذا الدير لطيف على شاطئ دجلة بقادسيّة سرّ من رأى وبين القادسيّة وسرّ من رأى أربعة فراسخ والمطيرة بينهما وهذه النواحي كلّها متنزّهات وبساتين وكروم. والناس يقصدون هذا الدير ويشربون في بساتينه وهو من مواطن السرور ومواضع القصف واللعب. ولابن المعتزّ فيه

يَا لَيَالِيَّ بِٱلْمَطِيرَةِ وَٱلْكَرْ خِ وَدَيْرِ ٱلسُّوسِيِّ بِٱللهِ عُودِي
كُنْتِ عِنْدِي أُنْمُوذَجَاتٍ مِنَ ٱلْجَنَّـةِ لٰكِنَّهَا بِغَيْرِ خُلُودِ

٢،١٤ والقادسيّة من أحسن المواضع وأنزهها وهي من معادن الشراب ومناخات المتطرّبين جامعة لما يطلب أهل البطالة والخسارة. وبالقادسيّة بنى المتوكّل قصره المعروف ببزكوارا ولمّا فرغ من بنائه وهبه لابنه المعتزّ وجعل إعذاره فيه وكان من أحسن أبنية المتوكّل وأجلّها وبلغت النفقة عليه عشرين ألف ألف درهم.

٣،١٤ قال ولمّا صحّ عزمه على إعذار أبي عبد الله المعتزّ أمر الفتح بن خاقان بالتأهّب له وأن يلتمس في خزائن الفرش بساطاً للإيوان في عرضه وطوله وكان طوله مائة ذراع وعرضه خمسين ذراعاً فلم يوجد إلّا فيما قبض عن بني أميّة فإنّه وجد في أمتعة هشام ابن عبد الملك على طول الإيوان وعرضه وكان بساطاً ابريسمياً غرز مذهّب مفروز مبطّن.[1] فلمّا رآه المتوكّل أُعجب به وأراد أن يعرف قيمته فجمع عليه التجّار وذكر أنّه قوّم على أوسط القيم عشرة آلاف دينار فبُسط في الإيوان. وبسط للخليفة في صدر

١ الأصل: (طول البساط مائة ذراع وعرضه ٥٠) وردت في الهامش.

Al-Sūsī's Monastery[101]

This is a pleasant monastery on the banks of the Tigris at Qādisiyyah, not far from Samarra. The two places are more than twelve miles (twenty kilometers) apart, and between them lies Maṭīrah. The whole area is one of parkland, orchards, and vineyards. People visit the monastery and drink in its grounds. It is a festive place, the scene of merrymaking and games. Ibn al-Muʿtazz mentions it in a couplet: 14.1

Nights at Maṭīrah and Karkh,
Nights at al-Sūsī's Monastery,
Come back!
You were like glimpses of Paradise,
But a paradise imprisoned in time.

Qādisiyyah is a fine, healthy place, a center of wine production and a venue for music lovers. In fact, it offers everything loafers and wastrels could want. It is where al-Mutawakkil built his palace called Barkuwārā. When he had finished building it, he gave it to his son al-Muʿtazz and organized his circumcision banquet there. It was one of the most beautiful and impressive of al-Mutawakkil's buildings, and it cost twenty million dirhams. 14.2

When al-Mutawakkil decided to celebrate Abū ʿAbdallāh al-Muʿtazz's circumcision[102] with a banquet,[103] he ordered al-Fatḥ ibn Khāqān to take care of the preparations, including looking in the furniture treasury for a carpet that would fit the width and breadth of the ceremonial hall, which measured fifty by one hundred cubits. No such carpet could be found except among the belongings confiscated from the Umayyads, where one of Hishām ibn ʿAbd al-Malik's carpets had the right dimensions. It was of floss silk woven with gold thread, with fringed borders and a lining. Al-Mutawakkil was amazed at the sight of it and wanted to know its value. He summoned the merchants to view it, and, so it is said, it was valued at around ten thousand dinars.[104] It was spread out in the ceremonial hall, and a throne was set up for the caliph in the place of honor. In front of it were placed four thousand gold stands studded with precious stones 14.3

الإيوان سرير ومدّ بين يديه أربعة آلاف مرفع ذهب مرصّعة بالجوهر فيها تماثيل العنبر والندّ والكافور وجُعلت بساطاً ممدوداً.

٤،١٤ وتغدّى المتوكّل والناس وجلس على السرير وأحضر الأمراء والقوّاد والندماء فأُجلسوا على مراتبهم وجعل بين صوانيهم والسماط فرجة وجاء الفرّاشون بزبل قد غشيت بأدم مملوءة دنانير ودراهم نصفين فصبّت في تلك الفرج حتّى ارتفعت. وقام الغلمان فوقها وأمروا الناس عن الخليفة بالشرب وأن ينتقل كلّ من يشرب بثلاث حفنات ما حملت يداه من ذلك المال فكان إذا نقل الواحد منهم ما اجتمع في كمّه أخرجه إلى غلمانه فدفعه إليهم وعاد إلى مجلسه وكلّما فرغ موضع أتى الفرّاشون بما يملؤونه حتّى يعود الى حاله. وخلع على سائر من حضر ثلاث خلع كلّ واحد وحُملوا عند انصرافهم على الأفراس والشهاريّ وأعتق المتوكّل عن المعتزّ ألف عبد وأمر لكلّ واحد منهم بمائة درهم وثلاثة أثواب.

٥،١٤ وكان في صحن الدار بين يدي الإيوان أربعمائة بُلّية عليهنّ أنواع الثياب وبين يديهنّ ألف نبيجة[1] خيزران فيها أنواع الفواكه من الأترج والنارنج على قلّته كان في ذلك الوقت والتفّاح الشاميّ والليمون[2] وخمسة آلاف باقة نرجس وعشرة آلاف باقة بنفسج وتقدّم إلى الفتح بأن ينثر على البلّيات وخدم الدار والحاشية ما كان أعدّه لهم وهو عشرون ألف ألف درهم فلم يقدم أحد على التقاط شيء فأخذ الفتح درهماً فأكبّت الجماعة على المال فنُهب. وكانت قبيحة قد تقدّمت بأن تضرب دراهم عليها بركة من الله لإعذار أبي عبد الله المعتزّ بالله فضُرب لها ألف ألف درهم نُثرت على المزيّن ومَن في حيّزه والغلمان والشاكريّة وقهارمة الدار والخدم الخاصّة من البيضان والسودان.

٦،١٤ وكان ممّن حضر المجلس ذلك اليوم محمّد المنتصر[3] وأبو أحمد وأبو سليمان ابنا الرشيد وأحمد والعبّاس ابنا المعتصم وموسى بن المأمون وابنا حمدون النديم وأحمد بن أبي رؤيم والحسين بن الضحّاك وعليّ بن الجهم وعليّ بن المنجّم وأخوه.

١ كذا في عوّاد؛ الأصل: بسجه (غير واضحة). ٢ الأصل: والليموه. ٣ كذا في عوّاد؛ الأصل: محمّد بن المنتصر.

and decorated with figurines of ambergris, solid perfume, and camphor. These stands were arranged to look like a carpet.

Al-Mutawakkil and the other people came in for the banquet and he took his place on the throne, while the princes, commanders, and court companions were seated according to their rank. There were open spaces between their trays and the cloth the food was placed on. The house servants came with leather-covered plaited palm-leaf bags filled half with dinars and half with dirhams, which were emptied until the spaces were piled high. Slave boys stood by, and they conveyed the caliph's order that the guests should drink and that everyone who drank should take three handfuls of coins, as much as his hands could hold. If anyone felt the coins he had stored in his sleeve[105] were too heavy, he took them out to his slaves, gave them to them, and returned to his place. When the spaces were empty, the house servants brought more coins to fill them up again. Three ceremonial robes were bestowed on each guest, and when they left, they were given thoroughbreds or grade horses to ride. Al-Mutawakkil freed a thousand slaves[106] in al-Muʿtazz's name and had each one given a hundred dirhams and cloth for three robes. 14.4

In the palace courtyard in front of the ceremonial hall were four hundred dancing girls from Ubullah wearing different costumes, with a thousand cane trays before them piled with citrons, oranges (although it was not the season for them), apples from Syria, and lemons, as well as five thousand bouquets of narcissi and ten thousand bouquets of violets. The caliph ordered al-Fatḥ to scatter among the dancing girls, the house servants, and the retinue the gift he had prepared for them: twenty million dirhams. When no one came forward to take anything, al-Fatḥ picked up a dirham, and then they all threw themselves on the money and snatched up every coin. 14.5

Qabīḥah had had dirhams minted on her own initiative with the inscription "A blessing from God. For Abū ʿAbdallāh al-Muʿtazz bi-llāh's circumcision feast." A million dirhams were struck and distributed to the barber who performed the operation and his assistants, the slave boys, the caliph's personal bodyguard,[107] the palace superintendents, and the black and white eunuchs of the household.

Among those who attended the ceremony that day were Muḥammad al-Muntaṣir; Abū Aḥmad and Abū Sulaymān, the sons of al-Rashīd; Aḥmad and al-ʿAbbās, the sons of al-Muʿtaṣim; Mūsā, the son of al-Maʾmūn;[108] Ḥamdūn the Companion's two sons; Aḥmad ibn Abī Ruʾaym; al-Ḥusayn ibn al-Ḍaḥḥāk; ʿAlī ibn al-Jahm; and ʿAlī ibn Yaḥyā the Astrologer and his brother. 14.6

ومن المغنّين[1] عمرو بن بانة أحمد بن أبي العلاء ابن الحفصيّ ابن المكّيّ سلمك عثعث سليمان الطبّال المسدود أبو حشيشة ابن القصار صالح[2] الدفّاف زنّام الزامر تفّاح الزامر. ومن المغنّيات عريب بدعة جاريتها سراب شارية وجواريها ندمان منعم نجلة تركيّة فريدة عرفان.

٧،١٤ قال إبراهيم بن المدبّر[3] لمّا طُهّر المعتزّ اجتمع مشايخ الكتّاب بين يدي المتوكّل وكان فيهم يحيى بن خاقان وابنه عبيد الله إذ ذاك الوزير وهو واقف موقف الخدم بقباء ومنطقة وكان يحيى لا يشرب النبيذ فقال المتوكّل لعبيد الله خذ قدحاً من تلك الأقداح واصبب فيه نبيذاً وصيّر على كفك منديلاً وامضِ إلى أبيك يحيى فضعه في كفّه قال ففعل فرفع يحيى رأسه الى ابنه فقال المتوكّل يا يحيى لا تردّه قال لا يا أمير المؤمنين ثمّ شربه وقال قد جلّت نعمتك عندنا يا أمير المؤمنين فهنّأك الله النعمة ولا سلبنا ما أنعم به علينا منك فقال يا يحيى إنّما أردت أن يخدمك وزير بين يدي خليفة في طهور وليّ عهد.

٨،١٤ وقال إبراهيم بن العبّاس سألت أبا حرملة المزيّن في هذا اليوم فقلت كم حصل لك إلى أن وُضع الطعام فقال نيّف وثمانون ألف دينار سوى الصياغات والخواتيم والجواهر والعدات. قال وأقام المتوكّل ببركوارا ثلاثة أيّام ثمّ أُصعد إلى قصره الجعفريّ وتقدّم بإحضار إبراهيم بن العبّاس وأمره أن يعمل له عملاً بما أنفق في هذا الإعذار ويعرضه عليه ففعل ذلك فاشتمل العمل على ستّة وثمانين ألف ألف درهم.

٩،١٤ وكان الناس يستكثرون ما أنفقه الحسن بن سهل في عُرس ابنته بوران حتى أُرّخ ذلك في الكتب وسُمّيت دعوة الإسلام ثمّ أتى من دعوة المتوكّل ما أنسى ذلك.

١ الأصل: المغنيين. ٢ الأصل: صلح. ٣ الأصل: (في ختان المعتزّ أمر المتوكّل الفتح بن يحيى بن خاقان أن يضع قدحًا مملوءًا نبيذًا في كفّ والده يحيى وكان لم يشربها) وردت في الهامش.

The musicians included ʿAmr ibn Bānah, Aḥmad ibn Abī l-ʿAlāʾ, Ibn al-Ḥafsī, Ibn al-Makkī, Salmak, ʿAthʿath, Sulaymān the Drummer, Masdūd of the blocked nose, Abū Ḥashīshah, Ibn al-Qaṣṣār, Ṣāliḥ the Tambourine Player, Zunām the Flautist, and his colleague Tuffāḥ.

Among the singing girls were ʿArīb and her slave girl Bidʿah; Sarāb; and Shāriyah and her slave girls Nadmān, Munʿim, Najlah, Turkiyyah, Farīdah, and ʿIrfān.

A recollection from Ibrāhīm ibn al-Mudabbir: When al-Muʿtazz was circumcised, the senior state secretaries met with al-Mutawakkil. Yaḥyā ibn Khāqān was there, as was his son, ʿUbaydallāh, who was the vizier then. ʿUbaydallāh, who was standing as a servant would, was wearing a robe and sash. Yaḥyā did not drink wine, but al-Mutawakkil said to ʿUbaydallāh, "Take one of those glasses, fill it with wine, put a napkin on your shoulder, go over to your father, and put the glass in his hand." He did so. Yaḥyā raised his head to look at his son, but then al-Mutawakkil said to him, "Yaḥyā, don't refuse it." "Certainly not, sire." When he had drunk it, he exclaimed, "How great are your favors to us, sire! May God give you joy with His bounty and not deprive us of what He has granted us through you." At which al-Mutawakkil rejoined, "Yaḥyā, all I wanted was for you to be served by a vizier in a caliph's presence at a crown prince's circumcision."[109] 14.7

Ibrāhīm ibn ʿAbbās said: I asked Abū Ḥarmalah the barber that day, "How much had you received by the time the food arrived?" "Some eighty thousand dinars," he said, "not counting the gold and silver jewelry, the rings, precious stones, and promissory notes." 14.8

He went on: Al-Mutawakkil stayed three days in Barkuwārā; then he was conveyed upstream to the Jaʿfarī Palace, which he had built. He summoned Ibrāhīm ibn ʿAbbās and ordered him to draw up a list of what had been spent on this circumcision celebration and to present him with the calculation. Ibrāhīm did so, and the amount came to eighty-six million dirhams.

People used to think that what al-Ḥasan ibn Sahl had spent on his daughter Būrān's wedding was a huge sum—it was recorded as such in books, and the celebration was known as "the Banquet of Islam." But what was spent on al-Mutawakkil's banquet consigned it to oblivion. 14.9

وكانت الدعوات المشهورة في الإسلام ثلاثاً لم يكن مثلها فمنها دعوة المعتزّ هذه ١٠،١٤
المذكورة. ومنها عرس زبيدة بنت جعفر بن أبي جعفر فإنّ المهديّ زوّج ابنه الرشيد بأمّ جعفر ابنة أخيه فاستعدّ لها ما لم يُستعدّ لامرأة قبلها من الآلة وصناديق الجوهر والحليّ والتيجان والأكاليل وقباب الفضّة والذهب والطيب والكسوة وأعطاها بدنة عبيدة ابنة عبد الله بن يزيد بن معاوية امرأة هشام ولم يُرَ في الإسلام مثلها ومثل الحَبّ الذي كان فيها وكان في ظهرها وصدرها خطّان ياقوت أحمر وباقيها من الدرّ الكبار الذي ليس مثله. ودخل بها الرشيد في المحرّم سنة خمس وستّين ومائة في قصره المعروف بالخلد وحشر الناس من الآفاق وفرّق فيهم من الأموال أمراً عظيماً[١] فكانت الدنانير تُجعل في جامات فضّة والدراهم في جامات ذهب ونوافج المسك وجماجم العنبر والغالية في بواطي زجاج ويفرّق ذلك على الناس ويخلع عليهم خلع الوشي المنسوجة. وأوقد بين يديه في تلك الليلة شمع العنبر في أتوار الذهب وأحضر نساء بني هاشم وكان يدفع إلى كلّ واحدة منهنّ كيساً فيه دنانير وكيساً[٢] فيه دراهم وصينيّة كبيرة فضّة فيها طيب ويخلع عليها خلعة وشي مثقل فلم يُرَ في الإسلام مثلها وبلغت النفقة في هذا العرس من بيت مال الخاصّة سوى ما أنفقه الرشيد من ماله خمسين ألف ألف درهم.

واسم زبيدة أمة العزيز وزبيدة لقب وكان أبو جعفر يرقّصها وهي صغيرة وكانت ١١،١٤
سمينة ويقول ما أنت إلّا زبيدة ما أنت إلّا زبيدة فمضى عليها هذا الاسم.

ومنها عرس المأمون ببوران ابنة الحسن بن سهل وكان ذلك بفم الصِلح وكانت النفقة ١٢،١٤
عليه أمراً عظيماً[٣] وسأل المأمون زبيدة عن تقدير النفقة في العرس فقالت ما بين خمسة وثلاثين ألف ألف إلى سبعة وثلاثين ألف ألف فبلغ الحسن بن سهل فقال كأنّ[٤] النفقة على يد زبيدة. أنفقنا خمسة وثلاثين ألف ألف وكان يجري في جملة الجرايات في كلّ يوم على نيف وثلاثين ألف ملّاح.

---

١ الأصل: عبيده. ٢ الأصل: كيس. . . وكيس. ٣ الأصل: امر عظيم. ٤ الأصل: كان.

There were three famous unparalleled banquets in Islam. One was this banquet for al-Muʿtazz's circumcision. The second was Zubaydah bint Jaʿfar ibn Abī Jaʿfar's wedding. Al-Mahdī married his son al-Rashīd to Zubaydah Umm Jaʿfar, his brother's daughter, providing her with a trousseau the likes of which no woman had had before. It included furnishings, caskets of precious stones, jewelry, coronets, tiaras, gold and silver palanquins, perfumes, and clothes. He also gave her the jewel-studded surcoat that had belonged to ʿAbdah, the daughter of ʿAbdallāh ibn Yazīd ibn Muʿāwiyah and wife of Hishām. Nothing like it, not even its pearls, had ever been seen in Islamic times. It had two rows of rubies on the front and back, and the rest was studded with pearls of unparalleled size and beauty. Al-Rashīd consummated the marriage with Zubaydah in Muharram 165 [November 781] in his palace of al-Khuld. He assembled people from far and wide and distributed quantities of costly gifts among them. Dinars had been put into silver bowls and dirhams into gold ones, while pouches of musk and wooden boxes of ambergris and perfume were ranged in glass bowls. He dealt them out to the attendees and gave them ceremonial robes of woven brocade. That night, candles of ambergris in golden candlesticks were lit in his presence. He summoned the Hashimite women and gave each one a purse of dinars, a purse of dirhams, and a large silver tray laden with perfumes, as well as a ceremonial robe of encrusted brocade. Nothing like that had ever been seen in Islamic times. The expenses for this wedding, which were paid from the private treasury, apart from what al-Rashīd spent of his own money, ran to fifty million dirhams. 14.10

Zubaydah's given name was Amat al-ʿAzīz; Zubaydah was her nickname. 14.11 Her grandfather Abū Jaʿfar used to dance her on his knees when she was little, and because she was plump he would say, "You're just a little butter pat (*zubaydah*), you're just a little butter pat," and the name stuck.

The third banquet was for al-Ma'mūn's wedding to Būrān at Fam al-Ṣilḥ. 14.12 It cost a huge amount. Al-Ma'mūn asked Zubaydah to estimate the expense of the wedding, and she replied, "Between thirty-five and thirty-seven million dirhams." Al-Ḥasan ibn Sahl learned of her comments, and objected, "As though Zubaydah was paying for everything! We spent thirty-five million, and the expenses every day included the pay for about thirty thousand sailors."[110]

وكان دخولها في المدينة التي بناها بفم الصلح على شاطئ دجلة لثمان خلون من شهر رمضان سنة عشر ومائتين.

قال وأمهر المأمون بوران مائة ألف دينار وخمسة آلاف ألف درهم وأوقد بين ١٣،١٤
يديه تلك الليلة ثلاث شمعات عنبر وكثر دخانها فقالت زبيدة إنّه فيما ظهر من المروءة لكفاية ارفعوا هذا الشمع العنبر وهاتوا الشمع.

قال ولمّا جُليت بوران على المأمون نثر عليها حبّاً كباراً كان في كمّه فوقع على حصير ذهب كان تحته فقال لله درّ الحسن بن هانئ حيث يقول[١]

كَأَنَّ صُغْرَى وَكُبْرَى مِنْ فَوَاقِعِهَا حَصْبَاءُ دُرٍّ عَلَى أَرْضٍ مِنَ ٱلذَّهَبِ

قال وامتنع من كان حاضراً أن يلتقط شيئاً فقال المأمون أكرمنها فمدّت زبيدة يدها فأخذت حبّة فالتقط مَن حضر الباقي.

وكان اسم بوران خديجة وكانت وفاتها في سنة إحدى وسبعين ومائتين في أيّام ١٤،١٤
المعتمد ولها ثمانون سنة ولبوران ترثي المأمون

أَسْعِدَانِي عَلَى ٱلْبُكَا مُقْلَتَيَّا صِرْتُ بَعْدَ ٱلْإِمَامِ لِلْهَمِّ فَيَّا
كُنْتُ أَسْطُو عَلَى ٱلزَّمَانِ فَلَمَّا مَاتَ صَارَ ٱلزَّمَانُ يَسْطُو عَلَيَّا

وذكر ابن خرداذبه أنّ المتوكّل أنفق على الأبنية التي بناها وهي بركوارا والشاة والعروس ١٥،١٤
والبركة والجوسق والمختار والجعفريّ والغريب والبديع والصبيح والمليح والسندان والقصر والجامع والقلاية والبرج وقصر المتوكّليّة والبهو واللؤلؤة مائتي ألف ألف

١ الأصل: (ما أعظمه من شاعر فصيح) وردت في الهامش.

The consummation took place in the city that al-Ma'mūn had built at Fam al-Ṣilḥ on the banks of the Tigris, on Ramadan 9, 210 [December 23, 825].

Al-Ma'mūn gave Būrān one hundred thousand dinars and five million dirhams as a bride-price. He had three ambergris candles lit in his presence that night. They produced a lot of fumes, so Zubaydah said, "Enough of this show of generosity! Remove these ambergris candles and bring wax ones." 14.13

When Būrān was unveiled in front of al-Ma'mūn, he scattered over her some huge pearls he had in his sleeve. They fell onto a golden rug beneath him, at which he exclaimed, "How splendid a poet Abū Nuwās was! And how eloquent when he said:[111]

Bubbles of air,
great and small,
on the surface of wine,
Like fine pearls
on a carpet of gold."[112]

Those who were present refrained from taking anything until al-Ma'mūn said, "Do her honor!" Then Zubaydah stretched out her hand and took a pearl, and the other women picked up the rest.

Būrān's given name was Khadījah. She died at the age of eighty in the year 271 [884], during al-Mu'tamid's reign. 14.14

She lamented al-Ma'mūn with these verses:

Eyes, give me tears to weep!
Our imam[113] has gone—
Grief's made me a shade.
I had lorded it over Fate.
Then he died—
And Fate became my lord.

Ibn Khurdādhbih reported that al-Mutawakkil spent 274 million dirhams and 100 million gold dinar coins on his buildings: Barkuwārā, the Ewe, the Bride, the Blessing, al-Jawsaq, the Choice, Ja'far's Palace, the Strange, the Original, the Comely, the Lovely, the Great Building, the Castle, the Mosque, the Chamber, the Tower, the Mutawakkiliyyah Palace, the Courtyard, and the Pearl.[114] 14.15

وأربعة وسبعين ألف ألف درهم ومن العين مائة ألف ألف دينار تكون قيمة الورق عيناً بصرف الوقت مع ما فيه من العين ثلاثة عشر ألف ألف دينار وخمسمائة ألف دينار وخمسة وعشرين ألف دينار.

١٤،١٦ قال شرب المتوكّل يوماً في بركوارا فقال لندمائه أرأيتم وإن[١] لم تكن أيّام الورد لا نعمل نحن شادكلاه[٢] قالوا يا أمير المؤمنين لا يكون الشادكلاه إلّا بالورد فقال بلى ادعوا لي عبيد الله بن يحيى فحضر فقال تقدّم بأن تضرب لي دراهم في كلّ درهم حبّتان قال كم المقدار يا أمير المؤمنين قال خمسة آلاف ألف درهم فتقدّم عبيد الله في ضربها فضربت وعرّفه الخبر فقال اصبغ منها الحمرة والصفرة والسواد واترك بعضها على حاله ففعل ثمّ تقدّم إلى الخدم والحاشية وكانوا سبعمائة أن يعدّ كلّ واحد منهم قباءً جديداً وقلنسوة على خلاف لون قباء الآخر وقلنسوته ففعلوا. ثمّ عمد إلى يوم تحرّكت فيه الريح فنُصبت له قبّة لها أربعون باباً فاضطجع فيها والندماء حوله ولبس الخدم الكسوة التي أعدّها وأمر بنثر الدراهم كما ينثر الورد فنثرت أوّلاً أوّلاً فكانت الريح تحمل الدراهم فتقف بين السماء والأرض كما يقف الورد فكان من أحسن أيّام المتوكّل وأظرفه.

١٤،١٧ وكان البرج من أحسن أبنيته فجعل فيه صوراً عظاماً من الذهب والفضّة وبركة عظيمة جعل فرشها ظاهرها وباطنها صفائح الفضّة وجعل عليها شجرة ذهب فيها كلّ طائر يصوّت ويصفر مكلّلة بالجوهر وسمّاها طوبى. وعُمل له سرير من الذهب كبير عليه صورتا سبعَين عظيمَين ودرج عليها صور السباع والنسور وغير ذلك على ما يوصف به سرير سليمان بن داود عليهما السلام وجعل حيطان القصر من داخل وخارج ملبّسة بالفسيفساء والرخام المذهّب فبلغت النفقة على هذا القصر ألف ألف وسبع مائة ألف دينار.

١٤،١٨ جلس فيه على السرير الذهب وعليه ثياب الوشي المثقلة وأمر ألّا يدخل عليه أحد إلّا في ثياب وشي منسوجة أو ديباج ظاهره. وكان جلوسه فيه في سنة تسع وثلاثين

١ الأصل: (و) ورد تحت السطر. ٢ الأصل: سادحلاه.

At the exchange rate for gold, the silver content of the dirhams was worth thirteen million five hundred and twenty-five thousand dinars at that time.

Ibn Khurdādhbīh went on: One day al-Mutawakkil settled down to drink 14.16
at Barkuwārā, and he turned to his courtiers. "What do you think? Even if it's not the season for roses, can't we hold a rose-petal-scattering session?"[115] "But sire, you need roses for petal scattering." "Indeed. Summon ʿUbaydallāh ibn Yaḥyā to me." When ʿUbaydallāh presented himself, al-Mutawakkil said to him, "Have dirhams struck for me, each one weighing two grams." "How many, sire?" "Five million."

ʿUbaydallāh arranged for the minting, and when the coins were struck he informed al-Mutawakkil, who said, "Now have them colored, some red, some yellow, some black, and leave some as they are." ʿUbaydallāh did so. Al-Mutawakkil had the servants and retainers, who numbered seven hundred, prepare new robes and caps, each a different color from the servant beside him. They did so. He chose a windy day and had a domed pavilion with forty doors set up. He began with a morning drink, surrounded by his courtiers, while the servants wore the clothes he'd had prepared. At his order, the dirhams were scattered apiece like roses. The wind caught them up and they floated between heaven and earth as if they were roses. It was among al-Mutawakkil's best and most entertaining days.

The Tower was one of his finest buildings. Inside, he had placed large pictures 14.17
in gold and silver and a great fishpond, silver-plated inside and out, with a golden tree just beside it. All kinds of birds chirped and sang in its bejeweled branches, and he named it the Tree of Bliss. A large golden throne was made for him with statues of two lions and images of lions, eagles, and suchlike on the steps up to it, along the lines of the description of the throne of Solomon son of David (eternal peace be theirs).[116] He had the walls of the palace set with mosaics and gilded marble. The outlay for it was 1.7 million dinars.

When al-Mutawakkil, attired in brocade heavy with gold, took his seat 14.18
upon the golden throne to inaugurate the palace, he ordered that only those wearing garments of woven silk or faced with embroidery were to be admitted. This ceremony took place in 239 [853]. When he called for the dishes to be brought, the courtiers, all the singers and musicians present, and everyone

ومائتين ثمّ دعا بالطعام وحضر الندماء وسائر المغنيّن والملهـيّين[1] وأكل الناس ورام النوم فما تهيّأ له فقال له الفتح يا مولاي ليس هذا يوم نوم. فجلس للشرب فلمّا كان الليل رام النوم فما أمكنه فدعا بدهن بنفسج فجعل منه شيئاً[2] على رأسه وتنشّقه فلم ينفعه. فمكث ثلاثة أيّام بلياليها لم ينم ثمّ حُمّ حمّى حادّة فانتقل إلى الهارونيّ قصر أخيه الواثق فأقام به ستّة أشهر عليلاً وأمر بهدم البرج وضرب تلك الحليّ عيناً.

١ الأصل: المغنيين والملهين. ٢ الأصل: شى.

else ate. Then he wanted to sleep, but sleep eluded him. Al-Fatḥ[117] said, "Sire, this is not a day for sleeping." So he had wine brought and drank until nightfall. Then he wanted to sleep but could not, so he called for oil of violets, put some on his head, and inhaled it. It did not help, and for three days and nights he did not sleep. Then he developed a high fever and was moved to the Hārūnī Palace, built by his brother al-Wāthiq, where he lay ill for six months. He ordered the Tower Palace to be razed and the adornments to be melted down.

ديـر مَرمـاري[1]

وهــذا الدير بسرّ من رأى عند قنطرة وصيف وهو دير عامر كثير الرهبان حوله كروم وشجر وهو من المواضع النزهة والبقاع الطيّبة الحسنة. وللفضل بن العبّاس ابن المأمون فيه ١،١٥

أَنْضَيْتُ فِي سُرَّ مَنْ رَأَى خَيْلَ لَذَّاتِي　　وَنِلْتُ فِيهَا مُنَى نَفْسِي وَشَهَوَاتِي
عَمَرْتُ فِيهَا بِقَاعَ ٱللَّهْوِ مُنْغَمِساً　　فِي ٱلْقَصْفِ مَا بَيْنَ أَنْهَارٍ وَجَنَّاتِ
بِدَيْرِ مَرْ مَارٍ إِذْ نُحْيِي ٱلصَّبُوحَ بِهِ　　وَنُعْمِلُ ٱلْكَأْسَ فِيهِ بِٱلْعَشِيَّاتِ
بَيْنَ ٱلنَّوَاقِيسِ وَٱلتَّقْدِيسِ آوِنَةً　　وَتَارَةً بَيْنَ عِيدَانٍ وَنَايَاتِ
وَكَمْ بِهِ مِنْ غَزَالٍ أَغْيَدٍ غَزِلٍ　　يَصِيدُنَا بِٱللِّحَاظِ ٱلْبَابِلِيَّاتِ

وذكر الفضل هذا أنّه خرج ذات يوم مع المعتزّ للصيد قال فانقطعنا عن الموكب ٢،١٥ أنا وهو ويونس بن بُغا فشكا المعتزّ العطش فقلت له يا أمير المؤمنين إنّ في هذا الدير راهباً أعرفه له مودّة حسنة وفيه آلات جميلة فهل لأمير المؤمنين أن نعدل إليه قال افعل. فصرنا إلى الديرانيّ فرحّب بنا وتلقّانا أجمل لقاء وجاءنا بماء بارد فشربنا وعرض علينا النزول عنده وقال تبتردون عندنا ونحضركم ما تيسّر في ديرنا فتنالون منه. فاستظرفه المعتزّ وقال انزل بنا إليه. فنزلنا فسألني الديرانيّ عن المعتزّ ويونس ابن بغا فقلت هما من أبناء الجند فقال بل مفلتان من أزواج الحور فقلت هذا ليس من دينك ولا اعتقادك. قال هو الآن من ديني واعتقادي. فضحك المعتزّ ثمّ جاءنا بخبز وأشاطير وما يكون مثله في الديارات فكان من أنظف طعام وأطيبه وأحسن آنية فأكلنا وغسلنا أيدينا. فقال لي المعتزّ قل له بينك وبينه من تحبّ أن يكون معك

١ الأصل: دير مر مار.

The Monastery of Mār Mārī

This monastery is in Samarra at the Waṣīf Bridge. It is prosperous, houses many monks, and is surrounded by vineyards and orchards. People go there on outings, as it is a pleasant and beautiful spot. 15.1

Al-Faḍl ibn al-ʿAbbās ibn al-Maʾmūn composed a short poem on it:

> I wore out the steeds of my pleasure in Samarra,
> fulfilling my wishes and my heart's desire,
> Bringing life to parks of pleasure, plunged into revelry
> between rivers and gardens at Mār Mārī Monastery.
> Again we drank the morning draft,
> and in the evening passed the cup around,
> At times to the rhythm of the clappers and the chants of priests,
> at times to the sound of lutes and plaintive pipes.
> And how many tender, flirtatious gazelles
> hunted us with their Babylonian glances!

Al-Faḍl went hunting with al-Muʿtazz one day. He recalled: Al-Muʿtazz, 15.2
Yūnus ibn Bughā, and I got separated from the rest of the company. Al-Muʿtazz complained of feeling thirsty so I said to him, "Sire, there is a monk in this monastery whom I know. He is a good friend and the monastery is well appointed. Would the Commander of the Faithful like us to turn off to it?" "Let's do that." We came to the abbot of the monastery, who welcomed us and gave us a fine reception. He brought us cold water to drink and then invited us to dismount and spend some time with him, saying, "You can cool off here and we will bring you such food as the monastery can offer."

Al-Muʿtazz took to him and said, "Let's dismount and follow him." When we had dismounted, the superior asked me about al-Muʿtazz and Yūnus. "They are army officers." "No," he retorted, "they are two husbands of houris[118] who have slipped away." "That isn't part of your religion and creed." "It is now," he answered, and al-Muʿtazz laughed. The abbot brought us bread and light food such as can be found in monasteries. It was very wholesome, tasty, and nicely

من هذين ولا يفارقك قال فقلت له فقال كلاهما وتمرًا. فضحك المعتزّ حتّى مال من الضحك. فقلت للديرانيّ لا بدّ من أن تختار فقال الاختيار في هذا دمار. ما خلق الله عقلاً يميّز بين هؤلاء.

٣.١٥ ثمّ لحقنا الموكب فارتاع الديرانيّ فقال له المعتزّ بحياتي لا تنقطع عمّا كنّا فيه فإنّي لمن ثمّ مولى ولمن ههنا صديق. فجلسنا ساعة وأمر له المعتزّ بخمسين ألف درهم فقال والله لا قبلتها إلّا على شرط. قال وما هو قال يكون أمير المؤمنين في دعوتي مع من أحبّ قال ذاك إليك. فاتّفقنا ليوم جئناه فيه على ما أحبّ فلم يُبق غاية وأقام بمن كان معه وجاء بأولاد النصارى فخدمونا أحسن خدمة. فسُرّ المعتزّ سرورًا ما رأيته سُرّ مثله ووصله في ذلك اليوم بمال كثير ولم يزل يطرقه إذا اجتاز به ويأكل عنده ويشرب مدّة أيّامه.

٤.١٥ قال وكان المعتزّ سمح الأخلاق واسع النفس له أدب وفهم ويقول شعرًا صالحًا وكان يحبّ يونس بن بغا هذا ولا يصبر عنه وكان هو ويونس بن بغا من أحسن الناس وجهًا وأجملهم ولم يكن في خلفاء بني العبّاس أحسن وجهًا من الأمين والمعتزّ وكان يُضرب بهما المثل في الحسن والجمال.

٥.١٥ قالت عريب كنت لمحمّد الأمين وصيفة في عداد الوصائف ألبس قباء ومنطقة وأقوم على رأسه وربّما سقيته وسنّي إذ ذاك سبع عشرة سنة وكان أحسن خلق الله لم يُرَ ذكر[1] ولا أنثى مثله جمالاً وحسناً مع حسن خلق. قال أحمد بن عبد الله بن إسماعيل المراكبيّ وهو ابن مولاها أين كان المعتزّ منه فقد رأيناه ولم نر الأمين قالت كان المعتزّ فيه لمحة منه وأمّا مثله فلم يكن.

٦.١٥ قال وكان إلف المعتزّ ليونس بن بغا إلف الصبا فلم يفارقه وهو لا يصبر عنه وله فيه أشعار كثيرة فمن ذلك

١ الأصل: ذكرًا.

served. We ate and washed our hands, and then al-Muʿtazz said to me, "Ask him privately which of us two he would like to be with him and stay here?" I passed on the question, and the abbot said, "Both of them and then some!"[119] Al-Muʿtazz laughed so much he leaned back against the wall. I said to the abbot, "You must choose." "In this matter, selection is perdition. God has created no mind that could distinguish between them."

The rest of the company caught up with us, and the abbot was alarmed. 15.3
Al-Muʿtazz said to him, "By my life, let's not interrupt what we were doing. I'm master of those people there, but friend to the people here." So we sat together for a while, and al-Muʿtazz ordered that the abbot be given fifty thousand dirhams. The abbot said, "By God, I'll only accept them on one condition." "What's that?" "That the Commander of the Faithful be my guest, together with whomever he likes." Al-Muʿtazz replied, "I grant you that." Then we agreed on a day when we would visit him as he requested. He took the utmost pains, involving his community in the preparations, and he provided young Christians, who served us very well. Al-Muʿtazz was happier than I had ever seen him. He gave the abbot a great deal of money that day, and as long as he lived, he regularly called on him when he passed the monastery to eat and drink there.

Al-Faḍl went on: Al-Muʿtazz had a generous spirit; he was broad-minded, 15.4
cultured, and intelligent. He was also a good poet. He loved Yūnus ibn Bughā and couldn't be without him. He and Yūnus were extremely good-looking and elegant; of all the Abbasid caliphs, none were more handsome than al-Amīn and al-Muʿtazz. In fact, their beauty and elegance were proverbial.

ʿArīb recalled: I was one of those in attendance on Muḥammad al-Amīn. I 15.5
used to wear a gorgeous belted robe and stand at his head, and I sometimes poured the wine for him. I was seventeen then. He was the handsomest man God made; we never saw a man or woman like him for beauty, elegance, and good character.

Aḥmad son of Ismāʿīl ibn ʿAbdallāh al-Marākibī, who was the son of ʿArīb's owner, once asked her: "How did al-Muʿtazz compare with him? After all, we've seen al-Muʿtazz but we haven't seen al-Amīn." "Al-Muʿtazz had something of al-Amīn about him," she replied, "but he didn't really look like him."

Al-Muʿtazz was passionately attached to Yūnus. He never left his side, and 15.6
couldn't bear to be away from him. He composed a lot of poetry about him, such as these verses:

إِنِّي عَرَفْتُ دَوَاءَ ٱلطِّبِّ مِنْ وَجَعِي ... وَمَا عَرَفْتُ دَوَاءَ ٱلْمَكْرِ وَٱلْخُدَعِ
جَزِعْتُ لِلْحُبِّ وَٱلْحُمَّى صَبَرْتُ لَهَا ... إِنِّي لَأَعْجَبُ مِنْ صَبْرِي وَمِنْ جَزَعِي
مَنْ كَانَ يَشْغَلُهُ عَنْ إِلْفِهِ وَجَعٌ ... فَلَيْسَ يَشْغَلُنِي عَنْ حُبِّكُمْ وَجَعِي

٧،١٥ وكان المعتزّ يشرب على بستان مملوء بالنمّام وبين النمّام شقائق فأقبل يونس بن بغا وعليه قباء أخضر فقال المعتزّ

شَبَّهْتُ حُمْرَةَ خَدِّهِ فِي ثَوْبِهِ ... بِشَقَائِقِ ٱلنُّعْمَانِ فِي ٱلنَّمَّامِ

ثمّ قال أجيزوا فيه فبدر بنان[1] المغنّي فقال

وَٱلْقَدَّ مِنْهُ إِذَا بَدَا مُتَثَنِّيًا ... بِٱلْغُصْنِ فِي لِينٍ وَحُسْنِ قَوَامِ

فقال غنّ فيه الآن فعمل فيه لحناً وغنّاه إيّاه.

٨،١٥ قال وشرب المعتزّ يوماً والجلساء بين يديه وقد أعدّ الخلع والجوائز فدخل بغا فقال يا سيّدي والدة عبدك يونس في الموت وهي تشتهي أن تراه فأذن له فخرج وفتر المعتزّ وتغيّر ثمّ نعس فنام ونام الجلساء فلمّا كان وقت المغرب عاد يونس وبين يديه الشمع فلمّا رآه المعتزّ دعا برطل فشربه وسقاه مثله ثمّ عاد الندماء ورجع المجلس إلى أحسن ممّا كان فيه فقال المعتزّ

تَغِيبُ فَلَا أَفْرَحُ ... فَلَيْتَكَ لَا تَبْرَحُ ... وَإِنْ كُنْتَ عَذَّبْتَنِي ... بِأَنَّكَ لَا تَسْمَحُ
فَأَصْبَحْتُ مَا بَيْنَ ذَيْـنِ لِي كَبِدٌ تُجْرَحُ ... عَلَى ذَاكَ يَا سَيِّدِي ... دُنُوُّكَ لِي أَصْلَحُ[2]

١ الأصل: رسان. ٢ الأصل: (هكذا في الأصل) وردت في الهامش.

The doctors' cure for pain I know;
  for cunning and deceit I know no remedy.
In love I'm restive, patient when I'm feverish;
  how strange to be both patient and impatient.
Pain may turn a man from his beloved;
  from love of you my pain will not distract me.

Al-Muʿtazz was drinking in a garden full of thyme with anemones growing among it. Then Yūnus ibn Bughā arrived wearing a green cape. Al-Muʿtazz said: 15.7

Red cheeks and a green cape, anemones in thyme.

"Cap it!" Bunān the Singer volunteered:

and his figure when he bends—a branch in supple beauty.

"Put it to music now," ordered al-Muʿtazz.

And Bunān composed a setting and sang it to the caliph.

Al-Muʿtazz was drinking one day with Yūnus ibn Bughā beside him to pour the wine for him and the courtiers in front of him. He had had ceremonial robes and rewards prepared. Then Bughā came in and announced: "Sire, your servant Yūnus's mother is at death's door and she wants to see her son." Al-Muʿtazz gave Yūnus leave to go. The caliph became listless, his mood changed, and then he became drowsy and fell asleep. The courtiers, too, fell asleep. When it was time for the evening prayer and al-Muʿtazz had returned to the gathering, Yūnus came back, with candles borne in front of him. At the sight of him, the caliph called for a goblet of wine, drank it, and gave him one like it. The courtiers came back and the gathering resumed, even better than it had been before. Al- Muʿtazz declaimed: 15.8

You're gone. I know no joy. Would you were still here.
Yet if you come you torture me, resist, and stay severe.
Between these two I feel my heart will perish.
Stay by me, master. Close to you I flourish.

٩،١٥ ثمّ قال غنّوا فيه فجعلوا يفكّرون فقال لابن القصّار ويلك ألحان الطنبور أصلح وأخفّ
فغنّ فيه فغنّاه فدفع إليه دنانير الخريطة وهي مائة دينار فيها مائتان مكتوب على كلّ
دينار منها ضُرب هذا الدينار بالجوسق لخريطة أمير المؤمنين المعتزّ بالله ثمّ دعا بالخلع
والجوائز لسائر الناس.

١٠،١٥ قال واصطبح المعتزّ يوماً ويونس بن بغا وما رئي[1] وجهان قطّ مثلهما حسناً فما
مضت ثلاث ساعات حتّى سكرا فقال المعتزّ

مَا إِنْ تَرَى مَنْظَرًا إِنْ شِئْتَهُ حَسَنًا   إِلَّا صَرِيعًا تَهَادَى بَيْنَ سُكْرَيْنِ
سُكْرِ ٱلشَّبَابِ وَسُكْرٍ مِنْ هَوَى رَشَإٍ[2]   تَخَالُهُ وَٱلَّذِي يَهْوَاهُ غُصْنَيْنِ

ومن شعره في يونس وفيه لحن في طريقة الرمل

عَلَّمُونِي كَيْفَ أَجْفُو   كَ عَلَى رَغْمٍ مِنَ ٱنْفِي
وَجَفَائِي لَكَ يَا يُو   نُسُ مَقْرُونٌ بِحَتْفِي
غَيْرَ أَنَّ ٱللَّهَ قَدْ يَعْلَمُ مَا أُبْدِي وَأُخْفِي
فَوَقَانِي ٱللَّهُ فِيكَ ٱلدْ   دَهْرَ أَنْ يَأْتِي بِصَرْفِ

١١،١٥ قال هارون بن عبد العزيز بن المعتمد حدّثني سعيد بن يوسف كاتب أبي قال كنت
أتقلّد خزائن الكسوة وكان إذا أمر المعتزّ ليونس بشيء أخذت له أجلّ ما في الخزائن
وأحسنه. وكان يبرّني فلا أقبل برّه وربّما دخل الخزانة فجرته ومازحته فقلت له يوماً يا
سيّدي أنا عبدك وموفّر لمالك وأنت تشرّف مسرور المعتصميّ بالتحيّة الحسنة ممّا يكون
بين يدي أمير المؤمنين وأنا فلا تشرّفني بمثل ذلك. فقال الليلة نوبتك فلمّا كان في الليل
بعث إليّ بوصيف الخادم ومعه صينيّة ذهب فيها خوخ فقلّ في نفسي ثمّ كبر إذ كان

[1] الأصل: رأى. [2] الأصل: رشاء.

He turned to the musicians who were present: "Set it to music." They put their minds to the task, but then he said to Ibn al-Qaṣṣār the Pandore Player, "Come on. Tunes on the pandore are better and lighter. You make a setting." And he did so. 15.9

Al-Muʿtazz gave him the dinars in the presentation purse, which held one hundred Meccan dinars and two hundred bearing the inscription "This dinar was minted in the Jawsaq Palace for the caliph al-Muʿtazz bi-llāh's presentation purse." Then he called for the ceremonial robes and jewels to be given to the other courtiers.

One morning al-Muʿtazz was drinking with Yūnus ibn Bughā; no faces more handsome had ever been seen. Within three hours, they were drunk. Al-Muʿtazz proclaimed: 15.10

No sight will you see more beautiful
    than a youth brought low by carousing,
Swaying from wine and the love of a gazelle.
    See them together, two branches entwined.

Another of al-Muʿtazz's poems on Yūnus runs:

They taught me to reject you against my will.
O Yūnus, if I spurn you it will bring on my death!
God alone knows what I tell and hold back.
May God protect us both from Fate's cruel blows.

It has a setting in the *ramal* rhythmic mode.

Hārūn ibn ʿAbd al-ʿAzīz ibn al-Muʿtamid related this incident told by Saʿīd ibn Yūsuf, his father's secretary: 15.11

I was in charge of the garment treasury, and when al-Muʿtazz gave the order for Yūnus to receive a gift I would bring out the most gorgeous and beautiful robe in it for him. He would try to tip me but I didn't let him. Occasionally he would come into the treasury and I would give him a tap on the head, making a joke of it. One day I said to him, "Sir, I am your servant and I work to increase your wealth. You do Masrūr al-Muʿtaṣimī the honor of greeting him politely, as is usual in the caliph's presence. But you don't do me the same honor."

"Tonight will be your turn." That evening Yūnus sent Waṣīf the eunuch to me bearing a golden tray with plums on it. At first they did not impress me, but

من مجلس الخليفة فأخذت واحدة فنظرتها فإذا هي قد شُقّت وأُخرج ما فيها وجُعل مكانه ندّ معجون على مقدار ما كان فيها فأخرجت ما في جميعه فكان شيئاً كثيراً.

وللمعتزّ في يونس وقد خرج وعاد ١٢،١٥

ٱللّٰهُ يَعْــلَمُ يَا حَـبِيبِي أَنَّنِي مُـذْ غِبْتَ عَنِّي هَائِمٌ مَكْرُوبُ
يَدْنُو ٱلسُّرُورُ إِذَا دَنَا بِكَ مَـنْزِلٌ وَيَغِيبُ صَفْوُ ٱلْعَيْشِ حِينَ تَغِيبُ

وكانت البيعة للمعتزّ يوم الخميس لثلاث خلون من المحرّم سنة اثنتين وخمسين ومائتين ١٣،١٥
وخُلع لثلاث بقين من رجب سنة خمس وخمسين ومائتين وقُتل بعد الخلع بخمسة أيّام وسنّه أربع وعشرون سنة وستّة أشهر وأربعة عشر يوماً.

قال وكانت قبيحة حرّضت المعتزّ على الأتراك وقالت يا بنيّ اقتلهم في كلّ مكان وأخرجت إليه قميص أبيه المتوكّل مخضّباً بدمائه فقال يا أمّه ارفعيه وإلّا صار القميص قميصين.

وذكر أحمد بن حمدون قال بنى المعتزّ في الجوسق في الصحن الكامل بيتاً قدّرته له ١٤،١٥
أمّه ومثّلت حيطانه وسقوفه فكان أحسن بيت رئي[١] قال فدعانا المعتزّ إليه فكنّا في أحسن يوم رئي[٢] سروراً وخلف الستارة مغنّية تغنّي أحسن غناء ليس لي بها عهد.

قال فنحن في ذاك إذ دخل علينا خادم في يده طبق عليه مكبّة فوضعه في وسط البيت وكان في يد المعتزّ قدح فشربه وشربنا ثمّ قال للخادم ارفع المكبّة فرفعها فإذا رأس المستعين في الطبق فلمّا رأيته شهقت وبكيت فقال لي المعتزّ يابن الفاعلة ما هذا كأنّك دخلتك له رقّة فثاب إليّ عقلي وتماسكت وقلت ما كان لرقّة ولكنّي ذكرت

١ الأصل: رُاى. ٢ الأصل: رُاى.

then they went up in my estimation since they came from the caliph's court. I took one and examined it, and saw that it had been split and the stone had been taken out and replaced with the same amount of precious perfume. I took the perfume out of all the plums and it came to a large amount.

More of al-Muʿtazz's verses on Yūnus, when he had gone away and then come back: 15.12

> God knows, my friend, that since you went
> I'm anxious and distressed.
> When you are near joy comes close;
> when you're away I live in torment.

The oath of allegiance was sworn to al-Muʿtazz on Thursday Muharram 4, 252 AH [January 26, 866], and he was deposed on Rajab 25, 255 AH [July 12, 869]. Five days later he was killed. He was twenty-four years, six months, and fourteen days old.[120] 15.13

Qabīḥah stirred him up against the Turks, saying, "My boy, kill them everywhere." She showed him his father al-Mutawakkil's shirt, stained with his blood. He replied, "Mother, take it away. Otherwise we will have two shirts instead of one."

Aḥmad ibn Ḥamdūn recounts: Al-Muʿtazz had a pavilion built in the Perfect Courtyard of the Jawsaq Palace. His mother had made the plans, comparing the dimensions of the walls and the roofs, and it was the loveliest building ever seen. He invited us there and we spent the most festive day, with a singing girl I did not know performing songs that were new to me. While we were enjoying ourselves, a servant came in carrying a covered dish, which he put down in the middle of the pavilion. Al-Muʿtazz was holding a goblet and he drank it. We drank too. Then he said to the servant, "Take off the cover." 15.14

And there was al-Mustaʿīn's head in the dish.

When I saw it, I gasped and started to weep. Al-Muʿtazz turned to me. "You bastard! What's the matter? You seem to have a soft spot for him."

I came to my senses, pulled myself together, and replied, "Not at all. But I was just reminded of death."

الموت. فأمر الغلام بردّ المكبّة ورفع الطبق فرفعه وكأنّ المعتزّ دخلته فترة وكذلك جميع من حضر وافترقنا عن الحال التي كنّا عليه من السرور.

١٥،١٥ قال فنحن كذلك إذ سمعنا وراء الستر ضجّة أفزعتنا فإذا امرأة تصيح وامرأة أخرى تشتم الصائحة والصائحة تقول يا قوم أخذتموني غصباً ثمّ تجيئوني[1] برأس مولاي فتضعونه بين يديّ فسمعنا صوت العود قد ضُرب به رأسها وكان الضارب لها والشاتم قبيحة وكانت الجارية من جواري المستعين قال فانصرفنا عن المجلس أقبح انصراف وقد تنغّص علينا ما كنّا فيه.

ولم تمضِ إلّا أيّام يسيرة حتّى وثب الأتراك على المعتزّ فقتلوه ثمّ دعي بنا لننظر إليه فدخلنا عليه في ذلك البيت فإذا هو ممدود في وسطه ميّتاً.

١ الأصل: تجيوني.

Al-Muʿtazz told the servant to replace the cover and take the dish away, which he did. Al-Muʿtazz seemed to have become listless, as had everyone present. The joy we had felt before had left us.

While we were in that state, we heard an outcry behind the curtain, star- 15.15
tling us. One woman was screaming and another woman was cursing her. The one who was screaming cried out, "Look, everyone! You seized me by force and now you bring me my master's head and put it in front of me!" Then we heard the sound of the lute striking her head. The woman cursing and using the lute as a weapon was Qabīḥah, and the girl was one of al-Mustaʿīn's slaves. We left the gathering in the gloomiest mood and the pleasure we had felt during it was ruined.

Only a few days later, the Turks attacked al-Muʿtazz and killed him. We were invited to view the corpse, and so we went into the pavilion and there he was, lying in the middle of it, dead.

دير مريحنّا

١٦،١ وهـذا الدير إلى جانب تكريت على دجلة وهو كبير عامر كثير القلّايات والرهبان مطروق مقصود لا يخلو من المتطرّبين المتنزّهين ولا من مسافر ينزله ولكلّ مَن طرقه مِن الناس ضيافة قائمة على قدر المضاف لا يخلّون بها. وله مزارع وغلّات كثيرة وبساتين وكروم وهو للنسطور وعلى بابه صومعة عبدون الراهب رجل من الملكيّة بنى الصومعة ونزلها فصارت تُعرف به وهو الآن المستولي على الدير والقيّم به وبمن فيه. وقد بنى إلى جانبه بناء ينزله المجتازون ويقيم لهم الضيافة ويحسن لهم القرى.

١٦،٢ وقد قيل في هذا الدير أشعار ووصف طيبه ونزهته فمن ذلك قول عمرو بن عبد الملك الورّاق

أَرَى قَلْبِيَ قَدْ حَنَّا   إِلَى دَيْرِ مَرِيحَنَّا
إِلَى غِيطَانِهِ ٱلْفِيحِ   إِلَى بِرْكَتِهِ ٱلْغَنَّا
إِلَى ظَبْيٍ مِنَ ٱلْإِنْسِ   يَصِيدُ ٱلْإِنْسَ وَٱلْجِنَّا
إِلَى غُصْنٍ مِنَ ٱلْبَانِ   بِهِ قَلْبِيَ قَدْ جُنَّا
إِلَى أَحْسَنِ خَلْقِ ٱللّٰـهِ   إِنْ قَدَّسَ أَوْ غَنَّى
فَلَمَّا ٱنْبَلَجَ ٱلصُّبْحُ   بَـرَزْنَا بَيْنَنَا دَنَّا
وَلَمَّا دَارَتِ ٱلْكَأْسُ   أَدَرْنَا بَيْنَنَا لَحْنَا
وَلَمَّا هَجَعَ ٱلسُّمَّا   رُ نِمْنَا وَتَعَانَقْنَا

١٦،٣ وكان عمرو هذا من الخلعاء المجّان المنهمكين في البطالة والخسارة والاستهتار بالمرد والتطرّح في الديارات وله شعر كثير في المجون ووصف الخمر. وقد ذكرنا منه ما يليق بالكتاب فمن شعره قوله

The Monastery of Mār Yuḥannā (Saint John)

This monastery lies on the Tigris near Takrit. It is large and prosperous and has many monks and hermits' cells. Passersby stop there and it attracts visitors. Singers often make music in it and people come to enjoy the surroundings. It puts up travelers, and whoever stops there invariably receives hospitality according to his state. 16.1

Round this monastery are orchards, vineyards, and fields planted with different kinds of crops. It belongs to the Nestorians.[121] At its entrance, however, is the hermitage belonging to Monk ʿAbdūn, a Melkite.[122] He built it and lives in it now, and it is named after him. He is the superior in charge of the monastery and its residents. Beside it he has built a house to lodge those who are passing though; he puts them up and feeds them very well.

Poems have been composed about this monastery, celebrating its good and healthy air, for instance these lines by ʿAmr ibn ʿAbd al-Malik al-Warrāq: 16.2

I feel my heart's yearning for Mār Yuḥannā's Monastery,
Its endless fields, its pool ringed with plants,
And a gazelle of a boy, hunter of men and jinn,
Pliant as a supple branch, who's put madness in my heart,
Handsomest of God's creatures when he chants or swings the censer.
At first light we broached a jar of wine,
And as the cups went round we tossed each other tunes
Till voices fell silent and we lay twined in each other's arms.

This ʿAmr was frivolous and dissolute, a playboy and wastrel attracted to beardless boys, who enjoyed having a good time in monasteries. He composed many poems celebrating debauchery and describing wine. We quote here a selection appropriate to this book. One such poem runs: 16.3

وَحَـظِيَّـةٍ[1] فِيهَا ٱلْعَـطَبْ   غَـالَيْتُ فِيهَـا بِٱلْعَـطَبْ
أَتْلَفْتُ فِـيهَا مَـا كَـسَبْـتُ وَمَا جَمَعْتُ مِنَ ٱلنَّشَبْ
مَـا زِلْتُ حَـتَّى نِلْتُهَـا   فِي بَيْتِ مُضْـطَرِبِ ٱلْخَشَبْ
وَمُـدَامَـةٍ كَـرْخِيَّـةٍ   حَـمْرَاءَ مِنْ مَـاءِ ٱلْعِنَبْ
عَـاقَـرْتُهَـا فِي فِتْيَـةٍ   لَيْسُوا عَـلَى دِينِ ٱلْعَـرَبْ
فِي مَعْشَـرٍ مَهَـرُوا ٱلْمَجَا   نَةَ فِي ٱللَّذَاذَةِ وَٱلطَّـرَبْ
جَـعَـلُوا ٱلْمَجَانَـةَ سُـتْرَةً   لِلْعَـاذِلِينَ عَـلَى ٱلرُّتَبْ
تَمْـضِي ٱلصَّـلَاةُ عَـلَيْهِمِ   وَٱلسُّكْرُ مِنْهُمْ فِي ٱلْعَـصَبْ
فَإِذَا تَنَبَّـهَ مَنْ تَنَبَّـهَ كَانَ مِنْهَا فِي طَـلَبْ
وَإِذَا مَـضَتْ صَـلَوَاتُهُمْ   صَلَّوْا جُمَادَى فِي رَجَبْ

ومن شعره في المجون أيضاً[2] ٤،١٦

أَيُّهَا ٱلسَّـائِـلُ عَـنِّي   لَسْتُ مِنْ أَهْلِ ٱلصَّلَاحِ
أَنَا إِنْسَـانٌ مُـرِيبٌ   أَشْـتَهِي نَيْكَ ٱلْمِلَاحِ
قَدْ قَسَمْتُ ٱلدَّهْـرَ يَوْمَيْـنِ لِفِسْـقٍ وَلِرَاحِ
لَا أُبَالِي مَنْ لَحَـانِي   لَا أُطِيعُ ٱلدَّهْـرَ لَاحِي

ومن مجونه أيضاً[3]

إِذَا أَنْتَ لَمْ تَشْرَبْ عُقَارًا وَلَمْ تَلُطْ   فَأَنْتَ لَعَـمْرِي وَٱلْحِمَـارُ سَوَاءُ ٥،١٦
وَلَمْ تَمْـلَ بَيْتًا مِنْ قِحَابٍ وَلَمْ يَبِتْ   فِرَاشُكَ أَرْضًـا مَا عَلَيْـهِ غِطَـاءُ
وَلَمْ تَكُ بِٱلشِّطْرَنْجِ عَبْدًا مُقَامِـرًا   وَفِي ٱلنَّرْدِ عِنْدَ ٱلْخَصْلِ[4] مِنْكَ وَفَـاءُ
وَلَمْ تَكُ فِي لَعِبِ ٱلنَّوَى مُتَمَاحِكًا   فَتُسْـلَبَ مَـالًا أَوْ يَكُـونَ بَوَاءُ

١ الأصل: خَطِيَّةٍ. ٢ الأصل: (قف على شعر عمرو بن عبد الملك الورّاق وعلى مذهبه) وردت في الهامش. ٣ الأصل: عَبْدٌ مُقَامِرٌ. ٤ الأصل: الحَضل.

A cosseted girl, soft as down,
Cost me the earth in earnings and fortune.
I shelled them all out, completely unhinged,
Until I possessed her.
Red wine from Karkh, blood of the grape,
I have drunk with youths not of my faith,
Companions expert in pleasure and music,
Folly their shield from censure and blame,
Far gone in drink, oblivious to prayers.
When they come to, they ask for more wine.
If ever they pray, they don't know what they say.[123]

Here is another of his poems on debauchery:[124] 16.4

If you want to know me,
  I'm not a man of virtue—
A dubious character,
  I like fucking beauties.
Time for me is just two days—
  one for fucking and one for drinking.
I don't care who blames me.
  For me, fucking's a duty.

And another: 16.5

If you don't drink wine and you don't fuck boys,
  by God, you're just like an ass.
If you don't fill your house with whores,
  make your bed on the bare earth,
Gamble at chess, or hedge your bets
  at backgammon,
Quarrel over knucklebones
  to win the stake or else draw,

وَلَمْ تَتَّخِذْ كَلْباً وَقَوْساً وَبُنْدُقاً وَبُرجَ حَمَامٍ لَمْ يُصِبكَ رَخاءُ
وَلَمْ تَدْرِ مَا عَيْشٌ وَلَمْ تَلْقَ لَذَّةً فَأَنْتَ حِمَارٌ لَيْسَ فِيكَ مِرَاءُ
فَإِنْ أَنْتَ لَمْ تَفْطَنْ لِعَيْشٍ جَهِلْتَهُ فَدُونَكَهُ مَا دَامَ فِيكَ بَقَاءُ
وَإِيَّاكَ أَنْ تَنْفَكَّ مِنْ سُكْرِ طَافِحٍ مَسَاؤُكَ صُبْحاً وَٱلصَّبَاحُ مَسَاءُ
وَنِكْ مَنْ لَقِيتَ ٱلدَّهْرَ مِنْهُمْ وَلَا يَكُنْ عَلَيْكَ إِذَا أَعْطَوْكَ مِنْكَ إِبَاءُ

Own a dovecote, hunt with a dog and pellet bow,
    you'll always miss out,
You won't know what life is,
    you'll have no fun;
No doubt about it, you'll be an ass.
    If you haven't seized what you've missed
In life, go for it now and for as long as you can.
    Take good care that you don't sober up,
That your morning's evening and your evening morn;
    fuck anyone you meet anytime you want.
No fault of yours if they ask you for more.

دير صبّاعي[1]

وهـذا الدير شرقيّ تكريت مقابل لها مشرف على دجلة وهو نزه عامر له ظاهر عجيب ١،١٧
فسيح ومزارع حوله على نهر يصبّ من دجلة إلى الإسحاقيّ وهو خليج كبير. فيقصد
هذا الدير مَن قرب منه في أعياده وأيّام الربيع وهو إذ ذاك منظر حسن فيه خلق كثير
من رهبانه وقسّانه. ولبعض الشعراء فيه

حَنَّ ٱلْفُؤَادُ إِلَى دَيْرٍ بِتَكْرِيتْ   بَيْنَ صَبَّاعِي وَقَسُّ ٱلدَّيْرِ عِفْرِيتْ

١ الأصل: ضُبَاعي.

The Monastery of Ṣabbāʿī[125]

This monastery lies to the east of Takrit, opposite to it and overlooking the Tigris. It is pleasant and well kept, with wonderful spacious grounds and surrounded by fields. It is on a side canal flowing from the Tigris into the Isḥāqī Canal,[126] which is a great waterway. People from the surrounding area visit this monastery on its feast days and in the spring. Then it is a beautiful sight. Many people, monks and priests, live there. A poet said of it: 17.1

For a monastery by Takrit yearning fills my breast,
Ṣabbāʿī's Convent—and its fiend of a priest.

دير الأعلى

هـذا الدير بالموصل يطلّ على دجلة والعروب[1] وهو دير كبير عامر فيه قلّايات كثيرة لرهبانه وله درجة منقورة في الجبل تفضي إلى دجلة نحو المائة مرقاة وعليها يُستقى الماء من دجلة. وتحت الدير عين كبيرة تصبّ إلى دجلة ولها وقت من السنة يقصدها الناس فيستحمّون منها ويذكرون أنها تبرئ من الجرب والحكّة وتنفع المقرعين والزمنى. ١٨،١

والشعانين في هذا الدير حسن يخرج إليه الناس فيقيمون فيه الأيّام يشربون ومن اجتاز بالموصل من الولاة نزله. وقد قالت الشعراء في هذا الدير ووصفت حسنه ونزهته وللثروانيّ فيه ١٨،٢

إِسْقِنِي ٱلرَّاحَ صَبَاحًا قَهْوَةً صَهْبَاءَ رَاحَا
وَٱصْطَبِحْ فِي ٱلدَّيْرِ ٱلْأَعْلَى فِي ٱلشَّعَانِينِ ٱصْطِبَاحَا
إِنَّ مَنْ لَمْ يَصْطَبِحْهَا ٱلْيَوْمَ لَمْ يَلْقَ نَجَاحَا
ثُمَّ قَلِّدْنِي مِنَ ٱلزَّيْتُونِ وَٱلْخُوصِ وِشَاحَا
فِي ٱلشَّعَانِينِ وَإِنْ لَا قَيْتَ فِي ذَاكَ ٱفْتِضَاحَا
عَظِّمِ ٱلْأَعْلَامَ وَٱلرُّهْبَانَ وَٱلصُّلْبَ ٱلْمِلَاحَا
وَٱجْعَلِ ٱلْبِيعَةَ وَٱلْقَصْرَ جَمِيعًا مُسْتَرَاحَا
لَا كَمَنْ يَمْزَحُ[2] بِٱلشُّهْرَةِ وَٱلْخَلْعِ مُزَاحَا
أَوْ دَعِ ٱلشَّهْوَةَ[3] وَٱلْزَمْ كُلَّ مَنْ يَهْوَى ٱلصَّلَاحَا
وَٱلْزَمِ ٱلْجُمْعَةَ وَٱلْبُكْرَةَ فِيهَا وَٱلرَّوَاحَا

١ الأصل: الغروب. ٢ الأصل: يمرح. ٣ عوّاد: الشهرة.

Al-Aʿlā Monastery[127]

This monastery is in Mosul, overlooking the Tigris and the ʿArūb River. It is large and flourishing, with many monks' cells. A staircase with about a hundred treads cut into the rock leads down to the Tigris, and that is how the monks draw water from the river. Under the monastery is a large spring whose water flows into the Tigris. At a certain time of the year, people come and bathe in it; they say it cures scabies and eczema and helps those with hair loss and the chronically ill. 18.1

Palm Sunday in this monastery is beautiful. People go there and spend several days drinking. Governors who pass through Mosul visit it. Poets have sung of it, describing its beauty and natural surroundings. Al-Tharwānī has the following verses: 18.2

Pour me wine in the morning, crimson, dark, and generous,
An early drink in al-Aʿlā's Convent, a cup on Palm Sunday.
He who doesn't drink today is a ne'er-do-well and hopeless.
Dress me in a garland of palms and olive leaves
To celebrate Palm Sunday, though you think it a scandal.
Honor the banners, the monks, and the fine crosses;
Make the church and the citadel a place to relax,
Not like those who make fun of fame and marks of honor.
Or else give up sensual pleasure, keep company with God-fearers,
Spend your day at the mosque, and attend the Friday prayers.

٣،١٨ وكان المأمون اجتاز بهذا الدير في خروجه إلى دمشق فأقام به أيّاماً ووافق نزوله عيد[١] الشعانين. فذكر أحمد بن صدقة قال خرجنا مع المأمون فنزلنا الدير الأعلى بالموصل لطيبه ونزهته وجاء عيد الشعانين فجلس المأمون في موضع منه حسن مشرف على دجلة والصحراء والبساتين ويشاهد منه مَن يدخل الدير. وزُيّن الدير في ذلك اليوم بأحسن زيّ وخرج رهبانه وقسّانه إلى المذبح وحولهم فتيانهم بأيديهم المجامر قد تقلّدوا الصلبان وتوشّحوا بالمناديل المنقوشة. فرأى المأمون ذلك فاستحسنه. ثمّ انصرف القوم إلى قلاليهم وقربانهم وعطف إلى المأمون من كان معهم من الجواري والغلمان بيد كلّ واحد منهم تحفة من رياحين وقتهم وبأيدي جماعة منهم كؤوس فيها أنواع الشراب فأدناهم وجعل يأخذ من هذا ومن هذه تحيّة وقد شغف بما رآه منهم وما فينا إلّا من هذه حاله. وهو في خلال ذلك يشرب والغناء يُعمل.

٤،١٨ ثمّ أمر بإخراج مَن معه من وصائفه المزنّرات فأُخرج إليه عشرون وصيفة كأنّهنّ البدور عليهنّ الديباج وفي أعناقهنّ صلبان الذهب بأيديهنّ الخوص والزيتون. فقال يا أحمد قد قلت في هؤلاء أبياتاً فغنّني[٢] بها وهي

ظِبَاءٌ كَٱلدَّنَانِيرِ مِلَاحٌ فِي ٱلْمَقَاصِيرِ
جَلَاهُنَّ ٱلشَّعَانِينُ عَلَيْنَا فِي ٱلزَّنَانِيرِ
وَقَدْ زَرْفَنَّ أَصْدَاغًا كَأَذْنَابِ ٱلزَّرَازِيرِ
وَأَقْبَلْنَ بِأَوْسَاطٍ كَأَوْسَاطِ[٣] ٱلزَّنَابِيرِ

ثمّ أخرج نعم جاريته وكانت وصيفة فغنّت

وَزَعَمْتِ أَنِّي ظَالِمٌ فَهَجَرْتِنِي وَرَمَيْتِ فِي كَبِدِي بِسَهْمٍ نَافِذِ
وَنَعَمْ ظَلَمْتُكِ فَٱصْفَحِي وَتَجَاوَزِي هٰذَا مَقَامُ ٱلْمُسْتَجِيرِ ٱلْعَائِذِ

١ الأصل: عند. ٢ الأصل: فغنيني. ٣ الأصل: كأوسط.

Al-Ma'mūn visited this monastery on his way to Damascus[128] and spent several days in it. His stay happened to coincide with Palm Sunday. Aḥmad ibn Ṣadaqah recalled: We had set out with al-Ma'mūn and we stopped at al-Aʿlā Monastery in Mosul because of its beauty and pleasant surroundings. When Palm Sunday came, al-Ma'mūn took his seat in a lovely spot looking out over the Tigris, the fields,[129] and the gardens, where he could see who came into the monastery. The monastery had been beautifully decorated that day. The monks and priests processed to the altar, accompanied by their servers with censers and wearing crosses and embroidered vestments. Al-Ma'mūn found it a beautiful scene to watch. Then those present retired to their cells and their festive offerings. The girls and boys who had accompanied them approached al-Ma'mūn, each with a bunch of freshly cut basil, and a group carrying glasses of different kinds of drink. He motioned to them to come closer, accepting a greeting from first one and then another, delighted at their behavior. All of us felt the same way. Meanwhile, he drank while the singers performed. 18.3

Then he summoned the girdled[130] servant girls who accompanied him, and twenty girls, lovely as full moons, clad in brocade with golden crosses round their necks and palm and olive branches in their hands, appeared. He turned to me. "I've made up some verses about them, so set them to music." These were the verses: 18.4

Palm Sunday revealed to us gazelles
like coins of gold, lovely in their chambers,
Resplendent in their girdles,
advancing, locks curled like starlings' tails,
Swaying, wasp-waisted.

Then he summoned his concubine, the singing girl Nuʿm,[131] and she sang:

You claimed I was unfair and broke with me,
aiming an arrow that pierced my heart.
Yes, I wronged you. But forget and forgive!
I'm begging for help. Won't you give me support?

وطرب وشرب واستعاد الصوت دفعات ثمّ قال لليزيديّ أرأيت أَحسن ممّا نحن ٥،١٨
فيه قال نعم يا أمير المؤمنين أن تشكر مَن خوّلك فيزيدك منه ويحفظه عليك. قال
بارك الله عليك فلقد ذكرت في موضع الذكرى ثمّ أمر بثلاثين ألف درهم فتصدّق
بها للوقت.

وإلى جانب هذا الدير مشهد عمرو بن الحَمِق الخزاعيّ ومسجد[1] بنته بنو حمدان يتّصل ٦،١٨
بالقبر. ولعمرو بن الحمق صحبة وكان من أصحاب عليّ بن أبي طالب صلوات الله عليه
وشهد معه مشاهده كلّها وكان معاوية طلبه دهرًا وهو ينتقل من مكان إلى مكان ثمّ
ظفر به بالموصل وكان قد سقي بطنه واشتدّت علّته فدلّ عليه عبد الرحمٰن بن أمّ الحكم
الثقفيّ وهو ابن أخت معاوية فكبسه في غار بالموصل وقتله وحمل رأسه إلى معاوية.
وهو أوّل رأس حُمل في الإسلام من بلد إلى بلد ودُفنت جثّته في هذا الموضع.
وكانت امرأته آمنة بنت الشريد بدمشق فحبسها معاوية حبسًا طويلاً فلمّا حُمل ٧،١٨
رأس عمرو إليه وجّه به إلى آمنة إلى السجن وقال للرسول أَلقه في حجرها واحفظ ما
تقول.[2] فلمّا أتاها ارتاعت له وأكبّت تقبّله ثمّ قالت واضيعتا في دار هوان. نفيتموه
طويلاً وأهديتموه إليّ قتيلاً فأهلاً وسهلاً بمن كنت له غير قالية وأنا له غير ناسية.
قل لمعاوية أيتم الله ولدك وأوحش منك أهلك ولا غفر لك ذنبك. فعاد الرسول بما
قالت فأمر بها فأُحضرت وعنده جماعة فيهم إياس بن شُرَحْبيل وكان في شدقيه
نتوء لعظم لسانه فقال معاوية لها يا عدوّة الله أنت صاحبة الكلام قالت نعم غير
نازعة عنه ولا معتذرة منه وقد لعمري اجتهدت في الدعاء وأنا أجتهد إن شاء الله
والله من وراء العباد. فأمسك معاوية فقال إياس اقتل هذه فما كان زوجها بأحقّ
بالقتل منها. فقالت ما لك ويلك بين شدقيك جثمان الضفدع وأنت تأمره بقتلي كما
قُتل بعلي ﴿إِن تُرِيدُ إِلَّآ أَن تَكُونَ جَبَّارًا فِى ٱلْأَرْضِ وَمَا تُرِيدُ أَن تَكُونَ
مِنَ ٱلْمُصْلِحِينَ﴾. فضحك معاوية والجماعة وبان الخجل في إياس.

---

١ الأصل: مسجدًا. ٢ الأصل: (مخاطبة آمنة بنت الشريد لمعاوية بعدما أُلقي إليها رأس زوجها) وردت في الهامش.

He was ecstatic and drank some wine, asking her to repeat the song several times. Then he asked al-Yazīdī, "Can you think of anything better than the situation we are in?" "Yes, Commander of the Faithful. Giving thanks to the One who has given you this power, so that He may increase it and preserve it for you." Al-Maʾmūn said, "God bless. It is entirely apposite of you to mention God." Then he called for thirty thousand dirhams, and gave them away on the spot. 18.5

Beside this monastery is the tomb of ʿAmr ibn al-Ḥamiq al-Khuzāʿī and a mosque connected to it built by the Banū Ḥamdān. ʿAmr ibn al-Ḥamiq was a Companion and one of ʿAlī ibn Abī Ṭālib's supporters, God's blessing be upon him. He was with ʿAlī during all his battles. Muʿāwiyah hunted for him for a long time as he moved from place to place, and finally captured him in Mosul. ʿAmr had developed dropsy and become seriously ill, and Muʿāwiyah's nephew ʿAbd al-Raḥmān ibn Umm al-Ḥakam, who had been told of his whereabouts, surprised him in a cave, killed him, and took his head to Muʿāwiyah. (It was the first head to be taken from one city to another in Islamic times.) His corpse was buried in this place. 18.6

His wife, Āminah bint al-Sharīd, was in Damascus, where Muʿāwiyah had kept her imprisoned for a long time. When ʿAmr's head was brought to him, he had it taken to Āminah in prison, instructing the messenger, "Drop it into her lap and take note of what she says."[132] She was shocked when he came. She bent to kiss the head and then cried out, "Woe is me in this abode of shame! You banished him for an age, then you brought him to me slain. Hail, hail this man I've never hated and will never forget! Say to Muʿāwiyah, 'May God make your children orphans, may He make your wives mourn your demise, and may He never forgive your sins.'" When the messenger reported back what she had said, Muʿāwiyah sent for her. He was with a group of men, among them Iyās ibn Shuraḥbīl, whose cheeks bulged because his tongue was so large. Muʿāwiyah asked her, "Enemy of God, are these your words?" "Yes. I take nothing back and do not apologize. I swear, I've dedicated myself to cursing and, God willing, I'll go on doing so. God is behind his servants." Muʿāwiyah held his tongue, but Iyās burst out, "Kill her! She deserves to be killed more than her husband." "What's the matter with you, damn you! You've got a dead toad in your mouth. You're telling him to kill me as he killed my husband. «You only want to be a tyrant in the land, not one of those who set things right.»"[133] Muʿāwiyah and the rest of the company laughed, while Iyās was visibly embarrassed. 18.7

٨،١٨ ثمّ قال لها معاوية اخرجي عنّي فلا أسمع بك في شيء من الشام. قالت سأخرج عنك فما الشام لي بوطن ولا أعرج فيه على حميم ولا سكن ولقد عظمت فيه مصيبتي وما قرّت به عيني وما أنا إليك بعائدة ولا لك حيث كنتُ حامدة. فأشار إليها بيده أن اخرجي فقالت عجباً لمعاوية يبسط عليّ غرب لسانه ويشير إليّ ببنانه. فلمّا خرجت قال معاوية يُحمل إليها ما يُقطَع به لسانها عنّي وتُخفّ به إلى بلدها فقبضت ما أمر لها به وخرجت تريد الكوفة فلمّا وصلت إلى حمص توفّيت بها.

Muʿāwiyah turned to her. "Leave here and go. I don't want to hear that you're still in Syria." "I'll leave you and go. Syria's not my country and I've neither relative nor sanctuary here. This is where I've suffered calamity and known no amity. I won't come back to you, and wherever I may be, I'll utter no praise of you." Muʿāwiyah gestured to her to leave, upon which she remarked, "Just look at Muʿāwiyah, unleashing his vicious tongue on me and pointing his finger at me!" When she had left, Muʿāwiyah said, "Give her enough to silence her attacks on me and enable her to get home." She accepted this and set out for Kufa, but died when she reached Homs. 18.8

ديـر يونس بن متّى

وهـذا الدير يُنسب إلى يونس بن متّى النبيّ صلّى الله عليه وعلى اسمه بُني وهو في ١،١٩
الجانب الشرقيّ من الموصل بينه وبين دجلة فرسخان وموضعه يُعرف بنينوى ونينوى هي مدينة يونس[١] عليه السلام. وأرضه كلّها نوّار وشقائق وله في أيّام الربيع ظاهر حسن مونق وهو مقصود. وتحت الدير عين تُعرف بعين يونس فالناس يقصدون هذا الموضع لخلال منها التنزّه واللعب ومنها التبرّك بموضعه ومنها الاغتسال من العين التي تحتها. وكان اليهود في أيّام الحسن[٢] بن عبد الله بن حمدان دسّوا واحداً منهم فدخل الهيكل وأحدث فيه واتّصل الخبر إلى ابن حمدان فجمع كلّ يهوديّ بالموصل فصادرهم على مال كثير أخذه منهم.

ولأبي شاس منير فيه ٢،١٩

يَا دَيْرَ يُونُسَ جَادَتْ صَوْبَكَ ٱلدِّيَمُ ... حَتَّى تُرَى نَاضِراً بِٱلنُّورِ تَبْتَسِمُ
لَمْ يَشْفِ فِي نَاجِرٍ[٣] مَاءٌ عَلَى ظَمَإٍ ... كَمَا شَفَى حَرَّ قَلْبِي مَاءُكَ ٱلشَّبِمُ
وَلَمْ يَحُلَّكَ مَحْزُونٌ بِهِ سَقَمٌ ... إِلَّا تَحَلَّلَ عَنْهُ ذٰلِكَ ٱلسَّقَمُ
أَسْتَغْفِرُ ٱللهَ مِنْ فَتْكٍ بِذِي غَنَجٍ ... جَرَى عَلَيَّ بِهِ فِي رَبْعِكَ ٱلْقَلَمُ

وكان أبو شاس هذا من أطبع الناس مليح الشعر كثير الوصف للخمر ملازماً للديارات ٣،١٩
متطرّحاً بها مفتوناً برهبانها ومَن فيها فمن شعره الذي وصف فيه الخمر وملح قوله

أَعَارَكَ ٱلْحِلْمُ وَٱلْوَقَارُ ... ثَوْبَاً مِنَ ٱلصَّمْتِ لَا يُعَارُ
فَقُمْ إِلَى ٱلْخَمْرِ فَٱمْتَحِنْهَا ... إِذَا ٱسْتَقَرَّتْ بِكَ ٱلدِّيَارُ

١ الأصل: نينوني. ٢ الأصل: الحسين. ٣ الأصل: ناخرٍ، مصحَّحة في الهامش.

The Monastery of Yūnus ibn Mattā (Jonah Son of Amittai)[134]

This monastery is linked to the prophet Yūnus ibn Mattā, God's blessings be upon him, and is called after him. It stands to the east of Mosul, some six miles (ten kilometers) from the Tigris, at a place called Nineveh. Nineveh is the city of Yūnus, peace be upon him. Its grounds are carpeted with flowers such as anemones. It looks lovely and delightful in spring, and attracts many visitors. Beneath the monastery is a spring known as Yūnus's Spring. People visit the place for various reasons, such as walking in the gardens, amusement, gaining blessing from the place, and washing in the spring below. 19.1

In the days of al-Ḥasan ibn ʿAbdallāh ibn Ḥamdān, the Jews had one of their people infiltrate the sanctuary and defecate there. When Ibn Ḥamdān heard of it, he rounded up all the Jews in Mosul and confiscated a large sum of money from them.

Here are verses by Abū Shās Munīr: 19.2

Convent of Yūnus! May the rains be kind to you,
make you radiant, smiling in the sunlight.
No draft for a thirsty man on a torrid day can equal
your cool water to quench my desire's heat.
The man of sorrow and sickness comes to you,
and is freed of his ills and healed.
I ask God's forgiveness for seducing a coquettish youth;
I let my pen run over him in your abode.

Abū Shās was very gifted and composed fine poetry. He often described wine, and used to frequent the monasteries for relaxation and because he was attracted by the monks and other people there. One of his beautiful poems describing wine is: 19.3

Insight and gravity have clothed you
In a mantle free from blame.

وَغَنَّتِ ٱلطَّيْرُ فِي رِيَاضٍ   زَيَّنَ عِيدَانَهَا ٱخْضِرَارُ
مِنَ ٱلَّتِي صَانَهَا مُلُوكٌ   هُمْ هُمُ ٱلسَّادَةُ ٱلْكِبَارُ
إِذَا بَدَتْ وَٱلدُّجَى مُقِيمٌ   صَارَ مَكَانَ ٱلدُّجَى نَهَارُ
كَأَنَّهُمْ وَٱلْمُدَامُ رَكْبٌ   يَؤُمُّهُمْ فِي ٱلظَّلَامِ نَارُ

٤،١٩ ومن مليح شعره أيضاً

لَا تَعْدِلَنَّ عَنِ ٱبْنَةِ ٱلْكَرْمِ   بِأَبِي فَفِيهَا صِحَّةُ ٱلْجِسْمِ
وَٱعْلَمْ بِأَنَّكَ إِنْ لَهِجْتَ بِغَيْرِهَا   هَطَلَتْ عَلَيْكَ سَحَائِبُ ٱلْهَمِّ
وَإِذَا شَرِبْتَ فَكُنْ لَهَا مُتَيَقِّظًا   حَتَّى تُبَيِّنَ طِيبَةَ ٱلطَّعْمِ
لَوْ لَمْ يَكُنْ فِي شُرْبِهَا مِنْ رَاحَةٍ   إِلَّا ٱلتَّخَلُّصُ مِنْ يَدِ ٱلْغَمِّ

٥،١٩ وقال أيضاً

أَعَاذِلَ مَا عَلَى مِثْلِي سَبِيلُ   وَعَذْلُكَ فِي ٱلْمُدَامَةِ مُسْتَحِيلُ
أَعَاذِلَ لَا تَلُمْنِي فِي هَوَاهَا   فَإِنَّ عِتَابَنَا فِيهَا طَوِيلُ
كِلَانَا يَدَّعِي فِي ٱلْخَمْرِ عِلْمًا   فَدَعْنِي لَا أَقُولُ وَلَا تَقُولُ
أَلَيْسَ مَطِيَّتِي حَقْوَيْ غُلَامٍ   وَوَصْلُ أَنَامِلِي كَأْسٌ شَمُولُ
إِذَا كَانَتْ بَنَاتُ ٱلْكَرْمِ شُرْبِي   وَنُقْلِي وَجْهُهُ ٱلْحَسَنُ ٱلْجَمِيلُ
أَمِنْتُ بِذَيْنِ عَاقِبَةَ ٱللَّيَالِي   وَهَانَ عَلَيَّ مَا قَالَ ٱلْعَذُولُ
وَمُعْتَذِرٍ إِلَيَّ بِشَطْرِ عَيْنٍ   لَهُ عَنْ كَسْرِ نَاظِرِهَا رَسُولُ
صَرَفْتُ ٱلْكَأْسَ عَنْهُ حِينَ غَنَّى   وَإِنَّ لِسَانَهُ مِنْهَا ثَقِيلُ
أَرِحْنِي قَدْ تَرَيَّعَتِ[1] ٱلثُّرَيَّا   وَغَالَتْ كُلَّ لَيْلِي عَنْكَ غُولُ

١ الأصل: يريع؛ عوّاد: ترفعت.

Come, taste the wine and savor it, now that you're settled
And the birds are singing in meadows of green branches.
It's wine kept by kings, true lords and mighty.
When it's poured in the dark, darkness turns to day—
They're night raiders guided by a wine like a fire.

Here is another of his good poems: **19.4**

Don't frown at the daughter of the vine—
by God, it ensures the body's health;
Don't doubt, if you've a passion for anything else,
clouds of care will descend and engulf you.
And when you drink, stay wide awake
to savor the wine's bouquet,
Even if drinking it brings no rest
except escape from distress and decay.

Another poem of his: **19.5**

Blamer! There's no way you can touch me.
To blame me for wine is absurd.
Blamer! Don't reproach me for love of it.
Your reproaches have gone on too long.
We both claim to know about wine,
so let me be, without any wrangling.
Don't I ride on the hips of a youth,
with a full cup at my fingertips?
If the vineyard's daughters are my drink,
and his beautiful face my nibbles,
I'm safe from the blows of destiny.
What blamers say I hold in contempt.
When he cast a glance of excuse at me,
sending a message from his downcast eyes,
I turned the cup away from him as he sang—
his tongue was already heavy from wine.
Let be! The Pleiades tremble in the sky
and my whole night is lost to you.

دير الشياطين

١،٢٠ وهـذا الدير غربيّ دجلة من أعمال بلد بين جبلين في فم الوادي له منظر حسن وموقع جليل. والناس يطرقونه للشرب به وهو من مطارح أهل البطالة ومواطن ذوي الخلاعة وللخبّاز البلديّ فيه

رُهْبَانُ دَيْرٍ سَقَوْنِي ٱلْخَمْرَ صَافِيَةً   مِثْلَ ٱلشَّيَاطِينِ فِي دَيْرِ ٱلشَّيَاطِينِ
مَشَوْا إِلَى ٱلرَّاحِ مَشْيَ ٱلرُّخِّ وَٱنْصَرَفُوا   وَٱلرَّاحُ تَمْشِي بِهِمْ مَشْيَ ٱلْفَرَازِينِ

٢،٢٠ وكان عُبادة لمّا نفاه المتوكّل إلى الموصل يمضي إلى دير الشياطين فيشرب فيه ولم يكن يفارقه فهوي غلاماً من الرهبان بالدير وكان من أحسن الناس وجهاً وقدّاً فهام به وجُنّ عليه ولزم الدير من أجله ولم يزل يخدعه ويلاطفه ويعطيه إلى أن سلخ الراهب من الدير وخرج معه. وفطن رهبان الدير بعبادة وما فعل من إفساده الغلام فأرادوا قتله بأن يرموه من أعلى الدير إلى الوادي ففطن بهم وهرب فلم يعد إلى الموضع.

٣،٢٠ وكان عبادة من أطيب الناس وأخفّهم روحاً وأحضرهم نادرة وكان أبوه من طبّاخي المأمون وكان معه فخرج حاذقاً بالطبيخ ثمّ مات أبوه فتخنّث وصار رأساً في العيارة والخلاعة. فوُصف للمأمون وهو إذ ذاك حدث فاستحضره فلمّا وقف بين يديه تنادر وحاكى ومازح فاستطابه المأمون. فقال امضوا به إلى زبيدة لتراه وتضحك منه فمضوا به إليها فلمّا دخل عليها وجدها على برذعة تاختج وعلى رأسها جارية تذبّ عنها بمذبّة خوص. فقال عبّادة يا ستّي كأنّك من ناطف البركة فضحكت منه واستطابته. فأقام عندها أيّاماً فوصلته وكسته وكانت لا تكاد تصبر عنه.

٤،٢٠ قال جلس المأمون في بعض الأيّام وأمر بأن تُحضر اللحوم والحيوان وما يُحتاج إليه من آلة الطبيخ وقال للندماء ليطبخ كلّ واحد منكم قدراً وطبخ هو أيضاً قدراً وطبخ أخوه

The Devils' Monastery[135]

This monastery stands to the west of the Tigris in the district of Balad, between two mountains at the entrance to the valley. It is beautiful and occupies a splendid site. People visit it to drink, and it is a place where loafers and profligates gather. Al-Khabbāz al-Baladī has these verses on it: 20.1

The monks poured me pure wine to drink,
like the devils in the Devils' Convent.
Like rooks they walked to the wine, and turned back
mincing like queens.[136]

When al-Mutawakkil exiled ʿUbbādah to Mosul, he would go to the Devils' Monastery to drink and stay there. He fell in love with a very handsome young monk who had a fine figure and became crazily infatuated with him. He stayed there because of him, deceiving and flattering him and giving him presents, until he prized him away from it and spirited him away. The monks, who realized what ʿUbbādah was up to and how he had debauched the youth, wanted to kill him by throwing him from the highest point of the monastery into the valley, but he guessed what they were planning and fled, never to return. 20.2

ʿUbbādah was one of the nicest people, witty and full of jokes. His father had been one of al-Ma'mūn's cooks, and through spending time with him he became an expert in cooking. When his father died, he came out and turned into a thorough vagabond and wastrel. He was mentioned to al-Ma'mūn when he was very young, so al-Ma'mūn summoned him. In the caliph's presence, ʿUbbādah started to tell funny stories, mimicking and cracking jokes. Al-Ma'mūn found him amusing and said, "Take him to Zubaydah for her to see him and laugh at him." When he entered her presence, he found her sitting on a Nīshāpūrī saddlecloth with a slave girl behind her fanning her with a palm-frond fan. ʿUbbādah said, "Madam, you look as if you were made of cream on top of pastry." She laughed. She liked him, and so he stayed for a few days with her. She gave him money and clothes, and could hardly let him out of her sight. 20.3

One day, al-Ma'mūn was holding audience. He ordered butchered meat and all the necessary cooking utensils. Then he said to his courtiers, "Let everyone 20.4

أبو إسحاق قدرًا ففاحت لها روائح غلبت على روائح قدورهم طيبًا وعطريّة فعجبوا من ذلك. وعبّادة حاضر فحسده فقال إن أردت أن تزيد في طيب قدرك فصُبّ فيها سُكرّجة كامخ فأخذ سُكرّجة كامخ كَبَر وصبّها في القدر فساعة صبّ السُّكرّجة فاحت لها روائح منتنة. فقال المأمون ويلكم ما هذه الرائحة المنتنة قال عبّادة رائحة قدر أخيك الطبّاخ قال ماذا طرحتَ فيها حتّى عادت بعد الطيب إلى هذه الرائحة فقال سُكرّجة كامخ كبر أشار بها عبّادة. فقال أما علمت أنّك إذا أدخلت جسمًا ميّتًا على جسم حيّ أفسده فحقدها المعتصم على عبّادة فلمّا ولي المعتصم أمر بقتله ثمّ قال ما لهذا الكلب من القدر ما يُقتل ولكن انفوه فنُفي. فلمّا ولي الواثق ردّه فكان معه ثمّ مع المتوكّل بعده ثمّ غضب عليه المتوكّل فنفاه إلى الموصل.

٥،٢٠ قال أبو حازم الفقيه وقد جرى ذكر عبّادة ما كان أظرفه. قيل وكيف قال كان المتوكّل نفاه فلمّا حصل بالموصل تبعه غرماؤه وطالبوه وقدّموه إلى عليّ بن إبراهيم الغَمريّ وهو قاضي الموصل فحلف لواحد ثمّ لآخر ثمّ لآخر فقال عليّ بن إبراهيم ويحك ترى هؤلاء أجمعوا على ظلمك فاتّق الله وارجع إلى نفسك فإن كانت عسرة كانت بإزائها نظرة. قال صدقت فديتك ليس كلّهم ادّعى الكذب ولا كلّهم ادّعى الصدق وإنّما دفعت ما لا أطيق. ثمّ ردّه المتوكّل.

٦،٢٠ وكان من أحضر الناس نادرةً وأسرعهم جوابًا وقال المتوكّل لعبّادة ذات يوم دع التخنيث حتّى أزوّجك. قال أَنت خليفة أَو دلّالة.

وقال له ابن حمدون يا عبّادة لو حججت لاكتسبت أجرًا ورآك الناس في مثل هذا الوجه المبارك فقال اسمعوا ويلكم إلى هذا العيّار يريد أن ينفيني من سامرّا على جمل.

وقال له دعبل يومًا والله لأهجونّك قال والله لئن فعلت لأخرجنّ أمّك في الخيال.

cook a potful." He cooked a pot, and so did his brother Abū Isḥāq. The smells that wafted from Abū Isḥāq's pot were delicious, more savory than the rest, and everyone was surprised at that. ʿUbbādah, who was present, was jealous. He said to him, "If you want to make your dish tastier, add half a cup of vinegar condiment." Abū Isḥāq took half a cup of vinegar sauce with capers and added it to the pot, and the moment he did so it produced a disgusting smell. Al-Ma'mūn exclaimed, "What's this filthy smell, damn it?" ʿUbbādah replied, "The smell of your brother the cook's pot." Al-Ma'mūn turned to his brother. "What did you add to turn the delicious smell into this?" "Vinegar sauce with capers. ʿUbbādah suggested it to me." Al-Ma'mūn commented, "Didn't you know that adding a 'dead' ingredient to a 'living' one ruins it?"[137]

Abū Isḥāq al-Muʿtaṣim held this against ʿUbbādah, and when he became caliph, he ordered his death. But then he said, "This dog is not important enough to deserve killing. Send him into exile." And exiled he was. When al-Wāthiq succeeded, he had ʿUbbādah brought back, and ʿUbbādah attended him, and attended al-Mutawakkil after him. Then he angered al-Mutawakkil, who exiled him to Mosul.

When the talk had turned to ʿUbbādah, Abū Ḥāzim the jurist said, "How witty he was!" The others asked, "In what way?" So he explained: After ʿUbbādah had reached Mosul, his creditors came after him, demanding he settle his debts. They presented him to ʿAlī ibn Ibrāhīm al-Ghamrī, the judge in Mosul, and he swore to one after the other that he had paid them. 20.5

"Damn it!" said ʿAlī ibn Ibrāhīm. "Do you think they've agreed among themselves to wrong you? For God's sake, come to your senses. And if you are in a real difficulty, we can look into it." "You're right, may I be your ransom. They are not all lying, and not all telling the truth. But by God, I've paid out more than I can bear." Later, al-Mutawakkil summoned him back.

He was brilliant at telling jokes and had the quickest repartee. Al-Mutawakkil said to him once, "Stop being effeminate so I can find you a wife." He retorted, "Are you a caliph or a matchmaker?" 20.6

Ibn Ḥamdūn suggested to him: "ʿUbbādah, if you were to perform the pilgrimage, you would earn recompense and people would see you in a blessed place like Mecca." "Listen to this rogue, damn it! He wants to expel me from Samarra on a camel."

Diʿbil warned him one day, "By God, I'll lampoon you without fail." He parried, "By God, if you do so, I'll put your mother into a shadow play."

٧،٢٠ قال سعد بن إبراهيم الكاتب قلت له يوماً يكون مخنّث بغير بغاء قال نعم ولكن لا يكون مليح يكون مثل قاضٍ بدون دنيّة.

وقال يوماً لأبي حرملة المزيّن حذّفني قال يا مخنّث أضع يدي على وجهك وأنا أضعها على وجه أمير المؤمنين قال فأنت أيضاً تضعها على باب استك كلّ يوم خمس مرّات.

قال ودخل عبّادة يوماً الحمّام بغير مئزر متبذّلاً غير محتشم وفي الحمّام شيخ جليل فقال له ويحك أما تستحي استتر بيدك فقال أيش أستر إنّما هي هديّة مكّة مقلتين ومسواك.

٨،٢٠ قال عليّ بن يحيى المنجّم قال عبّادة يوماً للمتوكّل ويحيى بن أكثم القاضي حاضر يا أمير المؤمنين قل ليحيى يعلّمني فرائض الصلب فقال المتوكّل ليحيى هو ذا تسمع فقال وقد علم أنّ المتوكّل غمز عليه عبّادة ليتنادر به سأل محالاً يا أمير المؤمنين قال وكيف قال لأنّ الشاعر يقول

وَإِنَّ مَنْ أَدَّبْتَهُ فِي ٱلصِّبَى كَٱلْعُودِ يُسْقَى ٱلْمَاءَ فِي غَرْسِهِ

وهذا شيخ لا ينجح فيه التعليم ولكن إن كان له ابن حدث ذكر فليأتني به أعلّمه فنظر إليه عبّادة وقال يا قاضي لو كنت من أهل صناعتنا ما قوي بك أحد فقال لست من أهل صناعتك وما بأحد عليّ قوّة.

٩،٢٠ قال وخرج عبّادة يوماً في السحر إلى الحمّام فلقي غلاماً من أولاد الأتراك فأعطاه عشرة دراهم وقال اقطع أمر عمّك فبينا الغلام فوقه خلف الدرب إذ أشرفت عجوز من غرفة لها فرأتهما فصاحت اللصوص فقال عبّادة يا عجوز السوء النقب في استي صياحك أنت من أيش.

١٠،٢٠ وذكر أبو حاتم القاضي قال كنت مقيماً بدمشق مع ابن مدبّر وكان لا يرد عليه كتاب إلّا أقرأنيه فورد عليه كتاب سعيد الرسح[١] خليفة له بسرّ من رأى فقرأه وتبسّم ولم يدفعه

[١] كذا في الأصل.

Sa'd ibn Ibrāhīm the secretary related: "I said to 'Ubbādah once, 'Can a queer exist without debauchery?' 'Yes,' he answered, 'but he won't be any fun. He'll be like a judge without a vice.'" 20.7

'Ubbādah told Abū Ḥarmalah the barber one day, "Give me a trim." "You queer, am I supposed to touch your face with the hand that touches the Commander of the Faithful's face?" "But you touch the hole in your butt with it five times a day."

'Ubbādah once went into the hammam without a loincloth, careless and without a shred of modesty. A venerable shaykh who was there exclaimed, "Have you no shame? Cover yourself with your hand." He flung back, "What should I cover? This is a gift from Mecca: two palm fruits and a toothpick."

According to 'Alī ibn Yaḥyā al-Munajjim, 'Ubbādah one day said to al-Mutawakkil when Judge Yaḥyā ibn Aktham was in attendance: "Commander of the Faithful, tell Yaḥyā to teach me the inheritance rules for direct descendants."[138] Al-Mutawakkil said to Yaḥyā, "You hear what he says?" Yaḥyā, who realized that al-Mutawakkil had put 'Ubbādah up to making fun of him, responded, "He's asked the impossible, Commander of the Faithful." "How's that?" "As the poet says: 20.8

Someone you've trained in his youth
is like a sapling watered when planted.

"This fellow is old and unteachable, but if he has a young son, I'll teach him." 'Ubbādah looked at him and said, "Judge, if you were in our profession, no one could get the better of you." At which Yaḥyā answered, "I'm not in your profession, but still no one has the whip hand over me."

Another anecdote 'Alī ibn Yaḥyā told: One early morning when 'Ubbādah was on his way to the hammam, he met a young Turkish servant. He gave him ten dirhams, saying, "Take care of your uncle's needs." While the boy was on top of him behind the door, an old woman saw them from her room. "Thieves!" she cried out. 'Ubbādah responded, "The disaster is the hole in my butt. Why are you shouting?" 20.9

Abū Ḥāzim the judge related: I was living in Damascus with Ibn al-Mudabbir. No letter arrived without him getting me to read it. But one day a letter came from Sa'īd al-Rasḥ, one of his deputies in Samarra. He read it and smiled, and didn't hand it to me. Then I asked him what it said. He replied, "Sa'īd wrote to say that he was standing at al-Mutawakkil's door when Mūsā ibn 20.10

إليّ فسألته ما فيه فقال كتب لي سعيد يذكر أنّه كان واقفاً بباب المتوكّل إذ خرج موسى ابن عبد الملك وهو متغيّر الوجه فقال لغلامه احمل إلى عبّادة ألف درهم وقل لا تعاود أن تكثر فضولك فسألت عن الخبر فقيل دخل موسى على المتوكّل وهو جالس على بركة السباع وعبّادة بين يديه يتكلّم ويعبث فقال المتوكّل يا موسى قد صدع رأسي عبّادة فما تريحني منه فقال يا أمير المؤمنين اطرحه في بركة الأسد فقال عبّادة نعم اطرحني أنا في بركة الأسد واحمله هو إلى أسد دمشق حتّى يستخرج لك الأموال منه فتغيّر موسى وقامت عليه القيامة وبعث إلى عبّادة بمال أسكته بـه.

'Abd al-Malik came out looking upset. Mūsā told his servant, 'Take 'Ubbādah a thousand dirhams and say to him, "Don't do me such great favors again."' I asked around about what had happened and was told that Mūsā had been admitted to al-Mutawakkil while he was sitting by the pool of the lions with 'Ubbādah in front of him talking and playing the fool. Al-Mutawakkil turned to Mūsā. 'Mūsā, 'Ubbādah's given me a headache. Can you get rid of him for me?' 'Commander of the Faithful,' he answered, 'throw him into the lions' pool.' 'Ubbādah retorted, 'Yes, throw me into the pool of the lions, and send him to the lion of Damascus to extort the revenues from him for you.' Mūsā's face fell, and he panicked and sent 'Ubbādah money to keep his mouth shut."

عُمر الزعفران

١،٢١ هـذا العمر بنصيبين ممّا يلي الجانب الشرقيّ منها في الجبل والجبل مشرف على البلد وهو من الديارات الموصوفة والمواضع المذكورة بالطيب والحسن وحوله الشجر والكروم وفيه عيون تتدفّق وهو كثير القلّايات والرهبان. وشرابه موصوف يُحمل إلى نصيبين وغيرها وليس يخلو من أهل القصف واللعب فهو وسائر بقاعه معمورة بمن يطرقها.

وبهذا الجبل ثلاثة[١] ديارات أُخر في صفّ واحد أحسن شيء منظرًا وأجلّه موقعًا وهي عمر الزعفران ومرأوجين[٢] ومر يوحنّا والعمر الكبير بالموضع أحد متنزّهات الدنيا. وأسفل الجبل الهِرماس وهو نهر نصيبين وعيون تتدفّق من أصل الجبل ويُعرف الموضع برأس الماء. وهذا الجبل أوّل طور عبدين وهو على ثلاثة فراسخ من نصيبين ويجري هذا النهر بين جبلين وعلى حافته الكروم والشجر فإذا وصل إلى نصيبين افترق فرقتين فمنه ما يجتاز بباب سنجار فيسقي ما هناك من البساتين ويصبّ في الخابور ومنه ما يعدل إلى شرقيّ البلد فيدير أرحية هناك ويسقي البساتين أيضًا وما هناك.

٢،٢١ ولمصعب الكاتب في دير عمر الزعفران

عُمِرَتْ بِقَاعُ عُمْرِ ٱلزَّعْفَرَانِ ... بِفِتْيَانٍ غَطَارِفَةٍ هِجَانِ
بِكُلِّ فَتًى يَحِنُّ إِلَى ٱلتَّصَابِي ... وَيَهْوَى شُرْبَ عَاتِقَةِ ٱلدِّنَانِ
بِكُلِّ فَتًى يَمِيلُ إِلَى ٱلْمَلَاهِي ... وَأَصْوَاتِ ٱلْمَثَالِثِ وَٱلْمَثَانِي
ظَلَلْنَا نُعْمِلُ ٱلْكَاسَاتِ فِيهِ ... عَلَى رَوْضٍ كَنَقْشِ ٱلْخُسْرَوَانِيّ
وَأَغْصَانٍ تَمِيلُ بِهَا ثِمَارٌ ... قَرِيبَاتٍ مِنَ ٱلْجَانِي دَوَانِي

---

١ الأصل: ثلث. ٢ كذا في عوّاد؛ الأصل: اوحي.

The Zaʿfarān (Saffron) Monastery

This monastery lies to the east of Nisibis on a mountain that overlooks Balad. It is often described and noted for its fragrance and beauty. It is surrounded by trees and vineyards and it has bubbling springs. It is the location of many cells and monks, and its wine, which is famous, is transported to Nisibis and other places. Pleasure-seekers and revelers frequent it, and its grounds are filled with visitors. 21.1

There are three other monasteries along this mountain ridge, all in a row, and they are a beautiful sight in impressive surroundings. Mār Awgīn's Monastery, Mār Yūḥannā's Monastery,[139] and the Great Monastery[140] together form one of the most memorable places to visit, besides the Zaʿfarān Monastery. Beneath the mountain flows Hirmās, the river on which Nisibis stands, while springs well up from the foot of the mountain in a place known as the Water's Head. The mountain is the beginning of the Ṭūr ʿAbdīn range and is about nine miles (fifteen kilometers) from Nisibis. The river flows between two mountains, its banks lined with vineyards and trees. When it reaches Nisibis, it divides. One stream passes the gateway to Sinjār, irrigating the orchards there and flowing into the Khābūr River. The other turns off to flow east of Balad, where it drives water mills and irrigates orchards and everything else there.

Muṣʿab the Secretary composed these verses on the Zaʿfarān Monastery: 21.2

Zaʿfarān Monastery, may your grounds
be thronged with men noble and proud,
Lovers in search of adventure
and of wine long matured in jars,
Men who turn to lighthearted play
as the plucked lutestrings vibrate.
How often we've passed the cups around
in meadows brocaded with flowers,
And branches heavily laden with fruit
within reach of hands to pluck it;

تُثَنِّيهَا ٱلرِّيَاحُ كَمَا تَثَنَّى بِحُسْنِ قَوَامِهِ مَاوِي جِنَانِ
وَأَنْهَارٍ تُسَلْسِلُ جَارِيَاتٍ يَلُوحُ بَيَاضُهَا كَٱللُّؤْلُؤَانِ
وَأَطْيَارٍ إِذَا غَنَّتْكَ أَغْنَتْ عَنِ ٱبْنِ ٱلْمَارِقِيِّ وَعَنْ بُنَانِ
تُجَاوِبُهَا إِذَا نَاحَتْ بِشَجْوٍ بِقَهْقَهَةِ ٱلْقَوَاقِزِ وَٱلْقَنَانِي
وَغِزْلَانٍ مَرَاتِعُهَا فُؤَادِي شَجَانِي مِنْهُمُ مَا قَدْ شَجَانِي
وشَمْعُونٌ[١] وَيُوحَنَّا وَشَعْيَا ذَوُو ٱلْإِحْسَانِ وَٱلصُّوَرِ ٱلْحِسَانِ
رَضِيتُ بِهِمْ مِنَ ٱلدُّنْيَا نَصِيبِي غَنِيتُ بِهِمْ عَنِ ٱلْبِيضِ ٱلْغَوَانِي
أُقَبِّلُ ذَا وَأَلْثِمُ خَدَّ هٰذَا وَهٰذَا مُسْعِدٌ سَلِسُ ٱلْعِنَانِ
فَهٰذَا ٱلْعَيْشُ لَا حَوْضٌ وَنُؤْيٌ وَلَا وَصْفُ ٱلْمَعَالِمِ وَٱلْمَغَانِي

٣،٢١ وكان مصعب هذا من أشدّ الناس تهتّكاً وأكثرهم خلاعة ومجوناً واستهتاراً بالمرد وتطرّحاً في الحانات والديارات وأشعاره كلّها في الغلمان لا تعدو هذا المعنى إلى غيره ونحن نورد من ذلك ما يُستطرف ويُستطاب ويُستملح من معانيه. ومن شعره قوله

أَنَا ٱلْمَاجِنُ ٱللُّوطِيُّ دِينِي وَاحِدٌ وَإِنِّي فِي كَسْبِ ٱلْمَعَاصِي لَرَاغِبُ
أَلُوطُ وَلَا أَزْنِي فَمَنْ كَانَ لَائِطًا فَإِنِّي لَهُ حَتَّى ٱلْقِيَامَةِ صَاحِبُ
أَدِينُ بِدِينِ ٱلشَّيْخِ يَحْيَى بْنِ أَكْثَمٍ وَإِنِّي عَنْ دِينِ ٱلزُّنَاةِ لَنَاكِبُ
وَمِثْلِ قَضِيبِ ٱلْبَانِ فِي زِيِّ شَاطِرٍ إِذَا مَا بَدَا لِلطَّرْفِ فَٱلْعَقْلُ عَازِبُ
لَهُ نَخْوَةٌ إِنْ قُلْتَ صِلْنِي بِزَوْرَةٍ تَشِيبُ لَهَا يَا بْنَ ٱلْكِرَامِ ٱلذَّوَائِبُ
دَعَوْتُ لَهُ مِنْ قَوْمِ لُوطٍ عِصَابَةً تَذِلُّ لَهُمْ فِي ٱلنَّائِبَاتِ ٱلْمَصَاعِبُ

١ الأصل: وسوهم.

The wind makes them bend like oryx cows
lovely in exquisite gardens.
Streams cascade there, and rivulets,
their drops gleaming white as pearls,
While birds sing songs so lovely
Māriqī's son and Bunān are eclipsed.
When their cooing becomes a lament,
we reply with chuckling cups and bottles.
How many gazelles, come to graze in my heart,
have shaken me to the core!
Shamʿūn, Yūḥannā, and Shaʿyā,
granting favors, well-favored themselves,
With them I've had all I hope for from life.
I've no need of fair maidens;
I stroke one's cheek, kiss another,
and the third, biddable, makes me happy.
This is life! Forget troughs and date pits,
and poems about landmarks and campsites.[141]

Muṣʿab was an extreme example of frivolity, dissoluteness, and debauchery. He was infatuated with young boys and spent his time in taverns and monasteries. All his poems are about boys; he never treats another theme. We will quote some pleasant, interesting, and attractive examples of his poetry and the motifs he develops. For instance: 21.3

I'm a rake and a pervert, it's all I believe in;
I want to earn a reward for my sins.
I go for boys, not girls, and anyone who's a perv
will have me as a friend till Judgment Day.
I follow the faith of Shaykh Yaḥyā ibn Aktham,
not for me the girl-fuckers' creed.
A willow-like boy, dressed as a scoundrel—
when he appears, I lose my mind.
He's got such an ass: when I say, "Pay me a visit,"
the sequel, my friend, will turn your hair white.
I called for a band of gays to meet him—
no mishap or calamity ever stops them

فَقَالَ وَقَدْ غَصَّ ٱلزُّنَارُ بِحَلْقِهِ ... مَقَالَةَ مَنْ أَعْيَتْ عَلَيْهِ ٱلْمَذَاهِبُ
كَرِيمٌ أَصَابَتْهُ مِنَ ٱلدَّهْرِ نَبْوَةٌ ... وَأَيُّ كَرِيمٍ لَمْ تُصِبْهُ ٱلنَّوَائِبُ

٤،٢١ ومن شعره أيضاً[١]

نَصِيحَةُ مَنْ حَوَى أُذْنًا وَطَرْفًا ... أَتَتْكَ وَسَوْفَ تَسْعَدُ إِنْ فَعَلْتَا
عَلَيْكَ إِذَا لَقِيتَ بِحُسْنِ بِشْرٍ ... وَكُنْ مِنْ أَكْثَرِ[٢] ٱلثَّقَلَيْنِ سَمْتَا
وَلَا تُخْلِ ٱلْأَصَابِعَ مِنْ عُقُودٍ ... وَغُتَّ ٱلنَّاسَ بِٱلْآثَارِ غَتَّا
وَعِظْهُمْ وَٱنْهَهُمْ عَنْ مُنْكَرَاتٍ ... وَلَا تَدَعِ ٱلْبُكَاءَ إِذَا وَعَظْتَا
وَوَاخِ أَبَا ٱلَّذِي تَهْوَاهُ كَيْمَا ... يُقَالُ أَخُو أَبِيهِ وَقَدْ ظَفِرْتَا
وَإِنْ أَبْصَرْتَ شَرْطَكَ بَيْنَ قَوْمٍ ... وَلَمْ تَصْبِرْ فَسَارِقْ إِنْ نَظَرْتَا
وَإِنْ فَطِنُوا فَأَطْرِقْ ثُمَّ فَكِّرْ ... كَأَنَّكَ لَمْ تَكُنْ نَظَرًا أَرَدْتَا
وَدَارِ ٱلْمُرْدَ مِنْكَ بِحُسْنِ لُطْفٍ ... وَلَا تَدَعِ ٱلدَّبِيبَ إِذَا سَكِرْتَا
وَصَاتِي يَا سَعِيدُ فَلَا تَدَعْهَا ... فَأَنْتَ مِنَ[٣] ٱلْفَلَاسِفِ إِنْ قَبِلْتَا

٥،٢١ وقال أيضاً

هَجَرْتُ مُجُونِي فَٱسْتَرَحْتُ مِنَ ٱلْعَذْلِ ... وَكُنْتُ وَمَا لِي فِي ٱلتَّمَادِي مِنْ مِثْلِ
فَيَا ٱبْنَ يَمَانٍ هَلْ سَمِعْتَ بِعَاشِقٍ ... يُعَدُّ مِنَ ٱلنُّسَّاكِ فِي مَنْ مَضَى قَبْلِي
أَلَمْ تَرَ أَنِّي حِينَ أَغْدُو مُسَبِّحًا ... بِسَمْتِ أَبِي ذَرٍّ وَفِسْقِ أَبِي جَهْلِ
وَأَخْشَعُ فِي مَشْيِي وَأَصْرِفُ نَاظِرِي ... وَسَجَّادَتِي فِي ٱلْوَجْهِ كَٱلدِّرْهَمِ ٱلْبَغْلِيِّ
وَآمُرُ بِٱلْمَعْرُوفِ لَا مِنْ تَقِيَّةٍ ... وَكَيْفَ وَقَوْلِي لَا يُصَدِّقُهُ فِعْلِي

١ الأصل: (قف على وصيّة مصعب الكاتب) وردت في الهامش. ٢ الأصل: (أحسن) وردت فوق هذه الكلمة.
٣ الأصل: (من) وردت في الهامش.

And he spoke, when the pincers were plunged in his arsehole,
the words of a person who sees no way out:
"An honorable man struck by a blow of fate—
and which honorable man doesn't suffer fate's blows?"[142]

Another of his poems:[143] **21.4**

Here's advice from one who's used his ears and eyes.
Follow it and you'll have good fortune.
Be cheerful at a meeting;
behave like the best of men and jinn,
Prayer beads slipping through your fingers;
smother the company with "The Prophet said . . . ,"
Preach to them, warn them against what's forbidden,
and accompany your sermon with tears.
Get close to the father of your object of love;
when his dad calls you friend, you're well on the way.
If you glimpse your proposition in a group
and can't control yourself, just steal a glance.
If they notice, drop your gaze, be lost in thought,
as if taking a look was the last thing you meant.
Hang around young boys, treat them kindly,
always creep up to them when you're tipsy.
Follow my advice, lucky fellow. If you take it,
you'll be a philosopher, sure as can be.

Here are further poems of his: **21.5**

I gave up debauchery, and my critics left me in peace.
I've taken the prize for perseverance.
Yamāni's son, did you ever hear before
of a lover who was reckoned an ascetic?
Haven't you seen me walking, praising God,
with the mien of Abū Dharr but debauched as Abū Jahl?
I walk humbly, with my eyes on the ground;
prostration's left a mark like a dirham on my forehead.
I enjoin what is good, but not out of piety;
how could I, when my deeds don't match my words?

أَقولُ إِذا مـا قُـلْتُ يَومـاً أَلا ٱتَّقِ   وَلَوْ عَـرَفوا حـالي لَحَلَّ لَهُمْ قَـتْلي
وَمَحْـبَرَتي رَأْسُ ٱلرِّيَاءِ وَدَفْـتَـري   وَنَعْلَيَ بِٱلْأَسْحارِ أَوْ رائِحاً رِجْلي
أَؤُمُّ فَقِـيهاً لَيسَ هَـمِّيَ فِـقْـهَـهُ   وَلٰكِنْ لَدَيْهِ ٱلْمُـرْدُ مُجْتَمِعُ ٱلشَّمْلِ
فَيَا رُبَّ مَغْـرُورٍ غَـرَرْتُ بِدَفْتَري   فَلَمّا ثَناهُ ٱلْحَـزْمُ عـارَضَهُ فِـعْلي
وَكَـمْ أَمْـرَدٍ قَدْ قَـالَ وَالِدُهُ لَهُ   عَلَيْكَ بِهٰذا إِنَّهُ مِنْ ذَوِي ٱلْعَـقْلِ
يَفِـرُّ بِهِ مِنْ أَنْ يُعاشِرَ شاطِراً   كَمَنْ فَرَّ مِنْ حَرِّ ٱلْجِراحِ إِلَى ٱلْقَـتْلِ
فَأَوْسَعْتُهُ نَيْكاً وَلَمْ أُلْفَ عـاجِزاً   وَكُنْتُ لَهُ فِي ٱلْحِفْظِ وَٱللِّينِ كَٱلْبَعْلِ
وَلَيَّـنْتُهُ بِٱلرِّفْقِ مِنْ بَعْـدِ عِـزَّةٍ   كَما لَيَّنَ ٱلرَّوّاضُ مُسْتَصْعَبَ ٱلْإِبْلِ

وقال أيضاً ٦،٢١

وَقَائِلَةٍ تَـرْجُو صَـلاحِي إِلَى مَـتَى   فَقُلْتُ لَهَا مَا دَامَ فِي ٱلْأَرْضِ أَمْـرَدُ
فَقَالَتْ لَقَدْ أَنْضَيْتَ فِي ٱلْغَيِّ جَاهِداً   رَكَائِبَ فِسْقٍ أَنْتَ فِيهَا تُـرَدِّدُ
أَتَبْكِي لِنَشْءٍ بَعْدَ نَشْءٍ فَمَا أَرَى   بُكَاءَكَ حَتَّى يَنْفَدَ ٱلدَّهْرُ يَنْفَدُ
أَعاذِلَ لَوْلَا ٱلْمُرْدُ أَصْبَحْتُ عَابِداً   هُمُ أَهْلَكُوا دِينِي عَلَيَّ وَأَفْسَدُوا
دَعَانِي أُنَاسٌ زَاهِداً حِينَ أَبْصَرُوا   خُشُوعِي أَلَا فِي ٱلزُّهْدِ أَصْبَحْتُ أَزْهَدُ
نَصَبْتُ لَهُمْ تَحْتَ ٱلْخُشُوعِ مَكَايِدِي   وَلِلرِّفْقِ أَحْيَاناً عَوَاقِبُ تُحْمَدُ
تَشَبَّهْتُ بِٱلزُّهَّادِ وَٱلْحَرْبُ خُدْعَةٌ   وَرَاءَيْتُ بِٱلتَّسْبِيحِ وَٱلْكَفُّ تُعْقَدُ

وقال أيضاً ٧،٢١

كُلُّ حَيَاةٍ بِلَا دِينٍ فَفَاسِدَةٌ   وَٱلْمُرْدُ يَا ٱبْنَ يَمَانٍ أَفْسَدُوا دِينِي
كَمْ تَوْبَةٍ بَعْدَهَا أُخْرَى ٱسْتَتَبْتُ بِهَا   فَلَيْسَ دَهْرِي عَلَى دِينِي بِمَأْمُونِ

If I say something once, I say, "Surely, you should fear God,"
but if they knew what I was like they'd have the right to kill me.
My inkwell and notebook are the height of hypocrisy,
my sandals at dawn and my feet on the move.
I frequent a jurist not for his rulings
but because he's collected a bevy of boys.
My scholarly comportment has fooled so many!
When resolution makes them bend, they're faced with my acts.
Many a boy has heard his father say,
"Let this man teach you, he's a superior intelligence."
He consents to his son going about with a rogue
like one who flees from wounding to certain death.
I've fucked him and fucked him, never found wanting;
I've been like a mule, holding back, then letting loose,
And I've treated him gently after rough handling,
as a trainer is gentle with an unruly camel.

Ask a woman who hopes to reform me, "How long still?" **21.6**
"I'll carry on as long as there are boys in the world."
"Your transgression's exhausted debauchery
returning to sin time and again.
Do you weep for one calf and then for another?
I guess you'll be weeping till the end of time."
"You blame me, but if not for boys I'd be a hermit;
they've brought me to sin and ruined my faith.
Men have called me ascetic, seeing my humility,
but I've renounced abstinence, I'm no ascetic.
Beneath humility's cloak I've set my snares.
Cunning can bring praiseworthy fruits.
I wear an ascetic's disguise, but 'deception's part of warfare.'[144]
While I seem to tell my beads, my hand's out for a deal."

Life without religion is corrupt, Yamāni's son, **21.7**
and boys have ruined my religion.
How many acts of repentance I've performed!
Yet my fate's not secure against my religion.

لَوْ أَمَّـنَتْنِي ٱلَّذِي نَفْسِي تُخَوِّفُـهُ   مِنْهُمْ بِبَغْدَادَ يَوْماً عُـذْتُ بِٱلصِّـينِ
وَقَدْ سَـأَلْتُ خَبِـيرًا مِنْ تُجَارِهِمِ   فَظَلَّ مِنْهُ بِحُسْنِ ٱلْوَصْفِ يُنْبِـيـنِي
فَقَـالَ بِٱلصِّـينِ أَلْوَانٌ تَلِينُ لَهَـا   صُلْبُ ٱلْقُـلُوبِ وَأَمْرٌ لَيْسَ بِٱلدُّونِ
وَقَـائِلٍ عُـذْ بِبَـيْتِ ٱللهِ قُلْتُ لَهُ   مَنْ لِي مِنَ ٱلْمُـرْدِ فِي ٱلْإِحْرَامِ يُنْجِينِي
إِذَا بَدَتْ كُثُبٌ لِيثَتْ بِهَا أُزُرٌ   وَقَفْتُ نَصْباً لِمَنْ بِٱللَّحْظِ يَرْمِيـنِي
مَنْ لِي إِذَا رَاحَمُونِي فِي طَوَافِهِمِ   هُنَاكَ يُبْدِي ضَمِيرِي كُلَّ مَكْنُونِ
مَا لِي مِنَ ٱلْمُرْدِ إِلَّا ٱللهُ يَعْصِمُنِي   رَبُّ ٱلْمَثَانِي وَطٰهٰ وَٱلطَّوَاسِـينِ
قَدْ كُنْتُ فِي ٱلنُّسْكِ قَبْلَ ٱلْيَوْمِ مُنْغَمِساً   يَشُوبُ حُبِّي لَهُمْ سَمْتُ ٱبْنِ سِـيرِينِ
أَدْنُو بِعَـيْنِ تَقِيٍّ حَشْوُ مُـقْلَتِهَـا   حُبٌّ لِكُلِّ تَقِيِّ ٱلْخَـدِّ ذِي لِينِ
فَٱلْآنَ تُبْتُ فَحَسْبِي مِنْهُمُ نَظَرِي   أَسْتَغْفِـرُ ٱللهَ وَٱلتَّقْبِيلَ فِي ٱلْحِينِ

وقال أيضاً ٨،٢١

إِنِّي بَكَيْتُ لِجِسْمٍ فِي تَنَقُّصِهِ   لَمْ أَبْكِ رَسْماً وَلَا رَبْعـاً وَلَا دَارَا
وَشَاطِرٍ ذِي ٱخْتِيَالٍ فِي تَكَرُّهِهِ   كَٱلْغُصْنِ يَأْلَفُ فُسَّاقاً وَشُطَّارَا
مَا زِلْتُ عَنْهُ بِمَكْرِي وَٱلْخِدَاعِ إِلَى   أَنْ صَارَ عِرْفَانُهُ لِلْحَقِّ إِنْكَارَا
قَاتَلْتُ[1] عَقْلَ ٱلْفَتَى بِٱلْكَأْسِ أَقْرَعُهَا   بِٱلْخَمْرِ أُتْبِعُهَا شِعْراً وَأَسْمَارَا
حَتَّى إِذَا مَا ٱسْتَعَارَ ٱللَّيْلُ مُهْجَتَهُ   وَقَبَضَ ٱلنَّوْمُ أَسْمَاعاً وَأَبْصَارَا
دَبَبْتُ أَمْشِي عَلَى ٱلْكَفَّيْنِ أَلْمَسُهُ   كَمَشْيِ مُسْتَرِقٍ لِلسَّمْعِ أَسْرَارَا
وَكَرَّ يَمْشُقُ فِي قِرْطَاسِهِ قَلَمِي   وَٱللَّيْلُ مُلْقٍ عَلَى ٱلْآفَاقِ أَسْتَارَا

١ الأصل: فاىلب؛ عوّاد: فَاتَلْتُ.

Were it to protect me from what I fear of them
in Baghdad, I'd seek refuge in China.
I asked a well-informed merchant about China.
He gave me a glowing description:
In China there are boys to soften any heart,
of every kind, and fine ones too.
Some have advised me, "Take refuge in God's House,"[145]
but who will save me from boys in pilgrim's garb?
When buttocks appear swathed in wrappers,
I stand erect if someone looks my way.
What can I do? If they crowd round me at the Kaaba,
all my secret thoughts are revealed.
What have I to do with boys? May God protect me,
Lord of the Qur'an, its surahs and verses.
I was immersed before in self-denial,
hiding my desire, as pious as Ibn Sīrīn.
My God-fearing eyes spoke of love as I approached
every supple boy with pure and pious cheeks.
Now repentant, I only look at them,
and, God forgive me, steal a kiss from time to time.

I don't cry over ruined campsites or pastures; **21.8**
I lament for my body as it declines.
A smart fellow, his distaste seductive,
a pliable branch, friend of perverts and scoundrels,
I kept at him with cunning and deceit
till the Truth he'd recognized he came to deny.
I fought with his mind, in my arms cups full of wine,
following them up with poems and sweet talk
Until the night had laid claim to his spirit
and sleep had closed his eyes and ears.
Then I crept my way toward him,
like someone stealing overheard secrets.
My pen ran back and forth in his parchment,
while night's curtains hid the horizon.

فَقَالَ لَمَّا ٱنْجَلَى عَنْ عَيْنِهِ وَسَنٌ وَقَدْ رَأَى تِكَّةً حُلَّتْ وَآثَارَا
يَا رَاقِدَ ٱللَّيْلِ مَسْرُورًا بِأَوَّلِهِ إِنَّ ٱلْحَوَادِثَ قَدْ يَطْرُقْنَ أَسْحَارَا

وله أيضاً ٩،٢١

وَمُغْفٍ عَلَى ٱلْكَأْسِ مِنْ سُكْرِهِ تَبَذَّلْتُ مَا صَانَ مِنْ ظَهْرِهِ
وَقَبَّلْتُهُ مِائَتَيْ قُبْلَةٍ وَلَمْ أَرْضَ إِلَّا عَلَى ثَغْرِهِ
وَأَعْزِزْ عَلَيَّ بِمَا سَرَّنِي مِنَ ٱلْإِقْتِدَارِ عَلَى أَمْرِهِ
فَلَمَّا تَنَبَّهَ أَبْصَرْتُهُ مِنَ ٱلْغَيْظِ يَخْرُجُ مِنْ قِشْرِهِ
وَقَدْ كَانَ فِي سَقْيِهِ كَادَنِي وَلٰكِنَّهُ رُدَّ فِي نَحْرِهِ

وله أيضاً ١٠،٢١

يَا أَيُّهَا ٱلْمُرْدُ قَدْ نَصَحْتُ لَكُمْ خَافُوا مِنَ ٱللهِ فَضْلَ نِقْمَتِهِ
إِذَا سَطَا أَمْرَدٌ وَتَاهَ عَلَى عَاشِقِهِ كَانَ غِبَّ سَطْوَتِهِ
أَنْ يَبْعَثَ ٱللهُ فِي مَحَاسِنِهِ شَعْرًا فَيُطْفِي ضِيَاءَ بَهْجَتِهِ
عُقُوبَةُ ٱلْأَمْرَدِ ٱلَّذِي كَثُرَتْ ذُنُوبُهُ فِي خُرُوجِ لِحْيَتِهِ
يُنْكِرُهُ ٱلنَّاسُ بَعْدَ مَعْرِفَةٍ وَقَدْ تَوَاصَوْا بِطُولِ جَفْوَتِهِ
هٰذَا نَبِيُّ ٱلْإِلٰهِ قَبْلَكُمُ قَدْ أَنْكَرَتْهُ عُيُونُ إِخْوَتِهِ
وَبَعْدَهُ أَيْنَ حُسْنُ وَجْهِ أَبِي بَكْرٍ وَأَلْحَاظُهُ بِفِتْنَتِهِ
وَأَيْنَ بَخْطَارُهُ وَنَخْوَتُهُ وَقَتْلُهُ ٱلْمُبْتَلَى بِنَبْوَتِهِ
قَدْ عَقْرَبَ ٱلصُّدْغُ فَوْقَ وَجْنَتِهِ عَلَى بَيَاضٍ مِنْ تَحْتِ حُمْرَتِهِ
صَارَ عَلَى ٱلنَّاسِ بَعْدَ عِزَّتِهِ مِثْلَ قُعَيْسٍ بِبَابِ عَمَّتِهِ

When the sleep cleared from his eyes
and he saw his undone pants and the stains,
He said, "You watcher, happy as night falls,
disasters may happen at dawn."[146]

A boy so drunk he lolled over his cup, 21.9
I paid out freely to keep him afloat.
I gave him kisses two hundred times,
accepting nothing but his mouth.
What joy it was when at last
I took him and possessed him.
When he came to, I saw that he
was beside himself with fury.
He'd tricked me when he poured the wine,
but he paid for it when he was slaughtered.

You beardless boys, here's some advice: 21.10
Fear God's engulfing vengeance.
If a boy's haughty and spurns his lover,
his power will come to an end
When God grows hair on his face,
dimming the light of his splendor.
The boy who's committed many sins
is punished with a beard,
People who knew him ignore him,
in league to give him the cold shoulder.
Long before you, the prophet of God
was looked down on by his brothers.[147]
And then Abū Bakr,[148] where's his lovely face,
and his so-seductive glances,
His swaying walk, his arrogance,
his murder of his lovers with rejection,
His locks curled scorpion-like over his temples,
his skin lily white with a hint of pink?
After his moment of glory, he's become
a wretch in the rain with nowhere to go.[149]

عُمر أَحْويشا

١،٢٢ وتفسير أَحْوِيشا بالسّريانيّة الحبيس وهذا العمر بسعرت وسعرت[١] مدينة كبيرة من ديار بكر بقرب أَرزن والعمر مطلّ على أرزن وهو كبير عظيم فيه أربعمائة راهب في قلالي وحوله بساتين وكروم وهو في نهاية العمارة وحسن الموقع وكثرة الفواكه والخمور ويُحمل منه الخمر إلى المدن المذكورة. وبقربه عين عظيمة تدير ثلاث أرحاء. وإلى جانبه نهر يُعرف بنهر الروم وهذا العمر مقصود من كلّ موضع للتنزّه فيه والشرب. والخلعاء والمتطرّبون أغلب عليه من أهله.

٢،٢٢ وللبّاديّ الشاعر فيه

وَفِتْيَانٍ كَهَمِّكَ مِنْ أُنَاسٍ ... خِفَافٍ فِي ٱلْغُدُوِّ وَفِي ٱلرَّوَاحِ
نَهَضْتُ بِهِمْ وَسِتْرُ ٱللَّيْلِ مُلْقًى ... وَضَوْءُ ٱلصُّبْحِ مَقْصُوصُ ٱلْجَنَاحِ
نَؤُمُّ بِدَيْرِ أَحْوِيشَا غَزَالًا ... غَرِيبَ ٱلْحُسْنِ كَٱلْقَمَرِ ٱللِّيَاحِ
وَكَابَدْنَا ٱلسُّرَى شَوْقًا إِلَيْهِ ... فَوَافَيْنَا ٱلصَّبَاحَ مَعَ ٱلصَّبَاحِ
نَزَلْنَا مَنْزِلًا حَسَنًا أَنِيقًا ... بِمَا نَهْوَاهُ مَعْمُورَ ٱلنَّوَاحِ
قَسَمْنَا ٱلْوَقْتَ فِيهِ لِٱغْتِبَاقٍ ... عَلَى ٱلْوَجْهِ ٱلْمَلِيحِ وَلِٱصْطِبَاحِ
ظَلَلْنَا[٢] بَيْنَ رَيْحَانٍ وَرَاحٍ ... وَأَوْتَارٍ تُسَاعِدُنَا فِصَاحِ
وَسَاعَفَنَا ٱلزَّمَانُ بِمَا أَرَدْنَا ... فَأُبْنَا بِٱلْفَلَاحِ وَبِٱلنَّجَاحِ

وكان هذا اللبّاديّ يُكنّى أبا بكر أحمد بن محمّد من طيّاب الناس وملاحهم وذوي المجانة والخلاعة. وسُمّي اللبّاديّ لأنّه كان يلبس أبدًا على ثيابه لبادًا أحمر.

١ الأصل: بسعوب وسعوب. ٢ كذا في عوّاد؛ الأصل: ظلنا.

The Monastery of Aḥwīshā (the Anchorite)

Aḥwīshā is a Syriac word meaning "anchorite." This monastery is by Siirt, a large town in the Diyarbakir region near Arzan, and it overlooks Arzan. It is enormous, with four hundred monks living in cells. Orchards and vineyards surround it; it is flourishing, beautifully situated, and well supplied with fruit and wines. The wine is sent to the cities mentioned above to be sold. Close to the monastery is a large spring whose water powers three mills, and next to it flows a river called the Byzantines' River.[150] People from all over visit this monastery to relax and drink, and revelers and pleasure-seekers in fact outnumber the residents. 22.1

The poet al-Lubbādī composed these verses on it: 22.2

With young men better than any,
light in their movements and cheerful,
I set off when night's curtain was drawn,
and the wings of the morning's light clipped.
We sought a gazelle at the Anchorite's Monastery,
of wondrous beauty, a silvery moon.
For longing for him we bore the night journey,
and we saw his matinal charm as dawn broke.
We lodged in a fine and elegant dwelling
richly supplied with all our needs.
We toasted his face in the morning;
in the evening we toasted it again,
Between scented basil, wine, and the lute,
its strings giving voice to our delight.
Fate granted us what we wanted;
success and prosperity were ours.

Al-Lubbādī's full name was Abū Bakr Aḥmad ibn Muḥammad. He was a very pleasant and good-looking fellow, frivolous and dissipated. He earned the nickname "al-Lubbādī" because he always wore a red felt over his clothes.

ذكر أبو عليّ الأوارجيّ أنّه كان يتقلّد أرْدبيل قال فقسّطت في وقت من الأوقات عشرين ألف دينار بالعدل فيهم على قدر أحوالهم فكان فيمن لحقه التقسيط اللبّاديّ هذا فكُتب باسمه عشرون ديناراً .قال فبينا أنا جالس في الديوان أستخرج إذ دخل عليّ رجل قد طيّن وجهه بطين أحمر وعليه لباد أحمر وعمامة حمراء وبيده عكّاز أحمر وفي رجليه خفّان أحمران فسلّم ووقف وبدأ ينشد في قصيدة عملها قال فيها ٣،٢٢

لَئِنْ كَانَ ٱلْأَمِيرُ بِهِ ٱفْتِقَارُ إِلَى ٱلشُّعَرَاءِ فِي كَرَمِ ٱلنِّصَابِ
لَقَدْ أَوْدَتْ بِهِ ٱلْأَيَّامُ حَتَّى لَقَدْ رَامَ ٱلْعِرَاقَ مِنَ ٱلْكِلَابِ

فقلت من هذا قالوا هذا أبو بكر اللبّاديّ الشاعر. فرفعته ثمّ سألته عن قصيدته في أحمد بن حسن الماذرائيّ وخبره معه.

فقال لي قصدته فوجدته سائراً نحو قزوين فوقفت له على طريقه خلف حجر بهذا الزيّ الذي تراه عليّ فلمّا أن دنا منّي خرجت إليه فقلت ٤،٢٢

كَمَا تَرَى صَيَّرَنِي

فقال ماذا.

فقلت

قَطْعِي قِفَارَ ٱلدِّمَنِ
أَقْطَعُهَا طَوْرًا وَطَوْ رًا بِٱلسُّرَى تَقْطَعُنِي
أَسْرِي عَلَى سَبَّاقَةٍ فِي سَيْرِهَا لَمْ تَخُنِ
لَا تَعْرِفُ ٱلذُّلَّ وَلَا قِيدَتْ بِثَنْيِ ٱلرَّسَنِ
أَسْعَى بِهَا مُعْتَسِفًا إِلَيْكَ يَا ابْنَ ٱلْحَسَنِ
مُسْتَعْدِيًا فَأَعْدِنِي عَلَى صُرُوفِ ٱلزَّمَنِ
فَقَدْ وَرَبِّ ٱلرُّكْنِ أَوْ هَى لِيَ مَشْيِي رُكُنِي

Abū ʿAlī al-Awārijī related that once, when he was governor of Ardabīl, he levied twenty thousand dinars, dividing the amount fairly according to the circumstances of the different individuals. He takes up the story: One of the people concerned was al-Lubbādī, and I assessed him for twenty dinars. While I was sitting in the office to receive the money, a man came in. He had plastered his face with red clay and was wearing a red felt and red turban. He had a red cane in his hand and was wearing red slippers. He greeted me, struck a pose, and began to recite from a poem he had composed: 22.3

> If the emir ever had need of poets of noble origin,
> Fate has brought him so low
> That he'd even take their gnawed bones
> from the dogs.

I asked, "Who on earth is this?" and was told that it was the poet Abū Bakr al-Lubbādī. I asked him to stop, and then inquired about his poem in praise of Aḥmad ibn al-Ḥasan al-Mādharāʾī and the meeting they'd had.

So he told me: "I set out to meet him and found him on the road to Qazvīn. I lay in wait for him on the road behind a rock, dressed as you see me. When he approached, I stepped out to meet him, declaiming: 22.4

> As you now see me, I'm wearied.

"'What?' he asked. So I went on:

> From crossing the wastes with their ruins.
> At times I traverse them with ease;
> at others the night journeys exhaust me,
> Mounted on a swift racing camel,
> who never falls short in her paces,
> Who knows no humiliation
> and has no need of a halter.
> With her I turn aside to meet you,
> Ḥasan's son, to ask your help.
> Support me, I beg you,
> against fickle time's changes!
> By the Lord of the Kaaba,
> my life's course has shaken my firm frame.

كَمْ جَرْعَةٍ جَرَّعَنِي وَغُصَّةٍ غَصَّصَنِي
كَأَنَّمَا يَطْلُبُنِي فِي مَرِّهِ بِٱلْإِحَنِ
فَٱلْحَمْدُ لِلّٰهِ ٱلَّذِي أَدَالَ مِنْ دَهْرِي ٱلدَّنِي
يَا ذَا ٱلَّذِي مِنْهُ ثِمَا رُ ٱلْجُودِ يَجْنِي ٱلْمُجْتَنِي
جُودُكَ مِنْ أَعْلَى ٱلذُّرَى يَدْعُو بِصَوْتٍ مُعْلِنِ
حَيَّ عَلَى ٱبْنِ ٱلْحَسَنِ حَيَّ عَلَى ٱلْبَدْرِ ٱلسَّنِي
حَيَّ عَلَى مَنْ جُودُهُ كَصَوْبِ ٱلْمَاءِ ٱلْمُزُنِ
فَجِئْتُ أَسْعَى وَٱلَّذِي مِنْ عَرْشِهِ وَفَّقَنِي
لِحُبِّ آلِ ٱلْمُصْطَفَى وَحُبُّهُمْ أَنْقَذَنِي
دُونَكَهَا قَوَافِيًا أَجَلْتُ فِيهَا فِطَنِي
لَبُسْكَهَا أَحْسَنُ مِنْ لُبْسِ نَسِيجِ عَدَنِي

قال فأمر لي بعشرة آلاف درهم وحملني على دابّة بسرجه ولجامه.

قال أبو عليّ فوقّعت إلى المستخرج بإعطائه براءة بما قسط عليه فأخذ البراءة وشكرني وانصرف.

٥،٢٢ ومدح اللبّاديّ أبا قاسم يوسف بن ديوداذ أبي الساج[١] فصار إلى داره فلمّا دخل الدهليز قال له الحاجب وأنكر زيّه ولبّاده أيّ شيء أنت قال شاعر وقد مدحت الأمير فقال لبعض من بين يديه زَبِّطْرَه فزبطره وانصرف. وكتب إلى أبي بكر محمّد بن أحمد كاتب الأفشين

١ الأصل: ديوداذ بن أبي الساج.

How many blows I've suffered,
how many sorrows I've had!
As though in the turns my life's taken
I've been attacked with hatred.
Praise be to God who
has deflected scandal from me.
You whose largesse bears
fruits that all may pluck,
Your generosity shouts
in ringing tones from the highest peak,
'Come to Ḥasan's son,
come to the radiant moon.
Come to the giver whose gifts
rain down from the clouds.'
So by the One who helped me
from His throne, I've come,
Brought by love of the Prophet
and of his family.
I offer these verses
over which I've long reflected.
They suit you better by far
than any brocade from Aden."

Al-Lubbādī continued: "He ordered me to receive ten thousand dirhams and gave me a mount with saddle and bridle."

Abū 'Alī said: So I sent a note with my signature to the receiver to give him an exemption from what he had been assessed for. He took the exemption, thanked me, and left.

Al-Lubbādī composed a panegyric on Yūsuf ibn Dīwdādh Abī al-Sāj and took it to his palace. When he entered the hallway, the porter, who didn't like the look of his clothes and his felt, said to him, "What are you?" "A poet," he answered, "and I've made a poem praising the emir." The porter turned to one of the bystanders. "Throw him out." He was thrown out, so he went off and wrote to Abū Bakr Muḥammad ibn Aḥmad, the Afshīn's[151] secretary: 22.5

مَدَحْتُ ٱلْأَمِيرَ أَبَا قَاسِمٍ   وَنَفْسِي لِجَدْوَاهُ مُسْتَنْظِرَهْ
بِمَدْحٍ كَوَشْيِ رِيَاضِ ٱلرَّبِيعِ غَلَّسَهُ ٱلطَّلُّ إِذْ بَاكَرَهْ
وَقَالُوا هُمَامٌ جَزِيلُ ٱلثَّنَاءِ   جَزِيلُ ٱلْأَيَادِي وَلَمَّا أَرَهْ
فَلَمَّا ٱنْتَهَيْتُ إِلَى دَارِهِ   جُزِيتُ عَلَى مَدْحِهِ زَنْطَرَهْ
فَأَنْكَرْتُ جَائِزَتِي مِنْهُمُ   وَكَانَتْ لَعَمْرَ[1] أَبِي مُنْكَرَهْ[2]
وَأَمْكَنْتُ نَفْسِي مِنَ ٱلْحَادِثَاتِ   وَأَيْقَنْتُ أَنِّي صَرِيعُ ٱلشَّرَهْ
فَبَكِّ عَلَى ٱلشِّعْرِ وَٱلْمُكْرُمَاتِ   وَنَادِ بِهِنَّ مِنَ ٱلْمَقْبَرَهْ
فَقَدْ أَسْخَنَ ٱللهُ عَيْنَ ٱمْرِئٍ   يُقَالُ لَهُ ٱلْآنَ مَا أَشْعَرَهْ
فَهَلْ يَا مُحَمَّدُ مِنْ نَائِلٍ   يَبُلُّ ٱللَّهَاةَ أَوَ ٱلْحَنْجَرَهْ
فَمَنْ يَفْعَلِ ٱلْخَيْرَ خَيْرًا يَرَهْ   وَمَنْ يَفْعَلِ ٱلشَّرَّ شَرًّا يَرَهْ

فقال أبو بكر أي والله وكرامة. ووجّه إليه توقيعاً بخمسين ديناراً[3] إلى الجهبذ فأبى الجهبذ أن يقبض التوقيع إلّا أن يقيم عنده فأقام عنده ودفع إليه الخمسين ديناراً[4] وخمسة من عنده. ثمّ أوصله أبو[5] بكر إلى أبي القاسم يوسف وحدّثه حديثه فضحك منه وسمع شعره وأعطاه وحمله وكساه.

١ الأصل: لعمرو. ٢ في الهامش الأبيات الأربعة الآتية: وَقَدْ أَبَى لِي مَعْدِنِي / أَنْ لَا أَكُونَ مَعَ دَنِي // وَالعِرْقُ مِن يَدِي دَنِي / يَأْنَفُ مِنْهُ دَيْدَنِي // وَلَسْتُ مِمَّنْ غَرَّهُ / فِي النَّاسِ خُضْرُ الدِّمَنِ // أَمُوتُ ظَمْآنًا وَلَا / أَشْرَبُ ماءَ الحُقَنِ. ٣ الأصل: دينار.
٤ الأصل: دينار. ٥ الأصل: إلى.

I praised the emir Abū Qāsim,
  and appealed to him for a gift,
With a poem bright as a meadow in spring,
  glistening at dawn, after night's dew.
They said: He's a hero, deserving high praise,
  a generous giver. I'd never seen him.
When I reached his palace, all I got
  for praising him was to be thrown out.
I didn't approve their reward,
  I swear by my father, blame it deserved,[152]
But I set my mind to reflect on it,
  and saw I'd fallen victim to greed.
Lament for poetry and generous deeds!
  Proclaim their fate from the graveyard!
A man who's much admired as a poet
  has wept hot tears of spite.
Is there any gift now in view, Muḥammad,
  to move throat and tongue to action?
He who does good, it's good he'll see;
  he who does evil will see evil.[153]

Abū Bakr responded, "Yes, certainly, by God." He sent a signed request for fifty dinars in favor of al-Lubbādī to the clerk of finances, who refused to honor it unless the poet spent some time with him. When al-Lubbādī did so, he received the fifty dinars and an extra five from the clerk. Then Abū Bakr brought him to Abū l-Qāsim Yūsuf, telling Abū l-Qāsim about him. Abū l-Qāsim laughed, listened to his poetry, and rewarded him with money, a mount, and clothes.

دير فيق

وهــذا الدير في ظهر عقبة فيق فيما بينها وبين بحيرة طبريّة في جبل يتّصل بالعقبة ١،٢٣
منقور في الحجر وهو عامر بمن فيه ومَن يطرقه من النصارى لجلالة قدره عندهم. وغيرهم
يقصده للتنزّه والشرب فيه. والنصارى يزعمون أنّه أوّل دير للنصرانيّة وأنّ المسيح صلّى
الله عليه كان يأوي إليه ومنه دعا الحواريّين وفيه حجر ذكروا أنّ المسيح كان يجلس عليه
فكلّ مَن دخل الموضع كسر قطعة من ذلك الحجر تبرّكًا به. وعُمل هذا الدير في الموضع
على اسم المسيح عليه السلام.

ولأبي نواس يذكره ٢،٢٣

بِحَجِّكَ قَاصِدًا مَاسَرْجِسَانِ　　فَدَيْرَ ٱلنَّوْبَهَارِ فَدَيْرَ فِيقِ

وهي قصيدة طريفة يخاطب فيها غلامًا نصرانيًا كان يهواه.[١] أوّلها

بِمَعْمُودِيَّةِ ٱلدَّيْرِ ٱلْعَتِيقِ　　بِمُطْرِنِيهَا بِٱلْجَاثَلِيقِ
بِشَمْعُونٍ بِيُوحَنَّا بِعِيسَى　　بِمَا سَرْجِيسَ بِٱلْقَسِّ ٱلشَّفِيقِ
بِمِيلَادِ ٱلْمَسِيحِ بِيَوْمِ دِنْحٍ　　بِبَاعُوثَا بِتَأْدِيَةِ ٱلْحُقُوقِ
بِأُشْمُونِي وَسَبْعٍ قَدَّمَتْهُمْ　　وَمَا حَادُوا جَمِيعًا عَنْ طَرِيقِ
بِمَارَتِ مَرْيَمٍ وَبِيَوْمِ فِصْحٍ　　وَبِٱلْقُرْبَانِ وَٱلْخَمْرِ ٱلْعَتِيقِ
وَبِٱلصُّلْبَانِ تَرْفَعُهَا رِمَاحٌ　　تَلَأْلَأُ حِينَ تُومِضُ بِٱلْبُرُوقِ
بِحَجِّكَ قَاصِدًا مَاسَرْجِسَانِ　　فَدَيْرَ ٱلنَّوْبَهَارِ فَدَيْرَ فِيقِ

---

١ الأصل: (من هذه القصيدة أخذ مدرك ما أخذه وخاطب به معشوقه عمرًا) وردت في الهامش.

The Fīq Monastery

This is a monastery behind the Fīq Pass,[154] between it and the Sea of Galilee, built into a mountain. It is well populated with residents and also with the Christians, who come to visit it because they venerate it so. Other people, too, visit it for recreation and to drink. According to the Christians, it was the first monastery to be established in Christianity. Christ, God bless him, used to spend time there, and it was there that he summoned the disciples. There is a rock upon which they say Christ sat, and everyone who visits the place chips off a piece of it to acquire blessing. The monastery was built there and called after Christ, peace be upon him. 23.1

Abū Nuwās mentions it in a line of poetry: 23.2

By your pilgrimage making for Mār Sirjisān
and the monasteries of Nawbahār and Fīq.[155]

It's an unusual poem, in which he addresses a Christian boy he was in love with, and it starts:

By the baptistery of the Old Monastery,
the catholicos and the bishops,
By Shimʿūn, Yūḥannā, and ʿĪsā,
by Mār Sarjīs and the compassionate priest,
By Christ's birth, by the Epiphany,
by Easter and the payment of church tithes,
By Ushmūnī and the seven she led—
none ever abandoned the true path—
By Mārt Maryam and the Resurrection,
the host and the wine grown old,
By the crosses raised upon lances,
shining as the lightning flashes,
By your pilgrimage making for Mār Sirjisān[156]
and the monasteries of Nawbahār[157] and Fīq,

بِهَيْكَلِ بَيْعَةِ ٱللُّدِّ ٱلْمُفَدَّى   وَقُسَّانٍ أَتَوْهُ مِنْ سَحِيقِ
وَبِٱلنَّاقُوسِ فِي ٱلْبِيَعِ ٱللَّوَاتِي   تُقَامُ بِهَا ٱلصَّلَاةُ لَدَى ٱلشُّرُوقِ
بِمَرْيَمَ بِٱلْمَسِيحِ وَكُلِّ حَبْرٍ   حَوَارِيٍّ عَلَى دِينٍ وَثِيقِ
بِرُهْبَانِ ٱلصَّوَامِعِ فِي ذُرَاهَا   أَقَامُوا ثُمَّ فِي جُهْدٍ وَضِيقِ
بِإِنْجِيلِ ٱلشَّعَانِينِ ٱلْمُفَدَّى[1]   وَشَمْعَلَةِ ٱلنَّصَارَى فِي ٱلطَّرِيقِ
وَبِٱلصُّلْبِ ٱلْعَظِيمَةِ حِينَ تَبْدُو   وَبِٱلزُّنَّارِ فِي ٱلْخَصْرِ ٱلدَّقِيقِ
وَبِٱلْحُسْنِ ٱلْمُرَكَّبِ فِيكَ إِلَّا   رَحِمْتَ تَحَرُّقِي وَجُفُوفَ رِيقِي
أَمَا وَٱلْقُرْبِ مِنْ بَعْدِ ٱلتَّنَائِي   يَمِينُ فَتًى لِقَاتِلِهِ[2] عَشِيقِ
لَقَدْ أَصْبَحْتَ زِينَةَ كُلِّ دَيْرٍ   وَعِيدٍ مَعَ جَفَائِكَ وَٱلْعُقُوقِ
وَأَذَّنَ عَاشِقُوكَ إِلَى ٱلنَّصَارَى   مِنَ ٱلْإِسْلَامِ طُرًّا بِٱلْمُرُوقِ

---

١ الأصل: ٱلْمُبَدَّا.   ٢ الأصل: لِقائِلِهِ.

By the altar of the church of Lydda the ransomed,[158]
    and priests who visit it from afar,
By the clappers resounding in the churches
    announcing the service at daybreak,
By Mary, by Christ, by all the disciples,
    wise men confessing a firm faith,
By monks in their cells on the summits
    living in struggle and hardship,
By the proclamation of the Palm Sunday gospel
    and the candles Christians carry in the road,
By the great crosses when they're brought out,
    and the girdle round the slender waist,[159]
By all the beauty you're made up of,
    pity my burning passion and parched mouth!
I swear by nearness after distance,
    as a lover of his killer swears an oath,
Though you scorn and disobey me,
    you grace every convent and every feast,
And all those Muslims who love you
    proclaim gratitude to Christians as their creed.

دير الطور

والطور جبل مستدير مستطيل واسع الأسفل مستدقّ الأعلى لا يتعلّق بشيء من الجبال وليس إليه إلّا طريق واحد وهو فيما بين طبريّة واللجون مشرف على الغور ومرج اللجون وعين تنبع بها والدير في نفس القلّة وحوله كروم تُعصر فالشراب عندهم كثير. ويُعرف أيضاً بدير التجلّي لأنّ المسيح صلّى الله عليه على زعمهم تجلّى لتلاميذه بعد أن رُفع حتّى أراهم نفسه وعرفوه. والناس يقصدونه من كلّ موضع فيقيمون به ويشربون فيه فموقعه حسن وهو من المواضع الطيّبة. ١،٢٤

ولمهلهل بن يموت بن المزرّع فيه ٢،٢٤

نَهَضْتُ إِلَى الطُّورِ فِي فِتْيَةٍ سِرَاعِ ٱلنُّهُوضِ إِلَى مَا أُحِبْ
كَهَمِّكَ مِنْ فِتْيَةٍ أَنْفَقُوا تِلَادَهُمُ فِي سَبِيلِ ٱلطَّرَبْ
كِرَامِ ٱلْجُدُودِ حِسَانِ ٱلْوُجُوهِ كُهُولِ ٱلْعُقُولِ شَبَابِ ٱللَّعِبْ
فَأَيُّ زَمَانٍ بِهِمْ لَمْ يُسَرّ وَأَيُّ مَكَانٍ بِهِمْ لَمْ يَطِبْ
أَنَخْتُ ٱلرِّكَابَ عَلَى دَيْرِهِ وَقَضَّيْتُ مِنْ حَقِّهِ مَا يَجِبْ
وَأَنْزَلْتُهُمْ وَسْطَ أَعْنَابِهِ أُسَقِّيهِمْ مِنْ عَصِيرِ ٱلْعِنَبْ
وَأَحْضَرْتُهُمْ قَمَرًا مُشْرِقًا تَمِيلُ ٱلْغُصُونُ بِهِ فِي ٱلْكُثُبْ
تَحُثُّ ٱلْكُؤُوسَ بِأَهْزَاجِهِ وَمَزْمُومِ أَرْمَالِهِ وَٱلنَّصَبْ
وَمَا بَيْنَ ذَاكَ حَدِيثٌ يَرُوقُ وَخَوْضٌ لَهُمْ فِي فُنُونِ ٱلْأَدَبْ

The Monastery of Mount Tabor

Tabor is a long mountain, round and extended, with a broad base and flattened summit. It stands alone with no other mountains near it, and can only be reached by one road. It lies between Tiberias and Lajjūn,[160] overlooking the Jordan Valley and the plain of Lajjūn, with a spring that rises in it. The monastery stands right on the summit, surrounded by vineyards from which wine is pressed. They produce a great deal of wine. The monastery is also known as the Monastery of the Transfiguration because, as the Christians claim, Christ, God bless him, appeared to his disciples after he was raised up, showing himself to them so they could recognize him.[161] People from all parts visit it, staying there and drinking. The setting is beautiful and it is a pleasant place. 24.1

Al-Muhalhil ibn Yamūt ibn al-Muzarriʿ mentions it in a poem: 24.2

I went up to Tabor with a company,
 swift to perform what I want,
Splendid fellows who'd spent their fortunes
 in the search for pleasure,
Of noble descent and handsome mien,
 wise in their thoughts but boys at play,
With them every hour's joyful,
 every place a delight.
I halted the column at the monastery,
 performing the rites it demands.
I settled them among the vines
 and poured the juice of the grape.
I brought them a shining moon,
 a swaying branch on a sandhill.
The cups made quick rounds
 with his songs, light, joyful, and solemn.
Our talk was a feast of the mind,
 touching on refinement and letters,

فَمَا شِئْتَ مِنْ مَثَلٍ سَائِرٍ ... وَمِنْ خَبَرٍ نَادِرٍ مُسْتَحَبْ
فَيَا طِيبَ ذَا ٱلْعَيْشِ لَوْ لَمْ يَزَلْ ... وَيَا حُسْنَ ذَا ٱلسَّعْدِ لَوْ لَمْ يَغِبْ

وكان مهلهل من المطبوعين في الشعر والمنهمكين في الخلاعة واللعب والتطرّح ٣،٢٤
في مواطن اللّٰهو والطرب ملازماً للحانات والديارات. ونحن نورد من شعره ما يليق
بكتابنا هذا.

فمن شعره في وصف الرياض والحثّ على الشرب قوله

لِجُنُونِ ٱلْهَوَى وَهَبْتُ جَنَانِي ... فَدَعَانِي يَا أَيُّهَا ٱلْعَاذِلَانِ
طَرَبِي زَائِدٌ فَفِي حَرَجٍ مَنْ ... لَامَنِي فِي خَلَاعَةٍ أَوْ نَهَانِي
قَدْ أَبَانَتْ لِيَ ٱلرِّيَاضُ مِنَ ٱلزَّهْـ ... ـرِ غَرِيبَ ٱلصُّنُوفِ وَٱلْأَلْوَانِ
وَبَدَا ٱلنَّرْجِسُ ٱلْمُفَتَّحُ يَرْنُو ... مِنْ جُفُونِ ٱلْكَافُورِ بِٱلزَّعْفَرَانِ
كَعُيُونٍ قَدْ حَدَّقَتْ بَاهِتَاتٍ ... نَاظِرَاتٍ إِلَى وُجُوهٍ حِسَانِ
يَتَثَنَّى زَبَرْجَدُ ٱلْقَضْبِ مِنْهُ ... طَرَبًا لِلْجَنِينِ وَٱلْعِقْيَانِ
وَقَفَ ٱلطَّلُّ فِي ٱلْمَحَاجِرِ مِنْهَا ... ثُمَّ مَاسَتْ فَٱنْهَلَّ مِثْلَ ٱلْجُمَانِ
يَا غُلَامُ ٱسْقِنِي فَقَدْ ضَحِكَ ٱلْوَقْـ ... ـتُ وَقَدْ تَمَّ طِيبُ هٰذَا ٱلزَّمَانِ
أَدْنِ مِنِّي ٱلدِّنَانَ صُفَّ ٱلْأَبَارِيـ ... ـقَ ٱسْتَحِثَّ ٱلْكُؤُوسَ صُفَّ ٱلْقَنَانِي
بَادِرِ ٱلْوَقْتَ وَٱغْتَنِمْ فُرَصَ ٱلْعَيْـ ... ـشِ وَلَا تَكْذِبَنَّ فَٱلْعُمْرُ فَانِي

ومن مليح شعره في هذا المعنى قوله ٤،٢٤

Proverbs, jokes, strange anecdotes,
all that one could enjoy.
What a wonderful life had it not ended;
what happiness were it not over!

Al-Muhalhil was a naturally gifted poet, given to dissipation and frivolity. He frequented places where people enjoyed themselves and made music, and he spent much time in taverns and monasteries. Here we will quote some of his poetry appropriate to this book. 24.3

This is one of his fine poems describing flowering meadows and encouraging drinking:

I've given myself over to the madness of love.
Leave me alone, you brace of blamers,
I'm in utter ecstasy. The sinner is he
who blames me or forbids me depravity.
The meadows have revealed flowers
of wondrous forms and colors,
The narcissi, as they open, gaze with eyes
of saffron surrounded by camphor,
Like eyes gazing in wonder
and contemplating beautiful faces.
Their emerald stems sway, dancing
in delight at gold and silver.
Their eyes are filled with dew till they move
and scatter it like pearls.
Boy, pour me a drink, for time is laughing,
and this age cannot be better.
Bring the wine jars close, line up the pitchers,
send the cups around, and the bottles.
Don't miss the moment, seize the chance to live,
don't disappoint. This life's not forever.

Another of his good poems on this theme is: 24.4

زَمَانُ ٱلرِّيَاضِ زَمَـانٌ أَنِيقُ ... وَعَيْشُ ٱلْخَلَاعَـةِ عَيْشٌ رَقِيقُ
وَقَـدْ جَمَعَ ٱلْوَقْتُ حَالَيْهِمَا ... فَمَنْ ذَا يَفِيقُ وَمَنْ يَسْتَفِيقُ
أَيَا مَنْ هُوَ ٱلسُّولُ لِي وَٱلْمُنَى ... وَمَنْ هُوَ بِٱلْحُبِّ مِنِّي حَقِيقُ
أَدِرْ لَحْظَ عَيْنِكَ أَمْرِجْهُ فِي ... مُرُوجِ ٱلرِّيَاضِ فَكُلٌّ يَرُوقُ
بِقَاعٌ تُنِيرُ وَمَاءٌ نَمِيرٌ ... وَرَوْضٌ نَضِيرٌ[1] وَزَهْرٌ أَنِيقُ
لَهُ نُسَخٌ حُرِّرَتْ فَٱسْتَنَارَتْ ... فَخَطٌّ جَلِيلٌ وَمَعْنًى دَقِيقُ
يُضَاحِكُ وَجْهَكَ وَجْهٌ عَشِيقٌ ... وَيَلْقَى مَشَمَّكَ مِسْكٌ فَتِيقُ
إِذَا ضَاحَكَ ٱلزَّهْرَ زَهْرُ ٱلرِّيَاضِ ... فَكَيْفَ ٱلْخَلَاصُ وَأَيْنَ ٱلطَّرِيقُ
بَهَارٌ بَهَرْتَ بِهِ غَيْرَهُ ... عَلَى نَرْجِسٍ وَشَقِيقٌ شَفِيقُ
فَذَا عَاشِقٌ وَجِلٌ خَائِفٌ ... وَذَا خَجِلٌ وَكَذَاكَ ٱلْعَشِيقُ
تَرُوقُكَ مِنْهُ عُيُونٌ تَرُوقُ ... بِأَلْحَاظِهَا وَخُدُودٌ تَشُوقُ
مَدَاهِنُ يَحْمِلْنَ طَلَّ ٱلنَّدَى ... فَهَاتِيكَ تِبْرٌ وَهٰذِي عَقِيقُ
تَضَمَّنُ أَوْرَاقُهَا دُرَّهُ ... وَيَنْشُرُ مِنْهُ ٱلَّذِي لَا يُطِيقُ
يَمِيلُ ٱلنَّسِيمُ بِأَغْصَانِهَا ... فَبَعْضٌ نَشَاوَى وَبَعْضٌ مُفِيقُ
فَبَادِرْ بِنَا حَادِثَاتِ ٱلزَّمَانِ ... فَوَجْهُ ٱلْحَوَادِثِ وَجْهٌ صَفِيقُ

ومن مليح شعره قوله ٥،٢٤

أَعِدْ شُرْبَكَ ٱلْكَأْسَ فِيمَا تُعِيدُ ... وَسَاعِدْ فَقَدْ شَمَلَتْنَا ٱلسُّعُودُ
وَحُثَّ ٱلصَّبُوحَ لِضَوْءِ ٱلصَّبَاحِ ... فَإِنَّ ٱلْحَوَادِثَ عَنَّا رُقُودُ

١ الأصل: نطيرٌ.

The season of meadows is a pretty time,
    the life of frivolity's a life that is fine.
Fate has brought these two together,
    now who will wake up, who will come to?
You whom I entreat, you whom I desire,
    you who are worthy of my love,
Look around you, turn your gaze
    on the fields flowering in all their beauty.
Blooming meadows, water that's clear,
    gardens all alike, blossoms fine and lovely
Like finely written texts that glisten,
    their script majestic and meaning delicate.
A beloved face greets you with a smile,
    your nose encounters a fragrant scent.
When the meadows' flowers laugh among their fellows,
    how to be free? Where's the path?
Beauty with which you surpass its like
    possessed by narcissi and tender anemones,
Here's a lover, timid and fearful;
    there's a violet, a bashful beloved.
You marvel at its eyes with delightful glances
    and at its cheeks, which fill you with desire.
Hollows in the rock bearing dawn's dewdrops,
    some gold and some carnelian,
Flowers with petals embracing pearls,
    which scatter in showers, far and wide,
When the breeze sways with its branches,
    some drunken, others alert.
Come, let us forestall the disasters of fate;
    such disasters have a shameless face.

Here is another good poem of his: **24.5**

Drink again from the cup, drink over and over,
    come to our help as we're swallowed in happiness.
Hasten the morn's drink to the light of dawn
    while fate sleeps, heedless of us.

أَمَا نَشْكُرُ ٱلْفِعْلَ مِنْ يَوْمِنَا   وَنَبْهَى بِمَا نَحْنُ فِيهِ خُلُودُ
سَمَاءٌ تَجُودُ وَرَوْضٌ نَضِيدُ   وَزَهْرٌ جَدِيدٌ وَغُصْنٌ يَمِيدُ
وَنَدٌّ يَفُوحُ وَرَاحٌ تُرِيحُ   وَسَاقٍ مَلِيحٌ وَنَايٌ وَعُودُ
وَصَوْتٌ يَشُوقُ وَزَمْرٌ رَفِيقٌ   وَعَيْشٌ أَنِيقٌ وَجَدٌّ سَعِيدُ
أَدَامَ ٱلْإِلٰهُ لَنَا عَيْشَنَا   وَلَا نَالَ مِنَّا مُنَاهُ ٱلْحَسُودُ

وقال في هذا المعنى وتغنّى فيه ٦،٢٤

قَدْ قُدِّمَتْ لِلسُّرُورِ أَنْفَالُ[1]   وَحَثَّ شَهْرَ ٱلصِّيَامِ شَوَّالُ
وَأَقْبَلَ ٱلْغَيْمُ لَابِسًا حُلَلًا   مِسْكِيَّةً مَا لَهُنَّ أَذْيَالُ
وَدَبَّجَ ٱلْأَرْضَ رَوْضُهَا فَغَدَا   يُنْشَرُ فِيهَا وَٱلْأَرْضُ تَخْتَالُ
وَٱهْتَزَّ عُودٌ وَحَنَّ مِنْ طَرَبٍ   نَايٌ وَعُمَّتْ بِٱلرَّاحِ أَرْطَالُ
وَبُوعِدَ ٱلْخَوْفُ مِنْ مَحَاذِرِهِ   وَقُرِّبَتْ لِلْقُلُوبِ آمَالُ
أَيَّامُنَا فِي ٱلْحَيَاةِ عَارِيَةٌ   تَحُثُّهَا لِلْفَنَاءِ آجَالُ
فَٱغْتَنِمُوا فُرْصَةَ ٱلزَّمَانِ وَلَا   تُفَرِّطُوا فَٱلزَّمَانُ مُغْتَالُ

ومّما ملح فيه قوله ٧،٢٤

زَمَنٌ كَٱلشَّبَابِ أَوْ كَٱلتَّرَاضِي   بَعْدَ طُولِ ٱلصُّدُودِ وَٱلْإِعْرَاضِ
أَلْقَحَ ٱلْغَيْثُ كُلَّ أَرْضٍ فَأَضْحَتْ   فِي وِلَادٍ وَبَعْضُهَا فِي مَخَاضِ
يَا غُلَامُ ٱسْقِنِي فَقَدْ ضَحِكَ ٱلْعَيْـشُ إِلَيْنَا وَهَشَّ بَعْدَ ٱنْقِبَاضِ
وَأَرَى لُؤْلُؤَ ٱلْحَبَابِ يُبَارِي   لُؤْلُؤَ ٱلطَّلِّ فَوْقَ زَهْرِ ٱلرِّيَاضِ

١ الأصل: انعال؛ عوّاد: أَثْقَالُ.

Let's give thanks for our doings today,
 and be joyful at what we may stay in forever,
A generous sky, a carpet-like meadow,
 fresh flowers, the swaying of branches,
Fragrant perfume, wine, which gives rest,
 a handsome cupbearer, a flute and reed pipe,
A voice full of longing, a gentle melody,
 a life of elegance and the favors of fate,
May God grant us this life the livelong day,
 and may the envious not rob us of our desires.

On the same theme, he also composed this poem, which was set to music: **24.6**

Gifts have been brought to celebrate,
 Shawwal[162] follows hard on the month of the fast.
Clouds cloaked in mantles of musk
 have arrived and have left no trail.
Gardens have woven brocade for the earth,
 who struts proudly in her new display.
The lutestrings quiver, the flute plays a yearning tone,
 wine's poured out, measure on measure.
Cautious men now get rid of their fear,
 hope's been brought to hearts—
Our days in this life are unarrayed,
 urged on at fixed times to destruction,
So seize any chance destiny offers—
 don't let it slip; fate will only deceive.

Another of his fine poems: **24.7**

A period like youth—or reconciliation
 after aversion and long-lasting rejection.
Rain has made the whole earth fertile:
 a part has given birth, a part's still in labor.
Boy, pour me a drink! Life has smiled on us,
 laughing and cheerful after dejection.
I see the pearl-like bubbles rivaling
 the pearls of dew on the garden's flowers.

وقال أيضاً ٨،٢٤

أَسْتَوْدِعُ ٱللّٰهَ مَنْ لَمْ يَرْوِ لِي[١] نَظَرِي لَمَّا مَضَى خَاطِرًا وَٱلرِّدْفُ يَجْذِبُهُ
يَحْكِيهِ مِنْ حَرَكَاتِ ٱلْغُصْنِ أَشْكَلُهَا وَمِنْ نَسِيمِ ذَكِيِّ ٱلْمِسْكِ أَطْيَبُهُ

وقال أيضاً

وَبَدِيعٍ يَكِلُّ عَنْ وَصْفِهِ ٱلْعَقْـلُ لِإِفْرَاطِ حَيْرَةِ ٱلْأَبْصَارِ
فَهْوَ كَٱلْخَاطِرِ ٱلَّذِي دَقَّ مَعْنَا هُ فَأَضْحَى يَجُولُ فِي ٱلْأَفْكَارِ

وقال أيضاً

كَأَنَّ أَجْفَانَهُ مِنْ جِسْمِ عَاشِقِهِ قَدْ رُكِّبَتْ فَهْيَ فِي ٱلْأَسْقَامِ تَحْكِيهِ
وَفِي صُدْغِهِ عَقْرَبٌ لِلْجِسْمِ لَادِغَةٌ دِرْيَاقُ لَدْغَتِهَا فِي ٱلرِّيقِ مِنْ فِيهِ

وقال في غلام نصرانيّ كان يحبّه ٩،٢٤

شَدَّ زُنَّارَهُ عَلَى دِقَّةِ ٱلْخَصْـرِ وَشَدَّ ٱلْقُلُوبَ فِي ٱلزُّنَّارِ
وَأَسَالَ ٱلْأَصْدَاغَ فَوْقَ عِذَارٍ أَنَا مِنْ عِشْقِهِ خَلِيعُ ٱلْعِذَارِ
وَبَدَتْ مِنْهُ طُرَّةٌ تُذْكِرُ ٱلنَّا ظِرَ لَيْلًا يَلُوحُ فَوْقَ نَهَارِ

وهو أبو نضلة مهلهل بن يموت بن المزرّع بن يموت بن موسى بن حكيم بن جبلة العبديّ. وحكيم هو الشهيد بالبصرة الذي منع عائشة وطلحة والزبير الدخول إليها وحاربهم حتّى قُتل. وكان من خبره ومقتله أنّه لمّا تمكّن طلحة والزبير من البصرة وقتلوا حرس بيت المال وهم سبعون رجلاً من غير ذنب ولا سبب وأخذوا عثمان بن حنيف ١٠،٢٤

١ الأصل: روني.

Here are three couplets: 24.8

I commend to God one not hidden from my eyes
as he walked past proudly, pulled at by a follower.
He's imitated by the loveliest swaying branch
and the most fragrant musk borne on the breeze.

A youth tiring the mind that wants to describe him,
for he leaves the eyes so distraught.
He's like an idea, subtle in meaning,
moving freely through one's thoughts.

His eyelids seem to be part of his lover's body,
for they copy him in their sickness.
From his forehead hangs a scorpion that stings the body;
its antidote is his mouth's saliva.

And he composed this poem on a Christian boy he loved: 24.9

He'd tied his belt fast round his slender waist,
and he tied many hearts into his belt;
His locks hung low in front of his cheeks.
I've the cheek to love him with no excuse.
At its parting his hair recalls
night looming over the light of day.

Muhalhil's full name is Abū Naḍlah Muhalhil ibn Yamūt ibn al-Muzarriʿ ibn 24.10
Yamūt ibn Mūsā ibn Ḥakīm ibn Jabalah al-ʿAbdī.

Ḥakīm was the martyr in Basra who prevented ʿĀʾishah, Ṭalḥah, and al-Zubayr from entering it, fighting to death. Apropos of his deeds and his death: Ṭalḥah and al-Zubayr, when they conquered Basra, killed the guards of the treasury, seventy men in all, for no wrong or reason. They seized ʿUthmān ibn Ḥunayf al-Anṣārī, the governor of Basra appointed by the Commander of the Faithful ʿAlī ibn Abī Ṭālib, God bless him, and plucked out his beard and were

الأنصاريّ عامل أمير المؤمنين عليّ بن أبي طالب صلوات الله عليه على البصرة ونتفوا لحيته وأرادوا قتله قام حكيم في قومه خطيباً فقال لهم يا قوم إنّ ابن حنيف دم مصون وأمانة مودّاة والله لو لم يكن علينا أميرًا لمنعناه لحقّ الجوار ومكانه من رسول الله صلّى الله عليه وسلّم فكيف وله الحقّ والولاية. إلّا أنّ الحيّ ميّت والميّت مسؤول. فإمّا أن تموتوا كراماً وإمّا أن تعيشوا أحراراً. فأجابوه إلى ما دعاهم إليه.[1] وقال في ذلك أبو أميّة الأصمّ وكان فارس القوم

مَعَاشِرَ عَبْدِ ٱلْقَيْسِ مُوتُوا عَلَى ٱلَّتِي تَسُرُّ عَلِيّاً وَٱحْذَرُوا سَبَّةَ ٱلْغَدْرِ
وَلَا تَرْهَبُوا فِي ٱللهِ لَوْمَةَ لَائِمٍ وَمُوتُوا كِرَاماً فَهْوَ أَشْرَفُ لِلذِّكْرِ

وغدا حكيم في ثلاثمائة رجل من أصحابه إلى العدوّ وهو يشتم[2] عائشة فخرج طلحة والزبير وحملا عائشة على الجمل وذلك اليوم يُسمّى يوم الجمل الأصغر. فقاتل حكيم قتالاً شديداً وجعل يقول إنّما تريدان أن تُصيبا من الدنيا حظّاً. اللّهمّ اقتلهما بمن قتلا ولا تعطهما ما سألا ولا تبلغهما ما أمّلا ولا تغفر لهما أبداً. وحمل عليهما وهم في عشر آلاف وهو في ثلاثمائة فهزمهم حتّى أدخلهم سكّة. وشدّ رجل من الأزد على حكيم وهو غافل فضربه على ساقه فقطع رجله فأخذ حكيم رجله فضرب بها الأزديّ فصرعه ثمّ جاء فقتله وأنشأ يقول ١١،٢٤

يَا نَفْسُ لَا تُرَاعِي
إِنْ قُطِعَتْ كُرَاعِي
إِنَّ مَعِي ذِرَاعِي

وقتل هو وثلاثة إخوة له وأخرجوا ربيعة من البصرة وأجلوهم عنها.

[1] كذا في عوّاد؛ الأصل: دعاهم وقال. [2] الأصل غير واضح.

intending to kill him. Then Ḥakīm stood up in the tribal assembly and delivered a speech: "Men, Ibn Ḥunayf's life must be protected, a trust we have been given. Even if he were not our governor, I swear by God we would defend him because of our duty to protect him and because of his standing with the blessed Messenger of God. So what about now, when he has both right and the governorship on his side? Every living person is bound to die, and every dead person will be asked to give account of his acts. Die as noblemen or live as free." They consented to his proposal.

Upon this, Abū Umayyah al-Aṣamm, the tribe's champion, composed verses:

> Tribe of ʿAbd Qays, die for what pleases ʿAlī,
> beware of being cursed for treachery.
> Don't fear any slur, by God, die as nobles,
> and earn respect for your memory.

Cursing[163] ʿĀʾishah, Ḥakīm faced the enemy with three hundred men 24.11
of his tribe, and Ṭalḥah and al-Zubayr came out to meet them. ʿĀʾishah had been mounted on a camel, and so that day is known as the lesser Battle of the Camel.[164] Ḥakīm fought fiercely, taunting his opponents: "You both are just out for worldly gain. God, kill them in revenge for those they killed, don't grant their request, don't fulfill their hopes, don't ever forgive them." With his three hundred men he charged their twelve thousand and routed them, making them flee into an alley. Then an Azdī attacked him, catching him unawares, and struck his leg and cut off his foot. Ḥakīm picked it up, struck the Azdī with it, and felled him to the ground. Then he turned and killed him, saying:

> My soul, fear not!
> Though my foot's been cut,
> my arm can still clout.

He and three of his brothers were killed, and Rabīʿah was driven out of Basra and forbidden to enter it.

ومن شعر يموت بن المزرّع في ابنه مهلهل ١٢،٢٤

مُهَلْهِلُ شَقَّنِي صِغَرُكْ وَأَسْبَلَ دَمْعَتِي عَسَرُكْ
لَدى أَكْنَافِ شَامِهِمِ أَمُوتُ فَيُمَّحَى أَثَرُكْ
وَلَوْ سُومِحْتُ فِي عُمْرِي لَجَلَّ لَدَيْهِمِ خَطَرُكْ
فَوَا أَسَفِي عَلَى لُمَّةٍ يَطُولُ إِلَيْهِمِ سَفَرُكْ
وَإِنْ أَهْلِكْ فَإِنَّ ٱللهَ دُونَ ٱلْخَلْقِ لِي وَزَرُكْ

وشعره وشعر ابنه مهلهل كثير في سائر فنون الشعر وإنّما ذكرنا ما احتمله الكتاب واقتضاه الشرط.

Here is part of a poem by Yamūt ibn al-Muzarriʿ addressing his son Muhalhil: **24.12**

Muhalhil, your youth rends my heart,
and I weep to see your distress.
If I die on Syria's slopes,
then you will have no honor left.
If I am granted life, you will enjoy
great prestige in their eyes.
Alas for the companions
to whom your road will be long.
If I perish, then God, not men,
will take care of you for me.

He and his son Muhalhil composed a great deal of poetry in the various genres, but here we have only mentioned what suits the book and corresponds to its purpose.

دير البُخت

١،٢٥ وهـذا الدير بدمشق على فرسخين منها وهو دير كبير حسن وكان يُسمّى دير ميخائيل فسُمّي بهذا الاسم لبُخت كانت لعبد الملك بن مروان مقيمة هناك فعُرف بها. وكان لعليّ بن عبد الله بن عبّاس بذلك الموضع جنينة مقدارها أربعة أجربة فكان يخرج إليها ويتنزّه فيها أيّام مقامه بدمشق.

٢،٢٥ فذكر عليّ بن محمّد بن أبي سيف المدائنيّ عن رجاله قال

اشترى عبد الله بن عبّاس بالمدينة أَمة صفراء بربريّة فولدت في منزل عبد الله غلاماً فسمّاه سليطاً ونشأ في منزله فخرج جلداً ظريفاً ثمّ شخص مع عليّ بن عبد الله إلى الشام فلم يزل في خدمته حتّى مات عبد الملك ووليَ الوليد ابنه فأظهر التحامل على عليّ بن عبد الله وعيّبه بحضرة الناس وسعى قوم من حسدة عليّ وأهل البغي فأفسدوا سليطاً وزيّنوا له ادّعاء ولادة عبد الله بن عبّاس وقالوا أنت شبيهه في جمالك وهيئتك فادّعى سليط أنّه ابن عبد الله بن عبّاس وخاصم عليّاً إلى الوليد. فأمر الوليد برفعهما إلى قاضي دمشق فأحضر سليط[1] قوماً شهدوا له على نسبه وأنهى ذلك إلى الوليد فألحقه بعبد الله بن العبّاس. فخاصم سليط عليّاً في الميراث وطلب منازعته إيّاه حتّى قاربه عليّ وصيّره في عياله فكان يقوم لعليّ بحوائجه وأموره.

٣،٢٥ فخرج عليّ يوماً إلى جنينته بدير البخت وكان له فيها قوم يعملون منهم أبو الدنّ من ولد أبي رافع مولى رسول الله صلّى الله عليه فوقعت بينهم وبين سليط مشاجرة. فوثبوا عليه فقتلوه بعد أن انصرف عليّ بن عبد الله إلى دمشق واحتفروا له حفرة بالجنينة فواروه فيها.

---

١ الأصل: سليطاً.

The Bactrians' Monastery

This monastery, large and beautiful, is about two and a half miles (four kilometers) from Damascus. It used to be called Mīkhā'īl's Monastery, but its name was changed because ʿAbd al-Malik's Bactrian camels were stabled there and then it was named after them. ʿAlī ibn ʿAbdallāh ibn ʿAbbās had a garden there of about ten acres (four hectares), which he used to visit and relax in when he was in Damascus. 25.1

ʿAlī ibn Muḥammad ibn Abī Sayf al-Madā'inī quoted his authorities as saying: 25.2

ʿAbdallāh ibn ʿAbbās bought a fair Berber slave girl in Mecca who gave birth to a boy in his house. He named him Salīṭ. Salīṭ grew up there, tough and likable; he accompanied ʿAbdallāh to Syria, and continued in his service until ʿAbd al-Malik died and his son al-Walīd succeeded him. When the new caliph showed hostility to ʿAbdallāh's son ʿAlī, and criticized him in public, people jealous of ʿAlī and other troublemakers worked on Salīṭ, suggesting that he claim to be ʿAbdallāh ibn ʿAbbās's son. For, as they said, he was handsome like him and had the look of him. Salīṭ then alleged that he was ʿAbdallāh's son and challenged ʿAlī before al-Walīd, who referred the question to the judge in Damascus. Salīṭ produced individuals who testified to his descent and he reported this to al-Walīd, who incorporated him in ʿAbdallāh ibn ʿAbbās's genealogy. Then Salīṭ challenged ʿAlī over the inheritance, demanding his share. But ʿAlī got on good terms with him, including him among his dependents, and he saw to ʿAlī's needs and affairs.

One day ʿAlī went out to his garden at the Bactrians' Monastery, where the people who worked for him included Abū l-Dann, a descendant of Abū Rāfiʿ, the freedman of the blessed Prophet. A dispute broke out between Salīṭ and the laborers, who attacked and killed him after ʿAlī had left for Damascus, and then dug a grave in the grounds, where they buried him. 25.3

فاحتبس سليط على أمّه فاسترابت فخرجت في طلبه فخُبرت أنّه دخل الجنينة ولم يخرج منها فأتت باب الوليد صارخةً فقال من تتّهمين قالت عليّ بن عبد الله. فقال أحضريني من يشهد على دخوله معه الجنينة فأحضرت شهوداً على ذلك فأرسل إليه[1] الوليد قوماً إلى الجنينة ينظرون هل يرون شيئاً أو أثراً. فأثاروا منها عدّة مواضع فلم يروا شيئاً. فقال لهم أكّار كان في الجنينة امخُروا عليها الماء حتّى يتبيّن لكم. فمخروها فانخسف الموضع فأثاروه فاستخرجوا سليطاً.

٤،٢٥ فبعث الوليد إلى عليّ فعنّفه وأغلظ له وقال والله لئن صحّ عندي أنّك قتلته لأقتلنّك به. فحلف أنّه ما قتله ولا أمر بقتله فحبسه الوليد وكتب إلى أمراء الأمصار وفقهائهم بقصّته وما اتّهم به وما شهد عليه. فكتب إليه عمر بن عبد العزيز من المدينة بأن يُضرب ويُلبس جبّة صوف ويطاف به. فدعا الوليد بعليّ بن عبد الله فضربه أحداً وستّين سوطاً ويقال مائة ثمّ أطافه وأقامه في الشمس وألبسه جبّة شعر وصبّ على رأسه ماءً فبلغ ذلك عبّاد بن زياد وكان صديقاً لعليّ بن عبد الله وكان أثيراً عند الوليد فجاء فألقى ثيابه على عليّ ودخل إليه فكلّمه فيه وقال يا أمير المؤمنين عليّ يُتّهم بالقتل عليّ أتقى لله وأفضل من أن يقتل أحداً. فأمر به الوليد فسُيّر إلى دَهلك. فلمّا أُخرج عن دمشق تكلّم فيه سليمان بن عبد الملك وقال يا أمير المؤمنين ردّه واحتبسه فبعث رسولاً فحبسه حيث أدركه. وكان أُدرك بالفرعاء فحُبس هناك في قرية منها حتّى مات الوليد ووليَ سليمان. فردّه فنزل الحميمة بالشراة من البلقاء. وباع[2] عليّ بستانه بدير البُخت من فاطمة بنت عبد الملك.

٥،٢٥ قال وكان عبد الملك عند وفاته وصّى الوليد بثلاثة نفر. قال له عليّ بن عبد الله في نسبه وقرابته وانقطاعه إلينا أكرمه واعرف حقّه وأخوك عبد الله أقرّه على مصر ولا تعزله عنها وعمّك محمّد بن مروان أقرّه على الجزيرة واعرف له موضعه. فأوّل

١ كذا في الأصل. ٢ الأصل: أباع.

Salīṭ's mother missed him and grew suspicious. She started to look for him and was told he had entered the estate and not left it. So, screaming, she came to the door of al-Walīd's palace. "Whom do you suspect?" he asked her. She replied, "'Alī ibn 'Abdallāh." "Bring me someone who can testify that Salīṭ entered the grounds with him." She produced witnesses, upon which al-Walīd sent people to the garden to see if they could find any clue or trace. They dug up various areas and found nothing, but then a laborer who worked there advised them, "Channel water over those places and then you'll see." They did so, and one area subsided, so they dug it up and brought out Salīṭ.

Al-Walīd sent for 'Alī, mishandled and insulted him, and said, "I will kill you 25.4
in revenge if it turns out that you killed him." 'Alī swore that he had neither killed him nor given an order to have him killed, but al-Walīd put him in prison.

He then wrote to the governors and legal authorities of the main cities about the accusations against 'Alī and the testimonies. From Medina, 'Umar ibn 'Abd al-'Azīz replied, "Beat him, dress him in a hair shirt, and have him paraded through the city." So al-Walīd summoned 'Alī ibn 'Abdallāh, gave him sixty-one lashes (some say one hundred), had him paraded through the city, exposed him in the sun dressed in a hair shirt, and poured water over his head.

When al-'Abbād ibn Ziyād, who was a friend of 'Alī and in favor with al-Walīd, heard, he came and threw his mantle over him. Then he appeared before the caliph to intercede for him, saying, "Commander of the Faithful, 'Alī is accused of murder. But he is too God-fearing and upright to kill anyone." So al-Walīd ordered 'Alī to be banished to Dahlak. After he had left Damascus, Sulaymān ibn 'Abd al-Malik mentioned his case to the caliph: "Commander of the Faithful, bring him back from Dahlak and detain him." Thereupon, al-Walīd sent a messenger, who had 'Alī imprisoned where he found him. That was in al-Far'ā'. So he was kept in detention in a village there until al-Walīd died and was succeeded by Sulaymān.

Sulaymān had 'Alī brought back to Syria. He settled in al-Ḥumaymah in the Sharāh Mountains in the Balqā' and sold his garden at the Bactrians' Monastery to Fāṭimah bint 'Abd al-Malik.

When 'Abd al-Malik was dying, he commended three people to al-Walīd 25.5
with these words: "Honor 'Alī ibn 'Abdallāh and recognize his rights because of his ancestry, his being a relative, and his loyalty to us. Confirm your brother 'Abdallāh as governor of Egypt and don't dismiss him. Confirm your uncle Muḥammad ibn Marwān as governor of the Jazīrah and recognize his position

ما بدأ بأخيه عزله عن مصر بقُرّة بن شريك وعزل عمّه عن الجزيرة وضرب عليّاً بالسوط مرّتين.

٦،٢٥ وكانت بنو العبّاس لمّا ولوا الأمر وجدوا في خزائن بني مروان كتاباً من سليمان بن عبد الملك إلى الوليد يسأله في عليّ بن عبد الله ويعرّفه حقّه فكان هذا الكتاب سبباً لترك سليمان في قبره بدابق لم ينبشوا عنه كما نبشوا عن إخوته وبني حرب.

٧،٢٥ وكان أبو مسلم صاحب دعوتهم يدّعي أنّه من ولد سليط بن عبد الله بن عبّاس. فكان ممّا قرعه به أبو جعفر وادّعيتَ أنّك ابن سليط بن عبد الله بن عبّاس. فكان هذا أوّل ما بدأ به من خطابه ثمّ تعريفه إيّاه بذنوبه فكتبت إلى أبي العبّاس تقول إنّ إبراهيم الإمام أقرّ بما استودعه إيّاه محمّد بن عليّ من نسبك وولادة عبد الله بن عبّاس إيّاك وأنّك عبد الرحمٰن بن سليط بن عبد الله بن عبّاس وأنّه وعدك إذا أتمّ الله هذه الدعوة وقتل الكفرة من بني أميّة أن يزوّجك أمّ عليّ بنت عليّ بن عبد الله فما كنت قائلاً لرسول الله صلّى الله عليه وأنت المجهول النسب علج من علوج إصبهان. قال يا أمير المؤمنين أخبرني بهذا أخوك إبراهيم بن محمّد. وكان هذا القول جرى بينهما في خطاب طويل قبل قتله إيّاه.

in the family." The first thing al-Walīd did was to dismiss his brother from the governorship of Egypt in favor of Qurrah ibn Sharīk. Then he dismissed his uncle from the Jazīrah and had ʿAlī whipped twice.

When the Abbasids took power, they found in the Marwanid treasury a letter from Sulaymān ibn ʿAbd al-Malik to al-Walīd, asking him to treat ʿAlī well and recognize his rights. This letter was the reason Sulaymān was left in his grave at Dābiq and not dug up like his brothers and the Banū Ḥarb. 25.6

Abū Muslim, who was in charge of Abbasid propaganda, used to claim that he was a son of Salīṭ ibn ʿAbdallāh ibn ʿAbbās, and this was one of the accusations Abū Jaʿfar al-Manṣūr leveled at him: "You've claimed that you are the son of Salīṭ ibn ʿAbdallāh ibn ʿAbbās." That was how he began his speech, before confronting him with his offences. "You wrote to Abū l-ʿAbbās saying that Imam Ibrāhīm accepted what Muḥammad ibn ʿAlī confided to him about your descent and ʿAbdallāh ibn ʿAbbās being your father, and so you are ʿAbd al-Raḥmān ibn Salīṭ ibn ʿAbdallāh ibn ʿAbbās. And you claim Ibrāhīm promised you that if God granted success to this propaganda and killed the Umayyad infidels, he would marry you to Umm ʿAlī, the daughter of ʿAlī ibn ʿAbdallāh. What would you say then to our blessed Messenger, with your unknown lineage, you uncouth pagan from Isfahan?" Abū Muslim answered, "Commander of the Faithful, it was your brother Ibrāhīm ibn Muḥammad who told me this." They traded words about these claims for a long time before al-Manṣūr killed Abū Muslim. 25.7

ديـر زكّـى

وهـذا الدير بالرقّة على الفرات وعن جنبيه نهر البليخ وهو من أحسن الديارات موقعاً ١،٢٦
وأنزهها موضعاً. وكانت الملوك إذا اجتازت به نزلته وأقامت فيه لأنّه يجتمع فيه كلّ
ما يريدونه من عمارته ونفاسة أبنيته وطيب المواضع التي به. ونُزهه ظاهرة لأنّ له
بقايا عجيبة. وبناحيته من الغزلان والأرانب وما شاكل ذلك ممّا يصطاد بالجارح من
طير الماء والحبارى وأصناف الطير. وفي الفرات بين يديه مطارح الشباك للسمك.
فهو جامع لكلّ ما يريد الملوك والسوقة. وليس يخلو من المتطرّبين لطيبه سيمّا أيّام الربيع
فإنّ له في ذلك الوقت منظرًا عجيباً.

للصنوبريّ فيه ٢،٢٦

أَرَاقَ سِجَالَهُ بِٱلرَّقَّتَيْنِ جَنُوبِيٌّ صَخُوبُ ٱلْجَانِبَيْنِ
وَأَهْدَى لِلرَّصِيفِ رَصِيفَ مُزْنٍ يُعَاوِدُهُ طَرِيرُ ٱلطُّرَّتَيْنِ
مَعَاهِدُ بَلْ مَآلِفُ بَاقِيَاتٌ بِأَكْرَمِ مَعْهَدَيْنِ وَمَأْلَفَيْنِ
يُضَاحِكُهَا ٱلْفُرَاتُ بِكُلِّ فَجٍّ فَيَضْحَكُ عَنْ نُضَارٍ أَوْ لُجَيْنِ
كَأَنَّ ٱلْأَرْضَ مِنْ صُفْرٍ وَحُمْرٍ عَرُوسٌ تُجْتَلَى فِي حُلَّتَيْنِ
كَأَنَّ عِنَاقَ نَهْرَيْ[1] دَيْرِ زَكًّى إِذَا ٱعْتَنَقَا عِنَاقُ مُتَيَّمَيْنِ
وَقَتْ ذَاكَ ٱلْبَلِيخَ يَدُ ٱللَّيَالِي وَذَاكَ ٱلنِّيلَ مِنْ مُتَجَاوِرَيْنِ
أَقَامَا كَٱلسِّوَارَيْنِ ٱسْتِدَارًا عَلَى كَتِفَيْهِ أَوْ كَٱلدُّمْلُجَيْنِ
أَيَا مُتَنَزَّهِي فِي دَيْرِ زَكَّى أَلَمْ تَكُ نُزْهَتِي بِكَ نُزْهَتَيْنِ
أُرَدِّدُ بَيْنَ وَرْدِ نَدَاكَ طَرْفًا يُرَدَّدُ بَيْنَ وَرْدِ ٱلْوَجْنَتَيْنِ

---

١ الأصل: نهرِ.

The Monastery of Zakkā (Zacchaeus)

This monastery stands above the Euphrates in Raqqa, with the Balīkh River flowing on both sides. It has one of the best and loveliest settings. Rulers used to stop and spend time there when they passed by, because it offered what they wanted.[165] It is well kept, with fine buildings and pleasant grounds, and it provides obvious attractions with amazing ruins, gazelles, and hares, as well as waterfowl, bustards, and such small game as are hunted with birds of prey. Before the monastery on the Euphrates are places where fishers cast their nets. It thus combines everything both high and low require. Pleasure-seekers visit it because of its attractiveness, especially in the spring, when it looks wonderful. 26.1

Al-Ṣanawbarī has a poem about it: 26.2

A south wind has rained on Raqqa and its surroundings,
torrents dashing down on all sides,
Covering the embankment with a blanket of rain,
a familiar friend to the plants on the banks.
Abodes well known, where meetings occur,
preserved in the noblest places where friends gather.
In its gorges the Euphrates smiles at them,
laughing with glistening gold and silver.
The earth clad in red and yellow flowers seems
a bride in her robes, her face revealed.
The river encircles Zakkā's Monastery
like the embrace of two rapturous lovers.
Destiny's hand has protected Balīkh
and the great river, neighbors both,
Like bracelets or armlets
around Zakkā's upper arms.
Oh Zakkā, when I strolled in your grounds,
didn't my delight in you take two forms?
I turned on the roses of your moist soil a gaze
that wandered to the roses in the cheeks,

وَمُبْتَسِمٍ كَنَظْمِ أُقْحُوَانٍ   جَلَاهُ ٱلطَّلُّ بَيْنَ شَقِيقَتَيْنِ
وَيَا سُفُنَ ٱلْفُرَاتِ بِحَيْثُ تَهْوَى   هَوِيَّ ٱلطَّيْرِ بَيْنَ ٱلْجَانِبَيْنِ
تُطَارِدُ مُقْبِلَاتٍ مُدْبِرَاتٍ   عَلَى عَجَلٍ تَطَارُدَ عَسْكَرَيْنِ
تُرَانَا وَاصِلِيكَ كَمَا عَهِدْنَا   وِصَالًا لَا نُنَغِّصُهُ بِبَيْنِ
أَلَا يَا صَاحِبَيَّ خُذَا عِنَانِيَ   هَوَايَ سَلِمْتُمَا مِنْ صَاحِبَيْنِ
لَقَدْ غَصَبَتْنِيَ ٱلْخَمْسُونَ فَتْكِي   وَقَامَتْ بَيْنَ لَذَّاتِي وَبَيْنِي
وَكَانَ ٱللَّهْوُ عِنْدِي كَٱبْنِ أُمِّي   فَصِرْنَا بَعْدَ ذَاكَ لِعَلَّتَيْنِ

ومن مليح شعره في وصف الرقّتين ٣،٢٦

أَمَّا ٱلرِّيَاضُ فَقَدْ بَدَتْ أَلْوَانُهَا   صَاغَتْ فُنُونَ حُلِيِّهَا أَفْنَانُهَا
رَقَّتْ مَعَانِيهَا وَرَقَّ نَسِيمُهَا   وَبَدَتْ مَحَاسِنُهَا وَطَابَ زَمَانُهَا
نُظِمَتْ قَلَائِدُ زَهْرِهَا كَجَوَاهِرٍ[1]   نُظِمَتْ زُمُرُّدُهَا إِلَى عِقْيَانِهَا
هٰذَا خُزَامَاهَا وَذَا قَيْصُومُهَا   هٰذَا شَقَائِقُهَا وَذَا حَوْذَانُهَا
لَوْ أَنَّ غُدْرَانَ ٱلسَّحَابِ تَوَاصَلَتْ   حُسْنًا إِذًا لَتَوَاصَلَتْ غُدْرَانُهَا
تَبْكِي عَلَيْهَا عَيْنُ كُلِّ سَحَابَةٍ   مَا أَنْ تَمَلَّ مِنَ ٱلْبُكَا أَجْفَانُهَا
مُنْقَادَةٌ طَوْعَ ٱلْجَنُوبِ إِذَا بَدَتْ   فَكَأَنَّمَا بِيَدِ ٱلْجَنُوبِ عِنَانُهَا
وَاهًا لِرَافِقَةِ ٱلْجَنُوبِ مَحَلَّةً   حَسُنَتْ بِهَا أَنْهَارُهَا وَجِنَانُهَا
يَا بَلْدَةً مَا زَالَ يَعْظُمُ قَدْرُهَا   فِي كُلِّ نَاحِيَةٍ وَيَعْظُمُ شَأْنُهَا
أَمَّا ٱلْفُرَاتُ فَإِنَّهُ ضَحْضَاحُهَا   أَمَّا ٱلْهَنِيُّ فَإِنَّهُ بُسْتَانُهَا

[1] الأصل: لجواهرٍ.

And a smile like two rows of chamomiles,
unveiled by a shower, between anemones.
Ships of the Euphrates! As you sail by,
speeding like birds between its banks,
Advancing and retreating
swiftly, like armies in maneuvers,
You see us coming, as is our custom,
in a meeting we'll not spoil with parting.
My friends, take over the reins of my love;
my friends, may harm never befall you;
Fifty years have robbed me of daring and
built a barrier between my pleasures and me.
Playful enjoyment was like my mother's son;
now we're sons of two different mothers.

Here is a fine poem of his describing the twin cities of Raqqa and Rāfiqah: 26.3

The meadows have seen their colors appear,
the branches have formed their many ornaments.
Their motifs are delicate, light as the breeze;
their beauty's displayed, their time's a delight.
Their gemlike flowers have been strung into necklaces
of jewels, with emeralds paired to carnelians.
Here's lavender, there's the southernwood plant.
Here are anemones, there water lilies.
If the pools of the clouds were to bring eternal rain,
then their pools too would form a chain.
The eyes of the clouds weep for them,
their lids never cease to shed tears,
Pliant, obeying the south wind when it blows,
as though the south wind had taken them in hand.
O for Rāfiqah, lying to the south,
whose rivers and gardens are full of yearning,
A town of ever-increasing importance,
enjoying high prestige everywhere.
The Euphrates is the pool before it,
the Hanī Canal is its garden.

وَكَأَنَّ أَيَّامَ ٱلصِّبَا أَيَّامُهَا　وَكَأَنَّ أَزْمَانَ ٱلْهَوَى أَزْمَانُهَا
مَهْمَا نَصِدْ غِزْلَانَهَا يَوْمًا فَقَدْ　ظَلَّتْ[1] تَصِيدُ قُلُوبَنَا غِزْلَانُهَا
حُثَّ ٱلْكُؤُوسَ فَإِنَّ هٰذَا وَقْتُهَا　وَصِلِ ٱلرِّيَاضَ فَإِنَّ ذَا إِبَّانُهَا
إِنَّ ٱلرَّبِيعَ يَجِلُّ قَدْرُ شُهُورِهِ　لٰكِنْ أَجَلُّ شُهُورِهِ نِيسَانُهَا

وله　٤،٢٦

إِنَّ ٱلزَّمَانَ غَدَا بِوَجْهٍ كَالِحٍ　مِنْ بَعْدِ مَا كُنَّا نَرَاهُ طَلِيقَا
أَيَّامَ أَسْحَبُ فَضْلَ أَيَّامِ ٱلصِّبَا　فِي ظِلِّ عَيْشٍ لَا يَزَالُ أَنِيقَا
بِٱلرَّقَّةِ ٱلْبَيْضَاءِ إِذْ تَرْعَى ٱلْمَهَا　حَقِّي وَلَا أَرْعَى لَهُنَّ حُقُوقَا
أَغْدُو عَلَى ٱللَّذَّاتِ غَيْرَ مُرَاقِبٍ　مَنْعًا وَلَا مُتَخَوِّفٍ تَعْوِيقَا
فِي فِتْيَةٍ خَلَعُوا أَعِنَّتَهُمْ فَمَا　يَأْلُونَ فِي طُرُقِ ٱلسَّدَادِ مُرُوقَا
نَازَعْتُهُمْ كَأْسًا كَأَنَّ نَسِيمَهَا　مِسْكٌ[2] تَضَوَّعَ فِي ٱلْإِنَاءِ فَتِيقَا
شَقَّتْ قِنَاعَ ٱللَّيْلِ لَمَّا غَادَرَتْ　كَفُّ ٱلنَّدِيمِ قِنَاعَهَا مَشْقُوقَا
صَبَغَتْ سَوَادَ دُجَاهُ حُمْرَةُ لَوْنِهَا　فَكَأَنَّهَا سَبَجٌ أُعِيدَ عَقِيقَا
وَلَقَدْ أَقُولُ لِصَاحِبَيَّ أَلَا صِلَا　لِي بِٱلصَّبُوحِ عَلَى ٱلْفُرَاتِ غَبُوقَا
إِنَّ ٱلْفُرَاتَ هُوَ ٱلرَّحِيقُ وَإِنَّمَا　تَتَعَاطَيَانِ عَلَى ٱلرَّحِيقِ رَحِيقَا

وله　٥،٢٦

قَدْ أَحْدَقَ ٱلْوَرْدُ بِٱلشَّقِيقِ　خِلَالَ بُسْتَانِكَ ٱلْأَنِيقِ
كَأَنَّهُ حَوْلَهُ وُجُوهٌ　مُسْتَشْرِفَاتٌ إِلَى حَرِيقِ
فَٱشْرَبْ عَلَى ذَا ٱلشَّقِيقِ كَأْسًا　تَشْرَبْ عَقِيقًا عَلَى عَقِيقِ

١ الأصل: ضَلَّتْ. ٢ الأصل: مِسْكًا.

Its days are like the days of youth;
methinks its seasons the seasons of love.
We hunt its gazelles for just one day;
they forever hunt our hearts.
Hurry on the cups, for this is their hour;
move to the meadows, for their time has come.
All the months of spring have their splendor,
but April is the most splendid month.

Here are several poems of his: 26.4

The face of fate has now turned somber,
when we'd been used to see it gladsome,
In days when I trailed the hem of youth
in the shadow of a life still graceful,
In fair Raqqa, where oryxes respected my rights,
though I respected no right of theirs,
Pursuing pleasure, heeding no taboo,
undismayed by any hindrance,
With fellows who'd thrown off all restraint,
at pains to press into the paths of obstruction.
With them I shared wine whose bouquet was musk,
spreading its sharp scent from the pitcher,
It tore night's veil when my friend's hand
tore the wine's veil in two.
Its ruddy hue dyed the darkness of night—
black shells turned to carnelian.
To my friends I said, "Join my morning cup
to my evening cup on the Euphrates.
The true wine's the Euphrates, so you'll simply
partake of one wine on another."

Roses gaze at anemones 26.5
on the borders of your fair garden,
As though around it were faces
gazing up at a fire.
Raise a cup to those anemones,
drink agate on carnelian.

وقال أيضاً ٦،٢٦

أَنَّ شَوْقًا وَلِلْمُحِبِّ أَنِينُ   حِينَ فَاضَتْ عَلَى ٱلْخُدُودِ ٱلْجُفُونُ
آهِ مِنْ زَفْرَةٍ يُنَشِّئُهَا ٱلشَّوْ   قُ وَدَاءٌ بَيْنَ ٱلضُّلُوعِ دَفِينُ
كَيْفَ يَسْلُو ٱلشَّجِيُّ أَمْ كَيْفَ يَنْسَى ٱلـ   ـصَّبُّ أَمْ كَيْفَ يَذْهَلُ ٱلْمَحْزُونُ
لَا تَلُمْنِي بِٱلرَّقَّتَيْنِ وَدَعْنِي   إِنَّ قَلْبِي بِٱلرَّقَّتَيْنِ رَهِينُ
يَا نَدِيمِي أَمَا تَحِنُّ إِلَى ٱلْقَصْـ   ـفِ فَهٰذَا أَوَانُ يَبْدُو ٱلْحَنِينُ
مَا تَرَى جَانِبَ ٱلْمُصَلَّى وَقَدْ أَشْـ   ـرَقَ مِنْهُ ظُهُورُهُ وَٱلْبُطُونُ
أُقْحُوَانٌ وَسَوْسَنٌ وَشَقِيـ   ـقٌ وَبَهَارٌ يُجْنَى وَآذَرِيُونُ
أَسْرَجَتْ فِي رِيَاضِهِ سُرُجَ ٱلْقَطْـ   ـرِ وَطَابَتْ سُهُولُهُ وَٱلْحُزُونُ
إِنَّ آذَارَ لَمْ يَذَرْ تَحْتَ بَطْنِ   ٱلْأَرْضِ شَيْئًا أَكَنَّهُ كَانُونُ
وَبَدَا ٱلنَّرْجِسُ ٱلْبَدِيعُ كَأَمْثَا   لِ عُيُونٍ تَرْنُو إِلَيْهَا عُيُونُ
مَا تَرَى جَانِبَ ٱلْهَنِيِّ وَقَدْ أَشْـ   ـرَقَ فِيهِ ٱلْخِيرِيُّ وَٱلنِّسْرِينُ
صَاحَ فِيهِ ٱلْهَزَارُ نَاحَ بِهِ ٱلْقُمْـ   ـرِيُّ غَنَّى فِي جَوِّهِ ٱلشَّفْنِينُ
فَلِهٰذَا قَيْصُومُهُ وَخُزَامَا   هُ وَذَا ٱلْوَرْدُ فِيهِ وَٱلْيَاسَمِينُ
وَكَأَنَّ ٱلْفُرَاتَ بَيْنَهُمَا عَيْـ   ـنُ لُجَيْنٍ يَعُومُ فِيهَا ٱلسَّفِينُ
كَبُطُونِ ٱلْحَيَّاتِ أَوْ كَظُهُورِ ٱلْـ   ـمَشْرَفِيَّاتِ أَخْلَصَتْهَا ٱلْقُيُونُ
مَا أَتَى ٱلنَّاسَ مِثْلُ ذَا ٱلْعَامِ عَامٌ   لَا وَلَا جَاءَ مِثْلُ ذَا ٱلْحِينِ حِينُ
بَلَدٌ مُشْرِقُ ٱلْأَزَاهِرِ مُوعٍ   وَسَحَابٌ جَمٌّ ٱلْعَزَالَى هَتُونُ
تَتَلَاقَى ٱلْمِيَاهُ مَاءٌ مِنَ ٱلْمُزْ   نِ وَمَاءٌ يَجْرِي وَمَاءٌ مَعِينُ

There's longing and a lover's groan 26.6
when eyelashes cover the cheeks.
Alas for a sigh born of desire
and a sickness hidden in the heart.
How can sorrow be consoled, the lover forget,
or the griever not remember?
Don't blame me about Raqqa and Rāfiqah! Let be!
My heart is pledged to Raqqa and her sister.
My friend, don't you long for revelry?
Now's the moment when longing appears.
Don't you look here at the side of the prayer place?
Within and without it's radiant.
Violets, windflowers, oxeye daisies,
lilies, anemones—all to be plucked.
In its gardens incense burners have been lit,
perfuming its flower beds and its paths.
March has brought from under the earth
all that December had kept concealed.
As if the lovely narcissus flowers
are eyes to which other eyes turn.
And look there by the Hanī Canal, where
jonquils and violets bloom,
With nightingales' warbling, the cooing of doves,
and pigeons' song in the air,
On the one side lemongrass and lavender,
roses and jasmine on the other,
And the Euphrates between them an eye of silver,
the ships swimming along it
Like serpents' bellies or the blades of swords
forged by silversmiths nearby.
No one has known a year like this,
nor a season.
A well-watered place, radiant with flowers,
where clouds empty well-filled waterskins,
A meeting of waters, rain from heaven,
the flowing river, and tears of relief.

كَمْ غَدَا نَحْوَ دَيْرِ زَكَّى مِنْ قَلْبٍ صَحِيحٍ فَرَاحَ وَهْوَ حَزِينُ
لَوْ عَلَى ٱلدَّيْرِ عُجْتَ يَوْمًا لَأَلْهَتْكَ فُنُونٌ وَأَطْرَبَتْكَ فُنُونُ
لَائِمِي فِي صَبَابَتِي قَدْكَ مَهْلًا لَا تَلُمْنِي إِنَّ ٱلْمَلَامَ جُنُونُ
كَمْ غَزَالٍ فِي كَفِّهِ ٱلْوَرْدُ مَبْذُو لٌ وَفِي ٱلْخَدِّ مِنْهُ وَرْدٌ مَصُونُ
فَإِذَا مَا أَجَلْتُ طَرْفِيَ فِي خَدْ دَيْهِ جَالَتْ فِي ٱلْقَلْبِ مِنِّي ٱلظُّنُونُ
لَا سَعِيدٌ مَنْ لَيْسَ يُسْعِدُهُ جَدْ دٌ سَعِيدٌ وَطَائِرٌ مَيْمُونُ
وَلِسَانٌ مِثْلَ ٱلْحُسَامِ وَقَلْبٌ صَادِقٌ عَزْمُهُ وَرَأْيٌ رَصِينُ

وقال أيضاً ٧،٢٦

مَنْ حَاكِمٌ بَيْنَ ٱلزَّمَانِ وَبَيْنِي مَا زَالَ حَتَّى رَاضَنِي بِٱلْبَيْنِ
فَأَمَا وَرَبْعَيَّ ٱللَّذَيْنِ تَأَبَّدَا لَا عُجْتُ بَعْدَهُمَا عَلَى رَبْعَيْنِ
مَا لِي نَأَيْتُ عَنِ ٱلْهَنِيِّ وَكُنْتُ لَا أَسْطِيعُ أَنْأَى عَنْهُ طَرْفَةَ عَيْنِ
يَا دَيْرَ زَكَّى كُنْتَ أَحْسَنَ مَأْلَفٍ[1] مَنَّ ٱلزَّمَانُ بِهِ عَلَى إِلْفَيْنِ
وَبِنَفْسِيَ ٱلْمَرْجُ ٱلَّذِي ٱبْتَسَمَتْ لَنَا جَنَبَاتُهُ عَنْ عَسْجَدٍ وَلُجَيْنِ
لَوْ حُمِّلَ ٱلثَّقَلَانِ مَا حُمِّلْتُ مِنْ شَوْقٍ لَأَثْقَلَ حَمْلُهُ ٱلثَّقَلَيْنِ

وقال أيضاً ٨،٢٦

وَإِلَى ٱلرَّقَّتَيْنِ أَطْوِي قُرَى ٱلْبِيدِ بِمَطْوِيَّةِ ٱلْقَرَا مِذْعَانِ
حَبَّذَا ٱلْكَرْخُ حَبَّذَا ٱلْعُمْرُ لَا بَلْ حَبَّذَا ٱلدَّيْرُ حَبَّذَا ٱلسَّرْوَتَانِ
قَدْ تَجَلَّى ٱلرَّبِيعُ فِي حُلَلِ ٱلزَّهْرِ وَصَاغَ ٱلْحَمَامُ حَلْيَ ٱلْأَغَانِي
أَلْبَسَتْهَا يَدُ ٱلرَّبِيعِ مِنَ ٱلْأَنْـ وَارِ بُرْدًا كَٱلْأَتْحَمِيِّ ٱلْيَمَانِي

[1] الأصل: مَأْلَفًا.

How many hearts have gone to Zakkā's Convent
healthy, and returned deeply afflicted!
If one day you turn aside to the monastery,
you'll find much to divert you, much to delight.
You who reprove me for my passion, stop!
Don't blame me, for blaming is madness.
Many a gazelle gives out roses with her hands
while the roses in her cheeks stay safe,
And if my glance wanders over her cheeks,
in my heart speculations arise.
No man is happy who receives no aid
from auspicious fate and a bird of good omen,
From a sword-keen tongue, a heart true of purpose,
and a judgment firm and composed.

Who will judge between me and destiny? 26.7
It's tamed me at last with separation.
By the spring encampments, now deserted
(may I never visit such encampments again),
Why did I ever quit and desert the Hanī,
when I couldn't take my eyes from it?
Zakkā's Convent, you were the best haunt
that fate could give two lovers.
I'd give my life for the gardens whose borders
smiled to us with silver and gold.
If men and jinn bore my burden of longing,
under its weight they'd be bowed.

Bound for the twin cities of Raqqa, I pass desert encampments, 26.8
on a docile mount, gaunt from traveling.
Would I were at Karkh or the cloister
or, better, the monastery with its cypress trees.
Spring has appeared, clad in robes of flowers;
doves have fashioned ornaments of song.
Spring's hand has unfurled cloaks brightly colored
like the brocades of Yemen and Tihāmah.

يَا خَلِيلَيَّ هٰتُمَا عَلِّلَانِي   عَاطِيَانِي ٱلصَّهْبَاءَ لَا تَذَرَانِي
أَبْعِدَا ٱلْمَاءَ أَبْعِدَا ٱلْمَاءَ قُومَا   أَدْنِيَا أَدْنِيَا بَنَاتِ ٱلدِّنَانِ
سَقِّيَانِي مِنْ كُلِّ لَوْنٍ مِنَ ٱلرَّا   حِ عَلَى كُلِّ هٰذِهِ ٱلْأَلْوَانِ
أَخْضَرِ ٱللَّوْنِ كَٱلزُّمُرُّدِ فِي أَحْـ   ـمَرَ صَافِي ٱلْأَدِيمِ كَٱلْأُرْجُوَانِ
وَأَقَاحٍ كَٱللُّؤْلُؤِ ٱلرَّطْبِ قَدْ فُصْـ   ـصِلَ بَيْنَ ٱلْعَقِيقِ بِٱلْمَرْجَانِ
وَبَهَارٍ مِثْلَ ٱلدَّنَانِيرِ مَحْفُو   فٍ بِزَهْرِ ٱلْخَيْرِيِّ وَٱلْحُوذَانِ
وَكَأَنَّ ٱلنُّعْمَانَ حَلَّ عَلَيْهَا   حُلَلًا مِنْ شَقَائِقِ ٱلنُّعْمَانِ

وللرشيد يذكر هذا الدير ٩،٢٦

سَلَامٌ عَلَى ٱلنَّازِحِ ٱلْمُغْتَرِبْ   تَحِيَّةُ صَبٍّ بِهِ مُكْتَئِبْ
غَزَالٌ مَرَاتِعُهُ بِٱلْبَلِيخِ   إِلَى دَيْرِ زَكَّى فَقَصْرِ ٱلْخَشَبْ
أَيَا مَنْ أَعَانَ عَلَى نَفْسِهِ   بِتَخْلِيفِهِ طَائِعًا مَنْ أَحَبْ
سَأَسْتُرُ وَٱلسَّتْرُ مِنْ شِيمَتِي   هَوَى مَنْ أُحِبُّ بِمَنْ لَا أُحِبْ

وكان عند مسيره من الرافقة إلى بغداد خلّف بها ماردة أمّ أبي إسحاق المعتصم ١٠،٢٦
فاشتاقها فكتب إليها بهذه الأبيات قال فلمّا ورد كتاب الرشيد عليها قالت لبعض من يقول الشعر أجبه فقال عن لسانها

أَتَانِي كِتَابُكَ يَا سَيِّدِي   وَفِيهِ مَعَ ٱلْفَضْلِ كُلُّ ٱلْعَجَبْ
أَتَزْعُمُ أَنَّكَ لِي عَاشِقٌ   وَأَنَّكَ بِي مُسْتَهَامٌ وَصَبْ
وَلَوْ كَانَ هٰذَا كَذَا لَمْ تَكُنْ   لِتَتْرُكَنِي نُهْزَةً لِلْكُرَبْ

Friends, come pour for me, give me
    a morning cup to drink, don't send me away!
Keep water at bay, keep water at bay,
    bring close the wine jars and their daughters!
Pour me to drink all kinds of wine,
    of every vintage and color,
An emerald's dark hue mingled with
    clear-surfaced reddish purple.
Here are chamomiles like soft pearls
    strung between coral and carnelian,
Oxeye daisies like gold coins surrounded
    by gillyflowers and lilies.
And King Nuʿmān has spread out there
    robes of his sisters, anemones.[166]

Hārūn al-Rashīd has verses in which he mentions this monastery: **26.9**

Greetings to the distant exile
    from one who loves her and grieves
For a gazelle who pastures by the Balīkh,
    the Zakkā Convent, and Khashab Palace.
I have wronged myself by willingly
    leaving behind the one I love;
Concealment's a trait of mine, so I'll hide
    my love for my darling behind one I don't love.

When al-Rashīd traveled from Rāfiqah to Baghdad, he left Māridah,[167] the mother of Abū Isḥāq al-Muʿtaṣim, at the Zakkā Monastery. Then he missed her and so he wrote these verses to her. When his letter arrived, she asked someone who could compose poetry to reply to him in her name: **26.10**

Sire, I received your letter,
    which with all its merits is wondrous.
Do you claim that you love me,
    that you're crazy with longing for me?
If this were true, you'd not have left me
    a prey to every torment.

وَأَنْتَ بِبَغْدَادَ تَرْعَى بِهَا   رِيَاضَ ٱللَّذَاذَةِ مَعَ مَنْ تُحِبّ
وَلَوْلَا ٱتِّقَاؤُكَ يَا سَيِّدِي   لَوَافَتْكَ بِي نَاجِيَاتُ ٱلنُّجُبْ

قال فلمّا قرأ كتابها وجّه يحدرها مِن وقتها إليه.

وذكر صالح التركيّ وكان المعتصم في حجره قال عشق الرشيد ماردة عشقاً مبرّحاً ١١،٢٦
فقال فيها

وَإِذَا نَظَرْتَ إِلَى مَحَاسِنِهَا   فَلِكُلِّ مَوْضِعِ نَظْرَةٍ نَبْلُ
وَتَنَالُ مِنْكَ بِحَدِّ نَاظِرِهَا   مَا لَا يَنَالُ بِحَدِّهِ ٱلنَّصْلُ
شَغَلَتْكَ وَهْيَ لِكُلِّ ذِي بَصَرٍ   لَاقَى مَحَاسِنَ وَجْهِهَا شُغُلُ
فَلِقَلْبِهَا حِلْمٌ يُبَاعِدُهَا   عَنْ ذِي ٱلْهَوَى وَلِطَرْفِهَا جَهْلُ
وَلِوَجْهِهَا مِنْ وَجْهِهَا قَمَرٌ   وَلِعَيْنِهَا مِنْ عَيْنِهَا كُحْلُ

وللرشيد شعر صالح وأبيات مفردات كان يتمثّل بها وأكثر شعره في جواريه ١٢،٢٦
وعشقه لهنّ. فمن قوله

مَلَكْتُ مَنْ أَصْبَحَ لِي مَالِكًا   لٰكِنَّهُ فِي مُلْكِهِ ظَالِمُ
لَوْ شِئْتُ لَٱسْتَاقَتْهُ لِي قُدْرَةٌ   وَلٰكِنَّ حُكْمَ ٱلْحُبِّ لِي لَازِمُ
أَحْبَبْتُهُ مِنْ بَيْنِ هٰذَا ٱلْوَرَى   وَهْوَ بِحُبِّي خَبِرٌ عَالِمُ
قَبِيحُ فِعْلٍ حَسَنٌ وَجْهُهُ   يَعْذِرُ فِي أَمْثَالِهِ ٱللَّائِمُ
أَحْسَنُ مَنْ أَبْصَرَهُ مُبْصِرٌ   لَوْ أَنَّهُ فِي حُسْنِهِ رَاحِمُ

وله

You're in Baghdad now, playing
in pleasure's grounds with your lover.
But for my fear of you, sire, swift camels
would have brought me to you.

When Hārūn read this letter, he immediately had her brought to Baghdad.

Ṣāliḥ al-Turkī, who was al-Muʿtaṣim's tutor, remembered: Al-Rashīd was passionately in love with Māridah and he composed this poem about her: 26.11

If you look at her beauties,
each one's a pointed arrow.
Her sharp glances cut you
deeper than any dagger.
She obsesses anyone who sees her beauty
as much as she obsesses you.
Her heart's reason keeps her far from lovers,
but there's folly in her gaze,
Her face has given itself moonlike beauty,
her eye's kohl comes from her eye.

Al-Rashīd composed sound poetry and stand-alone verses he loved to quote. Most of his poetry is about his slave girls and his love for them, for instance: 26.12

I own a girl who's now my owner,
and as an owner she's unjust.
I could force her to come, if I wanted,
but I obey the laws of love.
I love her above all mankind,
of my love she's well aware.
Ugly deeds and a lovely face,
blamers for her find excuses;
The most beautiful being ever seen—
if only, in her beauty,
she were to show mercy.

Another of his poems:

صَيَّرَنِي ٱلْحُبُّ إِلَى مَا تَرَى   أَنْحَلَ جِسْمِي وَلِقَلْبِي كَوَى
قَدْ كَتَبَ ٱلْحُبُّ عَلَى جَبْهَتِي   هٰذَا قَتِيلٌ فِي سَبِيلِ ٱلْهَوَى

قال وكان الرشيد قد أشخص هيلانة جارية أخيه الهادي وأحبّها حبّاً شديداً فخلّفها في بعض أسفاره ببغداد ثمّ اشتاقها فقال هذه الأبيات ١٣،٢٦

أَهْدَى ٱلْحَبِيبُ مَعَ ٱلْجَنُوبِ سَلَامَهُ   فَٱرْدُدْ عَلَيْهِ مَعَ ٱلشَّمَالِ سَلَامَا
وَٱعْرِفْ بِقَلْبِكَ مَا تَضَمَّنَ قَلْبُهُ   وَتَدَاوَلَا بِهَوَاكُمَا[1] ٱلْأَيَّامَا
مَهْمَا بَكَيْتَ لَهُ فَأَيْقِنْ أَنَّهُ   سَتَفِيضُ عَيْنَاهُ ٱلدُّمُوعَ[2] سِجَامَا
فَٱحْبِسْ دُمُوعَكَ رَحْمَةً لِدُمُوعِهِ   إِنْ كُنْتَ تَحْفَظُ أَوْ تَحُوطُ ذِمَامَا

ومن شعره في جواريه الثلاث ١٤،٢٦

إِنَّنِي وَزَّعْتُ حُبِّي طَائِعًا   بَيْنَ شَجْوٍ وَضِيَاءٍ وَخُنُثْ
يَتَنَازَعْنَ ٱلْهَوَى مِنْ ذِي هَوًى   آمِنَاتٍ عُقْدَةً لَا تَنْتَكِثْ
وَإِذَا شَجْوٌ أَتَتْ زَائِرَةً   كَشَفَتْ عَنِّيَ شَجْوٌ كُلَّ بَثّْ

قال وكان مولد الرشيد بالريّ أوّل سنة ثمان وأربعين ومائة ووُلد الفضل بن يحيى قبله بسبعة أيّام فأرضعته أمّ الفضل وبويع له بالخلافة ليلة السبت لأربع عشرة ليلة بقيت من شهر ربيع الأوّل سنة سبعين ومائة ووُلد في هذه الليلة عبد الله المأمون من جارية تُسمّى مراجل. في هذه الليلة مات خليفة ووليَ خليفة ووُلد خليفة وهذا من الاتّفاقات الطريفة. ١٥،٢٦

وتوفّي الرشيد بقرية[3] تُدعى سنداباذ من عمل طوس وله خمس وأربعون سنة يوم السبت لأربع خلون من جمادى الآخرة[4] سنة ثلاث وتسعين ومائة وكانت خلافته ثلاثاً وعشرين سنة وشهراً ونصفاً.[5]

---

١ الأصل: وَبَدَا وَلَا تَهوَاكُمَا. ٢ الأصل: منهُ للدّمُوع. ٣ كذا في عوّاد؛ الأصل: غرفة. ٤ الأصل: الآخر. ٥ الأصل: ونصف.

Love has rendered me as you see,
my body wasted, my heart seared.
Love has inscribed upon my forehead:
"A martyr on passion's field."

Al-Rashīd summoned Hīlānah,[168] his brother al-Hādī's slave, and he fell violently in love with her. He left her behind in Baghdad when he went on a journey, and missed her. So he composed these verses: 26.13

The lover sends his greetings borne by the south wind;
send back a greeting on the wind from the north.
Know in your heart what his heart hides;
let the days pass between you, united in passion.
Whenever you weep for him, have no doubt
he will be shedding a torrent of tears.
Hold back your tears from compassion for his
if you honor the duty you have to protect him.

Here is one of his poems on his three slaves: 26.14

I've divided my love submissively
between Shajw, Ḍiyā', and Khunth:[169]
They fight over their lover's passion,
trusting in a pact never broken.
When Shajw comes for a visit,
she brings out all my secret sorrows.

Al-Rashīd was born in Rayy at the beginning of 148 [765]. Al-Faḍl ibn Yaḥyā 26.15
was born a week before him and al-Faḍl's mother was his wet-nurse. He was acclaimed caliph on Saturday night, Rabi al-Awwal 17, 170 [September 9, 786]. That night a slave girl called Marājil[170] gave birth to ʿAbdallāh al-Ma'mūn. So, on the night a caliph died, a caliph assumed power and a caliph was born—an unusual coincidence.

Al-Rashīd died aged forty-five in a village called Sandābādh in the district of Ṭūs on Saturday, Jumada al-Thani 3,[171] 193 [March 24, 809]. His reign had lasted twenty-three years, one month and a half.

ديـر مـار[1] سرجيس

١،٢٧ وهــذا الدير بعانة وعانة مدينة على الفرات عامرة وبها هذا الدير وهو كبير حسن كثير الرهبان والناس يقصدونه للتنزّه فيه وهناك كروم ومعاصر وبساتين وشجر والموضع في نهاية الحسن جامع لما يحتاج إليه أهل التطرّب والتفرّج. ولابن أبي طالب المكفوف الواسطيّ فيه

رُبَّ صَهْبَاءَ مِنْ بَنَاتِ ٱلْمَجُوسِ　　قَهْوَةٍ بَابِلِيَّـةٍ خَـنْدَرِيسِ
قَـدْ تَحَسَّيْتُهَا بِنَـايٍ وَعُودٍ　　قَبْلَ قَرْعِ ٱلشَّمَّاسِ لِلنَّـاقُوسِ
وَغَـزَالٍ مُكَحَّـلٍ[2] ذِي دَلَالٍ　　سَاحِرِ ٱلطَّرْفِ سَامِرِيٍّ عَرُوسِ
دِينُهُ مُعْـلَنٌ لِدِينِ ٱلنَّصَارَى　　وَإِذَا مَا خَـلَا فَـدِينُ ٱلْمَجُوسِ
قَـدْ خَـلَوْنَا بِظَبْـيَةٍ نَجْتَلِيهِ[3]　　يَوْمَ سَبْتٍ إِلَى صَبَاحِ ٱلْخَمِيسِ
بَيْنَ وَرْدٍ وَنَـرْجِسٍ وَبَهَـارٍ　　وَسْطَ بُسْتَانِ دَيْرِمَا سَرْجِيسِ

٢،٢٧ وبهذا الموضع قبر أمّ الفضل بن يحيى بن خالد بن برمك وكان الرشيد لمّا شخص من الرقّة إلى بغداد يريد الحجّ شخص معه البرامكة فتوفّيت أمّ الفضل وكانت أرضعت الرشيد بلبن الفضل وكان يحبّها ويجلّها. وكان مولد الفضل قبل مولد الرشيد بسبعة أيّام فأمر الرشيد فاشتُريت لها عشرة أجربة من بستان عند وادي القناطر على شاطئ الفرات فدُفنت هناك وبُنيت عليها قبّة فهي تُعرف بقبّة البرمكيّـة.

١ الأصل: ما. ٢ الأصل: مكملٍ. ٣ كذا في الأصل.

The Monastery of Mār Sarjīs (Saint Sergius)

This monastery is situated in ʿĀnah, a flourishing city on the Euphrates. It is large and beautiful, and has many monks. People visit it for recreation, since it possesses vineyards, winepresses, gardens, and orchards, and is in an extremely beautiful setting, offering all that pleasure-seekers and fun-lovers could want. Here's a poem on it by Ibn Abī Ṭālib al-Makfūf al-Wāṣiṭī: 27.1

Many a ruby-colored wine, a Magians' daughter,
 a vintage from Babylon, long matured,
I've sipped to the sound of flute and lute,
 before the deacon struck the clappers.
A gazelle with kohl-rimmed eyes, coquettish,
 her gaze bewitching, a Sumerian bride,
Proclaiming that her faith is Christian,
 but in secret a follower of Zoroaster—
We unveiled her, fawn-like, to spend
 from Saturday to Thursday morn,
Alone among roses, narcissi, and daisies,
 in Mār Sarjīs's gardens.

The grave of Umm al-Faḍl, the mother of al-Faḍl ibn Yaḥyā ibn Khālid ibn Barmak, is here. The Barmakids accompanied al-Rashīd when he traveled from Raqqa to Baghdad on his way to the pilgrimage, and Umm al-Faḍl died here. Al-Rashīd was fond of her and honored her because she had suckled him with al-Faḍl's milk. (Al-Faḍl was born a week before al-Rashīd.) About twenty-five acres (ten hectares) of a garden were bought at the Valley of the Bridges on the banks of the Euphrates and she was buried there. A dome was built over her grave, which is known as the Dome of the Barmakid Lady. 27.2

ديـر ابن مزعوق

١،٢٨ وهـذا الدير بالحيرة في وسطها وهو دير كثير الرهبان حسن العمارة أحد المتنزّهات المقصودة والأماكن الموصوفة. ولمحمّد بن عبد الرحمٰن الثروانيّ فيه

هَلْ لَكَ فِي دَيْرِ مَارِ فَثْيُونَ[١] وَفِي ... دَيْرِ ٱبْنِ مَزْعُوقَ غَيْرِ مُخْتَصَرِ
وَنَسْأَلُ ٱلْأَرْضَ عَنْ مَنَابِتِهَا ... وَعَهْدِهَا بِٱلرَّبِيعِ وَٱلْمَطَرِ
يَا لَكَ طِيبًا وَشَمَّ رَائِحَةٍ ... كَٱلْمِسْكِ يَأْتِي بِنَفْحَةِ ٱلسَّحَرِ
فِي شُرْبِ خَمْرٍ وَسَمْعِ مُحْسِنَةٍ ... تُلْهِيكَ بَيْنَ ٱللِّسَانِ وَٱلْوَتَرِ
فَكُلُّ سَاقٍ كَأَنَّهُ قَمَرٌ ... بَلْ زَادَ فِي حُسْنِهِ عَلَى ٱلْقَمَرِ
لَمْ يَخْلُقِ ٱللّٰهُ مِثْلَهُ بَشَرًا ... فَهْوَ حَيَاةٌ وَمُنْيَةُ[٢] ٱلْبَشَرِ
فِي صُورَةٍ أُكْمِلَتْ إِذَا طَلَعَتْ ... دِينَ لَهَا بِٱلسُّجُودِ فِي ٱلصُّوَرِ

٢،٢٨ والثروانيّ هذا كوفيّ من المطبوعين في الشعر والمنهمكين في البطالات والمتطرّحين في الحانات والمدمنين لشرب الخمر والمغرقين في اتّباع المرد لا يعرف شيئًا غير ذلك ولا[٣] يوجد في شيء من أمر الدنيا إلّا فيه. وكان آخر أمره أن أُصيب في حانة خمّار بين زقّي خمر وهو ميّت. ومن مليح شعره قوله

أَتَاكَ عَلَى ٱلدُّخُولِ ٱلْمِهْرَجَانُ ... تُشَيِّعُهُ ٱلْمَعَازِفُ وَٱلْقِيَانُ
وَزُفَّتْ نَحْوَكَ ٱلصَّهْبَاءُ صِرْفًا ... تَسِيرُ بِهَا وَتَحْمِلُهَا ٱلدِّنَانُ
لِهٰذَا ٱلْيَوْمِ فَضْلٌ مُسْتَبِينٌ ... عَلَى ٱلْأَيَّامِ تَعْرِفُهُ وَشَانُ

١ كذا في عوّاد؛ الأصل: فاثور. ٢ الأصل: ومنته. ٣ الأصل: لا.

Ibn Mazʿūq's Monastery

This monastery stands in the middle of Ḥīrah. Many monks live there; it has fine buildings, and is a place people go to on excursions. Poets have often described it. Muḥammad ibn ʿAbd al-Raḥmān al-Tharwānī has these verses about it: 28.1

Shall we go to Mār Fāthyūn's Convent
  or Ibn Mazʿūq's, a leisurely walk?
We'll ask the earth about its plants
  and when it last saw spring and rain.
How perfumed you are, and fragrant
  as musk wafting on the dawn breeze!
A singer whose delightful song and lute
  accompanies the wine we drink,
Every cupbearer mirrors the moon—
  no, he's lovelier than it by far.
God has created no beings like them;
  they're the life and desire of mankind,
In a form perfected, and when they appear,
  we bow down before their images.

Al-Tharwānī came from Kufa. He was a naturally gifted poet, thoroughly dissolute, a frequenter of taverns, a compulsive drinker, and an obsessive pursuer of young boys. He had no other interests or ambition in life. He met his end in a wine cellar, being found dead between two jars of wine. This is one of his good poems: 28.2

The autumn festival[172] comes to greet you,
  to the sound of flutes and singers.
Pure wine is brought to meet you,
  borne by casks and pitchers—
This day is far above any other,
  and that you very well know.

إِذَا وَقَّرْتَهُ عَظَّمْتَ كِسْرَى   وَأَكْرَمَكَ ٱلشَّرِيفُ ٱلْهُرْمُزَانُ
وَأَصْفَاكَ ٱلْهَوَى بَهْرَامُ جُورٍ   وَسَارَعَ فِي رِضَاكَ ٱلْفَيْرُزَانُ
لِتَعْظِيمِ ٱلَّذِي قَدْ عَظَّمُوهُ   وَدَانَ بِهِ أَوَائِلُهُمْ وَدَانُوا
فَدَعْ عَنْكَ ٱلْخِلَافَ وَلَا وَحَتَّى   وَسَوْفَ أَجِيئُكُمْ وَنَعَمْ وَٱلْآنُ
خِلَافُكَ لَا يَجُوزُ عَلَى ٱلنَّدَامَى   وَلَا يَرْضَى بِذَاكَ ٱلْمِهْرَجَانُ

وقال أيضاً ٣،٢٨

تُقَلِّبُ طَرْفَ عَيْنِكَ مِنْ بَعِيدٍ   شَبِيهاً بِٱلْمَوَدَّةِ وَٱلْوَعِيدِ
تُقِرُّ بِطَرْفِ عَيْنِكَ لِي بِوَصْلٍ   وَفِعْلُكَ لِي مُقِرٌّ بِٱلْجُحُودِ
تُشَكِّكُنِي وَأَعْلَمُ أَنَّ هٰذَا   هَوًى بَيْنَ ٱلتَّعَطُّفِ وَٱلصُّدُودِ
هَوَاكَ هَوًى تُجَدِّدُهُ ٱللَّيَالِي   وَلَا يَبْلَى عَلَى مَرِّ ٱلْعُهُودِ

ومن شعره أيضاً

كَرَّ ٱلشَّرَابُ عَلَى نَشْوَانَ مُصْطَبِحِ   قَدْ هَبَّ يَشْرَبُهَا وَٱلدِّيكُ لَمْ يَصِحِ
وَاللَّيْلُ فِي عَسْكَرٍ جَمٍّ بَوَارِقُهُ   مِنَ ٱلنُّجُومِ وَضَوْءُ ٱلصُّبْحِ لَمْ يَضِحِ
وَٱلْعَيْشُ لَا عَيْشَ إِلَّا أَنْ تُبَارِكَهَا   صَهْبَاءُ تَقْتُلُ هَمَّ ٱلنَّفْسِ بِٱلْفَرَحِ
حَتَّى يَظَلَّ ٱلَّذِي قَدْ بَاتَ يَشْرَبُهَا   وَلَا مَرَاحَ بِهِ يَخْتَالُ كَٱلْمَرِحِ

Respect it and you honor Khosroes,
while the noble Hurmuzān will honor you,
Bahrām Gūr will be your true friend,
Fīruzān will speed to please you—
As you exalt the one they exalted and worshipped,
they and their fathers before them.
Stop arguing, saying "No" and "Until,"
"I'll come to you," "Yes," or "Now";
Such arguments don't work with friends,
and the festival won't accept them.

And here are two other poems of his: **28.3**

You turn your gaze to me from afar,
apparently loving or threatening;
Your looks assure me we'll meet,
but your actions proclaim rejection.
You leave me in doubt, knowing your love
wavers between affection and refusal.
Fate has renewed my love for you;
time's passing can never exhaust it.

A second round's poured for the merry fellow
who rose to drink before cockcrow,
While night was encamped with the flashing stars
and morning had not yet dawned.
This is the life! A life blessed by wine,
which kills cares with gaiety,
Till the worry-worn man who drank it
struts proudly, filled with joy.

دير سَرجس

١،٢٩ وهـذا الدير كان بطيزناباذ وهو بين الكوفة والقادسيّة على حافّة الطريق وبينها وبين القادسيّة ميل. وكانت محفوفة بالكروم والشجر والحانات وكانت إحدى[١] البقاع المقصودة والنزه الموصوفة وقد خربت وبطلت وعفت آثارها وتهدّمت آبارها ولم يبقَ من جميع رسومها إلّا قباب خراب وحجر على قارعة الطريق يسمّيه الناس معصرة أبي نواس. ولأبي نواس فيها

قَالُوا تَنَسَّكَ بَعْدَ ٱلْحَجِّ قُلْتُ لَهُمْ أَرْجُو ٱلْإِلٰهَ وَأَخْشَى طِيـزَنَابَاذَا
أَخْشَى قُضَيِّبَ كَرْمٍ أَنْ يُنَازِعَنِي رَأْسَ ٱلْخِطَامِ وَإِنْ أَسْرَعْتُ إِغْذَاذَا
فَإِنْ سَلِمْتُ وَمَا نَفْسِي عَلَى ثِقَةٍ مِنَ ٱلسَّلَامَةِ لَمْ أَسْلَمْ بِبَغْدَاذَا
مَا أَبْعَدَ ٱلرُّشْدَ مِنْ قَلْبٍ تَضَمَّنَهُ قُطْرُبُلٌ فَقُرَى بِنَا فَكَلْوَاذَا

٢،٢٩ وكان هذا الدير من أحسن الديارات عمارة وأنزهها موضعاً. وللحسين بن الضحّاك فيه

أَخَوَيَّ حَيَّ عَلَى ٱلصَّبُوحِ صَبَاحَا هُبَّا وَلَا تَعِدَا ٱلنَّدِيمَ رَوَاحَا
مَهْمَا أَقَامَ عَلَى ٱلصَّبُوحِ مُسَاعِدٌ وَعَلَى ٱلْغَبُوقِ فَلَنْ أُرِيدَ بَرَاحَا
عُودَا لِعَادَتِنَا صَبِيحَةَ أَمْسِنَا فَٱلْعَوْدُ أَحْمَدُ مُغْتَدًى وَمَرَاحَا
هَلْ تَعْذُرَانِ بِدَيْرِ سَرْجِسَ صَاحِبًا بِٱلصَّحْوِ أَوْ تَرَيَانِ ذَاكَ جُنَاحَا
إِنِّي أُعِيذُكُمَا بِأُلْفَةِ بَيْنِنَا أَنْ تَشْرَبَا بِقُرَى ٱلْفُرَاتِ قَرَاحَا
عَجَّتْ قَوَاقِزُنَا وَقَدَّسَ قَسُّنَا هَرَجًا وَأَصْخَبَنَا ٱلدَّجَاجُ صِيَاحَا

---

١ الأصل: أحد.

Sarjis's Monastery

This was a monastery at Ṭayzanābād, beside the road between Kufa and Qādisiyyah, a mile (less than two kilometers) from Qādisiyyah. It was surrounded by vineyards, orchards, and taverns; attracted many visitors; and was much spoken of. Now it is ruined and abandoned, its wells have fallen in, and no trace of it remains except tumbledown domes and stones at the edge of the road people call Abū Nuwās's winepress. 29.1

He mentions the place in this poem:

They ask, "Have you turned ascetic after the hajj?"
I say, "I put hope in God, I fear Ṭayzanābād."
However much I press my mount ahead, I fear
a branch of the vine will seize its bit and bridle.
If I stay safe, and I'm far from sure of that,
I won't escape the dangers of Baghdad.
Good sense is far from one who dwells
in Quṭrabbul, Binnā's hamlets, and Kalwādhā.

This monastery was very prosperous and in a most pleasant setting. 29.2
Al-Ḥusayn ibn al-Ḍaḥḥāk composed these verses on it:

Brothers, come early to the morning cup,
hurry! Don't promise your friend to come later.
Though many join us, drinking early or late,
I'll never have a mind to depart.
Let's go back to yesterday's custom;
to return is praiseworthy, whether you come or go.
Can you excuse a friend's sobriety
at Sarjis's Convent, or is it a sin?
I beg you, for our friendship's sake,
don't drink the pure water of the Euphrates.
Our goblets have clinked, our priest's prayer is in disorder,
our shouting has roused the hens to cackle.

لِلْجَاشِرِيَّةِ فَضْلُهَا فَتَعَجَّلَا إِنْ كُنْتُمَا تَرَيَانِ ذَاكَ صَلَاحَا
يَا رُبَّ مُلْتَبِسِ ٱلْجُفُونِ بِنَوْمَةٍ نَبَّهْتُهُ بِٱلرَّاحِ حِينَ أَرَاحَا
فَكَأَنَّ رَيَّا ٱلْكَأْسِ حِينَ نَدَبْتُهُ لِلْكَأْسِ أَنْهَضَ فِي حَشَاهُ جَنَاحَا
فَأَجَابَ يَعْثُرُ فِي فُضُولِ رِدَائِهِ عَجْلَانَ يَخْلِطُ بِٱلْعِثَارِ مَرَاحَا
فَهَتَكْتُ سِتْرَ مُجُونِهِ بِتَهَتُّكِي فِي كُلِّ مُلْهِيَةٍ وَبُحْتُ وَبَاحَا
مَا زَالَ يَضْحَكُ بِي وَيُضْحِكُنِي بِهِ مَا يَسْتَفِيقُ دُعَابَةً وَمُزَاحَا

The predawn drink has merits. Don't hold back,
  hurry, if you believe it's the right thing to do.
Many a friend, his eyelids confounded by sleep,
  I've woken with wine, after his rest.
And the scent from the cup when I've called him to drink
  has given him wings to go on.
He's responded, stumbling in the folds of his cloak,
  hurrying to cover his misstep with mirth.
Foolish myself, I've torn the veil from his folly,
  in games where we've both unburdened our hearts.
He's not stopped mocking me and inspiring me to mock him,
  never sobering up, with teasing and banter.

ديارات الأساقف

هذه الديارات بالنجف بظاهر الكوفة وهو أوّل الحيرة وهي قباب وقصور تُسمّى ديارات الأساقف وبحضرتها نهر يُعرف بالغدير عن يمينه قصر أبي الخصيب مولى أبي جعفر وعن شماله السدير وبين ذلك الديارات. وقصر أبي الخصيب هذا أحد متنزّهات الدنيا وهو مشرف على النجف وعلى ذلك الظهر ويصعد من أسفله على درجة طولها خمسون مرقاة إلى سطح حسن ومجلس. فيشرف الناظر على النجف والحيرة من ذلك الموضع. ثمّ يصعد منه على درجة أخرى طولها خمسون مرقاة إلى سطح أفيح ومجلس عجيب. وأبو الخصيب هذا مولى أبي جعفر المنصور وحاجبه. والسدير قصر عظيم من أبنية ملوك لخم في قديم الزمان. وما بقي الآن منه فهو ديارات وبيع للنصارى. ١،٣٠

٢،٣٠ ولعليّ بن محمّد الحمّانيّ العلويّ يذكر هذه المواضع

كَمْ وَقْفَةٍ لَكَ بِٱلْخَوَرْ نَقِ لَا تُوَازَى بِٱلْمَوَاقِفْ
بَيْنَ ٱلْغَدِيرِ إِلَى ٱلسَّدِيرِ إِلَى دِيَارَاتِ ٱلْأَسَاقِفْ
فَمَدَارِجِ ٱلرُّهْبَانِ فِي أَطْمَارِ خَائِفَةٍ وَخَائِفْ
دِمَنٌ كَأَنَّ رِيَاضَهَا يُكْسَيْنَ أَعْلَامَ ٱلْمَطَارِفْ
وَكَأَنَّمَا غُدْرَانُهَا فِيهَا عُشُورٌ فِي مَصَاحِفْ
وَكَأَنَّمَا أَنْوَارُهَا تَهْتَزُّ بِٱلرِّيحِ ٱلْعَوَاصِفْ
طُرَرُ ٱلْوَصَائِفِ يَلْتَقِينَ بِهَا إِلَى طُرَرِ ٱلْوَصَائِفْ
تَلْقَى أَوَائِلُهَا أَوَا خِرَهَا بِأَلْوَانِ ٱلزَّخَارِفْ
بَحْرِيَّةٌ شَتَوَاتُهَا بَرِّيَّةٌ فِيهَا ٱلْمَصَايِفْ

The Bishops' Monasteries

The Bishops' Monasteries are in Najaf, outside Kufa and close to Ḥīrah. They are a group of domes and palaces with a river, the Ghadīr, running between them. To the right is the palace of Abū l-Khaṣīb, Abū Jaʿfar's freedman, and to the left is al-Sadīr, with the monasteries in between. Abū l-Khaṣīb's palace is a truly memorable attraction for visitors. It looks out over Najaf and the open country, with a staircase of fifty steps leading up to a lovely terrace and place to sit. From there one looks toward Najaf and Ḥīrah. Another flight of fifty steps leads up to a vast terrace with a wonderful reception area. 30.1

Abū l-Khaṣīb was Abū Jaʿfar al-Manṣūr's freedman and his chamberlain.

Al-Sadīr was a great palace built by the Lakhmid kings in times past, but all that remains of it now are Christian monasteries and churches.

ʿAlī ibn Muḥammad al-Ḥimmānī al-ʿAlawī mentions these places in a poem: 30.2

How often you've stopped at al-Khawarnaq,
times that have no equal,
Between the Ghadīr, the Sadīr,
and the convents of the bishops,
And the paths of the monastics,
shabbily clad and fearful.
Ruins where the grass seems
to outrival silk brocade banners
And the pools to contain verses
of writing in sacred texts.
Imagine the palace lights
flickering in the gusts of stormy wind,
And carefully coiffured
servant girls coming and going,
Maidens meeting maidens
with ornaments in plenty,
Their winters spent on water,
their summers on the land.

دُرِّيَّةُ ٱلْحَصْبَاءِ كَا ... فُورِيَّةٌ فِيهَا ٱلْمَشَارِفْ
ثُمَّ ٱنْبَرَتْ سَحًّا كَبَا ... كِيَةٍ[1] بِأَرْبَعَةٍ ذَوَارِفْ

٣،٣٠ ولأبي نواس يذكر أيّامه بالسدير

عُدْنَ لِي بِٱلسَّدِيرِ أَيَّامُ قَصْفِ ... وَسُرُورٍ مَعَ ٱلنَّدَامَى وَعَزْفِ
وَعُيُونُ ٱلظِّبَاءِ تَرْنُو إِلَيْنَا ... مُنْعِمَاتٍ بِكُلِّ بِرٍّ وَلُطْفِ
وَرَخِيمِ ٱلْخُطَا يَكَادُ مِنَ ٱلرِّقَّةِ يُدْمِي أَدِيمَهُ كُلُّ طَرْفِ
حَلَّ مِنْهُ ٱلصَّلِيبُ فِي مَوْضِعِ ٱلْجِيدِ فَقَدْ خَصَّهُ عَلَى كُلِّ إِلْفِ
قَدْ أَدَرْنَا رَحَى ٱلنَّعِيمِ ثَلَاثًا ... وَوَصَلْنَا ٱلنَّعِيمَ كَفًّا بِكَفِّ

٤،٣٠ قال ولمّا نزل الرشيد الحيرة وقت منصرفه من الحجّ ركب جعفر بن يحيى إلى السدير فطافه ونظر إلى بنائه ثمّ وقعت عينه على كتاب في أعلاه فأمر من صعد إلى الموضع فقرأه. فقال في نفسه قد جعلته فألاً لما أخافه من الرشيد فقُرئ فإذا هو

إِنَّ بَنِي ٱلْمُنْذِرِ عَامَ ٱنْقَضَوْا ... بِحَيْثُ شَادَ ٱلْبِيعَةَ ٱلرَّاهِبُ
أَضْحَوْا وَلَا يَرْجُوهُمُ رَاغِبٌ ... يَوْماً وَلَا يَرْهَبُهُمْ رَاهِبُ
وَأَصْبَحُوا أُكْلاً لِدُودِ ٱلثَّرَى ... وَٱنْقَطَعَ ٱلْمَطْلُوبُ وَٱلطَّالِبُ

فحزن جعفر لذلك وصار[2] ينشد الأبيات ويقول ذهب والله أمرنا.

٥،٣٠ ومن هذه الأبنية المسقّطات وهو قصر فيه آزاج مستطيلة مسقّطة شرقيّ الحيرة على طريق الحاجّ ثمّ القصر[3] ثمّ كوّة البقّال ثمّ قصر العدسيّين ثمّ الأقصى الأبيض ثمّ

١ (بَاكِيَةٍ): ساقطة من الأصل. ٢ كذا في عوّاد؛ الأصل: لذلك ينشد. ٣ الأصل: الحاجّ القصر.

Pearl-like the stones of the palaces,
camphor white the hills.
Then the rain started pouring torrents,
emptying four waterskins.

Abū Nuwās has a poem recalling the days he spent at Sadīr: 30.3

Days of revelry at Sadīr I recall,
days of joy with companions and music,
Gazed at by the eyes of gazelles
adorned with gentleness and kindness.
A boy lightly stepping, so delicate
any look seems to wound his skin,
Set apart from all his friends
by the cross around his neck.
Three days we ground the mill of pleasure.
and pleasure we reached, hand in hand.

When al-Rashīd stopped at Ḥīrah on his way back from the pilgrimage,[173] 30.4
Jaʿfar ibn Yaḥyā rode over to Sadīr, walked around it, and looked at the buildings. He noted an inscription high up, so he ordered someone to climb up and read it, thinking it was a portent of what he feared from al-Rashīd. The inscription ran:

The sons of al-Mundhir, the year their rule ended—
the year the monk built the church—
Had no more visits from petitioners,
and inspired awe no longer.
They became food for worms in the earth,
seeking nothing and never sought after.

Jaʿfar grieved at these verses and used to recite them, saying, "We're finished, by God."

These buildings include al-Musaqqatāt, a palace with extensive porticoes with 30.5
encrusted decoration east of Ḥīrah on the Pilgrims' Road, and then Kuwwat al-Baqqāl, the ʿAdsī Palace, the Farther White Palace, and finally the Palace of Banū Buqaylah. This last palace belonged to ʿAbd al-Masīḥ ibn Buqaylah

قصر بني بُقيلة وكان هذا القصر لعبد المسيح بن بُقيلة الغسّانيّ وإنّما سُمّي بُقيلة لأنّه خرج يوماً على قومه في حلّتين خضراوين قد اتّزر بإحداهما[١] واشتمل بالأخرى فقال قومه ما هو إلّا بُقيلة فسُمّي بذلك. وعبد المسيح هذا هو ابن أخت سطيح الكاهن وكان كسرى أنفذه إلى سطيح بسبب الرؤيا التي رآها. فجاءه وهو يجود[٢] بنفسه. فقال أصمّ أم يسمع غطريف اليمن في أبيات. ففتح سطيح عينه وقال عبد المسيح على جمل مشيح جاء إلى سطيح وقد أوفى على الضريح من قبل ملك بني ساسان لارتجاس الإيوان وخمود النيران ورؤيا الموبذان. والخبر مشهور تركناه لشهرته.

٦،٣٠ فلمّا نزل خالد بن الوليد الحيرة خرج إليه عبد المسيح فقال له خالد من أين أقصى أثرك قال من صلب أبي. قال ما عن هذا سألتك قال ولا أجبت إلّا عمّا سألت عنه. قال ما أنتم قال عرب استنبطنا. قال فما بال هذه الحصون قال بنيناها نتحرّز بها من الجاهل إلى أن يجيء العاقل فيردعه. قال أتعقل قال نعم وأقيد. قال فما سنّك قال عظم. قال كم أتى عليك قال لو أتى عليّ شيء لقتلني. قال كم مضى من عمرك قال أربعمائة سنة قال فما رأيت من العجائب قال رأيت السفن وهي ترفئ في هذا الموضع ورأيت المرأة وهي تخرج من الحيرة إلى الشام بمغزلها في يدها ومكتلها على رأسها لا يروعها أحد وهي الآن خراب يباب. وذلك دأب الله في خلقه.

٧،٣٠ وكان في يده شيء يقلّبه. قال خالد ما هذا الذي في يدك قال سمّ ساعة. قال وما تصنع به قال إن أعطيتني ما أحبّ وإلّا قتلت نفسي به ولم أكن أوّل من أدخل الذلّ على قومه وساق إليهم ما يكرهون. فقال خالد هلمّه إليّ فناوله إيّاه فطرحه

---

١ الأصل: بأحدهما. ٢ الأصل: ورد التصحيح فوق (يكيد).

al-Ghassānī. Buqaylah acquired this name when he appeared before his clan one day clad in two green robes, one worn as a wrapper and the other as a cloak. They said, "He's just a green shoot (*buqaylah*)," and the name stuck.

ʿAbd al-Masīḥ was the son of Saṭīḥ the diviner's sister. Khosroes[174] sent him to Saṭīḥ to have his dreams interpreted, but when he arrived, Saṭīḥ was on the point of death. He recited some verses with the question "Is Yemen's lord deaf or can he hear?" at which Saṭīḥ opened his eyes and replied:

On a strong camel ʿAbd al-Masīḥ
has come to inquire of Saṭīḥ,
who's not yet in the earth.
Sent by the Sassanian king
whose palace is shaking,
his fire is dying
and his chief priests
see visions appearing.[175]

The story is so well known that we have not included it.

When Khālid ibn al-Walīd stopped in Ḥīrah, ʿAbd al-Masīḥ came out to greet him. "How far back do you trace your descent?" asked Khālid. "To my father's loins." "That's not what I asked you." "But I only answered what you'd asked," said ʿAbd al-Masīḥ. Khālid went on: "What kind of people are you?" ʿAbd al-Masīḥ replied, "Bedouin Arabs who've become Nabatean farmers."[176] "And what's the point of these fortifications?" "We built them to protect ourselves from the Ignorant until the Wise One would come and destroy them." "Are you in your right mind?"[177] "Yes, and I kill in revenge as well." "What's your age?"[178] "An ancient bone." "How much time have you lived through?"[179] "If anything finished me off it would kill me." "How many years have you lived?" "Four hundred." "And what amazing sights have you seen?" "I've seen boats mooring here. I've seen a woman setting out from Ḥīrah to Damascus with her spindle in her hand and her basket on her head, unmolested. And now it's dust and ruins. That is God's way with His creation." 30.6

ʿAbd al-Masīḥ was turning something in his hand, and Khālid asked, "What's that in your hand?" "Quick-working poison. If you grant me what I ask, fine. If not, I'll use it to kill myself. That way I won't be the first man to bring humiliation on his people and impose something abhorrent on them." "Give it here," said Khālid. Khālid took it from ʿAbd al-Masīḥ and, pouring the phial into his 30.7

في فيه وقال بسم الله وازدرده. فأخذته غشية ثمّ أفاق كأنّما نشط من عقال. فرجع عبد المسيح إلى قومه فقال جئتكم من عند رجل شرب سمّ ساعة وما ضرّه وحمل إليه مالاً صالحه عليه وانصرف عنهم.

ومن بعده دار عون ثمّ قبّة غصين[1] وهي ممّا يلي النجف فهذه قصور الحيرة الباقية الآن.

[1] الأصل: فيه عصر.

mouth with the words "In the name of God," he swallowed it. He fainted, but then he came round, lively as if he'd just been set free. ʿAbd al-Masīḥ went back to his people, saying, "Greetings. I come from a man who has drunk deadly poison and suffered no harm." Then he brought Khālid tribute, they made peace, and Khālid departed.

After the palace of Banū Buqaylah comes the residence of ʿAwn, and then Ghuṣayn's Dome, which is close by Najaf. These are the palaces of Ḥīrah that are still standing.

قبّة الشتيق

وهي من الأبنية القديمة بالحيرة على طريق الحاجّ وبإزائها قباب يقال لها الشكورة ١،٣١
جميعها للنصارى فيخرجون يوم عيدهم من الشكورة إلى القبّة في أحسن زيّ عليهم
الصلبان بأيديهم المجامر والشمامسة والقسّان معهم يقدّسون ويتبعهم خلق كثير من
متطرّبي المسلمين وأهل البطالة إلى أن يبلغوا قبّة الشتيق فيتقرّبون ويتعمّدون ثمّ يعودون
بمثل تلك الحال فهو منظر مليح.

ولبعض الشعراء فيه

وَٱلنَّصَارَى مُشَدَّدَاتُ[١] ٱلزَّنَانِيـرِ عَلَيْهِنَّ كُلُّ حَلْيٍ وَثِيقِ
يَتَمَشَّيْنَ مِنْ قِبَابِ ٱلشَّعَانِيـنِ إِلَى صَحْنِ قُبَّةِ ٱلشَّتِّيقِ
يَا خَلِيلِي فَلَا تُعَنِّفْنِي يَوْ مَ تَرَى ٱللَّهْوَ فِيهِ بِٱلتَّحْقِيقِ

ولبكر بن خارجة ٢،٣١

يَا خَلِيلَيَّ عَرِّجَا بِي إِلَى ٱلْحِيـرَةِ كَمْ كَمْ تُرَاقِبَانِ ٱلنُّجُومَا
وَٱسْقِيَانِي مِنْ بَيْتِ تَنُّومَ رَاحاً قَهْوَةً لَا تُمَاكِسَا تَنُّومَا
حَانَةٌ حَشْوُهَا ظِبَاءٌ مِلَاحٌ هَيَّجُوا بِٱلدَّلَالِ قَلْباً سَقِيمَا
وَإِذَا مَا سَقَيْتُمَانِي شَرَاباً خَنْدَرِيساً مُعَتَّقاً مَخْتُومَا
فَٱقْصِدَا قُبَّةَ ٱلشَّتِيقِ وَظَبْياً سَكَنَ ٱلدَّيْرَ قَدْ سَبَانِي رَخِيمَا
عَقْدُ زُنَّارِهِ تَوَصَّلَ بِٱلْقَلْـبِ وَأَمْسَى بَيْنَ ٱلْحَشَا مَحْزُومَا

١ الأصل: مُشَدَّدِين.

The Shrine of al-Shatīq[180]

This is one of the ancient buildings in Ḥīrah. It stands on the Pilgrims' Road, and opposite it is a group of shrines known as al-Shukūrah.[181] They all belong to the Christians, who process from al-Shukūrah to the shrine on their feast day in their best clothes, wearing crosses and with censers in their hands. The deacons and priests celebrate the liturgy and a crowd of pleasure-loving Muslims and idlers follow them until they reach the Shrine of al-Shatīq, where they receive communion and baptisms are performed. Then they go back the same way. It is a lovely sight, and a poet has composed these verses on it: **31.1**

Christian girls, with their tightly tied
 sashes and their jewels finely set,
Walking from the Shrines of the Palms
 to the court of the Shrine of al-Shatīq.
Friend, on a day when you see
 joy fulfilled, don't ever reproach me.

This poem is by Bakr ibn Khārijah: **31.2**

Friends, come with me to Ḥīrah!
 How often we've watched the stars.
Now pour me wine from Tanḥūm's[182] cellar.
 Don't haggle with him over the price
In a tavern filled with lovely gazelles,
 their coyness stirring the suffering heart.
And when you've poured me
 a night-dark aged wine, untouched,
Let's make for Shatīq's shrine and convent,
 where a slender fawn's enslaved me.
He's tied his belt around my heart—
 my bosom is bound.

وبكر بن خارجة هذا من أهل الكوفة وكان من المنهمكين في الخمر والمستهترين ٣،٣١
بالتطرّح في الحانات والديارات وكان أكثر شعره في ذلك. فمن شعره أيضاً

رَاحَ مِنَ ٱلحَانَةِ سَكْرَانَا فَـزَادَنِي هَـمّاً وَأَحْـزَانَا
حَانَةِ تَنْحُومَ ٱلَّتِي صَيَّرَتْ مِنْ حُبِّهَا فِي ٱلْقَلْبِ نِيرَانَا
يَرْنُو بِعَيْنَيْ شَادِنٍ أَحْوَرَ تَخَالُهُ لِلسُّكْرِ وَسْـنَانَا
مَا رَأَتِ ٱلْعَيْنَانِ شِبْهاً لَهُ إِنْساً إِذَا عُـدَّ وَلَا جَانَّا
مَعَاقِدُ ٱلزُّنَّارِ فِي خَصْرِهِ عَـذَّبْتَـنِي بِٱلْحُبِّ أَلْوَانَا
كَتَمْتُ حُبِّي وَهَوَايَ لَهُ دَهْـراً وَأَحْوَالاً وَأَزْمَـانَا
حَتَّى تَوَلَّى جَسَدِي لِلْبِلَى فَمَا أُطِيقُ ٱلْيَوْمَ كِتْمَانَا

Bakr ibn Khārijah was a Kufan, a compulsive drinker, and given to debauchery in taverns and monasteries. Most of his poetry is on that subject. Here is another piece: 31.3

He left the tavern drunk,
  filling me with worry and grief:
Tanḥūm's tavern—
  for love of it my heart is on fire—
His eyes those of a black-eyed fawn,
  drowsy through drink.
His like has never been seen
  among men, no, nor among jinn.
The sash knotted round his waist
  torments me with all kinds of love.
For a week I hid my passion for him,
  and then for months, for years,
Till my body wasted away,
  and now I cannot conceal it.

دير هند بنت النعمان بن المنذر

١،٣٢ بَنَت هند هذا الدير بالحيرة وترهّبت فيه وسكنته وعاشت دهرًا طويلاً ثمّ عميت.
وهذا الدير من أعظم ديارات الحيرة وأعمرها وهو بين الخندق وحاضرة[1] بكر.

٢،٣٢ ولمّا قدم الحجّاج الكوفة في سنة أربع وسبعين قيل له إنّ بين الحيرة والكوفة ديرًا
لهند بنت النعمان وهي فيه وهي متمكّنة[2] من رأيها وعقلها فانظر إليها فإنّها تقيّة. فركب والناس معه حتّى أتى الدير فقيل لها هذا الأمير الحجّاج بالباب فاطّلعت من ناحية الدير. فقال لها[3] يا هند ما أعجب ما رأيت. قالت خروج مثلي إلى مثلك. فلا تغترّ يا حجّاج بالدنيا فإنّا أصبحنا ونحن كما قال النابغة

رَأَيْتُكَ مَنْ تَعْـقِـدْ لَهُ حَبْـلَ ذِمَّـةٍ   مِنَ ٱلنَّاسِ يَأْمَنْ سَرْحُهُ حَيْثُ أَرْبَعَا

ولم نمسِ إلّا ونحن أذلّ الناس وقلّ إناء امتلأ إلّا انكفأ.

٣،٣٢ فانصرف الحجّاج مغضباً وبعث إليها من يُخرجها من الدير ويستأديها الخراج.
فأُخرجت مع ثلاث جوار من أهلها فقالت إحداهنّ في خروجها

خَارِجَاتٌ يُسَقْنَ مِنْ دَيْرِ هِنْدٍ   مُـذْعَـنَاتٌ بِـذِلَّةٍ وَهَوَانِ
لَيْتَ شِعْرِي أَأَوَّلُ ٱلْحَشْرِ هٰذَا   أَمْ مَحَا ٱلدَّهْرُ غَيْرَةَ ٱلْفِتْيَانِ

فشدّ فتى من أهل الكوفة على فرسه فاستنقذهنّ من أشراط الحجّاج وتغيّب. فبلغ الحجّاج شعرها وفعل الفتى فقال إن أتانا فهو آمن وإن ظفرنا به قتلناه. فأتاه الفتى فقال

---

١ الأصل: وحصراه. ٢ الأصل: وهي فيه من رأيها. ٣ الأصل: (مخاطبة الحجّاج الثقفيّ لهند بنت المنذر) وردت في الهامش.

The Monastery of Hind, Daughter of al-Nuʿmān ibn al-Mundhir

Hind built this monastery in Ḥīrah, took the veil, and lived there. At the end of her long life, she went blind. It is one of the largest and most flourishing monasteries in Ḥīrah, standing between the Trench and Bakr's settlement. 32.1

When al-Ḥajjāj came to Kufa in the year 74 [693–94], he was told that between Ḥīrah and Kufa there was a monastery founded by Hind bint al-Nuʿmān, where she was living. She was pious, in full command of her wits, and worth visiting. So he set off for Hind's Monastery with his retinue. When he arrived, she was informed that Commander al-Ḥajjāj ibn Yūsuf was at the gate. She came out from round the side of the monastery, and al-Ḥajjāj asked her,[183] "Hind, what's the most extraordinary thing you have experienced?" She replied, "Someone like me coming out to someone like you. Ḥajjāj, don't set any store by this world. We used to be as al-Nābighah says: 32.2

When you extend the hand of protection to someone,
I've seen how his flocks are safe wherever they graze.[184]

"But now we have become the most wretched of people. Seldom is a vessel filled without being broken. "

Al-Ḥajjāj left in a rage, sent some guards to make her leave the monastery, and demanded she pay the tax. She was forced to leave, taking three young relatives with her, and as they left one of them declaimed these verses: 32.3

We leave, driven from Hind's Monastery,
suffering insult and humiliation!
Is this perchance the start of Judgment Day?
Has fate erased all sense of honor?

A Kufan saddled his horse, rode to rescue them from al-Ḥajjāj's guards, and then disappeared. Al-Ḥajjāj heard of the girl's poetry and the man's action, and declared, "If he comes to us of his free will, he will have safe conduct. But if we arrest him, we'll kill him." The man presented himself, and al-Ḥajjāj asked him,

له ما حملك على ما صنعت قال الغيرة فوصله وخلّاه.

٤،٣٢ وكان سعد بن أبي وقّاص حين فتح العراق أتى هند إلى ديرها فخرجت إليه فأكرمها وعرض عليها نفسه في حوائجها فقالت سأحيّيك بتحيّة كانت أملاكنا تُحيّا بها مسّتك يد نالها فقر بعد غنى ولا مسّتك يد نالها غنًى بعد فقر ولا جعل الله لك إلى لئيم حاجة ولا نزع الله عن كريم نعمة إلّا جعلك سبباً لردّها عليه.

٥،٣٢ ثمّ جاءها المغيرة[١] لمّا ولّاه معاوية الكوفة فاستأذن عليها فقيل لها أمير هذه المدرة بالباب فقالت قولوا له من أولاد جبلة بن الأيهم أنت قال لا. قالت فمن ولد المنذر بن ماء السماء قال لا. قالت فمن أنت قال المغيرة بن شعبة الثقفيّ. قالت فما حاجتك قال جئتك خاطباً. قالت لو جئتني لجمال أو حال لأجبتك ولكن أردت أن تتشرّف بي في محافل العرب فتقول نكحت بنت النعمان بن المنذر وإلّا فأيّ فخر في اجتماع أعور وعمياء.

٦،٣٢ فبعث إليها قال كيف كان أمركم قالت سأختصر لك الجواب أمسينا مساءً وليس في الأرض عربيّ إلّا وهو يرغب إلينا ويرهبنا ثمّ أصبحنا وليس أحد إلّا ونحن نرغب إليه ونرهبه. قال فما كان أبوك يقول في ثقيف قالت اختصم إليه رجلان منهم في شيء أحدهما ينتمي إلى إياد والآخر إلى بكر بن هوازن فقضى به للإياديّ وقال

إِنَّ ثَقِيفاً لَمْ يَكُنْ هَوَازِنَا وَلَمْ يُنَاسِبْ عَامِرًا وَمَازِنَا

فقال المغيرة أمّا نحن فمن بكر بن هوازن فليقل أبوك ما شاء.

١ الأصل: (حضور المغيرة بن شعبة إلى هند بنت المنذر يخطبها لزواجها وامتناعها) وردت في الهامش.

"What made you do what you did?" "My sense of honor." Al-Ḥajjāj rewarded him and let him go.

When Saʿd ibn Abī Waqqāṣ conquered Iraq,[185] he went to visit Hind in her monastery. She came out to him, and he showed her honor and offered to supply her needs. "I will give you the greeting our kings used to use," she said. "May you receive gratitude from those afflicted by poverty after wealth, not from those enriched after poverty. May God preserve you from seeking a base man's help. May God not strip fortune from a noble man unless He makes you the instrument of its return to Him." 32.4

Then al-Mughīrah came to her,[186] after Muʿāwiyah had appointed him governor of Kufa. He asked permission to speak to her and she was told, "The commander of this city is at the gate." She replied, "Ask him if he's a son of Jabalah ibn al-Ayham." He said, "No." "Or descended from al-Mundhir ibn Māʾ al-Samāʾ." "No." "So who are you?" she asked. "Al-Mughīrah ibn Shuʿbah al-Thaqafī." She asked, "What's your business?" He answered, "I've come to ask your hand in marriage." "If you'd come to me for my beauty or wealth, I would have agreed. But you just want to win honor when the Arabs muster by saying you've married the daughter of al-Nuʿmān ibn al-Mundhir. What's there to boast about if a one-eyed man and a blind woman come together?" 32.5

He sent a messenger to ask her about her family's status and she replied, "I'll answer in a few words. One night there was no Arab who did not petition us and fear us, and the next day there was no one we did not petition or fear." "And what did your father say about Thaqīf?" "Two Bedouins of Thaqīf asked him to arbitrate between them—one was from Iyād and the other from Bakr ibn Hawāzin. He decided in favor of the Iyādī and commented: 32.6

Thaqīf's not Hawāzin,
nor the equal of ʿĀmir and Māzin."

Whereupon al-Mughīrah said, "We're from Bakr ibn Hawāzin. Your father can say what he likes."[187]

ديـر زُرارة

وهو دير حسن بين جسر الكوفة وحمّام أعين ناحية عن الطريق على يمين الخارج من بغداد إلى الكوفة وهو موضع نزه حسن كثير الحانات والشراب عامر بمن يطرقه لا يخلو ممّن يطلب اللعب واللّهو ويؤثر البطالة وهو من المواطن المستصلحة لذلك. ١،٣٣

قال خرج يحيى بن زياد ومطيع بن إياس حاجّين فلمّا قربا من دير زرارة قال أحدهما لصاحبه هل لك أن نقدّم أثقالنا ونمضي إلى زرارة فنشرب في ديرها ليلتنا ونتزوّد من مردها وخمرها ما يكفينا إلى العودة ثمّ نلحق بأثقالنا ففعلا وسار الناس وأقاما فلم يزل ذلك دأبهما إلى أن انصرف الحاجّ فلمّا وصلا إلى الكوفة حلقا رؤوسهما[١] وركبا بعيرين ودخلا مع الحاجّ فقال مطيع ٢،٣٣

أَلَمْ تَـرَنِي وَيَحْيَى إِذْ حَجَجْنَا   وَكَانَ ٱلْحَجُّ مِنْ خَيْرِ ٱلتِّجَارَهْ
خَرَجْنَا طَالِبَيْ حَجٍّ وَدِينٍ   فَمَالَ بِنَا ٱلطَّرِيقُ إِلَى زُرَارَهْ
فَآبَ ٱلنَّاسُ قَدْ غَنِمُوا وَحَجُّوا   وَأُبْنَا مُوقَرِينَ مِنَ ٱلْخَسَارَهْ

ثمّ قال فيه أيضاً وفيه لحن وقيل إنّ الأبيات لأبي عليّ البصير ٣،٣٣

خَرَجْنَا نَبْتَغِي مَكَّـةَ حُجَّاجاً وَزُوَّارَا
فَلَمَّا قَدِمَ ٱلْحِيرَ   ةَ حَادِي جَمَلِي حَارَا
وَقَدْ كَادَ يَغُورُ ٱلنَّجْـمُ لِلْإِصْبَاحِ أَوْ غَارَا
فَقُلْتُ ٱحْطُطْ بِهَا رَحْلِي   وَلَا تَحْفِلْ بِمَنْ سَارَا
فَجَدَّدْنَا عُهُوداً سَلَفَتْ مِنَّا وَآثَارَا
وَقَضَّيْنَا لُبَانَاتٍ   لَنَا كَانَتْ وَأَوْطَارَا

١ كذا في الأصل.

The Zurārah[188] Monastery

This is a fine monastery between the embankment of Kufa and Aʿyan's Bath,[189] some way from the road on the right as you go from Baghdad to Kufa. It is a pretty, attractive place, well supplied with taverns and wine, and full of visitors. Many go there for pleasure and entertainment or to pass the time, and it is an excellent place for that. 33.1

Yaḥyā ibn Ziyād and Muṭīʿ ibn Iyās set out on the pilgrimage, but when they 33.2
approached the Zurārah Monastery, one of them said to the other, "What do you think? Let's send our baggage on ahead, go to Zurārah, and spend tonight drinking in the monastery. We'll have had enough boys and wine to keep us going till we come back, and we'll catch up with our baggage afterward." The rest of the caravan continued on its way while they stayed there, spending the time as they had proposed, until the pilgrims returned. Then they went to Kufa, shaved their heads, mounted two camels, and entered Baghdad with the pilgrim caravan. Muṭīʿ composed a poem about it:

Have you seen how Yaḥyā and I went on hajj?
What a splendid deal it was.
We set out as pilgrims to fulfill our duty
but the road took us to Zurārah.
The others came back, profiting from the hajj,
while we were laden with loss.

He made another poem, which was set to music. Some say the author was 33.3
Abū ʿAlī al-Baṣīr:

We set out for Mecca, visitors and pilgrims,
But when he reached Ḥīrah,
My camel driver faltered.
The stars had almost set as daylight dawned,
So I said, "Let's stop. Forget who's going on."
We saw old friends, revisited old haunts,
Fulfilled all the wishes and desires we had,

وَصَاحَبْنَا بِهَا دَيْرًا   وَقِسِّيسًا وَخَمَّارَا
وَظَبْيًا عَاقِدًا بَيْنَ   ٱلنَّقَا وَٱلْخَصْرِ زُنَّارَا
شَرَحْنَا لَكَ أَخْبَارًا   وَأَدْمَجْنَاكَ أَخْبَارَا

ولأبي نواس في هذا المعنى ٤،٣٣

وَقَائِلٍ هَلْ تُرِيدُ ٱلْحَجَّ قُلْتُ لَهُ   نَعَمْ إِذَا فَنِيَتْ لَذَّاتُ بَغْدَاذِ
أَمَا وَقُطْرَبُّلٍ مِنْهَا بِحَيْثُ تَرَى   فَقُبَّةِ ٱلْفِرْكِ مِنْ أَكْنَافِ كَلْوَاذِي
فَٱلصَّالِحِيَّةِ فَٱلْكَرْخِ ٱلَّذِي ٱجْتَمَعَتْ   شُذَّاذُ بَغْدَادَ لِي فِيهِ بِشُذَّاذِي
وَكَيْفَ بِٱلْحَجِّ لِي مَا دُمْتُ مُنْغَمِسًا   فِي بَيْتِ قَوَّادَةٍ أَوْ بَيْتِ نَبَّاذِ
وَهَبْكَ مِنْ قَصْفِ بَغْدَادٍ تُخَلِّصُنِي   كَيْفَ ٱلتَّخَلُّصُ لِي مِنْ طِيزَنَابَاذِ

وممّن فعلَ فعْلَ مطيع سليمان بن محمد الأمويّ وكان قد أعدّ البخاتيّ للحجّ وصنعها طول ٥،٣٣
سنته فلمّا وصل إلى الكوفة بدا له وأقام وقال

حِرْصِي عَلَى ٱلْحَجِّ أَفْسَدَ ٱلْحِجَا   إِذْ لَمْ أَجِدْ مَهْرَبًا وَلَا مَنْجَا
تُبْتُ إِلَيْهِ مِنَ ٱلذُّنُوبِ وَمِنْ   عَرْضٍ بَرِيءٍ بِمُنْكَرٍ يُهْجَا
فَرَدَّنِي خَاسِئًا إِلَى قَدَحِي   وَقَوْلِ شِعْرٍ وَعَفْوُهُ يُرْجَا
بِحَيْثُ تُضْحِي ٱلزِّقَاقُ خَاضِعَةً   تَحْسَبُهَا مِنْ سَوَادِهَا زَنْجَا
إِذَا وَضَعْنَا لِلزِّقِّ بَاطِيَةً   وَحُلَّ عَنْهُ رِبَاطُهُ مَجَّا
زَادِي إِلَى ٱلْحَجِّ صَارَ مُنْتَقِلًا   لِمَا ٱحْتَسَيْتُ ٱلْمُدَامَةَ ٱلزَّلْجَا
وَمَضْجَعِي زُكْرَتِي نَعِمْتُ بِهَا   مَمْلُوءَةً مَا تُفَارِقُ ٱلْخُرُجَا
كَذَاكَ مَنْ يَطْلُبُ ٱلثَّوَابَ وَلَا   يَنْهَضُ إِلَّا بِنِيَّةٍ عَرْجَا

Taking in the convent, the priest and taverner,
And a gazelle, his sash tied between hip and waist.
Some things we've told you, others hidden.

Abū Nuwās has a poem on the same theme: 33.4

I'm often asked if I want to go on hajj.
Yes, say I, when Baghdad's empty of pleasure.
But by the Quṭrabbul quarter, as you see,
the Firk Dome behind Kalwādhā,
Ṣāliḥiyyah, and Karkh, where Baghdad's misfits
meet with the misfit I am,
How can I make hajj while I'm stuck
in the house of a wine seller or a pimp?
And even if you rescued me from the revelry of Baghdad,
how to rescue me from Ṭayzanābād?

Another poet who acted like Muṭīʿ was Sulaymān ibn Muḥammad al-Umawī. 33.5
He had acquired Bactrian camels for the hajj and spent a year feeding them up, but when he reached Kufa he changed his mind and stopped there. He made verses about it:

Longing to be a pilgrim ruined my wits,
I couldn't find a way to get out of it;
For the hajj I repented of my sins
and of harmless exchanges meanly maligned.
But it spurned me and sent me back to my cups
and my verses, though I hope for forgiveness.
I saw the wineskins submissive and humble,
so dark they looked like black men.
Then we set a jug to the wineskin,
broke the seal and let it pour;
My hajj provisions changed direction
when the wine slipped down my throat.
I slept in bliss where my wineskin was
in the saddlebag, full and to hand—
Here's one who seeks a reward from God,
but starts off, his intention twisted.

٦،٣٣ وخرج أبو المضرجيّ وسلّام بن غالب بن شمّاس وأبو عليّ البصير[١] الشاعر يريدون الحجّ فلمّا قدموا الكوفة بدا لأبي عليّ البصير[٢] ولسلّام ثمّ مضى أبو المضرجيّ فقال أبو عليّ البصير[٣] يخاطب سلّاماً

خُذْ بِرَأْسِ ٱلْقِطَارِ[٤] وَٱسْتَخِرِ ٱللّٰـهَ إِلَى دَارِ قَيْنَةِ ٱلرَّمَّاحِ
حَيْثُ لَا تُنْكَرُ ٱلْمَعَازِفُ وَٱلْخَمْرُ وَوَضْعُ ٱلْأَيْدِي عَلَى ٱلْأَقْدَاحِ

٧،٣٣ وكان مطيع بن إياس من أظرف الناس وأحسنهم شعراً وأكثرهم نادرة وأشدّهم مجوناً وخلاعة وكان لا يغبّ الشرب واللّعب والانهماك في الخسارة والتطرّح في مواضع اللذّات. وكان مطيع ويحيى بن زياد وحمّاد عجرد وحمّاد الراوية لا يفترقون وكان جميعهم على منهاج واحد في الخلاعة وكلّهم مُتّهَم بالزندقة.

٨،٣٣ فذكر العتبيّ عن أبيه قال قدم علينا شيخ من أهل الكوفة لم أر قطّ أحسن منه حديثاً فكان يحدّثني عن مطيع والحمّادين وعن ظرفاء أهل الكوفة وعجائبهم. فلم يكن يحدّث عن أحد منهم بأحسن ممّا يحدّثني به عن مطيع بن إياس فقلت له كنت والله أشتهي أن أرى مطيعاً. فقال والله لو رأيته للقيت منه بلاءً عظيماً. فقلت وكيف قال كنت ترى رجلاً لا يصبر عنه العاقل إذا رآه ولا يصحبه أحد إلّا افتضح به.

٩،٣٣ وذكر ابن حبيب قال رأيت رجلاً من أهل الكوفة فسألته عن مطيع وكان قد صحبه فقال لا ترد أن تسأل عنه. قلت ولِمَ ذاك قال ما سؤالك عن رجل إذا حضرك ملكك وإذا غاب عنك شاقك وإذا عرفت بصحبته فضحك.

١٠،٣٣ وكان مطيع من مخضرمي الدولتين الأمويّة والعبّاسيّة وقد مدح الوليد بن يزيد ونادمه ومدح أخاه وخصّ به.

١١،٣٣ قال حضر مطيع بن إياس وشراعة بن الزندبوذ[٥] ويحيى بن زياد ووالبة بن الحباب وعبد الله بن عيّاش المنتوف وحمّاد عجرد بمجلس بعض الأمراء بالكوفة فاجتمعوا كلّهم

١ الأصل: أبو البصير. ٢ الأصل: أبو البصير. ٣ الأصل: أبو البصير. ٤ الأصل: القطَا. ٥ الأصل: الرند بود.

Abū l-Miḍrajī, Sallām ibn Ghālib ibn Shammās, and Abū al-Baṣīr the poet set out on the pilgrimage, but when they reached Kufa, Abū al-Baṣīr and Sallām changed their minds, while Abū l-Miḍrajī went on. So Abū al-Baṣīr said to Sallām: 33.6

Take the caravan's head and ask God's guidance
  to lead us to al-Rammāḥ's singing girl's house,
Where music and wine are not frowned on,
  nor is putting a hand on someone's pussy.

Muṭīʿ ibn Iyās was a most delightful person, a fine poet, a store of witty anecdotes, frivolous and dissolute. He was always engaged in drinking and having fun, a thoroughly depraved haunter of places of pleasure. He, Yaḥyā ibn Ziyād, Ḥammād ʿAjrad, and Ḥammād al-Rāwiyah were inseparable—all were equally dissolute, and all were accused of unbelief. 33.7

Al-ʿUtbī said, quoting his father: There was a certain shaykh who came to us from Kufa, and I never encountered a more entertaining talker. He used to tell me about Muṭīʿ, the two Ḥammāds, and the wits of Kufa and their amazing doings. The best incidents he related were about Muṭīʿ, so I said to him, "I'd really like to see Muṭīʿ." "By God," he replied, "it would be disastrous for you if you were to see him." "Why?" "You'd see a man that intelligent people can't bear to be away from once they've met him, but if they keep him company they get a bad name." 33.8

This anecdote comes from Ibn Ḥabīb: I met someone from Kufa and asked him about Muṭīʿ, who was a friend of his. He replied, "You shouldn't ask about him." "Why not?" "What's the point of asking about a person who dominates you if he's with you, makes you long for him if he's absent, and exposes you to infamy if you're seen in his company?" 33.9

Muṭīʿ was one of those who composed poetry under the Umayyads and the Abbasids. He made panegyrics of al-Walīd ibn Yazīd and became a companion of his; he also praised al-Walīd's brother and was closely associated with him. 33.10

Muṭīʿ; Shurāʿah ibn al-Zandabūdh; Yaḥyā ibn Ziyād; Wālibah ibn al-Ḥubāb; ʿAbdallāh ibn ʿAyyāsh, he of the plucked beard; and Ḥammād ʿAjrad were attending the court of one of the governors of Kufa. The others all got together 33.11

على مطيع فكايدوه وهجوه فغلبهم كلّهم ثمّ بدههم فقال

وَخَمْسَةٍ قَدْ أَبَانُوا لِي عَدَاوَتَهُمْ　　وَقَدْ تَلَظَّى لَهُمْ مِقْلًى وَطَنْجِيرُ
لَوْ يَقْدِرُونَ عَلَى لَحْمِي تَقَسَّمَهُ　　قِرْدٌ وَكَلْبٌ وَجِرْوَاءُ وَخِنْزِيرُ

فقطعهم وأقرّوا له.

١٢،٣٣ قال واجتمعوا يشربون فأقاموا على ذلك أيّاماً فقال لهم يحيى بن زياد ليلة وهم سكارى ويحكم ما صلّينا منذ ثلاثة أيّام فقوموا بنا حتّى نصلّي. فقالوا نعم فقام مطيع فأذّن وأقام ثمّ قال للمغنّية تقدّمي فصلّي بنا فتقدّمت وكانت بلا سراويل وعليها غلالة رقيقة. فلمّا سجدت انكشف متاعها فوثب إليها مطيع فقبّله ثمّ قال

وَلَمَّا بَدَا هٰنُهَا جَاثِمًا　　كَرَأْسِ حَلِيقٍ وَلَمْ تَعْتَمِدْ
سَجَدْتُ عَلَيْهِ وَقَبَّلْتُهُ　　كَمَا يَفْعَلُ ٱلْعَابِدُ ٱلْمُجْتَهِدْ

فقطعوا صلاتهم بالضحك ثمّ عادوا إلى ما كانوا عليه.

١٣،٣٣ قال كتب يحيى بن زياد يوماً إلى مطيع أنا نشيط للشرب فإن كنت فارغاً فصر إليّ وإن كان عندك نبيذ طيّب وغناء جئتك. فجاءته الرقعة وعنده حمّاد الراوية وحكم الوادي وغلام أمرد فأجابه

نَعَمْ لَنَا نَبِيذٌ　　وَعِنْدَنَا حَمَّادُ
وَعِنْدَنَا وَادِينَا　　وَهْوَ لَنَا عِمَادُ
وَخَيْرُنَا كَثِيرٌ　　وَٱلْخَيْرُ يُسْتَزَادُ
وَلَهْوُنَا لَذِيذٌ　　لَمْ تَلْهُهُ ٱلْعِبَادُ
أَوْ تَشْتَهِي فَسَادًا　　فَعِنْدَنَا فَسَادُ

to set a trap for Muṭīʿ and lampoon him, but he got the better of them, and then he improvised:

Five have shown me their enmity,
with a frying pan and saucepan on the fire;
If they could seize my flesh, they'd divvy it up—
ape, mangy camel, pig, and dog.

With that he silenced them and they admitted he'd gotten the better of them.

Once they had a drinking session that lasted several days. One night when 33.12
they were drunk, Yaḥyā ibn Ziyād exclaimed, "Shame on us. We haven't prayed for three days. Let's get up and perform the prayer." "Yes," they said. Muṭīʿ stood up and gave the call for prayer, then stopped. He turned to the singing girl. "Come to the front and lead the prayer for us." She came forward. She was not wearing drawers and she had a thin tunic on, so when she prostrated herself her private parts could be seen. Muṭīʿ sprang forward to kiss them, and then he said:

When she showed her pussy unwittingly,
and it looked like a shaven pate;
I bowed low and kissed it,
as prayerful as a hermit.

Laughing, they broke off their prayer and went back to what they had been doing.

One day Yaḥyā ibn Ziyād sent a note to Muṭīʿ: "I feel like a drink. If you're 33.13
free, come to me. But if you've got fine wine and some good music, I'll come to you." The note arrived when Ḥammād al-Rāwiyah, Ḥakam al-Wādī, and a young boy were with him, so Muṭīʿ replied:

We've wine, Ḥammād,
and our mainstay, our Wādī,
And many other good things,
but we won't say no to more,
We're having loads of fun,
which the pious ignore.
If you want dissipation,
we've got what you want;

أَوْ تَشْتَهِي غُلَامًا   فَعِنْدَنَا زِيَادُ
مَا إِنْ بِهِ ٱلْتِوَاءٌ   عَنَّا وَلَا بِعَادُ

فلمّا قرأ الرقعة صار إليهم فتمّموا بقيّة يومهم.

وقال يحيى بن زياد له انطلق بنا إلى فلانة المغنّية وكان يهواها فإنّ بيننا مغاضبة فلعلّك أن تصلح بيني وبينها وبئس المصلح والله أنت. فدخلا إليها فأقبل يحيى يعاتبها ومطيع ساكت فقال له ما يسكتك أسكت الله نأمتك. فقال مطيع ١٤،٣٣

أَنْتِ مُعْتَلَّةٌ عَلَيْهِ وَمَا زَا   لَ مُهِينًا لِنَفْسِهِ فِي هَوَاكِ

فأعجب يحيى ما قاله وهشّ له وقال هيه فقال

فَدَعِيهِ وَوَاصِلِي ٱبْنَ إِيَاسٍ   جُعِلَتْ نَفْسُهُ ٱلْغَدَاةَ فِدَاكِ

فقام إليه يحيى بالوسادة يجلد بها رأسه وقال ألهذا دعوتك يا ابن الفاعلة.

قال وكان بالكوفة مقيّن يقال له أبو الأصبغ وكان له ابن يقال له أصبغ أحسن الناس وجهاً وكان مطيع بن إياس ويحيى بن زياد وحمّاد عجرد يغشون منزله ويعشقون ابنه ولا يقدرون عليه فعزم أبو الأصبغ على أن يصطبح يوماً مع يحيى بن زياد فأهدى إليه يحيى من الليل جداء ودجاجاً وفراخاً وفاكهةً وشراباً. فقال أبو الأصبغ لجواريه إنّ يحيى بن زياد عندنا فأصلحوا له ما يشتهيه[1] فلمّا فرغ من الطعام لم يجد رسولاً يبعث به إليه سوى ابنه أصبغ فقال له لا تبرح إلّا ويحيى معك. فلمّا جاءه أصبغ قال للغلام أدخله وتنحَّ أنت وأغلق الباب فإن أراد الخروج فامنعه. فلمّا دخل إليه أصبغ وأدّى الرسالة راوده يحيى عن نفسه فامتنع فثاوره يحيى فصرعه ورام حلّ تكّته فلم يقدر على ١٥،٣٣

[1] كذا في عوّاد؛ الأصل: يشبهه.

If you desire a boy,
 we can let you have Ziyād—
He's not standoffish,
 from us he never turns away.

When he read the note, he joined them, and they spent the rest of the day together.

Yaḥyā ibn Ziyād suggested to Muṭīʿ, "Let's go and see so-and-so the 33.14
singer"—he was in love with her—"because we've had a quarrel, and perhaps you can make peace between us, though you're a poor peacemaker, by God." At her house, Yaḥyā started to reproach her while Muṭīʿ kept silent. So Yaḥyā turned on him. "Why don't you say anything, God stop your mouth?" So he said:

You find excuses to annoy him,
 while he demeans himself with your love.

Yaḥyā was delighted and said, "Go on."

Leave him and come to Ibn Iyās,
 who would give his life for you.

At which Yaḥyā got up, seized the cushion, and beat him about the head with it, saying, "That's not why I invited you, you bastard!"[190]

There was a dealer in singing girls in Kufa called Abū l-Aṣbagh who had a 33.15
very good-looking son, Aṣbagh. Muṭīʿ ibn Iyās, Yaḥyā ibn Ziyād, and Ḥammād ʿAjrad used to visit his house frequently. They all wanted his son but couldn't get anywhere with him. Abū l-Aṣbagh decided to invite Yaḥyā ibn Ziyād for a morning drink, because the evening before Yaḥyā had sent him kids, poultry, chickens, fruit, and wine. Abū l-Aṣbagh said to his slave girls, "Yaḥyā ibn Ziyād will be with us, so prepare what's appropriate for him." After he had dealt with the question of food, he couldn't find anyone to send to Yaḥyā except his son Aṣbagh, and he instructed him, "Don't come back without Yaḥyā."

When Aṣbagh reached the house, Yaḥyā said to his servant, "Let him in, leave him alone with me, and lock the door. And if Aṣbagh wants to leave, stop him." When the boy arrived and delivered the message, Yayḥā tried to seduce him but he resisted. He threw himself on him and wrestled him to the ground. Then he tried to undo the cord of his drawers and couldn't, so he cut it. When

ذلك فقطعها يحيى فلمّا فرغ أعطاه أربعين ديناراً كانت تحت مصلّاه فأخذها. وقال له يحيى امضِ فأنا على أثرك.

١٦،٣٣ فخرج أصبغ من عنده واغتسل يحيى وجلس يتزيّن ويتبخّر. فدخل إليه مطيع فرأى ما هو فيه فقال له كيف أصبحت فلم يجبه وشمخ بأنفه وقطّب حاجبه فقال له أراك تتزيّن وتتبخّر أين عزمت فلم يجبه فقال ويحك ما لك نزل عليك الوحي أوكلّمتك الملائكة أو بويع لك بالخلافة وهو يومئ برأسه لا لا. قال فأراك قد تهت علينا فما تكلّم حتّى كأنّك قد نكتّ أصبغ بن أبي أصبغ. فقال أي والله الساعة وأعطيته أربعين ديناراً. قال فإلى أين تمضي قال إلى دعوة أبيه فقال مطيع امرأته طالق إن فارقتُك أو أقبّل أيرك فأبداه يحيى له فقبّله. ثمّ قال له كيف قدرت عليه فحدّثه حديثه وقام ليمضي إلى منزل أبي الأصبغ. فأتبعه مطيع وصبر ساعة ثمّ دقّ الباب واستأذن فخرج إليه الرسول فقال له إنّه اليوم على شغل لا يتفرّغ لك فتعذر. قال فابعث إليّ دواة وقرطاساً[١] فكتب مطيع إلى أبي الأصبغ بهذه الأبيات

يَا أَبَا ٱلْأَصْبَغِ لَا زِلْتَ عَلَى ... كُلِّ حَالٍ عَالِيًا مُمْتَنِعَا
لَا تُصَيِّرُنِي فِي ٱلْوُدِّ كَمَنْ[٢] ... قَطَعَ ٱلتِّكَّةَ قَطْعًا شَنِعَا
وَأَتَى مَا يَشْتَهِي لَا يَنْتَهِي ... خِيفَةً أَوْ حِفْظَ حَقٍّ ضُيِّعَا
لَوْ تَرَى ٱلْأَصْبَغَ مُلْقًى تَحْتَهُ ... مُسْتَكِينًا خَجِلًا قَدْ خَضَعَا
وَلَهُ دَفْعٌ عَلَيْهِ عَجِلٌ ... شَبَقًا سَاءَكَ مَا قَدْ صَنَعَا
فَٱدْعُ بِٱلْأَصْبَغِ فَٱعْرِفْ حَالَهُ ... سَتَرَى أَمْرًا قَبِيحًا فَظِعَا

١ الأصل: وقرطاس. ٢ كذا في الأصل.

he'd finished, he took forty dinars from under a prayer carpet and gave them to the boy, who accepted them. Then he said to him, "Go back home. I'll follow you."

After Aṣbagh left, Yaḥyā washed. He was sitting preening himself and perfuming himself with incense when Muṭīʿ arrived. He noticed the state Yaḥyā was in and asked, "How are you this morning?" Yaḥyā didn't answer but just turned up his nose and frowned. So Muṭīʿ said, "I can see you've been grooming and perfuming yourself. Where are you off to?" He still didn't answer, so Muṭīʿ said, "What's the matter with you, damn you? Have you received a revelation? Have the angels spoken to you? Have you become caliph and received the oath of allegiance?" Each time, Yaḥyā just gestured with his head to say no. "I see you're too high and mighty to speak to us. You're acting as though you'd fucked Aṣbagh." "Yes, by God, that's just what I've done, an hour ago. And I gave him forty dinars." "And where are you going now?" "To his father's house. He's invited me." Muṭīʿ exclaimed, "May he divorce his wife if I leave you without kissing your dick." Upon which Yaḥyā took it out and he kissed it. Then he asked, "How did you get the better of him?" So Yaḥyā told him the story. Then he got up to go to Abū l-Aṣbagh's house. Muṭīʿ followed him, waited for a while, and then knocked at the door to be let in. A servant came out and told him, "He's busy today and has no time for you. Please excuse him." Muṭīʿ asked for a piece of parchment and an inkwell and wrote these verses to Abū l-Aṣbagh: 33.16

Abū l-Aṣbagh, may you always enjoy
  honor and respect,
And not treat me, your friend,
  as the villain who cut the cord,
Doing what he wanted, unrestrained
  by fear or deference to any right.
Had you seen Aṣbagh prostrate
  beneath him, submissive and ashamed,
And him, goatishly screwing him,
  the sight would have shocked you.
Call Aṣbagh, ask him what happened:
  you'll hear a disgusting tale.

١٧،٣٣ فقال أبو الأصبغ ليحيى فعلتها يا ابن الزانية قال لا فضرب بيده إلى تكّة ابنه فوجدها مقطوعة فأيقن بالفضيحة فقال يحيى قد كان الذي كان وسعى إليك مطيع ابن الزانية. وهذا ابني وهو أفره من ابنك وأنا وهو عربيّ ابن عربيّة وابنك نبطيّ ابن نبطيّة. فنك ابني عشرًا مكان المرّة التي نكتُ ابنك فتكون قد ربحت الدنانير وللواحد عشرة. فضحك أبو الأصبغ وقال لابنه هات الدنانير يابن الفاعلة فرمى بها إليه وقام خجلاً. فقال يحيى والله لا دخل مطيع ابن الزانية فقال أبو الأصبغ وجواريه والله ليدخلنّ إلينا فقد فضحنا. فأدخل وجلس يشرب معهم ويحيى يشتمه بكلّ لسان ومطيع يضحك.

١٨،٣٣ ولمطيع أخبار كثيرة طريفة منع من إيرادها خوف الإطالة وما تدعو إليه من الملالة. وله شعر حسن مليح ويتغنّى في شعره فمن ذلك قوله

وَاهـًا لِظَـبْيٍ رَجَوْتُ نَائِلَهُ حَتَّى ٱنْثَنَى لِي بِوُدِّهِ صَـلَفَـا
لَانَتْ حَوَاشِيهِ لِي وَأَطْمَعَنِي حَتَّى إِذَا قُلْتُ نِلْتُهُ ٱنْصَرَفَـا

وقال أيضاً وله فيه غناء

خَلِيـلِي مُخْـلِفُ أَبَـدَا يُمَـنِّيني غَـدًا فَغَـدَا
وَبَعْـدَ غَدٍ وبَعْدَ غَـدٍ كَذَا لَا يَنْقَضِي أَبَـدَا
وَلَيسَ بِلَابِثٍ جَمْـرُ ٱلْـغَضَا أَنْ يَحْرِقَ ٱلْكَبِدَا

ومن مليح شعره قوله

اِخْلَعْ عِذَارَكَ فِي ٱلْهَوَى وَٱشْرَبْ مُعَتَّقَةَ ٱلدِّنَانِ
وَصِلِ ٱلْقِيَانَ مُجَاهِرًا فَٱلْعَيْشُ فِي وَصْلِ ٱلْقِيَانِ
لَا يُلْهِيَنَّكَ غَيْرُ مَا تَهْوَى فَإِنَّ ٱلْعُمْرَ فَانِي

Abū l-Aṣbagh asked Yaḥyā, "Did you do this, you son of a bitch?" "No." 33.17
So Abū l-Aṣbagh felt the cord of his son's drawers, found it was cut, and realized they had been disgraced.

Then Yaḥyā said, "What's happened has happened. Muṭīʿ, that bastard, has told on me. Here's my son, who's fresher than yours. He and I are Arabs son of Arabs, while your son's a Nabatean, son of a Nabatean mother. Fuck my son ten times for the one time I fucked your son, and you'll have won the dinars and the ten fucks for the price of one." Abū l-Aṣbagh laughed and said to his son, "Give me the dinars, you son of a bitch." The boy gave them to him and got up to go, ashamed. Yaḥyā begged, "Don't allow Muṭīʿ in." But Abū l-Aṣbagh and his slave girls protested, "Let him come in. He's given us good advice." So he was invited in and sat drinking with them while Yaḥyā cursed him, calling him every name he could think of, and he just laughed.[191]

There are many entertaining stories about Muṭīʿ, which have not been 33.18
included because they would go on too long and might bore the reader. He has excellent, beautiful poetry, some of it set to music. Here is one poem:

Alas for a gazelle whom I hoped to possess;
when he seemed to be slightly friendly,
The affection he showed led me to hope,
but just when I thought I'd caught him, he scarpered.

This poem has a setting:

My love is always putting me off:
tomorrow, she says, and tomorrow,
The day after, the day after,
the day after, on and on forever.
The embers of her refusal
will soon sear my heart and liver.

And here is another fine poem of his:

Throw shame to the winds, make love,
drink mature, full-bodied wine,
Spend time with singing girls,
don't try to hide, that's what living's about.
Don't let anything deflect you,
for life passes all too quickly.

وكان مطيع يبغض أباه ويهجوه وهو من بني كنانة وكان يوماً يذكر قبائل قريش والعرب ١٩،٣٣
ويصف قوماً قوماً فقال له بعض من حضر فأين بنو كنانة فقال غير متمهّل بفلسطين
يحسنون الركوب. أراد قول الشاعر

حَلَقٌ مِنْ بَنِي كِنَانَةَ حَوْلِي   بِفِلَسْطِينَ يُحْسِنُونَ ٱلرُّكُوبَا

Muṭīʿ hated his father and composed lampoons on him. He belonged to the Banū Kinānah. One day he was talking about Quraysh and the other Arab tribes, mentioning them one by one, and someone present asked him, "What about Banū Kinānah?" He answered straight off, "In Palestine, swift mounted horsemen." He was alluding to what the poet said: 33.19

Around me a circle of Banū Kinānah—
in Palestine, swift mounted horsemen.[192]

عُمر مر يونان

وهـذا العُمر بالأنبار على الفرات وهو عُمر حسن كثير القلّايات والرهبان وعليه سور ١،٣٤
محكم البناء فهو كالحصن له والجامع ملاصقه. ولا يخلو من المتنزّهين والمتظرّفين وله
ظاهر حسن ومنظر عجيب سيّما في أيّام الربيع لأنّ صحاريه وسائر أراضيه تكون كالحلل
لكثرة طرائف زهره وفنون أنواره. ومن اجتاز بالأنبار من الخلفاء ومَن دونهم ينزله
مدّة مقامه. وقد وصفته الشعراء وذكرته في أشعارها. وللحسين بن الضحّاك فيه

آذَنَكَ ٱلنَّـاقُوسُ بِٱلْفَجْـرِ   وَغَـرَّدَ ٱلرَّاهِبُ فِي ٱلْعُـمْرِ
وَٱطَّرَدَتْ عَيْنَاكَ فِي رَوْضَةٍ   تَضْحَكُ عَنْ حُمْرٍ وَعَنْ صُفْرِ
وَحَنَّ مَخْـمُورٌ إِلَى خَـمْرِهِ   وَجَاءَتِ ٱلْكَأْسُ عَلَى قَـدْرِ
فَٱرْغَبْ عَنِ ٱلنَّوْمِ إِلَى شُرْبِهَا   تَرْغَبْ عَنِ ٱلْمَوْتِ إِلَى ٱلنَّشْرِ

ولكشاجم فيه ٢،٣٤

أُغْـدُ يَا صَاحِبِي إِلَى ٱلْأَنْبَارِ   تَشْرَبِ ٱلرَّاحَ فِي شَبَابِ ٱلنَّهَارِ
وَٱعْمُـرِ ٱلْعُـمْرَ بِٱللَّذَاذَةِ وَٱلْقَصْـفِ   وَحَثِّ ٱلْكُؤُوسِ وَٱلْأَوْتَـارِ
مَا تَـرَى ٱلدَّهْرَ قَدْ أَتَاكَ بِوَجْـهٍ   طَـلِقٍ بَعْـدَ نَبْوَةٍ وَٱزْوِرَارِ
لَابِسًا حُـلَّةً مِنَ ٱلزَّهْـرِ كَانَتْ   قَبْـلُ مَحْجُوبَـةً عَنِ ٱلْأَبْصَـارِ
نَـرْجِسٌ كَٱلْعُيُونِ يَـرْقُبُ مَنْ يَهْـوَاهُ مِنْ غَـيْرِ رِقْبَةٍ أَوْ حِـذَارِ

The Monastery of Mār Yawnān

This monastery, which lies on the Euphrates at al-Anbār, is a large and beautiful building with many cells and monks, surrounded by a thick wall so it looks like a fortress. The mosque abuts it. Many people come to visit it on outings or in search of pleasure. The surrounding area is lovely and presents a wonderful sight, especially in spring, when, because of the myriad flowers and blossoms, the steppe and the rest of the land round it look like decorated robes. Caliphs and lesser notables who have to pass through al-Anbār put up there for the length of their stay. It has been mentioned and described by poets, for instance in these verses by al-Ḥusayn ibn al-Ḍaḥḥāk: 34.1

> The clappers at dawn and the monks' chant
>   in the convent have called you to prayer.
> You've let your eyes stray
>   over meadows, joyful in yellow and red;
> A tipsy man's longed for his wine,
>   and the cup's come just as he wanted.
> So turn from sleep to drain it,
>   and you'll turn from death back to life.

Kushājim has this poem on it: 34.2

> Let's go to Anbār to drink wine
>   in the youthful hours of the day;
> Let's furnish the convent with delights,
>   revelry, drinking, and songs.
> See! Fate comes toward us
>   bright-faced, after haughty aversion,
> Clad in a robe of flowers
>   hidden from view until now.
> Narcissi like bold eyes watch
>   the beloved without precaution,

وَإِذَا مَا بَدَا ٱلشَّقَائِقُ فِيهَا   خَالَهُ ٱلنَّاظِرُونَ شُعْلَةَ نَارِ
أَوْ كَمَا نُشِّرَتْ مَطَارِدُ حُمْرٌ   لِأَمِيرٍ فِي جَحْفَلٍ جَرَّارِ
وَكَأَنَّ ٱلْبَنَفْسَجَ ٱلْغَضَّ فِيهَا   أَثَرُ ٱلْقَرْصِ فِي خُدُودِ ٱلْجَوَارِي
وَتَرَى ٱلْخُرَّمَ ٱلسَّمَائِيَّ فِيهَا   كَٱلْيَوَاقِيتِ نُظِّمَتْ فِي ٱلْمَدَارِي
وَكَأَنَّ ٱلْمَنْثُورَ حُلَّةُ وَشْيٍ   مِثْلَهَا مَا حَوَتْ تُخُوتُ ٱلتِّجَارِ
فِي طِرَازِ ٱلرَّبِيعِ حِيكَتْ وَلٰكِنْ   نَمَّقَتْ وَشْيَهَا يَدُ ٱلْأَمْطَارِ
أُقْحُوَانٌ وَسَوْسَنٌ حَسَنُ ٱلنَّوْ   رِ وَشِيحٌ مُنَمْنَمٌ مَعْ بَهَارِ
فَٱغْتَنِمْ غَفْلَةَ ٱلزَّمَانِ وَبَادِرْ   وَٱفْتَرِصْ لَذَّةَ ٱللَّيَالِي ٱلْقِصَارِ

وكشاجم أبو الفتح محمود بن الحسين الكاتب مليح الشعر رقيق الطبع حسن الوصف له ٣،٣٤
كتب كثيرة وتأليفات طريفة. فمن شعره في بعض من كان يألفه قوله

مَنْ عَذِيرِي مِنْ عِذَارَيْ رَشَأٍ[١]   عَرَّضَ ٱلْقَلْبَ لِأَسْبَابِ ٱلتَّلَفْ
قَمَرٌ جَالَ نَعِيمُ ٱلْحُسْنِ فِي   مَاءِ خَدَّيْهِ عَلَى مَاءِ ٱلتَّرَفْ
وَلَهُ خَطُّ عِذَارٍ خَطَّهُ   رَوْنَقُ ٱلْعِزِّ بِأَقْلَامِ ٱلشَّرَفْ
حِكْمَةٌ فِي نِعْمَةٍ قَدْ طُرِّزَتْ   بِطِرَازٍ لَمْ يَجُزْ حَدَّ ٱلشُّنُفْ
جَمَّشَا خَدَّيْهِ ثُمَّ ٱنْعَطَفَا   آهِ مَا أَحْسَنَ ذَاكَ ٱلْمُنْعَطَفْ
عَلِمَ ٱلشَّعْرُ ٱلَّذِي عَاجَلَهُ   أَنَّهُ جَارَ عَلَيْهِ فَوَقَفْ
فَهْوَ فِي وَقْفَتِهِ مُعْتَرِفٌ   بِٱلتَّنَاهِي فِي ٱلتَّعَدِّي وَٱلسَّرَفْ

١ الأصل: رَشَاءٍ.

The anemones when they bloom
flash like fire,
Or red javelins deployed
for a commander's mighty host.
The tender violets recall the mark
of love bites on slave girls' cheeks,
The blue lavender flowers are sapphires
threaded on the prongs of a flail,
Wallflowers are brocade cloth
such as merchants keep in their chests,
Woven on the looms of spring
but cuffed by the hand of the rains.
Chamomile and lilies with lovely flowers,
wormwood stippled with daisies—
Hurry while fate's distracted, drink to the lees
the pleasures of nights all too brief.

Kushājim's name was Abū l-Fatḥ Maḥmūd ibn al-Ḥusayn. He was a secretary and a good poet, sensitive and gifted in description. He wrote many books, some of them remarkable. Here is a poem of his about someone he loved: 34.3

Who'll excuse me for the down
on a fawn's cheeks, exposing my heart to ruin,
A moon whose fresh face with its graceful
beauty floats on pure luxury.
With a noble pen, majesty's splendor
has traced his mustache's fine line,
An embroidered epigram of grace;
it's not reached the scroll of the ears.
It burdens his cheeks, then curves—
ah, what a lovely curve!
The hair has grown swiftly
but knows it's wronged him and stopped—
And, stopping, admits it's gone
too far and committed many a fault.

وله في صفة عود[1] ٤،٣٤

جاءَتْ بِعُودٍ كَأَنَّ نَغْمَتَهُ   صَوْتُ فَتاةٍ تَشْكُو فِراقَ فَتَى
مُحَفَّفٌ حَفَّتِ ٱلنُّفُوسُ بِهِ   كَأَنَّمَا ٱلزَّهْرُ حَوْلَهُ نَبَتَا
دارَتْ مَلاوِيهِ فِيهِ وَٱخْتَلَفَتْ   مِثْلَ ٱخْتِلافِ ٱلْكَفَّيْنِ شُبِّكَتَا
لَو حَرَّكَتْهُ وَراءَ مُنْهَزِمٍ   عَلَى بَرِيدٍ لَعَاجَ وَٱلْتَفَتَا
يا حُسْنَ صَوْتَيْهِما كَأَنَّهُما   أُخْتانِ فِي صَنْعَةٍ تَراسَلَتَا
وَهْوَ عَلَى ذَا يَنُوبُ إِنْ سَكَتَتْ   عَنْهَا وَعَنْهُ يَنُوبُ إِنْ سَكَتَا

وله في ذلك ٥،٣٤

وَمُسْمِعَةٍ تَحْنُو عَلَى مُتَرَنِّمٍ   لَهُ زَجَلٌ عالٍ وَلَيْسَ لَهُ سِحْرُ
إِذَا ما تَأَمَّلْتَ ٱلْحَشَى مِنْهُ خِلْتَهُ   تَضَمَّنَ شِعْباً وَهْوَ مُنْخَرِقٌ صِفْرُ
لَهُ نَغَمٌ يُفْضِينَ[2] مِنْ كُلِّ سامِعٍ   إِلَى حَيْثُ لَا تُفْضِي بِشارِبِها ٱلْخَمْرُ
إِذَا طَرَقَتْهُ بِٱلْأَنامِلِ وَٱلْتَقَى   عَلَى جِسْمِهِ مِنْ جِسْمِها ٱلنَّحْرُ وَٱلصَّدْرُ
بَكَى طَرَباً فَٱسْتَضْحَكَ ٱللَّهْوَ نَحْوَهُ   وَفُضَّتْ عُرَى ٱلْأَسْبابِ وَٱسْتُلِبَ ٱلصَّبْرُ
وَتَمْنَحُهُ ٱلْيُمْنَى حِساباً مُفَصَّلاً   فَتُحْمَلُ فِيهِ ٱلْخَمْسُ وَٱلسِّتُّ وَٱلْعَشْرُ
فَمُتْ صَرِيعَ ٱلسُّكْرِ أَطْيَبَ مَيْتَةٍ   وَمَا ٱلْحِلْمُ إِلَّا أَنْ يُسَفِّهَكَ ٱلسُّكْرُ

---

١ الأصل: (قف على وصف العود) وردت في الهامش. ٢ الأصل: نعصين.

Here is a poem of his on a lute:[193] 34.4

She came with a lute whose song
was of a girl lamenting separation,
Well wrapped, with hearts around it,
like a flower in a garden of plants.
She turned the pegs and they argued,
as two hands twined together will.
A fugitive on a swift horse would stop
and listen if he heard her playing.
Singer and lute, how lovely their voices,
like sisters communing in their art.
If she's silent, it takes her place,
and if it's silent, she gives voice.

And another poem on this theme: 34.5

A singer bows over a chanter,
loud-voiced but without magic.
Look inside and you think it's solid,
but in fact it's hollow and void.
Its melody transports the listener
to a place beyond wine.
If her fingers pluck it and their bodies
meet, its neck on her breast,
It weeps for joy, summoning
pleasure to laugh,
And friends forget friends,
all patience gone.
Her right hand explores
all the notes of the scale
And I die, felled by drink—
an excellent death;
True wisdom dictates
that drink makes men fools.

ومن مليح شعره ٦،٣٤

يَقُولُونَ تُبْ وَٱلْكَأْسُ فِي يَدِ أَغْيَدٍ وَصَوْتُ ٱلْمَثَانِي وَٱلْمَثَالِثِ عَالِي
فَقُلْتُ لَهُمْ لَوْ كُنْتُ أَضْمَرْتُ تَوْبَةً وَأَبْصَرْتُ هٰذَا كُلَّهُ لَبَدَا لِي

وله يصف معزفة

مُعَلَّقَةُ ٱلْأَوْتَارِ صَخَّابَةٌ لَهَا حَنِينٌ كَحَنِينِ ٱلْغَرِيبْ
زَادَتْ عَلَى ٱلْمِزْهَرِ طِيباً وَقَدْ تَاهَتْ عَلَى ٱلنَّايِ بِخَلْقٍ عَجِيبْ
مَكْسُوَّةٌ أَحْشَاؤُهَا جِلْدَةً بَيْضَاءَ مِنْ جِلْدِ غَزَالٍ رَبِيبْ
كَأَنَّمَا تِسْعَةُ أَوْتَارِهَا نُصِبْنَ أَشْرَاكاً لِصَيْدِ ٱلْقُلُوبْ

وله في مضراب ٧،٣٤

يَا أَيُّهَا ٱلصَّلِفُ ٱلْمُدِلُّ بِحُسْنِهِ جُدْ لِلْمُحِبِّ فَأَنْتَ أَهْلُ ٱلْجُودِ
بِقُبُولِ مِضْرَابٍ حَكَاكَ بِحُسْنِهِ حَسَنِ ٱلتَّعَطُّفِ مُخْطَفٍ مَقْدُودِ
مُتَشَبِّهٌ بِكَ حِينَ تَخْطُو لَاهِياً وَتَمِيسُ بَيْنَ مَجَاسِدٍ وَعُقُودِ
لَا تُشْمِتَنَّ بِيَ ٱلْحَسُودَ بِرَدِّهِ يَفْدِيكَ كُلُّ حَسُودَةٍ وَحَسُودِ
لَمْ أُهْدِهِ لَكَ يَا مُنَايَ وَإِنَّمَا أَهْدَيْتُهُ مُتَقَرِّباً لِلْعُودِ[1]

وله يرثي قدحاً كان له انكسر ٨،٣٤

وَعِنْدِي فَجَائِعُ لِلنَّائِبَاتِ وَلَيْسَ كَفَجْعَتِنَا بِٱلْقَدَحْ
وِعَاءُ ٱلْمُدَامِ وَتَاجُ ٱلْبَنَانِ وَخِدْنُ ٱلسُّرُورِ وَمُقْصِي ٱلتَّرَحْ

[1] ورد البيت في الهامش.

Here are some more attractive verses: 34.6

They say, "Repent!"
Here's a slender youth
with a cup in his hand
and the lute's ravishing sounds.
I reply, "If I were minded
to repent and saw all this,
I'd certainly change my mind."

Here he describes a lyre:[194]

With its strings tightened, it cries out,
loud as a stranger's lament,
Lovelier than the lute, outdoing the flute
with its wondrous sweetness,
Clad inside in white leather
from the skin of a young gazelle.
Its nine cords resemble
a net cast to trap hearts.

And here a plectrum: 34.7

You haughty fellow, coquettish in beauty,
be generous to your lover—you're one to be generous,
By accepting a plectrum whose beauty copies yours,
nicely turned, slender waisted, slim,
It looks like you as you playfully prance
in your saffron robes and necklaces.
Don't reject it and make the envious gloat!
May all the envious be your ransom.
I've not given it to you, my hope and desire;
I've given it to the lute, to bring me nearer.

In this poem, he mourns a cup of his that had broken: 34.8

I've suffered disasters fit to be mourned,
but nothing to equal the loss of this cup,
A vessel for wine, a jewel in the hands,
a friend to joy, banishing sorrow.

يَرُدُّ عَلَى ٱلشَّخْصِ تِمْثَالَهُ فَلَوْ تَتَّخِذْهُ مَرَاةً صَلَحْ
يَكَادُ مَعَ ٱلْمَاءِ إِنْ مَسَّهُ لِمَا فِيهِ مِنْ شِبْهِهِ يَنْسَفِحْ
فَأَفْقَدَنِيهِ عَلَى ضِنَّةٍ بِهِ لِلزَّمَانِ غَرِيمٌ مُلِحْ
كَأَنَّ لَهُ نَاظِرًا يَنْتَقِي فَمَا يَتَعَمَّدُ غَيْرَ ٱلْمُلَحْ
فَلَا تَبْعَدَنَّ فَكَمْ مِنْ حَشًى عَلَيْكَ كَلِيمٍ وَقَلْبٍ قَرِحْ

وله في النيل ٩،٣٤

كَأَنَّ ٱلنِّيلَ حِينَ أَتَى بِمِصْرٍ وَفَاضَ بِهَا وَكُسِّرَتِ ٱلتِّرَاعُ
وَأَحْدَقَ بِٱلْقُرَى مِنْ كُلِّ وَجْهٍ سَمَاوَاتٌ كَوَاكِبُهَا ضِيَاعُ

وقال في البطّيخ

وَطَيِّبٍ أَهْدَى لَنَا طَيِّبًا فَدَلَّنَا ٱلْمُهْدَى عَلَى ٱلْمُهْدِي
يَا جَانِيَ ٱلْبِطِّيخِ مِنْ غَرْسِهِ جَنَيْتَ مِنْهُ ثَمَرَ ٱلْحَمْدِ
لَمْ يَأْتِنَا حَتَّى أَتَتْنَا بِهِ رَوَائِحٌ أَغْنَتْ عَنِ ٱلنَّدِّ
كَأَنَّمَا تَكْشِفُ مِنْهُ ٱلْمُدَى عَنْ زَعْفَرَانٍ دِيفَ فِي شَهْدِ
كَأَنَّمَا فِي جَوْفِهِ قَهْوَةٌ يُنْقَعُ فِيهَا مَنْدَلٌ هِنْدِي

وفيما أتينا به من طريف شعره وغريب صفاته كفاية تفي بالشرط ولا تتجاوز الحدّ.

It gave back to its holder his likeness;
if you wanted, it would make a fine mirror.
If crystalline water was poured into it,
like crystal it melted into water.
Though I guarded it jealously from fate,
a pestering rival made me lose it.
It seems he was watching, on the lookout,
his sights set on things of beauty.
If only you had not perished! How many mourn you!
How many wounded hearts miss you!

He composed these verses on the Nile: **34.9**

The Nile, when it floods Egypt,
breaking down the embankments,
Surrounding the villages on every side,
is like a sky with hamlets for stars.

And these on a watermelon:

Someone good gave us something good,
and the gift told us who was the giver.
When you plucked the watermelon
from its tendril, you plucked a fruit of praise.
Until you brought it, we didn't know
There are perfumes more fragrant than ambergris.
Under the knife its flesh appears
as saffron mingled with honey,
As if it has wine in its heart,
mixed with sandalwood oil.

These passages we have quoted of his amazing and unusual poetry are enough for the book's purpose.

ديـر قُنّى
ويُعرف أيضاً بدير مـر مـاري السـليح

١،٣٥ وهـذا الدير على ستّة عشر فرسخاً من بغداد منحدراً في الجانب الشرقيّ. بينه وبين دجلة ميل ونصف وبينه وبين دير العاقول بريد. وهو دير حسن نزه عامر وفيه مائة قلاّية لرهبانه والمتبتّلين فيه. لكلّ راهب قلاّية وهم يتبايعون هذه القلالي بينهم من ألف دينار إلى مائتي دينار إلى خمسين ديناراً.[1] وحول كلّ قلاّية بستان فيه من جميع الثمار والنخل والزيتون وتُباع غلّته من مائتي دينار إلى خمسين ديناراً.[2] وعليه سور عظيم يحيط به وفي وسطه نهر جارٍ. وعيده الذي يجتمع الناس إليه عيد الصليب.

٢،٣٥ وقد وصفته الشعراء ولابن جمهور فيه

يَا مَـنْزِلَ ٱللَّهْوِ بِـدَيْـرِ قُـنَّا ... قَلْبِي إِلَى تِلْكَ ٱلرُّبَى قَدْ حَـنَّا
سُـقْـيًا لِأَيَّامِكَ لَمَّـا كُـنَّا ... نَمْـتَارُ مِـنْكَ لَذَّةً وَحُسْـنَا
أَيَّامِ لَا أَنْعَـمَ عَـيْشٍ مِـنَّا ... إِذَا ٱنْتَشَيْنَـا وَصَحَوْنَا عُـدْنَا
وَإِنْ فَـنَى دَنٌّ بَـزَلْنَـا[3] دَنَّا ... حَـتَّى يُظَنَّ أَنَّنَـا جُنِـنَّا
وَمُسْـعِدٍ فِي كُـلِّ مَا أَرَدْنَا ... يَحْكِي لَنَا ٱلْغُصْنَ ٱلرَّطِيبَ ٱللَّدْنَا
أَحْسَنِ خَـلْقِ ٱللهِ أَدَّى لَحْـنَا ... وَجَسَّ زِيـرَ عُودِهِ وَغَـنَّى
بِٱللهِ يَا قَسِـيسَ يَا مَـا قُـنَّى ... مَـتَى رَأَيْتَ ٱلرَّشَـأَ ٱلْأَغَـنَّا
مَـتَى رَأَيْتَ فِـتْنَتِي يُوحَـنَّا ... آهٍ إِذَا مَـا مَـاسَ أَوْ تَـثَـنَّى

١ الأصل: دينار. ٢ الأصل: دينار. ٣ الأصل: نزلنا.

Qunnā's Monastery, Also Known as the Monastery of Mār Mārī the Apostle[195]

This monastery lies some twenty-five miles (forty kilometers) downriver from Baghdad to the east and nearly two miles (about three kilometers) from the Tigris. It is one post stage distant from the ʿĀqūl Monastery. It is a beautiful, well kept, and flourishing monastery, with a hundred cells for the monks and ascetics who live there. Each monk owns a cell and they exchange these cells among them for prices that range from fifty to two hundred to one thousand dinars. Each cell is set in a garden with all kinds of fruit, palm trees, and olives, and the sale of the produce brings in between fifty and two hundred dinars. The monastery is surrounded by a massive wall, and a stream flows through the middle of it. The feast when people come to visit it is the Feast of the Cross.[196] 35.1

Various poets have described it, among them Ibn Jamhūr: 35.2

Qunnā's Convent, home of enjoyment,
my heart's filled with longing for those haunts;
The memory's fresh of those days when
you plied us with beauty and pleasure,
A time when life held nothing finer than
drinking and getting sober again and again.
When one jar was exhausted, we brought out another
till you'd think we'd gone crazy.
We had a helper for all we needed,
like a fresh branch, supple and lissome,
The best of mankind in performing a tune,
plucking the lutestrings and singing.
By God, you priest of Mār Mārī at Qunnā,
did you ever see such a soft-spoken fawn?
Did you ever see the entrancing Yūḥannā,
how he walked tall yet swayed back and forth!

يَا مُنْيَةَ ٱلْقَلْبِ إِذَا تَمَنَّى فَتَكْتَ بِٱلصَّبِّ بِكَ ٱلْمُعَنَّى
ثُمَّ قَلَبْتَ فِي ٱلْهَوَى ٱلْمِجَنَّا عَذَّبْتَهُ بِٱلْحُبِّ فَنًّا فَنَّا
وَصَارَتِ ٱلْأَرْضُ عَلَيْهِ سِجْنَا فَمَا يُلَاقِي ٱلْجَفْنُ مِنْهُ جَفْنَا
أَفْدِيكَ لَمْ تَهْجُرْ صَبًّا مُضْنَى قَدْ كَانَ مِنْ غَدْرِكَ مُطْمَئِنَّا
أَسَأْتُ إِذْ أَحْسَنْتُ فِيكَ ٱلظَّنَّا وَصَارَ قَلْبِي فِي يَدَيْكَ رَهْنَا

وقال فيه أيضاً ٣،٣٥

وَكَمْ وَقْفَةٍ فِي دَيْرِ قُنَّى وَقَفْتُهَا أُغَازِلُ فِيهِ فَاتِنَ ٱلطَّرْفِ أَحْوَرَا
وَكَمْ فَتْكَةٍ لِي فِيهِ لَمْ أَنْسَ طِيبَهَا أَمَتُّ بِهَا عُرْفًا وَأَحْيَيْتُ مُنْكَرَا

٤،٣٥ وهو أبو عليّ محمّد بن الحسين بن جمهور العمّيّ[1] وكان أبوه من رواة أهل البيت صلوات الله عليهم وحاملي الأثر عنهم. وكان أبو عليّ ظريفاً متأدّباً مليح الشعر والكتابة وقد سافر في طلب العلم وتطرّح في مواطن اللعب وعاشر أهل الخلاعة وطرق الحانات والديارات. ثمّ أقام بالبصرة وحسنت حاله بها وصارت له نعمة كثيرة.

ومن شعره في جارية كانت في القيان تُعرف بزاذمهر جارية المنصوريّة وكانت له معها في القيان أحاديث طريفة ثمّ تأتّى له أن اشتراها قوله

رُبَّمَا ٱسْتَصْعَبَ وَٱسْتَبْعَدَ أَمْرٌ وَهْوَ دَانِي
يَفْعَلُ[2] ٱلْإِنْسَانُ مَا يَهْوَاهُ فِي صَفْوِ ٱلزَّمَانِ
فَيَرَى ٱلْمُسْتَخْذِيَ ٱلْآ يِسَ مِنْ نَيْلِ ٱلْأَمَانِي
قَدْ حَوَى مَا كَانَ يَرْجُو فِي ٱغْتِبَاطٍ وَأَمَانِ

١ الأصل: القمّيّ. ٢ كذا في عوّاد؛ الأصل: يأتي.

Heart's desire, if ever the heart had a wish,
you've slain the lover tormented by your love,
You've dealt craftily with the one who adores you,
inflicting on him all kinds of torture.
The world has closed in on him like a prison—
a prison in which his eyes never close.
I beg you, don't abandon this suffering lover,
who was certain you would not betray him.
In thinking well of you I was mistaken—
in your hands, my heart became a pawn.

He also composed these verses on the monastery: 35.3

How often I've stopped in Qunnā's Convent,
flirting with an entrancing black-eyed boy,
Taking liberties with him—how sweet they were—
burying decency, breathing life into infamy.

This poet's full name was Abū ʿAlī Muḥammad ibn al-Ḥusayn ibn Jamhūr 35.4
al-ʿAmmī. His father was one of the transmitters of information about the Prophet's family, God bless them, and the bearers of traditions originating with them. Abū ʿAlī was witty, cultivated, and a good poet and writer. He traveled to various cities to study, frequented places of amusement, moved in frivolous circles, and visited taverns and monasteries. Then he settled in Basra, his material situation improved, and he acquired great wealth. He composed poetry on a girl called Zādmahr, the servant of the singer al-Manṣūriyyah.[197] There are many amusing stories about his relationship with her while she was with the singing slaves; later on he had the opportunity to buy her. Here are verses of his about her:

At times a thing seems out of reach
when really it's close by;
When fortune smiles,
a man may do exactly as he will—
He who's meek and despairs
of getting what he wants
Finds rapture and security
when his hope's fulfilled.

وقال أيضاً

كَمْ قَدْ أَرَتْنَا صُرُوفُ ٱلدَّهْرِ مِنْ عَجَبِ وَمِنْ مُحِبٍّ شَدِيدِ ٱلسُّقْمِ وَٱلْوَصَبِ
صَفَا لَهُ ٱلدَّهْرُ حَتَّى نَالَ بُغْيَتَهُ مِمَّنْ تَعَشَّقَهُ فِي أَيْسَرِ ٱلطَّلَبِ

وأخباره معها ومع غيرها من القيان عجيبة. ٥،٣٥

قالت له زاذَمهر هذه وهي في القيان وقد دعاها خذ لي الطالع في شيء أضمرته. فأخذ الطالع وزرقها فقال سألت عن رجل عليل القلب شديد الكرب دائم الفكر طويل الحيرة قد أشفى على أمر عظيم في طاعة إنسان عزيز. فضحكت ثمّ قالت مسرعة على بظر أمّ الكاذب. والله ما سألت إلّا عن الثوب المصمت الذي وعدتني به. متى تبعث به إليّ فخجل وبعث به إليها.

وطرّز مرّة منديلاً بهذه الأبيات وأنفذه إليها ٦،٣٥

أَنَا رَسُولٌ مِنْ فَتًى عَاشِقٍ أَدْمُعُهُ مِنْ خَدِّهِ جَارِيَهْ
هٰذَا ٱبْنُ جُمْهُورٍ فَجُودِي لَهُ مِنْكِ بِمَا يَهْوَاهُ يَا قَاسِيَهْ
وَلَيْسَتِ ٱلنَّفْسُ وَإِنْ شَفَّهَا حُبُّكِ يَا مَوْلَاتَهُ سَالِيَهْ

فردّت المنديل وقد طرّزت في وسطه

أُمُّ مَنْ يَسْخَرُ بِنَا حَتَّى يَنِيكَنَا زَانِيَهْ

٧،٣٥ وكتب إليها وقد كانت هجرته يا سيّدةَ عبدها والله إنّ الذي بلغك باطل لكنّي أعترف به طاعة لك وأقول كما قال ربيعة الأسديّ

And here are other verses:

Many a strange turn of fate we've seen,
many a lover sorely tried and sick,
Till destiny helped him gain his wish
of his beloved—without him even asking!

There are splendid anecdotes about Abū ʿAlī with Zādmahr and with other singing girls. One day when he invited Zādmahr with the singing girls, she said to him, "Cast a horoscope. What's in the stars for me?" but did not say why. He did so and looked at her intently, saying, "You've asked about a man who's sick at heart, burdened with cares, always pensive, ever regretful. A terrible fate will befall him because he's yielded to someone he loves." She burst out laughing and replied immediately, "Fuck the liar's mother! By God, I was only asking about the velvet robe you promised me. When will you send it to me?" Embarrassed, he sent it to her. 35.5

One day he sent her a handkerchief on which he'd had the following verses embroidered: 35.6

I bear a message from a young lover
whose tears flow down his cheeks.
It's Ibn Jamhūr. Be generous,
give him what he wants, cruel one.
Though love for you, mistress,
wore him out, he'd never be consoled.

She returned the handkerchief after she had embroidered in the middle of it:

If anyone mocks me
until he fucks me,
his mother's a whore.

When she was avoiding him, he wrote to her: "Mistress of her slave, what you have heard about me is untrue, but I'll admit to it just to obey you. I'll say, quoting Rabīʿah al-Asadī: 35.7

هَبِينِي ٱمْرَءًا أَذْنَبْتُ ذَنْبًا جَهِلْتُـهُ   وَلَمْ آتِـهِ عَمْدًا وَذُو ٱلْحِلْمِ يَجْهَـلُ
عَفَا ٱللّٰهُ عَمَّا قَدْ مَضَى لَسْتُ عَائِدًا   وَهَـا أَنَا ذَا مِنْ سُخْـطِكُمْ أَتَنَصَّلُ

وقد قلت أيضاً

أَمَـلِي إِنْ كُنْتُ أَخْطَأْ   تُ رَشَادِي فِي هَوَالِـكِ
فَلَقَـدْ أَسْهَرْتُ عَيْنًا   أَرِقَتْ عِنْـــدَ كَرَالِـكِ
فَٱصْفَحِي عَنِّي وَجُودِي   جُعِلَتْ نَفْسِي فِـدَالِـكِ

فوقّعت على ظهر الرقعة ما لك تغمّ نفسك وتتنطّع في كتب الأشعار. وجّه إليّ الغلالة وقد اصطلحنا.

وله فيها ٨،٣٥

بَاتَتْ عِـدَاكَ كَمَا أَبِيتُ   وَلَقِي حَسُودُكَ مَـا لَقِـيتُ
يَا مَنْ شَـقِـيتُ بِحُـبِّهِ   صِلْ لَا شَقِيتَ كَمَا شَقِيتُ
لَا خُنْتُ عَهْـدَكَ مَا حَيِيتُ   وَلَا قَـطَـعْـتُ وَلَا نَسِـيتُ
كُنْ كَـيْفَ شِـئْتَ فَإِنَّنِي   أَرْعَى وِدَادَكَ مَـا بَقِـيتُ

وقال لها يوماً يا قحبة قالت له يا ابن القحبتين. فقال لها ويلك أقول لك يا قحبة فتقولين لي يا ابن القحبتين فقالت نعم أنا شموص أردّ بالزوج.

٩،٣٥ وكنّا نحضر مجلسه بالبصرة فيملي أخبار أهل البيت عليهم السلام وغيرها فإذا فرغ من الإملاء ابتدأ جواريه فقرأن بألحان ثمّ قلن القصائد الزهديّات فإذا فرغن من ذلك انصرف من انصرف واحتبس عنده من يأنس به وعمل الغناء والشرب.

Suppose I'm someone who's sinned
without knowing,
Unintentionally—even the wise make mistakes;
may God forgive what has passed!—
I'll not sin again, and my repentance
will wash away your anger.

"And I've composed some verses too:

If I've been wrong, I hope to find
my right mind in your love.
My eyes have been wide open,
sleepless while you slept;
Forgive me and be generous.
I'd give my life for you."

So she wrote on the back of the message: "Why do you wear yourself out thumbing through books of poetry? Send me the under-tunic and we'll be friends again."

This is another poem of his about her: 35.8

Your enemies and I are in the same state;
those who envy you experience my fate.
You for whose love I've suffered much,
receive me! May you never suffer like me.
I won't betray your trust while I'm alive,
or cut you or forget you.
Be as you will—as long as I live,
I'll stay your faithful lover.

Once he cursed her: "You whore!" She replied, "You son of two whores." "Damn you," he said, "I say to you, 'you whore,' and you answer, 'you son of two whores.'" "Yes, I'm difficult. I reply with the double."

We used to attend his receptions in Basra, where he dictated reports about 35.9
the Prophet's family, peace be upon them, and other subjects. When he had finished dictating, his slave girls would come and chant surahs of the Qur'an, and then sing ascetic poems. People would leave when they finished, except for those he asked to stay because he felt at ease with them, and then the singing and drinking would start.

قال وكان عبدون بن مَخلد أخو صاعد بن مخلد عند وفاة أخيه وإطلاقه من الحبس صار إلى دير قنّى فأقام فيه وتعبّد وكان عبدون هذا ناقص الصنعة شديد التخلّف وبلغ مع ذلك مبلغاً عظيماً في أيّام أخيه. قال فأهدت ريق المغنّية إلى عبدون فاكهة مبكّرة فيها تين ورمّان وغيرهما فقال لكاتبه اكتب إليها جواب رقعتها بشعر فحلف أنّه ما قال شعراً قطّ فغضب عبدون غضباً شديداً وقال أنت بين يديّ منذ سنين لا تحسن قصائد السبع يا حمار اكتب إليها ١٠،٣٥

قَـدْ أَتَتْنَـا هَــدِيَّتَـانِكْ
فِي يَوْمِ مَـهْـرَجَـانِكْ
وَأَكَلْنَـا مِنْ رُمَّـانِكْ
لِأَنَّكِ جَانْجَانُنَا وَنَحْنُ جَانْجَانُكْ

وكان صاعد من رجالات الناس حزماً وضبطاً وكفايةً وكرماً ونبلاً وكان كثير الصدقات والصلوات ليلاً ونهاراً وكان في أيّام وزارته للموفّق يركب إلى دار الموفّق فيقيم بحضرته أربع ساعات ثمّ ينصرف إلى منزله فينظر في حوائج الناس وأمور الحاضر والغائب إلى الظهر ثمّ يتغدّى وينام ثمّ يجلس بالعشيّ فينظر في الأعمال السلطانيّة إلى عشاء الآخرة لا يبرح أو يحصّل جميع الأموال ما حُمل منها وما أُنفق وما بقي. ويعمل له بذلك عملاً في كلّ يوم ويعرض عليه وما يخفى عنه شيء ممّا يجري في الأعمال كلّ يوم ثمّ ينظر في أمرضياعه وأسبابه ويتقدّم إلى وكلائه وخاصّته بما يحتاج إليه ثمّ يتشاغل بعد ذلك مع نديم يتشاغل بحديثه ويأنس به ثمّ ينام ويقوم في آخر الليل فلا يزال يصلّي إلى طلوع الفجر ثمّ يأذن للناس فيسلّمون عليه ثمّ يركب إلى دار الموفّق. ١١،٣٥

قال ولمّا انصرف صاعد من فارس شكا إليه الموفّق أمر عمرو بن الليث وقلّة الأموال وما يحتاج إليه لإنهاض العسكر والتمس منه احتيال مال يُخرج به راشداً إلى الصفّار. فقال والله ما لي حيلة أكثر من حظر النفقات ومنع المرتزقين. فقال الموفّق ١٢،٣٥

When Ṣā'id ibn Makhlad died, his brother 'Abdūn ibn Makhlad was released from prison. He went to the Qunnā Monastery and lived an ascetic life. He was not properly qualified as a secretary and was not quick on the uptake, yet he reached a high position during his brother's time in office. 35.10

Rayyiq the singer offered him some early fruits once—figs, pomegranates, and other things—so he said to his secretary, "Write a reply to her note in poetry." The secretary swore that he had never composed verses, which infuriated 'Abdūn. "You've been working for me for years and you don't even know the Poems of the Seven,"[198] he said. "You ass, write to her:

> We've got your presents,
> on the day of your phaste,[199]
> We've eaten of your pomegranate,
> you're our beloved *amorosa*
> and we're your adoring *amoroso*."[200]

Ṣā'id was an outstanding personality: decisive, precise, competent, generous, and high-minded. He regularly gave alms and prayed day and night. When he was al-Muwaffaq's vizier, he would ride to the prince's palace, spend four hours with him on business, and then return home, where he would look into petitions and the affairs of those far and near until midday. Then he had lunch, took a siesta, and in the evening dealt with affairs of state until the night prayer. He would not leave until he had checked all the finances, income, expenses, and balance. Accounts were drawn up and presented to him every day, and nothing escaped him. Subsequently, he would look into the situation of his estates and other property, pointing out to his agents and close aides what should be done. He would spend some time with one of his companions, enjoying conversation with him, and relaxing before going to bed. Then he would get up at the end of the night to pray until daybreak, give permission for his attendants to come in and greet him, and ride off to al-Muwaffaq's palace. 35.11

When Ṣā'id left Fars, al-Muwaffaq complained to him about the threat posed by 'Amr ibn al-Layth al-Ṣaffār, mentioning how short he was of money and how much was needed to refit the army. He asked him to think of a plan to raise money to finance sending Rāshid to fight 'Amr. Ṣā'id responded, "By God, the only plan I can think of is to reduce expenses and dock pensions." "That's not what I need," said al-Muwaffaq. "I want you to take a loan from the 35.12

أين يقع ذلك ممّا أحتاج والذي أريد أن تأخذ من التجّار قرضاً وتوظّف عليهم وعليك وعلى الكتّاب والعمّال مالاً نستعين به على إخراج راشد فإذا اتّسعنا رددناه عليهم. فاستوحش صاعد من ذلك وأراد إعمال الحيلة في التباعد عنه فقال أمّا بواسط فلا يتهيّأ لي ولكن إن أذن لي الأمير في المصير إلى مدينة السلام رجوت أن أحتال له ما يريد. فقال اعزم على ذلك وكتب إلى أبي العبّاس ابنه بالقبض على ما لصاعد بسرّ من رأى وبغداد وجميع أسبابه.

١٣،٣٥ قال إسحاق بن إبراهيم الكاتب فرأيت صاعداً في اليوم الذي قُبض عليه فيه متثاقلاً عن المصير إلى الموفّق فلم أزل به إلى أن قعد في الطيّارة وهو على غاية الكراهة ووصل إلى حضرة الموفّق وقد واقف الموفّق راشداً[1] أن يسير إلى دار صاعد عند حصوله بين يديه فيقبض على ما فيها وعلى ابنه وأسبابه فلمّا رأى صاعد عند مسيره الجيش على الجسر قال ما هذا أعزّ الله الأمير قال استأذنني راشد في عرض رجاله الذين يخرجون معه إلى فارس وقد مضى لعرضهم. قال فأقوم وأمضي نحوهم وأحضر عرض الرجال معه. قال افعل فوثب صاعد ليمضي فعُدل به إلى الحجرة التي أُعدّت له ووكل به وقبض على ما كان له بواسط وعلى عبدون أخيه وجميع أموالهما في يوم واحد. وحصل ممّا قُبض عنه وعن أخيه وابنه من الضياع ما مقدار ارتفاعه ألف ألف دينار ووُجد لهم من المتاع والكسوة والطيب والجوهر والفرش والآلات ما لا قيمة له كثرةً ونحو أربعة آلاف رأس من الدوابّ والبغال وأربعة آلاف غلام بين فحل وخادم ولم يوجد له ممّا ظهر من المال إلّا نحو مائتي ألف دينار ثمّ وضع يده في كشف أموالهم وودائعهم ومصادرات أسبابهم فكان ذلك أمراً عظيماً.

١٤،٣٥ ولم يزل محبوساً إلى سنة خمس وسبعين[2] ومائتين ثمّ نُقل إلى دار ابن طاهر فمات هناك من خلفة أصابته فدُفن بإزاء الدار المعروفة به.

ومات أخوه عبدون وهو مترهّب بدير قنّى في سنة عشر وثلاثمائة.

[1] الأصل: واقف راشداً الموفّق. [2] الأصل: وتسعين.

merchants and collect a levy from them, from yourself, and from the secretaries and administrators to finance Rāshid's expedition. When things become easier, we'll pay them back."

Ṣāʿid found the idea odious and he started to think of a way to distance himself from the prince. "I won't be able to manage that in Wāsiṭ," he said, "but if the prince allows me to go to Baghdad, I hope I could find a way to get him what he wants." "Do that," said al-Muwaffaq. At the same time, he wrote to his son Abū l-ʿAbbās[201] to seize Ṣāʿid's property in Samarra and Baghdad and all his possessions.

Isḥāq ibn Ibrāhīm the secretary recalled: I saw Ṣāʿid on the day he was arrested 35.13
hanging back from going to al-Muwaffaq, and I persuaded him to take his seat in the skiff, though he was extremely unwilling. When he was admitted into al-Muwaffaq's presence, the prince had already agreed with Rāshid to go to his residence as soon as he arrived, confiscate everything there, and put his son and his household under arrest. Ṣāʿid saw the army drawn up by the bridge and said, "What's this, God preserve the prince?" "Rāshid asked my permission to parade the men who accompany him to Fars, and he's gone off to inspect them." "Let me go and join them and see the parade with him." "Very well." Ṣāʿid sprang up to leave, but was seized, taken to the room prepared for him, and put under guard. His property in Wāsiṭ was seized, his brother ʿAbdūn was arrested, and everything they owned was confiscated, all in one day.

The estates belonging to him, his brother, and his son that were confiscated were worth a million dinars. Their utensils, clothes, perfumes, jewels, furnishings, and vessels were too numerous to be valued. They had around four thousand beasts of burden and mules and four thousand male slaves, uncastrated and eunuchs. On first inspection, they had only two hundred thousand dinars in cash, but when al-Muwaffaq got his hands on the inventory of their wealth and deposits and the confiscations of their household, it came to a huge amount.

Ṣāʿid remained in prison until the year 275 [889], when he was transferred 35.14
to Ibn Ṭāhir's palace, where he died from dementia. He was buried opposite the palace called after him.

His brother ʿAbdūn died in 310 [922–23] in the Qunnā Monastery, where he had become a monk.

عمر كسكر

١،٣٦ وهو أسفل من واسط في الجانب الشرقيّ منها بالقرية المعروفة بيرجونيّ[١] وفيه كرسيّ المطران وهو عمر كبير عظيم حسن البناء محكم الصنعة حوله قلّايات كثيرة كلّ قلّاية منها لراهب وسبيلها سبيل القلّايات الّتي بدير قنّى. ويحيط بالموضع بساتين كثيرة فيها الشجر والنخل وسائر الثمار فكلّ ذي ظرف يطرقه وكلّ ذي شجن يتسلّى به.

٢،٣٦ ولمحمّد بن حازم فيه وكان قصده أيّام مقام الحسن بن سهل بواسط ومدح الحسن ابن سهل وله معه حديث نذكره بعقب الشعر

بِعُمْرِ وَاسِطَ طَابَ ٱللَّهْوُ وَٱلطَّرَبُ ... وَٱلِٱدِّكَارَاتُ وَٱلْأَذْوَارُ وَٱلنُّخَبُ
وَفِتْيَةٍ بَذَلُوا لِلْكَأْسِ أَنْفُسَهُمْ ... وَأَوْجَبُوا لِرَضِيعِ ٱلْكَأْسِ مَا يَجِبُ
وَأَنْفَقُوا فِي سَبِيلِ ٱلْقَصْفِ مَا وَجَدُوا ... وَأَنْهَبُوا مَا لَهُمْ فِيهَا وَمَا ٱكْتَسَبُوا
مُحَافِظِينَ إِنِ ٱسْتَنْجَدْتَهُمْ دَفَعُوا ... وَأَسْخِيَاءَ إِنِ ٱسْتَوْهَبْتَهُمْ وَهَبُوا
نَادَمْتُ مِنْهُمْ كِرَامًا سَادَةً نُجُبًا ... مُهَذَّبِينَ نَمَتْهُمْ سَادَةٌ نُجُبُ
فَلَمْ نَزَلْ فِي رِيَاضِ ٱلْعُمْرِ نَعْمُرُهَا ... قَصْفًا وَتَغْمُرُنَا ٱللَّذَّاتُ وَٱلطَّرَبُ
وَٱلزَّهْرُ يَضْحَكُ وَٱلْأَنْوَاءُ بَاكِيَةٌ ... وَٱلنَّايُ يُسْعِدُ وَٱلْأَوْتَارُ تَصْطَخِبُ
وَٱلْكَأْسُ فِي فَلَكِ ٱللَّذَّاتِ دَائِرَةٌ ... تَجْرِي وَنَحْنُ لَهَا فِي دَوْرِهَا قُطُبُ
وَٱلدَّهْرُ قَدْ طُرِفَتْ عَنَّا نَوَاظِرُهُ ... فَمَا تُرَوِّعُنَا ٱلْأَحْدَاثُ وَٱلنُّوَبُ

٣،٣٦ وكان محمّد بن حازم أحد الشعراء المطبوعين يجيد كلّ فنّ يركبه ويأتي بالمعاني التي تستغلق على غيره وكان أكثر شعره في القناعة ومدح التصوّن وذمّ الحرص والطمع.

---

١ الأصل: بيرحوى.

The Monastery of Kaskar

This is a monastery below Wāsiṭ, lying to the east of it in the village called Barjūnī. It is large and imposing, well and solidly built, and surrounded by numerous cells. Each cell belongs to a monk, and they exchange them as the monks do the cells in Qunnā's Monastery. Round it are many gardens with trees, palms, and all kinds of fruit. It is visited by men of refinement, who have a good time, and by men experiencing grief, who find solace there. 36.1

Muḥammad ibn Ḥāzim composed this poem about it: he had visited it when al-Ḥasan ibn Sahl was residing at Wāsiṭ and he went to recite a panegyric to him. Their story will be told after the poetry: 36.2

Fine pleasure and music Wāsiṭ's Convent
offered, memories, songs, and toasts;
A company devoted to the cup,
giving their due to those weaned on the glass,
Spending all they had on revelry,
surrendering wealth and gains;
Protective: if you sought their help, they gave it;
generous: if you asked for a gift, you received it.
My companions they were, noble lords,
well born, the cultured sons of noble fathers.
We reveled in the convent's gardens—
gardens that drowned us in music and pleasure.
The flowers laughed as the setting stars wept,
while the flute played joyfully and music filled the air.
The cup revolved slowly in pleasure's firmament,
and we were its poles as it revolved.
Destiny had averted its eyes from us,
and so we feared no reversal or blow.

Muḥammad ibn Ḥāzim was a naturally gifted poet who excelled in every genre he practiced. He employed images and motifs that others did not 36.3

وذكر محمّد بن حازم هذا قال عرضت لي حاجة في عسكر الحسن بن سهل فأتيته وقد كنت قلت في السفينة شعرًا فدخلت إلى محمّد بن سعيد بن سالم الباهليّ فانتسبت فعرفني وأنزلني وأكرم مثواي ثمّ قال لي ما قلت في الأمير قلت لم أقل بعد شيئًا. فقال رجل كان معي في السفينة بلى قد قال أبياتًا فسألني أن أنشده إيّاها فأنشدته

وَقَالُوا لِي مَدَحْتَ فَتًى كَرِيمًا فَقُلْتُ وَكَيْفَ لِي بِفَتًى كَرِيمِ
بَلَوْتُ ٱلنَّاسَ مُذْ خَمْسِينَ[1] عَامًا وَحَسْبُكَ بِٱلْمُجَرِّبِ مِنْ عَلِيمِ
فَمَا أَحَدٌ يُعَدُّ لِيَوْمِ خَيْرٍ وَلَا أَحَدٌ يَعُودُ عَلَى حَمِيمِ
وَيُعْجِبُنِي ٱلْفَتَى وَأَظُنُّ خَيْرًا فَأَكْشِفُ مِنْهُ عَنْ رَجُلٍ لَئِيمِ
تَقَبَّلَ بَعْضُهُمْ بَعْضًا فَأَضْحَوْا بَنِي أَبَوَيْنِ قَدًّا مِنْ أَدِيمِ
فَطَافَ ٱلنَّاسُ بِٱلْحَسَنِ بْنِ سَهْلٍ طَوَافَهُمُ بِزَمْزَمَ وَٱلْحَطِيمِ
وَقَالُوا سَيِّدًا[2] يُعْطِي جَزِيلًا وَيَكْشِفُ كُرْبَةَ ٱلرَّجُلِ ٱلْكَظِيمِ
فَقُلْتُ مَضَى بِذَمِّ ٱلْقَوْمِ شِعْرِي وَقَدْ يُؤْتَى ٱلْبَرِيءُ مِنَ ٱلسَّقِيمِ
وَمَا خَبَرٌ تُرَجِّمُهُ ظُنُونٌ بِأَشْفَى مِنْ مُعَايَنَةِ ٱلْحَكِيمِ
فَإِنْ يَكُ مَا تَنَشَّرَ عَنْهُ حَقًّا رَجَعْتُ بِأُهْبَةِ ٱلرَّجُلِ ٱلْمُقِيمِ
وَإِنْ يَكُ غَيْرَ ذَاكَ حَمِدْتُ رَبِّي وَزَالَ ٱلشَّكُّ عَنْ رَجُلٍ حَلِيمِ
وَلَيْسَ ٱلْمَالُ يَعْطِفُنِي عَلَيْهِ وَلَٰكِنَّ ٱلْكَرِيمَ أَخُو ٱلْكَرِيمِ

١ الأصل: خمسون. ٢ كذا في الأصل.

understand. Most of his poetry was on contentment with one's lot or in praise of the virtuous life and condemnation of greed and ambition.

He himself told the following story: I went to al-Ḥasan ibn Sahl's camp because I had some business there. On the boat going there I composed some verses, so when I arrived I went to see Muḥammad ibn Saʿīd ibn Sālim al-Bāhilī.[202] I introduced myself, and when he realized who I was, he gave me a lodging and treated me well. He asked me, "What verses have you composed about the prince?" "I haven't composed anything yet." But a man who was on the boat with me butted in: "Oh yes, he has composed a poem." Muḥammad asked me to recite it, and I did so:

They asked, "Have you ever praised a man of nobility?"
  I answered, "Where can I find such a man?"
For fifty long years I've tried out people,
  and you know experience is the best teacher.
No one can be relied on when things go well;
  no one bestows favors on relatives.
I may like a man and think highly of him,
  but then I discover he's base and mean.
Some people throw their arms around each other
  and become brothers, chips off the same block.
Pilgrims circle around al-Ḥasan ibn Sahl
  as they do round Ḥaṭīm and Zamzam's well.[203]
They say, "A chief who's openhanded,
  relieving the sorrow of those who conceal it."
And I, "My verses have always been lampoons,
  but what's sick may produce something healthy.
No hearsay arising from suspicions
  is more effective than a wise man's witness.
If what's told of him is true, I'll receive
  the help of a man who sets things right.
If it turns out otherwise, I'll praise my Lord,
  and a man of insight will have lost his doubts.
Wealth will not make me turn to him,
  but one noble man is another noble's brother."

فلمّا أنشدته الشعر قال بمثل هذا تلقى الأمير والله لو كان نظيرك لما جاز لك أن ٤،٣٦
تخاطبه بهذا. قلت صدقت ولذلك قلت إنّي لم أمدحه. ولكنّي سأمدحه مدحة تشبهه. قال افعل. ودخل إلى الحسن فأخبره الخبر وأنشده الشعر وعجبه من جودة البيت الأخير. فأمر بإدخالي عليه لغير مدح. فأُدخلت فأمرني أن أنشده الشعر فاستعفيته فلم يُعفني وقال قد قنعت بهذا العذر إذ لم تدخلني في جملة من ذممت ومع هذا فعلينا حسن مكافأتك فأنشدته فضحك وقال ويحك ما لك وللناس تعمّهم بالهجاء حسبك الآن من هذا النمط وأبق عليهم فقلت قد وهبتهم للأمير قال قد قبلت وأنا أطالبك بالوفاء مطالبة من أهديت له هديّة فقبلها ثمّ وصلني فأجزل.

فقلت فيه وأنشدته ٥،٣٦

وَهَبْتُ ٱلْقَوْمَ لِلْحَسَنِ بْنِ سَهْلٍ فَعَوَّضَنِي ٱلْجَزِيلَ مِنَ ٱلثَّوَابِ
وَقَالَ دَعِ ٱلْهِجَاءَ وَقُلْ جَمِيلاً فَإِنَّ ٱلْقَصْدَ أَقْرَبُ لِلصَّوَابِ
فَقُلْتُ لَهُ بَرِئْتُ إِلَيْكَ مِنْهُمْ فَلَيْتَهُمُ بِمُنْقَطِعِ ٱلتُّرَابِ
وَلَوْلَا نِعْمَةُ ٱلْحَسَنِ بْنِ سَهْلٍ عَلَيَّ لَسُمْتُهُمْ سُوءَ ٱلْعَذَابِ
أَكِيدُهُمُ مُكَايَدَةَ ٱلْأَعَادِي وَأَخْتِلُهُمْ مُخَاتَلَةَ ٱلذِّئَابِ
وَمَا مُسِخُوا كِلَاباً غَيْرَ أَنِّي رَأَيْتُ ٱلْقَوْمَ أَشْبَاهَ ٱلْكِلَابِ

فضحك ثمّ قال ويلك الساعة ابتدأت بهجائهم وما أفلتوا منك بعد فقلت هذه بقيّة طفت على قلبي وأنا كافّ عنهم ما أبقى الله الأمير.

When I recited his poem to him, he said, "Is this the kind of poetry you will confront the prince with? By God, it wouldn't be suitable for you to address him like this even if he were your equal." "That's right," I said, "and that's why I said that I hadn't composed a eulogy. But I'll produce a panegyric appropriate to him." "Do so," said Muḥammad ibn Saʿīd. 36.4

Then he went in to see al-Ḥasan and told him the story, reciting the poem and pointing out how good the last verse was. Al-Ḥasan ordered that I be admitted, but without praising him. So I was allowed in and he ordered me to recite the poem. I asked to be excused, but he did not agree, saying, "Since you haven't included me among the people you've cursed, I accept your excuse. All the same, you deserve a good reward from me." So I recited him the poem and he laughed, saying, "Damn it, what's your problem with people? You make them all targets of your lampoons. Enough of that. Let them live!" I replied, "I'll grant the prince their lives." "I accept. And as someone to whom you've made a gift, which he has accepted, I demand you keep faith." And he rewarded me generously.

Then I composed this poem, which I recited to him: 36.5

I granted men's lives to al-Ḥasan ibn Sahl,
    and generous was his reward.
"Leave satire," he said, "and speak fair.
    That way you're close to the mark."
And I, "I've given them to you.
    Would that they lay in an abyss.
But for al-Ḥasan's favor to me,
    I'd mete them out a horrid punishment,
With the stratagems of a foe,
    creeping up on them like a wolf.
They haven't been transformed
    into dogs, but that's how they look."

He laughed. "Damn you, you've started to lampoon them immediately. They haven't escaped you yet." I answered, "This is the last thing I had in my heart. Now, while God grants life to the prince, I won't attack them again."

قال وكان محمّد بن حازم قد نسك وترك شرب النبيذ فدخل يوماً على إبراهيم بن شكلة ٦،٣٦
فحادثه وأكل معه وجلس إبراهيم للشرب وسأله أن يشرب معه فامتنع وقال

أَبَعْدَ خَمْسِينَ أَصْبُو   وَٱلشَّيْبُ لِلْجَهْلِ حَرْبُ
سِنٌّ وَشَيْبٌ وَجَهْلٌ   أَمْرٌ لَعَمْرُكَ صَعْبُ
يَا ٱبْنَ ٱلْإِمَامِ فَهَلَّا   أَيَّامُ عُودِي رَطْبُ
وَشَيْبُ رَأْسِي قَلِيلٌ   وَمَنْهَلُ ٱلْحُبِّ عَذْبُ
وَإِذْ سِهَامِي صِيَابٌ   وَنَصْلُ سَيْفِي عَضْبُ
وَإِذْ شِفَاءُ ٱلْغَوَانِي   مِنِّي حَدِيثٌ وَقُرْبُ
فَٱلْآنَ لَمَّا رَأَى بِي   ٱلْعُذَّالُ مَا قَدْ أَحَبُّوا
وَآنَسَ ٱلرُّشْدَ مِنِّي   قَوْمٌ أُعَابُ وَأَصْبُو
آلَيْتُ أَشْرَبُ كَأْسًا   مَا حَجَّ لِلّٰهِ رَكْبُ

وذكرحمدان بن يحيى قال آخرما فارقت عليه محمّد بن حازم أنّه قال لي لم يبق عليّ ٧،٣٦
شيء من اللذّات إلّا بيع السنانير. فقلت له أسخن الله عينك أيش لك في بيع
السنانير قال تجيني العجوز الرعناء تخاصمني وتقول هذا سنوري سُرق منّي فأقول لها
كذبتِ ثمّ تشتمني وأشتمها وتخاصمني وأخاصمها. قال وأنشدني

صِلْ خَمْرَةً بِخُمَارٍ   وَصِلْ خُمَارًا بِخَمْرِ
وَخُذْ بِحَظِّكَ مِنْهَا   زَادًا إِلَى حَيْثُ تَدْرِي

فقلت إلى أين فقال إلى الهاوية يا رقيع.

After Muḥammad ibn Ḥāzim had embraced asceticism and renounced wine, he presented himself one day at Ibrāhīm ibn Shaklah's.[204] They talked and ate together, and then Ibrāhīm settled down to drink. He asked Muḥammad to join him but he declined, saying: 36.6

At over fifty, should I behave like a boy?
   White hair's the enemy of folly.
Believe me, old age, white hair,
   and folly don't make good partners.
Son of the Imam, tell me,
   will the fresh days of yore come back,
When my hair was scarcely gray
   and the source of love ran sweet,
When my arrows found their mark
   and my blade was keen,
And the company and chatter
   of young beauties was balm to my heart?
Now, when my behavior finds
   approval with the critics,
And they've gotten used to my wisdom,
   should I earn blame with folly?
I've sworn never to drink wine
   as long as pilgrims ride to Mecca.

Ḥamdān ibn Yaḥyā[205] related: The last time I saw Muḥammad ibn Ḥāzim, he said, "Selling cats is the only pleasure I have left in life." "May God afflict you! What pleasure can you have in selling cats?" "I like it when a stupid old woman argues with me and says, 'This is my cat, which was stolen from me.' I say, 'Liar!' She curses me, I curse her back; she argues with me and I with her." 36.7

And he recited to me:

Put wine and a tavern together,
   a tavern keeper and wine;
Take your share as supplies
   for where you decide to go.

"Where's that?" I asked. "The bottomless pit, you idiot."

ومن مليح شعره قوله ٨،٣٦

أَيَا ٱبْنَ سَعِيدٍ جُزْتَ بِي غَايَةَ ٱلْبِرِّ وَحَمَّلْتَنِي مَا لَا أُطِيقُ مِنَ ٱلشُّكْرِ
وَإِنَّ ٱمْرَءًا أَعْطَاكَ مَجْهُودَ شُكْرِهِ وَفُتَّ وَلَمْ يَبْلُغْ مَدَاكَ لَفِي عُذْرِ
تُقَلَّبُ حَالٌ لِلْفَتَى بَعْدَ حَالَةٍ وَتَبْقَى أَيَادٍ حُرَّةٌ لِفَتًى حُرِّ

ومن جيّد شعره قوله

وَإِنِّي لَذُو وُدٍّ لِمَنْ دَامَ وُدُّهُ وَجَافٍ لِمَنْ رَامَ ٱلْجَفَاءَ مَلُولُ
وَإِنَّ ٱمْرَءًا يَأْوِي إِلَى دَارِ ذِلَّةٍ تَعَبَّدَهُ فِيهَا ٱلرَّجَاءُ ذَلِيلُ
وَفِي ٱلْيَأْسِ مِنْ ذُلِّ ٱلْمَطَامِعِ رَاحَةٌ وَفِي ٱلنَّاسِ مِمَّنْ لَا تُحِبُّ بَدِيلُ

وقال في القناعة ٩،٣٦

ٱللهَ أَحْمَدُ شَاكِرًا فَبَلَاؤُهُ حَسَنٌ جَمِيلُ
أَصْبَحْتُ مَسْتُورًا مُعَا فًى بَيْنَ أَنْعُمِهِ أَجُولُ
خِلْوًا مِنَ ٱلْأَحْزَانِ خِفَّ ٱلظَّهْرِ يُقْنِعُنِي ٱلْقَلِيلُ
لَمْ يُشْقِنِي طَمَعٌ وَلَا حِرْصٌ وَلَا أَمَلٌ طَوِيلُ
سِيَّانِ عِنْدِي ذُو ٱلْغِنَى ٱلْمِتْلَافُ وَٱلرَّجُلُ ٱلْبَخِيلُ
وَنَفَيْتُ بِٱلْيَأْسِ ٱلْمُنَى عَنِّي فَطَابَ لِيَ ٱلْمَقِيلُ
وَٱلنَّاسُ كُلُّهُمُ لِمَنْ خَفَّتْ مَؤُونَتُهُ خَلِيلُ

قال محمّد بن حازم بعث إليّ بعض الطاهريّة وكنت قد بالغت في هجوه وأفرطت بألف ١٠،٣٦
درهم وتخت ثياب وقال أما ما قد مضى فلا سبيل إلى ردّه ولكنّي أحبّ ألّا تزيد عليه

Here is one of his good poems: 36.8

You've been more than generous with me, Ibn Saʿīd,
and loaded me with a huge burden of thanks;
A man can be excused if he gives you
all the gratitude he can, but it still falls short.
Circumstances may change from one day to the next,
but noble favors from a man of honor live on.

And this is an excellent piece:

I show affection to those whose love is lasting;
indifferent, I cold-shoulder those who snub me.
To enter the abode of ignominy,
a slave to hope, is to be mortified.
Renounce the yoke of ambition, find rest.
When you don't like someone, you can find someone else.

This poem is about contentment with one's lot: 36.9

I praise and give thanks to God,
for His blessings are many and fine,
My needs are taken care of.
Protected, I go from favor to favor,
Free from sorrows, lighthearted,
contented with very little,
Untroubled by ambition,
avarice, or far-fetched hope.
The rich spendthrift
and the miser to me are alike.
I've banished desires with despair;
taking rest agrees with me.
When a man lives on little,
everyone's his friend.

Muḥammad ibn Ḥāzim related the following: After I'd lampooned a member of the Ṭāhirid family ferociously, he sent me a thousand dirhams and a set of clothes with the message: "What's past is past and cannot be recalled. But I'd 36.10

شيئاً. فرددت الدراهم والثياب وكتبت إليه

لَا أَلْبَسُ ٱلنَّعْمَاءَ مِنْ رَجُلٍ   أَلْبَسْتُهُ عَارًا عَلَى ٱلدَّهْرِ

ثمّ أمسكت عن هجائه.

قال وكان سعيد بن مسعود القطربّليّ صديقاً لي فسألته حاجة فردّني عنها ١١،٣٦
فانقطعت عنه فبعث إليّ بألف درهم وترضّاني فرددتها وكتبت إليه

مُتَسِّعُ ٱلصَّدْرِ رَحِيبٌ لِمَا   يَضِيقُ عَنْهُ ٱلْحُوَّلُ ٱلْقُلَّبُ
رَاجِعَ بِٱلْعُتْبَى فَأَعْتَبْتُهُ   وَرُبَّمَا أَعْتَبَكَ ٱلْمُذْنِبُ
أَجَلْ وَفِى ٱلدَّهْرِ عَلَى أَنَّهُ   مُوَكَّلٌ بِٱلْبَيْنِ مُسْتَعْتَبُ
سُقْيًا وَرُعْيًا لِزَمَانٍ مَضَى   عَنِّي وَسَهْمُ ٱلشَّامِتِ ٱلْأَخْيَبُ
قَدْ جَاءَنِي مِنْكَ مُوَيْلٌ فَلَمْ   أَعْرِضْ لَهُ وَٱلْحُرُّ لَا يَكْذِبُ
أَخْذِيَ مَالًا مِنْكَ بَعْدَ ٱلَّذِي   أَوْلَيْتَنِيهِ مَرْكَبٌ يَصْعُبُ
أَنِفْتُ أَنْ أَشْرَبَ عِنْدَ ٱلرِّضَا   وَٱلسُّخْطِ إِلَّا مَشْرَبًا يَعْذُبُ
أَعَزَّنِي ٱلْيَأْسُ وَأَغْنَى فَمَا   أَرْجُو سِوَى ٱللهِ وَلَا أَرْهَبُ
قَارُونُ عِنْدِي فِي ٱلْغِنَى مُعْدِمٌ   وَهِمَّتِي مَا فَوْقَهَا مَذْهَبُ
فَأَيُّ هَاتَيْنِ تَرَانِي بِهَا   أَصْبُو إِلَى مَالِكَ أَوْ أَرْغَبُ

ومن شعره في القناعة قوله ١٢،٣٦

rather you did not carry on with such attacks." I sent back the dirhams and the clothes with this verse:

I'll not wear the clothes of a man
  whom I've clothed in shame for eternity.

Then I stopped lampooning him.

Saʿīd ibn Masʿūd al-Quṭrabbulī was a friend of mine. I requested something 36.11
from him and he refused me, so I broke off relations. Then he sent me a thousand dirhams to placate me but I sent them back with this poem:

A greathearted generous man,
  abhorred by the fickle and inconstant,
Changed his mind to please me—
  at times an offense makes you see reason—
Ever faithful through forced separation,
  and when I asked him to relent.
Ah, for the memory of a time gone by
  when the gloater drew the short straw.
You've sent me a paltry sum,
  but I've not touched it—
  a noble man does not lie—
To accept your money
  after how you treated me
Is a course too hard to follow.
Whether anger flares or contentment ensues,
  I'll only partake of what's pleasant.
Despair has given me riches and strength,
  I hope in God; I've no fear of Him.
For all his wealth, in my eyes
  Qārūn[206] has nothing,
No road rises beyond my ambition.
So, what do you think my state of mind is?
Do I yearn for your money or reject it?

Here is one of his poems on contentment: 36.12

مَنْ أَعْمَلَ ٱلْيَأْسَ كَانَ ٱلْيَأْسُ جَاعِلَهُ   مُعَظَّماً أَبَداً فِي أَعْيُنِ ٱلنَّاسِ
وَمَنْ رَمَاهُمْ بِعَيْنِ ٱلطَّامِعِينَ رَأَى   ذُلًّا وَحَسُّوهُ مُرَّ ٱلْمَنْعِ فِي كَاسِ
ٱلْيَأْسُ خَيْرٌ وَمَا لِلْيَأْسِ مِنْ ثَمَرٍ   هَاتِ ٱمْرَءاً ذَلَّ بَعْدَ ٱلْيَأْسِ لِلنَّاسِ

وقال في هذا المعنى

جَعَلْتُ مَطِيَّةَ ٱلْآمَالِ يَأْساً   فَآوَانِي إِلَى كَنَفٍ وَدِيعِ
فَتِلْكَ مَطِيَّةُ ٱلْآمَالِ غُفْلٌ   بِلَا رَحْلٍ يُشَدُّ وَلَا نُسُوعِ
لَعَمْرُكَ لَلْقَلِيلُ أَصُونُ وَجْهِي   بِهِ فِي ٱلْأَوْحَدِينَ وَفِي ٱلْجَمِيعِ
أَحَبُّ إِلَيَّ مِنْ طَلَبِي كَثِيراً   تُمَدُّ إِلَيْهِ أَعْنَاقُ ٱلْخُضُوعِ
فَعِشْ بِٱلْقُوتِ يَوْماً بَعْدَ يَوْمٍ   كَمَصِّ ٱلطِّفْلِ فِيقَاتِ ٱلضُّرُوعِ
وَلَا تَرْغَبْ إِلَى أَحَدٍ بِحِرْصٍ   رَفِيعٍ فِي ٱلْأَنَامِ وَلَا وَضِيعِ
وَقَدْ رَحَلَ ٱلشَّبَابُ وَحَلَّ شَيْبٌ   فَهَلْ لَكَ مِنْ شَبَابِكَ مِنْ رُجُوعِ

١٣،٣٦ قال محمد بن حازم دخلت على المأمون فلمّا مثلت بين يديه قال كيف بصرك بأيّام الناس وأخبار العرب قلت أنا على الميدان فليطلق من عناني. قال أنشد ما بدا لك. فتركت ما أومأ إليه وعملت في صلاح شأني وقلت مجلس خلافة ولست آمن نبوة فأنشدته

رُزِقْتُ عَقْلاً وَلَمْ أُرْزَقْ مُرُوءَتَهُ   وَمَا ٱلْمُرُوءَةُ إِلَّا كَثْرَةُ ٱلْمَالِ
إِذَا أَرَدْتُ مُسَامَاةً تَقَاعَدَ بِي   عَمَّا يُنَوِّهُ بِٱسْمِي رِقَّةُ ٱلْحَالِ

When a man adopts despair, despair will make him
a great man forever in people's eyes.
While he who approaches them with requests
will drink from humiliation's bitter cup.
Despair is best, though it bears no fruit;
a man who expects nothing is never brought low.

And on the same theme:

I've loaded my hopes on the mount of despair,
and it's brought me to a haven of calm.
That mount bears no owner's brand;
it carries no saddle, no straps fasten its load.
I swear, the little I need to preserve my repute
whether I'm with few or among a crowd,
Has my favor. I'd rather not seek for wealth
at which the lowly will crane their necks.
Take your food as it comes, day by day,
just as the suckling seeks milk in the breast.
Pin no hopes, request no favors
from anyone, high or low.
Youth has departed, gray hair's appeared;
do you think your youth will come again?

Muḥammad ibn Ḥāzim also recounted: I was admitted to al-Ma'mūn's presence, and when I appeared before him, he asked, "How do you see the course of destiny and the Arabs' past?" "I'm lined up to race," I replied, "so give the signal for me to be off." Then he said, "Recite what you think fit." But, ignoring his suggestion, I decided to act in my own interest, thinking that this was a caliphal audience and I couldn't be sure something disagreeable wouldn't happen. So I recited to him: **36.13**

I was given a mind, but wasn't given nobility,
because nobility comes only with wealth.
If I want to rise up in the world, I'm held back
from a great reputation by my slender means.

قال المأمون الشيخ يشكو رقّة الحال فليُدفع إليه ألف درهم وتبسّم فقلت ما وراء التبسّم إلّا خير فأنشدته

أَنْتَ سَمَاءٌ وَيَدِي أَرْضُهَا   وَٱلْأَرْضُ قَدْ تَأْمُلُ غَيْثَ ٱلسَّمَا
فَٱزْرَعْ يَداً عِنْدِي مَحْمُودَةً   تَحْصُدْ بِهَا فِي ٱلنَّاسِ حُسْنَ ٱلثَّنَا

١٤،٣٦ قال هذا المعنى أقوى من الأوّل وأمر لي بألفي درهم ثمّ قال خدعتني قلت قد حضرني بيتان في الخديعة فقال وما هما فأنشدته

وَإِذَا ٱلْكَرِيمُ أَتَيْتَهُ بِخَدِيعَةٍ   فَرَأَيْتَهُ فِيمَا تَرُومُ يُسَارِعُ
فَٱعْلَمْ بِأَنَّكَ لَمْ تُخَادِعْ جَاهِلاً   إِنَّ ٱلْكَرِيمَ بِفِعْلِهِ يَتَخَادَعُ

فقال هما والله أحسن من الأوّل وأمر لي بمثل ما أمر به وسألني أن أنشده فأنشدته

لَا تَرْهَقَنَّكَ ضَجْرَةٌ مِنْ سَائِلٍ   فَلَخَيْرُ دَهْرِكَ أَنْ تُرَى مَسْؤُولَا
لَا تَجْبَهَنْ بِٱلْمَنْعِ وَجْهَ مُؤَمِّلٍ   فَبَقَاءُ عِزِّكَ أَنْ تُرَى مَأْمُولَا
وَٱعْلَمْ بِأَنَّكَ عَنْ قَلِيلٍ صَائِرٌ[1]   خَبَراً فَكُنْ خَبَراً يَرُوقُ جَمِيلَا
يُلْقَى ٱلْكَرِيمُ فَيُسْتَدَلُّ بِبِشْرِهِ   وَتَرَى ٱلْعُبُوسَ عَلَى ٱللَّئِيمِ دَلِيلَا

فقال لله درّك ما أحسن معانيك. يا غلام صكّ له بمثل ما أعطيناه.

١٥،٣٦ وله من هذا الفنّ وغيره كلّ شيء حسن ولولا خروج الكتاب عن حدّه المرسوم وخوف الإطالة لأوردت من غرر شعره ومحاسنه ما يلتذّ به سامعه. وفيما أوردناه كفاية.

١ الأصل: صَائِرًا.

Al-Ma'mūn remarked, "The old man's complaining about his poverty. Let him be given a thousand dirhams," and he smiled. I thought to myself, "What's behind that smile of his just now?" And I declaimed:

You are the heaven, my hand is your earth,
 and the earth can hope for rain from the clouds.
Sow there a good seed of favors and gifts;
 you'll garner fine praise from the people around.

Al-Ma'mūn remarked, "This motif is more effective than the first one," 36.14
and he ordered me to be given two thousand dirhams. Then he said, "You've deceived me." I responded, "I've just thought of two verses about being deceived." "And what are they?" So I declaimed:

If you come with a lie to a generous man,
 and you see him hurry to fulfill your request,
Be sure you haven't really fooled a fool;
 he's pretending to be fooled to do your behest.

"They're both better than the first efforts," al-Ma'mūn said. He ordered me to be given the same as before and asked me to recite something else, so I did:

Don't let petitioners drive you crazy;
 to get requests is the best you could want.
Don't frown in the face of any hopeful;
 hopes pinned on you prove your worth.
Soon you'll be gone but people will talk of you.
 Make sure what they say is praise and honor;
The sign of a giver is his cheerful mien,
 a miser's betrayed by his gloom and frown.

Al-Ma'mūn was enthusiastic. "Well done! How well you develop this theme. Servant! Write him an order of payment for the same amount as we've given him."

Muḥammad ibn Ḥāzim composed excellent poetry on all kinds of themes. 36.15
If they had not taken up more space than the book foresees, I would have included gems of his poetry and anecdotes to delight their hearers. But what I have mentioned is enough.

ديارات مصر التي تقصد للشرب فيها والتنزّه بها فمنها

دير القصير

وهذا الدير في أعلى الجبل على سطح في قلّته وهو دير حسن البناء محكم الصنعة نزه البقعة فيه رهبان مقيمون به وله بئر منقورة في الحجر يُستقى الماء له منها وفي هيكله صورة مريم في حجرها صورة المسيح عليه السلام والناس يقصدون الموضع للنظر إلى هذه الصورة. وفي أعلاه غرفة بناها أبو الجيش خمارَويه بن أحمد بن طولون لها أربع طاقات إلى أربع جهات وكان كثير الغشيان لهذا الدير معجباً بالصورة التي فيه يشرب على النظر إليها. ١،٣٧

وفي الطريق إلى هذا الدير من جهة مصر صعوبة فأمّا من قِبْليّه فسهل الصعود والنزول وإلى جانبه صومعة لا تخلو من حبيس يكون فيها وهو مطلّ على القرية المعروفة بشهران وعلى الصحراء والبحر. وهذه القرية المذكورة قرية كبيرة عامرة على شاطئ البحر ويذكرون أنّ موسى صلّى الله عليه وُلد فيها ومنها ألقته أمّه إلى البحر في التابوت. ٢،٣٧

فدير القصير هذا أحد الديارات المقصودة لحسن موقعه وإشرافه على مصر وأعمالها. وقد قال فيه شعراء مصر وذكروا طيبه ونزهته ولأبي هريرة ابن أبي العصام فيه

كَمْ لِي بِدَيْرِ ٱلْقُصَيْرِ مِنْ قَصَفِ مَعْ كُلِّ ذِي صَبْوَةٍ وَذِي ظَرَفِ
لَهَوْتُ فِيهِ بِشَادِنٍ غَنِجٍ تَقْصُرُ عَنْهُ بَدَائِعُ ٱلْوَصَفِ

وقال فيه أيضاً

The Monasteries of Egypt That People Visit for Drink and Recreation

The Quṣayr[207] Monastery

This monastery stands high on the mountain,[208] on a terrace at the summit. It is well and solidly built and has a pleasant setting. There are monks living there, and it has a well hewn in the rock from which they draw water. In the altar[209] stands an icon of Mary with the image of Christ, peace be upon Him, on her lap, and people visit the place to look at it. Above it is a hall built by Abū l-Jaysh Khumārawayh ibn Aḥmad ibn Ṭūlūn, with four arches on the four sides. He used to visit this monastery often because he loved this icon, and he would sit drinking and looking at it. 37.1

From the city of Cairo, the monastery is hard to reach, but from the south the ascent and descent are easy. Beside it is a cell where there is always a hermit living. The monastery looks out over the village called Shahrān, the desert, and the Nile. Shahrān is a large, prosperous village on the banks of the Nile. They say it is where Moses, God bless him, was born and where his mother cast him into the Nile in a casket. 37.2

The Quṣayr Monastery attracts visitors because of its beautiful situation, looking out over Cairo and its surroundings. Egyptian poets have celebrated it, mentioning its beauty and the entertainment it offers. Here is Abū Hurayrah ibn Abī al-ʿIṣām:

What times I've had at Quṣayr's Convent,
 with friends of folly and distinction.
I had lots of fun with a coy young thing
 whose beauty defies description.

And this poem is also by him:

أَذْكَرْتَنِي يَا دَيْرُ مَنْ قَدْ مَضَى   مِنْ أَهْلِ وُدِّي وَمُصَافَاتِي
كَمْ كَانَ لِي فِيكَ وَفِيهِمْ مَعًا   مِنْ طِيبِ أَيَّامٍ وَلَيْلَاتِ
أَشْكُو إِلَى ٱللَّهِ مُصَابِي بِهِمْ   وَفَقْدَنَا أَهْلَ ٱلْمُرُوءَاتِ

ولمحمّد بن عاصم في هذا الدير ٣،٣٧

إِنَّ دَيْرَ ٱلْقُصَيْرِ هَاجَ ٱدِّكَارِي   لِهَوَ أَيَّامِيَ ٱلْحِسَانِ ٱلْقِصَارِ
وَزَمَانًا مَضَى حَمِيدًا سَرِيعًا   وَشَبَابًا مِثْلَ ٱلرِّدَاءِ ٱلْمُعَارِ
عَرَّفَتْنِي رُبُوعُهُ بَعْدَ نُكْرٍ   فَعَرَفْتُ ٱلرُّبُوعَ بِٱلْإِنْكَارِ
فَلَوَ ٱنَّ ٱلدِّيَارَ تَشْكُو ٱشْتِيَاقًا   لَشَكَتْ جَفْوَتِي وَبُعْدَ مَزَارِي
وَلَكَادَتْ نَحْوِي تَسِيرُ لِمَا قَدْ   كُنْتُ فِيهَا سَيَّرْتُ مِنْ أَشْعَارِي
فَكَأَنِّي إِذْ زُرْتُهُ بَعْدَ هَجْرٍ   لَمْ يَكُنْ مِنْ مَنَازِلِي وَدِيَارِي
إِذْ صُعُودِي عَلَى ٱلْجِيَادِ إِلَيْهِ   وَٱنْحِدَارِي فِي ٱلْمُعْنِقَاتِ ٱلْجَوَارِي
بِصُقُورٍ إِلَى ٱلدِّمَاءِ صَوَادٍ   وَكِلَابٍ عَلَى ٱلْوُحُوشِ ضَوَارِي
مَنْزِلًا لَسْتُ مُحْصِيًا مَا لِقَلْبِي   وَلِنَفْسِي فِيهِ مِنَ ٱلْأَوْطَارِ
مَنْزِلًا مِنْ عُلُوِّهِ كَسَمَاءٍ   وَٱلْمَصَابِيحُ حَوْلَهُ كَٱلدَّرَارِي
وَكَأَنَّ ٱلرُّهْبَانَ فِي ٱلشَّعَرِ ٱلْأَسْوَدِ سُودُ ٱلْغِرْبَانِ فِي ٱلْأَوْكَارِ
غَرْبُهُ ذُو ٱلْبِحَارِ وَٱلْأَنْهَارِ   فِي ثِيَابٍ مِنْ سُنْدُسٍ ذِي ٱخْضِرَارِ
غَرَّدَتْ بَيْنَهَا[1] ٱلطُّيُورُ فَطَارَتْ   بِفُؤَادِ ٱلْمُتَيَّمِ ٱلْمُسْتَطَارِ
كَمْ خَلَعْتُ ٱلْعِذَارَ فِيهِ وَلَمْ أَرْ   عَ مَشِيبًا بِمَفْرِقِي وَعِذَارِي

[1] الأصل: بيننا.

You remind me, cloister, of those passed away,
 people I loved and felt good with;
How many splendid nights and days
 I spent with them in your grounds.
I lament to God of what befell me
 when I lost those noble companions.

Muḥammad ibn ʿĀṣim composed a poem on this monastery: 37.3

Quṣayr's Monastery has aroused my memories
 of fine days of pleasure,
A blessed time too quickly gone,
 my youth like a borrowed gown.
It left its mark on me forever,
 and I knew the place after I'd denied it.
If places would complain from longing,
 it would say I'd gone off and shunned it.
It almost set out to find me
 because I'd put it in so many verses,
But when I visited it after an absence,
 I felt I'd never been in its houses,
When I rode up to it on a good mount,
 then came down through a series of passes,
With falcons thirsty for blood, and hounds
 who'd been trained for the chase.
It's a place where my heart and soul
 have more desires than I'll ever tell.
Buildings as high as the heavens,
 lit by lights shining like pearls,
The monks in their coarse black habits,
 like crows in their lofty nest,
To the west a land of rivers and streams,
 a cloth of green silk spread like brocade.
The birds warbled, stealing the lover's
 volatile heart in flight;
How often did I let myself go, heedless
 of threads of gray on my head or beard;

كَمْ شَرِبْنَا عَلَى ٱلتَّصَاوِيرِ فِيهِ   بِصِغَارٍ مَحْثُوثَةٍ وَكِبَارِ
صُورَةٌ مِنْ مُصَوِّرٍ فِيهِ ظَلَّتْ   فِتْنَةً لِلْقُلُوبِ وَٱلْأَبْصَارِ
أَطْرَبَتْنَا بِغَيْرِ شَدْوٍ فَأَغْنَتْ   عَنْ سَمَاعِ ٱلْعِيدَانِ وَٱلْمِزْمَارِ
يَفْتُرُ ٱلْجِسْمُ حِينَ تَرْمِيهِ حُسْنًا   بِفُنُونٍ مِنْ طَرْفِهَا ٱلسَّحَّارِ
وَإِشَارَاتِهَا إِلَى مَنْ رَآهَا   بِخُضُوعٍ وَذِلَّةٍ وَٱنْكِسَارِ
لَا وَحُسْنِ ٱلْعَيْنَيْنِ وَٱلشَّفَةِ ٱللَّمْيَاءِ مِنْهَا وَخَدِّهَا ٱلْجُلَّنَارِي
لَا تَخَلَّفْتُ عَنْ مَزَارِي لِدَيْرٍ   هِيَ فِيهِ وَلَوْ نَأَى بِي مَزَارِي
فَٱقْصِرَا عَنْ مَلَامِيَ ٱلْيَوْمَ إِنِّي   غَيْرُ ذِي سَلْوَةٍ وَلَا إِقْصَارِ
فَسَقَى ٱللّٰهُ أَرْضَ حُلْوَانَ فَٱلنَّخْلَ فَدَيْرَ ٱلْقُصَيْرِ صَوْبَ ٱلْقِطَارِ[1]
كَمْ تَنَبَّهْتُ مِنْ لَذَاذَةِ نَوْمِي   بِنَعِيرِ ٱلرُّهْبَانِ فِي ٱلْأَسْحَارِ
وَٱلنَّوَاقِيسُ صَائِحَاتٌ تُنَادِي   حَيَّ يَا نَائِمًا عَلَى ٱلِٱبْتِكَارِ
قَبْلَ أَنْ يُبْلِيَ ٱلْجَدِيدَ ٱلْجَدِيدَا   نِ بِلَيْلٍ مُعَاقِبٍ لِنَهَارِ
إِنَّمَا هٰذِهِ ٱلْحَيَاةُ عَوَارٍ   وَعَلَى ٱلْمُسْتَعِيرِ رَدُّ ٱلْمُعَارِ

٤،٣٧ ولابن الزنبقيّ المصريّ في دير القصير من شعر طويل

يَا حَسْرَةً فِي ٱلْقَلْبِ مَا أَقْتَلَهَا   كَأَنَّهَا فِي ٱلْقَلْبِ أَطْرَافُ ٱلْأَسَلْ
كَمْ كَمْ وَكَمْ مِنْ لَيْلَةٍ أَحْيَيْتُهَا   يَا صَاحِبِي بِٱلدَّيْرِ فِي خَيْرِ مَحَلّْ
دَيْرِ ٱلْقُصَيْرِ ٱلْفَرْدِ فِي صِفَاتِهِ   يَا مَنْ رَأَى ٱلْجَنَّةَ فِي رَأْسِ جَبَلْ

١ الأصل: (العشار) وردت فوق هذه الكلمة.

How often we raised to its images
cups quickly drained, great and small.
An icon, the work of an artist,
utter delight for heart and eyes,
Enthralled us despite its silence.
We were deaf to lutes and oboes.
Our bodies grew weak from its beauty
as it gazed at us so bewitchingly,
Beckoning humbly to those who saw it,
meekly and in submission.
No! By the beauty of its eyes,
its delicate mouth, and rose-red cheeks,
I'll not stay away from its convent home,
though the journey to reach it is long.
Now, cut short your reproaches.
I'll not be consoled or silenced.
May God bless Ḥulwān, its palm trees,
and Quṣayr looking out on the caravans.
How often sweet sleep was broken
by the gruff chant of the monks at matins,
While the clappers loudly called,
"Come, you sleeper, to morning prayer,
Before the new day passes,
overtaken by a new night and day."
This life is on loan to us,
and he who borrows must repay.

Here is part of a long poem by the Egyptian Ibn al-Zanbaqī where he mentions the Quṣayr Monastery: 37.4

Alas! The grief in my heart
is killing me with the tips of lances!
How many, many nights we enlivened,
friend, in that convent, the best of places.
Quṣayr's Monastery, unique of its kind.
Whoever saw Paradise on a hilltop?

أَشْرَبُهَا رَاحًا شَمُولاً قَرْقَفًا ‏ ‏ تَدِبُّ فِي ٱلْجِسْمِ صَبَاحِي وَٱلْأُصُلْ
يُدِيرُهَا ذُو غُنُجٍ بِطَرْفِهِ ‏ ‏ يُحْيِي مَنْ شَاءَ وَمَنْ شَاءَ قَتَلْ
كَأَنَّهُ غُصْنٌ مِنَ ٱلْبَانِ وَقَدْ ‏ ‏ زَادَ عَلَيْهِ بِٱلْقَوَامِ ٱلْمُعْتَدِلْ
أَلْثَغُ حَتْفُ ٱلنَّاسِ فِي لُثْغَتِهِ ‏ ‏ تَاهَ بِهَا عَلَى ٱلْوَرَى تِيهَ مُدِلّْ
إِنْ قَالَ نَارٌ قَالَ نَاغٌ أَو يَقُلْ ‏ ‏ نُورٌ يَقُلْ نُوغٌ بِدَلٍّ وَغَزَلْ
وَضَرَبَ ٱلنَّاقُوسَ فِيهِ رَاهِبٌ ‏ ‏ ضَرْبًا عَلَى رَيْثٍ وَضَرْبًا بِعَجَلْ
فَٱحْثُثْ كُؤُوسَ ٱلرَّاحِ يَا سَاقِيَنَا ‏ ‏ وَٱغْتَنِمِ ٱلدَّهْرَ فَلِلدَّهْرِ دُوَلْ
مِنْ قَبْلِ أَنْ يَطْرُقَنَا بَيْنٌ فَلَا ‏ ‏ يَنْفَعُ عِنْدَ ٱلْبَيْنِ لَيْتٌ وَلَعَلّْ

دير مرحنّا

وهذا الدير على شاطئ بركة الحبش قريب من البحر وإلى جانبه بساتين أنشأ بعضها الأمير تميم أخو أمير المؤمنين العزيز بالله عليهما السلام ومجلس على عمد حسن البناء مليح الصنعة مصوَّر أنشأه الأمير تميم أيضاً. وبقرب هذا الدير بئر تُعرف ببئر نجاتيّ عليها جميّزة يجتمع الناس إليها ويشربون عندها. فهذا الموضع من مواضع اللعب ومواطن اللّهو والطرب نزه في أيّام النيل وزيادته وامتلاء البركة حسن المنظر نزه البقاع وكذلك في أيّام الزرع والنوّار. ولا يكاد يخلو من المتطرّحين والمتنزّهين. ١،٣٨

وقد ذكرت الشعراء حسنه وطيبه ولابن عاصم فيه ٢،٣٨

I've drunk wine there so cold it sends
  shivers through the body night and morn,
Poured by a coquettish boy
  who can kill you or make you reborn.
He's like a slender branch,
  but lovelier because better balanced.
His guttural *r*'s drive men crazy
  and he proudly shows them off,
With "fighe" for "fire" and "lyghe"
  for "lyre," such coquetry and charm.
A monk has plied the clappers on him,
  now quickly, then taking his time.
Hurry, cupbearer, fill the cups,
  let's enjoy the moment while fate smiles,
Before we're forced to part,
  and "perhaps" or "if only" are in vain.

The Monastery of Mār Ḥannā (Saint John)

This monastery stands on the banks of the pool known as the Ethiopians' Pool, close to the Nile. It is flanked by gardens, some of which were laid out by Prince Tamīm, the brother of the Commander of the Faithful al-ʿAzīz bi-llāh, peace be upon them both. He also put up a meeting room on columns, well built, of fine craftsmanship and decorated with frescoes. Near the monastery is a well, known as Najātī's Well, under a sycamore tree, and people gather there to drink. It is a place where entertainment, revelry, and exquisite music-making happen, and it is delightful when the Nile rises and floods. When the pool floods, it is a beautiful sight in a lovely setting, as it is at seedtime and with spring blossoms. It is seldom without revelers and people seeking entertainment. 38.1

Poets have described its beauty and attractiveness, among them Ibn ʿĀṣim: 38.2

يَا طِيبَ أَيَّامٍ سَفَحْتُ مَعَ ٱلصِّبَى   طَوْعَ ٱلْهَوَى فِيهَا بِسَفْحِ ٱلْمَنْظَرِ
فَٱلْبِرْكَةُ ٱلْغَنَّاءُ فَٱلدَّيْرُ ٱلَّذِي   قَدْ هَاجَ فَرْطَ صَبَابَتِي وَتَفَكُّرِي
فَٱحْثُثْ كُؤُوسَكَ يَا غُلَامُ وَأَعْفِنِي   فَلَقَدْ سَكِرْتُ وَخَمْرُ طَرْفِكَ مُسْكِرِي
وَأَرَى ٱلثُّرَيَّا فِي ٱلسَّمَاءِ كَأَنَّهَا   تَاجٌ تَفَصَّلَ جَانِبَاهُ بِجَوْهَرِ
فَٱشْرَبْ عَلَى حُسْنِ ٱلرِّيَاضِ وَغَنِّنِي   أُنْظُرْ إِلَى ٱلسَّاقِي ٱلْأَغَنِّ ٱلْأَحْوَرِ
فَلَعَلَّ أَيَّامَ ٱلْحَيَاةِ قَلِيلَةٌ   وَلَعَلَّنِي قَدَّرْتُ مَا لَمْ يُقْدَرِ

وقال أيضاً ٣،٣٨

عَرِّجْ بِجُمَيْزَةِ ٱلْعَرْجَا مَطِيَّاتِي   بِسَفْحِ حُلْوَانَ فَٱلْمِمْ بِٱلتُّوَيْتَاتِ
وَٱلْمِمْ بِقَصْرِ ٱبْنِ بِسْطَامَ فَرُبَّتَمَا   سُعِدْتُ فِيهِ بِأَيَّامِي وَلَيْلَاتِي
وَٱقْرَأْ عَلَى دَيْرِ مَرْحَنَّا ٱلسَّلَامَ فَقَدْ   أَبْدَى تَذَكُّرُهُ مِنِّي صَبَابَاتِي
وَبِرْكَةُ ٱلْحَبَشِ ٱللَّاتِي بِبَهْجَتِهَا   أَدْرَكْتُ مَا شِئْتُ مِنْ لَهْوِي وَلَذَّاتِي
كَأَنَّ أَجْبَالَهَا مِنْ حَوْلِهَا سُحُبٌ   تَقَشَّعَتْ بَعْدَ قَطْرٍ عَنْ سَمَاوَاتِ
كَأَنَّ أَذْنَابَ مَا قَدْ كَانَ صِيدَ لَنَا   مِنْ أَبْرَمِيسَ وَرَايٍ بِٱلشُّبَيْكَاتِ
أَسِنَّةٌ خُضِبَتْ أَطْرَافُهَا بِدَمٍ   أَوْ دَسْتَجٌ نَزَعُوهُ مِنْ جِرَاحَاتِ
مَنَازِلًا كُنْتُ أَغْشَاهَا وَأَطْرُقُهَا   وَكُنَّ قِدْمًا مَوَاخِيرِي وَحَانَاتِي

وقال أيضاً ٤،٣٨

أَأَيَّامِي بِشَاطِي ٱلْبِرْكَتَيْنِ   سَقَاكِ ٱللهُ نَوْءَ ٱلْمِرْزَمَيْنِ
لَقَدْ أَذْكَرْتِنِي طَرَبِي وَلَهْوِي   وَوَكَّلْتِ ٱلْفُؤَادَ بِلَوْعَتَيْنِ
تُرَى أَيَّامُنَا فِيكِ ٱلْمَوَاضِي   يَعُودُ وِصَالُهَا مِنْ بَعْدِ بَيْنِ

How sweet the days I spent in my youth,
  obedient to love, gazing on beauty,
On that gorgeous garden and convent,
  which aroused my fervent longing and memories.
Quick, boy, fill the cups and forgive me.
  I'm drunk from the wine of your gaze.
The Pleiades in the sky
  are like a bejeweled crown.
Drink to the meadows' beauty! Sing!
  Gaze at the dark-eyed, sweet-voiced cupbearer.
Life's days may be few. But I may
  have foreseen something not predestined.

Here are two more poems of his: **38.3**

Turn aside at Najātī's sycamore by Ḥulwān's foot;
  make for the mulberry bushes,
For Ibn Bisṭām's palace. Often my days
  and nights there were happy.
Greet Mār Ḥannā's Convent.
  Memories of it arouse my longing,
And the lovely Ethiopians' Pool,
  where I had my fill of fun and pleasure.
The surrounding hills resembled
  clouds, scattered after rain;
The tails of the tilapia and perch when landed
  were lances, with bloodied points,
  or swords drawn from wounds.
These were places I visited,
  my brothels and taverns of old.

May God refresh with rain **38.4**
  my memories of days at the twin pools!
They recall ecstasy and fill
  my heart with longing—
Will the days spent there
  delight us again after separation?

سَقَى ٱللّٰهُ ٱلْبِقَاعَ مُلِثَّ قَطْرٍ وَأَعْطَشَ مَنْزِلاً بِٱلْجِلْهَتَيْنِ
وَطَلَّ ٱلطَّيْلَسَانَ بِصَوْبِ طَلٍّ إِلَى ٱلنَّخَلَاتِ فَٱلْجُمَّيْزَتَيْنِ
وَدَارَ عَلَى ٱلْمَدَارِ رِهَامُ مُزْنٍ تَسِيرُ إِلَى جِنَانِ ٱلسَّرْوَتَيْنِ
وَخَصَّ ٱلرَّبْوَتَيْنِ فَكَمْ غَزَالٍ رَبِيبٍ بَيْنَ تِلْكَ ٱلرَّبْوَتَيْنِ
مَنَازِلُ قَدْ شَهِدْنَا ٱللَّهْوَ فِيهَا بِأَكْرَمِ مَعْهَدَيْنِ وَمَأْلَفَيْنِ
وَكَمْ مِنْ بَيْعَةٍ عُقِدَتْ لِقَصْفٍ وَعَزْفٍ فِي رِيَاضِ ٱلْبُقْعَتَيْنِ
وَكَمْ مِنْ مُذْنِفٍ قَدْ حَازَ وَصْلاً وَنَالَ مُنَاهُ وَسْطَ ٱلْمُنْيَتَيْنِ

وللعبّاس بن البصريّ[1] من قصيدة ٥،٣٨

يَا حَامِلَ ٱلْكَأْسِ أَدِرْهَا وَٱسْقِنِي قَدْ ذَعَرَ ٱلشَّوْقُ فُؤَادِي فَٱنْذَعَرْ
أَمَا تَرَى ٱلْبِرْكَةَ مَا أَحْسَنَهَا إِذَا تَدَاعَى ٱلطَّيْرُ فِيهَا فَصَفَرْ
أَمَا تَرَى نُوَّارَهَا أَمَا تَرَى حُسْنَ مَسِيلِ مَائِهَا إِذَا ٱنْحَدَرْ
كَأَنَّمَا صُفْرُ ٱلدَّنَانِيرِ بِهَا مَبْذُولَةٌ لَيْسَ بِهَا مِنْ مُتَّجَرْ
كَأَنَّمَا ٱلْجَوْهَرُ فِي أَلْوَانِهَا نُثِّرَ فِي تِلْكَ ٱلنَّوَاحِي فَٱنْتَثَرْ
كَأَنَّمَا كَفُّ جَوَادٍ وَلَعَتْ فِي ذٰلِكَ ٱلرَّوْضِ بِتَبْدِيدِ ٱلْبِدَرْ
وَأَبْيَضُ ٱلنَّرْجِسِ فِي أَجْفَانِهِ دَمْعُ ٱلنَّدَى لَوْلَا ٱلتَّشَاجِي لَقَطَرْ
وَنَظْرَةُ ٱلْوَرْدِ إِلَى أَتْرَابِهِ نَظْرَةُ مَعْشُوقٍ بِلَحْظٍ مُنْكَسِرْ
دَعْنِي فَمَا أَهْلِكُ إِلَّا بِٱلْجَوَى مَا عِيشَةُ ٱلْعَاشِقِ إِلَّا فِي كَدَرْ

ولصالح بن موسى مولى بني تميم يذكر البركة ٦،٣٨

[1] الأصل: عبّاس بن البصريّ.

May God send it shower upon shower—
  and drought to the desert camp—
Watering the fields of flowers
  like brocade, the sycamores and palm trees.
Let it drizzle throughout the year,
  falling in the cypress gardens
And on the two hills where so many
  young gazelles have been raised.
We reveled in those places
  with the noblest allies and friends.
How many oaths were sworn
  to carouse and make music in the meadows;
How many wan lovers fulfilled
  their wish of meeting their beloveds.

This is part of a poem by Ibn al-ʿAbbās al-Baṣrī: 38.5

Fill the cup you bear and give me a drink,
  for longing has struck fear in my heart.
See how lovely the pool is
  when the birds round it sing to each other.
Look at its flowers, at its beauty,
  with the stream flowing downhill,
As though gold dinars had been strewn
  on its surface, beyond the merchant's grasp;
As though many-colored jewels
  had been scattered there and lay unclaimed,
As though an openhanded man
  reveled in sowing purses in that meadow.
The white narcissi have dewdrop tears
  in their lashes, held back in their grief.
The roses exchange lovers' glances,
  their eyes meekly lowered.
Leave me! Passion alone will kill me.
  A lover's life is truly one of sorrow.

Ṣāliḥ ibn Mūsā, the client of Banū Tamīm, composed this poem on the pool: 38.6

وَحَسْبُكَ ٱلْبِرْكَةُ مَرْأًى لَا يُمَلّ   تَبْذُلُ وَشْيًا لَمْ يَكُنْ بِمُبْتَذَلْ
مُتَّصِلَ ٱلْأَطْرَافِ غَيْرَ مُنْفَصِلْ   مِنْ شَاطِئِ ٱلنِّيلِ إِلَى سَفْحِ ٱلْجَبَلْ
أَكْرِمْ بِتِلْكَ مَنْزِلًا لِمَنْ نَزَلْ   قَدْ نَشِطَتْ أَطْيَارُهُ بَعْدَ ٱلْكَسَلْ
وَسَجَعَتْ وَرَجَعَتْ عَلَى مَهَلْ   بَيْنَ ٱلثَّقِيلِ وَٱلْخَفِيفِ وَٱلرَّمَلْ
كَأَنَّهُنَّ فِي مِرَاءٍ وَجَدَلْ   يَنُحْنَ لَا لِلْحُزْنِ لٰكِنْ لِلْجَذَلْ
يُذَكِّرْنَنَا أَيَّامَنَا ٱلْغُرَّ ٱلْأُوَلْ

٧،٣٨ وقال أيضاً يذكر الدير والبركة

إِنِّي لِمِثْلِكَ نَاصِحٌ   فَٱجْنَحْ إِلَيَّ وَلَا تَغُرْ
بَكِّرْ إِلَى دَيْرِ ٱلْمُعَا   فِرِ آنَ أَوْقَاتُ ٱلْبُكَرْ
أَوَمَا تَرَى حُسْنَ ٱلرِّيَا   ضِ وَمَا ٱكْتَسَيْنَ مِنَ ٱلزَّهَرْ
وَجْهُ ٱلرَّبِيعِ وَحَبَّذَا   وَجْهُ ٱلرَّبِيعِ إِذَا ظَهَرْ
ٱلْوَشْيُ يُنْشَرُ وَٱلْمَلَا   حِفُ وَٱلْمَطَارِفُ وَٱلْحِبَرْ
هٰذَا ٱلْبَنَفْسَجُ فِي ٱلْحِدَا   دِ بِغَيْرِ حُزْنٍ قَدْ ظَهَرْ
وَأَتَى ٱلْبَهَارُ بِصُفْرَةٍ   فَلِكُلِّ حُسْنٍ قَدْ بَهَرْ
وَكَأَنَّ آذَرْيُونَهُ   كَاسَاتُ خَمْرٍ تَبْتَدِرْ
وَكَأَنَّمَا ٱلْمَنْثُورُ عِقْدٌ فِي جَوَانِبِهِ ٱنْتَثَرْ
وَٱلْأُقْحُوَانُ فَضَاحِكٌ   عَنْ عَسْجَدٍ فِيهِ دُرَرْ
وَشَقَائِقُ ٱلنُّعْمَانِ كَٱلْأَعْلَامِ ثَمَّ[1] لِمَنْ نَظَرْ
وَتَوَرَّدَ ٱلْوَرْدُ ٱلذَّكِيُّ   وَفَاحَ مِسْكًا فِي ٱلسَّحَرْ
وَتَجَاوَبَتْ طَيْرُ ٱلْغُصُو   نِ بِكُلِّ لَحْنٍ مُشْتَهَرْ
فَمُغَرِّدٌ حَسَنُ ٱلْغِنَا   ءِ شَدَا وَآخَرُ قَدْ زَمَرْ
وَتَسَرَّقَتْ أَنْفَاسُنَا   بِنَسِيمِ أَنْفَاسِ ٱلسَّحَرْ

١ الأصل: ثُمّ.

The pool's a sight you never tire of,
Clad in unworn brocade.
Its edges run even and unbroken
From the banks of the Nile to the mountain.
What a splendid place to stop at.
The birds, idle for a while, are lively,
Warbling and cooing, unrushed,
In various rhythms, heavy and light,
As though engaging in dispute,
Plaintive not from sorrow but joy,
Reminding us of splendid days now past.

And this is a poem of his on the monastery and the pool: 38.7

I'll give you some advice, so listen and pay attention:
Go early to the Maʿāfir[210] Convent, it's time for a morning meeting.
Don't you see the lovely gardens clad in flowers,
The face of spring's revealed. Ah! The splendid face of spring,
With shot silk in drapes, cloaks, veils, and robes,
Violets in mourning colors yet untouched by grief
Yellow oxeyes, their beauty unsurpassed,
Marigolds like cups of wine rushed to relieve a drinker,
Gillyflowers like a necklace adorning the garden's walls,
Daisies with laughing faces of gold set with pearls,
Anemones like signs pointing the way to such beauty,
Fragrant roses blushing, wafting musk in the rays of dawn,
Birds serenading each other with tunes well known,
Sweet-voiced nightingales and warblers with fluted tone.
The early morning breezes have stolen our breath away.

دير نَهْيا

ونَهْيا بالجيزة وديرها من أحسن الديارات وأنزهها وأطيبها عامر برهبانه وسكّانه. ١،٣٩
وله في النيل منظر عجيب لأنّ الماء يحيط به من جميع جهاته فإذا انصرف الماء وزُرع أظهرت أراضيه غرائب النوّار وأصناف الزهر فهو من المتنزّهات الموصوفة والبقاع المشهورة. وله خليج يجتمع إليه سائر الطيور فهو أيضاً متصيّد حسن وقد وصفته الشعراء وذكرت حسنه وطيب موضعه.

وللعبّاس[1] بن البصريّ فيه ٢،٣٩

يَا مَنْ إِذَا سَكِرَ ٱلنَّدِيمُ بِكَأْسِهِ غَرِيَتْ لَوَاحِظُهُ بِسُكْرِ ٱلْفُيَّقِ
طَلَعَ ٱلصَّبَاحُ فَسَقِّنِي تِلْكَ ٱلَّتِي ظُلِمَتْ فَشُبِّهَ لَوْنُهَا بِٱلزَّنْبَقِ
وَٱلْقَ ٱلصَّبَاحَ بِنُورِ وَجْهِكَ إِنَّهُ لَا يَلْتَقِي ٱلْفَرَحَانِ حَتَّى يَلْتَقِي
قَلْبِي ٱلَّذِي لَمْ يُبْقِ فِيهِ هَوَاكُمُ إِلَّا بَقِيَّةَ نَارِ شَوْقٍ قَدْ بَقِي
أَوَمَا تَرَى وَجْهَ ٱلرَّبِيعِ وَقَدْ زَهَتْ أَنْوَارُهُ بِنَهَارِهِ ٱلْمُتَأَلِّقِ
وَتَجَاوَبَتْ أَطْيَارُهُ وَتَبَسَّمَتْ أَشْجَارُهُ عَنْ ثَغْرِ زَهْرٍ مُونِقِ
لَمْ يَغْذُهَا طَلُّ ٱلرَّذَاذِ بِبَرْدِهِ حَتَّى تَفَتَّحَ كُلُّ جَفْنٍ مُطْبَقِ
وَٱلْبَدْرُ فِي وَسَطِ ٱلسَّمَاءِ كَأَنَّهُ وَجْهٌ مَلِيحٌ فِي قِنَاعٍ أَزْرَقِ
يَا لِلدِّيَارَاتِ ٱلْمِلَاحِ وَمَا بِهَا مِنْ طِيبِ يَوْمٍ مَرَّ لِي بِتَشَوُّقِ
أَيَّامَ كُنْتُ وَكَانَ لِي شُغُلٌ بِهَا وَأَسِيرُ شَوْقِ صَبَابَتِي لَمْ يُطْلَقِ
يَا دَيْرَ نَهْيَا مَا ذَكَرْتُكَ سَاعَةً إِلَّا تَذَكَّرْتُ ٱلشَّبَابَ بِمَفْرِقِي

١ الأصل: ولعبّاس.

The Nahyā Monastery

Nahyā is near Giza. Its monastery is most beautiful, pleasant, agreeable, and flourishing with its monks and those dwelling there. It is an amazing sight when the Nile floods, for it is surrounded by water on all sides, and when the water recedes and its grounds are sown, they produce an amazing variety of blossoms and flowers. It is a famous place, a well-known destination for outings. A canal attracts all manner of waterfowl, so it is a good place for hunting. There are many descriptions of it in poetry, celebrating its attractive and lovely setting. 39.1

Here are two poems by al-ʿAbbās ibn al-Baṣrī: 39.2

When my friend's drunk from the wine in his cup,
  and your eyes are fixed on the second round,
Morning's come! Pour me a draft of the nectar
  in which the color of the lily's not to be found.
Greet the morning with a bright face,
  good things happen when they meet;
In my heart your love has left no trace
  but embers of the fire of a longing ever discreet.
See! The face of spring shines full of light,
  bright with radiant oxeye daisies;
Its birds sing in chorus, its trees sway and smile,
  flowering with blossoms like young beauties,
Nourished by the cool dew and drizzle,
  and opening their eyes to reveal their petals.
The moon, high in the heaven, looks down
  like a lovely face draped in a midnight-blue surround.
Oh, for the fine convents and wonderful days
  I spent there, a prey to longing and desire,
A time when its people filled my thoughts
  and the prisoner of my passion was not set free.
Nahyā's Convent, whenever I remember you
  I recall my youth and my hair, not yet gray,

وَٱلدَّهْرُ غَضٌّ وَٱلزَّمَانُ مُسَاعِدٌ　　وَمَقَامُنَا وَمَبِيتُنَا بِٱلْجَوْسَقِ
وَإِذَا سُئِلْتَ عَنِ ٱلطُّيُورِ وَصَيْدِهَا　　وَجُنُوسِهَا فَٱصْدُقْ وَإِنْ لَمْ تَصْدُقِ
فَٱلْغُرُّ فَٱلْكَرَوَانُ فَٱلْفَارُورُ إِذْ　　يُشْجِيكَ فِي طَيَرَانِهِ ٱلْمُتَحَلِّقِ
أَشَهِدْتَ حَرْبَ ٱلطَّيْرِ فِي غِيطَانِهِ　　لَمَّا تَجَوَّقَ مِنْهُ كُلُّ مُجَوَّقِ
وَٱلزُّمَّجَ ٱلْغَضْبَانَ فِي رَهْطٍ لَهُ　　يَنْحَطُّ بَيْنَ مُرَعِّدٍ وَمُبَرِّقِ
وَرَأَيْتُ لِلْبَازِيِّ سَطْوَةَ مُوسِرٍ　　وَلِغَيْرِهِ ذُلَّ ٱلْفَقِيرِ ٱلْمُمْلِقِ
كَمْ قَدْ صَبَوْتُ بِغِرَّتِي فِي شِرَّتِي　　وَقَطَعْتُ أَوْقَاتِي بِرَمْيِ ٱلْبُنْدُقِ
وَخَلَعْتُ فِي طَلَبِ ٱلْمُجُونِ حَبَائِلِي　　حَتَّى نُسِبْتُ إِلَى فِعَالِ ٱلْأَخْرَقِ
وَمُهَاجِرٍ وَمُكَاثِرٍ وَمُنَافِرٍ　　قَلِقَ ٱلْفُؤَادُ بِهِ وَإِنْ لَمْ يَقْلَقِ
لَوْ عَايَنَ ٱلتُّفَّاحُ حُمْرَةَ خَدِّهِ　　لَصَبَا إِلَى دِيبَاجِ ذَاكَ ٱلرَّوْنَقِ
يَا حَامِلَ ٱلسَّيْفِ ٱلْغَدَاةَ وَطَرْفُهُ　　أَمْضَى مِنَ ٱلسَّيْفِ ٱلْحُسَامِ ٱلْمُطْلَقِ
ٱرْفُقْ بِعَبْدِكَ لَا تُطِلْ أَشْجَانَهُ　　وَٱرْفُقْ بِهِ يَا صَاحِبَ ٱلثَّغْرِ ٱلنَّقِي

وقال أيضاً ٣،٣٩

أَتَنْشَطُ لِلشُّرْبِ يَا سَيِّدِي　　فَيَوْمُكَ هٰذَا دَقِيقُ ٱلدُّرُوزِ
فَعِنْدِي لَكَ ٱلْيَوْمَ مَشْوِيَّتَانِ　　سَرَقْتُهُمَا مِنْ دَجَاجِ ٱلْعَجُوزِ
وَخَمْسُونَ بَيْضَهْ[1] مِثْلُ ٱلنُّجُومِ　　خَبَتْهُنَّ مِنِّيَ فِي جَوْفِ كُوزِ
فَغَافَلْتُهَا وَتَنَاوَلْتُهُنَّ　　وَلَمْ تَنْتَفِعْ بِٱلْمَكَانِ ٱلْحَرِيزِ
أَتَنْشَطُ عِنْدِي عَلَى نَبْقَتَيْنِ　　عَلَى لَوْزَتَيْنِ عَلَى قَطْرَمِيزِ

[1] كذا في الأصل.

When time was young and fate on my side,
    and the Jawsaq Palace was where I stayed.
Nahyā's Convent, when I recall you
    I speed toward you at a swift steed's pace.
If you're asked about birds in all their breeds,
    speak the truth, though you won't be believed,
The coot, the water hen, the plover
    fill one with pleasure as they circle in flight.
Have you seen the birds battle in the fields,
    as they caw and squawk, caught up in their fight?
And the angry buzzard, swooping down on a group,
    now like a thunderbolt, now a flash of lightning.
I've seen the hawk wax arrogant, like a rich man,
    while other birds, poor underlings, bow down.
How often I've played, with a young man's ardor,
    passing the time with pellet bow;
I sprang all my traps in the hunt for frivolity,
    till my actions gave me the name of a fool.
My beloved, often defiant, contentious,
    who troubles the heart, but is untroubled,
Your cheek would be the envy of an apple
    for the smooth beauty of its rich color;
You carry a sword in the morning,
    though your glance cuts deeper than a sword;
Pity your slave, put an end to his sorrows,
    mercy, you whose mouth breathes delight.

Are you keen for a drink, sir? 39.3
    Today your wish will come true.
I've got two roasted birds,
    nicked from the old woman's hen coop.
Fifty eggs like stars, which she hid
    from me deep in a jar,
Filched without her knowing,
    the "safe place" was no bar.
Come, get busy at my place,
    with grape juice, almonds, and a pitcher,

وَنَقْصُدُ نَهْيَا وَدَيْرًا لَهَا ... بِهِ مَطْرَحُ ٱلْوَرْدِ وَٱلْمَرْزَنجُوزِ
وَنَشْرَبُ مِنْهَا بِرَطْلٍ وَجَامٍ ... وَكَبَّرَةٍ وَٱنْتِخَابٍ بِكُوزِ
فَأَمَّا ٱلطُّيُورُ لِفَرْطِ ٱلسُّرُورِ ... فَبَيْنَ ٱلرِّيَاضِ وَبَيْنَ ٱلْغُرُوزِ
فَهٰذَا يَصِيحُ عَلَى ٱلْحَادِثَاتِ ... تَنَحَّ وَهٰذَا[1] بِنَا لَا تَجُوزِي
وَخَشْفٍ أَتَانَا رَخِيمِ ٱلدَّلَالِ ... نَشَا فِي ٱلنَّعِيمِ وَلُبْسِ ٱلْخُزُوزِ
يُحِبُّ ٱلنَّدَامَى وَأَشْعَارَهُمْ ... وَيُخْبِي وَدَائِعَهُمْ فِي ٱلْكُنُوزِ
فَزُرْنِي تَجِدْنِي وَفِيَّ ٱلْمَقَالِ ... وَإِلَّا أَفِي فَٱكْسِعِ ٱلْيَوْمَ طِيزِي

وكان ابن البصريّ هذا من الخلعاء المجّان وله شعر يجري مجرى الهزل والطيب. ٤،٣٩
وخدم أبا القاسم أُونوجور بن الإخشيد فأحسن إليه وكساه وصار يركب معه وكان يلبس طيلسانًا أزرق يتشبّه بالقضاة وكان أونوجور قد حمله على برذون أصفر غليظ بطيء السير فكان إذا سار مع أقوام من إخوانه قال لهم صِفوا لي موضعكم حتّى ألحق بكم. وكان مليح المجالسة كثير النادرة وكان يبيع الصيدلة في مسجد عبد الله بمصر.

ديرطَمّويه

وطَمّويه في الغرب بإزاء حلوان والدير راكب البحر وحوله الكروم والبساتين والنخل ١،٤٠
والشجر فهو نزه عامر آهل وله في النيل منظر حسن وحين تخضرّ الأرض فإنّه يكون بين بساتين من البحر والزرع. وهو أحد متنزّهات مصر المذكورة ومواضع لهوها المشهورة.

[1] الأصل: وهذا يقول.

And let's make for Nahyā's Convent,
with its roses and acacias,
To drink measures of wine in goblets,
toasting with vintage sorts,
The birds, crazed with joy,
between meadow and vine stock,
Sing, "Be off" to destiny,
telling it to keep its distance.
A fawn comes, sweetly coy,
clad in silks and reared in riches,
Loving your friends' poems
and hiding their assets in his rocks.
Visit me, you'll find I'm telling the truth.
If not, my bum's yours for the knocks.

Ibn al-Baṣrī was frivolous and dissolute. His poems were on amusing and pleasant themes. He served Abū l-Qāsim Ūnūjūr ibn al-Ikhshīd, who treated him well and rewarded him with garments. He accompanied the prince when he rode out, wearing a blue headdress like that worn by judges. Ūnūjūr had given him a pale, sturdy horse with a slow gait, and when he went out riding with some of his friends he would say, "Tell me where you're going so I can catch up with you." He was good company and a mine of anecdotes. He used to sell medicinal drugs at the mosque of ʿAbdallāh[211] in Cairo. 39.4

The Monastery of Ṭamwayh

Ṭamwayh is on the west bank of the Nile opposite Ḥulwān. The monastery is just by the river, surrounded by vineyards, gardens, palm groves, and trees. It is pleasant, flourishing, and well populated. When reflected in the Nile, it looks beautiful. When the ground turns green in spring, it lies between two carpets, the river and the crops. It is a notable destination for an outing from Cairo and a well-known place of diversion. 40.1

ولابن عاصم فيه ٢،٤٠

أَقْصِرَا عَنْ مَلَامِي ٱلْيَوْمَ إِنِّي   غَيْرُ ذِي سَلْوَةٍ وَلَا إِقْصَارِ
فَسَقَى ٱللهُ دَيْرَ طَمْوَيْهِ غَيْثًا   بِغَوَادٍ مَوْصُولَةٍ بِسَوَارِي
كَمْ لَيَالٍ نَبَهْتُ مِنْ نَوْمِ سُكْرِي   بِنَعِيرِ ٱلرُّهْبَانِ فِي ٱلْأَسْحَارِ
وَٱلنَّوَاقِيسُ صَائِحَاتٌ تُنَادِي   حَيَّ يَا نَائِمًا عَلَى ٱلِٱبْتِكَارِ

وقال فيه أيضاً ٣،٤٠

وَٱشْرَبْ بِطَمْوَيْهِ مِنْ صَهْبَاءَ صَافِيَةٍ   تُزْرِي بِخَمْرِ قُرَى هِيتٍ وَعَانَاتِ
عَلَى رِيَاضٍ مِنَ ٱلنَّوَّارِ زَاهِرَةٍ   تَجْرِي ٱلْجَدَاوِلُ مِنْهَا بَيْنَ جَنَّاتِ
كَأَنَّ نَبْتَ ٱلشَّقِيقِ ٱلْعُصْفُرِيِّ بِهَا   كَاسَاتُ خَمْرٍ بَدَتْ فِي إِثْرِ كَاسَاتِ
كَأَنَّ نَرْجِسَهَا فِي حُسْنِهِ حَدَقٌ   فِي خَفْيَةٍ تَتَنَاجَى بِٱلْإِشَارَاتِ
كَأَنَّمَا ٱلنِّيلُ فِي مَرِّ ٱلنَّسِيمِ بِهَا   مُسْتَلْئِمٌ فِي دُرُوعٍ سَابِرِيَّاتِ
مَنَازِلًا كُنْتُ مَفْتُونًا بِهَا يَفَعًا   وَكُنَّ قِدْمًا مَوَاخِيرِي وَحَانَاتِي
إِذْ لَا أَزَالُ مُلِحًّا بِٱلصَّبُوحِ عَلَى   ضَرْبِ ٱلنَّوَاقِيسِ صَبًّا بِٱلدِّيَارَاتِ

Ibn ʿĀṣim composed this poem on it: 40.2

Stop blaming me today,
I'll not be consoled or silenced.
May God send rain morn
and night to Ṭamwayh's Convent.
Often I was dragged from a drunken stupor
by the monks' gruff chanting,
While the clappers loudly called,
"Come, sleeper, wake up for matins."

Here is another of his poems: 40.3

At Ṭamwayh drink a pure red nectar,
which scoffs at the wine of Hīt and ʿĀnah
In meadows like Paradise, brilliant
with blossoms, crisscrossed by streams,
Where the carmine anemones
are like cups of wine in succession,
The lovely narcissi like eyes
secretly communicating through their sparkles.
When the breeze passes over,
the Nile shimmers in Shapur's armor.
These places charmed me in my youth;
they were my brothels and taverns of old.
The cup at the sound of the clappers
and love for the convent have not lost their hold.

الديارات المعروفة بالعجائب على ما ذكره أهلها ووصفوه عنها فمنها

دير الخنافس

وهو بين الموصل وبلد كبير كثير الرهبان له يوم في السنة يجتمع الناس إليه من كلّ ١،٤١
موضع فتظهر فيه الخنافس ذلك اليوم حتّى تغطّي حيطانه وسقوفه وأرضه ويسودّ
جميعه منها. فإذا كان اليوم الثاني وهو عيد الدير اجتمعوا إلى الهيكل فقدّسوا[١]
وتقرّبوا وانصرفوا وقد غابت الخنافس حتّى لا يُرى منها شيء إلى ذلك الوقت.

دير الكلب

وهو بين الموصل وبلد. يُعالج فيه من عضّه كلب كَلِب. فمن عضّه كلب كَلِب بادر ١،٤٢
إليه فعالجوه منه برأ ومن مضت له أربعون يوماً من العضّة لم ينجع فيه العلاج.

١ الأصل: فقسّوا.

The Monasteries Where Miracles Are Performed According to What Those Living There Have Said and Described

The Scarabs' Monastery

This is a large monastery between Mosul and Balad, with many monks. On one day in the year, people assemble there from all over, and that is when the scarabs appear. They cover its walls, roofs, and ground, turning the whole place black. The next day, which is the monastery's patronal festival, people gather in the church, celebrate the liturgy, receive communion, and then leave. By then, the scarabs have disappeared and nothing more is seen of them until the same time the following year. 41.1

The Rabies Monastery[212]

This lies between Mosul and Balad. People who are bitten by rabid dogs are treated there. Anyone bitten by a rabid dog who goes there quickly to be treated will be cured. But the treatment will have no effect on anyone who waits forty days after being bitten. 42.1

دير القيّارة

وهو لليعقوبيّة على أربع فراسخ من الموصل في الجانب الغربيّ من أعمال الحديثة مشرف ١،٤٣
على دجلة تحته عين قير وهي عين تفور بماء جارٍ تصبّ في دجلة ويخرج منه القير فما
دام القير في مائه فهو لين يمتدّ فإذا فارق الماء وبرد جفّ. وهناك قوم يجتمعون فيجمعون
هذا القير يغرفونه من مائه بالقفاف ويطرحونه على الأرض ولهم قدور حديد كبار
ويُنخل له الرمل فيُطرح عليه بمقدار يعرفونه ويوقد تحته حتّى يذوب ويختلط بالرمل وهم
يحرّكونه تحريكاً دائماً فإذا بلغ حدّ استحكامه قُلب على الأرض قطعاً مجدّدةً ويُصلب ويُحمل
إلى البلدان فمنه تُقيّر السفن والحمّامات وغير ذلك ممّا يُستعمل فيه القير.

والناس يكثرون القصد لهذا الموضع للتنزّه فيه والشرب ويستحمّون من ذلك الماء ٢،٤٣
الذي يخرج معه القير لأنّه يقوم مقام الحمّات في قلع البثور.

وله قائم وكلّ دير لليعقوبيّة والملكيّة فعنده قائم فأمّا ديارات النسطور فلا قائم لها.

دير مر[١] قوما

وهذا الدير بميّافارقين على فرسخين منها في جبل عالٍ له عيد يجتمع الناس من كلّ ١،٤٤
موضع ويقصده أهل البطالة والخلاعة للشرب فيه وتحته برك يجتمع فيها ماء الأمطار
ومر[٢] قوما هذا هو الشاهد الذي فيه يزعم النصارى أنّ له سبع مائة سنة وأنّه ممّن
شهد المسيح. وهو في خزانة خشب لها أبواب تُفتح أيّام أعيادهم فيظهر منه نصفه

١ كذا في عوّاد؛ الأصل: برقوما. ٢ الأصل: برقوما.

The Tar Spring Monastery

This monastery belongs to the Jacobites. It lies some fourteen miles (twenty-four kilometers) from Mosul in the western part of the district of Ḥadīthah, looking out over the Tigris. Beneath it is a tar spring—that is, a spring of hot water flowing into the Tigris from which tar is extracted. The tar stays soft in the water and can be manipulated, but becomes brittle when it is taken out and cools. There are people who gather to collect the tar. They scoop it out of the water in baskets and put it on the ground. They place a little sand in big iron cauldrons, then add a specific quantity of the tar and keep a fire going under the cauldron, stirring all the time, until the tar melts and mixes with the sand. When it has reached the right consistency, it is poured out on the ground, becomes solid, and hardens. Then it is exported and is used to tar ships and baths and for other uses tar is put to. 43.1

Many people visit this place to enjoy themselves and have a drink. They bathe in the water from which the tar is extracted because it is as efficacious at removing pustules as mud baths. 43.2

The monastery has an administrator; unlike the Nestorian monasteries, all the Jacobite and Melkite monasteries have administrators.

The Monastery of Mār Tūmā (Saint Thomas)

This is a monastery some six miles (ten kilometers) from Mayyāfāriqīn on a high mountain. People gather from all over for its patronal festival, and it attracts lovers of fun and depravity to drink there. Beneath the monastery is a pool where rainwater gathers. Mār Tūmā was a martyr who, according to the Christians, lived for seven hundred years. He was one of those who saw Christ. His body is kept in a wooden casket, which has doors that are opened during their festivals. Then the upper part of his body appears, upright. His 44.1

الأعلى وهو قائم وأنفه وشفته العليا مقطوعان. وذلك أنّ امرأة احتالت حتّى قطعت أنفه وشفته ومضت بهما[1] فبنت عليهما ديرًا في البرّيّة في طريق تكريت.

دير باطا

١،٤٥ وهذا الدير بالشرق[2] وهو دير حسن عامر نزه في أيّام الربيع ويُسمّى أيضًا دير الحمار وشاهده يُعرف بمر بكس[3] وهو ناءٍ عن دجلة وعن المدينة. وله باب حجر ذكر النصارى أنّ هذا الباب يفتحه الواحد والاثنان حتّى يتجاوز السبعة فإن تجاوز السبعة لم يقدر أحد منهم على فتحه ولا يفتحه حينئذ إلّا سبعة.

وذكروا أيضًا أنّ فيه غِرْبان تتناسل هناك لا يخلو منها فربّما طرقه اللصوص فدخلوه فإن حصل فيه أحد منهم صعد الغرابان على برج[4] الدير فإذا أقبل إليه أحد ممّن يطرقه أو يقصده تلقّاه الغرابان يصيحان في وجهه كالمنذرين له فيعلم أنّ في الدير قومًا فيرجع فإن لم يكن في الدير أحد لم يفعلا شيئًا من ذلك.

دير مارشمعون[5] بنواحي السنّ[6]

١،٤٦ في هذا الدير كرسيّ الأسقف وفيه أيضًا بئر فمن لحقه بَهَق قصده واغتسل من البئر لم يبرح حتّى يزول عنه.

---

١ الأصل: بها. ٢ كذا في الأصل. ٣ كذا في عوّاد؛ الأصل: مر يكس. ٤ الأصل: مرج. ٥ كذا في عوّاد. الأصل: دير ربارسون. الأصل: (هكذا في الأصل) وردت في الهامش. ٦ الأصل: السِ، الأصل: (هكذا في الأصل) وردت في الهامش.

nose and his upper lip have been amputated. A woman contrived to cut them off, took them away, and built a monastery over them in the desert on the road to Takrit.

The Bāṭā Monastery

This is a monastery in the east, beautiful, flourishing, and pleasant in spring. 45.1
It is also known as the Donkey's Monastery. It is dedicated to the martyr Mār Bākhūs. It is a long way from the Tigris and Baghdad.[213] It has a stone door, which the Christians say can be opened by as many as seven people, but cannot be opened by more than seven.

They also say there are two ravens that breed there and never leave. The ravens fly onto the monastery tower if robbers turn up and manage to gain entry to the monastery. When the intruder reaches the tower, the ravens fly and squawk in his face as if to warn him, and make it known that the monastery is inhabited, at which the robbers retreat. The ravens would not behave like this if the monastery was uninhabited.

The Monastery of Mār Shim'ūn (Saint Simeon) near Sinn

This monastery houses the bishop's seat. It also has a well, and anyone with 46.1
a skin complaint who goes there and washes in the well will be cured before he leaves.

ديرالعجّاج

١٠٤٧ وهـذا الدير بين تكريت وهيت عامركثير الرهبان وخارجه عين ماء تصبّ إلى بركة هناك وفي البركة سمك أسود وهو طيّب عذب الطعم. وحوله مزارع وخضر تُسق من تلك العين.

ديرالجوديّ

١٠٤٨ والجوديّ هو الجبل الذي استقرّت عليه السفينة وبين هذا الجبل وجزيرة ابن عمر سبعة فراسخ. وهذا الديرمبنيّ على قلّة الجبل يُقال إنّه بُني منذ أيّام نوح عليه السلام. ويزعمون أنّ فيه أعجوبة حدّثني بها بعض نصارى الجزيرة وهي أنّ سطحه يُشبر فيكون عشرين شبرًا ثمّ يُعاود قياسه فيكون ثمانية[١] عشر شبرًا ثمّ يُعاود فيكون اثنين[٤] وعشرين شبرًا وفي كلّ دفعة يُشبر يختلف عدده وإنّه اعتبر ذلك وقاسه فوجده كما ذكر.

كنيسة الطور

١٠٤٩ وطور سينا هو الجبل الذي تُجلّي فيه لموسى عليه السلام وصُعق فيه. والكنيسة في أعلى الجبل مبنيّة بحجر أسود وعرض حصنه سبعة أذرع وله ثلاثة أبواب حديد وفي

١ الأصل: ثماني. ٤ الأصل: اثنان.

The ʿAjjāj[214] Monastery

This monastery lies between Takrit and Hīt. It is flourishing and houses many monks. Outside there is a spring whose water flows into a pool containing black fish. They are good and tasty. Round the monastery are fields growing vegetables irrigated from the spring. 47.1

The Jūdī Monastery

Jūdī[215] is the name of the mountain on which the ark came to rest. It is about twenty-five miles (forty kilometers) from Jazīrat Ibn ʿUmar. The monastery is built on the summit and is said to have been constructed in the time of Noah, peace be upon him. They say there is something extraordinary there, which a Christian of the Jazīrah told me about. When its roof terrace is measured, sometimes it is twenty spans[216] long, sometimes eighteen spans, sometimes twenty-two spans. Each time it is measured, the number changes. He himself had tried measuring it and found that what they said was accurate. 48.1

The Church of Mount Sinai

Mount Sinai is the mountain where Moses, peace be upon him, experienced the revelation and fell down thunderstruck.[217] The church, built of black stone, is at the top of the mountain. Its fortifications are seven cubits thick. It has three iron doors, and on the west side there is a small door with a stone in front 49.1

غربيّه باب لطيف قدّامه حجر لهم إذا أرادوا رفعه رفعوه وإن قصدهم أحد أرسلوه فانطبق على الموضع فلم يُعرف مكان الباب. وداخلها عين ماء وخارجها عين أخرى. وزعم النصارى أنّ بها ناراً من نوع النار الجديدة التي كانت بالبيت المقدّس يوقدون[1] منها في كلّ عشيّة وهي بيضاء ضعيفة الحرّ لا تحرق ثمّ تقوى إذا أُوقد منها السرج. وهو عامر بالرهبان والناس يقصدونه لأنّه من الديارات الموصوفة.

ولابن عاصم فيه ٢،٤٩

يَا رَاهِبَ ٱلدَّيْرِ مَاذَا ٱلضَّوْءُ وَٱلنُّورُ ... فَقَدْ أَضَاءَ بِهِ فِي دَيْرِكَ ٱلطُّورُ
هَلْ حَلَّتِ ٱلشَّمْسُ فِيهِ دُونَ أَبْرُجِهَا ... أَوْ غُيِّبَ ٱلْبَدْرُ عَنْهُ فَهْوَ مَسْتُورُ
فَقَالَ مَا حَلَّهُ شَمْسٌ وَلَا قَمَرٌ ... لٰكِنْ تَقَرَّبَ فِيهِ ٱلْيَوْمَ قَوْرِيرُ

بيعة أبي هور

١،٥٠ وهذه البيعة بِسرياقوس من أعمال مصر عامرة كثيرة الرهبان لها أعياد يقصدها الناس. وفيها[2] على ما ذكره أهلها أعجوبة وهي أنّ من كانت به خنازير يقصد هذا الموضع ليُعالج به فيأخذه رئيس الموضع فيضجعه ويأتيه بخنزير فيرسله على موضع الوجع فيأكل الخنزير الذي فيه لا يتعدّى ذلك الموضع فإذا تنظّف الموضع ذرّ عليه من رماد خنزير فعل مثل هذا الفعل من قبل ومن زيت قنديل البيعة فيبرأ ثمّ يؤخذ ذلك الخنزير فيُذبح ويُحرق ويُعدّ رماده لمثل هذه الحال.

١ الأصل: يقدون. ٢ الأصل: فيه.

of it. When they want to, they raise the stone, but if attacked, they let it down and it covers the place so no one knows where the door is. There is a spring inside the monastery and one outside as well. The Christians claim that there is a fire in the church like the New Fire in Jerusalem.[218] Each evening, they light their lamps from it. It is white and does not give out much heat or burn fiercely, but it flares up when lamps are lighted from it. There are many monks living there and people visit it because it is a much-talked-of monastery.

Ibn ʿĀṣim composed this poem on it: 49.2

You monk of Sinai, what's this light and radiance
the mountain has lit in your convent?
Has the sun abandoned the planets to live there,
or the moon sought shelter as a migrant?
"No, neither moon nor sun have come near,
but Qawzīr[219] took communion here."

The Priory of Abū Hūr

This priory is in Siryāqūs on the outskirts of Cairo. It is flourishing and houses 50.1
many monks, and it has several festivals, which people flock to. It is said that a particular miracle happens there. A person suffering from scrofula[220] goes there for treatment. The superior of the priory takes him, makes him lie down, and brings a pig, which he directs to the affected part. The pig eats the patient's scrofula but nothing else. The patient recovers when the wound has been cleaned, and the ashes of a pig who had performed this operation earlier are sprinkled on it, together with oil from the priory lamp. Then the pig is slaughtered and burned, and its ashes are kept for a subsequent case.

دير يُحَنَّس

١،٥١ هـذا الدير بدمنهور من أعمال مصر. إذا كان يوم عيده أُخرج شاهده من الدير في تابوت فيسير التابوت على وجه الأرض لا يقدر أحد أن يمسكه ولا يحبسه حتّى يرد البحر فيغطس فيه ثمّ يرجع إلى مكانه.

بيعة إتريب

١،٥٢ وعيدها اليوم الحادي والعشرون من بؤونة.[١] يذكرون أنّ حمامة بيضاء تجيئهم في ذلك العيد فتدخل المذبح لا يدرون من أين جاءت ثمّ لا يرونها إلى يوم مثله.

ودير بنواحي أخميم

١،٥٣ دير كبير عامر يُقصد من كلّ موضع وهو بقرب الجبل المعروف بجبل الكهف وفي موضع من الجبل شقّ إذا كان يوم عيد هذا الدير لم يبقَ من الطير المعروف ببوقير شيء في ذلك المكان وهم به كثير حتّى يجيء إلى الموضع فيكون أمرًا عظيمًا لكثرته واجتماعهم وصياحهم عند ذلك الشقّ ثمّ لا يزالون واحدًا بعد واحد يدخل رأسه في ذلك الشقّ ويصيح ويخرج ويجيء غيره فيفعل فعله إلى أن يعلق رأس أحدهم وينشب في الموضع فيضطرب حتّى يموت فحينئذ يتفرّق الباقون ويرجعون إلى مواضعهم.[٢]

١ الأصل: بونه. ٢ أضافت يدٌ أُخرى بخطّ رديء: فلا يبقى منها طاير والله أعلم.

The Monastery of Yuḥannas

This monastery is in Damanhur, a town in Egypt. On its feast day its patron saint is brought out of the monastery in a casket, and it travels along the ground, and no one is able to restrain it or stop it until it reaches the Nile. It plunges into the water and then goes back to its place in the monastery. 51.1

The Priory of Itrīb

Its feast day is on the twenty-first of Ba'ūnah [June 28].[221] It is said that on that day a white dove comes and enters the altar. They do not know where it comes from and they do not see it again until the same day the following year. 52.1

The Monastery in the Region of Akhmīm

Near Akhmīm there is a large monastery that attracts visitors from everywhere; it lies close to the Mountain of the Cave. In this mountain is a crevice, and on the monastery's feast day all the hornbills from the surrounding areas (and there are a great many of them) collect there. It is a splendid sight to see them gathered at the crevice, cawing. 53.1

Each hornbill puts its head into the crevice, caws, and takes it out, to be followed by another who does the same thing. This goes on until one puts its head into the crevice and it sticks fast. The bird struggles until it dies, at which point the others separate and return to where they came from. So there are no birds left there. And God is all-knowing.

Notes

1 Because the first part of the manuscript is lost, this section starts shortly after the monastery has been named, in the middle of the passage describing its situation and surroundings.

2 It was common practice to swear to divorce one's wife and free one's concubines if one was lying, to emphasize the truth of what one was saying or to give force to a vow.

3 The postal service (*barīd*) consisted of couriers who transmitted messages; it also served as a spy network.

4 Cropping an ear was a punishment for offences such as stealing or vagrancy in both the premodern Muslim world and Europe.

5 This line is not in Marwān ibn Abī Ḥafṣah's diwan.

6 A purse containing either ten thousand dirhams or seven thousand dinars. The dinar was a gold coin weighing 4.25 grams; it was the basis of the monetary system.

7 ʿUbayd is a diminutive of ʿAbdallāh as well as meaning "little slave." By addressing Abū ʿAbdallāh as Abū ʿUbayd, al-Mutawakkil reminded him of his mutilated state.

8 The name means "companion."

9 The name means "courage" but also "snake."

10 One or two folios are missing from the manuscript here. The continuation is from Yāqūt's *Dictionary of Writers* (*Muʿjam al-udabāʾ*, 167–68).

11 Where the manuscript resumes, the Ibrāhīm mentioned is a member of the Banū Ḥamdūn family, not Ibrāhīm ibn Muḥammad ibn (al-)Mudabbir.

12 Drinking played an important part in libertine and some palace circles. Wine was usually made from grapes but sometimes from dates. It was often mixed with water. The best times for drinking were considered to be early in the morning or in the evening after dinner.

13 The dirham was a silver coin that originally weighed a little less than three grams. It was worth one-tenth of a dinar in the eighth century but its value fell sharply in the ninth century.

14 At least one word is missing because of damage to the folio.

15 These two lines are part of a different poem.

16 Foxes' basilicum (*rayḥān al-thaʿālib*) is a fragrant plant of the genus *Artemisia*.

17 This revolt of slaves working on the land in southern Iraq broke out in AD 869 and lasted until AD 884. The slaves, from East Africa, were known as "Zanj." Their leader, ʿAlī ibn Muḥammad, whom al-Shābushtī does not mention by name, was of obscure origin and born in Iran.

18 The catholicos was the head of the Church of the East (Nestorian Church).

19 Musical settings were indicated by the rhythmic mode, here light *ramal*, and sometimes by the melodic mode as well. See Wright, "Music and Verse," and for more detail Sawa, *Music Performance Practice in the Early ʿAbbāsid Era 132–320 AH / 750–932 AD*, 35–107.

20 The pandore (Ar: *ṭunbūr*) is a long-necked lute with two strings. It is not clear from this anecdote whether the Baghdadi or the more elaborate Khurasani pandore is meant (cf. Sawa, *Musical and Socio-Cultural Anecdotes from Kitāb al-aghānī al-kabīr*, 56, 418–19).

21 These two verses were previously mentioned in §3.8, on the Monastery of the Foxes, where they are attributed to al-Nāshiʾ al-Akbar.

22 Arabic *mudyān* from Syriac *mawdyānī*. This translation is proposed by ʿAwwād.

23 The perfumed dye paste (*khalūq*) mentioned here was one of many varieties of perfume used by men and women of the wealthy classes. Perfumes and their erotic significance are discussed in King, "The Importance of Imported Aromatics in Arabic Culture: Illustrations from Pre-Islamic and Early Islamic Poetry."

24 Q Quraysh 106:4.

25 The false accusation of adultery, like adultery itself, is subject to a penalty mandated in the Qur'an (Q Nūr 24:4).

26 Comment in the margin: "May Almighty God be merciful to the Commander of the Faithful ʿAbdallāh al-Ma'mūn. How wise he was and how well he managed his affairs, including appointing Abū ʿAlī to lead the prayers at the funerals of members of the caliphal family."

27 Masked players, *sammājah*, are attested at festivals at the court in Baghdad, though whether they performed mimes, slapstick comedy, or dances is not clear. See Moreh, *Live Theatre and Dramatic Literature in the Medieval Arabic World*, 45–48.

28 Robes of honor (sing. *khilʿah*) were luxury garments or ensembles presented by rulers to their subjects as a reward or sign of distinction.

29 Literally "I won't catch any game."

30 Travel in Iraq was generally by boat, either on the Euphrates, the Tigris, or one of the many canals.

31 Comment in the margin: "The Lady Zubaydah's passing Isḥāq's dwelling, with her entering it to examine his generosity."

32 The clappers (Gk. *semantron*) consist of a piece of wood beaten with a mallet, used to summon monastics to chapel. They are used in monasteries in the Near East, the Balkans, and Russia. See the survey in Debié, "Livres et monastères en Syrie-Mésopotamie d'après les sources syriaques."

33 The name means "gold."

34 It is unlikely that this monastery was named after any of the Sassanian rulers called Shapur. Two bishops called Sābūr are known to have lived in the fourth and seventh centuries, and one of them may have founded it (Fiey, *Assyrie chrétienne: Contribution à l'étude de l'histoire et de la géographie ecclésiastique et monastique du Nord de l'Iraq*, 3:297).

35 Comment in the margin: "I say: Consider the ethics of al-Muʿtaṣim's act along with his nobility. He was afraid to upset his circle with a disaster if one of his companions were to drown, so he himself rescued him and supported him from his saddle, not asking any of his followers to do it."

36 The name means "ease" or "prosperity."

37 A waxy substance produced in the stomach of sperm whales that, when dried, becomes fragrant. It is much used in perfumes.

38 A day at the end of the month of Shaban when the sky is overcast, hiding the new moon, and so it is not certain whether the fast of Ramadan, the next month, has begun.

39 Qūṭā may be the name of an otherwise unrecorded village. In Syriac, however, it can mean "troop," "herd," or "flock." (I thank Salam Rassi for this suggestion.) Some monasteries had nicknames, for instance, the Foxes' Monastery or the Devils' Monastery.

40 The name means "tender branches."

41 A well-known singing girl. The name means "reed pen."

42 The name means "lights."

43 The name means "enthralled (by love)."

44 After the end of Shaban, the fast will start.

45 Comment in the margin: "The witty anecdotes in [the section on] this monastery are delightful. A conversationalist needs to commit them to memory and keep them in mind, for the doings of men of excellence elevate the mind."

46 Syriac: *rabban*.

47 This joke and several of the following ones have Abū l-ʿAynāʾ as the protagonist here but are attached to other personalities or anonymous figures in other collections of anecdotes. See, for this joke, Marzolph, *Arabia ridens: Die humoristische Kurzprosa der frühen adab-Literatur im internationalen Traditionsgeflecht*, vol. 2, no. 767; and, for the joke in §10.11, no. 830.

48 The fast includes abstaining from sexual intercourse during the day.

49 Presumably, ʿAlī ibn al-Jahm was making a song and dance about reciting his poem and Abū l-ʿAynāʾ laughed at him. The call to prayer would not normally be recited except to introduce the ritual prayer.

50 This refers to the division of estates according to Islamic inheritance law.

51 This is an oblique reference to the dispute between Abbasids and ʿAlids about the right to lead the Community, the Abbasids being descendants of Muḥammad's uncle and thus more distantly related to him than the ʿAlids, his direct descendants.

52 That is, ʿUmar ibn al-Khaṭṭāb, the second "rightly guided" caliph.

53 The context was ʿUmar's being stabbed to death, and the grammatical point concerns the voweling of the particle before "God" and "the Muslims." In the first case it is *la-*, entreating God's help, and in the second *li-*, rallying the Muslims. See al-Khaṭīb al-Baghdādī, *Tārīkh Baghdād*, 3:172.

54 Q Ṣād 38:30, 38:44, referring to Solomon and Job.

55 Q Qalam 68:11–13, referring to opponents of Muḥammad in Mecca.

56 Apparently an inaccurate reference to a tradition of the Prophet, who is reported to have said when a scorpion stung him during prayer: "May God curse the scorpion, for it does not spare anyone, whether he is praying or not" (Ibn Mājah, *Sunan Ibn Mājah*, book 5, #1246).

57 This refers to the fact that the uprising against the Umayyads, in which both descendants of ʿAlī ibn Abī Ṭālib and descendants of the Prophet's uncle al-ʿAbbās took part, originally foresaw a caliph from the Prophet's family, an ambiguous expression embracing both lineages.

58 A sweet-and-sour dish of lamb with vinegar and dried fruit.

59 Q Muʾminūn 23:108. God is replying to unbelievers in hell.

60 A belief developed among Muslims that the Night of Māshūsh was a time of uninhibited licentiousness and promiscuity among Christians, monks, nuns, and laity; see Tannous, *The Making of the Medieval Middle East*, 470–71, and the references there. See also §13.2. The idea that monasteries and convents were hotbeds of corruption and promiscuity was not confined to the Near East, as can be seen from several stories in Boccaccio's *Decameron* and Chaucer's *Canterbury Tales*.

61 Unidentified singer.

62 The last two lines are added from Yāqūt, *Muʿjam al-buldān*, 523, to complete the sense.

63 Palm Sunday falls at the end of March or in April, and Epiphany is on January 6, which implies nearly a year's stay at the monastery. But the poet may have inverted the feasts for the sake of the rhyme.

64 Arabic poetry traditionally has rhyme and quantitative meter. It has been suggested that since al-Muʿtamid could compose metrically, his nonmetrical poetry was experimental (van Gelder, *Sound and Sense in Classical Arabic Poetry*, 147–49).

65 Arabic music traditionally has rhythmic modes or patterns. Some of them have names resembling those of poetic meters but they are not identical with them.

66 "Badr," meaning "full moon," was a common name for a servant. "Jullanār" means "pomegranate blossom."

67 Jacob the Coppersmith refers to Yaʿqūb ibn al-Layth al-Ṣaffār (see his entry in the Glossary). The "coppersmith on the cross" is possibly a reference to Yaʿqūb's brother ʿAmr, who was captured, taken to Baghdad, and publicly humiliated before he died in prison.

68 Several of the words in the manuscript lack pointing and are incomprehensible. The poem might be a subversive invitation to eat during the day in Ramadan.

69 Several monasteries of this name existed in Iraq and Syria apart from the two al-Shābushtī mentions here.

70 Fiey traces the origin of this story to Ḥīrah and substitutes young girls for nuns. The fast occurred shortly after Epiphany (*Assyrie chrétienne*, 3:122–23).

71 The device described in the text was a hydraulic organ (Farmer, *The Organ of the Ancients from Eastern Sources (Hebrew, Syriac and Arabic)*, 85–116).

72 Q Anbiyāʾ 21:89.

73 Q Baqarah 2:156.

74 Conjectured translation. The text appears to be faulty.

75 He was afraid the caliph would seize her from him. For another example of a more powerful or socially superior person confiscating a singer, see above, §12.8, where a leading Turkish general appropriates one of the caliph's singers.

76 The first three lines of this poem also appear in §2.11.

77 This was in 289/902, when al-Muktafī processed to Baghdad on succeeding his father as caliph.

78 Comment in the margin: "I say this is not specific to the ruler, but every great man must be kept company in perfect manners and discretion."

79 Q Baqarah 2:74, 85, 140, 144, 149 (slightly modified).

80 An echo of Q Ṭalāq 65:7.

81 The name means "discord."

82 Different towns were known for the cloth they produced. Al-Ḥaẓīrah near Baghdad was famous for fine cotton weaves.

83 Comment in the margin: "Ibn Abī Fanan composed sublime poetry."

84 Comment in the margin: "This should be committed to memory."

85 Robes of honor made of luxurious material were awarded by rulers to mark an investiture or as a reward.

86 Most of this line of poetry has been scratched out. It is supplied from al-Marzubānī, *Muʿjam al-shuʿarāʾ*, 463. The poem is falsely attributed to Ibn al-Rūmī; it comes from an elegy of the ʿAlid ruler of Ṭabaristān, al-Ḥasan ibn Zayd, by his secretary.

87 "Eighth" in the text.

88 Black was the color associated with the Abbasids. It is not certain that this was the first instance of black banners being deployed in a battle.

89 Comment in the margin: "When al-Maʾmūn vanquished Naṣr ibn Shabath."

90 The prayer carpet spread out over the caliph's divan was regarded as an insignia of royalty; a special official was in charge of it.

91 From the caliph's point of view, anyone who refused allegiance to him was a heretic, because they called into question the God-given order he represented.

92 Modified quotation of a line by Abū l-ʿAtāhiyah, *Dīwān*, 22:45.

93 Hostility may have existed between al-Muʿtaṣim and ʿAbdallāh ibn Ṭāhir on account of the caliph's suspicions of his powerful lieutenant in the east, but it was embroidered upon in works of belles lettres, as here. See *The History of al-Ṭabarī*, vol. 23, *Storm and Stress*, 137n181, and Kaabi, *Les Tahirides: Étude historico-littéraire de la dynastie des Banū Ṭāhir ibn al-Ḥusayn au Ḫurasān et en Iraq au IIIe s. de l'Hégire IXème s. J. C.*, 1:147–53.

94 Q Ḥāqqah 69:45.

95 Al-Shammākh ibn Ḍirār al-Ghaṭafānī (d. after 651), *Dīwān*, 336.

96 Not to be confused with the famous poet of the Jahiliya.

97 That is, al-Faḍl ibn Sahl. The name "Dhū al-Riyāsatayn" means "holder of the dual leadership."

98 In fact Monday.

99 During the Friday sermon (*khuṭbah*), the caliph was named and prayed for by the preacher, generally the most important dignitary in the town. To leave his name out was a sign of rebellion.

100 Al-Shābushtī's taste for sensationalism is reflected here. Other reasons for Ṭāhir's appointment as governor of Khurasan and reports that he died a natural death are discussed in Kaabi, *Les Tahirides*, 1:184–85, and Daniel, "Taherids," *Encyclopaedia Iranica* (online version).

101 Also known as Mary's Monastery (Yāqūt, *Muʿjam al-buldān*, 2:672). The monastery was founded by a monk from Sūs (southwestern Iran) (Fiey, *Assyrie chrétienne*, 3:119).

102 Circumcision is an obligatory ritual for Muslim boys, a sign of their belonging to the Islamic community. It is carried out by a barber at any age before puberty and is an occasion for rejoicing.

103 This celebration, one of three famous lavish ceremonial banquets, is frequently cited. For another version, with more explanation of the objects involved, see al-Qaddūmī, *Book of Gifts and Rarities*, 136–41.

104 Comment in the margin: "The carpet was one hundred cubits long and fifty cubits broad. It was valued at ten thousand dinars."

105 Sleeves were often wide and could be used as pockets. Sometimes extensions were added to them, increasing their capacity.

106 Freeing slaves was a pious act often performed to mark an important occasion.

107 The Arabic term *shākiriyyah* is somewhat obscure but refers to freeborn professional soldiers, probably of central Asian origin (Gordon, *The Breaking of a Thousand Swords: A History of the Turkish Military of Samarra (A.H. 200–275/815–889 C.E.)*, 40–42).

108 The guest list at the ceremony starts with princes of the Abbasid family. Apart from al-Muntaṣir, they do not appear elsewhere in the book and are otherwise unmemorable, so they have not been included in the Glossary.

109 Comment in the margin: "At al-Mu'tazz's circumcision, al-Mutawakkil ordered al-Fatḥ ibn Yaḥyā [*sic*] ibn Khāqān to put a cup full of wine in his father's hand, although he didn't drink." Al-Mutawakkil clearly sought to impose his authority on an elderly man in front of his professional colleagues (*mashāyikh al-kuttāb*), forcing him to act against his principles. Conceivably, the caliph wanted to show the secretaries that he could make them obey him even though he infringed the shariah. See Samer M. Ali, "Early Islam—Monotheism or Henotheism? A View from the Court," 16–17, who however understands the *mashāyikh* as "pious elders."

110 The guests were transported by boat from Baghdad.

111 Comment in the margin: "What an immensely eloquent poet he is."

112 Abū Nuwās al-Ḥasan ibn Hāni', *Dīwān*, 3:36.

113 "Imam," leader of the Muslim community, was a title of the caliph.

114 Of the palaces in and around Samarra listed here, only Balkuwārā, al-Jawsaq, and the Mutawakkiliyyah Palace occur elsewhere in the text; they are mentioned separately in the Glossary. For the others, see Alastair Northedge, "The Palaces of the 'Abbasids at Samarra."

115 The Persian festivity *shad-gulī* (rose joy), more often termed *gul-afshānī* (rose-strewing), was an occasion when rose petals, sometimes mixed with light coins and perfume, were scattered during a drinking party. It is mentioned in several poems in Arabic and Persian (Ṭabāṭabā'ī, "Gul-i surkh u bāda-yi gulgūn: Bāz-khwānī-yi abyātī az dīwān-I Abū Nuwās bar pāya-yi āyīn-i kuhan-i shādgulī." I thank Anna-Livia Beelaert for tracking down and summarizing this reference.)

116 Cf. OT I Kings 11:18–20. Solomon (Sulaymān) is mentioned in the Qur'an as a ruler and a prophet with magical powers, the material about him being chiefly rabbinic in origin.

117 That is, al-Fatḥ ibn Khāqān.

118 The bearing of the two noble beings suggests they are more than human, like husbands of the fabled beauties who, according to the Qur'an, inhabit Paradise.

119 The Arabic original is the proverb "Both of them and dates too" (al-Maydānī, *Majmaʿ al-amthāl* #3079: *kilāhumā wa-tamran*).

120 For the background to the brief caliphates and violent deaths of al-Mustaʿīn and al-Muʿtazz, see Gordon, *The Breaking of a Thousand Swords*, 95–101.

121 This and the following ecclesiastical term are discussed in Tannous, *The Making of the Medieval Middle East*, 12–14, with further references. "The Church of the East" is the designation the Nestorians use for themselves, and is generally accepted today.

122 For a comment on this unusual state of affairs, see Tannous, *The Making of the Medieval Middle East*, 122–36 and n. 44.

123 Literally "they pray Jumada during Rajab." Rajab follows Jumada al-Thani. It is one of the four sacred months during which special prayers are said, but these drunkards are behind with the calendar for prayers.

124 Comment in the margin: "Take note of ʿAmr ibn ʿAbd al-Malik al-Warrāq's poetry and his manner."

125 This monastery was dedicated to Shimʿūn bar Ṣabbāʿé, martyred in 329.

126 So called because it was dug by Isḥāq ibn Ibrāhīm ibn Muṣʿab.

127 Al-Aʿlā Monastery was built in the highest part of Mosul, hence its name, *aʿlā* ("higher" or "highest").

128 In 215/830.

129 For this translation of *ṣaḥrāʾ* see Bray, "Figures in a Landscape: The Inhabitants of the Silver Village," 80–81.

130 These girdles (*zunnār*) were a distinguishing mark of Christian dress.

131 The name means "prosperity."

132 Comment in the margin: "Āminah bint al-Sharīd's address to Muʿāwiyah after he cast her husband's head at her."

133 Q Qaṣaṣ 28:19.

134 The monastery is said to have been founded in the fourth century, at the site of ancient Nineveh. It seems to have disappeared by the end of the thirteenth century (Fiey, *Assyrie chrétienne*, 2:497–504).

135 Unlike other monasteries named for a saint, a founder, or the place where they are located, "Devils" appears to be a nickname. Unfortunately, al-Shābushtī does not comment on it.

136 The image is from chess. According to the rules in this period, the queen only moved one square at a time.

137 I have not found a satisfactory explanation of al-Ma'mūn's remark and the distinction he makes between "dead" and "living" ingredients.

138 The phrase also means "the religious obligations linked to getting hard," hence the subsequent exchange.

139 Probably the monastery of Saint John at Zāz in Ṭūr ʿAbdīn, founded at the end of the sixth century (Ṣādir, *Mawsūʿat al-adyirah al-naṣrāniyyah fī al-bilād al-mashriqiyyah ḥattā nihāyat al-ʿuṣūr al-ʿabbāsiyyah*, 347, quoting Barṣūm, *Tārīkh Ṭūr ʿAbdīn*, 217).

140 Monastery of Saint Abraham the Great of Kashkar (Kaskar), reviver of East Syrian monasticism in the sixth century.

141 An allusion to motifs of pre-Islamic poetry still employed in some conventional Abbasid poetry.

142 A proverbial expression adapted from a line by the pre-Islamic poet Labīd.

143 Comment in the margin: "Take note of Muṣʿab al-Kātib's counsel."

144 Literally "War is deception," a saying attributed to the Prophet in Sunni and Shiʿi hadith collections (e.g., al-Bukhārī, *Ṣaḥīḥ al-Bukhārī*, #3028, #3029; Muslim, *Ṣaḥīḥ Muslim*, #1739, #1740; al-Qāḍī al-Nuʿmān, *Sharḥ al-akhbār fī faḍāʾil al-aʾimmah al-aṭhār*, 1:297.

145 "God's House" is the Kaaba in Mecca. This and the subsequent verses allude to rituals of the pilgrimage to Mecca.

146 Muḥammad ibn Ḥāzim al-Bāhilī, *Dīwān*, 56. *Pace* ʿAwwād, the line is not found in Ibn al-Rūmī's diwan.

147 An allusion to the story of Joseph in the Qur'an (Surah 12). In Islamic tradition, his beauty is proverbial.

148 Not the first caliph in Islam, but an otherwise unknown ninth-century rent boy. The fluctuation between religious and profane references is typical of this poet's work.

149 Literally "Quʿays at his aunt's door," a proverbial expression.

150 Known to the Arab geographers as Nahr al-Sarbaṭ.

151 Afshīn was a title that was used not only by a famous commander of al-Muʿtaṣim but also by the Sājid rulers of Azerbaijan in the early tenth century, including Yūsuf.

152 Addition to the poem in the margin: "My origin prevents me from not standing by my friends, / An ignoble man's favor I'm not wont to accept; / I'm not fooled by those whose fine appearance masks filth; / I'd rather die of thirst than slake it with clyster water."

153 Echoing Q Zalzalah 99:7–8: «Whoever does an atom's weight of good will see it. Whoever does an atom's weight of evil will see it».

154 The pass leading down from the Golan to the Jordan Valley. The village of Fīq was an important stage on the road from Damascus to Jerusalem (Sharon, "An Arabic Inscription from the Time of the Caliph ʿAbd al-Malik," 369).

155 Comment in the margin: "From this poem Mudrik took certain verses to address his beloved ʿAmr." As ʿAwwād points out, this poem is not in Abū Nuwās's printed poetry. The Mudrik mentioned is Mudrik ibn ʿAlī al-Shaybānī (early tenth century).

156 A monastery near Wāsiṭ, possibly dedicated to saints Sarjīs (Sergius) and Bākhūs (Bacchus), warrior martyrs whose names are often linked. Sirjisān means "the two Sergiuses."

157 This is a reference to the Nawbahār temple in Balkh, most likely a Manichean center (Kamoliddin, "On the Religion of the Nawbahar Temple in Balkh").

158 Perhaps a reference to the Islamic legend that the Antichrist will be vanquished before the door of the church in Lydda (Lod).

159 The girdle said to have been worn by the Virgin Mary and given to the apostle Thomas. It is an important relic in the Syriac Christian tradition. Here it forms a transition to the poet's addressing his beloved.

160 Lajjūn was built on hills southwest of the Jezreel Valley. After 1948 it was destroyed by the Israelis, who built the kibbutz of Megiddo on the land.

161 According to the Gospels, the Transfiguration happened before the Crucifixion and the Ascension: Mt 17:1–9; Mk 9:2–13; Lk 9:28–36. Al-Shābushtī appears to be confusing the Transfiguration with Christ's appearances after the Resurrection.

162 That is, the month following Ramadan.

163 "Cursing" has been partially erased in the manuscript. See the Introduction for the reflections in *The Book of Monasteries* of the confessional strife between Sunnis and Shiʿis.

164 The Battle of the Camel between ʿAlī and his supporters on one side and ʿĀʾishah, Ṭalḥah, and al-Zubayr on the other took place over two days, the first of which, when ʿAlī had not yet arrived, is termed the lesser one.

165 It was the residence of the Syrian Orthodox patriarch in the seventh century.

166 This is the literal meaning of the Arabic name for anemones, *shaqāʾiq nuʿmān*.

167 The name means "rebellious."

168 Helena, not to be confused with Haylānah, the slave girl al-Rashīd acquired from Jaʿfar the Barmakid, mentioned by Ibn al-Sāʿī in *Consorts of the Caliphs: Women and the Court of Baghdad*, 22.

169 Respectively, "Emotion," "Brightness," and "Softness."

170 The name means "Yemeni brocades."

171 Not 5, as in the manuscript.

172 The autumn festival, in Arabic (from Persian) *Mihrajān*, is the autumn counterpart to Nauruz, for which see the Glossary. "Mihrajān" has come to mean "festival" in general, without being specific to a season.

173 This pilgrimage was in 187/803. While in Mecca, al-Rashīd, who was becoming increasingly independent of his supporters, the Barmakids, arranged the question of his succession, and it was after that that he turned against the Barmakids. See Kennedy, *The Prophet and the Age of the Caliphates*, 141–44.

174 Here the sixth-century Khosroes Anūshirwān is meant.

175 ʿAbd al-Masīḥ had been asked to interpret the king's dream and could not, so he turned to his uncle. In the context of Zoroastrianism with its cult of fire worship, the mention of the dying fire has a symbolic meaning, pointing to the replacement of the ancient Persian religion with Islam. Short and obscure rhyming phrases are typical of the speech associated with pre-Islamic soothsayers.

176 In this context, "Nabatean" designates Aramaic speakers.

177 Or: "do you pay blood money?," playing on two senses of *ʿaqala*.

178 Or: "what is your tooth?," playing on two senses of *sinn*.

179 Or: "How much has finished you off?," playing on two senses of *atā ʿalā*.

180 Probably from the Syriac *shatīqā*, meaning "silent" (al-Shābushtī, *Diyārāt*, ed. ʿAwwād, 241n1).

181 Possibly the Syriac *shakūrā*, "flowers, roses" (al-Shābushtī, *Diyārāt*, ed. ʿAwwād, 241n2).

182 I thank Liran Yadgar for suggesting this Jewish name, attested in late Antiquity and the Middle Ages.

183 Comment in the margin: "Al-Ḥajjāj al-Thaqafī's conversation with Hind bint al-Nuʿmān ibn al-Mundhir."

184 This line is absent from the diwans of both al-Nābighah al-Dhubyānī (late sixth century) and the younger al-Nābighah al-Jaʿdī (seventh century). The former is the probable author, since he was the court poet of Hind's father, the ruler of Ḥīrah.

185 The decisive battle was at Qādisiyyah in 15/636.

186 Comment in the margin: "Al-Mughīrah ibn Shuʿbah's visit to Hind bint al-Nuʿmān ibn al-Mundhir to ask for her hand in marriage and her refusal."

187 The tribal confederation Hawāzin in the Hijaz included ʿĀmir ibn Ṣaʿṣaʿah and Māzin ibn Ṣaʿṣaʿah. The tribe of Thaqīf, based in Ṭāʾif, traced its lineage back either to Hawāzin or to Iyād (al-Yaʿqūbī, *The Works of Ibn Wāḍiḥ al-Yaʿqūbī*, 2:539–41). Whether this anecdote is genuine or made up by Hind on the spur of the moment, the aim was to give al-Mughīrah his comeuppance.

188 This monastery was established on the estate of Zurārah ibn Yazīd ibn ʿAmr of the Banū l-Bukkāʾ ibn Rabīʿah, from which it took its name (al-Shābushtī, *Diyārāt*, ed. ʿAwwād, 247; al-Ṭurayḥī, *al-Diyārāt wa-l-amkinah al-naṣrāniyyah fī al-Kūfah wa-ḍawāḥīhā*, 109–10).

189 So called after a freedman of Saʿd ibn Abī Waqqāṣ, conqueror of Iraq.

190 A parallel version of this anecdote has the same situation and poetry, but the protagonists are Ḥammād ʿAjrad, the spurned lover, and Muṭīʿ ibn Iyās, who is proposing to replace him in the girl's affections (Ibn al-Muʿtazz, *Ṭabaqāt al-shuʿarāʾ al-muḥdathīn*, 253–54).

191 In this striking anecdote, peer rivalry, concepts of masculinity and femininity, and social differentiation are all present. Empathy with the victim of the rape, which a modern reader tends to expect, is absent. See Lagrange, "Une affair de viol," for an illuminating discussion of the text. The translation he provides is, however, not from al-Shābushtī but from another unspecified *adab* work.

192 The line is from a poem by Ibn Qays al-Ruqayyāt (*Dīwān*, 109).

193 Comment in the margin: "Note the description of the lute."

194 Examples of the use of this instrument are given in Sawa, *Musical and Socio-Cultural Anecdotes*, 55, 170.

195 According to legend, Qunnā was a noblewoman whom the first-century apostle Mārī cured of leprosy, and in gratitude she gave him the land for the monastery. The monastery was destroyed by the Sassanians in the fifth century but was later rebuilt. It became a flourishing center of learning of the Church of the East and provided secretaries for the Abbasid administration.

196 It falls on September 14.

197 Al-Manṣūriyyah means "slave or freedwoman of al-Manṣūr."

198 The Seven Poems, often known as the *Muʿallaqāt*, are the most famous collection of pre-Islamic poetry. The first efforts to assemble this canonical anthology go back to the second/eighth century.

199 The spelling mistake is intentional.

200 ʿAbdūn uses a Persian word here and abandons any semblance of meter.

201 The later Caliph al-Muʿtaḍid.

202 Muḥammad ibn Ḥāzim went to the otherwise unidentified Muḥammad ibn Saʿīd, an attendant on al-Ḥasan ibn Sahl, as a member of the same tribe, Bāḥilah.

203 The well of Zamzam is in the Holy Mosque of Mecca. Al-Ḥaṭīm is a low wall close to the Kaaba.

204 That is, Ibrāhīm ibn al-Mahdī.

205 Al-Shābushtī has pruned the chain of transmission of this anecdote, which has four names in the *Kitāb al-Aghānī* (14:101), leaving only the penultimate name, Ḥamdān ibn Yaḥyā (Ḥammād ibn Yaḥyā in the *Aghānī*).

206 Qārūn is the Qur'anic counterpart of Korah in the Old Testament. A contemporary and opponent of Moses, he was fabulously wealthy, arrogant, and unjust (Q Qaṣaṣ 28:76–82).

207 The name means "little fortress." It was built in the fifth century and is also known as the Monastery of Saint Arsenios the Great.

208 The Moqattam Hills.

209 In the Eastern churches, this refers to the area known in the West as the sanctuary.

210 The Maʿāfir Pool was another name for the Ethiopians' Pool, and the Monastery of Saint John was thus also called the Maʿāfir Monastery.

211 Presumably the mosque of ʿAbdallāh ibn ʿAbd al-Malik ibn Marwān, in the area between Darb al-Maʿāṣir and Bāb al-Ṣafā (Ibn Duqmāq, *Kitāb al-Intiṣār li-wāsiṭat ʿiqd al-amṣār*, 4:91).

212 Al-ʿUmarī, *Masālik al-abṣār*, 1:698, apparently reproducing information of the Khālidīs, describes the setting of this monastery in terms very like those al-Shābushtī has used for monasteries in the main part of the book. It contrasts with al-Shābushtī's laconic presentation. ʿAwwād, however, following a communication from J. M. Fiey, gives the location as at Maʿlathāyā close to Dohuk, and I have adopted this.

213 Literally "the city," *al-Madīnah*. While *al-Madīnah* normally refers to the famous city in the Hijaz, it could also refer to *Madīnat al-salām*, the City of Peace, another name for Baghdad. But the geographical indications are problematic.

214 The name is a contraction of ʿAyn Jājj, the spring of Jājj. It was founded in the seventh century and dedicated to Saint Sergius.

215 Mount Jūdī is mentioned in the Qur'an (Q Hūd 11:44) as the site where Noah's ark came to rest after the flood. Its location (in southeastern Turkey near the Syrian and Iraqi borders) reflects Mesopotamian tradition. The location further north on Mount Ararat appears in about the tenth century.

216 A span is 23.1 centimeters.

217 An allusion to the story of Moses in the Qur'an (Q Aʿrāf 7:143).

218 Presumably the Holy Fire, whose descent in Christ's tomb is celebrated on Holy Saturday.

219 I have not been able to discover a satisfactory meaning for this word. In the context of Ibn ʿĀṣim's poem, it seems likely to be a personal name (cf. al-Najjār, *Shuʿarāʾ ʿabbāsiyūn mansiyyūn*, 6:28–29). The manuscript has "Qawzīr," but ʿAwwād, followed by al-Najjār, transcribes it "Qawrīr."

220 Scrofula, also known as king's evil, is an infection of the lymph nodes in the neck often connected with tuberculosis. The name is the diminutive of Latin *scrofa*, meaning a brood sow; the Arabic name, *khanāzīr*, means "pigs."

221 Ba'ūnah is the commemoration of the first church dedicated to the Virgin Mary in Caesarea Philippi. *Pace* ʿAwwād (al-Shābushtī, *Diyārāt*, 313n2), it is not the Feast of the Dormition (August 15), which in the Coptic calendar is Mesori 16.

Glossary

ʿAbbād ibn Ziyād ibn Abī Sufyān (d. 100/718) son of Muʿāwiyah's adopted brother. He served as general and governor under Umayyad caliphs.

al-ʿAbbās ibn al-Baṣrī (fl. mid-fourth/tenth century) poet at the Ikhshīdid court in Egypt, probably of Iraqi origin.

al-ʿAbbās ibn al-Maʾmūn (d. 223/838) al-Maʾmūn's eldest son, leader of military expeditions. He died in prison after a failed conspiracy against his uncle al-Muʿtaṣim.

ʿAbd al-ʿAzīz ibn ʿAbdallāh ibn Ṭāhir (mid-third/ninth century) unremarkable youngest son of ʿAbdallāh ibn Ṭāhir.

ʿAbd al-Malik ibn Marwān ibn al-Ḥakam (ca. 23–86/644–705) second caliph of the Marwanid branch of the Umayyad dynasty, succeeded 65/685.

ʿAbd al-Malik ibn Muḥammad al-Hāshimī, Abū al-Faḍl (fl. third/ninth century) unidentified descendant of the Prophet.

ʿAbd al-Masīḥ ibn Buqaylah al-Ghassānī (fl. early seventh century AD) member of a prominent and long-established family of Ḥīrah, around whom many legends were woven.

ʿAbd al-Raḥmān ibn Fahm (fl. third/ninth century) obscure transmitter.

ʿAbd al-Raḥmān ibn Umm al-Ḥakam (fl. late first/seventh century) governor of Kufa for Muʿāwiyah, his mother's brother.

ʿAbdah bint ʿAbdallāh ibn Yazīd ibn Muʿāwwiyah (early second/eighth century) granddaughter of the second Umayyad caliph, Yazīd ibn Muʿāwiyah, and wife of the tenth Umayyad caliph, Hishām ibn ʿAbd al-Malik.

ʿAbdallāh ibn ʿAbbās (d. 68/619–87) cousin of the Prophet and revered transmitter of traditions about him.

ʿAbdallāh ibn ʿAbbās ibn al-Faḍl ibn al-Rabīʿ (d. 247/861) grandson of the chamberlain al-Faḍl ibn al-Rabīʿ, courtier, poet, and musician. Began his career at court by performing before al-Rashīd.

ʿAbdallāh ibn ʿAbd al-Malik ibn Marwān (ca. 57–131/677–749) Umayyad general and governor of Egypt.

ʿAbdallāh ibn ʿAyyāsh (d. 171/788) Kufan transmitter of poetry and historical accounts.

ʿAbdallāh ibn Dāwud al-Khuraybī (d. 211/826) Hadith transmitter of Kufan origin who settled in Basra.

ʿAbdallāh ibn Khurdādhbih (fl. early third/ninth century) Khurasanian commander, governor of Ṭabaristān, the Iranian province south of the Caspian Sea.

ʿAbdallāh ibn Manṣūr (fl. mid-third/ninth century) influential state secretary in Samarra, briefly vizier under al-Mustaʿīn.

ʿAbdallāh ibn al-Muʿtazz see Ibn al-Muʿtazz.

ʿAbdallāh ibn Ṭāhir ibn al-Ḥusayn (182–229/798–844) governor of Egypt and then Khurasan under al-Maʾmūn and al-Muʿtaṣim. He was a patron, man of letters, poet, and musician.

ʿAbdūn ibn Makhlad (d. 310/922) Nestorian state scribe, brother of the vizier Ṣāʿid, who occupied important positions until his brother's fall from favor.

Abū l-ʿAbbās ibn al-Furāt (d. 291/904) influential state scribe in charge of land department under al-Muʿtaḍid.

Abu l-ʿAbbās al-Saffāḥ ʿAbdallāh ibn Muḥammad (d. 136/754) grandson of ʿAlī ibn ʿAbdallāh, brother of Ibrāhīm the Imam. First Abbasid caliph from 132/750.

Abū ʿAbdallāh ibn Ḥamdūn see Ibn Ḥamdūn.

Abū Aḥmad ʿUbaydallāh ibn ʿAbdallāh ibn Ṭāhir see ʿUbaydallāh ibn ʿAbdallāh ibn Ṭāhir.

Abū ʿAlī al-Awārijī, Hārūn ibn ʿAbd al- ʿAzīz (d. 344/955) state scribe and administrator.

Abū ʿAlī al-Baṣīr al-Faḍl ibn Jaʿfar (d. ca. 252/866) blind poet and man of letters, much admired at Baghdad and Samarra courts.

Abū ʿAlī ibn al-Rashīd (d. 230/845) unremarkable son of Hārūn al-Rashīd.

Abū ʿAlī Muḥammad ibn al-ʿAlāʾ al-Shajarī (fl. late third/ninth century) unidentified state scribe.

Abū l-Aṣbagh (fl. late second/eighth century) owner and seller of singing slave girls in Kufa.

Abū l-ʿAtāhiyah, Ismāʿīl ibn al-Qāsim (130–211/748–826) poet at al-Mahdī's court, famous for his love poems and later his ascetic verses.

Abū l-ʿAynāʾ Muḥammad ibn al-Qāsim Abū ʿAbdallāh (d. ca. 283/896) man of letters and courtier in Basra and Baghdad, a renowned wit around whom many humorous anecdotes collected.

Abū Bakr Muḥammad ibn al-Qāsim ibn al-Anbārī see Ibn al-Anbārī.

Abū l-Barq (fl. third/ninth century) obscure poet, client of Isḥāq ibn Ibrāhīm al-Ṭāhirī.

Abū l-Dann (fl. early second/eighth century) obscure laborer, descended from a freedman of the Prophet.

Abū Dharr al-Ghifārī (d. 31/652) Companion of the Prophet Muḥammad, one of the earliest converts to Islam.

Abū Ḥarmalah (fl. mid-third/ninth century) al-Mutawakkil's barber.

Abū Ḥashīshah Muḥammad ibn ʿAlī ibn Umayyah (d. before 279/892) court companion and musician, virtuoso on the pandore (long-necked lute), and author of two books on music.

Abū Ḥāzim (fl. mid-third/ninth century) jurist.

Abū Hūr Coptic saint, probably a martyr executed during the persecutions of the late third and early fourth centuries AD in Egypt.

Abū Hurayrah ibn Abī al-ʿIṣām (fl. early fourth/tenth century) Egyptian poet.

Abū Isḥāq ibn al-Rashīd see al-Muʿtaṣim bi-llāh.

Abū Jaʿfar al-Manṣūr (d. 158/775) second Abbasid caliph, grandson of ʿAlī ibn ʿAbdallāh and brother of Ibrāhīm the Imam, succeeded 137/755. Founder of Baghdad.

Abū Jafnah al-Qurashī obscure Iraqi poet of the Abbasid period.

Abū Jahl ʿAmr ibn Hishām (d. 2/624) contemporary of Prophet Muḥammad, notable of the powerful Makhzūm clan and leader of the Meccan opposition to the Prophet. Killed at the battle of Badr.

Abū al-Jaysh Khumārawayh ibn Aḥmad ibn Ṭūlūn (250–83/864–96) son of Aḥmad ibn Ṭūlūn, a Turkish general who established himself as the autonomous ruler of Egypt in 254/868. Succeeded his father in 270/884.

Abū l-Khaṣīb Marzūq (fl. second/eight century) freedman and chamberlain of al-Manṣūr.

Abū l-Miḍrajī (fl. late second/eighth century) Iraqi libertine.

Abū Muslim ʿAbd al-Raḥmān ibn Muslim al-Khurāsānī (d. 137/755) of Persian origin, leader of the revolution that overthrew the Umayyads and brought the Abbasids to power.

Abū Nuwās al-Ḥasan ibn Hāniʾ (ca. 139–99/757–815) leading "modern" poet especially famous for his wine songs. Panegyrist of al-Rashīd, companion of al-Amīn.

Abū l-Qāsim ʿAbdallāh al-Mawṣilī (fl. third/ninth century) obscure individual who was probably a state scribe.

Abū al-Qāsim Ūnūjūr ibn al-Ikhshīd (d. 349/960) succeeded his father, Muḥammad ibn Tughj al-Ikhshīd, as ruler of Egypt in 334/946. *Al-Ikhshīd*, the title of the kings of Ferghānah (where the family originated), was bestowed on Muḥammad ibn Tughj for his successful resistance to the Fatimids.

Abū l-Ṣaqr Ismāʿīl ibn Bulbul (ca. 229–79/844–92) state scribe and vizier to al-Muʿtamid and al-Muwaffaq, imprisoned by al-Muʿtaḍid.

Abū Shās Munīr al-Ghiṭrīf ibn Ḥuṣayn ibn Ḥanash (fl. mid-third/ninth century) poet and man of letters connected with al-Muʿtaṣim's army.

Abū l-Shibl al-Burjumī, ʿĀṣim ibn Wahb (fl. third/ninth century) poet from Basra, active in Baghdad and Samarra.

Abū l-ʿUmaythil ʿAbdallāh ibn Khulayd (d. 239/854) tutor of ʿAbdallāh ibn Ṭāhir's sons, poet and man of letters.

Aḥmad ibn Abī Duʾād (d. 239/854) companion of al-Maʾmūn, chief judge in Baghdad under al-Muʿtaṣim and al-Wāthiq, responsible for imposing the doctrine of the created Qurʾan.

Aḥmad ibn Abī l-ʿAlāʾ (fl. mid-third/ninth century) son of a court musician, excellent singer.

Aḥmad ibn Abī Khālid (d. 211/826) state scribe and close companion of al-Maʾmūn who headed the administration after al-Faḍl ibn Sahl's death.

Aḥmad ibn Abī Ruʾaym (fl. mid-third/ninth century) court companion of al-Mutawakkil.

Aḥmad ibn Buwayh (302–56/915–67) member of a Shiʿi family from Daylam in northwestern Iran who took power in various regions of the eastern Muslim world in the tenth century. Better known as Muʿizz al-Dawlah, he occupied Baghdad in 333/945 and ruled as emir under the Sunni caliph.

Aḥmad ibn al-Ḥasan al-Mādharāʾī (fl. late third/ninth century) member of an influential family of state secretaries and finance officials in Iraq and Egypt, originally from Mādharā, a village near Wāsiṭ.

Aḥmad ibn Isrāʾīl, Abū Jaʿfar (207–83/823–96) state scribe of Nestorian origin, vizier of al-Muʿtazz, tortured to death by Ṣāliḥ ibn Waṣīf under al-Muhtadī.

Aḥmad ibn Khālid al-Ṣarīfīnī (fl. mid-third/ninth century) fiscal prefect of Egypt in 255–56/840–41 and briefly al-Mutawakkil's vizier in 232–33/847–48.

Aḥmad ibn Mūsā ibn Shākir (fl. third/ninth century) one of the three Banū Mūsā brothers known for their writings on astronomy, geometry, and mechanical devices.

Aḥmad ibn Ṣadaqah (fl. third/ninth century) from a family of musicians, he sang at the courts of al-Ma'mūn and al-Mutawakkil.

Aḥmad ibn Yūsuf (d. ca. 213/828) private secretary, companion, and vizier of al-Ma'mūn, famed for his literary gifts.

ʿĀ'ishah bint Abī Bakr (d. 58/678) youngest wife of the Prophet, transmitter of hadiths. After opposing the third caliph, ʿUthmān, she was one of those who sought to avenge his killing and led the army that fought against ʿAlī in the Battle of the Camel.

Akhmīm town on the east bank of the Nile in Upper Egypt, opposite Sohag.

Alexander the Great (356–323) Greek conqueror of much of Asia, symbol of royal power.

ʿAlī ibn ʿAbdallāh ibn ʿAbbās (ca. 40–118/661–736) grandson of the Prophet's uncle ʿAbbās and grandfather of the first two Abbasid caliphs, al-Saffāḥ and al-Manṣūr.

ʿAlī ibn Abī Ṭālib (d. 40/661) cousin and son-in-law of Prophet Muḥammad, fourth rightly guided caliph (according to the Sunni view); first caliph after Muḥammad (according to the Shiʿi view). Attacked by Muʿāwiyah for not punishing the killers of the third rightly guided caliph, ʿUthmān, he was murdered by a Kharijite.

ʿAlī ibn Hishām (d. 217/832) cousin of Ṭāhir ibn al-Ḥusayn, one of al-Ma'mūn's generals. A music lover, he was the commander in the campaign against Bābak, and was subsequently disgraced and executed.

ʿAlī ibn Ibrāhīm al-Ghamrī (fl. third/ninth century) judge in Mosul.

ʿAlī ibn ʿĪsā ibn Māhān (d. 195/811) governor of Khurasan under al-Rashīd. He championed al-Amīn's cause against al-Ma'mūn and was killed in battle against al-Ma'mūn's forces led by Ṭāhir ibn al-Ḥusayn.

ʿAlī ibn al-Jahm (ca. 188–249/804–63) poet and man of letters who was al-Mutawakkil's court companion for a time.

ʿAlī ibn Muḥammad al-Ḥimmānī al-ʿAlawī (d. 260/874) descendant of ʿAlī ibn Abī Ṭālib from Kufa, composer of elegies on his Shiʿi relatives and on the passing of youth.

ʿAlī ibn Muḥammad ibn Abī Sayf al-Madā'inī see al-Madā'inī.

ʿAlī ibn Ṣāliḥ (fl. early third/ninth century) freedman of al-Ma'mūn, his chamberlain and Master of the Prayer Carpet, controlling access to him.

ʿAlī ibn Yaḥyā al-Munajjim (199–274/815–88) member of the cultivated Banū l-Munajjim family, man of letters, poet, musician, and author, patron of poets and writers, court companion of caliphs from al-Mutawakkil to al-Muʿtamid.

ʿAlids descendants of the Prophet's cousin and son-in-law, ʿAlī ibn Abī Ṭālib.

ʿAllūya, ʿAlī ibn ʿAbdallāh (d. 235/850) singer at court from the time of al-Amīn to al-Mutawakkil.

ʿAlth village about four and a half miles (seven kilometers) northwest of Balad on the east bank of the old course of the Tigris.

al-Amīn, Abū Mūsā Muḥammad (170–98/787–813) sixth Abbasid caliph, succeeded 193/809, generous patron of poets. He tried to restore Baghdad's authority over Khurasan, his brother al-Ma'mūn's province, and was defeated and killed by him.

Āminah bint al-Sharīd (d. ca. 50/670) one of the women of the early Umayyad period renowned for their eloquence in debate and repartee.

ʿAmr ibn ʿAbd al-Malik al-Warrāq (fl. early third/ninth century) dissolute poet in Baghdad who composed poems on the siege of Baghdad during the civil war between al-Amīn and al-Ma'mūn, lamenting the city's destruction.

ʿAmr ibn Bānah (d. 278/891) son of a secretary, singer at court from the time of al-Ma'mūn.

ʿAmr ibn al-Ḥamiq al-Khuzāʿī (d. 50/670) Companion of the Prophet. Involved in the murder of ʿUthmān, he supported ʿAlī and fought on his side against Muʿāwiyah at Ṣiffīn (36/657).

ʿAmr ibn al-Layth al-Ṣaffār (d. 289/902) succeeded his brother Yaʿqūb ibn al-Layth as ruler of much of Iran, while pursuing a more conciliatory policy toward the caliph. He was defeated by the Sāmānid ruler of Transoxiana and sent to Baghdad as a prisoner.

ʿĀnah town on the Euphrates on a major trade route between the Mediterranean and the Persian Gulf.

ʿĀqūl Monastery on the Tigris south of Baghdad, site of the Abbasid victory over Yaʿqūb al-Ṣaffār in 262/876. It flourished at least until the end of the tenth century.

ʿArīb (181–277/797–890) leading singer at court, poet, and courtier. She was owned by al-Amīn and al-Ma'mūn and freed by al-Muʿtaṣim; she also performed for later caliphs. The name means "ardent."

Arzan town to the east of Mayyāfāriqīn (present-day Silvan), prosperous up to the tenth century but now in ruins.

ʿAsālij singing girl belonging to Ruqayyah bint al-Faḍl ibn al-Rabīʿ (fl. early third/ninth century). The name means "tender branches."

al-Aṣmaʿī, ʿAbd al-Malik ibn Qurayb (123–213/740–828) Basran philologist and grammarian, collector of pre-Islamic poetry.

ʿAthʿath (fl. mid-third/ninth century) a black slave and gifted musician, he witnessed al-Mutawakkil's murder. The name means "softy."

Awānā village near the town of Dujayl, about forty miles (sixty-five kilometers) north of Baghdad.

ʿAwf ibn Muḥallim al-Khuzāʿī (d. ca. 215/830) poet, man of letters, and companion of Ṭāhir and his son ʿAbdallāh.

Awgīn (Eugene), Saint (d. AD 363) Egyptian monk said to have brought monasticism to Mesopotamia.

al-ʿAzīz (fl. early third/ninth century) freedman of ʿAbdallāh ibn Ṭāhir.

al-ʿAzīz bi-llāh, Abū Manṣūr Nizār (344–386/955–96) fifth Fatimid caliph, and al-Shābushtī's employer. He succeeded in 364/975.

ʿAzzūn ibn ʿAbd al-ʿAzīz al-Anṣārī (fl. third/ninth century) court companion of al-Muʿtaṣim, al-Wāthiq, and al-Mutawakkil.

Bābak (ca. 175–223/795–838) leader of resistance to Muslim settlers in northwestern Iran, defeated and executed in Samarra.

Badhl (fl. early third/ninth century) singer trained in Basra and owned by al-Amīn. She was vastly knowledgeable about the musical repertoire. The name means "giving."

Badr (d. 289/902) chief of police in Baghdad and later commander-in-chief of al-Muʿtaḍid's armies. He was named "al-Muʿtaḍidī" because of his influence over the caliph. "Badr," meaning "full moon," was a common name for a servant.

Badr al-Jullanār (fl. mid-third/ninth century) slave and favorite of al-Muʿtamid. "Jullanār" means "pomegranate blossom."

Bakr ibn Hawāzin, Banū major tribal grouping based in the Hijaz to which the tribe of Thaqīf belonged.

Bakr ibn Khārijah (fl. first half third/ninth century) notorious drinker who composed wine songs and love songs.

Bakr ibn Wāʾil, Banū important tribe settled mostly in Iraq. Many inhabitants of Ḥīrah belonged to it.

Balad (1) town some twenty-five miles (forty kilometers) northwest of Mosul. (2) Town fifty miles (eighty kilometers) north of Baghdad.

Balashkur village between Baradān and Baghdad on the east bank of the Tigris.

Balīkh River tributary of the Euphrates, which it joins at Raqqa.

Balkuwārā Palace palace on the Tigris south of Samarra, built by al-Mutawakkil for his son al-Mu'tazz around 239/854.

Baradān town twenty-two miles (thirty-five kilometers) north of Baghdad to the east of the Tigris.

Bārī village in the neighborhood of Kalwādhā.

Barmakids a family of viziers and administrators, originally Buddhists from Balkh, who served the first five Abbasid caliphs. They fell from favor in 187/803, when al-Rashīd executed or imprisoned many of them.

Bāshahrā monastery between Baghdad and Samarra. The name means "House of Vigils."

Bazūghī village to the north of Shammāsiyyah, some seven miles (eleven kilometers) from Baghdad.

Bidʿah (ca. 241–302/856–915) singer, pupil, and confidante of ʿArīb. She sang before al-Muʿtazz and al-Muʿtaḍid. The name means "nova."

Bunān (fl. mid-third/ninth century) singer and famous lutenist at the courts of al-Mutawakkil, al-Muntaṣir, and al-Muʿtazz.

Būrān (191–270/807–84) daughter of al-Ḥasan ibn Sahl, married to al-Ma'mūn.

Buṣrā village near Baghdad. Not the town in Syria.

Catholicos Patriarch of the Church of the East (Nestorian Church). In this period, he had his seat in Baghdad.

Companion A person belonging to the first generation of followers of the Prophet Muḥammad.

Dābiq locality north of Aleppo close to the Byzantine frontier.

Dahlak archipelago in the Red Sea not far from Massawa (present-day Eritrea).

Darius the son of Darius last king of the Achaemenid dynasty in Persia, defeated by Alexander the Great in 330. A symbol of royal greatness.

Dāwud Siyāh al-Khwārizmī (fl. early third/ninth century) commander in Ṭāhir ibn al-Ḥusayn's army.

Diʿbil ibn ʿAlī al-Khuzaʿī (148–246/765–860) Shiʿi poet from Kufa at court of al-Rashīd and al-Ma'mūn, famous for his panegyrics and satires.

Durmālis Monastery in the Shammāsiyyah quarter of northeast Baghdad.

Fabrūniyā (Febronia) saint martyred in Nisibin during the persecution of Diocletian AD 303–13.

al-Faḍl ibn al-ʿAbbās ibn al-Ma'mūn (fl. late third/ninth century) grandson of al-Ma'mūn who was a cultivated poet and governor of Medina.

al-Faḍl ibn Marwān (d. 250/864) state scribe of Christian origin. An expert in land taxation, he was briefly vizier under al-Muʿtaṣim.

al-Faḍl ibn al-Rabīʿ (139–207/757–823) vizier of al-Rashīd and al-Amīn, whom he supported against al-Maʾmūn.

al-Faḍl ibn Sahl (ca. 153–202/770–818) counselor and later briefly vizier of al-Maʾmūn. He bore the title *Dhū al-Riyāsatayn*: Holder of the Two (civil and military) Commands.

al-Faḍl ibn Yaḥyā al-Barmakī (148–92/765–808) eldest son of Yaḥyā al-Barmakī, very influential at court, tutor to al-Amīn, disgraced when his brother Jaʿfar was executed.

Fam al-Ṣilḥ town on the Tigris at its confluence with the Ṣilḥ Canal, to the south of modern Kūt al-ʿAmārah.

al-Farʿāʾ region in the southwest of the Arabian Peninsula, north of Yemen.

Farīdah (fl. mid-third/ninth century) slave girl owned by the singer ʿAmr ibn Bānah, who gave her to al-Wāthiq. After his death, she was acquired by al-Mutawakkil, who married her. She had a beautiful voice and was an excellent performer. The name means "solitaire."

al-Fatḥ ibn Khāqān son of a Turkish army commander, state scribe and companion of al-Mutawakkil, man of letters, and patron of poets. He was murdered with al-Mutawakkil in 247/861.

Fāthiyūn (Pethion), Mār (d. AD 448) saint martyred in Persia.

Fāṭimah bint ʿAbd al-Malik (fl. late second/eighth century) daughter of the caliph ʿAbd al-Malik ibn Marwān and wife of the caliph ʿUmar ibn ʿAbd al-ʿAzīz ibn Marwān.

Ghassān ibn ʿAbbād (fl. third/ninth century) cousin of al-Ḥasan ibn Sahl. Governor of Khurasan under al-Maʾmūn until replaced by Ṭāhir ibn al-Ḥusayn, subsequently governor of Sind.

Ghuṣayn monk after whom a dome in Ḥīrah was named.

al-Hādī, Abū Jaʿfar Mūsā (147–69/764–86; succeeded 168/785) fourth Abbasid caliph. He died unexpectedly, and was succeeded by al-Rashīd.

Ḥadīthah village on the Tigris not far from the Great Zab.

al-Ḥajjāj ibn Yūsuf al-Thaqafī (41–100/661–714) capable and ruthless governor of Iraq under ʿAbd al-Malik.

Ḥakam al-Wādī (fl. second half second/eighth century) singer from Wādī l-Qurā north of Medina, performed before al-Walīd ibn Yazīd and al-Mahdī.

Ḥakīm ibn Jabalah al-ʿAbdī (d. 35/656) Companion of the Prophet, partisan of ʿAlī ibn Abī Ṭālib.

Ḥamdān, Banū clan of the Banū Taghlib, which produced two Shiʿi dynasties that ruled in Mosul and Aleppo in the tenth century.

Ḥamdūn, Banū (fl. third/ninth century) family of courtiers serving al-Muʿtaṣim, al-Wāthiq, and al-Mutawakkil, and on occasion occupying administrative positions.

Ḥammād ʿAjrad (d. ca. 158/775) notoriously dissolute poet from Kufa, famous for his satires.

Ḥammād al-Rāwiyah (75–155/695–772) collector of poetry, courtier, and libertine from Kufa.

Ḥanīfah, Banū important tribe from central Arabia. After the Muslim conquests, many of them settled in Iraqi cities such as Kufa.

Ḥarb, Banū Abū Sufyān ibn Ḥarb ibn Umayyah and his descendants, including the caliphs Muʿāwiyah and Yazīd ibn Muʿāwiyah.

al-Ḥarīrī (fl. late third/ninth century) libertine, friend of the poet al-Numayrī. Not to be confused with the author of the *Maqāmāt*.

Harīsah dish of wheat or other grains simmered with meat and flavored with cinnamon and sugar.

Hārūn ibn ʿAbd al-ʿAzīz ibn al-Muʿtamid (fl. early fourth/tenth century) grandson of al-Muʿtamid.

Hārūn al-Rashīd see al-Rashīd, Hārūn.

al-Ḥasan ibn ʿAbdallāh ibn Ḥamdān Nāṣir al-Dawlah (303–58/916–69) second Ḥamdānid ruler of Mosul and the Jazīrah.

al-Ḥasan ibn Makhlad (207–68/823–82) state scribe of Christian origin who twice served as vizier under al-Muʿtamid and died in exile.

al-Ḥasan ibn Rajāʾ, Abū ʿAlī (fl. mid-third/ninth century) state scribe, son-in-law of al-Faḍl ibn Sahl, who held administrative posts in Baghdad and Iran. He was a poet and patron of poets.

al-Ḥasan ibn Sahl (d. 235/850) served al-Maʾmūn as secretary and head of taxation, then withdrew from public life after the assassination of his brother al-Faḍl. Married his daughter Būrān to al-Maʾmūn in a lavish ceremony in 210/825.

al-Ḥasan ibn Wahb, Abū ʿAlī (d. ca. 248/862) state scribe and poet who occupied important posts at Samarra.

Hāshimite member of the Banu Hāshim, the clan of the Quraysh tribe to which the Prophet Muḥammad and his descendants and also the descendants of his uncle ʿAbbās belonged.

Ḥātim al-Ṭāʾī warrior in ʿAlī ibn ʿĪsā ibn Māhān's army at Rayy. Not to be confused with the pre-Islamic poet.

Ḥawāzin important tribal confederation in the Hijaz to which Thaqīf is sometimes counted as belonging.

Hazār (fl. mid-third/ninth century) singing girl belonging to al-Muʿtamid. The name means "nightingale."

Ḥaẓīrah large village on the Tigris to the south of Balad, famous for its fine cotton cloth.

Hīlānah (fl. late second/eighth century) slave girl of al-Hādī and then al-Rashīd, not to be confused with Haylānah, the slave girl he acquired from Jaʿfar al-Barmakī. Hīlānah is an Arabized form of Helena.

Hind bint al-Nuʿmān ibn al-Mundhir (d. ca. 22/643) daughter of the last king of Ḥīrah, retired to a convent.

Ḥīrah ancient and wealthy city in Iraq just south of present-day Kufa. It was the capital of the Lakhmid kings and the center of Christianity in pre-Islamic Iraq.

Hishām ibn ʿAbd al-Malik (71–125/691–743) tenth Umayyad caliph, capable ruler and strict administrator.

Hishām ibn Muʿāwiyah al-Ḍarīr al-Naḥwī (d. 209/824) from Kufa, al-Maʾmūn's grammar teacher.

al-Hudāhidī (fl. late third/ninth century) possibly the owner of a slave girl called Sharwīn in Baghdad.

Ḥulwān town just south of Cairo.

al-Ḥumaymah village some thirty-seven miles (sixty kilometers) north of Aqaba, home of the Abbasids before they established their caliphate in Baghdad.

Ḥusayn the Eunuch (early third/ninth century) trusted attendant of al-Rashīd, al-Amīn, and al-Maʾmūn.

al-Ḥusayn ibn al-Ḍaḥḥāk (155–250/772–864) poet and profligate from Basra who frequented caliphal courts from al-Rashīd on and was known especially for his wine poetry.

al-Ḥusayn ibn Muṣʿab (d. 198/814) father of Ṭāhir ibn al-Ḥusayn, ruler of Būshang, a small principality in Khurasan.

Ibn ʿAbbās, ʿAbdallāh (d. 68/688) cousin of the Prophet, grandfather of the first Abbasids, leading early transmitter of Muslim traditions.

Ibn Abī Fanan, Abū ʿAbd al-Raḥmān Aḥmad (d. between 260/874 and 269/883) state scribe and respected poet in Baghdad.

Ibn Abī Ṭālib al-Makfūf al-Wāṣiṭī (fl. early third/ninth century) poet, possibly author of poetry on the siege of Baghdad by al-Maʾmūn.

Ibn al-Anbārī, Abū Bakr Muḥammad ibn al-Qāsim (271–327/885–939) grammarian and lexicographer in Baghdad, famous for his amazing memory.

Ibn al-Aʿrābī, Abū ʿAbdallāh Muḥammad (150–230/767–845) Kufan philologist, later in Baghdad and Samarra, authority on poetry, genealogies, grammar, and lexicography.

Ibn ʿĀṣim al-Mawqifī al-Miṣrī, Muḥammad (fl. late third/ninth century) poet and probably state scribe.

Ibn Badr (fl. third/ninth century) contemporary of Abū l-ʿAynāʾ.

Ibn Bisṭām, Aḥmad ibn Muḥammad (fl. late third/ninth and early fourth/tenth centuries) administrator and tax collector in Egypt.

Ibn Dihqānah al-Hāshimī, Muḥammad ibn ʿUmar (d. 278/891) governor of Basra and court companion.

Ibn Faraj al-Taghlibī (early third/ninth century) possibly a singer and transmitter of anecdotes.

Ibn Ḥabīb, Muḥammad (d. 246/860) Baghdadi transmitter of poetry, scholar of history and genealogy.

Ibn al-Ḥafṣī (fl. mid-third/ninth century) court singer and companion of al-Mutawakkil.

Ibn Ḥamdūn, Abū ʿAbdallāh Aḥmad (d. 254/868) poet and member of the Banū Ḥamdūn family of courtiers. He was a companion of caliphs from al-Mutawakkil to al-Muʿtamid.

Ibn Ḥamdūn, Abū Muḥammad ʿAbdallāh ibn Aḥmad (fl. late third/ninth century) son of the above, court companion of the caliphs from al-Mutawakkil to al-Muʿtaḍid.

Ibn Jaddān (late third/ninth century?) obscure transmitter of historical accounts.

Ibn Jahshiyār, Abū l-Ḥasan ʿAlī (late third/ninth century) chamberlain of al-Muwaffaq.

Ibn Jamhūr, Muḥammad ibn al-Ḥusayn al-ʿAmmī (d. 210/825) man of letters and transmitter of traditions in Basra.

Ibn Khurdādhbih, ʿUbaydallāh ibn ʿAbdallāh (d. 229/844) administrator, geographer, and courtier. Son of ʿAbdallāh ibn Khurdādhbih.

Ibn al-Makkī, Aḥmad ibn Yaḥyā (d. 248/862) son of a famous singer, court musician from the time of al-Maʾmūn on.

Ibn al-Māriqī, ʿAlī (fl. third/ninth century) singer at court under al-Mutawakkil and earlier.

Ibn al-Mudabbir, Aḥmad ibn Muḥammad (d. 269/883) state scribe, fiscal administrator, and man of letters.

Ibn al-Muʿtazz, ʿAbdallāh (247–95/861–908) Abbasid prince, poet, musician, patron, author of books on poetry and criticism. Caliph for a day, he was killed in the struggles over the succession to the caliphate.

Ibn al-Qaṣṣār, Sulaymān ibn ʿAlī (d. ca. 255/869) singer and lutenist at court from al-Muʿtaṣim's reign on.

Ibn Qudāmah, Jaʿfar (d. ca. 319/931) state scribe, man of letters, and poet, member of Ibn al-Muʿtazz's circle.

Ibn al-Rūmī, ʿAlī ibn al-ʿAbbās (221–83/836–96) a leading poet of his time who excelled in many genres. He lived in Baghdad but was never a court poet.

Ibn al-Sarī ibn al-Ḥakam, ʿUbaydallāh (d. 251/865) governor of Egypt 206–11/822–26. He sought to make himself independent by withholding taxes from the caliph in Baghdad and was ousted by ʿAbdallāh ibn Ṭāhir.

Ibn Sīrīn, Abū Bakr Muḥammad (33–110/654–728) transmitter of traditions, renowned for his piety, and author of a book of interpretation of dreams.

Ibn Tarkhān (early third/ninth century) slave trader, probably in Baghdad, specializing in singing girls.

Ibn Thawābah, Abū l-ʿAbbās Aḥmad ibn Muḥammad (d. 272/886 or 277/890) state secretary, assistant to viziers, talented stylist and poet, socially inept.

Ibn al-Zanbaqī (d. after 384/994) Egyptian poet.

Ibrāhīm ibn al-ʿAbbās al-Ṣūlī (178–243/792–857) state scribe and highly regarded poet, official and courtier under several caliphs from al-Maʾmūn onward.

Ibrāhīm ibn Abī ʿUbays (fl. late third/ninth century) probably member of the Banū Ḥamdūn family, fine singer.

Ibrāhīm ibn al-Mahdī (162–224/779–839) prince, singer, composer, and poet. Briefly counter-caliph when his nephew al-Maʾmūn was in Marw, then resigned, and was later pardoned. Subsequently concentrated on musical activities.

Ibrāhīm ibn al-Mudabbir see Ibrāhīm ibn Muḥammad ibn al-Mudabbir.

Ibrāhīm (the Imam) ibn Muḥammad ibn ʿAlī ibn ʿAbdallāh ibn al-ʿAbbās (82–131/701–49) descendant of the Prophet's uncle, al-ʿAbbās, resident in al-Ḥumaymah, leader of the Abbasid faction until his execution by the Umayyads.

Ibrāhīm ibn Muḥammad ibn al-Mudabbir (ca. 214–80/829–93) state scribe, poet, and man of letters who occupied important administrative posts and was a companion of al-Mutawakkil.

Ibrāhīm ibn al-Qāsim ibn Zarzūr (fl. early fourth/tenth century) court singer of al-Muqtadir who was a member of a family of musicians.

ʿIrfān (fl. early third/ninth century) singer belonging originally to Shāriyah. Her name means "knowledge."

Iron Gate on the west side of Baghdad leading to the Dujayl Road.

Isḥāq ibn Ibrāhīm (fl. end third/ninth century) obscure state scribe.

Isḥāq ibn Ibrāhīm al-Mawṣilī (150–235/767–850) the greatest musician of his time, leader of the "classical" school of performance, poet, courtier, man of letters, and author of books on music.

Isḥāq ibn Ibrāhīm ibn Muṣʿab al-Ṭāhirī, Abū al-Ḥusayn (d. 235/850) member of the powerful Ṭāhirid family, long-time police chief in Baghdad and the caliph's representative there.

Isḥāq ibn Murawwiḥ (fl. late third/ninth century) courtier.

Itrīb monastery near Banhā, an important town thirty miles (forty-eight kilometers) north of Cairo.

Iyād Arab tribe that in pre-Islamic times migrated from the Hijaz to Iraq.

Iyās ibn Shuraḥbīl (fl. mid-first/seventh century) son of a commander of the Arab armies that conquered Syria; companion of Muʿāwiyah.

Jabalah ibn al-Ayham al-Ghassānī (d. 24/645) last of the Ghassānid rulers in Syria, allies of the Byzantines and twice defeated by Muslim armies.

Jabhān al-Shīʿī (fl. late second/eighth century) notable in Khurasan.

Jacobites members of the Syrian Orthodox (pre-Chalcedonian) Church.

Jaʿfar ibn Yaḥyā al-Barmakī (d. 187/803) member of the Barmakid family, minister and close friend of al-Rashīd for ten years before al-Rashīd had him executed.

al-Jaʿfari Palace built by al-Mutawakkil in 245–47/859–61 at the north end of Samarra. It is the largest palace ever built in the Islamic world (521 acres or 211 hectares).

al-Jāḥiẓ, ʿAmr ibn Baḥr Abū ʿUthmān (159–272/776–868) major prose writer, author of works of literature, theology, and religious-political polemics.

Jaḥẓah al-Barmakī (ca. 224–324/839–936) member of the Barmakid family of ministers. Poet, musician, and court companion.

al-Jallūdī, ʿĪsā ibn Yazīd (fl. early third/ninth century) one of al-Maʾmūn's commanders, he succeeded ʿAbdallāh ibn Ṭāhir as governor of Egypt.

al-Jammāsh (fl. third/ninth century) obscure poet in Baghdad.

Jarīr ibn ʿAṭiyyah (ca. 32–111/653–729) famous poet of Bedouin origin, author of panegyrics and love poetry, renowned for his flytings with al-Farazdaq.

Jarjūth unidentified place near Quṭrabbul.

Jawsaq Palace one of the two principal palaces at Samarra, it was the residence of the caliphs and their families.

Jazīrah area between the Euphrates and the Tigris, in present-day northern Iraq, northeastern Syria, and southeastern Turkey.

Jazīrat Ibn ʿUmar town in southeastern Turkey, known today as Cizre.

Kalwādhā township on the eastern bank of the Tigris just south of Baghdad.

Karkh large suburb and commercial area to the south of the Round City of Baghdad.

Karkhāyā Canal branching off from the ʿĪsā Canal (called "great" in the text), which is a tributary of the Euphrates. A major waterway, it flowed through the western quarter of Karkh and rejoined the ʿĪsā Canal to flow into the Tigris.

Kashkar town opposite Wāsiṭ on the Tigris, seat of the senior bishopric of the Church of the East.

Kaysūm village in the upper Euphrates region, southwest of Adıyaman.

al-Khabbāz al-Baladī, Abū Bakr Muḥammad (fl. fourth/tenth century) noted poet from Balad.

Khālid ibn al-Walīd (d. 21/642) converted to Islam before the conquest of Mecca, commander during the early Muslim conquests who led armies in Iraq and Syria.

Khālid al-Kātib (d. ca. 262/876) state scribe from Baghdad and companion of leading officials. The author mainly of brief poems of love and longing, he finally lost his mind.

Khansāʾ (fl. ninth century) singer and poet. The name means "snub-nosed."

Kharijites various separatist groups in early Islamic history who believed that anyone could rule the Muslim community if he held the right beliefs and behaved piously, and who attacked the ruling establishment as unbelievers.

al-Khawarnaq and al-Sadīr two magnificent palaces built by the Arab king of Ḥīrah around AD 400.

Khosroes (Ar. Kisrā) generic term for Sassanian rulers, symbols of Persian high culture.

al-Khujistānī, Aḥmad ibn ʿAbdallāh (d. 268/882) military commander in Khurasan, briefly ruler of Nīshāpūr.

Khuld Palace caliphal palace built by al-Manṣūr in 158/775 to the northeast of the Round City of Baghdad. The name refers to the Eternal (*khuld*) Paradise mentioned in Q Furqān 25:15.

Khurasan region that includes today's northeastern Iran, Afghanistan, and parts of central Asia.

Kinānah, Banū tribe originally from the region south of Mecca.

Kulthūm ibn Thābit ibn Abī Saʿd (fl. early third/ninth century) head of the postal and intelligence service in Khurasan, originally from the Marw oasis.

Kurdiyyah singer belonging to Muḥammad ibn Rajāʾ. Her name means "Kurdish girl."

Kushājim, Abū l-Fatḥ Maḥmūd (d. ca. 359/970) poet and man of letters at the Ḥamdānid courts of Mosul and Aleppo, a founder of the genre of nature poetry.

Lākahkīfī (fl. early tenth century) obscure singer.

Lakhmids Arab dynasty that ruled in Ḥīrah from about AD 300 to 602, often allied with the Sassanian kings against the Byzantines.

al-Lubbādī, Abū Bakr Aḥmad ibn Muḥammad (fl. late third/ninth century) poet and eccentric in northwestern Iran.

al-Madāʾinī, ʿAlī ibn Muḥammad ibn Abī Sayf (d. ca. 228/843) important early compiler of historical and literary traditions who worked in Baghdad.

Mahdī Canal one of the main canals watering northeastern Baghdad.

Maḥmūd ibn Ḥasan al-Warrāq (d. ca. 230/845) courtier, known for admonitory and gnomic poetry.

al-Maʾmūn, ʿAbdallāh (169–218/786–833) seventh Abbasid caliph. Declared second successor by Hārūn al-Rashīd after his brother al-Amīn, he defeated al-Amīn in a civil war and was proclaimed caliph in 196/812. A patron of poets and scholars, he encouraged the translation movement.

Manichaean pertaining to the religion of Mānī, a third-century AD Iranian prophet whose extreme dualistic views about the struggle between the two principles of good and evil (Manichaeism) spread widely in western and central Asia as far as China.

Mār Sirjisān monastery near Wāsiṭ, possibly dedicated to Saints Sarjīs (Sergius) and Bākhūs (Bacchus) (known as the two Sergiuses), warrior martyrs whose names are often linked.

Marājil (fl. late second/eighth century) slave of al-Rashīd and mother of al-Maʾmūn. The name means "Yemeni brocades."

Mārī, Mār (d. ca. AD 121) disciple of Addai (Thaddeus/Judas), one of the apostles mentioned in the Acts of the Apostles (1:13). The two are regarded in the Syriac tradition as the evangelizers of Edessa and Iraq.

Māridah (fl. late second/eighth century) slave girl belonging to al-Rashīd. The name means "rebellious."

Marwān ibn Abī Ḥafṣah al-Aṣghar ibn Abī al-Janūb (d. after 247/861) panegyrist of caliphs from al-Ma'mūn to al-Mutawakkil and author of lampoons.

Marwān ibn Jabghūyah (fl. early third/ninth century) state scribe of central Asian origin.

Marwānids branch of the Umayyad family descended from Marwān ibn al-Ḥakam.

Maṣābīḥ (fl. mid-third/ninth century) singing girl belonging to al-Aḥdab. The name means "lamps."

Masdūd, Abū ʿAlī al-Ḥasan (fl. mid-third/ninth century) singer and famous player of the pandore. "Masdūd" is a nickname meaning "blocked nose."

Masrūr al-Balkhī (d. 280/893) senior military officer, leading armies against Yaʿqūb ibn al-Layth and the Zanj.

Masrūr al-Muʿtaṣimī (fl. mid-third/ninth century) servant acquired by al-Muʿtaṣim. His name means "delighted."

Maṭīrah a pleasure ground south of Samarra, first laid out by al-Ma'mūn.

Mayyāfāriqīn town east of Diyarbakir in eastern Anatolia, known today as Silvan.

Maymūn ibn Ḥammād (fl. mid-third/ninth century) unidentified man of letters.

Maymūn ibn Ibrāhīm (late third/ninth century) from the Mādharā'ī family of state secretaries, employed in the land tax department under ʿUbaydallāh ibn Sulaymān and as head of the postal-cum-intelligence service.

Mazrafah large village some ten miles (sixteen kilometers) north of Baghdad on the west bank of the Tigris.

Melkite (in this period) Christians accepting the Council of Chalcedon (AD 451).

Moqattam Hills range of hills located in southeast Cairo.

Muʿāwiyah ibn Abī Sufyān (d. 60/680) first caliph of the Umayyad dynasty. A member of this powerful clan of the Prophet's tribe, Quraysh, he converted to Islam in 8/630 and played a leading role in the conquest of Syria. Governor of Syria for the caliphs ʿUmar and ʿUthmān, he sought to avenge the latter's murder and clashed with ʿAlī. In 40/660 he established himself in Damascus as leader of the Muslim community.

Mufliḥ al-Turkī, Abū Isḥāq (d. 257/871) commander of al-Muʿtamid's army, killed fighting the Zanj.

al-Mughīrah ibn Shuʿbah al-Thaqafī (d. ca. 48/668) a convert to Islam in ca. 3/625. Despite many scandals, he became governor of Kufa under Muʿāwiyah in 41/661.

al-Muhalhil ibn Yamūt ibn al-Muzarriʿ (d. ca. 331/943) great-nephew of al-Jāḥiẓ, and a highly regarded poet.

Muḥammad ibn ʿAbd al-Malik al-Hāshimī (fl. mid-third/ninth century) poet and man of letters.

Muḥammad ibn ʿAbd al-Malik al-Zayyāt (131–233/749–848) state scribe, man of letters, and vizier of al-Muʿtaṣim and al-Wāthiq. He was executed under al-Mutawakkil.

Muḥammad ibn ʿAbdallāh ibn Ṭāhir (209–53/824–67) governor of Baghdad who quelled various ʿAlid uprisings. He was a poet, and a patron of scholars and singers.

Muḥammad ibn Abī l-ʿAbbās al-Ṭūsī (fl. early third/ninth century) Khurasanian commander in al-Ma'mūn's army, brother-in-law of Ṭāhir ibn al-Ḥusayn.

Muḥammad ibn Abī Umayyah (fl. early third/ninth century) state scribe and poet in the time of al-Ma'mūn.

Muḥammad ibn ʿAlī (fl. late third/ninth century) poet and state scribe known as "Aubergine."

Muḥammad ibn ʿAlī ibn ʿAbdallāh (d. ca. 126/744) descended from the Prophet's uncle ʿAbbās, and father of Ibrāhīm the Imam, Abu l-ʿAbbās al-Saffāḥ, and Abū Jaʿfar al-Manṣūr.

Muḥammad ibn al-Ḥārith ibn Buskhunnar (fl. mid-third/ninth century) son of a music-loving governor, he was a singer and the owner of singing girls.

Muḥammad ibn Hārūn (fl. early third/ninth century) secretary of Ḥusayn the Eunuch.

Muḥammad ibn al-Ḥasan ibn Muṣʿab (fl. early third/ninth century) cousin of Ṭāhir ibn al-Ḥusayn.

Muḥammad ibn Ḥāzim al-Bāhilī (fl. early third/ninth century) miserly poet from Basra. He worked in Baghdad, composing poems of invective and poems preaching contentment with one's lot.

Muḥammad ibn Marwān (d. 100/719) half brother of ʿAbd al-Malik. He was a successful general, and governor of the Jazīrah, Armenia, and Azerbaijan.

Muḥammad ibn al-Mu'ammil al-Ṭā'ī (fl. late second/eighth century) friend of Abū l-ʿAtāhiyah.

Muḥammad ibn Mukarram (fl. third/ninth century) sparring partner of the wit Abū l-ʿAynā'.

Muḥammad ibn Rajā' (fl. mid-third/ninth century) army commander. He took part in the campaign against the Byzantines in 248/862 and was governor of Basra in 254/868.

Muḥammad ibn Rāshid (fl. mid-third/ninth century) court companion of al-Muʿtaṣim and executioner.

Muḥammad ibn al-Sarī al-Sarrāj Abū Bakr (d. 316/928) important grammarian, applying the rules of logic to grammar.

Muḥammad ibn Ṭāhir ibn ʿAbdallāh ibn Ṭāhir (d. 297/910) governor of Khurasan. Driven out by Yaʿqūb ibn al-Layth, he was subsequently appointed governor of Baghdad, replacing his uncle ʿUbaydallāh ibn ʿAbdallāh.

Muḥammad ibn ʿUbaydallāh ibn Yaḥyā ibn Khāqān see ʿUbaydallāh ibn Yaḥyā ibn Khāqān.

Muḥammad ibn ʿUmar (fl. mid-third/ninth century) falconer and court companion of al-Mutawakkil.

Muḥammadiyyah village also known as Ītākhiyyah on the east bank of the Tigris north of Balashkur.

Muḥawwal suburb on the western side of Baghdad.

al-Muhtadī, Muḥammad ibn Hārūn al-Wāthiq (d. 256/870) fourteenth Abbasid caliph. He succeeded in 255/869 and instituted a pious style of life, but fell victim to the intrigues and discontent of Turkish soldiers.

Muʿizz al-Dawlah see Aḥmad ibn Buwayh.

Mukhāriq ibn Yaḥyā (d. 230/845) leading singer trained by Ibrāhīm al-Mawṣilī, famed for his beautiful voice.

al-Muktafī, Abū Aḥmad ʿAlī (263–96/877–908) seventeenth Abbasid caliph. Succeeded 289/902. A cultured ruler and patron of poets, he continued his father al-Muʿtaḍid's policy of restoring Abbasid power.

al-Mundhir ibn al-Nuʿmān (d. AD 554) also known as al-Mundhir ibn Mā' al-Samā', king of al-Ḥīrah during the first half of the sixth century. He was succeeded by his three sons.

Munʿim (fl. mid-third/ninth century) singer whose name means "benefactor."

al-Muntaṣir bi-llāh, Abū Jaʿfar Muḥammad (222–48/837–62) eleventh Abbasid caliph.

Mūsā ibn ʿAbd al-Malik (d. 245/859) official in charge of the land-tax office under al-Mutawakkil.

Mūsā ibn Bughā (d. 263/877) son of a Turkish general of al-Muʿtaṣim, close associate of al-Muwaffaq. He was the most powerful general from 256/870 until his death.

Mūsā ibn Ṣāliḥ ibn Shaykh (d. 256/870) poet, man of letters, companion of Isḥāq ibn Ibrāhīm al-Ṭāhirī.

Muṣʿab ibn al-Ḥusayn al-Baṣrī (fl. third/ninth century) state scribe, bookseller, and libertine poet.

al-Mustaʿīn bi-llāh, Aḥmad (d. 252/866) twelfth Abbasid caliph. Chosen by Turkish commanders to succeed al-Muntaṣir in 248/862, he abdicated in favor of al-Muʿtazz in 251/866 and was murdered shortly after.

al-Muʿtaḍid bi-llāh, Abū l-ʿAbbās Aḥmad (243–89/857–902) sixteenth Abbasid caliph. Son of al-Muwaffaq, he succeeded in 279/892.

al-Muʿtamid ʿalā Allāh, Abū l-ʿAbbās Aḥmad (ca. 229–79/843–92; succeeded 256/870) fifteenth Abbasid caliph. He served mainly as a figurehead for his brother al-Muwaffaq, the regent.

al-Muʿtaṣim bi-llāh, Muḥammad (ca. 191–227/807–42; succeeded 218/833) eighth Abbasid caliph. Before becoming caliph, he governed Egypt for his brother al-Maʾmūn. He organized campaigns against rebels and the Byzantines, founded Samarra, and continued al-Maʾmūn's support for the doctrine of the created Qurʾan.

al-Mutawakkil ʿalā Allāh, Jaʿfar (207–47/822–61; succeeded 233/847) tenth Abbasid caliph. Hostile to the Shiʿah, he was inclined to unrefined extravagance. He sought to break the power of the Turkish military and was murdered by Turkish soldiers.

Mutayyam al-Hishāmiyyah (fl. early third/ninth century) concubine of ʿAlī ibn Hishām, singer and composer. The name means "enthralled by love."

al-Muʿtazz, Abū ʿAbdallāh Muḥammad (231–55/845–69; succeeded 252/866) thirteenth Abbasid caliph. Unable to master events in Baghdad and Samarra, he was deposed and killed.

Muṭīʿ ibn Iyās (d. 169/785) Kufan poet and libertine, companion of princes, who composed wine songs and poems in other genres in both refined and vulgar styles.

al-Muwaffaq, Abū Aḥmad Ṭalḥah (227–78/842–91) brother of al-Muʿtamid, he ruled as his regent and started the restoration of Abbasid power, defeating the Ṣaffārid Yaʿqūb ibn al-Layth and the Zanj.

al-Nābighah al-Dhubyānī (fl. end sixth century AD) leading poet of Bedouin origin in the pre-Islamic period, he composed memorable panegyrics of al-Nuʿmān ibn al-Mundhir.

Nadmān (fl. mid-third/ninth century) singer in Samarra. Her name means "regretful."

Najaf town five and a half miles (nine kilometers) from Kufa, the site of ʿAlī's shrine and presently a major pilgrimage destination and center of Shiʿi learning.

Najāḥ ibn Salamah (d. 246/860) powerful state scribe in charge of the Bureau of Registering and Supervising Government Officials. He fell from favor and was put to death under al-Mutawakkil.

al-Nājim Abū ʿUthmān Saʿd ibn al-Ḥasan (d. 314/926) friend of Ibn al-Rūmī and transmitter of his poetry.

Najlah (fl. mid-third/ninth century) singer in Samarra. Her name means "wide-eyed."

al-Nāshiʾ al-Akbar ʿAbdallāh (d. 292/905) poet and scholar from al-Anbār who worked in Baghdad and Cairo.

Naṣr ibn Shabath al-ʿUqaylī (fl. 196–201/811–25) leader of a tribal revolt in northern Iraq, northeastern Syria, and southern Anatolia during the civil war between al-Amīn and al-Maʾmūn. He was defeated by ʿAbdallāh ibn Ṭāhir.

Nauruz festival of Iranian origin to celebrate the solar New Year on March 21.

Nawbahār Monastery Manichaean monastery in Balkh.

Nestorians name often used for the members of the Church of the East, mistakenly believed to follow teachings about Christ's natures ascribed to the fifth-century bishop Nestorius.

Nuʿm (fl. early third/ninth century) singing girl belonging to al-Maʾmūn. The name means "prosperity."

al-Nuʿmān ibn al-Mundhir (r. ca. AD 580–602) member of the Lakhmid dynasty, last king of Ḥīrah.

al-Numayrī, Abū l-Ṭayyib Muḥammad ibn al-Qāsim (fl. third/ninth century) well-born poet and friend of Ibn al-Muʿtazz.

Qabīḥah (d. 254/868) Byzantine slave of al-Mutawakkil, mother of al-Muʿtazz. She was famous for her beauty, hence her apotropaic nickname meaning "ugly."

Qabīṣah village near Samarra.

Qādisiyyah village near Samarra. Not the same as Qādisiyyah south of Baghdad, where the Persian army was defeated by the Muslims in 15/636.

Qalam al-Ṣāliḥiyyah (fl. mid-third/ninth century) owned by a high official, bought by al-Wāthiq. Singer and composer. Her name means "reed."

al-Qāsim ibn ʿUbaydallāh (258–91/872–904) son of ʿUbaydallāh ibn Sulaymān ibn Wahb, vizier of al-Muʿtaḍid and al-Muktafī.

Qāsim ibn Zarzūr (d. 297/909 at a great age) court singer and flautist under al-Muʿtamid and al-Muʿtaḍid.

Qaṣr see ʿAlth.

Qāṭūl canal dug by Khusraw Anūshirwān (mid-sixth century) near Samar.

Quraysh, Banū the tribe to which the Prophet Muḥammad belonged. Subsequently, rulers of the Muslim community, including the Umayyads, Abbasids, and Fatimids, belonged to this tribe.

Qurrah ibn Sharīk (d. 97/715) tribal noble related to al-Walīd ibn ʿAbd al-Malik and effective governor of Egypt.

Qūṭā, Mār (late sixth century AD) tree-dwelling saint from Mayyāfāriqīn.

Quṭrabbul area famed for its vineyards to the west of the Tigris and north of the Round City of Baghdad.

Rabīʿah al-Asadī al-Raqqī (d. 199/814) blind poet from Raqqa, panegyrist and courtier of al-Mahdī and al-Rashīd.

al-Rāḍī bi-llāh, ʿAbdallāh (d. 329/940) twentieth Abbasid caliph, succeeded 320/932.

al-Rāfiqah garrison town beside Raqqa established by Abū Jaʿfar al-Manṣūr as his capital before he founded Baghdad.

Rāshid (fl. late third/ninth century) freedman and general of al-Muwaffaq.

al-Rashīd, Hārūn ibn al-Mahdī (146–94/763–809; succeeded 170/786) fifth Abbasid caliph. At first, he left administration to the Barmakids, but after their fall he took over the government. He divided his empire between his sons al-Amīn and al-Maʾmūn. He was a patron of poets, writers, scholars, and singers.

Rayy important ancient city, close to modern-day Tehran.

Rayyiq (early third/ninth century) prominent singer taught by Ibrāhīm ibn al-Mahdī, whose style she propagated. She had vast knowledge of his repertoire.

Ruqayyah bint al-Faḍl ibn al-Rabīʿ (fl. early third/ninth century) daughter of al-Rashīd's and al-Amīn's vizier al-Faḍl. She was the owner of singing girls.

Ṣabbāʿī, Shimʿūn bar (d. AD 339) martyred during the persecution of the Christians by the Sassanian emperor Shapur II.

Saʿd ibn Abī Waqqāṣ (d. ca. 256/870) companion of the Prophet, commander of the Arab armies during the conquest of Iraq.

Saʿd ibn Ibrāhīm (fl. third/ninth century) state scribe.

al-Sadīr castle by Ḥīrah said to have been built by the Persians, a symbol of Lakhmid power.

Ṣāʿid ibn Makhlad (d. 276/889) convert to Islam from Nestorian Christianity, he was the chief minister to al-Muʿtamid and al-Muwaffaq in 265/878, fell from power in 272/885, and died in prison.

Saʿīd ibn Masʿūd al-Quṭrabbulī (fl. early third/ninth century) scribe working for the Nūshajānī family, notables from eastern Khurasan.

Saʿīd ibn Yūsuf (fl. late third/ninth century) secretary of al-Muʿtamid's son.

Saʿīd al-Rasḥ (?) (fl. third/ninth century) secretary employed by Aḥmad ibn al-Mudabbir.

Ṣāliḥ ibn Mūsā (probably third/ninth century) Egyptian poet.

Ṣāliḥ ibn al-Rashīd (fl. early third/ninth century) brother of al-Amīn. He governed Egypt for his half brother al-Maʾmūn and tried to reconcile him with al-Ḥusayn ibn al-Ḍaḥḥāk.

Ṣāliḥ the Tambourine Player (fl. mid-third/ninth century) instrumentalist.

Ṣāliḥiyyah quarter of Baghdad. Possibly the concession originally belonging to Ṣāliḥ, a son of al-Manṣūr.

Salīṭ (fl. early second/eighth century) putative son of ʿAbdallāh ibn ʿAbbās.

Sallām ibn Ghālib ibn Shammās (fl. late second/eighth century) friend of Muṭīʿ ibn Iyās.

Salmak (fl. early third/ninth century) Persian singer from Rayy.

Samālū Monastery occupied extensive grounds in the Shammāsiyyah quarter. Samālū, a town on the Armenian frontier, was captured by al-Rashīd and its inhabitants were transported to Baghdad. The monastery took the name of their hometown.

Samarra city on the east bank of the Tigris sixty-two miles (one hundred kilometers) north of Baghdad, founded by al-Muʿtaṣim in 221/836 as a new capital. In 279/892 the capital returned to Baghdad.

al-Ṣanawbarī, Abū Bakr Aḥmad (ca. 273–334/886–945) poet at the court of Sayf al-Dawlah in Aleppo, famous for his poetry on nature and gardens in a mannerist style.

Sarāb (fl. mid-third/ninth century) singer in Samarra. Her name means "mirage."

Saṭīḥ ibn Rabīʿah legendary pre-Islamic diviner, whose name is connected with prophecies of the coming of Islam.

Shadhr (fl. late second/eighth century) slave girl belonging to al-Rashīd, mother of Umm Abīhā. Her name means "vivacity."

al-Shāh ibn Mīkāl (fl. late third/ninth century) general and governor serving the Ṭāhirids.

Shājī (fl. ninth century) gifted singer and composer, and beloved wife of ʿUbaydallāh ibn ʿAbdallāh ibn Ṭāhir. Her name means "heartrending."

Shajw (fl. late second/eighth century) one of a trio of slave girls belonging to al-Rashīd, her name means "emotion." Her companions were Ḍiyāʾ ("brightness") and Khunth ("softness").

Shammāsiyyah quarter in northeast Baghdad. The name derives from *shammās* (deacon). The quarter was originally home to several monasteries, the most important of which were Durmālis and Samālū.

Shamʿūn, Mār (Saint Simeon) (fl. end sixth and early seventh century AD) monk and founder of the monastery of Sinn of the Church of the East, which was also the seat of a bishopric.

Shapur name of three Sassanian emperors, one of the third century and two of the fourth century. Probably Shapur II the Great (AD 309–79) is meant.

Sharāh mountainous region southwest of Amman.

Shāriyah (fl. early third/ninth century) singer, trained by Ibrāhīm ibn al-Mahdī and adept of his style, who had many pupils. Her name means "quarrelsome."

Shihrī a horse of mixed breed, with the sire being Arabian and the dam non-Arabian. They were highly valued.

Shikl (fl. late eighth century) slave girl belonging to al-Rashīd, mother of Abū ʿAlī ibn al-Rashīd. Her name means "coquetry."

Shimʿūn, Mār (Saint Simeon) (fl. end sixth and early seventh centuries AD) monk and founder of the monastery of Sinn of the Church of the East, which was also the seat of a bishopric.

Shujāʿ slave girl from Khwārizm (a large oasis lying between modern Kazakhstan, Uzbekistan, and Turkmenistan), mother of al-Mutawakkil. Her name means "courage" but also "snake."

Shurāʿah ibn al-Zandabūdh (fl. late second/eighth century) Kufan libertine.

Siʿird town in eastern Turkey southwest of Lake Van, known today as Siirt.

Sirjīs/Sirjiyūs, Mār (Saint Sergius) Roman army officer martyred in the early fourth century AD in Syria when he was discovered to be Christian. Ruṣāfah (Sergiopolis), where he and his companion Bacchus were buried, was a major pilgrimage center, and many monasteries and churches were dedicated to him.

Sulaymān ibn ʿAbd al-Malik ibn Marwān (55–99/675–717) seventh Umayyad caliph. Governor of Palestine, succeeded 97/715.

Sulaymān ibn ʿAbdallāh ibn Ṭāhir (d. 266/879) after governing Ṭabaristān (south of the Caspian Sea), Sulaymān replaced his brother ʿUbaydallāh in 255/869 as security chief in Baghdad at a time of great turmoil and remained in that position till his death.

Sulaymān ibn Muḥammad al-Umawī (fl. late second/eighth century?) descendant of the Umayyads, libertine and poet.

Sulaymān the Drummer (fl. mid-third/ninth century) player of the hand drum (*ṭabl*) in Samarra.

al-Ṣūlī, Abū Bakr Muḥammad (ca. 261–335/874–946) man of letters, court companion of three caliphs, writer on court life and "modern" poets, chess master.

Sūrā city east of the Euphrates and south of Baghdad. A center of Torah studies and the site of an important Jewish academy.

Taghlib, Banū important seminomadic tribe in northern Iraq, southeastern Turkey, and eastern Syria, mainly Christian until the mid-ninth century.

Ṭāhir ibn al-Ḥusayn ibn Muṣʿab (160–207/776–822) general of al-Maʾmūn's army fighting al-Amīn, commander of police in Baghdad, then governor of Khurasan. Patron of poets and prose writer.

Ṭāhir ibn Ibrāhīm ibn Mudrik (fl. early third/ninth century) officer of ʿAbdallāh ibn Ṭāhir's army in the campaign against Naṣr ibn Shabath and later in Tabaristān.

Ṭalḥah ibn ʿUbaydallāh ibn ʿUthmān (d. 35/656) Companion of the Prophet who was killed fighting against ʿAlī ibn Abī Ṭālib at the Battle of the Camel.

Tamīm ibn al-Muʿizz al-Fāṭimī (336–74/948–84 or '85) eldest son of the caliph al-Muʿizz li-Dīn Allāh. He was a poet and man of letters.

Tanḥūm (fl. early ninth century) Jewish tavern keeper in Ḥīrah.

Thaqīf tribe sometimes considered as part of the Ḥawāzin confederation settled round Ṭāʾif south of Mecca.

al-Tharwānī, Muḥammad ibn ʿAbd al-Raḥmān (fl. third/ninth century) obscure libertine poet.

Tibr (fl. third/ninth century) slave girl belonging to Abū l-Shibl. Her name means "gold."

Tuffāḥ (fl. mid-third/ninth century) instrumentalist at court. His name means "apples."

al-Ṭūlūnī two villages, Lesser and Greater, on the east bank of the Tigris, probably estates of Aḥmad ibn Ṭūlūn, who established himself as ruler of Egypt in 258/872.

Tūmā, Mār (Saint Thomas) one of the Twelve Apostles, believed to have evangelized the Parthians and even to have reached India. He is particularly venerated in the Church of the East.

Turkiyyah (fl. mid-third/ninth century) singer owned by Umm Jaʿfar, al-Mutawakkil's mother. Her name means "Turkish girl."

ʿUbaydallāh ibn ʿAbdallāh ibn Ṭāhir (223–300/838–913) son of ʿAbdallāh ibn Ṭāhir, police chief in Baghdad, highly cultivated patron, author, poet, and musician.

ʿUbaydallāh ibn Sulaymān ibn Wahb (225–88/840–901) son of a vizier and himself vizier under al-Muʿtamid and al-Muʿtaḍid.

ʿUbaydallāh ibn Yaḥyā ibn Khāqān Abū l-Ḥasan (d. 263/877) served as vizier of al-Mutawakkil and al-Muʿtamid.

ʿUbbādah (d. ca. 250/864) homosexual court entertainer and buffoon, around whom many humorous anecdotes collected.

Ubullah a town near Basra, famous for dancing girls.

ʿUkbarā a town between Baghdad and Samarra on the west bank of the Tigris.

ʿUmar ibn ʿAbd al-ʿAzīz ibn Marwān (ca. 60–101/680–720) eighth Umayyad caliph. He was previously governor of Hijaz and is remembered as a model of piety.

ʿUmar ibn al-Khaṭṭāb (d. 23/644) Companion of the Prophet, second of the rightly guided caliphs, succeeded 13/634. He is regarded in Sunni tradition as the model of a just ruler and paragon of virtues.

Umayyads first Muslim dynasty, ruling from Damascus 40–132/660–750. They were overthrown by the Abbasids.

Umm Abīhā (fl. early third/ninth century) daughter of Hārūn al-Rashīd by a concubine called Shadhr.

Ushmūnī (fl. second century BC) mother of the seven Maccabean brothers. In the Eastern Churches they are all honored as martyrs. Ushmūnī is her name in Syriac.

al-ʿUtbī, Abū ʿAbd al-Raḥmān Muḥammad (d. 227/842) poet and historian from Basra. He worked in Baghdad.

ʿUthmān ibn Ḥunayf al-Anṣārī (d. after 40/660) Companion of the Prophet and governor of Basra under ʿAlī. He fought on ʿAlī's side in the Battle of Ṣiffīn.

Wālibah ibn al-Ḥubāb (fl. late second/eighth century) poet and libertine from Kufa. Not accepted at court, he composed mainly on wine and boys.

al-Walīd ibn ʿAbd al-Malik ibn Marwān (ca. 54–96/674–715) sixth Umayyad caliph, succeeded 86/705.

al-Walīd ibn Yazīd ibn ʿAbd al-Malik (90–126/709–744) eleventh Umayyad caliph, succeeded 125/743. He was a poet and patron of poets, famous for his dissolute lifestyle.

Waṣīf (1) (d. 253/867) Turkish slave acquired by al-Muʿtaṣim. He served as army commander and later as chamberlain to al-Wāthiq and al-Mutawakkil. He took part in al-Mutawakkil's murder but was later killed by another Turkish faction. (2) (fl. late ninth century) Eunuch, client, and general under Yūsuf ibn Dīwdādh Abī al-Sāj in northwestern Iran and Armenia.

Wāsiṭ city in Iraq on the Tigris between Basra and Kufa, founded in 83/702. Important center of road and river communication.

al-Wāthiq bi-llāh, Hārūn (ca. 198–232/814–47, succeeded 227/842) ninth Abbasid caliph. Continued his father al-Muʿtaṣim's policies, including support for the doctrine of the created Qur'an. He was a composer and musician.

Yaḥyā ibn Aktham (d. 243/857) chief judge in Baghdad and counselor of al-Ma'mūn.

Yaḥyā ibn Kāmil (fl. early third/ninth century) obscure poet in Baghdad.

Yaḥyā ibn Khāqān al-Khurāsānī (fl. mid-third/ninth century) brother of al-Fatḥ ibn Khāqān, secretary of al-Ḥasan ibn Sahl, later head of the Bureau of Taxation.

Yaḥyā ibn Ziyād al-Ḥārithī (fl. mid-second/eighth century) poet from Kufa, panegyrist of early Abbasids and libertine.

Yamāmah region in the center of the Arabian Peninsula, part of what is now Nejd.

Yamūt ibn al-Muzarriʿ (d. ca. 302/914) man of letters and grammarian, nephew of al-Jāḥiẓ.

Ya'qūb ibn al-Layth al-Ṣaffār (225–65/840–79) led an uprising in the eastern Iranian region of Sistan, conquered much of Afghanistan, Iran, and Central Asia, but was defeated when he invaded Iraq.

al-Yazīdī, Abū Muḥammad Yaḥyā (d. 201/817) grammarian and man of letters from Basra, he tutored al-Ma'mūn and other princes, and was the founder of a dynasty of scholar-poets.

Yūnān, Mār (fl. fourth century AD) disciple of Saint Awgīn, who lived as a hermit in the region of Anbār.

Yūnus ibn Bughā favorite of al-Mu'tazz and son of Bughā the Younger, a Turkish military leader who held power under two previous caliphs, al-Muntaṣir and al-Musta'īn.

Yūnus ibn Mattā (Jonah the son of Amittai) (fl. eighth century BC) Old Testament prophet who is also venerated in Christianity and Islam. He was sent to Nineveh to prophesy about God's punishment for its inhabitants' wickedness.

Yusr slave at the court of al-Mutawakkil. The name means "ease" or "prosperity."

Yūsuf Abū l-Qāsim ibn Dīwdādh Abī al-Sāj (d. 316/928) army commander of Soghdian origin. He governed Azerbaijan and northwestern Iran in 288–306/901–19 and 310–16/922–28.

Zakkā, Mār (fl. end sixth century AD) Syrian Orthodox monk, staunch opponent of the Nestorians.

Zandaward Monastery in eastern Baghdad, south of the caliphal palaces. It took its name from the Zandaward Canal.

Zanj black slaves from East Africa working in gangs on the salt flats east of Basra under terrible conditions. In their uprising in 255–69/869–83, they controlled the main cities of southern Iraq for several years.

Zanjī, Abū 'Abdallāh Muḥammad ibn Ismā'īl (d. 333/945) state scribe influential in the period from al-Mu'taḍid to al-Rāḍī.

Zayd ibn Ṣā'id (fl. third/ninth century) obscure acquaintance of Abū l-'Aynā'.

Zoroastrianism Iranian religion looking back to the prophet Zarathustra (between 1500 and 500), which in the third century AD became the state religion in Iran. It teaches that in the struggle between Ahura Mazda, the creator and good spirit, and Ahriman, the evil spirit, good will eventually win. Fire as a symbol of purity plays a major role in the rituals of Zoroastrians, who are often called "fire worshippers."

Zubaydah, Amat al-ʿAzīz bint Jaʿfar (ca. 146–216/763–831) cousin and wife of al-Rashīd, mother of al-Amīn, later reconciled with al-Maʾmūn. Patron of poets, scholars, and musicians, and generous funder of public works.

al-Zubayr ibn al-ʿAwwām (d. 35/656) cousin and Companion of the Prophet, one of those seeking to avenge ʿUthmān's murder, killed shortly after the Battle of the Camel.

Zunām the Flute Player (fl. first half third/ninth century) court musician from the reign of al-Rashīd to al-Muʿtazz. The name means "calamity."

Zurāfah (d. ca. 252/866) one of al-Mutawakkil's chamberlains. He was involved in his murder and died later in Cairo.

Zurayqiyyah monastery in Baghdad in the Shammāsiyyah quarter.

Bibliography

Abū l-ʿAtāhiyah Ismāʿīl ibn Qāsim. *Dīwān*. Beirut: Al-Maṭbaʿah al-Kāthūlīkiyyah, 1406/1888.

Abū Nuwās al-Ḥasan ibn Hāniʾ. *Dīwān*. Vol. 3, edited by Ewald Wagner. Wiesbaden, Germany: Franz Steiner, 1988.

Ali, Samer M. "Early Islam—Monotheism or Henotheism? A View from the Court." *Journal of Arabic Literature* 39 (2008): 14–37.

Allard, Michel. "Les Chrétiens à Baġdād." Special issue, *Arabica* 9 (1962): 375–88.

Arazi, Albert. *Amour divin et amour profane dans l'Islam médiéval à travers le Dīwān de Khālid al-Kātib*. Paris: G.-P. Maisonneuve et Larose, 1990.

Atiya, Aziz Suryal. "Some Egyptian Monasteries According to the Unpublished MS. of al-Shābushtī's *Kitāb al-diyārāt*." *Bulletin de la Société d'archéologie copte* 5 (1939): 1–28.

Al-ʿAṭiyyah, Jalīl, ed. *Al-Diyārāt li-Abī al-Faraj al-Iṣbahānī*. London: Riad El-Rayyes Books, 1991.

Al-Bāhilī, Muḥammad ibn Ḥāzim. *Dīwān*. Edited by Muḥammad Khayr al-Biqāʿī. Damascus: Dār Qutaybah li-l-Ṭibāʿah wa-l-Nashr wa-l-Tawzīʿ, 1401–02/1981–82.

Baumer, Christoph. *The Church of the East: An Illustrated History of Assyrian Christianity*. London: I. B. Tauris, 2006.

Bray, Julia Ashtiany. "Figures in a Landscape: The Inhabitants of the Silver Village." In *Storytelling in the Framework of Non-fictional Arabic Literature*, edited by Stefan Leder, 79–93. Wiesbaden, Germany: Harrassowitz Verlag, 1998.

Al-Bukhārī, Muḥammad ibn Ismāʿīl. *Ṣaḥīḥ al-Bukhārī*, edited by ʿAbdallāh Muḥammad Aḥmad Khalīl. Beirut: Dār al-Kutub al-ʿIlmiyyah, 2014.

The Coptic Encyclopedia. Edited by Aziz Suryal Atiya. New York: Macmillan, 1991.

Débié, Muriel. "Livres et monastères en Syrie-Mésopotamie d'après les sources syriaques." In *Le monachisme syriaque*, edited by F. Jullien, 123–68. Paris: Geuthner, 2010.

Dmitriev, Kirill. "The Symbolism of Wine in Early Arabic Love Poetry: Observations on the Poetry of Abū Ṣakhr al-Hudhalī." In *Insatiable Appetite: Food as Cultural Signifier in the Middle East and Beyond*, edited by Kirill Dmitriev, Julia Hauser, and Bilal Orfali, 165–89. Leiden, Netherlands: Brill, 2019.

Ellenblum, Ronnie. "Demography, Geography, and the Accelerated Islamisation of the Eastern Mediterranean." In *Religious Conversion: History Experience and Meaning*, edited by Ira Katzenelson and Miri Rubin, 61–80. Farnham, UK: Ashgate, 2014.

Encyclopedia of Arabic Literature. Edited by Julie Scott Meisami and Paul Starkey. 2 vols. London: Routledge, 1998.

Encyclopaedia Iranica. Online edition. New York, 1996–. https://www.iranicaonline.org.

The Encyclopedia of Islam, Second Edition. Edited by P. Bearman, Th. Bianquis, C. E. Bosworth, E. van Donzel, and W. P. Heinrichs. Brill Online.

Farmer, Henry George. *The Organ of the Ancients from Eastern Sources (Hebrew, Syriac and Arabic)*. London: W. Reeves, 1931.

Fiey, Jean Maurice. *Assyrie chrétienne: Contribution à l'étude de l'histoire et de la géographie ecclésiastique et monastique du Nord de l'Iraq*. Vols. 1 and 2, Beirut: Imprimerie Catholique, 1965; vol. 3, *Bét̲ Garmaï, Bét̲ Aramāyé et Maišān nestoriens*, Beirut: Dār al-Mashriq, 1968.

———. *Chrétiens syriaques sous les Abbasides surtout à Bagdad (749–1258)*. Louvain, Belgium: Secrétariat du CSCO, 1980.

———. *Mossoul chrétienne: Essai sur l'histoire, l'archéologie et l'état actuel des monuments chrétiens de la ville de Mossoul*. Beirut: Imprimerie Catholique, 1959.

Ghālib, Idwār. *Al-mawsūʿah fī ʿulūm a-ṭabīʿah*. 3 vols. Beirut: Al-Maṭbaʿah al-Kāthūlīkiyyah, 1965.

Gil, Moshe. *A History of Palestine 634–1099*. Cambridge: Cambridge University Press, 1992.

Gordon, Matthew S. *The Breaking of a Thousand Swords: A History of the Turkish Military of Samarra (A.H. 200–275/815–889 C.E.)*. Albany: State University of New York Press, 2001.

Gorgias Encyclopedic Dictionary of the Syriac Heritage. Edited by Sebastian P. Brock et al. Piscataway, NJ: Gorgias Press, 2011.

Gruendler, Beatrice. "Verse and Taxes: The Function of Poetry in Selected Literary *Akhbār* of the Third/Ninth Century." In *On Fiction and Adab in Medieval Arabic Literature*, edited by Philip F. Kennedy, 85–124. Wiesbaden, Germany: Harrassowitz Verlag, 2005.

Harvey, S. H. "Monasticism." In *Gorgias Encyclopedic Dictionary of the Syriac Heritage*, edited by Sebastian P. Brock et al., 293–94. Piscataway, NJ: Gorgias Press, 2011.

Ibn Duqmāq, Ibrāhīm ibn Muḥammad. *Kitāb al-Intiṣār li-wāsiṭat ʿiqd al-amṣār*. Vols. 4 and 5, edited by Karl Vollers. Būlāq, Egypt: al-Maṭbaʿah al-Kubrā al-Amīriyyah, 1309/1893.

Ibn Khallikān, Abū l-ʿAbbās Shams al-Dīn ibn Muḥammad. *Wafayāt al-aʿyān*. Edited by Iḥsān ʿAbbās. 8 vols. Beirut: Dār Ṣādir, 1968–72.

Ibn Mājah, Muḥammad ibn Yazīd. *Sunan Ibn Mājah*. Edited by M. F. ʿAbd al-Bāqī. 2 vols. Cairo: Dār Iḥyāʾ al-Kutub al-ʿArabiyyah, 1952–53.

Ibn al-Muʿtazz, ʿAbdallāh. *Ṭabaqāt al-shuʿarāʾ al-muḥdathīn*. Edited by ʿAbd al-Sattār Aḥmad Farrāj. Cairo: Dār al-Maʿārif, 1956.

Ibn al-Nadīm. *Al-Fihrist*. Edited by Riḍā Tajaddud. 3rd ed. Beirut: Dār al-Masīrah, 1988.

Ibn Qays al-Ruqayyāt, ʿUbaydallāh. *Dīwān*. Edited by Muḥammad Yūsuf Najm. Beirut: Dār Ṣādir, 1958.

Ibn al-Sāʿī. *Consorts of the Caliphs: Women and the Court of Baghdad*. Edited and translated by Shawkat Toorawa et al. New York: New York University Press, 2015.

ʿInānī, Muḥammad Muḥammad. *Ṭuyūr Miṣr*. Cairo: Al-Hay'ah al-Miṣriyyah al-ʿĀmmah li-l-Kitāb, 1993.

Al-Iṣbahānī, Abū l-Faraj ʿAlī ibn al-Ḥusayn. *Kitāb al-Aghānī*. Vols. 1–16. Cairo: Dār al-Kutub, 1927–61. Vols. 17–24. Cairo: Al-Hay'ah al-Miṣriyyah al-ʿĀmmah li-l-Ta'līf wa-l-Nashr, 1970–74.

Jullien, Florence. "S'affirmer en s'opposant: Les polémistes du Grand Monastère (VIe–VIIe siècle)." In "Controverses des chrétiens dans l'Iran sassanide," edited by Christelle Jullien. Special issue, *Studia Iranica* 36 (2008): 29–40.

Kaabi, Mongi. *Les Tahirides: Étude historico-littéraire de la dynastie des Banū Ṭāhir ibn al-Ḥusayn au Ḫurasān et en Iraq au IIIe s. de l'Hégire IXème s. J. C.* 2 vols. Paris: Université de Paris Sorbonne, Faculté des lettres et sciences humaines, 1983.

Kamoliddin, Shamsiddin. "On the Religion of the Nawbahar Temple in Balkh." *O'zbekiston: Til va madaniyat / Uzbekistan: Language and Culture* 1 (2020): 62–74.

Kennedy, Hugh. *The Prophet and the Age of the Caliphs: The Islamic Near East from the Sixth to the Eleventh Century*. 3rd ed. London: Routledge, 2016.

Khalidi, Tarif, and Maher Jarrar. "Death and the *Badīʿ* in Early ʿAbbāsid Poetry: The Elegy for al-Numayrī by ʿAbd Allāh ibn al-Muʿtazz." *Al-Abḥāth* 54 (2006): 35–47.

Al-Khaṭīb al-Baghdādī, Aḥmad ibn ʿAlī. *Kitāb Tārīkh Baghdād*. 14 vols. Cairo: Maktabat al-Khānjī, 1931.

Kilpatrick, Hilary. *Making the Great Book of Songs: Composition and the Author's Craft in Abū l-Faraj al-Iṣbahānī's Kitāb al-Aghānī*. London: RoutledgeCurzon, 2003.

King, Anya. "The Importance of Imported Aromatics in Arabic Culture: Illustrations from Pre-Islamic and Early Islamic Poetry." *Journal of Near Eastern Studies* 67 (2008): 175–89.

Kushājim, Maḥmūd ibn al-Ḥusayn. *Dīwān*. Edited by al-Nabawī ʿAbd al-Wāḥid Shaʿlān. Cairo: Maktabat al-Khānjī, 1996.

Lagrange, Frédéric. "Une affaire de viol." *Tumultes* 41 (2013): 61–70.

Lassner, Jacob. *The Topography of Baghdad in the Early Middle Ages: Text and Studies*. Detroit, MI: Wayne State University Press, 1970.

Leder, Stefan, and Hilary Kilpatrick. "Classical Arabic Prose Literature: A Researchers' Sketch Map." *Journal of Arabic Literature* 23 (1992): 2–26.

Le Strange, G. *Baghdad during the Abbasid Caliphate: From Contemporary Arabic and Persian Sources*. Oxford: Clarendon Press, 1900.

———. *The Lands of the Eastern Caliphate: Mesopotamia, Persia and Central Asia from the Moslem Conquest to the Time of Timur.* Cambridge: Cambridge University Press, 1930.

———. *Palestine under the Moslems: A Description of Syria and the Holy Land from A.D. 650 to 1500.* London: Alexander P. Watt, 1890.

Marzolph, Ulrich. *Arabia ridens: Die humoristische Kurzprosa der frühen adab-Literatur im internationalen Traditionsgeflecht.* 2 vols. Frankfurt am Main: Vittorio Klostermann, 1992.

Al-Marzūbānī, Abū ʿUbaydallāh Muḥammad ibn ʿImrān. *Muʿjam al-shuʿarāʾ.* Edited by ʿAbd al-Sattār Aḥmad Farāj. Damascus: Manshūrāt al-Nūrī, n.d.

Al-Masʿūdī, ʿAlī ibn al-Ḥusayn. *Murūj al-dhahab wa-maʿādin al-jawhar.* Edited by Charles Pellat. 7 vols. Beirut: Publications de l'Université Libanaise, 1965–79.

Al-Maydānī, Aḥmad ibn Muḥammad. *Majmaʿ al-amthāl.* Edited by Muḥammad Abū l-Faḍl Ibrāhīm. 4 vols. Beirut: Dār al-Jīl, 1987.

Melling, David J., and Ken Parry. "Christology." In *The Blackwell Dictionary of Eastern Christianity,* edited by Ken Parry et al., 119–21. Malden, MA: Blackwell Publishing, 2001.

Moreh, Shmuel. *Live Theatre and Dramatic Literature in the Medieval Arabic World.* New York: New York University Press, 1992.

Mourad, Suleiman A. "Christian Monks in Islamic Literature: A Preliminary Report on Some Arabic *Apothegmata Patrum.*" *Bulletin of the Royal Institute for Inter-Faith Studies* 6, no. 2 (2004): 81–98.

Muslim ibn al-Ḥajjāj. *Ṣaḥīḥ Muslim.* Edited by Rāʾid ibn Ṣabrī ibn Abī ʿAlfah. Riyad: Dār al-Ḥaḍārah li-l-Nashr wa-l-Tawzīʿ, 2015.

Al-Najjār, Ibrāhīm. *Shuʿarāʾ ʿabbāsiyūn mansiyyūn.* 7 vols. Beirut: Dār al-Gharb al-Islāmī, 1997.

Neubauer, Eckhard. "Musiker am Hof der frühen ʿAbbāsiden." Dissertation, Frankfurt am Main, 1965.

Northedge, Alastair. "The Palaces of the ʿAbbasids at Samarra." In *A Medieval Islamic City Reconsidered.* Oxford Studies in Islamic Art 14, edited by Chase Robinson, 29–67. Oxford: Oxford University Press, 2001.

Orfali, Bilal. *The Anthologist's Art: Abū Manṣūr al-Thaʿālibī and His Yatīmat al-dahr.* Leiden, Netherlands: Brill, 2016.

Orfali, Bilal, and Nadia Maria El Cheikh, eds. *Approaches to the Study of Pre-Modern Arabic Anthologies.* Leiden, Netherlands: Brill, 2021.

Özkan, Hakan. "Wine Poetry in the Dīwān of Ibrāhīm al-Miʿmār." In *"Passed Around by a Crescent": Wine Poetry in the Literary Traditions of the Islamic World,* edited by Kirill Dmitriev and Christine van Ruymbeke, 97–119. Beirut: Ergon Verlag in Kommission, 2022.

Al-Qaddūmī, Ghāda al-Hijjāwī. *Book of Gifts and Rarities: Kitāb al-Hadāyā wa al-Tuḥaf.* Cambridge, MA: Harvard University Press, 1996.

Al-Qāḍī al-Nuʿmān ibn Muḥammad. *Sharḥ al-akhbār fī faḍā'il al-a'immah al-aṭhār.* Vol 1. Beirut: Mu'assasat al-aʿlamī li-l-maṭbūʿāt, 1427/2006.

Ṣādir, Kārīn. *Mawsūʿat al-adyirah al-naṣrāniyyah fī al-bilād al-mashriqiyyah ḥattā nihāyat al-ʿuṣūr al-ʿabbāsiyyah.* Beirut: Dār al-Mashriq, 2018.

Sachau, Eduard. *Vom Klosterbuch des Šâbuštî.* Abhandlungen der Preussischen Akademie der Wissenschaften. Berlin: Verlag der Akademie der Wissenschaften, 1919.

Sawa, George Dimitri. *Music Performance Practice in the Early ʿAbbāsid Era 132–320 AH / 750–932 AD.* Toronto: Pontifical Institute of Mediaeval Studies, 1989.

Sawa, George Dimitri. *Musical and Socio-Cultural Anecdotes from Kitāb al-aghānī al-kabīr: Annotated Translations and Commentaries.* Leiden, Netherlands: Brill, 2019.

Sezgin, Fuat. *Geschichte des arabischen Schrifttums.* Vol. 1: *Qur'ānwissenschaften, Ḥadīṯ, Geschichte, Fiqh, Dogmatik, Mystik bis ca. 430 H.*; vol. 2: *Poesie bis ca. 430 H.* 1975; vol. 9: *Grammatik bis ca. 430 H.* Leiden, Netherlands: Brill, 1967, 1975, 1984.

Al-Shābushtī, ʿAlī ibn Muḥammad. *Kitāb al-Diyārāt.* Edited and annotated by Kūrkīs ʿAwwād. 2nd ed. Baghdad: Maṭbaʿat al-Maʿārif, 1386/1966.

Al-Shammākh ibn Ḍirār al-Dhubyānī. *Dīwān.* Edited by Ṣalāḥ al-Dīn al-Hādī. Cairo: Dār al-Maʿārif, 1968.

Sharon, Moshe. "An Arabic Inscription from the Time of the Caliph ʿAbd al-Malik." *Bulletin of the School of Oriental and African Studies* 29 (1966): 367–72.

Al-Shīrwānī, Aḥmad ibn Muḥammad. *Ḥadīqat al-afrāḥ li-izāḥat al-aṭrāḥ.* Bulaq: Dār al-Ṭibāʿah al-ʿĀmirah, 1228/1866.

Sizgorich, Thomas. "The Dancing Martyr: Violence, Identity, and the Abbasid Postcolonial." *History of Religions* 57 (2017): 2–27.

Sourdel, Dominique. *Le vizirate ʿAbbāside de 749 à 936 (132 à 324 de l'Hégire).* Damascus: Publications de l'Institut français de Damas, 1959.

Stigelbauer, Michael. *Die Sängerinnen am Abbasidenhof um die Zeit des Kalifen Al-Mutawakkil: Nach dem Kitāb al-Aġānī des Abū-l-Faraǧ al-Iṣbahānī und anderen Quellen dargestellt.* Vienna: Verband der wissenschaftlichen Gesellschaften Österreichs, 1975.

Al-Sūdānī, Muzhir. *Jaḥẓah al-Barmakī: Al-adīb al-shāʿir.* Najaf: Maṭbaʿat al-Nuʿmān, 1397/1977.

Al-Ṭabarī, Muḥammad ibn Jarīr. *Tārīkh al-rusul wa-l-mulūk.* Edited by Muḥammad Abū al-Faḍl Ibrāhīm. 11 vols. Cairo: Dār al-Maʿārif, 1960.

———. *The History of al-Ṭabarī.* Vol. 32, *The Reunification of the ʿAbbāsid Caliphate.* Translated by C. E. Bosworth. New York: State University of New York Press, 1987.

———. *The History of al-Ṭabarī*. Vol. 23, *Storm and Stress along the Northern Frontiers of the ʿAbbāsid Caliphate*. Translated by C. E. Bosworth. New York: State University of New York Press, 1991.

———. *The History of al-Ṭabarī*. Vol. 34, *Incipient Decline*. Translated by Joel L. Kraemer. New York: State University of New York Press, 1989.

———. *The History of al-Ṭabarī*. Vol. 35, *The Crisis of the ʿAbbāsid Caliphate*. Translated by George Saliba. New York: State University of New York Press, 1985.

Ṭabāṭabāʾī, Sumayya al-Sādāt. "Gul-i surkh u bāda-yi gulgūn: Bāz-khwānī-yi abyātī az dīwān-I Abū Nuwās bar pāya-yi āyīn-i kuhan-i shādgulī" ("The Red Rose and Rose-Red Wine: A Re-Appraisal of Some Verses from the *Dīwān* of Abū Nuwās on the Basis of the Ancient Custom of *shādgulī*"). *Adab-i ʿarabī* 11, no. 2 (2019): 209–29.

Tamari, Steve. "The Bible Came from Lebanon: Sacred Land and Worldly Delights in a Seventeenth-Century Journey to the Valley of the Prophets." In *In the House of Understanding: Histories in Memory of Kamal S. Salibi*, edited by Abdul Rahim Abu Husayn, 405–21. Beirut: American University of Beirut Press, 2017.

Tannous, Jack. *The Making of the Medieval Middle East: Religion, Society and Simple Believers*. Princeton: Princeton University Press, 2018.

Al-Tanūkhī, al-Muḥassin ibn ʿAlī. *Stories of Piety and Prayer: Deliverance Follows Adversity*. Edited and translated by Julia Bray. New York: New York University Press, 2019.

Al-Tawḥīdī, Abū Ḥayyān. *Al-Baṣāʾir wa-l-dhakhāʾir*. Edited by Widād al-Qāḍī. 10 vols. Beirut: Dār Ṣādir, 1988.

Toral-Niehoff, Isabel. *Al-Ḥīra, eine arabische Kulturmetropole im spätantiken Kontext*. Leiden, Netherlands: Brill, 2014.

Al-Ṭurayḥī, Muḥammad Saʿīd. *Al-Diyārāt wa-l-amkinah al-naṣrāniyyah fī al-Kūfah wa-ḍawāḥīhā*. Beirut: Maṭbaʿat al-Mutanabbī, 1401/1981.

Al-ʿUmarī, Ibn Faḍl Allāh. *Masālik al-abṣār fī mamālik al-amṣār*. Edited by Aḥmad Zakī. 2 vols. Cairo: Dār al-Kutub al-Miṣriyyah, 1924.

Van Gelder, Geert Jan. *Sound and Sense in Classical Arabic Poetry*. Wiesbaden, Germany: Harrassowitz Verlag, 2012.

Winkler, Dietmar. "Terminology." In Wilhelm Baum and Dietmar Winkler, *The Church of the East: A Concise History*, 3–5. London: RoutledgeCurzon, 2003.

Wright, Owen. "Music and Verse." In *Arabic Literature to the End of the Umayyad Period (The Cambridge History of Arabic Literature)*, edited by A. F. L. Beeston et al., 433–59. Cambridge: Cambridge University Press, 1983.

Yaiche, Salah. *Les "livres des couvents," un genre littéraire arabe médiéval: L'élite musulman et le couvent chrétien*. Saarbrücken, Germany: Éditions universitaires européennes, 2012.

Al-Yaʿqūbī, Ibn Wāḍiḥ. *The Works of Ibn Wāḍiḥ al-Yaʿqūbī*. Vol. 2. Edited by Matthew S. Gordon et al. Leiden, Netherlands: Brill, 2018.

Yāqūt al-Ḥamawī. *Al-Khazal wa-l-daʾl bayn al-dūr wa-l-dārāt wa-l-diyarah*. Edited by Yaḥyā Zakariyyā ʿAbbādah and Muḥammad Adīb Jumrān. 2 vols. Damascus: Manshūrāt Wizārat al-Thaqāfah, 1998.

———. *Muʿjam al-buldān*. 5 vols. Beirut: Dār Ṣādir, 1965.

———. *Muʿjam al-udabāʾ*. Edited by Iḥsān ʿAbbās. Beirut: Dār al-Gharb al-Islāmī, 1993.

Zakharia, Katia. "Le moine et l'échanson, ou le *Kitāb al-diyārāt* d'al-Šābuštī et ses lecteurs: Une certaine représentation du couvent chrétien dans le monde musulman médiéval." *Bulletin d'Études Orientales* 53–54 (2001–02): 59–74.

———. "'Un paradis sans éternité': Note sur la poésie et les poètes cités dans le *Kitāb al-Diyārāt* (Livre sur les couvents) de Šābuštī (m. 388/998)." Unpublished paper.

Further Reading

Political and Social History

Gordon, Matthew S. *The Breaking of a Thousand Swords: A History of the Turkish Military of Samarra (A.H. 200–275/815/889 C.E.).* Albany: State University of New York Press, 2001.

Kennedy, Hugh. *The Court of the Caliphs: When Baghdad Ruled the Muslim World.* London: Weidenfeld and Nicholson, 2004.

Kennedy, Hugh. *The Prophet and the Age of the Caliphs: The Islamic Near East from the Sixth to the Eleventh Century.* 3rd ed. London: Routledge, 2016.

Lagrange, Frédéric. "Une affaire de viol." *Tumultes* 41 (2013): 61–70.

Al-Qaddūmī, Ghāda al-Hijjāwī, trans. and ann. *Book of Gifts and Rarities: Kitāb al-Hadāyā wa al-Tuḥaf.* Cambridge, MA: Harvard University Press, 1996.

Robinson, Chase, ed. *A Medieval Islamic City Reconsidered: An Interdisciplinary Approach to Samarra.* Oxford Studies in Islamic Art 14. Oxford: Oxford University Press, 2001.

Szombathy, Zoltan. *Mujūn: Libertinism in Mediaeval Muslim Society and Literature.* Cambridge, UK: Gibb Memorial Trust, 2013.

Toral-Niehoff, Isabel. *Al-Ḥīra, eine arabische Kulturmetropole im spätantiken Kontext.* Leiden, Netherlands: Brill, 2014.

Christianity

Allard, Michel. "Les Chrétiens à Baġdād." Special issue, *Arabica* 9 (1962): 375–88.

Baumer, Christoph. *The Church of the East: An Illustrated History of Assyrian Christianity.* London: I. B. Tauris, 2006.

Cannuyer, Christian. *Les Coptes: Fils d'Abraham.* 2nd ed. Turnhout, Belgium: Brepols, 1996.

Parry, Ken, ed. *The Blackwell Companion to Eastern Christianity.* Malden, MA: John Wiley, 2007.

Ṣādir, Kārīn. *Mawsūʿat al-adyirah al-naṣrāniyyah fī l-bilād al-mashriqiyyah ḥattā nihāyat al-ʿuṣūr al-ʿabbāsiyyah.* Beirut: Dār al-Mashriq, 2018.

Sélis, Claude. *Les Syriens orthodoxes et catholiques: Fils d'Abraham.* Turnhout, Belgium: Brepols, 1988.

Tannous, Jack. *The Making of the Medieval Middle East: Religion, Society and Simple Believers*. Princeton, NJ: Princeton University Press, 2018.

Thomas, David, ed. *Christians at the Heart of Islamic Rule: Church Life and Scholarship in ʿAbbasid Iraq*. Leiden, Netherlands: Brill, 2003.

Literature

Bencheikh, Jamal Eddine. *Poétique arabe*. Paris: Gallimard, 1989.

Cooperson, Michael, and Shawkat M. Toorawa, eds. *Arabic Literary Culture* 500–925. Detroit: Thomson Gale, 2005.

Dmitriev, Kirill. "The Symbolism of Wine in Early Arabic Love Poetry: Observations on the Poetry of Abū Ṣakhr al-Hudhalī." In *Insatiable Appetite: Food as Cultural Signifier in the Middle East and Beyond*, edited by Kirill Dmitriev, Julia Hauser, and Bilal Orfali, 165–89. Leiden, Netherlands: Brill, 2019.

Gruendler, Beatrice. "Verse and Taxes: The Function of Poetry in Selected Literary Akhbār of the Third/Ninth Century." In *On Fiction and Adab in Medieval Arabic Literature*, edited by Philip F. Kennedy, 85–124. Wiesbaden, Germany: Harrassowitz Verlag, 2005.

Kennedy, Philip F. *The Wine Song in Classical Arabic Poetry: Abū Nuwās and the Literary Tradition*. Oxford: The Clarendon Press, 1997.

Leder, Stefan, and Hilary Kilpatrick. "Classical Arabic Prose Literature: A Researchers' Sketch Map." *Journal of Arabic Literature* 23 (1992): 2–26.

Ya'iche, Salah. *Les «livres des couvents», un genre littéraire arabe médiéval: L'élite musulman et le couvent chrétien*. Saarbrücken, Germany: Éditions universitaires européennes, 2012.

Zakharia, Katia. "Le moine et l'échanson, ou le Kitāb al-diyārāt d'al-Šābuštī et ses lecteurs: Une certaine représentation du couvent chrétien dans le monde musulman médiéval." *Bulletin d'Études Orientales* 53–54 (2001–02): 59–74.

Index of Arabic Poetry

Section	Poet	Lines	Meter	Rhyme
		ء		
§4.8	Muḥammad ibn Abī Umayyah	3	*khafīf*	خَضْرَاءُ
§16.5	ʿAmr ibn ʿAbd al-Malik al-Warrāq	9	*ṭawīl*	سَوَاءُ
		ب		
§1.9	Abū ʿAbdallāh ibn Ḥamdūn	3	*rajaz*	اَلْعَجَائِبَا
§2.4	Khālid al-Kātib	1	*munsariḥ*	سَبَبِكْ
§2.10	Khālid al-Kātib	4	*khafīf*	اَلْقُلُوبُ
§2.10	Khālid al-Kātib	2	*ṭawīl*	قَــلْبِي
§4.4	Muḥammad ibn Abī Umayyah	3	*khafīf*	اَلْحَبِيبِ
§4.5	Muḥammad ibn Abī Umayyah	4	*khafīf*	اَلنَّحِيبِ
§4.7	Muḥammad ibn Abī Umayyah	3	*ṭawīl*	جَنْبِ
§4.9	Muḥammad ibn Abī Umayyah	2	*ṭawīl*	قَاضِبِ
§6.11	Abū l-Shibl al-Burjumī	3	*munsariḥ*	لَعِبِ
§8.2	ʿAbdallāh ibn ʿAbbās ibn al-Faḍl ibn al-Rabīʿ	11	*basīṭ*	وَاَلْكُرَبَا
§9.4	Abū Jafnah al-Qurashī	5	*ṭawīl*	تَغْضَبَا
§9.10	al-Numayrī	3	*ṭawīl*	بِعَاتِبِ
§9.13	al-Numayrī	4	*sarīʿ*	قُـرْبِي
§9.14	al-Numayrī	2	*ṭawīl*	وَاَلْقَلْبُ
§9.14	ʿAbdallāh ibn al-Muʿtazz	2	*ṭawīl*	اَلذَّنْبُ
§12.4	al-Muʿtamid	2	*mujtathth*	قَلْبِي
§12.4	al-Muʿtamid	3	*mutaqārib*	تُرْبَهْ
§12.5	al-Muʿtamid	4	*ramal*	وَاَكْتِئَابِي
§12.13	al-Muʿtamid	4	—	اَلْمَحْلُوبُ
§13.8	ʿUbaydallāh ibn ʿAbdallāh ibn Ṭāhir	2	*ṭawīl*	اَلْعَذْبِ
§13.15	ʿUbaydallāh ibn ʿAbdallāh ibn Ṭāhir	1	*ṭawīl*	وَيُنْدَبُ
§13.19	ʿUbaydallāh ibn ʿAbdallāh ibn Ṭāhir	2	*ṭawīl*	لَعَازِبُ
§13.32	Ibn al-Rūmī (attributed)	4	*kāmil*	بِهِ
§13.48	al-Maʾmūn	3	*ṭawīl*	سُكُوبُ

Section	Poet	Lines	Meter	Rhyme
§14.13	Abū Nuwās	1	*basīṭ*	ٱلذَّهَبِ
§15.12	al-Muʿtazz	2	*kāmil*	مَكْرُوبُ
§16.3	ʿAmr ibn ʿAbd al-Malik al-Warrāq	10	*ṭawīl*	بِٱلْعَطَبْ
§21.3	Muṣʿab al-Kātib	8	*ṭawīl*	لَرَاغِبُ
§22.3	al-Lubbādī	2	*wāfir*	ٱلنِّصَابِ
§24.2	al-Muhalhil ibn Yamūt ibn al-Muzarriʿ	11	*mutaqārib*	أُحِبْ
§24.8	al-Muhalhil ibn Yamūt ibn al-Muzarriʿ	2	*basīṭ*	يَجْذِبُهُ
§26.9	al-Rashīd	4	*mutaqārib*	مُكْتَئِبْ
§26.10	unidentified poet	5	*mutaqārib*	ٱلْعَجَبْ
§30.4	unidentified poet	3	*sarīʿ*	ٱلرَّاهِبُ
§33.19	Ibn Qays al-Ruqayyāt	1	*khafīf*	ٱلرُّكُوبَا
§34.6	Kushājim	4	*sarīʿ*	ٱلْغَرِيبْ
§35.4	Ibn Jamḥūr	2	*basīṭ*	وَٱلْوَصَبِ
§36.2	Muḥammad ibn Ḥāzim	9	*basīṭ*	وَٱلنُّخَبُ
§36.5	Muḥammad ibn Ḥāzim	6	*wāfir*	ٱلثَّوَابِ
§36.6	Muḥammad ibn Ḥāzim	9	*mujtathth*	حَرْبُ
§36.11	Muḥammad ibn Ḥāzim	10	*sarīʿ*	ٱلْقُلَّبُ

ت

Section	Poet	Lines	Meter	Rhyme
§6.2	Jaḥẓah	3	*sarīʿ*	جَنَّاتِهَا
§8.7	ʿAbdallāh ibn ʿAbbās ibn al-Faḍl ibn al-Rabīʿ	4	*kāmil*	عَدُوَّتِي
§9.2	Abū Jafnah al-Qurashī	8	*munsariḥ*	أَزِمَّتِهِ
§15.1	al-Faḍl ibn al-ʿAbbās ibn al-Maʾmūn	5	*basīṭ*	وَشَهْوَاتِي
§17.1	unidentified poet	1	*basīṭ*	عِفْرِيتْ
§21.4	Muṣʿab al-Kātib	9	*wāfir*	فَعَلْتَا
§21.10	Muṣʿab al-Kātib	10	*munsariḥ*	نِقْمَتِهِ
§34.4	Kushājim	6	*munsariḥ*	فَتَى
§35.8	Ibn Jamḥūr	4	*kāmil*	لَقِيتُ
§37.2	Abū Hurayrah ibn Abī al-ʿIṣām	3	*sarīʿ*	وَمُصَافَاتِي
§38.3	Muḥammad ibn ʿĀṣim	8	*basīṭ*	بِٱلتُّوَيْتَاتِ
§40.3	Muḥammad ibn ʿĀṣim	7	*basīṭ*	وَعَانَاتِ

ث

Section	Poet	Lines	Meter	Rhyme
§26.14	al-Rashīd	3	*ramal*	وَخُنُثْ

ذ

ر

Section	Poet	Lines	Meter	Rhyme
§13.15	ʿUbaydallāh ibn ʿAbdallāh ibn Ṭāhir	2	*ṭawīl*	ٱلْمَقَابِرِ
§13.24	ʿAbdallāh ibn al-Muʿtazz	3	*ṭawīl*	ٱلدَّهْرُ
§13.24	ʿUbaydallāh ibn ʿAbdallāh ibn Ṭāhir	2	*ṭawīl*	وَٱلْعُذْرُ
§13.29	Ibn Abī Fanan	8	*kāmil*	ٱلْأَمِيرِ
§13.30	Muḥammad ibn ʿAbdallāh ibn Ṭāhir	4	*basīṭ*	بَصَرِي
§13.34	al-Muʿtazz	2	*khafīf*	ٱلْقُبُورِ
§13.40	ʿAbd al-ʿAzīz ibn ʿAbdallāh ibn Ṭāhir	2	*kāmil*	ٱلْبَاهِرُ
§13.41	ʿAbd al-ʿAzīz ibn ʿAbdallāh ibn Ṭāhir	5	*sarīʿ*	ٱلشِّعْرَى
§13.45	ʿAwf ibn Muḥallim al-Khuzāʿī	1	*basīṭ*	وَٱلظَّفَرِ
§18.4	al-Maʾmūn	4	*hazaj*	ٱلْمَقَاصِيرِ
§19.3	Abū Shās Munīr	6	*munsariḥ*	يُعَارُ
§21.8	Muṣʿab al-Kātib	9	*basīṭ*	دَارَا
§21.9	Muṣʿab al-Kātib	5	*mutaqārib*	ظَهْرِهِ
§22.5	al-Lubbādī	10	*mutaqārib*	مُسْتَنْظِرَهْ
§24.8	al-Muhalhil ibn Yamūt ibn al-Muzarriʿ	2	*khafīf*	ٱلْأَبْصَارِ
§24.9	al-Muhalhil ibn Yamūt ibn al-Muzarriʿ	3	*khafīf*	ٱلزُّنَّارِ
§24.10	Abū Umayyah al-Aṣamm	2	*ṭawīl*	ٱلْغَدْرِ
§28.1	al-Tharwānī	7	*munsariḥ*	مُخْتَصَرِ
§33.2	Muṭīʿ ibn Iyās	3	*wāfir*	ٱلتِّجَارَهْ
§33.3	Muṭīʿ ibn Iyās/Abū ʿAlī al-Baṣīr	9	*hazaj*	وَزُوَّارَا
§33.11	Muṭīʿ ibn Iyās	2	*wāfir*	وَطَنْجِيرُ
§34.1	al-Ḥusayn ibn al-Ḍaḥḥāk	4	*sarīʿ*	ٱلْعُمْرِ
§34.2	Kushājim	13	*khafīf*	ٱلنَّهَارِ
§34.5	Kushājim	7	*ṭawīl*	سِحْرُ
§35.3	Ibn Jamhūr	2	*ṭawīl*	أَحْوَرَا
§36.7	Muḥammad ibn Ḥāzim	2	*mujtathth*	بِخَمْرِ
§36.8	Muḥammad ibn Ḥāzim	3	*ṭawīl*	ٱلشُّكْرِ
§36.10	Muḥammad ibn Ḥāzim	1	*sarīʿ*	ٱلدَّهْرِ
§37.3	Muḥammad ibn ʿĀṣim	27	*khafīf*	ٱلْقِصَارِ
§38.2	Muḥammad ibn ʿĀṣim	6	*kāmil*	ٱلْمَنْظَرِ
§38.5	Ibn al-ʿAbbās al-Baṣrī	9	*sarīʿ*	فَٱنْذَعَرْ
§38.7	Ṣāliḥ ibn Mūsā	15	*kāmil*	تَغُرْ
§39.3	Ibn al-ʿAbbās al-Baṣrī	12	*mutaqārib*	ٱلدُّرُوزِ
§40.2	Muḥammad ibn ʿĀṣim	4	*khafīf*	إِقْصَارِ
§49.2	Muḥammad ibn ʿĀṣim	3	*basīṭ*	ٱلطُّورُ

Section	Poet	Lines	Meter	Rhyme
		س		
§2.16	Jaḥẓah	4	*mutaqārib*	نُكْسِهِ
§4.9	Muḥammad ibn Abī Umayyah	4	*wāfir*	نَعَسَا
§6.5	al-Tharwānī	5	*sarīʿ*	بِتَغْلِيسِ
§12.11	Muḥammad ibn ʿAlī	3	*ramal*	مُوسَى
§12.11	al-Muʿtamid	3	*ramal*	مُوسَى
§13.10	ʿUbaydallāh ibn ʿAbdallāh ibn Ṭāhir	2	*ṭawīl*	وَلِلنُّكْسِ
§20.8	unidentified poet	1	*sarīʿ*	غَرْسِهِ
§27.1	Ibn Abī Ṭālib al-Makfūf	6	*khafīf*	خَنْدَرِيسِ
§36.12	Muḥammad ibn Ḥāzim	3	*basīṭ*	ٱلنَّاسِ
		ص		
§13.33	ʿUbaydallāh ibn ʿAbdallāh ibn Ṭāhir	2	*ṭawīl*	وَتَنْقُصُ
		ض		
§2.5	Khālid al-Kātib	4	*ṭawīl*	بِٱلْأَرْضِ
§2.12	Khālid al-Kātib	4	*ramal*	مَرَضِي
§24.7	al-Muhalhil ibn Yamūt ibn al-Muzarriʿ	4	*khafīf*	وَٱلْإِعْرَاضِ
		ط		
§2.13	ʿUbaydallāh ibn ʿAbdallāh ibn Ṭāhir	1	*kāmil*	ٱلْقِيرَاطْ
§6.3	unidentified poet	2	*mutaqārib*	يُسَاطْ
		ع		
§3.6	Ibn Dihqānah al-Hāshimī	2	*mutaqārib*	يَجْزَعُ
§4.2	Muḥammad ibn Abī Umayyah	6	*ṭawīl*	وَأَسْعَفَا
§9.7	al-Numayrī	3	*ṭawīl*	مُمْتِعُ
§9.15	ʿAbdallāh ibn al-Muʿtazz	2	*mujtathth*	طَاعَهْ
§11.5	Abū ʿUthmān al-Nājim	4	*ramal*	دُمُوعَا
§13.10	ʿUbaydallāh ibn ʿAbdallāh ibn Ṭāhir	2	*ṭawīl*	شَاسِعَا
§13.11	ʿAbdallāh ibn al-Muʿtazz	2	*ṭawīl*	تَسْجَعْ
§13.23	ʿUbaydallāh ibn ʿAbdallāh ibn Ṭāhir	3	*ṭawīl*	ٱلْمَدَامِعُ
§15.6	al-Muʿtazz	2	*basīṭ*	وَٱلْخُدَعِ
§24.11	Ḥakīm ibn Jabalah al-ʿAbdī	3	*rajaz*	تُرَاعِي
§32.2	al-Nābighah al-Dhubyānī	1	*ṭawīl*	أَرْبَعَا

Section	Poet	Lines	Meter	Rhyme
§33.16	Muṭīʿ ibn Iyās	6	*basīṭ*	مُمْتَنِعَا
§34.9	Kushājim	2	*wāfir*	ٱلتَّرَاعُ
§36.12	Muḥammad ibn Ḥāzim	7	*wāfir*	وَدِيعِ
§36.14	Muḥammad ibn Ḥāzim	2	*kāmil*	يُسَارِعُ

ف

Section	Poet	Lines	Meter	Rhyme
§2.8	Khālid al-Kātib	2	*mutaqārib*	تَذْرِفُ
§4.2	Muḥammad ibn Abī Umayyah	6	*ṭawīl*	وَأَسْعَفَا
§7.3	al-Ḥusayn ibn al-Ḍaḥḥāk	2	*kāmil*	ٱلتَّلَفُ
§9.13	ʿAbdallāh ibn al-Muʿtazz	4	*sarīʿ*	ٱلظَّرِفِ
§9.18	al-Numayrī	3	*mutaqārib*	تَنْطَفِي
§10.7	Abū l-ʿAynāʾ	3	*khafīf*	لَطَفْ
§12.4	al-Muʿtamid	2	*mutaqārib*	ٱلْجَفَاءِ
§13.20	Abū Bakr ibn al-Sarrāj	2	*kāmil*	تَفِي
§13.32	Ibn al-Rūmī	3	*kāmil*	يَكْسِفُ
§15.10	al-Muʿtazz	4	*ramal*	أَنْفِي
§30.2	ʿAlī ibn Muḥammad al-Ḥimmānī	11	*kāmil*	بِٱلْمَوَاقِفْ
§30.3	Abū Nuwās	5	*khafīf*	وَعَزْفِ
§33.18	Muṭīʿ ibn Iyās	2	*munsariḥ*	صَلَفَا
§34.3	Kushājim	7	*ramal*	ٱلتَّلَفْ
§37.2	Abū Hurayrah ibn Abī al-ʿIṣām	2	*munsariḥ*	ظَرْفِ

ق

Section	Poet	Lines	Meter	Rhyme
§4.6	Muḥammad ibn Abī Umayyah	4	*basīṭ*	مَعْشُوقِ
§9.19	al-Numayrī	3	*mujtathth*	بِعِشْقِكْ
§12.5	al-Muʿtamid	3	*ramal*	حُرَقَهْ
§12.12	al-Muʿtamid	4	—	أَحْمَقْ
§12.12	al-Rāḍī	2	*ramal*	أَحْمَقْ
§12.14	al-Muʿtamid	5	*rajaz*	ٱلْجَوْسَقَا
§23.2	Abū Nuwās (?)	1	*wāfir*	فِيقِ
§23.2	Abū Nuwās (?)	17	*wāfir*	بِٱلْجَاثَلِيقِ
§24.4	al-Muhalhil ibn Yamūt ibn al-Muzarriʿ	15	*mutaqārib*	رَقِيقْ
§26.4	al-Ṣanawbarī	10	*kāmil*	طَلِيقَا
§26.5	al-Ṣanawbarī	3	*mujtathth*	ٱلْأَنِيقِ
§31.1	unidentified poet	3	*khafīf*	وَثِيقِ
§39.2	Ibn al-ʿAbbās al-Baṣrī	23	*kāmil*	ٱلْفُتُقِ

Section	Poet	Lines	Meter	Rhyme
				ك
§7.9	al-Ḥusayn ibn al-Ḍaḥḥāk	4	*khafīf*	أَرَاكَا
§24.12	Yamūt ibn al-Muzarriʿ	5	*wāfir*	عَسَرُكْ
§33.14	Muṭīʿ ibn Iyās	2	*khafīf*	هَوَاكِ
§35.7	Ibn Jamḥūr	3	*ramal*	هَوَاكِ
				ل
§1.5	Abū ʿAbdallāh ibn Ḥamdūn	3	*ṭawīl*	تَسِيلُ
§1.12	Abū ʿAbdallāh ibn Ḥamdūn	2	*mujtathth*	حَالِي
§2.3	Khālid al-Kātib	3	*munsariḥ*	ٱنْتِقَالُ
§2.6	Khālid al-Kātib	4	*kāmil*	تَقْبَلُ
§2.7	Khālid al-Kātib	3	*basīṭ*	وَاصِلِي
§2.13	Jaḥẓah	1	*mujtathth*	نَعْلِي
§2.14	Jaḥẓah	4	*kāmil*	ٱلْعَقْلِ
§3.2	Ibn Dihqānah al-Hāshimī	5	*kāmil*	وَغَزَالِ
§3.3	Ibn Dihqānah al-Hāshimī	3	*mutaqārib*	أَبْخَلِ
§4.4	Muḥammad ibn Abī Umayyah	4	*basīṭ*	تَفْعَلِ
§6.6	Yaḥyā ibn Kāmil	2	*sarīʿ*	ٱلظِّلّ
§8.3	ʿAbdallāh ibn ʿAbbās ibn al-Faḍl ibn al-Rabīʿ	2	*mujtathth*	قَتْلِي
§8.5	ʿAbdallāh ibn ʿAbbās ibn al-Faḍl ibn al-Rabīʿ	2	*khafīf*	وَقِيلَا
§9.5	al-Numayrī	5	*ṭawīl*	لِي
§9.12	al-Numayrī	4	*wāfir*	ٱلْجَلِيلِ
§9.12	al-Numayrī	1	*mujtathth*	لَكْ
§9.16	ʿAbdallāh ibn al-Muʿtazz	3	*mujtathth*	فِعْلَكْ
§9.16	al-Numayrī	2	*mujtathth*	بِفَضْلِكْ
§11.4	Abū ʿUthmān al-Nājim	2	*munsariḥ*	نُعْمِلُهَا
§12.6	al-Muʿtamid	1	*mujtathth*	حَالَكْ
§12.6	al-Muʿtamid	3	*sarīʿ*	ذِلَّهْ
§12.12	al-Muʿtamid	3	—	بِمَالِي
§13.39	ʿAbd al-ʿAzīz ibn ʿAbdallāh ibn Ṭāhir	6	*basīṭ*	جَبَلِ
§13.50	ʿAbdallāh ibn Ṭāhir	1	*basīṭ*	حَالِ
§19.5	Abū Shās Munīr	9	*wāfir*	مُسْتَحِيلُ
§21.5	Muṣʿab al-Kātib	13	*ṭawīl*	مِثْلِ
§24.6	al-Muhalhil ibn Yamūt ibn al-Muzarriʿ	7	*munsariḥ*	شَوَّالُ
§26.11	al-Rashīd	5	*kāmil*	نَبْلُ

Section	Poet	Lines	Meter	Rhyme
§34.6	Kushājim	2	*ṭawīl*	عَالِي
§35.7	Rabīʿah al-Raqqī al-Asadī	2	*ṭawīl*	يَجْهَلُ
§36.8	Muḥammad ibn Ḥāzim	3	*ṭawīl*	مَلُولُ
§36.9	Muḥammad ibn Ḥāzim	7	*kāmil*	جَمِيلُ
§36.13	Muḥammad ibn Ḥāzim	2	*basīṭ*	ٱلْمَالِ
§36.14	Muḥammad ibn Ḥāzim	4	*kāmil*	مَسْؤُولَا
§37.4	Ibn al-Zanbaqī	11	*sarīʿ*	ٱلْأَسَلْ
§38.6	Ṣāliḥ ibn Mūsā	11	*rajaz*	يُمَلْ

م

Section	Poet	Lines	Meter	Rhyme
§1.7	Marwān ibn Abī Ḥafṣah (attributed)	1	*kāmil*	بِشَمَّهْ
§2.12	Khālid al-Kātib	2	*ṭawīl*	إِلَيْكُمُ
§3.4	Jaḥẓah	1	*ṭawīl*	وَٱلدَّمَا
§7.10	al-Ḥasan ibn Rajāʾ	4	*wāfir*	ٱلصِّيَامِ
§9.10	al-Numayrī	2	*wāfir*	ٱلصِّيَامِ
§10.11	Abū l-ʿAynāʾ	2	*ṭawīl*	جِسْمُ
§10.15	unidentified poet	2	*ṭawīl*	ٱلْمُذَمَّمَا
§10.17	Abū l-ʿAynāʾ	1	*ṭawīl*	لِئَامُهَا
§12.14	al-Muʿtamid	3	*mutaqārib*	صُرُمْ
§12.15	al-Muʿtamid	2	—	ٱلْقَدَمْ
§13.2	unidentified poet	4	*mutaqārib*	حَرَامُ
§13.6	unidentified poet	1	*mutaqārib*	ٱلْمِعْصَمِ
§13.6	unidentified poet	1	*ṭawīl*	حَمَائِمُ
§13.17	unidentified poet	2	*ṭawīl*	تَغَشُّمَا
§13.18	ʿUbaydallāh ibn ʿAbdallāh ibn Ṭāhir	2	*ṭawīl*	وَنُعْظِمُ
§13.23	ʿUbaydallāh ibn ʿAbdallāh ibn Ṭāhir	2	*ṭawīl*	كِرَامِهَا
§13.50	ʿAbdallāh ibn Ṭāhir	1	*sarīʿ*	عَنَمْ
§15.7	al-Muʿtazz	1	*kāmil*	ٱلتَّمَامِ
§15.7	Bunān the Singer	1	*kāmil*	قَوَامِ
§19.2	Abū Shās Munīr	4	*basīṭ*	تَبْتَسِمُ
§19.4	Abū Shās Munīr	4	*kāmil*	ٱلْجِسْمِ
§26.12	al-Rashīd	5	*sarīʿ*	ظَالِمُ
§26.13	al-Rashīd	4	*kāmil*	سَلَامَا
§31.2	Bakr ibn Khārijah	6	*khafīf*	ٱلنُّجُومَا
§36.3	Muḥammad ibn Ḥāzim	12	*wāfir*	كَرِيمِ

Section	Poet	Lines	Meter	Rhyme
				ن
§1.3	Abū ʿAbdallāh ibn Ḥamdūn	4	*sarīʿ*	أَفْتَنَكْ
§1.10	Abū ʿAbdallāh ibn Ḥamdūn	4	*munsariḥ*	وَيَصْرِمُنِي
§1.14	Jaḥẓah	2	*wāfir*	تَغَنَّتْ
§2.2	Muḥammad ibn ʿAbd al-Malik al-Hāshimī	7	*kāmil*	أَحْزَانُهُ
§3.8	al-Nāshiʾ	2	*kāmil*	مَكَانُ
§4.1	Muḥammad ibn Abī Umayyah	2	*basīṭ*	ٱلشَّيَاطِينِ
§4.3	Muḥammad ibn Abī Umayyah	2	*wāfir*	وَلِلْقَرِينِ
§4.3	Muḥammad ibn Abī Umayyah	2	*kāmil*	مَكَانُ
§4.6	Muḥammad ibn Abī Umayyah	2	*sarīʿ*	أَمِينْ
§4.9	Muḥammad ibn Abī Umayyah	2	*sarīʿ*	ٱلظُّنُونْ
§5.2	al-Ḥusayn ibn al-Ḍaḥḥāk	7	*basīṭ*	أَحْيَانَا
§5.16	ʿAbbās ibn al-Aḥnaf	2	*khafīf*	ٱلْهِجْرَانِ
§7.4	al-Ḥusayn ibn al-Ḍaḥḥāk	6	*munsariḥ*	وَسِتِّينَا
§7.11	Muḥammad ibn al-Ḥārith ibn Buskhunnar	6	*ramal*	لُجَيْنِ
§8.7	ʿAbdallāh ibn ʿAbbās ibn al-Faḍl ibn al-Rabīʿ	2	*munsariḥ*	بِكُرْكِينِ
§8.8	ʿAbdallāh ibn ʿAbbās ibn al-Faḍl ibn al-Rabīʿ	2	*kāmil*	بَقِينَا
§8.9	ʿAbdallāh ibn ʿAbbās ibn al-Faḍl ibn al-Rabīʿ	7	*ramal*	لُجَيْنِ
§9.12	ʿAbdallāh ibn al-Muʿtazz	3	*rajaz*	وَعِصْيَانْ
§9.16	ʿAbdallāh ibn al-Muʿtazz	2	*basīṭ*	بِٱلدُّونِ
§9.19	ʿAbdallāh ibn al-Muʿtazz	2	*mujtathth*	وَعَيْنِ
§10.12	Abū l-ʿAynāʾ	2	*ṭawīl*	فَأَذَنَا
§12.2	Jaḥẓah	10	*khafīf*	وَٱلسُّكَانَا
§13.9	ʿUbaydallāh ibn ʿAbdallāh ibn Ṭāhir	2	*ṭawīl*	وَرَعَانِي
§13.22	ʿUbaydallāh ibn ʿAbdallāh ibn Ṭāhir	2	*ṭawīl*	يَخْتَلِفَانِ
§13.55	al-Shammākh ibn Ḍirār	1	*wāfir*	بِٱلْيَمِينِ
§15.10	al-Muʿtazz	2	*basīṭ*	سُكْرَيْنِ
§16.2	ʿAmr ibn ʿAbd al-Malik al-Warrāq	8	*hazaj*	مَرِيحَنَّا
§20.1	al-Khabbāz al-Baladī	2	*basīṭ*	ٱلشَّيَاطِينِ
§21.2	Muṣʿab al-Kātib	14	*wāfir*	هِجَانِ
§21.7	Muṣʿab al-Kātib	12	*basīṭ*	دِينِي
§22.4	al-Lubbādī	17	*rajaz*	صَيَّرَنِي
§24.3	al-Muhalhil ibn Yamūt ibn al-Muzarriʿ	10	*khafīf*	ٱلْعَاذِلَانِ
§26.2	al-Ṣanawbarī	17	*wāfir*	ٱلْجَانِبَيْنِ
§26.3	al-Ṣanawbarī	14	*kāmil*	أَفْنَانُهَا

Section	Poet	Lines	Meter	Rhyme
§26.6	al-Ṣanawbarī	25	*khafīf*	ٱلْجُفُونُ
§26.7	al-Ṣanawbarī	6	*kāmil*	بِٱلْبَيْنِ
§26.8	al-Ṣanawbarī	11	*khafīf*	مِذْعَانِ
§28.2	al-Tharwānī	8	*wāfir*	وَٱلْقِيَانُ
§31.3	Bakr ibn Khārijah	7	*sarīʿ*	وَأَحْزَانَا
§32.3	unidentified poet	2	*khafīf*	وَهَوَانِ
§32.6	al-Nuʿmān ibn al-Mundhir	2	*rajaz*	هَوَازِنَا
§33.18	Muṭīʿ ibn Iyās	3	*kāmil*	ٱلدِّنَانِ
§35.2	Ibn Jamhūr	26	*rajaz*	قُنَّا
§35.4	Ibn Jamhūr	4	*ramal*	دَانِي
§35.10	ʿAbdūn ibn Makhlad	2	*rajaz mushawwah*	هَـدِيَّتَانِكِ
§38.4	Muḥammad ibn ʿĀṣim	10	*wāfir*	ٱلْمِزْرَمَيْنِ

ه

Section	Poet	Lines	Meter	Rhyme
§9.17	ʿAbdallāh ibn al-Muʿtazz	2	*rajaz*	سَاهِي
§9.18	ʿAbdallāh ibn al-Muʿtazz	1	*sarīʿ*	بِـٱللّٰهِ
§9.18	al-Numayrī	2	*sarīʿ*	بِـٱللّٰهِ

ى

Section	Poet	Lines	Meter	Rhyme
§8.5	ʿAbdallāh ibn ʿAbbās ibn al-Faḍl ibn al-Rabīʿ	3	*sarīʿ*	صَافِيَهْ
§12.7	al-Muʿtamid	3	*wāfir*	عَلَيْهِ
§13.14	ʿUbaydallāh ibn ʿAbdallāh ibn Ṭāhir	2	*ṭawīl*	بَالِيَا
§13.22	ʿUbaydallāh ibn ʿAbdallāh ibn Ṭāhir	2	*ṭawīl*	سَوَا
§13.38	ʿUbaydallāh ibn ʿAbdallāh ibn Ṭāhir	2	*basīṭ*	مَجَارِيهَا
§14.14	Būrān	2	*khafīf*	فِيَّا
§24.8	al-Muhalhil ibn Yamūt ibn al-Muzarriʿ	2	*basīṭ*	تَحْكِيهِ
§26.12	al-Rashīd	2	*sarīʿ*	كَوَى
§35.6	Ibn Jamḥūr	3	*sarīʿ*	جَارِيَهْ
§36.13	Muḥammad ibn Ḥāzim	2	*sarīʿ*	ٱلسَّمَا

Index

About the NYU Abu Dhabi Institute

The Library of Arabic Literature is supported by a grant from the NYU Abu Dhabi Institute, a major hub of intellectual and creative activity and advanced research. The Institute hosts academic conferences, workshops, lectures, film series, performances, and other public programs directed both to audiences within the UAE and to the worldwide academic and research community. It is a center of the scholarly community for Abu Dhabi, bringing together faculty and researchers from institutions of higher learning throughout the region.

NYU Abu Dhabi, through the NYU Abu Dhabi Institute, is a world-class center of cutting-edge research, scholarship, and cultural activity. The Institute creates singular opportunities for leading researchers from across the arts, humanities, social sciences, sciences, engineering, and the professions to carry out creative scholarship and conduct research on issues of major disciplinary, multidisciplinary, and global significance.

About the Typefaces

The Arabic body text is set in DecoType Naskh, designed by Thomas Milo and Mirjam Somers, based on an analysis of five centuries of Ottoman manuscript practice. The exceptionally legible result is the first and only typeface in a style that fully implements the principles of script grammar (*qawāʿid al-khaṭṭ*).

The Arabic footnote text is set in DecoType Emiri, drawn by Mirjam Somers, based on the metal typeface in the naskh style that was cut for the 1924 Cairo edition of the Qur'an.

Both Arabic typefaces in this series are controlled by a dedicated font layout engine. ACE, the Arabic Calligraphic Engine, invented by Peter Somers, Thomas Milo, and Mirjam Somers of DecoType, first operational in 1985, pioneered the principle followed by later smart font layout technologies such as OpenType, which is used for all other typefaces in this series.

The Arabic text was set with WinSoft Tasmeem, a sophisticated user interface for DecoType ACE inside Adobe InDesign. Tasmeem was conceived and created by Thomas Milo (DecoType) and Pascal Rubini (WinSoft) in 2005.

The English text is set in Adobe Text, a new and versatile text typeface family designed by Robert Slimbach for Western (Latin, Greek, Cyrillic) typesetting. Its workhorse qualities make it perfect for a wide variety of applications, especially for longer passages of text where legibility and economy are important. Adobe Text bridges the gap between calligraphic Renaissance types of the 15th and 16th centuries and high-contrast Modern styles of the 18th century, taking many of its design cues from early post-Renaissance Baroque transitional types cut by designers such as Christoffel van Dijck, Nicolaus Kis, and William Caslon. While grounded in classical form, Adobe Text is also a statement of contemporary utilitarian design, well suited to a wide variety of print and on-screen applications.

Titles Published by the Library of Arabic Literature

For more details on individual titles, visit www.libraryofarabicliterature.org

Classical Arabic Literature: A Library of Arabic Literature Anthology
Selected and translated by Geert Jan van Gelder (2012)

A Treasury of Virtues: Sayings, Sermons, and Teachings of ʿAlī, by al-Qāḍī al-Quḍāʿī, with the **One Hundred Proverbs** attributed to al-Jāḥiẓ
Edited and translated by Tahera Qutbuddin (2013)

The Epistle on Legal Theory, by al-Shāfiʿī
Edited and translated by Joseph E. Lowry (2013)

Leg over Leg, by Aḥmad Fāris al-Shidyāq
Edited and translated by Humphrey Davies (**4 volumes**; 2013–14)

Virtues of the Imām Aḥmad ibn Ḥanbal, by Ibn al-Jawzī
Edited and translated by Michael Cooperson (**2 volumes**; 2013–15)

The Epistle of Forgiveness, by Abū l-ʿAlāʾ al-Maʿarrī
Edited and translated by Geert Jan van Gelder and Gregor Schoeler (**2 volumes**; 2013–14)

The Principles of Sufism, by ʿĀʾishah al-Bāʿūniyyah
Edited and translated by Th. Emil Homerin (2014)

The Expeditions: An Early Biography of Muḥammad, by Maʿmar ibn Rāshid
Edited and translated by Sean W. Anthony (2014)

Two Arabic Travel Books
Accounts of China and India, by Abū Zayd al-Sīrāfī
Edited and translated by Tim Mackintosh-Smith (2014)
Mission to the Volga, by Aḥmad ibn Faḍlān
Edited and translated by James Montgomery (2014)

Disagreements of the Jurists: A Manual of Islamic Legal Theory, by al-Qāḍī al-Nuʿmān
Edited and translated by Devin J. Stewart (2015)

Consorts of the Caliphs: Women and the Court of Baghdad, by Ibn al-Sāʿī
Edited by Shawkat M. Toorawa and translated by the Editors of the Library of Arabic Literature **(2015)**

What ʿĪsā ibn Hishām Told Us, by Muḥammad al-Muwayliḥī
Edited and translated by Roger Allen **(2 volumes; 2015)**

The Life and Times of Abū Tammām, by Abū Bakr Muḥammad ibn Yaḥyā al-Ṣūlī
Edited and translated by Beatrice Gruendler **(2015)**

The Sword of Ambition: Bureaucratic Rivalry in Medieval Egypt, by ʿUthmān ibn Ibrāhīm al-Nābulusī
Edited and translated by Luke Yarbrough **(2016)**

Brains Confounded by the Ode of Abū Shādūf Expounded, by Yūsuf al-Shirbīnī
Edited and translated by Humphrey Davies **(2 volumes; 2016)**

Light in the Heavens: Sayings of the Prophet Muḥammad, by al-Qāḍī al-Quḍāʿī
Edited and translated by Tahera Qutbuddin **(2016)**

Risible Rhymes, by Muḥammad ibn Maḥfūẓ al-Sanhūrī
Edited and translated by Humphrey Davies **(2016)**

A Hundred and One Nights
Edited and translated by Bruce Fudge **(2016)**

The Excellence of the Arabs, by Ibn Qutaybah
Edited by James E. Montgomery and Peter Webb
Translated by Sarah Bowen Savant and Peter Webb **(2017)**

Scents and Flavors: A Syrian Cookbook
Edited and translated by Charles Perry **(2017)**

Arabian Satire: Poetry from 18th-Century Najd, by Ḥmēdān al-Shwēʿir
Edited and translated by Marcel Kurpershoek **(2017)**

In Darfur: An Account of the Sultanate and Its People, by Muḥammad ibn ʿUmar al-Tūnisī
Edited and translated by Humphrey Davies **(2 volumes; 2018)**

War Songs, by ʿAntarah ibn Shaddād
Edited by James E. Montgomery
Translated by James E. Montgomery with Richard Sieburth **(2018)**

Arabian Romantic: Poems on Bedouin Life and Love, by ʿAbdallāh ibn Sbayyil
Edited and translated by Marcel Kurpershoek **(2018)**

Dīwān ʿAntarah ibn Shaddād: A Literary-Historical Study
By James E. Montgomery **(2018)**

Stories of Piety and Prayer: Deliverance Follows Adversity, by al-Muḥassin ibn ʿAlī al-Tanūkhī
Edited and translated by Julia Bray **(2019)**

The Philosopher Responds: An Intellectual Correspondence from the Tenth Century, by Abū Ḥayyān al-Tawḥīdī and Abū ʿAlī Miskawayh
Edited by Bilal Orfali and Maurice A. Pomerantz
Translated by Sophia Vasalou and James E. Montgomery **(2 volumes; 2019)**

Tajrīd sayf al-himmah li-stikhrāj mā fī dhimmat al-dhimmah: A Scholarly Edition of ʿUthmān ibn Ibrāhīm al-Nābulusī's Text
By Luke Yarbrough **(2020)**

The Discourses: Reflections on History, Sufism, Theology, and Literature—Volume One, by al-Ḥasan al-Yūsī
Edited and translated by Justin Stearns **(2020)**

Impostures, by al-Ḥarīrī
Translated by Michael Cooperson **(2020)**

Maqāmāt Abī Zayd al-Sarūjī, by al-Ḥarīrī
Edited by Michael Cooperson **(2020)**

The Yoga Sutras of Patañjali, by Abū Rayḥān al-Bīrūnī
Edited and translated by Mario Kozah **(2020)**

The Book of Charlatans, by Jamāl al-Dīn ʿAbd al-Raḥīm al-Jawbarī
Edited by Manuela Dengler
Translated by Humphrey Davies **(2020)**

A Physician on the Nile: A Description of Egypt and Journal of the Famine Years, by ʿAbd al-Laṭīf al-Baghdādī
Edited and translated by Tim Mackintosh-Smith **(2021)**

The Book of Travels, by Ḥannā Diyāb
Edited by Johannes Stephan
Translated by Elias Muhanna **(2 volumes; 2021)**

Kalīlah and Dimnah: Fables of Virtue and Vice, by Ibn al-Muqaffaʿ
Edited by Michael Fishbein
Translated by Michael Fishbein and James E. Montgomery **(2021)**

Love, Death, Fame: Poetry and Lore from the Emirati Oral Tradition, by al-Māyidī ibn Ẓāhir
Edited and translated by Marcel Kurpershoek **(2022)**

The Essence of Reality: A Defense of Philosophical Sufism, by ʿAyn al-Quḍāt
Edited and translated by Mohammed Rustom **(2022)**

The Requirements of the Sufi Path: A Defense of the Mystical Tradition, by Ibn Khaldūn
Edited and translated by Carolyn Baugh **(2022)**

The Doctors' Dinner Party, by Ibn Buṭlān
Edited and translated by Philip F. Kennedy and Jeremy Farrell **(2023)**

Fate the Hunter: Early Arabic Hunting Poems
Edited and translated by James E. Montgomery **(2023)**

The Book of Monasteries, by al-Shābushtī
Edited and translated by Hilary Kilpatrick **(2023)**

English-only Paperbacks

Leg over Leg, by Aḥmad Fāris al-Shidyāq **(2 volumes; 2015)**
The Expeditions: An Early Biography of Muḥammad, by Maʿmar ibn Rāshid **(2015)**
The Epistle on Legal Theory: A Translation of al-Shāfiʿī's *Risālah*, by al-Shāfiʿī **(2015)**
The Epistle of Forgiveness, by Abū l-ʿAlāʾ al-Maʿarrī **(2016)**
The Principles of Sufism, by ʿĀʾishah al-Bāʿūniyyah **(2016)**

A Treasury of Virtues: Sayings, Sermons, and Teachings of ʿAlī, by al-Qāḍī al-Quḍāʿī, with the **One Hundred Proverbs** attributed to al-Jāḥiẓ **(2016)**

The Life of Ibn Ḥanbal, by Ibn al-Jawzī **(2016)**

Mission to the Volga, by Ibn Faḍlān **(2017)**

Accounts of China and India, by Abū Zayd al-Sīrāfī **(2017)**

A Hundred and One Nights (2017)

Consorts of the Caliphs: Women and the Court of Baghdad, by Ibn al-Sāʿī **(2017)**

Disagreements of the Jurists: A Manual of Islamic Legal Theory, by al-Qāḍī al-Nuʿmān **(2017)**

What ʿĪsā ibn Hishām Told Us, by Muḥammad al-Muwayliḥī **(2018)**

War Songs, by ʿAntarah ibn Shaddād **(2018)**

The Life and Times of Abū Tammām, by Abū Bakr Muḥammad ibn Yaḥyā al-Ṣūlī **(2018)**

The Sword of Ambition, by ʿUthmān ibn Ibrāhīm al-Nābulusī **(2019)**

Brains Confounded by the Ode of Abū Shādūf Expounded: Volume One, by Yūsuf al-Shirbīnī **(2019)**

Brains Confounded by the Ode of Abū Shādūf Expounded: Volume Two, by Yūsuf al-Shirbīnī and **Risible Rhymes**, by Muḥammad ibn Maḥfūẓ al-Sanhūrī **(2019)**

The Excellence of the Arabs, by Ibn Qutaybah **(2019)**

Light in the Heavens: Sayings of the Prophet Muḥammad, by al-Qāḍī al-Quḍāʿī **(2019)**

Scents and Flavors: A Syrian Cookbook (2020)

Arabian Satire: Poetry from 18th-Century Najd, by Ḥmēdān al-Shwēʿir **(2020)**

In Darfur: An Account of the Sultanate and Its People, by Muḥammad al-Tūnisī **(2020)**

Arabian Romantic: Poems on Bedouin Life and Love, by ʿAbdallāh ibn Sbayyil **(2020)**

The Philosopher Responds, by Abū Ḥayyān al-Tawḥīdī and Abū ʿAlī Miskawayh **(2021)**

Impostures, by al-Ḥarīrī **(2021)**

The Discourses: Reflections on History, Sufism, Theology, and Literature—Volume One, by al-Ḥasan al-Yūsī **(2021)**

The Book of Charlatans, by Jamāl al-Dīn ʿAbd al-Raḥīm al-Jawbarī **(2022)**

The Yoga Sutras of Patañjali, by Abū Rayḥān al-Bīrūnī **(2022)**

The Book of Travels, by Ḥannā Diyāb **(2022)**

A Physician on the Nile: A Description of Egypt and Journal of the Famine Years, by ʿAbd al-Laṭīf al-Baghdādī (2022)

Kalīlah and Dimnah: Fables of Virtue and Vice, by Ibn al-Muqaffaʿ (2023)

Love, Death, Fame: Poetry and Lore from the Emirati Oral Tradition, by al-Māyidī ibn Ẓāhir (2023)

About the Editor–Translator

Hilary Kilpatrick received her DPhil from Oxford. She has taught at universities in the UK, the Netherlands, the US, and Switzerland and is now an independent scholar based in Lausanne, Switzerland. She has published a study of al-Iṣbahānī's *Book of Songs* and many articles on modern, classical, and Ottoman Arabic literature. Her other major translation is of Ghassan Kanafani's novella *Men in the Sun.*